MACROECONOMICS

The Irwin Series in Economics

Consulting Editor   LLOYD G. REYNOLDS   Yale University

MACROECONOMICS

Paul Wonnacott
University of Maryland

1978   Revised Edition

RICHARD D. IRWIN, INC.   Homewood, Illinois   60430
Irwin-Dorsey Limited   Georgetown, Ontario   L7G 4B3

ISBN 0-256-02032-9
Library of Congress Catalog Card No. 77–085811
Printed in the United States of America

3 4 5 6 7 8 9 0 K 5 4 3 2 1 0

Preface

Much has happened since the first edition of this book was written: the increases in international prices of oil, the most severe recession of recent decades, and a worsening of the twin problems of unemployment and inflation. Both the statistical data and the theoretical discussion have been extensively updated to reflect the changes of the past four years. Out-of-date topics have been culled to make room for new material, in order to prevent a proliferation of pages.

In addition to updating, several major changes have been made. First, a new chapter (Chapter 10) has been introduced on the relationships between monetary and fiscal policies: how accommodative monetary policies can increase the impact of fiscal policies; how a sharing of restraint between fiscal and monetary policies can reduce the strains on particular sectors of the economy (such as housing) ; and how offsetting policies (of monetary expansion combined with fiscal restraint, or vice versa) can be used to achieve secondary goals of growth or balance of payments. This, of course, introduces standard material on the "theory of policy," as enunciated by Tinbergen and others. In the first edition, I shied away from this topic, dealing with it only briefly. This was not because of the unimportance of the theory of policy; after all, we live in a complex world, in which the policy-maker must consider a multitude of objectives. Rather, it was because of a concern about leaving students with an unwarranted impression of precision. With a set of equations, it is easy to demonstrate that, with N independent policy tools, N goals can be achieved. Yet, while this powerful conclusion moves toward the real world in one important aspect—in terms of a number of objectives—it moves away from it in another. Policy makers do not hold a set of precise equations in their hands. They are uncertain regarding the effects of monetary and fiscal policies, and consequently are able to fulfill their goals only imperfectly. (Furthermore, uncertainty regarding the achievement of a primary goal reduces the advisability of pursuing secondary goals.)

Thus, I had hesitated to deal with the theory of policy unless uncertainty was also considered. And this seemed to be too much to ask of an intermediate undergraduate. If a world of many objectives is messy, the world of uncertainty is messier still. After much experimenting, however, I am satisfied that some of the main propositions concerning uncertainty can be illustrated (though not proved) in a relatively simple and straightforward way. Thus, Chapter 10 involves a discussion of the interrelationships between fiscal and monetary policies in a world of numerous goals, and in a world of uncertainty. I believe that this represents a major addition.

A second major change involves the discussion of fiscal policy, which has been simplified, and presented in more detail in Chapter 4.

The third major organizational change is the elimination of the separate chapter on the relationship between the international economy and macroeconomic policy. This is not because international economics is unimportant. Indeed, as international economics is my first love, I consider such a view heresy. The problem is to get around to international economics in a one-semester course. Particularly when the international chapter is put toward the end of the book, it may be considered expendable. Yet, the events of the past decade cannot be understood in a one-country vacuum. Therefore, international issues have been integrated into the other chapters. For example, oil prices play an important role in Chapter 13.

But, while changes have been made, I have attempted once again to fulfill the major objective of the first edition; that is, to provide a sense of excitement over Macroeconomics as a study of big, controversial policy questions. What are the relative merits of fiscal and monetary policies as a means of controlling aggregate demand? Which is more effective? What are the practical problems and what are the delays in the operation of fiscal and monetary policies? What are the standards of performance which may reasonably be achieved? To what extent should policy makers attempt to "fine tune" the economy? What are the strengths and weaknesses of Keynesian theory as an approach to Macroeconomics?

In discussing uncertainty and controversy, I acknowledge that I am forfeiting some of the assured authority which is the hallmark of textbooks. Having been presented with several opinions, the student may make up his own mind; or he may end up with considerable doubts as to the proper course of action. While this is in some ways less satisfying than ending a course with a list of "correct answers," it is an important part of the educational process. The constraints on macroeconomic policies—particularly in the difficult 1970s—provide an important message for the student. There is, of course, a danger that the student will resent the economist's tendency toward the balanced argument, "on the one hand . . . ; on the other hand . . . ." Like President Truman, he may even long for a one-armed economist. But he will have to yearn; in the present state of the world, I am unable to play the amputee.

A major problem in the design of a course is the age-old tradeoff between depth and breadth. While I believe that this book can be covered in a one-semester course, some teachers will prefer to cut back on the coverage in order to treat some topics in greater depth. The book has been designed so that the appendixes can be skipped without loss of continuity. Where chapters have been deleted because of the pressure of time, I would recommend that the deletions be chosen from Chapters 12, 15, 16, and perhaps 17. I would strongly recommend keeping Chapter 13; no course can come to grips with the problems of current policy making without considering the simultaneous existence of high rates of unemployment and high rates of inflation. (Chapter 13 is rather long, but after much thought I decided against dividing it. If it were made into two chapters, I feared that some teachers would be tempted to deal only with the simple Phillips Curve, and skip the problems of shifts in Phillips Curves. Yet, in my view, it is impossible to understand what in the world is going on in current policy debates without dealing with these shifts.)

In the preparation of this edition, I have again shamelessly accumulated intellectual debts to my undergraduate and graduate students at the University of Maryland, and to an extensive list of colleagues. I should particularly like to thank Lloyd Atkinson of American University, Gillian Garcia of the University of California (Berkeley), G. W. Olson of the University of Missouri (Kansas City), and Ron and Tom Wonnacott of the University of Western Ontario; and a number of colleagues at the University of Maryland:

Roger Betancourt, Charles Brown, Colette Claude, Eric Howe, Charles Lieberman, Paul Meyer, Mancur Olson, Charles Schultze, and Craig West. Finally, I acknowledge Aunt Betty's suggestion: to have more introductory quotations, and "cut out all that dull stuff in between." I gave this some thought, Aunt Betty, but after all, this *is* a textbook.

January 1978   PAUL WONNACOTT

Contents

ployment. Shifts in the aggregate demand function: The multiplier. *An algebraic derivation.* Equilibrium income: The balance between "injections" and "leakages."

The multiplier: A single government expenditure versus continuing expenditures. *A single government expenditure. A continuing injection of government spending.* Taxation: The effects on the consumption function. *A lump-sum tax. The balanced budget multiplier. A tax proportional to income.* The multiplier in an economy with taxes. Automatic stabilizers. . . . . . .And fiscal drag. A policy trap: The annually balanced budget. The problem of the appropriate measure of fiscal policy: The full-employment budget concept. Appendix: More complex multipliers.

The investment demand function: The marginal efficiency of investment. The rate of interest. The simple Keynesian system: Unemployment equilibrium in the face of an increasing supply of money. Appendix: Unemployment with flexible wages and prices and a fixed nominal money supply.

Saving and investment in the classical system. *Keynes' objection.* A Keynesian-classical synthesis. *Equilibrium in the goods market: The investment-saving curve. Equilibrium in the financial sector: The LM curve. The equilibrium income and interest rate.* Fiscal policy in the *IS/LM* framework. Monetary policy: Shifts in the *LM* curve. Appendix: An algebraic version of the *IS/LM* framework.

The quantity theory and the real-balance effect. *The real-balance effect and the* IS/LM *analysis.* Say's Law and the inconsistency in classical theory. The multiplier and the real-balance effect. *Wealth and the size of the multiplier: A classical interpretation.* Stocks and flows and the problem of the Keynesian equilibrium. Problems with the Keynesian equilibrium and with the multiplier analysis: Their significance. *Keynesian economics: The long run and the short.* Appendix: The *General Theory* as the economics of disequilibrium: Clower and Leijonhufvud.

PART THREE
AGGREGATE DEMAND POLICIES IN A DYNAMIC AND UNCERTAIN ENVIRONMENT

during the Great Depression. *Federal Reserve policy. A crisis of confidence and withdrawals of deposits. Gold.* More recent experiences. *The pegging of interest rates in the 1940s. The early 1970s.* Appendix: Interest rates and the quantity of money in the *IS/LM* framework.

PART FOUR
CONSUMPTION, INVESTMENT, AND
AGGREGATE SUPPLY: A CLOSER LOOK

PART FIVE
THE MEASUREMENT OF ECONOMIC AGGREGATES

batable cases. Government. Investment. The GNP price deflator and other price indexes. The significance of the Gross National Product.

PART ONE

INTRODUCTION

I want, so to speak, to raise a dust; because it is only out of the controversy that will arise that what I am saying will be understood.

John Maynard Keynes, in a letter to Roy Harrod

Chapter 1

Economic goals and the performance of the economy

Economy is the art of making the most out of life.

George Bernard Shaw

Since the Industrial Revolution, growth has been the most conspicuous feature of the economies of Europe and North America. The total production of goods and services has grown to give us an unprecedented level of economic welfare.

But there have been problems. Periodically, our economies have suffered from recession, with able-bodied people unable to find jobs in spite of their eagerness to work. In 1933, at the depth of the Great Depression, the unemployment rate in the United States rose to 25 percent of the labor force, and the annual unemployment rate never fell below 14 percent during the whole decade from 1931 to 1940. There was a tremendous economic loss: people out of work producing nothing, while basic economic needs went unmet. There was a tremendous social cost: people out of work, feeling useless, in a trap of frustration and despair. And there were unmeasurable, but perhaps even greater, political consequences: the international depres-

3

sion was one of the factors bringing Hitler to power, with his promises of full employment and military conquest.

The disasters of the interwar period laid the foundation for modern macroeconomics. "Never again" was the determination of the economic scholar, the politician, and the man on the street alike. This determination was clearly reflected in the Employment Act of 1946, in which the Congress declared that "it is the continuing responsibility of the Federal Government to use all practicable means . . . to promote maximum employment, production, and purchasing power." And politicians and economic scholars have worked together to see that the 1930s did not happen again. Economic problems since 1946 have been mild compared to those of the decade prior to World War II.

But, in spite of successes, problems have remained. After the successful conversion to a peacetime economy in 1946–48, the economy paused in 1949, and the unemployment rate rose to 5.9 percent (compared to the average of about 4 percent in the preceding three years). Again in 1954, there was a pause, with a 5.5 percent unemployment rate. Then, during the late 1950s and early 1960s, there was an extended period of softness in the economy, with annual unemployment rising almost to 7 percent in 1958, and never falling below 5.5 percent until the Vietnam war began to escalate in 1964–65. Nor has economic performance been improving in recent years. During the past decade, there have been two economic downturns ("recessions")—in 1970 and 1974–75. Indeed, the 1974–75 recession was the worst since the Depression of the 1930s, with the unemployment rate rising to 8.5 percent of the labor force in 1975.

MACROECONOMICS AND MACROECONOMIC GOALS

Economics is divided into two basic categories: macroeconomics and microeconomics. Macroeconomics is the study of economic aggregates: the total amount of employment, the level of aggregate output, the growth of aggregate output, and changes in the average level of prices. Microeconomics, on the other hand, deals with the detailed behavior of individual economic units. How does a business firm maximize its profits? What forces determine the prices of individual goods? What determines the amount of a particular good that will be produced?

As they deal with different levels of aggregation, macroeconomics and microeconomics naturally focus on different economic objectives. Macroeconomic policy objectives are *full employment, stable prices,* and a *satisfactory rate of economic growth.* The key micro-economic objective is the efficient use of productive resources.

Macroeconomic policies and economic goals: The simple case

*For extreme illnesses, extreme treatments are most fitting.**

Hippocrates

At times, the economy falls so short of an important objective that policymakers should clearly concentrate on that objective. This was most obviously the case during the 1930s, when the economy was operating far short of capacity output, and labor and machines were idle. It has also been the case in countries suffering from hyper-inflation (very rapid rates of inflation), such as Germany in the early 1920s.

An important policy conclusion of macroeconomics is that *aggregate demand* (that is, total spending for the goods and services produced in the economy) should be changed in the event of such overwhelming pathological conditions. If the economy is suffering from a 1930s-type depression, then aggregate demand should be expanded, and quickly! Large-scale unemployment was a sign that there was insufficient total demand; an increase in the demand for goods and services was needed to put people back to work. On the other extreme, the hyperinflation in Germany in the 1920s was a result of a rise in aggregate demand that was much too rapid. Too much demand was chasing too few goods. The appropriate policy in those circumstances is to cut down the rate of growth of aggregate demand.

Two major policy levers are available to the authorities to control aggregate demand:

1. *Fiscal policy* involves changes in government spending or in taxation. If aggregate demand is inadequate, then expansive fiscal policies are in order—the expansion of government spending and/or the reduction of taxes. The effects of government spending are most easily seen: If the government builds additional roads or dams, then people will be put to work. For a tax cut, the effects are less direct. If taxes are reduced, then people will have more disposable income after taxes are paid, and their spending will rise; they will buy more clothing, housing, cars, and so on. Again, people will be put to work

---

* From *Aphorisms.*

to produce the clothing, housing, cars, and other goods as demand increases.

Historically, wars have constituted the most conspicuous occasion for increases in government spending, leading some observers to conclude mistakenly that military spending is necessary for the prosperity of a capitalist economy. This conclusion is incorrect: While government spending on guns will pull a depressed economy up toward full employment, it is the *spending*, not the guns, which is important. Stimulus could alternatively be provided by public works or other forms of government spending.

2. *Monetary policy* constitutes the second policy lever for influencing the level of aggregate demand. As the stock of money held by the public rises, there will be a tendency for aggregate demand to increase. Thus, to ease the problems of depression, the money stock should be increased; to restrain inflation, the rate of increase in the money stock should be reduced.

Macroeconomic policies and economic goals: Some complications

This important central lesson of macroeconomics deserves repeating: Changes in aggregate demand are the key to dealing with major problems of depression or hyperinflation. This lesson has been well learned. As a result, a repeat of the tragic experiences of the interwar years has been avoided. There have been no depressions even to approach the collapse of the 1930s, and no economically advanced country has suffered inflation rates comparable to those of Germany in the early 1920s.

But the continuing difficulties—such as the periodic unemployment rates in excess of 5 percent—suggest that there are more complex and intractable problems which do not lend themselves to simple solution by a straightforward application of monetary and fiscal policies. Policymakers do not face the simple (but profoundly depressing) problem of the 1930s, or of Germany during the hyperinflation. They are not in a position that clearly requires a large change in the path of aggregate demand; they are not in a position where they should clearly push hard on the monetary and fiscal accelerator in order to speed up the economy, or on the monetary and fiscal brakes in order to restrain runaway inflation.

There are two major complications that inhibit a vigorous manipulation of aggregate demand.

1. During the postwar period, there has been no tendency for the

level of aggregate demand to be clearly excessive or clearly inadequate for long periods of time. Rather, there have been periodic recessions—1949, 1954, 1958, 1960, 1970, and 1974—interspersed with periods of inflation—particularly 1946–47, 1950–51, 1957, and since 1965. This sequence of events must give policymakers pause. If they step too hard on the gas in order to eliminate unemployment, will they be laying the groundwork for the next inflation? Alternatively, if they step on the brakes to stop inflation, will they be contributing to the next recession? In the face of relatively mild cyclical movements, policymakers need more than a general notion of the monetary and fiscal accelerator and brake pedals. For an improved performance of the economy, they need a rather precise knowledge of the *strength* of monetary and fiscal policies, and the *timing* of their effects. *How much* change in aggregate demand will result from a particular proposed change in fiscal or monetary policy? *When* will the changes in aggregate demand take place? To a significant degree, the failure of the economy to perform better during the postwar period has been the result of ignorance of economists (and others) regarding the precise answers to those two questions.

2. The policymaker is concerned with more than one objective, and different objectives may give conflicting signals as to the appropriate course of aggregate demand. During the 1970s, for example, the U.S. economy suffered unemployment rates higher than the rates of the late 1960s, and, at the same time, prices stubbornly continued their upward march. On the basis of the high unemployment rate, we might conclude that aggregate demand should be expanded in order to increase the levels of production and employment. But the opposite conclusion was indicated by the continuing inflation: demand should be reduced in order to decrease the rate of price increase. In situations such as this, aggregate demand policies cannot be adjusted to insure the simultaneous achievement of the twin goals of full employment and price stability. At this point, macroeconomics broadens out from its focus on aggregate demand policies; complications on the supply side become very important. Why do producers continue to raise prices even when they have large excess capacity? Why do workers insist on higher wages even in the face of large-scale unemployment?

A PREVIEW

There are three major themes in this book, growing out of the preceding section on economic goals.

1. The first, simple theme: Aggregate demand is important in dealing with the major problems of depression and hyperinflation. While this theme runs through the book, it is not continuously repeated because of its basic simplicity. But much of the value of macroeconomics comes from that simple lesson. Unless this basic point is kept firmly in mind, there is not much to be gained from a study of the more detailed and complex macro relationships in the economy.

2. The second, more complex theme: To deal with more moderate, temporary problems of recession or inflation, it is important to know not only the *direction,* but also the *strength* and *timing* of the effects of monetary or fiscal actions on the level of aggregate demand.

While economists have learned much about the detailed consequences of monetary or fiscal actions, there is unfortunately still a considerable area of ignorance. The answers provided by economic theory and statistical evidence must be considered tentative. There is still controversy as to the relative strength and importance of fiscal and monetary policies. The operation of both these policies is considered in detail in Parts Two and Three, with fiscal policy being the particular focus of attention in Chapters 4 and 6, and monetary policy in Chapters 8, 9, and 11. Questions of strength and timing, and the relationships *between* fiscal and monetary policies, are studied in Chapters 10 and 12.

3. The third theme: Conflicts arise among economic goals, conflicts that cannot be solved by a simple increase or decrease in aggregate demand. Most notably, inflation and unemployment have existed simultaneously during much of recent history. This difficult dilemma has become more painful during the 1970s, and macroeconomics has consequently been broadened from its early preoccupation with aggregate demand. The inflation-unemployment dilemma is studied in Chapter 13.

The economics of J. M. Keynes

> *In one sense, we are all Keynesians now;*
> *in another, no one is a Keynesian any longer.**
>
> Milton Friedman

Modern macroeconomics dates from the Depression of the 1930s, and, in particular, from the appearance in 1936 of *The General*

---

* From *Dollars and Deficits* (Englewood Cliffs, N.J.: Prentice-Hall, 1968) , p. 15.

Theory of Employment, Interest and Money, by British economist John Maynard Keynes. Keynes' most important contribution was his focus on the management of aggregate demand. It was he who established a central theme of macroeconomics, that the stimulation of aggregate demand is the way to get out of a depression.

That is not to suggest that this point was entirely absent from the writings of Keynes' predecessors. The proposition that management of demand is a key to continuing prosperity may, indeed, be found running through the economics literature of the 1920s. But, on this point, "classical"[1] literature was hopelessly confused. It also contained, in very strong form, the proposition that the way to get out of a depression was to sit tight and wait for the normal forces of the market to restore full employment. Worse still, classical economists sometimes seemed to suggest that the depression provided a healthy purging of unsound businesses and would leave the economy ultimately stronger.

Confusion over the desirability of an increase in aggregate demand led to fiscal and monetary policies which at times were the direct opposites of those needed to get the economy out of the depression. In the fall of 1932, the Hoover administration recommended to Congress an *increase* in taxes of over $900 million—about *one third* as much as all existing taxes. This recommendation resulted in the Revenue Act of 1932, involving the greatest peacetime increase in taxes in U.S. history. The result was an extraction of spendable income from the public, with depressing effects on their total spending. Nor were things better on the monetary side. Monetary policy was more closely attuned to the balance of international payments than to the needs of the domestic economy, and no continuing vigorous action was taken by the Federal Reserve to prevent the *decline* of the money supply by more than one third between the business peak in August 1929 and the trough of the depression in March 1933.

Through the utter confusion regarding demand policies, Keynes cut with his powerful focus on an increase in aggregate demand as a solution to the depression. Since the *General Theory,* economics has never been the same; Keynes was the father of modern macroeconomics. Any modern study of macroeconomics is Keynesian, in

---

[1] In economics, as elsewhere, "classical" is a word with an ever-changing meaning. In this book, "classical" is used as Keynes used it, to refer to the accepted body of economics prior to the appearance of the *General Theory.*

the sense that it gives an important role to aggregate demand. We are all Keynesians now.

A second major policy conclusion stands out in the *General Theory:* Fiscal policy is the way to control aggregate demand. To illustrate this conclusion, Keynes presented a persuasive model of the operation of the economy (see Chapters 3–5). There were, however, problems with this model. In particular, in illustrating the effectiveness of fiscal policy, it tended to submerge monetary policy as a weapon for controlling aggregate demand. Thus, while the simple Keynesian model was adequate as a guide to prevent the repetition of the problems in the 1930s, it was increasingly seen to be less than satisfactory as a guide to the more complex problems of controlling the relatively mild aberrations of the postwar economy. The result was an elaboration of a more sophisticated Keynesian model, with greater focus on money and interest rates (see Chapter 6). In terms of a model applicable to the current world, nobody is a simple Keynesian any more.

But this is not all. A fundamental question arises as to whether the simple Keynesian model of the economy—with its focus on fiscal policy and its downgrading of monetary policy—can be patched up; whether, in other words, the fiscal bias shines through in spite of the polishing and adjustment. This point is hotly disputed among economists. Those on the anti-Keynesian side argue that the Keynesian model is beyond redemption (see Chapter 7), and they fall back on a pre-Keynesian, monetary model as a starting point in looking for the detailed determinants of aggregate demand.

While both the Keynesian and monetary models provide significant insights into the operation of the economy, neither is entirely adequate to the needs of the day. The Keynesian model inherently stresses fiscal policy; the monetary model inherently draws attention to monetary policy. If we are to become equipped for the subtleties of demand policies during a period of relatively modest deviation from a full-employment path, it is important to know the strengths and weaknesses of each of these models. Thus, Parts Two and Three provide a detailed explanation of the Keynesian and classical models of aggregate demand. In order to give a preliminary overview, the two models are briefly summarized and compared in Chapter 2. Before we turn to this summary, however, it is appropriate to provide a context for the later chapters, in the form of a review of major changes in economic aggregates during recent decades.

THE ECONOMIC AGGREGATES: NATIONAL PRODUCT

National product is defined:

$$Y \equiv C + I + G + X - Z \qquad (1\text{–}1)$$

where

Y is national product, or national income.[2]
C is consumption expenditures.
I is private domestic investment.
G is government expenditures for goods and services.
X represents exports of goods and services.
Z represents imports of goods and services (Z is used for imports, since I stands for investment and M for money).
$\equiv$ means "is defined equal to," or "is always equal to."

More will be said about the details of the national income accounts in Chapter 17.[3] Here, only a few of the highlights are touched upon.

National income includes not only the goods that have been produced during the year (food, clothing, etc.), but also the services, such as haircuts and medical services. The government component of national income includes only government purchases of goods and services. Government transfer payments (for example, social security payments to the elderly) are not included (although the resulting consumption expenditures of social security recipients *are* included, as part of the consumption component). The reason for excluding transfer payments is this: When the government collects social security payments from some individuals and makes payments to others, nothing has been produced in the process (although the distribution of income has obviously been affected). In contrast, when the government contracts for a road to be built, something is produced. The transfers are therefore excluded from national income; the construction of roads is included in national income.

In national income, all goods and services produced in the economy should be included—but *only once.* Thus, the production of shirts is included in national income, but the production of the cloth that went into those shirts is not included separately. To do

---

[2] "National income" is a broad term, frequently used interchangeably with "national product." It also has a narrower, more specific meaning described in Chapter 17.

[3] Chapter 17 is not dependent on Chapters 2–16 and may be studied directly after Chapter 1.

so would involve double counting: The cloth would be included both as cloth and as part of the total value of the shirts.

But, in excluding the cloth that went into the shirts, we do not exclude *all* intermediate goods that are useful as inputs in the production of final goods. Reconsider the cloth example. Suppose that 1 billion square yards are produced and that 900 million are used in the production of shirts. Cloth production has been sufficient not only for the production of shirts, but also for an addition of 100 million square yards to inventories of cloth. National product will include not only the shirts, but also the additional 100 million units of cloth that we have produced during the year. *Increases* in inventories of cloth and other goods during the year are included in national product, as part of the investment component. (Clearly it is possible for inventories to be smaller at the end of the year than at the beginning; in this case, inventory investment will appear as a negative item in the national income accounts.)

The same general line of argument applies to the other components of investment, namely equipment and buildings. The additions to equipment and buildings during the year should be included in national income. Here, however, we run into a problem. The increase in plant and equipment during the year is equal to our production of these things, *less* the amount by which plant and equipment has worn out or become obsolete. Thus,

$$I_n \equiv I_g - D \tag{1–2}$$

where

- I_n is *net* investment (that is, the increase in the stock of plant and equipment during the year or other accounting period, plus increases in inventories).
- I_g is *gross* investment (that is, the production of plant and equipment during the year, plus increases in inventories).
- D is depreciation (that is, the deterioration and obsolescence of plant and equipment during the year).

To measure national income—the net production during the year— we should include *net* investment. This gives one of the two major specific definitions of national income:

$$NNP \equiv C + I_n + G + X - Z \tag{1–3}$$

where

NNP is net national product.

The difficulty is that, while information may readily be gathered on the production of plant and equipment, depreciation is not easily observable, and, indeed, it is difficult to define precisely. (How is the obsolescence of a computer to be determined? Its market value may fall more rapidly than the rate at which it deteriorates physically, as new inventions are made and better computers come along. The cost of making calculations with computers has been dropping by about 15 percent per annum.) Nor is the change in the stock of capital (I_n) directly observable. Thus, while NNP is the key conceptual magnitude, economists generally settle for a second best when dealing with statistics, because of the difficulties of an accurate, meaningful estimate of depreciation. The second best definition of national product:

$$GNP \equiv C + I_g + G + X - Z \qquad (1\text{--}4)$$

where

GNP is gross national product

and

$$NNP \equiv GNP - \text{depreciation} \qquad (1\text{--}5)$$

Investment, it should be noted, is used in a very specific sense in macroeconomics. It means the production of buildings[4] and equipment, and the net accumulation of inventories. While it is common, everyday usage to say that an individual "invests" in a government bond or a corporate stock, such transactions do *not* involve *investment* as the term is used in macroeconomics. These transactions involve *transfers* of assets from one individual or institution to another; they do not involve the *production* of capital goods.

THE PERFORMANCE OF THE U.S. ECONOMY

National product may be measured in the prices currently in existence—with 1970 product measured in 1970 prices, 1976 product measured in 1976 prices, and so on. However, if we wish to judge the performance of the economy, current-dollar GNP figures are severely defective, since they can increase for two quite different

---

[4] In the national income accounts, the construction of houses and apartments is included in the investment category, while consumer durables such as automobiles and refrigerators are included in consumption.

reasons. First, they may rise because the economy is producing more food, clothing, housing, and so on. Second, they may rise because the general level of prices is rising. In practice, both changes in real output and changes in prices may, of course, occur at the same time. Between 1970 and 1976, for example, current dollar *GNP* rose from $982 billion to $1,692 billion, or by 72 percent. Only a quarter of this increase reflected changes in the quantities of goods and services being produced; the rest reflected a rise in prices.

A rise in real output is generally desirable; a rise in prices is not. In evaluating the performance of the economy, it is therefore essential to separate the effect of rising prices from the increases in *GNP* which reflect a rise in the quantities of goods and services produced. This can be done by measuring *GNP* for the various years, not at current prices but at the prices in existence during a single base year (such as 1972). In Figure 1–1, *GNP* and its major[5] components are shown, measured at 1972 prices. The lower half of the diagram provides indicators related to the three major macroeconomic objectives of high employment, price stability, and growth.

For the half-century shown in this diagram, several major points stand out:

1. There has been a very large increase in output. Measured in constant (1972) prices, *GNP* more than quadrupled during this half-century.
2. The growth of output has, however, been uneven. There was a very large decrease—almost 30 percent—in constant-dollar or "real" *GNP* as the economy plunged into the worst depression in U.S. history between 1929 and 1933.
3. The unemployment rate was very high during the 1930s, hitting its peak of almost 25 percent of the labor force in 1933. As production fell, large numbers of people were thrown out of work.
4. Prices fell during the early depression. However, with one minor exception, prices have risen since that time. (Price changes in Figure 1–1 show the changes in the implicit *GNP* deflator; this price index is calculated by dividing the current-dollar *GNP* by the constant-dollar *GNP*.)

Of the major components of *GNP*, investment and government spending have shown the most year-to-year variability. During the Depression, spending for gross private domestic investment fell

---

[5] Net exports (that is, exports minus imports) are too small to show up significantly in Figure 1–1, and are therefore omitted.

Figure 1–1
The performance of the economy, 1929–1976

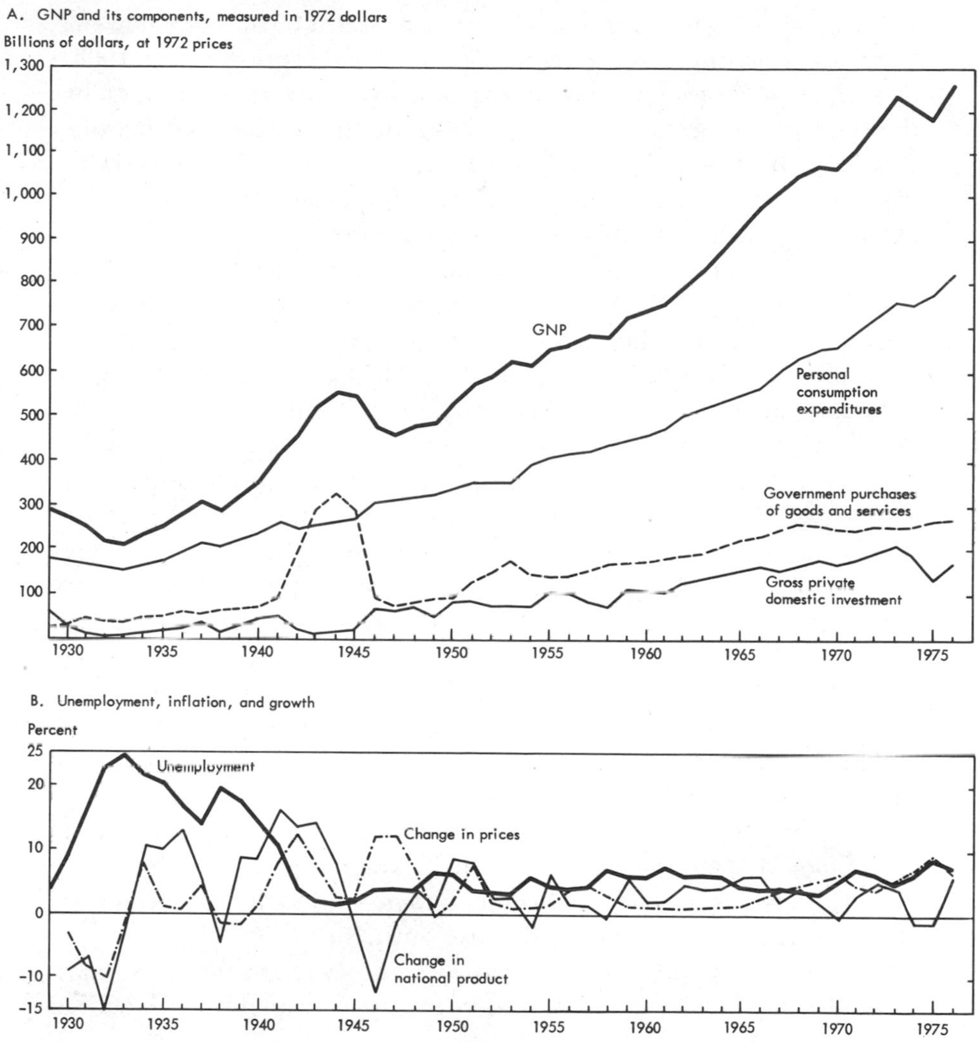

A. GNP and its components, measured in 1972 dollars

Billions of dollars, at 1972 prices

B. Unemployment, inflation, and growth

Percent

The largest fall in output and the highest rate of unemployment occurred during the Depression of the 1930s. The most rapid inflation occurred during and shortly after World War II, and during the middle 1970s.

from $16.2 billion in 1929 to $0.9 billion in 1933. And, on a *net* basis, investment fell from $7.6 billion in 1929 to −$6.2 billion in 1933; during the depths of the Depression, the amount spent on capital formation was much less than the depreciation of existing equipment.

The biggest changes in government spending took place as a result of World War II, first rising very rapidly as the country mobilized, and then falling almost as sharply after the defeat of the Axis powers. Perhaps surprisingly in the light of popular conception of the 1930s as a time of large government expenditures, the expenditures by the total public sector rose relatively gradually during that decade, from $9.2 billion in 1930 to $14.1 billion in 1940. This total, however, hides a major shift in the relative importance of federal government spending. In 1930, the federal government spent only $1.4 billion, with state and local governments accounting for the other $7.8 billion; by 1940, federal government spending had risen to $6.2 billion, while the state and local share remained relatively unchanged at $7.9 billion. During World War II, the federal government's role expanded dramatically as the resources of the nation were directed toward combat.

Breakdowns of the components of *GNP* during the past quarter-century are shown in Figure 1–2. Note that the trend of the depression and world war has been reversed. State and local government purchases have risen much more rapidly than federal government purchases, with states and local governments as a group becoming larger than the federal government during the late 1960s.

(It should be reiterated that *GNP* data include government spending only for goods and services—such as highways, schools, hospitals, defense, and so on; transfer payments are excluded since nothing is being "produced" by the recipient in return. If transfer payments—such as social security—were included, then total federal government spending would be much larger than shown in Figure 1–2. Indeed, with such inclusions, federal nondefense outlays are about three times as large as defense outlays.)

Of the volatile investment sector, inventory changes are the most volatile. Note also the substantial year-to-year changes in residential construction.

The recent performance of the economy on a seasonally adjusted, quarterly basis is given in Figure 1–3. By standards of the 1930s, the upward movement of real production has been remarkably stable and strong. But unemployment has been a problem, both during short-run downturns in the economy (1954) and during longer periods (1958–65, and in recent years). And rising prices have been a nagging difficulty. Furthermore, the nature of the inflation problem seems to have changed. Prior to World War II, periodic inflation (increases in prices) was interspersed with periodic defla-

Figure 1–2
Breakdown of components of *GNP* (billions of 1972 dollars)

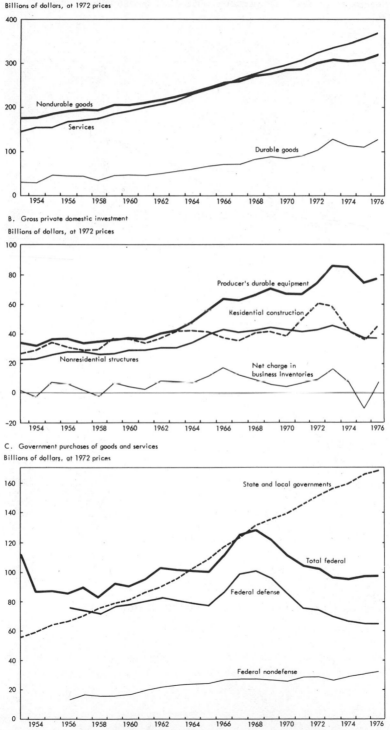

A. Personal consumption expenditures
Billions of dollars, at 1972 prices

B. Gross private domestic investment
Billions of dollars, at 1972 prices

C. Government purchases of goods and services
Billions of dollars, at 1972 prices

Figure 1–3
The performance of the economy quarterly, 1953–1977 (seasonally adjusted annual rates)

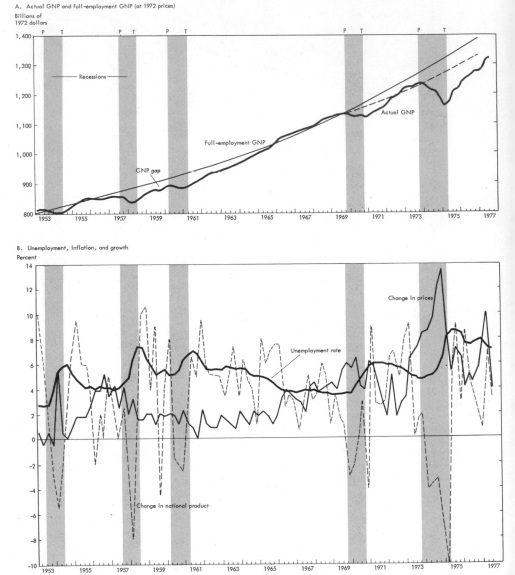

During recessions, output falls and the unemployment rate rises.

tion (declines in prices), and during the early postwar recessions, prices also showed some weakness. During the past 25 years, however, the average level of prices has moved only one way—inexorably up—during good times and bad.

In Figure 1–3, two additional sets of information are given: the business cycle peaks and troughs, and the full-employment or potential level of *GNP*. Each is used in evaluating the performance of the economy, although each represents a quite different emphasis and approach to the macroeconomic problems of unemployment and stable prices.

A business cycle has four phases: the *peak* of economic activity followed by a downward movement or *recession,* then a *trough* of activity, and finally an *expansion* phase. Not all downward movements of the economy are strong and pronounced. Indeed, they may be quite mild and of short duration. The problem then arises as to whether the downturn has been strong enough to be classified as a "recession."

The National Bureau of Economic Research (NBER) is the guardian of the definition of recessions; it decides what shall and shall not officially be called a recession. Basically, the NBER uses an historical approach in defining recessions. A downward movement is a recession if it is as pronounced as previous downturns that have been classified as recessions.[6] As a rule of thumb, a recession is said

---

[6] This historical approach raised a problem in mid-1970. There had been a downward movement of real *GNP* in 1969–IV and 1970–I totalling 1.1 percent of *GNP*. Then *GNP* became practically level. This was a decline less severe than any that had ever been called a recession in the past. (The NBER uses a number of other measures of activity in addition to real *GNP;* but they also confirmed this picture.) On the other hand, it was more severe than anything that had escaped the recession label in the past. With no clear guide from historical precedent, the NBER hedged. As the most conspicuous feature of early 1970 was the interruption of the growth of the economy rather than any large decline, Solomon Fabricant of the NBER in mid-1970 applied the label of "growth recession" to the then current state of economic activity.

The use of the term "recession" obviously has major political implications. In a speech to the NBER on September 24, 1970, Herbert Stein of the President's Council of Economic Advisers jokingly suggested that, as the bureau would soon be able to elect or diselect a president by declaring or not declaring a recession, he foresaw "a drive for direct public election of members of the board of the National Bureau." Stein also twitted Solomon Fabricant on his declaration of a "growth" recession:

> "I was prepared for this finding by a conversation I had with Sol Fabricant a few weeks ago. I met him on Madison Avenue walking a small poodle, or so I thought.
> 'That's a cute dog,' I said.
> 'That's no dog,' he replied; 'it's a horse.'
> 'It looks just like a dog to me,' I resisted.
> 'Yes, but it has many attributes of a horse,' was his explanation.
> (cont. on p. 20)

to have occurred if seasonally adjusted real *GNP* declines for two or more quarters. (The slight—0.2 percent—downward movement of real *GNP* for only one quarter at the beginning of 1967 was not classified as a recession by the NBER; it is frequently referred to as a "mini-recession.")

Potential *GNP* is calculated as the real amount that could be produced with the labor force 96 percent employed and working normal hours at normal productivity. The *GNP* "gap" is the difference between potential *GNP* and actual *GNP*, both in real terms. The emphasis here is not so much on stabilizing the growth of *GNP* as on getting the economy up to the full-employment level, defined as 4 percent unemployment. ("Full employment" obviously cannot mean that *nobody* is unemployed; there are always those who have left one job and are looking for another, or those who are shopping around for their first job. As long as such individuals have prospects of getting a reasonably satisfactory job within a reasonable time period, the economy may be considered to be "fully employed"; the full-employment concept does not rule out "frictional" unemployment.) There is little to be gained in stabilizing the economy at a high level of unemployment. Therefore, argue the proponents of the potential *GNP* approach, the emphasis should not be so much on stabilization per se, but rather on the continuous achievement of the desirable and feasible goal of full employment. (In contrast, the business cycle approach focuses attention on the objective of reducing cyclicals wings and stabilizing the economy.) The potential *GNP* approach has, however, been questioned in recent years, particularly since 1973. During that year, inflationary forces gathered momentum, even though the economy was below the potential *GNP* as usually defined. Some economists therefore argue that potential *GNP* should be revised downward, to the dashed curve. The concept of potential *GNP,* or economic capacity, is perhaps even more troublesome than the concept of "recession."

'But Sol,' I cried, 'it's so small.'
'I know,' he answered. 'That's why I call it a growth horse.' "

Humor soon became irrelevant. After increasing slightly in the middle two quarters of 1970, real *GNP* fell off in the fourth quarter to a level 1.5 percent below the high established in the third quarter of 1969. A recession had rather clearly taken place, although one which was mild by historical standards.

There was a sequel several years later, when Arthur Okun (who had been Johnson's chairman of the Council of Economic Advisers) concluded that the economy must be in trouble, since Stein was again quibbling over the definition of recession.

KEY POINTS

1. There are three goals of macroeconomic policy.
   a. Full employment (commonly defined in the United States as existing when unemployment is no more than 4 percent of the labor force).
   b. A stable average level of prices.
   c. A satisfactory rate of economic growth.
2. Changes in aggregate demand are an important determinant of employment and the rate of change of prices.
   a. During periods of high unemployment (such as the 1930s), aggregate demand should be *increased* to stimulate the economy toward the full employment level.
   b. During periods of runaway inflation, the rate of increase of aggregate demand should be slowed down.
3. There are two major policies for the control of aggregate demand.
   a. Fiscal policy. An expansive fiscal policy involves an increase in government spending, and/or a decrease in tax rates.
   b. Monetary policy. An expansive monetary policy involves an increase in the rate of growth of the quantity of money.
4. While it is clearly appropriate for aggregate demand policies to be expansive during depressions and restrictive during hyperinflations, in less extreme situations the desirable path of aggregate demand policies is more debatable for two reasons.
   a. Periods of inadequate demand and excess demand frequently follow one another. Thus, the policymaker should be concerned with *lags* in the operation of policy. Stimulative policies initiated during periods of economic slack may have their major effect during an ensuing period of boom.
   b. The policymaker may receive conflicting signals. It is possible for unemployment to be quite high (suggesting the need for expansive policies), while prices are simultaneously rising (suggesting the desirability of restrictive policies). This simultaneous existence of high unemployment and high inflation has plagued the U.S. economy (and many foreign economies) during the 1970s.
5. Much of the macroeconomic literature grows out of the 1936 book by British economist John Maynard Keynes, *The General*

Theory of Employment, Interest and Money. Two "Keynesian" policy propositions are particularly important.

a. The stimulation of aggregate demand is the way to get out of a depression, and governmental authorities have the responsibility to manage aggregate demand.

b. Fiscal policy is the most important tool for controlling aggregate demand. This proposition has been challenged by a number of economists who believe that monetary policy is the key determinant of aggregate demand.

QUESTION

1. What has happened recently to the variables considered in this chapter: unemployment, *GNP*, consumption, prices, etc.? (Recent data may be found in the *Survey of Current Business*, published monthly by the U.S. Department of Commerce.)

SUGGESTED READINGS

John Kenneth Galbraith, *The Great Crash, 1929* (Boston: Houghton Mifflin, 1961).

Robert Aaron Gordon, *Economic Instability and Growth: The American Record* (New York: Harper & Row, 1974).

Chapter 2

Keynesian economics and classical economics

*Those, who are strongly wedded to what
I shall call "the classical theory,"
will fluctuate, I suspect, between a
belief that I am quite wrong and a
belief that I am saying nothing new.**

John Maynard Keynes

The appearance of Keynes' *General Theory* in 1936 marked the beginning of modern macroeconomics. Keynes was appalled by the costs of the Depression and by the "do nothing" attitude of many of his contemporaries. He was particularly frustrated by the tendency of economists to argue, in the tradition of Adam Smith, that a "laissez-faire" policy was best—that the government should leave the economy alone. Indeed, the view of some contemporary economists, that there was no major demand problem and that the natural recuperative powers of the economy would in due time restore prosperity, led Keynes to attack the foundations of the accepted "classical" body of economic doctrine. His theory was intended to be revolutionary, and so it proved. Since the 1930s, Keynes' ideas have dominated the discussion of aggregate economic problems.

---

* From *The General Theory of Employment, Interest, and Money* (London: Macmillan, 1936), p. v.

The *General Theory* is a difficult book to read, full of subtle and complex argumentation. Nevertheless, three major propositions stand out. There were two key policy conclusions (previously noted in Chapter 1):

1. The way to get out of a depression is to stimulate aggregate demand. The control of aggregate demand is a central responsibility of public policymakers.
2. *Fiscal policies*—in the form of increased government spending or tax cuts (or both)—constitute the key policy weapon for stimulating the economy toward full employment. Monetary policy was held to be of secondary importance. Indeed, monetary policy might be useless as a means for stimulating the economy out of a deep depression.

And, in addition, there was a central theoretical proposition:

3. The economy has no strong natural tendency toward full employment, and can reach an equilibrium at less than full employment.[1]

The first of these propositions is valid; it forms one cornerstone of modern macroeconomics. The confusions of pre-Keynesian literature on this point are of interest to the historian of economic thought, but are not relevant to the development of current macroeconomic policies. In this respect, modern macroeconomics is unabashedly Keynesian.

The second point is, however, open to debate. During the past two decades, there has been a resurgence of interest in monetary policy. Because money was the focus of pre-Keynesian classical economics, this revival of interest in monetary policy has inspired talk of a "counterrevolution" in macroeconomics.[2] If the current

---

[1] Because of the subtlety and obscurity of some passages of the *General Theory*, not all economists agree that the basic models and propositions which are generally taken to represent Keynesian theory do in fact reflect the views of Keynes himself. See Axel Leijonhufvud, *On Keynesian Economics and the Economics of Keynes* (New York: Oxford University Press, 1968).

In my opinion, Chapters 3–5—which present the standard textbook version of Keynesian theory—do accurately reflect the central theme of the *General Theory*, especially its summary, Chapter 18, entitled "The General Theory of Employment Restated."

This is not to deny, however, that there are complex and sometimes contradictory strands in the *General Theory*. (Some of the complexities—and Leijonhufvud's interpretation of Keynesian economics—will be considered in the appendix to Chapter 7.)

[2] Harry G. Johnson, "The Keynesian Revolution and the Monetarist Counterrevolution," *American Economic Review*, May 1971, pp. 1–14.

problems were similar to those of the 1930s, with a very large increase in aggregate demand needed to restore full employment, then this fiscal-monetary debate would be of little immediate relevance. A vigorous application of both monetary and fiscal expansion would be in order. In a depression, the fine points can be ignored, and strong use should be made of all policies which will stimulate employment. In the modern world, however, with its more modest problems and its need for more subtle policymaking, the monetary-fiscal debate takes on importance. If demand is going to be accurately controlled, it is important to know with as much precision as possible the detailed determinants of aggregate demand. Unfortunately, there are only two major models for the analysis of aggregate demand: the Keynesian model, with its intrinsic focus on fiscal changes, and the classical model, with its focus on money. To get a balanced view of monetary and fiscal policy, both the Keynesian and monetary (classical) models must be investigated; this is done in the chapters that follow.

In his third conclusion, Keynes was in error. More precisely, the existence of an unemployment equilibrium in his theoretical system requires the implausible assumption that consumption behavior is completely unaffected by the public's holding of money or other forms of wealth. (This problem in Keynes' theory will be explained in Chapter 7.) The equilibrium debate is highly abstract, and would be of little interest for policymaking if it were not for one important consideration. The debate between Keynesian and classical economists over the nature of economic equilibrium is closely related to the debate over the relative importance of monetary and fiscal policies. The fiscal-monetary debate is therefore introduced with a description of Keynesian and classical theories of economic equilibrium.

CLASSICAL ECONOMICS: A BRIEF OUTLINE

Keynesian economics was built on a single, monumental work, the *General Theory*. It therefore forms a relatively coherent and specific set of propositions, in spite of some ambiguities on a number of important points in the *General Theory*. Classical literature, on the other hand, has no such single unified "bible." There were many classical economists writing on all sorts of subjects. They did not always present a coherent, consistent set of views on theory, much less on policy. Thus, any brief summary of classical views will of necessity be debatable. Keynes' *General Theory* was an attack on views which he represented as those of the classicists; there has been much disagreement as to whether Keynes fairly presented the classical position, or whether he constructed a straw man to ease the process of demolition. Indeed, in referring to the *General Theory,* J. R. Hicks (a sympathetic commentator) [3] observed that

> it is . . . clear that many readers have been left very bewildered by this Dunciad. Even if they are convinced by Mr. Keynes' arguments and humbly acknowledge themselves to have been "classical economists" in the past, they find it hard to remember that they believed in their unregenerate days the things Mr. Keynes said they believed.[4]

What the classicists "really" said is an important matter—perhaps one of the two or three most important subjects in any study of the history of economic thought. Here, however, we must short-circuit this question. What will be presented, rather, is a coherent alternative view to the Keynesian position, and one that is broadly in line with the thinking of a substantial group of classical economists.

Classical economics: The equilibrium of aggregate demand and aggregate supply

For a specific good, such as wheat, equilibrium occurs where the demand and supply curves intersect. If initially the quantity of wheat demanded falls short of the quantity supplied, the price of wheat will fall toward the equilibrium point, where the demand and supply curves intersect.

The question is: Does a similar proposition also apply to demand and supply in the aggregate? If total demand for goods and services falls short of the total amount which the economy can produce, and

---

[3] A less sympathetic observer, Harry G. Johnson, accused Keynes of doing much to implant a modern style of debate which "posits a nameless horde of faceless orthodox nincompoops, among whom a few recognizable faces can be discerned, and proceeds to ridicule a travesty of their published, presumed, or imputed views." (From Johnson's memoir, "How Good was Keynes' Cambridge?" *Encounter,* August 1976, p. 90.)

[4] J. R. Hicks, "Mr. Keynes and the 'Classics'; a Suggested Interpretation," *Econometrica,* April 1937, p. 147. This article is reprinted in Hicks, *Critical Essays in Monetary Theory* (Oxford: Clarendon, 1967). On the modification of Hicks' views since the appearance of his 1937 essay, see Hicks, "Recollections and Documents," *Economica,* February 1973, pp. 2–11.

if the general level of prices falls, will equilibrium be established with full employment? The classical answer is yes, it will. At least, it will in time.

This is not to say that the demand and supply curves for the economy as a whole are closely similar to demand and supply for a single product. The supply curve for wheat is drawn on the assumption that the price of wheat is the *only* price that changes; when drawing a supply curve for wheat, the prices of all other goods are assumed to be fixed. Thus, a rise in the price of wheat represents a rise in the price of wheat *compared to the prices* of all other goods, including oats, soybeans, and corn. If the price of wheat increases, farmers have an incentive to *shift* out of the production of these other crops and into the production of wheat. Thus, as the price of wheat rises, more wheat is supplied; the supply curve slopes upward to the right.

For the economy as a whole, a rise in the level of all prices cannot draw productive resources in from "other crops"; there are no such "other crops." If all prices were to rise—to, say, twice their initial level—then this would not automatically increase the amount of goods and services which the economy can produce. Thus, the aggregate supply curve—showing the quantity of all goods and services that producers will be willing to supply at various price levels—is vertical at the quantity of goods and services that can be produced at full employment (Figure 2–1).

On the vertical axis of this diagram, the average level of prices of all goods and services is shown. In order to simplify the discussion, it is usually assumed that the prices of all goods and services rise or fall *in the same proportion* as we move up or down the vertical axis. With this assumption, it is possible to rule out complications which may arise because of changes in the *relative* prices of specific goods.

In classical theory, total spending depends primarily on the quantity of money. The aggregate demand curve in Figure 2–1 is based on the assumption that the quantity of money in the economy is fixed. At a high level of prices, the fixed quantity of dollars will buy only a small amount of goods or services; as prices fall, the fixed quantity of money will buy more and more goods and services. Thus, said classical economists, the aggregate demand curve slopes downward to the right. Equilibrium occurs at *E*, where the aggregate demand and supply curves intersect, and where there is full employment.

Figure 2–1
Aggregate supply and aggregate demand in classical theory

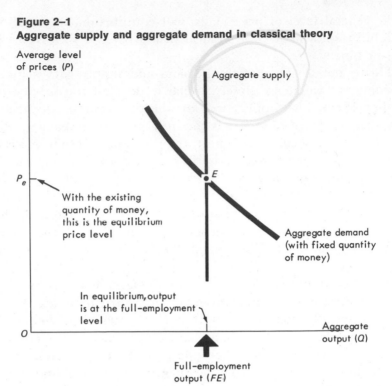

In classical theory, aggregate supply is vertical at the full-employment level of output.

Aggregate demand depends primarily on the quantity of money. At a lower average level of prices, the existing quantity of money in the economy will buy more goods and services. Thus, the aggregate demand curve slopes downward to the right.

The equation of exchange

In presenting their theory of full employment, classical economists relied on an important equation—*the equation of exchange.* Formally, this is written:

$$MV \equiv PQ \qquad (2\text{--}1)$$

where:

M is the quantity of money in the hands of the public.
Q is the total quantity of output (goods and services).
P is the average price level of this output.

V is the income velocity of money, hereafter known simply as "velocity."[5]

Specifically, V is *defined* as being equal to PQ/M.

Consider a simple illustration. Suppose that 10 billion units of output are purchased in an economy at an average price of $2. Then total spending is $20 billion. These goods and services are bought with money. Observe, however, that there does not have to be a full $20 billion in money in the economy for all these goods to be sold during the year. Why? Because, in the course of a year, a single $1 bill may be spent many times. When you go to the movies, you buy your ticket with four $1 bills. But these $1 bills do not remain in the cash register. Some are used to rent the film, others go to pay the ushers, and so on. The ushers, in turn, use the dollars to buy groceries or pay the rent. The landlord, in turn, uses the dollars to buy a new car or another item. Around and around the dollars go. Thus, if the average dollar is spent four times during the year, the total spending of $20 billion can occur with a money supply of only $5 billion.

Observe that velocity is defined in such a way that Equation (2–1) *must* be true. It is true by definition; it is beyond debate.

The equation of exchange and classical theory:
The quantity theory of money

The classical theory is built on this equation, and this theory *is* open to debate. (Indeed, it was attacked by Keynes.) This theory— *the quantity theory of money*—is based on the proposition that

---

[5] There were two versions of the equation of exchange. The first—shown as Equation (2–1)—was known as the "income" version, and concentrated on the total output of the economy (Q). But classical economists were also interested in another version. Money is used to buy not only the final output of the economy (Q) but also intermediate products. That is, money is used to purchase not only automobiles, but also the steel that goes into the production of automobiles, the coal that goes into the production of steel, and so on. Thus, classical economists also used a "total transactions" version of the equation of exchange:

$$MV_t \equiv PT \qquad (2-2)$$

where

T represents total transactions, both final and intermediate

and

V_t is the transactions velocity and is defined as being equal to PT/M.

Because we are interested in national output in this book, we will use Equation (2–1) as the equation of exchange.

velocity is stable. Thus, if the money supply (*M*) increases with velocity (*V*) remaining stable, then total spending (*PQ*) will rise. *Money,* in other words, *is a key determinant of aggregate demand.*

Note how the quantity theory is reflected in the demand curve shown in Figure 2–1. The total quantity of output that will be demanded (*Q,* measured horizontally to the demand curve in Figure 2–1) is:

$$Q = \frac{MV}{P} \qquad (2\text{–}3)$$

So long as the quantity of money is fixed, and so long as velocity is stable, then the numerator *MV* is stable. The quantity of output purchased (*Q*) will therefore rise as *P* falls; the aggregate demand curve slopes downward to the right.

CLASSICAL ECONOMICS AND UNEMPLOYMENT

Unemployment cannot exist *in equilibrium* in the classical system; the equilibrium point *E* in Figure 2–1 is one of full employment. Therefore, when classical economists came to deal with the phenomenon of unemployment, they considered patterns of change, disequilibrium, and adjustment in the economy. Specifically, classical unemployment theory centered on the phenomenon of the "business cycle." And, not surprisingly, *monetary disturbances* were seen as an important element in the business cycle; R. G. Hawtrey's theory of the cycle is a prime example. Hawtrey saw the business cycle as the result of swings in aggregate demand which were caused by swings in the quantity of money. Fluctuations in the quantity of money might be caused by a number of disturbances, including gold flows under the old international gold standard. (Under the old gold standard, a gold inflow tended to cause an increase in the quantity of money.)

Observe how a decline in the quantity of money might cause temporary unemployment (Figure 2–2). Initially, assume that the economy is in equilibrium at E_1, with aggregate demand D_1. Now, suppose that the money supply falls. Because demand depends importantly on the quantity of money, it will likewise decline, to D_2. Even so, there could still be full employment at the new equilibrium E_2, if prices and wages fell enough. But wages and prices are sticky; they do not fall quickly. Thus, in response to the shift in the demand curve to D_2, prices initially will fall only to P_A. At this level—

Figure 2–2
The classical theory of unemployment

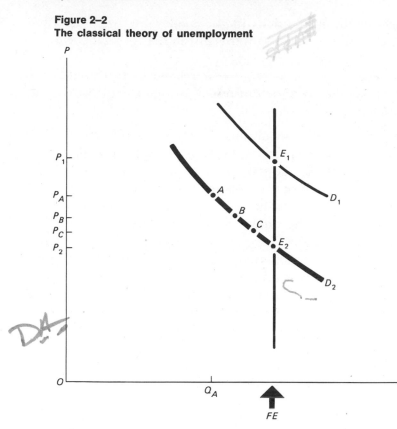

According to classical economics, unemployment can exist if there is a shock to the economy. If the money stock falls and aggregate demand decreases from D_1 to D_2, then the full-employment equilibrium will move to E_2. The economy may move toward E_2 only slowly, however. If wages and prices are sticky in a downward direction, then the economy will move initially to a point such as A, and only gradually move to B, C, and finally to E_2. During the transition, while the economy is at A, B, and C, there will be unemployment.

which exceeds the equilibrium price level—total demand is not enough to buy all the goods that producers are willing to make, and output (at Q_A) falls below the full-employment level (labelled FE). This unemployment represents a temporary disequilibrium condition. As prices fall further, the economy will move down the aggregate demand function, to B, C, and finally to the new full-employment equilibrium of E_2.

This classical framework suggests either (or both) of two ways to deal with the unemployment problem:

1. Smooth out the fluctuations in the money supply, thus eliminating the cause of the downward shift in the aggregate demand curve.
2. Speed up the adjustment process by removing institutional restraints which hamper the downward movement of prices and wages.

The former has the clear advantage of being consistent with a relatively stable price level; it has the even greater advantage of removing what was seen as the root cause of unemployment. It was, however, perceived to have the disadvantage of being inconsistent with the international gold standard and the maintenance of fixed exchange rates among the different national currencies. (An exchange rate is the price of one national currency in terms of another.) Partly because of international considerations, the second policy had significant support among classical economists; but both prescriptions may be found in classical literature.[6]

With the economic disasters of the 1930s, quantity theorists came increasingly to emphasize the desirability of controlling the quantity of money in order to provide for a level of demand consistent with full employment and relatively stable prices. Once full employment was reached, argued quantity theorists, the appropriate policy was a steady growth in the money supply in order to provide the steady increase in demand required for full employment and reasonably stable prices. (As time passes, the productive capacity of the economy increases. Thus, the aggregate supply function of Figure 2–1 shifts to the right. If prices are to remain stable, the aggregate demand function must move to the right at the same speed.) Thus, as a result of the Depression, "classical" monetary economists increasingly emphasized the desirability of an appropriate level of aggregate demand (Proposal 1). But this relatively quiet revolution became inconspicuous in the bright glare of the spotlight which Keynes focused on his theory of aggregate demand—which cast fiscal policies rather than money in the starring role.

In shifting their emphasis from price flexibility (Proposal 2) to a smoothing of aggregate demand (Proposal 1), classical economists ran into a problem on the international front. Policies to smooth out demand might be inconsistent with the maintenance of the interna-

---

[6] Keynes concentrated his fire on the second proposal as representing *the* classical position. This is somewhat surprising, as he had himself proposed the smoothing out of demand during his unregenerate classical days, when he wrote his work on *Monetary Reform* (New York: Harcourt, Brace and London: Macmillan, 1924).

tional gold standard. Keynes, in his *Monetary Reform* (1924), had had a very simple solution to this quandary: Reject the international gold standard and permit an adjustment in exchange rates when existing rates were inappropriate.

> If, therefore, the external [foreign] price level lies outside our control, we must submit either to our own internal price level or to our exchanges being pulled about by external influences. If the external price level is unstable, we cannot keep *both* our own price level *and* our exchanges stable. . . .
>
>   *   *   *   *   *
>
> The right choice is not necessarily the same for all countries. . . . Nevertheless, there does seem to be in almost every case a presumption in favor of the stability of prices, if only it can be achieved.[7]

Interestingly enough, somewhat similar proposals—a smooth growth in the money supply, and flexible exchange rates—are key proposals of the best-known present-day monetarist, Professor Milton Friedman of the University of Chicago. Friedman, in the classical tradition, places monetary disturbances in a central role in explaining unemployment. In particular, he argues that the Depression of the 1930s can be explained only in the light of the great banking disruptions of 1929–33.[8]

Classical economists insisted that full employment must exist *in equilibrium;* but many classical economists also held the view that changes in the quantity of money can affect the level of economic activity *during periods of adjustment.* This view may be traced back to the very beginnings of the quantity theory. In the middle of the 18th century, British philosopher David Hume wrote:

> Money is not, properly speaking, one of the subjects of commerce; but only the instrument which men have agreed upon to facilitate the exchange of one commodity for another. It is not of the wheels of trade: It is the oil which renders the motion of the wheels smooth and easy. If we consider any one kingdom by itself, it is evident, that the greater or less plenty of money is of no consequence; since the prices of commodities are always proportioned to the plenty of money. . . .
>
>   *   *   *   *   *

---

[7] Keynes, *Monetary Reform,* pp. 167–69. (Italics in original.)

[8] Milton Friedman and Anna Schwartz, *A Monetary History of the United States, 1867–1960* (Princeton: Princeton University Press, 1963), chap. 7. For a different view, see Peter Temin, *Did Monetary Forces Cause the Great Depression?* (New York: Norton, 1976).

But notwithstanding this conclusion, which must be allowed just, it is certain, that, since the discovery of the mines in America, industry has increased in all the nations of Europe. . . .

To account, then, for this phenomenon, we must consider, that though the high price of commodities be a necessary consequence of the encrease of gold and silver, yet it follows not immediately upon that encrease; but some time is required before the money . . . makes its effect be felt. . . . In my opinion, it is only in this interval or intermediate period, between the acquisition of money and the rise of prices, that the encreasing quantity of gold and silver is favourable to industry.[9]

In other words, while the *equilibrium* of full employment could result from either an increase in the quantity of money or a general fall in prices and wages, there might, in practice, be a world of difference between a period with a rising money stock and a period with deflation (falling prices). A direct increase in the quantity of money during a recession would be relatively painless, involving a quick and smooth increase in the demand for goods and in employment. On the other hand, the process of deflation might be slow and painful; in general, this was a bad way to move toward the full-employment equilibrium. While there was much confusion and disagreement on this point in classical literature, there were grounds in the classical theory for preferring option 1 (a smooth growth in the quantity of money) to option 2 (deflation) as a way of preventing unemployment.

One final point should be noted regarding classical theory. Classical economists generally believed that the private economy is *basically stable,* and will be severely disturbed from a position of full employment only when there are severe monetary disruptions. Thus, classical economists (both before and after Keynes) tend to be less interventionist than Keynesian economists, who see unemployment as a probable outcome unless the government takes a strongly active role. Classical economists, in contrast, tend toward the view that the government and particularly the central bank are responsible for establishing a stable milieu for the private economy, but should not continuously tinker with demand. Something of this debate has carried over into the political arena: Democratic members of the Council of Economic Advisers talk in terms of "fine tuning" the level of aggregate demand in order to stabilize the economy at a high

---

[9] David Hume, "Of Money," in *Essays Moral, Political and Literary* (Oxford University Press, 1963), pp. 289–94. (First published in 1741–42.)

level of employment and stable prices; Republican advisers talk in terms of an "even-handed" approach to demand management in order to achieve the same goals.

CLASSICAL ECONOMICS AND FISCAL POLICY

The quantity theory was a main theme running through classical literature; classical economists were united by the view that the velocity of money was stable. But the strength with which this view was held varied considerably. Some classical economists argued that velocity was *highly* stable and that therefore forces other than the quantity of money were relatively unimportant as determinants of aggregate demand.[10] Such "other forces" include fiscal policy. Other classical economists argued that, while velocity was reasonably stable, it could be affected by a host of factors—including fiscal policy. According to this weaker classical view, fiscal policy could be a useful tool for demand management.

Classical views on fiscal policy thus varied widely. Beginning with the strongest classical position, we may summarize these views:

1. Government spending is unlikely to have a significant stimulative effect on the economy, at least not unless it is accompanied by monetary expansion. This is because velocity is very stable. An increase in government spending financed by borrowing on the financial markets will tend to crowd out a more or less equivalent amount of expenditures elsewhere. (This was the British Treasury view of the early depression, against which Keynes' *General Theory* was directed.)

---

[10] Classical economists also elaborated a *highly abstract* theoretical model in which *nothing* was allowed to change but the quantity of money. For example, the tastes of individuals do not change, nor does technology. In such a world, *if only equilibrium positions are considered,* then velocity is not only stable—it is *constant.* An increase in money will lead to a proportional increase in aggregate demand. More specifically, since unemployment cannot exist *in equilibrium* in such a model, then an increase in the money supply will lead to an equivalent increase in equilibrium *prices.* The very narrow, theoretical basis of this argument was stressed by the title given to the model by classical economists, namely, *The Classical Stationary State,* a state in which the equilibrium was so narrowly defined that not only were there no changes in tastes, but there was no net investment or growth either. Whether economists describing this model would argue that velocity is constant in the real world in response to actual policy changes is quite another matter. ["The Classical Stationary State" was the title of an article by A. C. Pigou in the *Economic Journal,* December 1943, pp. 343–51, in which he responded to Keynes' attack on the classicists. The most complete statement of the formal static classical model is Don Patinkin, *Money, Interest, and Prices: An Integration of Monetary and Value Theory,* 2d ed. (New York: Harper & Row, 1965). This book is pretty stiff going for any but the most advanced undergraduates; the same is true of the Pigou article.]

2. Fiscal policy is likely to have a significant effect on aggregate demand, but primarily because it is likely to have a significant effect on the quantity of money in the economy. When the government increases spending and the central bank attempts to keep the interest rate level reasonably stable, the bank will find itself buying up the additional government debt in order to keep interest rates from rising. These purchases will involve an increase in the money supply. (This is explained in detail in Chapter 11.) As a consequence, demand will increase.

If such combined policies are pursued, with the central bank in effect financing additional government spending with newly created money, then a semantic problem will arise as to whether the resulting increase in expenditure should be attributed to "monetary" or "fiscal" policy. As this is a definitional matter, there is no "right" answer. But the question is important, since it is one of the major reasons why Keynesians and monetarists tend to talk right past one another when interpreting statistical evidence, particularly the evidence from periods when fiscal expansion was accompanied by money creation. In the heat of debate, a major substantive point gets lost—namely, that government expenditures financed by monetary expansion will unquestionably expand aggregate demand. As to whether this should be called fiscal or monetary policy—you take your choice.

3. If there is a really deep depression, such as in the 1930s, expansive fiscal policy may be *essential* to get up to the level of aggregate demand needed to get back to full employment reasonably promptly. This is because normal monetary policy working through open market operations may be ineffective as a means of quickly expanding the money supply. (This is explained in Chapter 9.) In such circumstances, fiscal policy is required as a tool for monetary expansion. The government can borrow from the central bank and spend the newly printed money, thus increasing the quantity of money in the hands of the public.

4. Expansive fiscal policy is effective in its own right, even if unaccompanied by an expansion in the money supply. In quantity theory terms, increases in government spending will lead to an increase in velocity, thus increasing aggregate demand.

These four views fade into one another at the edges, and it may be difficult in practice to identify which view is held by a specific classical writer. That a classical economist may favor fiscal expansion during periods of unemployment is, however, beyond doubt. In early 1933, Jacob Viner—who could not by any stretch of the imagination be considered a Keynesian—argued that:

> taxes have been an increasing burden on industry and have, more-over, had a perverse flexibility, rising during the depression period when it was peculiarly urgent that they should fall. . . .

* * * *

> The outstanding though unintentional achievement of the Hoover Administration in counteracting the depression has in fact been its deficits of the last two years. . . . Had the government and the business magnates retained their mental balance, there would have been less cause to fear net ill effects during a depression than during the war from even a *ten billion dollar deficit.*[11]

Gross national product at that time was $56 billion. While Keynesian theory is more conducive to fiscal policy activism than is classical theory, there is nothing in the classical theory which requires an economist to sit on his hands while the world disintegrates around him.[12]

KEYNESIAN ECONOMICS: A BRIEF OUTLINE

Keynes objected both to the classical aggregate supply function and to the classical aggregate demand function of Figure 2–1. First,

---

[11] Jacob Viner, *Balanced Deflation, Inflation, or More Depression* (Minneapolis: University of Minnesota Press, Day and Hour Series, 1933), pp. 8, 18–19 (italics added). Viner did, however, have some worries about the desirability of great fiscal expansion, hinted at in the above quotation. The Hoover administration had carried on a campaign stressing the need for "sound" finance and the desirability of a balanced federal budget. As a result of this stress on fiscal "soundness," Viner was concerned regarding the effects of large government spending programs on confidence. (As investment depends on the *expected* future profitability of business, it can be sensitive to changes in confidence.) In order to make the criticism bipartisan, it might be pointed out that Franklin Roosevelt in 1932 ran on a platform of balancing the federal budget. (In a speech on July 30, 1932, for example, Roosevelt urged: "Let us have the courage to stop borrowing to meet continuing deficits. Stop the deficits.")

[12] Indeed, Leijonhufvud argues that Keynes exaggerated the influence among classical economists of the British Treasury view—that fiscal policy was useless as a way of alleviating the depression. According to Leijonhufvud, "it may at least be questioned whether it (the Treasury view) was held anywhere outside London." See Axel Leijonhufvud, *Keynes and the Classics* (London: Institute of Economic Affairs, 1971), pp. 9–10.

Regarding classical views on fiscal policy, see also J. R. Davis, "Chicago Economists, Budget Deficits, and the Early 1930s," *American Economic Review,* June 1968; J. T. W. Hutchison, *Economics and Economic Policy in Britain* (London: Allen and Unwin, 1968); and Herbert Stein, *The Fiscal Revolution in America* (Chicago: University of Chicago Press, 1969).

while some classical economists had recognized the possibility of price stickiness, and had used this stickiness to explain *transitional* periods of unemployment following a downward shift of the aggregate demand curve, Keynes emphasized the length of time which prices could stay at or near their existing level even in the face of large-scale unemployment. In other words, the vertical aggregate supply function of classical economics did not represent the actual responses of the modern economy. Rather, a more realistic representation of aggregate supply—at least as a first approximation[13]— was a function that formed the reversed "L" of Figure 2–3. If aggregate demand is more than enough to provide full employment at

Figure 2–3
The simple Keynesian aggregate supply function

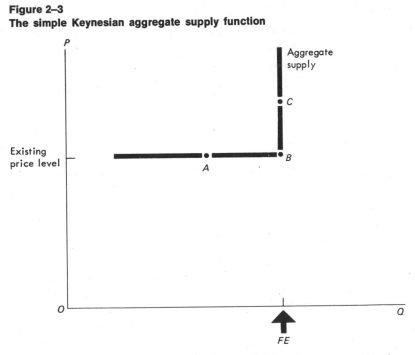

In Keynesian theory, downward inflexibility of wages and prices is persistent. Therefore, the aggregate supply function forms a reversed "L." In section *AB*—which is horizontal at the existing price level—changes in aggregate demand will result in a change in the equilibrium quantity of output, not in a change in prices.

---

[13] This is a simplified version, which is adequate to explain the major differences between Keynesian and classical economics. We will consider a more complex version of the Keynesian aggregate supply function in the appendix to Chapter 13.

the current price level, then prices will rise; the economy will move up the vertical section (*BC*) of the aggregate supply function. In this range, the Keynesian view corresponds to the classical view: too much demand will cause inflation. But, if aggregate demand falls short of the productive capacity at the existing price level, then unemployment will result. The economy will come to rest at a point (such as *A*) on the horizontal section of the aggregate supply function. Decreases in aggregate demand will cause the economy to move to the left, with higher rates of unemployment. Increases in aggregate demand will cause the economy to move to the right, toward the point of full employment, *B*. Thus, we come to a central proposition of the Keynesian revolution: Policymakers should forget about downward price flexibility and concentrate on demand management as a way of restoring full employment.

On the demand side, Keynes' objections to classical theory were equally strong. Of course, Keynes did not deny the equation of exchange. How could he, as it was true by definition? Rather, he denied that it was an *enlightening* place to begin the analysis of aggregate demand. Specifically, he denied the central proposition of the quantity theory—that velocity is stable. According to Keynes, velocity is pliable and elastic, particularly during a depression. An increase in the quantity of money might simply result in a decrease in velocity, with total demand remaining unchanged. Thus, it is not to the quantity of money that we should turn our attention.

Rather, the most enlightening way of studying aggregate demand is to study its major components. If we ignore the international sector for simplicity,[14] then aggregate demand is the sum of: (1) con-

---

[14] This is a standard simplifying assumption, which was made by Keynes himself in the *General Theory*. For the U.S. economy, in which the international sector is small, this simplifying assumption provides a reasonable starting point. (Even for the United States, however, the international sector can be quite important at times. For example, it is impossible to provide an adequate explanation of the path of the economy in the early 1970s without reference to international events, particularly the increase in the price of imported oil.)

It is perhaps surprising that Keynes abstracted from the international sector in the *General Theory*, since trade was relatively much more important for his British audience than for the United States. Furthermore, Keynes had himself shown very close interest in international economic affairs in his earlier works, particularly *The Economic Consequences of the Peace* (1919), which denounced the attempt by the victorious powers to extract reparations from Germany, and *The Economic Consequences of Mr. Churchill* (1925), which denounced the decision by the then Chancellor of the Exchequer, Mr. Winston Churchill, to return to the gold standard at the prewar price for gold in terms of sterling.

sumption demand, (2) investment demand, and (3) government demand.

1. *Consumption demand.* Of the three components of aggregate demand, consumption is by far the largest. In 1930, for example, consumption demand was 78 percent of the total; in 1975, it was 64 percent of the total. Consumption and its determinants therefore play a central role in Keynesian theory.

Keynes argued that consumption is determined primarily by the level of disposable income—that is, by take-home pay after such deductions as income taxes and social security taxes. In Chapter 3, we will explain the important role of consumption in Keynes' theory of aggregate demand.

2. *Investment demand.* Although investment demand is much smaller than consumption demand, it too plays a very important role in Keynesian theory. Indeed, it can be important precisely because it can be quite low. How can this be; how can a small size make something important? Because, said Keynes, if investment demand is low, then total demand in the private sectors of the economy— investment and consumption—may be too low to ensure full employment. A market economy, unaided by active government policies, can reach a point of large-scale unemployment. Moreover, during a depression, business executives are pessimistic; they are hesitant to undertake new investments in machinery and buildings. Large-scale unemployment may be a *lasting phenomenon* in a market economy.

Furthermore, said Keynes, even if investment demand does become great enough to ensure full employment, this happy outcome may be temporary. Why? Because willingness to invest depends on *business confidence;* and confidence is fragile. Investment responds sensitively to expectations and to the prospects for future sales. [Recall from Chapter 1 (Figure 1–1) that investment is a relatively volatile component of the economy.]

Thus, Keynes argued that the market economy might suffer from two major diseases. It might reach a lasting condition of unemployment—that is, an *unemployment equilibrium*—because of an insufficiency of investment demand. And, even if it did reach full employment, the economy might be *highly unstable.*

While both of these problems were prominent themes in *General Theory*, it is the equilibrium argument which is featured in textbook interpretations of Keynesian economics. And so it is here. The unemployment equilibrium argument is explained in Chapters 3 and 4, and the problem of investment and instability is deferred until Chapter 15.

3. Government demand. Because of the defects of the market economy, Keynesian theory placed two major responsibilities on the government. First, during a depression, the government should engage in public works and other spending projects to move the economy toward full employment. Then, once full employment is reached, the government has the responsibility to *stabilize* the economy, tightening up on fiscal policy when inflation threatens, and moving toward a more expansive policy when a recession is expected. (The role of fiscal policy is outlined in Chapter 4.)

FISCAL ACTIVISM AND THE TWO THEORIES OF DEMAND

Both the Keynesian and classical theories have considerable intrinsic appeal, as witnessed by their continuing vitality in the face of extensive attack. Each theory has its attractions, and each contains certain features which tend to repel some economists.

Each of the simple theories has the attraction of forming a simple, sensible, and coherent framework which may be used as a point of reference in interpreting the complex workings of the economy. Each theory, in short, provides a sensible framework for the orderly investigation of economic developments. It is precisely this intrinsic plausibility of each of the theories that argues against making either the exclusive focus of an introductory study. When plausible arguments are presented regarding the working of an economy, it is important that plausible arguments pointing in different directions also be presented.

Keynesian economics grew out of the Depression, and provided a coherent set of policy recommendations—centering on fiscal policy —to deal with the problem of unemployment. It is natural that whenever unemployment becomes a pressing problem, the appeal of Keynesian economics will rise. Keynesian economics, with its stress on the need for intervention in the economy to prevent business cycles, has a natural appeal for the activist economist who wishes to use the fiscal power of the government to increase the level of economic activity. The alternative classical theory seems to many economists to be a do-nothing theory.

Keynesian economics, moreover, has an appeal to those who feel that the natural public dislike of taxation puts an undue restraint on the level of government spending, and who would like to see a reallocation of resources away from the private sector of the economy toward government spending on hospitals, schools, welfare, and so on. Keynesian theory, with its assumption that the economy may slip into unemployment and stagnation in the absence of government action, and its basic policy recommendation that additional government spending is the best way to prevent this stagnation, is obviously a promising starting point for those who wish to see additional government spending. On the other hand, for economists who have reservations about the merit of a reallocation of resources toward the government sector, the Keynesian intellectual framework is likely to have little appeal, and, indeed, may be considered an easy and invalid way of creating a climate for additional government spending without presenting the detailed (and debatable?) case for the specific programs in question. To such economists, there is a natural appeal in the alternative classical framework, with its presumption that the economy will remain at relatively stable full-employment conditions if the government and central bank provide the appropriate stable monetary conditions; there is no general need for additional government spending to provide full employment.

But if there is a natural tendency for those who favor a reallocation of resources toward government spending to rally to the Keynesian banner, while those who are skeptical regarding the desirability of government spending adhere to classical economics, there is no logical *necessity* for those who favor additional government spending to adhere to Keynesian economics, or for those who oppose additional government spending to adhere to classical economics. That is, a "good Keynesian" can, without logical contradiction, take the view that government spending should not as a general proposition be increased, and that stimulation to the economy should be provided where necessary by a reduction in tax rates. A classical economist, on the other hand, taking the position that the provision of an orderly monetary expansion is the most important prerequisite for a relatively full-employment level of demand, may nevertheless with perfect logic take the view that the marginal social return to various government programs is high and that, therefore, additional resources should be committed to such programs.

Because of the general tendency for Keynesians to favor additional government spending and for classical economists to in general oppose it, it is particularly important that this distinction—between what is needed for the maintenance of a *full-employment* level of demand, and what is a desirable *allocation* of resources between the public and private sectors of the economy—be sharply drawn. There are two logically separable issues—the maintenance of an appropriate level of total demand, and the allocation of resources between the private and public sectors. The focus of this book is on the first of these questions; the allocation of resources is mentioned only peripherally and is left for detailed consideration in courses on taxation and government spending.

KEYNESIAN ECONOMICS AND CLASSICAL ECONOMICS: A SUMMARY

The main points of disagreement between Keynesian and classical economists are summarized in Table 2–1. A major purpose of this book is to investigate the reasons for these views and why disagreements exist. Part Two (Chapters 3–7) will explain the Keynesian unemployment equilibrium, the role of fiscal policy, and classical objections to the Keynesian theory of an unemployment equilibrium (Issues 2 and 5 in Table 2–1). Part Three investigates the role of monetary policy as a determinant of aggregate demand (Issue 6) and some of the causes of economic instability (Issues 3 and 4).

Through Parts Two and Three, we concentrate on aggregate demand because this was the major focus of the Keynesian revolution, and because differences regarding aggregate demand have been a major bone of contention between Keynesian and classical economists. In Part Four, we turn to aggregate supply (Issue 1 in Table 2–1). There, we must tackle one of the most bothersome problems of the past decade—the simultaneous existence of inflation and a high level of unemployment. Neither the Keynesian nor the classical aggregate supply function sheds much light on this question—at least not in their simple forms (Figures 2–1 and 2–3). In the simple versions of both theories, inflation occurs only when aggregate demand is "too high," that is, when the economy is producing at its full-employment capacity and still is incapable of satisfying aggregate demand at the existing price level. In Part Four, we also look at some of the additional complexities of the economy, including the causes of economic instability (Issue 3).

Table 2–1
Keynesian economics and classical economics: A comparison

Issue	*Keynesian*	*Classical*
1. Aggregate supply	Prices are downwardly inflexible; aggregate supply is a reversed "L" (Figure 2–3).	Although prices are sticky during periods of transition, they are flexible in the long run. The long-run aggregate supply function is vertical (Figure 2–1).
2. Equilibrium	There can be an equilibrium with large-scale unemployment.	Equilibrium involves full employment.
3. Stability	The market economy is highly unstable because of of the volatility of investment demand.	The market economy is by no means perfectly stable, but it shows a high degree of stability *provided the quantity of money grows steadily*.
4. The causes of the Great Depression of the 1930s	To explain the collapse of the economy, we should investigate why investment demand collapsed between 1929 and 1933.	To explain the collapse, we should investigate why financial institutions were so unstable, and why the money supply fell between 1929 and 1933.
5. Fiscal policy	Fiscal policy is the main policy tool to control aggregate demand, and thus the main tool for the attainment and maintenance of full employment.	There was a great variety of views among classical economists regarding the desirability of using fiscal policy to help achieve prosperity.
6. Monetary policy	When the economy is relatively close to full employment, monetary policy can play an important role in support of fiscal policy. However, it may be of little value—or even useless—as a way of stimulating the economy out of a depression.	Changes in the quantity of money are the key to changes in aggregate demand. From this basic proposition, classical economics breaks into two subdivisions: *a.* Monetary policy should be used as the central tool for stabilization policy. *b.* The monetary authorities should aim for a fixed, steady rate of growth of the money stock. Because of the basic stability of the market economy (see Issue 3), this will result in a reasonable stable economy.

QUESTIONS

1. Following Keynesian theory, suppose that unemployment can exist when the economy is in equilibrium. Suppose further that aggregate demand is completely unresponsive to increases in *M;* such increases do not cause an increase in the nominal national income. What does this imply about the fundamental classical equation, Equation (2–1), and about the quantity theory? (*Hint:* Specifically, what does it imply about velocity?)

2. Suppose, within the classical system, it is argued that an increase in government spending unaccompanied by an increase in the quantity of money will stimulate aggregate demand. What does this imply about the effect of fiscal policy on velocity? Why might fiscal policy be expected to affect velocity in this manner?

SUGGESTED READINGS

Milton Friedman and Walter W. Heller, *Monetary vs. Fiscal Policy: A Dialogue* (New York: W. W. Norton, 1969).

Herbert Stein, *The Fiscal Revolution in America* (Chicago: University of Chicago Press, 1969).

Dudley Dillard, *The Economics of John Maynard Keynes* (Englewood Cliffs, N.J.: Prentice-Hall, 1948), chaps. 1 and 3.

PART TWO

MODELS OF MACROECONOMIC EQUILIBRIUM

In particular, it is an outstanding characteristic of the economic system in which we live that, whilst it is subject to severe fluctuations in respect of output and employment, it is not violently unstable. Indeed it seems capable of remaining in a chronic condition of sub-normal activity for a considerable period without any marked tendency either towards recovery or towards complete collapse. Moreover, the evidence indicates that full, or even approximately full employment is of rare and short-lived occurrence.

John Maynard Keynes

Chapter 3

An introduction to Keynesian theory: The consumption function, equilibrium income, and the simple multiplier

Old men are always advising young men to save money. This is bad advice. . . . I never saved a dollar until I was forty.

Henry Ford

Since the appearance of Keynes' *General Theory*, the principal focus of macroeconomics has been on the determinants of aggregate demand. Yet in macroeconomics, as in microeconomics (which deals with the theory of the firm), it is necessary to have both a demand *and* a supply function to establish an equilibrium. Keynes provided a simple aggregate supply function—the "backward L" described in Chapter 2 (Figure 2–3).[1] This simple function lay behind most of the early Keynesian literature—whether the authors took the time to specify this function or not.

---

[1] As will be shown in the more detailed discussion of aggregate supply in Chapter 13, Keynes believed that for more sophisticated analysis, the aggregate supply function shown in Figure 2–3 should be modified.

Keynes' *General Theory* was written during a period of high unemployment; its major theme was the need to increase aggregate demand in order to increase the level of output. The basic Keynesian model was one in which there were unemployed resources, with increases (or decreases) in aggregate demand leading to changes in real output rather than changes in prices. (This is represented by the horizontal section *AB* of the aggregate supply function in Figure 2–3.) It was, of course, recognized that demand might be increased to the point of full employment—indeed, this was the purpose of Keynesian policy prescriptions—at which time further increases in demand would lead to increases in prices rather than increases in real output (the vertical section *BC* in Figure 2–3). Throughout this chapter, we will assume the simple Keynesian aggregate supply function and, furthermore, concentrate on the horizontal segment. Changes in aggregate demand lead to changes in real output, with the price level remaining unchanged. Thus, in the diagrams in this chapter, *no prices are shown: Since prices are assumed not to change, we may ignore them.*

THE CONSUMPTION FUNCTION

As we noted in Chapter 2, Keynes believed that the most enlightening way to investigate aggregate demand was to look at its components. When the international sector is excluded for simplicity, then:

$$\text{Aggregate demand} \equiv \text{Consumption demand} \\ + \text{Investment demand} \\ + \text{Government demand} \qquad (3\text{–}1)$$

Government spending constitutes the primary policy variable; it is by changes in this variable that the government can manipulate demand toward the full-employment level. The appropriate level of government spending, therefore, cannot be determined until we have looked at the other two components of aggregate demand and determined what level of spending is needed to bring aggregate demand up to the full-employment level. We will therefore defer consideration of the government sector for the time being. Thus, we initially consider a very simple two-sector economy, with only consumption and investment. Taxes will also be excluded from the introductory discussion. To simplify our analysis further, we will make the assumption—admittedly unrealistic—that we can take investment demand as a given constant.

That leaves us with consumption, the subject of the present chapter. Following Keynes, it seems reasonable to expect that consumption (C) depends on disposable income (Y_d), that is, on the amount of income people have left after taxes. (Since we are considering a very simple economy with no taxes, disposable income in this case is equal to total national income, Y.) Specifically, as people's incomes rise, they will consume more, but their consumption will not rise by as much as their income increases. The fraction of their additional disposable income that they consume is known as the marginal propensity to consume (MPC). Formally, we define

$$MPC = \frac{\Delta C}{\Delta Y_d} \qquad (3\text{--}2)$$

where

Δ means "the change in."

If, for simplicity, the MPC is assumed constant, this gives a consumption schedule of the type shown in the first two columns of Table 3–1, which is shown graphically in Figure 3–1. The same information may be written in the form of an equation:

$$C = 0.8Y + 200 \qquad (3\text{--}3)$$

In our simple world with no government spending, no taxation, and no international sector, saving is defined as the difference between income and consumption:

$$S \equiv Y - C \qquad (3\text{--}4)$$

Table 3–1
Consumption and saving (taxes assumed to be zero; Y, C, and S in $ billions at constant prices)

Y Income	C Consumption	MPC marginal propensity to consume $(\Delta C/\Delta Y)$	S Saving $(Y - C)$	MPS marginal propensity to save $(\Delta S/\Delta Y = 1 - MPC)$
500	600		−100	
		$\frac{400}{500} = 0.8$		$\frac{100}{500} = 0.2$
1,000	1,000		0	
		$\frac{400}{500} = 0.8$		$\frac{100}{500} = 0.2$
1,500	1,400		+100	
		$\frac{400}{500} = 0.8$		$\frac{100}{500} = 0.2$
2,000	1,800		+200	

Figure 3–1
The consumption function ($ billions)

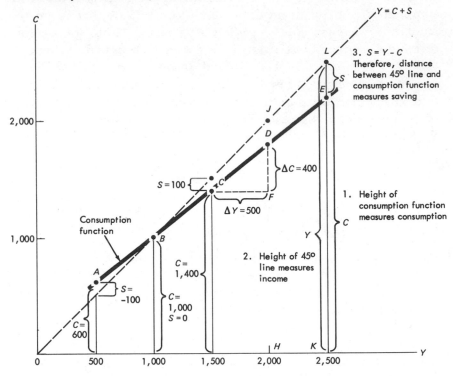

With a constant marginal propensity to consume, the consumption function is a straight line.

Figure 3–2
The saving function ($ billions)

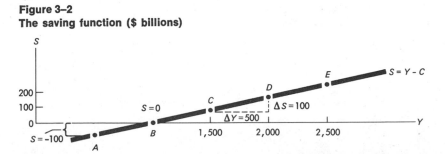

Since $S \equiv Y - C$, the saving function can be derived directly from the consumption function of Figure 3–1. At any level of income, the height of the saving function is equal to the vertical distance between the consumption function and the 45° line.

With this definition, saving can readily be derived from the first two columns of Table 3–1; this is done in column 4. Also, from Equations (3–3) and (3–4), a saving equation may be derived:

$$S = 0.2Y - 200 \qquad (3–5)$$

Likewise, a saving diagram may be derived from Figure 3–1. To aid in this process, a 45° line is drawn from the origin in Figure 3–1. This line has an obvious property—it represents all points equidistant from the two axes. If any point on the 45° line—such as *J*— is chosen, then the vertical distance to the 45° line (*HJ*) is equal to the level of income (*OH*). Thus, in this diagram, income may be measured either *horizontally* along the axis (*OH*), or *vertically* to the 45° line (*HJ*). Hence, both the horizontal axis and the 45° line are labeled as measuring income (*Y*). But, by rearranging Equation (3–4), we know that income is the sum of consumption plus saving. Thus, the vertical distance to the 45° line, *Y*, is also equal to *C* + *S*, and it is so labeled.

Now consider the situation when income is at *K* ($2,500 billion). The height of the consumption function (*KE*) indicates the amount of consumption at that income. But the total vertical distance to the 45° line—*KL*—measures income. Income less consumption—or *EL* —is a measure of saving. In general, the *vertical distance between the consumption function and the 45° line measures saving.* Thus, the saving function of Figure 3–2 may be derived directly from the consumption function. *Figures 3–1 and 3–2 represent precisely the same information presented in two different ways.*

It should be reiterated that, in presenting this simplified form of the consumption function, we have made a number of assumptions. First, we have assumed that the marginal propensity to consume is constant throughout; that is, we have assumed that the consumption function forms a straight line—an assumption that obviously makes graphical presentation easier and is even more important for a simple, algebraic formulation of the consumption function (Equation 3–3). Keynes, however, had some doubts about the constancy of the marginal propensity to consume, suggesting that it might decline as incomes rise.[2] This is a matter of some importance, but the detailed study of the consumption function will be deferred to Chapter 14 in order to keep the analysis simple.

The second thing that should be noted in writing the consumption function in this form is that we have tacitly assumed that there

---

[2] Keynes, *General Theory*, p. 31.

are unemployed resources and stable prices. Consumption behavior is primarily dependent on real income, not on money income. Thus, if a change in money income from \$1,000 billion to \$2,000 billion were to represent simply a doubling of prices rather than a doubling of real income, we would expect money consumption to rise to \$2,000 billion (that is, 2 times the initial consumption of \$1,000) rather than the \$1,800 billion shown in Table 3–1. The \$1,800 billion assumes that changes in money income represent changes in real income, that is, it assumes price stability. Clearly, if we wish to consider situations of excess demand and inflation, modifications will have to be made in the manner of presenting the consumption function.

But let us skip over these qualifications and consider the implications of the simple consumption function.

EQUILIBRIUM: THE SIMPLEST FORM

Equilibrium may be illustrated in its simplest form—although not very realistically—by assuming that there are only two major components of total demand, consumption and investment, with government spending being deferred for later consideration. In order to explain equilibrium output, we will need to distinguish sharply between *measured* magnitudes and *demanded* magnitudes. *Actual or measured* magnitudes—the quantities which show up in the national income accounts—are represented simply by capital letters. Thus, in our basic two-sector economy,

$$Y \equiv C + I \qquad \text{(3–6; from 1–1)}$$

where

Y is measured national income.
C is measured consumption.
I is measured investment.

Desired or demanded magnitudes are indicated with asterisks:

$$Y^* \equiv C^* + I^* \qquad \text{(3–7; from 3–1)}$$

where

Y^* is aggregate demand.
C^* is consumption demand.
I^* is investment demand.

If we assume—as we are assuming prior to Chapter 5—that investment demand is a given constant, say, $100 billion, then aggregate demand becomes:

$$Y^* = C^* + I^*$$
$$= 0.8Y + 200 + 100 = 0.8Y + 300 \qquad (3\text{--}8)$$

The information in Equation (3–8) may be depicted graphically in Figure 3–3. Equilibrium occurs at $1,500 billion, where the total aggregate demand function crosses the 45° line, that is, where aggregate demand is equal to national product (or national income). Using the alternative formulation in terms of a saving function, equilibrium occurs when saving equals the investment demand, again at $1,500 billion (Figure 3–4).

To see why this is the equilibrium point, it is helpful to suppose that, for some reason, total production is not at the $1,500 billion level. Suppose, for example, that production is running at the rate of $2,000 billion. What will happen then?

In this event, producers would be putting out $2,000 billion worth of goods and services, while there would be a demand for only $1,900 billion (consisting of $1,800 billion of consumption and $100 billion of investment). As a result, inventories of unsold goods would pile up; there would be *undesired* inventory investment. As a result, merchants would cut back on their orders, and production schedules would be cut back. The result would be a reduction in production to the $1,500 billion level. (In practice, production might fall *below* the $1,500 billion level while the unwanted inventory accumulation is worked off, after which it would recover to the $1,500 billion level. However, we are now beginning to get into dynamic questions which will be deferred to Chapter 15.)

During the period prior to the adjustment, production will be running at the disequilibrium rate of $2,000 billion. All production —the whole $2,000 billion—must go into either the consumption or investment category (since we have excluded the government and foreign sectors for the time being). But how can there be $2,000 billion of consumption and investment when the total consumption and investment *demand* is less than this?

To answer this question, we must go back to the distinction between *desired* investment and *actual* investment. Actual investment represents increases in plant, equipment, and inventories—*whether that inventory accumulation is desired or not*. With production running at $2,000 billion, consumer demand would be $1,800 billion.

Figure 3–3
Equilibrium income ($ billions)

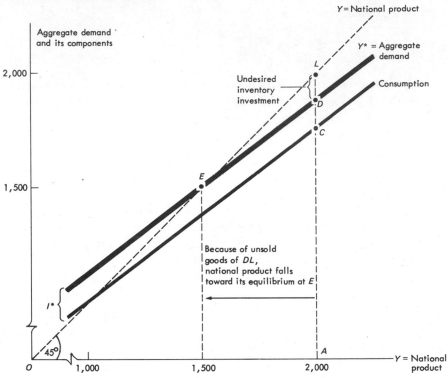

Note: Breaks in the axes allow the relevant part of the diagram to be enlarged.

Equilibrium occurs where the aggregate demand function cuts the 45°
line.

If income is at *A*, greater than the equilibrium income, total demand
will fall short of actual output. Unsold goods (amounting to *DL*) will pile
up and businesses will cut back on production.

Figure 3–4
Equilibrium of saving and investment ($ billions)

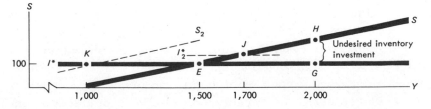

At equilibrium (*E*), investment demand (*I**) and saving are equal.

Actual investment would be $200 billion. But *desired* investment—*investment demand,* that is—would amount to only $100 billion. At the $2,000 billion level of production, therefore, there would be an *undesired* inventory investment of $100 billion. As noted above, it is this undesired accumulation of inventories which will lead to a reduction in production toward the equilibrium level of $1,500 billion.

A formal statement of the condition for equilibrium

The condition for equilibrium may therefore be stated in several alternative ways. Equilibrium occurs when aggregate demand equals output; when

$$Y^* = Y \qquad\qquad (3\text{--}9)$$

(This condition was illustrated in Figure 3–3.)

Consumers cannot be *forced* to purchase goods; we may assume that actual consumption equals consumption demand:[3]

$$C = C^* \qquad\qquad (3\text{--}10)$$

Thus, equilibrium occurs when desired investment equals actual investment:

$$I^* = I \qquad\qquad (3\text{--}11)$$

[This equation may readily be derived from Equations (3–9) and (3–10).[4] It also follows from our earlier discussion of undesired

---

[3] This assumption need not be valid during a wartime period of shortages and rationing. In such circumstances, consumers cannot buy all they want; consumption demand exceeds actual consumption. These circumstances have little relevance to the world which concerned Keynes, when there were plenty of goods to be bought but few buyers. In the Keynesian world, Equation (3–10) is eminently reasonable. Indeed, C and C^* can be used interchangeably without causing confusion. It is the distinction between actual investment (I) and investment demand (I^*) and between actual output (Y) and aggregate demand (Y^*) which are important in explaining the Keynesian equilibrium.

[4] From Equations (3–6) and (3–7), it follows that,

if

$$Y^* = Y \qquad\qquad (3\text{--}9)$$

and

$$C^* = C \qquad\qquad (3\text{--}10)$$

then

$$I^* = I \qquad\qquad (3\text{--}11)$$

inventory accumulation, which equals zero when Equation (3–11) is fulfilled.]

Furthermore, in our government-free economy, income goes into either consumption or saving:

$$Y \equiv C + S \qquad \text{(reordering of 3–4)}$$

Comparing this equation to Equation (3–6), it may be seen that, *by definition,* saving (S) and *actual* investment (I) are *identical* in this simple world; that is:

$$S \equiv I \qquad (3\text{–}12)$$

Thus, the condition for equilibrium (Equation 3–11) may be rewritten. Equilibrium occurs when saving and *desired* investment are equal:

$$\boxed{I^* = S} \qquad (3\text{–}13)$$

This is illustrated in Figure 3–4.

Thus, there are three different (but equivalent) ways of stating the equilibrium condition; namely, Equation (3–9), (3–11), or (3–13).

To illustrate the equilibrium level of $1,500 billion, we began by assuming that actual production exceeded that level, running at $2,000 billion. A similar illustration could be run through, assuming that the initial level of income is less than the equilibrium level. Suppose, for example, that it was initially $1,000 billion. In this case, total demand would be $1,100 billion, and therefore there would be an undesired running down of inventories by $100 billion. Orders would increase and production would increase to the equilibrium point of $1,500 billion.

SAVING AND INVESTMENT: THE PARADOX OF THRIFT

Stated in terms of the saving-investment diagram (Figure 3–4), equilibrium occurs when saving equals desired investment. And, behind this general statement, there is an important secondary proposition. Although saving and desired investment are *equal* in equilibrium, the saving and desired investment schedules are determined independently, and *saving does not cause investment.* Saving is what is left over from income after consumption has taken place. Desired investment depends on the expected profitability of new plant and equipment and inventories (as we shall see in

Chapter 5). If there is a tendency for saving to exceed desired investment—for example, if the initial level of income were at the disequilibrium level of $2,000 billion—then the level of income would fall until saving and desired investment are brought into equality. It is much more accurate to say that *desired investment causes saving* than the other way around, *at least in an economy with large-scale unemployment,* bumping along in the horizontal range of the aggregate supply function (*AB* in Figure 2–3). If desired investment were to increase—to say, $140 billion (as shown by the dashed line I_2^* in Figure 3–4)—then equilibrium income would increase to $1,700 billion and equilibrium saving would increase to $140 billion, at point *J*. (Observe that this increase in saving involves a *movement along* the saving function. An increase in investment demand causes a higher income and, with this higher income, people want to save more.) This relationship between desired investment and saving is fundamental to the Keynesian argument: Keynes was here attacking those classical economists who argued that additional *saving* automatically *causes* additional *investment*.

One further point of note: If, for some reason, there is an increase in the desire of the public to save rather than to consume, this can be illustrated as an upward shift in the saving function to the dashed line S_2 in Figure 3–4. What will happen in this case? Equilibrium saving will not actually increase, but rather *income and employment will fall until the public is satisfied with the preexisting level of saving;* with desired investment at $100 billion, income would fall to $1,000 billion in our illustration. *Increases in the desire to save do not lead to an increase in the equilibrium quantity of saving, but rather to a fall in the level of income.*

Indeed, the case can be put even more strongly. If the demand for investment rises with a rising income so that the investment function slopes upward to the right as shown in Figure 3–5, then an increase in the desire to save (that is, an upward shift to the saving function) will cause a *fall* in the equilibrium quantity of saving. An upward shift in the saving function from S_1 to S_2 will initially result in an attempt by consumers to increase their saving from *GA* to *GH* (Figure 3–5). But this attempt will cause unsold goods to pile up, as production exceeds aggregate demand. Income will consequently fall toward its new equilibrium level, *OJ*. Actual saving will *fall* from *GA* to *JB*, as a result of the *increase* in the desire to *save*. This is the *paradox of thrift.* An increase in the desire to save does not cause an increase in saving, but rather the opposite. It must be

Figure 3–5
The paradox of thrift

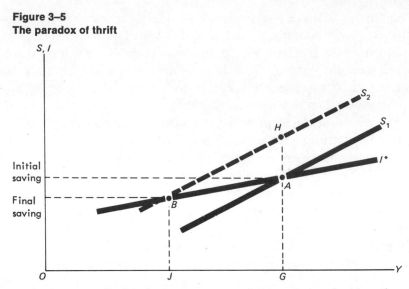

An increase in the *desire* to save —shifting the saving function up from S_1 to S_2—can cause a *fall* in the quantity of saving (from *GA* to *JB*).

emphasized that the paradox of thrift applies to an economy with large-scale unemployment (moving along the horizontal section of the aggregate supply function). In an economy with excess demand and rapid inflation, a fall in consumer demand will release resources for investment. An increase in the desire to save can thus cause an *increase* in investment and saving in equilibrium.

EQUILIBRIUM AT LESS THAN FULL EMPLOYMENT

The simple Keynesian diagrams (Figures 3–3 and 3–4) illustrate how the *equilibrium* level of national income is determined. It is most important to stress that the *equilibrium* income need not involve full employment. Indeed, the whole point of the Keynesian presentation is to demonstrate that *there may be a divergence between equilibrium income and the full-employment level of income.* The full-employment level of income at any period of time is determined by such factors as the size of the work force, the state of technology, and the amount of productive plant and equipment in place. A great unemployment problem would arise if these determinants of productive capacity combined to give a full-employment level of output significantly greater than the equilibrium level of income. This would be the case, for example, if the full-employment level of income were at the $2,000 billion level shown in Figure 3–6.

If the equilibrium level of income ($1,500 billion in our illustration) is less than the full-employment level of income ($2,000 billion), then aggregate demand will be inadequate to maintain full employment. Even if full employment were to exist temporarily, it would be an unsustainable level of output, since aggregate demand at that level of income would be less than the total full-employment level of production of $2,000 billion. Specifically, demand would total only $1,900 billion (composed of $1,800 billion of consumption demand and $100 billion of investment demand). This gap

Figure 3–6
Equilibrium income and the recessionary gap

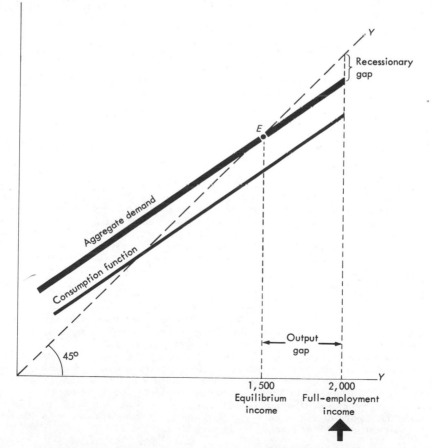

In equilibrium, national income may fall short of the level required for full employment.

between full-employment output ($2,000 billion) and the level of aggregate demand at that output ($1,900 billion) is known as the *recessionary gap* or the *deflationary gap*.[5] As a result of this recessionary gap—of $100 billion in our illustration—there would be undesired inventory accumulation and a reduction of production back to the $1,500 billion equilibrium level.

If aggregate demand exceeds output when output is at the full-employment level, then an "inflationary gap" exists. It is the vertical distance between the aggregate demand line and the 45° line at the full-employment level of national income.

SHIFTS IN THE AGGREGATE DEMAND FUNCTION: THE MULTIPLIER

So long as the consumption function and investment demand remain stable, then equilibrium national income will remain unchanged. But, from time to time, investment demand will in fact change. Investment depends on expectations regarding the future profitability of new buildings, machines, and equipment, and these expectations are subject to change as time passes.

Suppose that the outlook brightens and that investment demand consequently increases by $100 billion. Then, the aggregate demand function will shift up by the $100 billion, as shown in Figure 3–7. Observe that, as a result of the increase of $100 billion in investment spending, equilibrium national income will rise by much more than $100 billion; indeed, it will rise by $500 billion. How can that be? As businesses decide to build more factories or acquire more ma-

---

[5] Neither of these terms conveys precisely the right connotation. "Recessionary gap" implies a downward swing—or recession—in economic activity. Keynesian analysis, however, emphasized that large-scale unemployment might represent an *equilibrium*, with no tendency toward recovery but no continuing downward movement either. (This view is illustrated by the quotation from Keynes' *General Theory* which introduced Part Two of this book.)

"Deflationary gap" is even less satisfactory, since Keynesian analysis is based on the assumption that a deficiency of aggregate demand will result in unemployment and not deflation. ("Deflation" means a fall in prices; "inflation" means an increase in prices.) In drawing diagrams such as Figure 3–6, it is assumed that the economy is to the left of full-employment point *B* in Figure 2–3; changes in aggregate demand result in changes in real output, with prices remaining stable.

(The shape of the functions can change when aggregate demand moves beyond the point of full employment and inflation begins. Consumption, for example, responds differently to changes in prices and changes in real income. Strictly speaking, the aggregate demand function should not be extended beyond the full-employment output in Figure 3–6. However, this fine point is not always observed. In order to make the diagrams easier to follow, the functions are sometimes run beyond the full-employment output—for example, in Figures 3–7 and 3–8.)

Figure 3–7
A change in investment demand: The multiplier ($ billions)

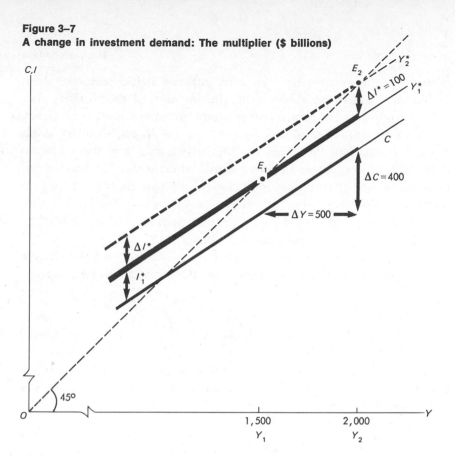

As a result of an increase of $100 billion in investment demand, equilibrium national income rises by $500 billion. This reflects the $100 billion increase in investment, plus $400 billion of additional consumption. The change in investment reflects a *shift* of the investment demand function. The change in consumption involves a movement *along* the consumption function as income rises.

Figure 3–8
The multiplier: An alternative presentation

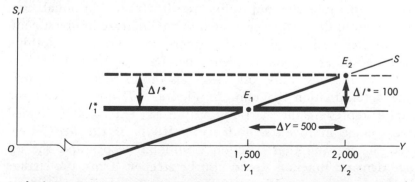

An increase in investment demand causes the equilibrium income to rise from Y_1 to Y_2. The new equilibrium is reached when income has increased enough to cause saving to rise by an amount equal to the new investment. Observe that the multiplier, $\Delta Y / \Delta I^*$, is equal to $1/s$.

chines, people are put back to work making bricks, cement, steel, machinery, and so on. As a result, the incomes of the workers rise. They respond by consuming more: they buy more food, cars, shoes, shirts, and so on. In turn, the farmers, auto workers, clothing workers, and others find their incomes increasing, and they also consume more as a consequence. In other words, the increase in investment demand causes an increase in income, and this in turn causes an increase in consumption. Indeed, we can see from Figure 3–7 that an increase of $100 billion in investment demand induces a total of $400 billion in additional consumption.

The relationship between the change in income and the change in investment demand is known as the *investment multiplier*. Formally,

$$\text{Investment multiplier} = \frac{\Delta Y}{\Delta I^*} \qquad (3\text{--}14)$$

In our example, with an *MPC* of 0.8, income rises by $500 billion as a result of the $100 billion increase in investment demand; the multiplier is thus 5.

In general,

$$\text{Multiplier} = \frac{1}{1-c} \qquad (3\text{--}15)$$

where

   c is the marginal propensity to consume.

Note that a rise in the *MPC* will cause an increase in the size of the multiplier. Because the multiplier results from additional consumption out of the income generated by the increase in investment, the multiplier will be higher if farmers, auto workers, clothing workers, and other income recipients spend a large fraction of their increases in income. This conclusion also follows from the basic income determination diagram. In Figure 3–7, observe that the multiplier represents the change in output $(Y_2 - Y_1 = 500)$ divided by the change in investment demand (100). If the *MPC* were greater, the consumption function would be steeper and the aggregate demand function would also be steeper. Thus, the change in income associated with any increase in investment would be larger.

An algebraic derivation

More formally, the multiplier equation (3–15) may be derived algebraically. Recall that the condition for equilibrium is that actual output equals aggregate demand:

$$Y = C^* + I^* \tag{3–16}$$

and hence,

$$\Delta Y = \Delta C^* + \Delta I^* \tag{3–17}$$

But we know that the marginal propensity to consume (c) is defined:

$$c \equiv \frac{\Delta C^*}{\Delta Y} \tag{3–18}$$

Thus

$$\Delta C^* = c\Delta Y \tag{3–19}$$

From Equations (3–17) and (3–19) it follows that

$$\Delta Y = c\Delta Y + \Delta I^* \tag{3–20}$$
$$\therefore \quad (1 - c)\Delta Y = \Delta I^* \tag{3–21}$$

From Equations (3–14) and (3–21), the equation for the multiplier (3–15) follows directly.

Furthermore, additional income is either consumed or saved. Thus,

$$s \equiv 1 - c \tag{3–22}$$

where

s is the marginal propensity to save.

Consequently, the equation for the multiplier (3–15) may alternatively be written:

$$\text{Multiplier} = \frac{1}{s} \tag{3–23}$$

This relationship is shown in Figure 3–8.

It must be stressed that the two equations for the multiplier— (3–15) and (3–23) —*apply only to the very simple economy* we have been considering so far. In particular, these simple formulations of the multiplier *do not apply in a more complex economy in which there is taxation or international trade.*

EQUILIBRIUM INCOME: THE BALANCE BETWEEN "INJECTIONS" AND "LEAKAGES"

The multiplier process results from the *circular flow of income:* When one individual spends, this provides income for a second person; from this income, the second person buys consumer goods and services, thereby providing income to a third person; and so on.

This circular flow of income may be illustrated most simply in the most basic of all economies; one in which there is no government and no investment demand—where, in other words, consumption is the sole component of demand. Such an economy is shown in Figure 3–1. The equilibrium level of income occurs where the consumption function cuts the 45° line, that is, at point *B,* with $1,000 billion in income. The level of national income is so low and people are so poor that they spend all their $1,000 billion in income on consumption.[6] The $1,000 billion spent on consumption goes to the producers of the consumer goods in the form of wages, salaries, and other payments. Again receiving $1,000 billion in income, people again consume the full $1,000 billion. Round and round the $1,000 billion circulates in the economy; and the economy remains at the equilibrium level of income of $1,000 billion (Figure 3–9).

Now, suppose that new inventions are made, the outlook brightens, and businesses decide to invest at the rate of $100 billion per period. Equilibrium national income rises to $1,500 billion, as shown in Figure 3–3. Alternatively, the results are illustrated in Figure 3–10. The $100 billion of investment represents an *injection* of spending into the income stream. Initially, with only $1,000 billion of consumption, the added $100 billion of investment causes an increase in income to $1,100 billion. But, with this higher level of income, consumers decide to spend more. How much more depends on the marginal propensity to consume. In our illustration, with an *MPC* of 0.80, consumers spend $80 billion more, adding to the size of the spending stream. What happens to the remaining $20

---

[6] Here, a distinction may be made between the *average* propensity to consume (*APC*)—defined as *C/Y*—and the marginal propensity to consume (*MPC*). Where the consumption function cuts the 45° line, the *APC* is 1; people consume all their income (point *B* in Figure 3–1). However, observe that the *MPC* is less than 1 at this point—the consumption function has a slope of less than 1. For the simple linear consumption function that we have been using, the *MPC* is constant. However, the *APC* becomes smaller as income rises. (For example, the *APC* is 1 at point *B* in Figure 3–1, and 0.9 at point *D*.)

Figure 3–9
The circular flow of income and expenditures: The simplest economy

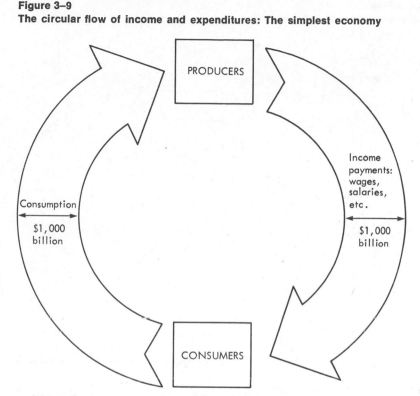

This simple economy, with no investment and no government spending, reaches equilibrium when people are willing to consume all their incomes (corresponding to point *B* in Figure 3–1).

billion? It is saved, not spent; it does not circulate round and round, rather it *leaks* from the spending stream.

With the $80 billion in additional consumption, the incomes of producers will rise. Again, they will respond to the higher incomes by consuming more, again the spending stream will broaden. And, as incomes continue to rise, saving will also rise. The process of expansion will go on until the leakages—in the form of saving—are equal to the injections—in the form of $100 billion in investment each period. Leakages will come to equal injections when national income has risen to its equilibrium of $1,500 billion. The equilibrium between investment demand and saving may be looked on as an equilibrium between injections into the spending stream and leakages from it. The amount by which the spending stream broad-

Figure 3–10
The circular flow: Investment added

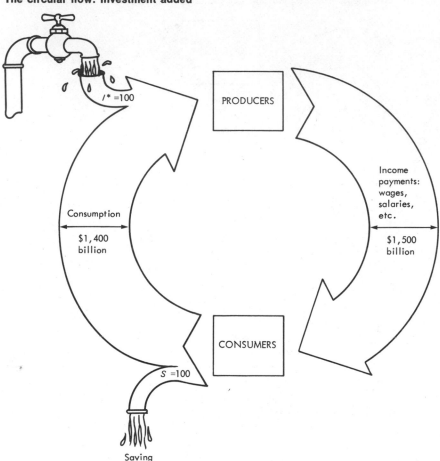

/* =100	PRODUCERS
Consumption	Income payments: wages, salaries, etc.
$1,400 billion	$1,500 billion
	CONSUMERS
S =100	

Saving

With the injection of $100 billion of investment into the spending stream, equilibrium national income rises to $1,500 billion (corresponding to point *E* in Figure 3–3).

ens depends on the "marginal rate of leakages," in this case, on the marginal propensity to save. As the multiplier formula indicates, the spending stream broadens by $1/s$ times the additional investment (Figure 3–8).

Other injections into the spending stream also have an expansive effect, for example, increases in government spending or in exports.

And there also are other leakages that affect the size of the multiplier. Of these other leakages, taxation is the most important. In the coming chapter, we will study additional injections and additional leakages, most notably those resulting from the direct activities of the government.

KEY POINTS

1. In simple Keynesian theory, it is customary to assume that changes in aggregate demand up to the full-employment level will lead to changes in (real) output, with no change in prices. Increases in demand beyond the full-employment level will result in increases in prices, and no change in output.

2. The most important determinant of consumption is income. In its simplest general form, $C = a + cY$.

3. Equilibrium occurs when total output is equal to aggregate demand. In the simplest economic system with no government and no international sector, equilibrium occurs when total output is equal to the sum of consumption demand and investment demand.

4. When output differs from the equilibrium level, undesired changes in inventories generate pressures to move toward the equilibrium level. If aggregate demand falls short of total output, there is an undesired buildup of inventories. Orders are cut back and production falls. On the other hand, if aggregate demand exceeds total output, inventories fall short of their desired levels. Orders are increased and output rises.

5. Equilibrium income may fall short of the full-employment level of output, in which case there will be unemployment. If aggregate demand exceeds the value of output at the full-employment level, then prices will rise. (This is an application of Point 1 above.)

6. An increase in investment demand will raise incomes and therefore stimulate consumption. Thus, the total effects on aggregate demand will be greater than the increase in investment demand (the multiplier).

QUESTION

1. In a simple economy with no government and no international sector,

    Total national income $\equiv$ Consumption $+$ Investment

    But, in addition, income is either consumed or saved, and thus

    Total national income $\equiv$ Consumption $+$ Saving

    These two equations are always true, whether the economy is at equilibrium or not (as shown by $\equiv$). Therefore, saving is always equal to investment. How can this be reconciled with Figure 3–4, which shows that saving and investment are equal only when the economy is in equilibrium?

SUGGESTED READING

Walter W. Heller, *New Dimensions in Political Economy* (New York: W. W. Norton, 1967), chap. 2, "The Promise of Modern Economic Policy."

Chapter 4

Fiscal policy

. . . Fiscal policy has to be put on constant . . . alert. . . . The management of prosperity is a full-time job.*

Walter W. Heller

The private components of demand—consumption and investment—may be sufficiently high to ensure the full-employment level of output. This possibility was illustrated in the final example of Chapter 3 (point E_2 in Figure 3–7). But there is no guarantee that market forces will lead to this happy result. Investment may remain at a low level, and consequently an unemployment equilibrium may persist. In this case, Keynes' principal policy prescription becomes relevant: *The government should spend enough to push the economy to the full-employment level.*

In order to increase aggregate demand to the full-employment level, the government should undertake additional spending *equal*

---

* From "The Promise of Modern Economic Policy," in Heller, *New Dimensions of Political Economy* (New York: W. W. Norton, 1967), p. 69.

to the size of the original recessionary gap.[1] (In a situation of *excess* aggregate demand and inflationary pressures, the appropriate policy is a *cut* in government spending equal to the inflationary gap.)

Let us reconsider the unemployment equilibrium described in Chapter 3 (Figure 3–6). In this illustration, the recessionary gap was $100 billion; $100 billion is therefore the appropriate amount of government spending. Aggregate demand is the sum of consumption, investment, and government demand. Thus, when government demand is introduced, we can simply add it vertically to the original consumption and investment demand. This is done in Figure 4–1. (The alternative injections-leakages formulation is presented in Figure 4–2. Here, there is only one leakage—saving—since taxes have not yet been introduced. There are two injections: investment and government spending.) Observe that when government spending of $100 billion is added, then equilibrium national income increases by $500 billion; the multiplier process and the basic multiplier formulas $(1/1 - c$ or $1/s)$ also apply to government spending (although we may now speak of the "government multiplier," defined as $\Delta Y/\Delta G^*$).

Once more, we should stress that the multiplier in this simple form $(1/1 - c$ or $1/s)$ applies only to a world with *no taxation and no international transactions.* How can such a simple world possibly be worth considering? How can the government spend without taxing? The answer is that the government can engage in *deficit spending;* that is, the government can borrow to finance its expenditures. Indeed, this is a fundamental proposition of Keynesian economics: *If the government wants to create a large increase in aggregate demand* and national income by government spending, *it should not raise taxes to finance that spending, but borrow instead.* As we shall see shortly, an increase in taxation to pay for the spending would tend to offset the stimulative effect of the government expenditures.

THE MULTIPLIER: A SINGLE GOVERNMENT EXPENDITURE VERSUS CONTINUING EXPENDITURES

If there is an unemployment equilibrium, then the policy objective is to *move* to full employment and *stay* there; there is a need

---

[1] In the example introduced in Chapter 3, we considered a situation where there was no government spending initially. In this simple case, "additional" government spending and total government spending are obviously the same thing. In the more realistic case where there is some government spending to begin with, government spending should be *increased* by the amount of the deflationary gap.

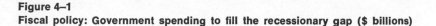

Figure 4–1
Fiscal policy: Government spending to fill the recessionary gap ($ billions)

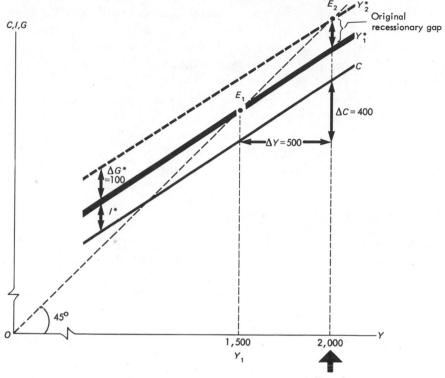

In an economy caught in an unemployment equilibrium, the government should increase spending by enough to fill the original recessionary gap. Observe that as a result of $\Delta G^* = \$100$ billion, consumption increases by $400 billion and income rises by $500 billion.

Figure 4–2
Fiscal policy: The injections-leakages formulation ($ billions)

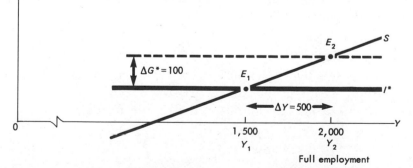

Note: In this simple illustration, there is government spending but no taxation.

The information in Figure 4–1 may be shown in this alternative diagram.

for a *permanent* increase in aggregate demand. In order to provide for such a permanent increase, the government will have to raise spending and *keep it at the higher level*. In the above example (Figure 4–1), we assumed just such a permanent government spending program; the aggregate demand function shifts permanently up to Y_2^*.

If, in contrast, the government engages just in a single expenditure, spending $100 billion during one period but nothing in following periods, then the economy will gradually fall back to its original equilibrium. In order to contrast sharply the effects of a single and a continuing expenditure, we will consider each in detail.

A single government expenditure

If the government spends $100 billion on the purchase of goods and services during an initial time period (t_1), then workers and suppliers of equipment and materials will find their incomes increased by the $100 billion. They will therefore be in a position to increase their consumption, and they may be expected to do so. It is, however, reasonable to expect some *lag* between the increase in income and the increase in consumption; thus, for example, the income of time t_1 may affect consumption in the next period (t_2). With a marginal propensity to consume of 0.8, the recipients of income during period 1 will increase their consumption by $80 billion during t_2; they will buy more shoes, shirts, cars, and so on. The producers of shoes, shirts, and cars will therefore find that their incomes rise by $80 billion and, with an *MPC* of 0.8, they in turn will increase their consumption by $64 billion during the third time period; and so on. This will give a stream of spending as shown in Table 4–1. The total effects of the original government expenditure are the series shown in the last column: 100, 80, 64. . . . This is a series of the general form

$$k + kc + kc^2 + \cdots + kc^{n-1} + \cdots \qquad (4\text{–}1)$$

As long as c is less than 1 (which it clearly is in this case, being 0.8), the sum of this geometric progression taken to an infinite number of periods may be found by the simple formula:

$$\text{Sum} = \frac{k}{1 - c} \qquad (4\text{–}2)$$

where

k is the initial injection ($100 billion in the example).

Applying this formula to the series in the last column of Table 4–1, we get the $500 billion sum shown at the bottom of the column.

Once again we see the multiplier process at work. But here there is a difference from our earlier examples. The multiplier in the present case does not represent the relationship between the change

Table 4–1
The multiplier effects of a single government expenditure ($ billions)

Time period	Assumed government spending G	Effects on spending for: C	I	Total
1	100	0	0	100
2	0	80	0	80
3	0	64	0	64
4	0	51.2	0	51.2
.	.	.	.	.
.	.	.	.	.
n	0	$100 \times 0.8^{n-1}$	0	$100 \times 0.8^{n-1}$
.	.	.	.	.
.	.	.	.	.
$\to \infty$	0	$\to 0$	0	$\to 0$
Sum	100	400	0	500

in the *equilibrium* level of national income and the change in the *permanent* level of government spending. Rather, it represents the relationship between the *total flow of income* into the indefinite future which results from a *single* government expenditure. But, after this distinction is made, the same basic multiplier equations (3–15) and (3–23) can be applied. In the present example, with an *MPC* of 0.8, the total effect on income is $500 billion as a result of the initial government expenditure of $100 billion.

The basic proposition here—that a single-shot government expenditure will lead to a series of consumption expenditures but will not permanently change the equilibrium national income—is illustrated in Figure 4–3, which shows the expenditure effects in the last column of Table 4–1.

Figure 4–3
The multiplier: A single government expenditure

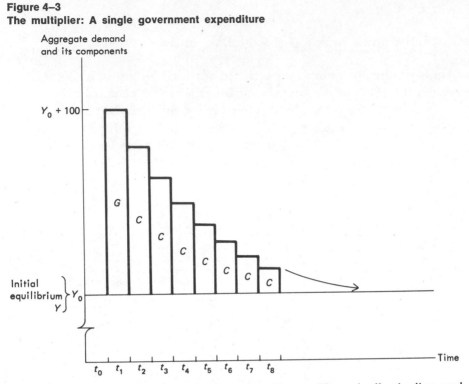

The effects of a single government expenditure will gradually decline and the economy will fall back toward its initial equilibrium.

A continuing injection of government spending

If the economy is at an equilibrium at less than full employment, a single, short-run program of government expenditures does not provide a solution; we have seen that the effects of the single government expenditure will peter out as time passes. Although there was much talk of government "pump priming" during the depression of the 1930s, the simple Keynesian model suggests that something more fundamental than pump priming may be needed. The indicated solution is rather a *continuing* program of government expenditures.

Consider a *continuing* program of government expenditures of $100 billion in *each* time period. In the first period, as before, aggregate demand will be increased by the $100 billion. In the second period, consumers as a result will spend $80 billion more; there will, moreover, be a second government expenditure of $100

Figure 4–4
The multiplier: A continuous injection of government spending

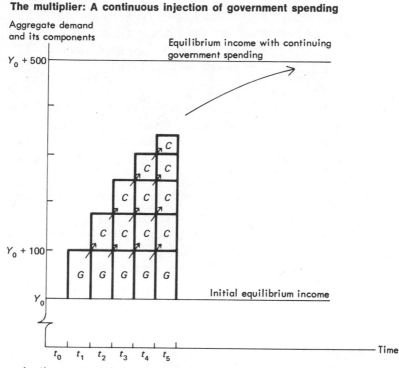

Aggregate demand
and its components

Equilibrium income with continuing
government spending

$Y_0 + 500$

$Y_0 + 100$

Y_0

Initial equilibrium income

Time

t_0 t_1 t_2 t_3 t_4 t_5

In the event of *continuing* government spending, the economy
will approach a new, higher equilibrium, up by the amount of government spending times the multiplier.

billion. Aggregate demand will therefore be increased by a total of
$180 billion in the second period. In the third period, the effects
on aggregate demand will be the sum of three components:

1. The $100 billion in new government spending.
2. Consumption of $80 billion, resulting from the $100 billion in
    incomes flowing from the government spending in the second
    period.
3. Consumption of $64 billion, resulting from the $80 billion con-
    sumption of the second period, which in turn was a result of the
    government spending of $100 billion in the initial period.

This gives a pattern of expenditure as shown in Figure 4–4. In this
case of a continuing expenditure, the multiplier gives the relationship between the increase in *equilibrium* income ($500 billion in
our illustration) and the government spending per period.

TAXATION: THE EFFECTS ON THE CONSUMPTION FUNCTION

*There is one difference between a tax collector and
a taxidermist—the taxidermist leaves the hide.*

Mortimer Caplin, Commissioner of
Internal Revenue, 1963

Thus far, the simplifying assumption has been made that only one side of fiscal actions is considered, namely, government spending. But taxes, alas, cannot be avoided forever. Not only are they miserable to pay, but they add a messy complication to the simple illustrations of income determination and the multiplier principle. The complication is that a distinction must now be drawn between total income and disposable income; consumption depends on the disposable income of the consuming public.

What this means is that, when taxes are imposed, the consumption and saving functions must be moved as functions of total income. Two simple illustrations may be used to show the effects of two different types of tax.

A lump-sum tax

First, consider the case—admittedly unrealistic—where taxes are collected as a lump sum (of, say, $100 billion) *regardless of the level of income of the taxpayers.* How does this affect the consumption function? Consider the example shown in Table 4–2 and illustrated

Table 4–2
Consumption with a lump-sum tax ($ billions)

A. Before tax

Consumption	National income (equals disposable income when taxes are zero)	Point in Figure 4–5
1,800	2,000	*J*
1,880	2,100	*K*

B. After tax of $100 billion

For consumption to be	Disposable income must be	Which means national income (before tax) must be	Point in Figure 4–5
1,800	2,000	2,100	*L*
1,880	2,100	2,200	*M*

With $100 tax (in Part B), national income must be $100 greater to maintain any given level of consumption.

in Figure 4–5. Prior to the imposition of taxes, disposable income and national income are identical. For consumption of $1,800 billion, disposable income and national income must be $2,000 billion (point J). For the same rate of consumption *after* the imposition of taxes, disposable income must still be $2,000 billion. But now, with the tax ($T = \$100$ billion), national income must be $2,100 billion in order for consumers to pay the $100 billion tax and still have $2,000 billion in disposable income. Thus, the tax causes point J to shift to the *right* by the amount of the tax, to point L. The same is true for every other point on the consumption function; the function *shifts to the right by the amount of the tax.*

This effect of taxation may alternatively be described as a *down-ward* shift of the consumption function. Observe, however, that the downward shift is not a full $100 billion. With an *MPC* of 0.8, point L is only $80 billion below point K. In general, the tax causes the consumption function to *shift down by the tax times the MPC.*

Thus, taxes are almost as powerful a tool for affecting aggregate demand as are changes in government spending. Almost, but not quite. Recall that $100 billion of government purchases will shift the aggregate demand function up by the full $100 billion (Figure

Figure 4–5
A lump-sum tax ($ billions)

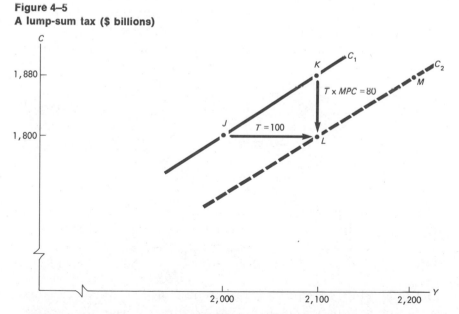

With a lump-sum tax, the consumption function shifts down by the tax times the *MPC*.

4–1). A $100 billion cut in taxation will shift the consumption function—and therefore the whole aggregate demand function—up by only $80 billion (with an *MPC* of 0.8). But, although they are less effective, tax changes may in practice have a major advantage over changes in spending as a fiscal policy tool: Tax changes may be less controversial. Thus, changes in taxation have in fact played an important role in fiscal policy. For example, taxes were cut in 1964 and again in 1975, with the explicit intention of stimulating aggregate demand. In 1968, taxes were increased to restrain aggregate demand and reduce the inflationary pressures associated with the war in Vietnam. Finally, President Carter suggested a tax rebate early in 1977, in order to provide stimulus to the economy and reduce the amount of unemployment. The rebate proposal was, however, withdrawn in April 1977, when inflation showed signs of accelerating (and when substantial opposition to the proposed rebate developed in Congress).

The balanced budget multiplier

Because the effect of $1 of government spending is somewhat larger than the effect of $1 of taxation, there is a small net effect if G and T are changed by the same amount. The change in government spending causes aggregate demand to shift up by ΔG; the tax causes a downward shift by $\Delta T \times MPC$. Thus, for a *balanced budget change*, with $\Delta G = \Delta T$, there is a net upward shift in the aggregate demand function of:

$$\Delta G - \Delta T \times MPC \qquad (4\text{--}3)$$

or

$$\Delta G - \Delta G \times MPC \qquad (4\text{--}4)$$

that is

$$\Delta G(1 - MPC) \qquad (4\text{--}5)$$

The multiplier process works on this shift in the aggregate demand function, just like it works on other shifts. In the simple case,

$$\text{Multiplier} = \frac{1}{1 - MPC} \qquad (4\text{--}6; \text{repeat of } 3\text{--}15)$$

The total effect on equilibrium national income therefore equals (4–5) times Equation (4–6), or ΔG. Thus, we have the *balanced budget theorem:* A balanced change of both G and T causes national income to go up by ΔG. The balanced budget multiplier, $\Delta Y/\Delta G$,

therefore is *one*. (At least, it is one in this simple theoretical framework.)

A tax proportional to income

Although a lump-sum tax allows us to consider a very simple case,
it is unrealistic. In the real world, taxes rise as incomes rise. Consider
a case where taxes are a constant fraction of pretax income, for
example, 25 percent. Then the effects on the consumption function
are illustrated in Table 4–3 and Figure 4–6. Just as a constant, lump-

Table 4–3
Consumption and saving schedules with proportional taxation ($ billions)

Figure 4–6 Point	National income (Y)	Disposable income $(Y_d = 0.75Y)$	Consumption $(C = 0.8Y_d + 200;$ $C = 0.6Y + 200)$	Personal saving $(S = Y_d - C)$
A............	500	375	500	−125
B............	1,000	750	800	− 50
C............	1,500	1,125	1,100	+ 25

sum tax shifts each point on the consumption function to the right
by a *constant* amount, so a proportionate tax moves each point on
the consumption function to the right by a *proportionate* amount.
In other words, the proportionate tax causes consumption (as a
function of national income) to rotate clockwise about the intercept
on the vertical axis (point *D* in Figure 4–6).

Observe that a proportional tax has two effects:

1. The tax causes a downward rotation of the consumption function. Thus, the *imposition* of the tax causes a *fall* in equilibrium
   national income.
2. The tax makes the consumption function *flatter*. As a consequence, the *existence* of the tax makes the *multiplier smaller*.
   And the *higher* the marginal tax rate, the *lower* will be the
   multiplier. (The *marginal tax rate* is defined as the change in
   tax collections as a fraction of the change in national income,
   that is, $\Delta T / \Delta Y$.)

THE MULTIPLIER IN AN ECONOMY WITH TAXES

In an economy with a marginal tax rate, *t*, an increase of $100
in total income will cause an increase in disposable income of

Figure 4–6
Consumption function with a proportional tax ($ billions)

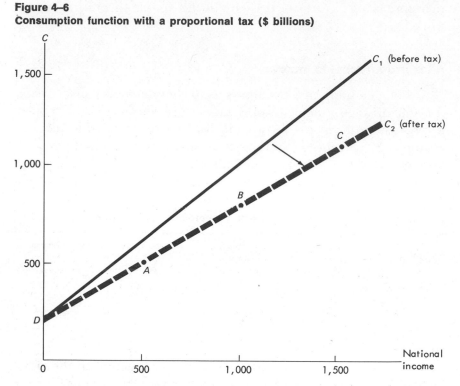

A proportional tax causes a clockwise rotation of consumption, as a function of national income.

$(1 - t) \times \$100$. With an *MPC* of *c,* the consumption resulting from this increase in income will be $c(1 - t) \times \$100$. Thus, in Figure 4–6, the slope of the consumption function is $c(1 - t)$. But the slope of this line determines the size of the multiplier. In the very simple economy without taxes, the slope of the consumption function is equal to *c* and the multiplier is $1/(1 - c)$. By analogy,[2] we may conclude that in an economy with taxes and with a consumption function having a slope of $c(1 - t)$,

$$\text{Multiplier} = \frac{1}{1 - c(1 - t)} \qquad (4\text{–}7)$$

---

[2] It may be proved algebraically in a manner similar to that used in Chapter 3 to derive the simple multiplier.

$$\Delta Y = \Delta C^* + \Delta I^* + \Delta G^* \qquad (4\text{–}8)$$

While this multiplier is beginning to become complex, it should be stressed that Equation (4–7) nevertheless still applies only to a *very* simple economy. The international sector has not yet been included, and complications such as corporation saving have been ignored. (International trade is discussed in the appendix to this chapter.) One thing does, however, stand out even from this initial introduction of a single complication into the multiplier: With the introduction of taxation, the multiplier becomes smaller. For example, in our illustration in which a marginal tax rate of 25 percent is introduced into a system with an *MPC* of 0.8, the multiplier drops from 5 to 2.5 (Table 4–4).

AUTOMATIC STABILIZERS . . .

Because taxes reduce the size of the multiplier, they add stability to the economy. Consider the effects of an upswing in investment demand. Because investment spending raises the incomes of those who produce capital goods, it will stimulate consumption; a multi-

---

Let us consider the multiplier $(\Delta Y / \Delta I^*)$ following a change in investment demand. We thus set

$$\Delta G^* = 0 \tag{4–9}$$

The marginal propensity to consume is defined:

$$c = \frac{\Delta C}{\Delta Y_d} \tag{4–10}$$

Thus

$$\Delta C^* = c \Delta Y_d \tag{4–11}$$

The change in disposable income is:

$$\Delta Y_d = \Delta Y - \Delta T \tag{4–12}$$

The marginal tax rate, t, is defined:

$$t = \frac{\Delta T}{\Delta Y} \tag{4–13}$$

that is,

$$\Delta T = t \Delta Y \tag{4–14}$$

From Equations (4–12) and (4–14),

$$\begin{aligned} \Delta Y_d &= \Delta Y - t \Delta Y \\ &= (1 - t) \Delta Y \end{aligned} \tag{4–15}$$

From Equations (4–8), (4–9), 4–11), and (4–15), it follows that

$$\Delta Y = c[(1 - t)\Delta Y] + \Delta I^* \tag{4–16}$$
$$\Delta Y [1 - c(1 - t)] = \Delta I^* \tag{4–17}$$

From which we readily derive the multiplier equation shown above:

$$\text{Multiplier} = \frac{\Delta Y}{\Delta I^*} = \frac{1}{1 - c(1 - t)} \tag{4–7}$$

Table 4–4
The multiplier*

	Economy with zero taxes		Economy with taxes $= tY$	
	In numbers	In symbols	In numbers	In symbols
1. A change in income of $100 means a change in Y_d of:.................	$100	$100	$75	$100(1 - t)$
2. This involves a change in C of:	$ 80	$100 \times c$	$60	$100 \times c(1 - t)$
3. Thus, the slope of the consumption function is:	0.8	c	0.6	$c(1 - t)$
4. And the multiplier is: ...	5	$\dfrac{1}{1 - c}$	2.5	$\dfrac{1}{1 - c(1 - t)}$

* Assumptions: $c = 0.8$ and $t = 0.25$.

plier process will be set in motion. But with leakages out of the spending stream in the form of taxation, the upswing will be weakened. Similarly, when investment declines, the existence of taxation will moderate the downswing; tax collections will *automatically* tend to fall, moving the budget into deficit.

While almost any tax system will have some built-in stabilizing character, the *degree* to which tax collections respond to changes in income will vary with the specific characteristics of the taxes. A progressive income tax exerts a high degree of built-in stabilization. The social security tax involves a weak built-in stabilization. (Social security taxes are a flat 11.7 percent on wages and salaries up to a maximum of $16,500 per worker. The 11.7 percent is collected in halves, one from the employer and one from the employee. On incomes greater than $16,500, no tax is collected. Thus, an upswing in personal incomes during a boom leads to a less-than-proportional increase in tax collections, and consequently results in a weak automatic stabilization.) [3] General sales taxes are in the middle of the spectrum, changing roughly in proportion to changes in aggregate demand.

The expenditure side may also involve built-in stabilization. Certain expenditures—of which payments to the unemployed are

[3] The maximum income subject to social security tax—amounting to $16,500 in 1977—has been repeatedly raised and is expected to reach $27,900 by the mid-1980s. These increases in the maximum reflect primarily the need for additional revenues to finance higher social security benefits. (This attention to the social security tax is warranted because the tax has become an increasingly important component of total taxation, rising during the past two decades from about 15 percent of total federal government revenues to about 30 percent.)

the most obvious—will rise during recessions and fall during booms, thus cushioning the change in aggregate demand. *Unlike the taxation side, however, there is no general presumption that government expenditures will tend to stabilize the economy;* indeed, the government itself may be a major source of economic instability. Most clearly, when governments become involved in wars, they spend large amounts in an inflationary and destabilizing manner.[4]

In the period following World War II, economists gave considerable thought to the improvement of automatic stabilizers. The sense of urgency was heightened by fears that the postwar economy might be subject to major fluctuations and perhaps even to a repeat of the disaster of the 1930s. However, when the postwar economy proved to be more stable—at high rates of employment—than economists generally had anticipated, the sense of urgency was reduced.

. . . AND FISCAL DRAG

Then, during the 1960s, the automatic stabilization function of taxes fell into partial disrepute. Automatic stabilizers reduce *fluctuations* in the economy. But, in the early 1960s, the problem was seen *not* so much as one of *instability,* but rather one of getting aggregate demand up to the level needed for full employment; aggregate demand was reasonably *stable but inadequate.*

In a discussion that was soon to become quaintly dated, economists worried about *fiscal drag*—the tendency of tax receipts to rise as business expands, thus acting as a drag on the growth of aggregate demand needed for full employment in an expanding economy. The rise in tax receipts tends to move the government's budget into a surplus; that is, a *fiscal dividend* is created. President Kennedy's advisers stressed the importance of using the fiscal dividend to undertake new spending programs or to cut taxes. In either case, the fiscal drag would be removed and the basis laid for a healthy expansion of aggregate demand. Thus, the tax cut of 1964 was a way of using the fiscal dividend and of reducing the fiscal drag on aggregate demand.

---

[4] The problem of destabilizing fiscal actions has not, however, been confined to wartime periods. For the experience prior to the extensive involvement in the Vietnam war, see Wilfred Lewis, Jr., *Federal Fiscal Policy in the Postwar Recessions* (Washington, D.C.: Brookings Institution, 1962). Lewis concluded (p. 18) that "discretionary fiscal actions of the federal government were sharply contractionary during the recession of 1953–54, were mildly expansionary in 1948–49, and were approximately neutral during the other recessions. The story during the recovery phases is less favorable. . . ."

As it turned out, strong forces were being unleashed on the spending side, which would have wiped out the fiscal dividend even in the absence of the tax cut of 1964. Most conspicuously, the rapid escalation of the war in Vietnam involved large expenditures; to a significant degree, the fiscal dividend was blown up in southeast Asia. Furthermore, the big new domestic spending programs of President Johnson's Great Society put additional strain on the budget. As it turned out, there was no strong tendency for the budget to move into surplus as the expansion continued in the mid-1960s. On the contrary, government spending was creating a dangerously inflationary situation by 1966; a tax *increase* by that time had become appropriate as a means of cooling off the overheated economy. But President Johnson was unwilling to accept the political costs of a tax increase; the income tax surcharge was delayed until 1968.

But that was not the end of the story. In 1974–75, the U.S. economy suffered its most severe and persistent recession since the 1930s. Even as the recovery began, there were fears that a high level of employment might not be restored until 1980—or even later. Once again, concerns of fiscal drag and a lasting inadequacy of aggregate demand came to the fore. As a consequence, taxes were cut in 1975.

One final point should be emphasized. Although they carry quite different connotations, "fiscal drag" and "automatic stabilizer" are two different terms for exactly the same phenomenon: the built-in tendency for the tax system to stabilize the economy. Two different terms are used, not because of differences in the way the tax system works, but because of differences in the underlying conditions in the economy. *If* the problem is one of *short-term fluctuations* in aggregate demand, then fiscal arrangements that smooth out changes are desirable. A positive-sounding term is appropriate, and the term "automatic stabilizer" is used. *But if* the problem is one of a *persistent inadequacy* of aggregate demand, then the tendency of the tax system to stabilize the economy at a low level is undesirable; the term "fiscal drag" is in order.

A POLICY TRAP: THE ANNUALLY BALANCED BUDGET

The public finance system provides automatic stability to the economy, with falling tax collections helping to maintain the disposable incomes of consumers during recessions. These falling revenues, of course, tend to cause deficits in the government's budget.

And herein lies a major policy trap. If policymakers follow the superficially plausible rule of *balancing the budget, then they will cancel out the automatic stabilization of the budget; the economy will be destabilized.* During a recession, when tax collections fall as a result of declining incomes, governments may cut back spending in order to balance the budget. But this is precisely when an *increase* in spending is desirable—to soften the recession. Alternatively, tax rates may be increased with the same objective of balancing the budget. Again, the effects will be perverse: Aggregate demand will be suppressed and the recession deepened. The Hoover administration fell into this policy trap. The Depression was made worse by strong efforts to balance the budget—including a major increase in tax rates in 1932. If a balanced budget is taken as a rule of thumb, then inflationary booms may also be worsened. Constraints on government spending will tend to be relaxed as government revenues rise during a boom. But this is precisely the time when government restraint is particularly needed.

One of the major contributions of Keynesian economics was to warn against this dangerous policy trap. Government expenditures and taxes should not be tailored to a balanced budget, said Keynes. Rather, they should be tailored to the desired path of aggregate demand, aiming at the avoidance of large-scale unemployment on the one hand, and inflation on the other.

THE PROBLEM OF THE APPROPRIATE MEASURE OF FISCAL POLICY: THE FULL-EMPLOYMENT BUDGET CONCEPT

A major policy conclusion of Keynesian economics is that expansive fiscal policy—in the form of either additional government spending or tax cuts—is the appropriate response to conditions of inadequate demand and unemployment. A superficial look at economic history suggests, however, that there is a paradox in this policy prescription, since government deficits have tended to be high during periods of depression and recession. How can this be, if deficit spending is indeed a stimulus to economic activity?

The answer lies in the two-way causation between government deficits and economic activity. Steps taken to increase the government deficit—additional spending or tax cuts—will tend to stimulate the economy. There is, however, also a line of causation running in the opposite direction: A slowdown in economic activity will reduce tax revenues flowing to the government and cause a deficit in the government budget. It is this effect of economic activity on tax revenues that lies behind the discussion of automatic stabilization, and it is this effect that is responsible for the historical association of government deficits with economic recessions.

What this means is that, in interpreting historical or current budgetary data, we cannot take the size of the actual government deficit as an *indicator* of fiscal policy. A large deficit may not reflect *policies* taken to stimulate the economy, but rather the effects of an economic downturn on tax revenues.

What is needed, then, if we are to *measure* the expansive or contractionary nature of fiscal policies, is something other than the *actual* budgetary position of deficit or surplus. The indicator of fiscal policy used to avoid this difficulty is the *full-employment surplus* (or deficit). What the full-employment budget measures is not the difference between actual government revenues and expenditures, but rather the difference between revenues and expenditures that *would exist if the economy were operating at full employment.* Specifically, it represents the difference between:

1. Federal revenues that would be collected with the existing tax rates if the economy were at full employment, and
2. Federal expenditures that would occur with the existing spending programs if the economy were at full employment. (This is equivalent to actual federal expenditures, less those expenditures—such as payments to the unemployed—associated with unemployment in excess of the "full-employment" level, usually taken to be 4 percent of the labor force.)

While the full-employment budget concept avoids the gross problems that would arise if the actual budgetary position were taken as the indicator of fiscal policy, it is not without its limitations. Specifically, the following criticisms have been made of the full employment budget as a measure of fiscal policy:[5]

1. The rate of inflation affects tax revenues. Why is this so? Because the income tax law has progressive rates (that is, taxes rise as a percentage of income, as income rises), and taxes are

---

[5] For a discussion, see Joint Economic Committee, U.S. Congress, *The Impact of Inflation on the Full Employment Budget,* July 30, 1975. This pamphlet includes studies by Murray L. Weidenbaum, "Shortcomings in the Full Employment Budget"; Nancy H. Teeters, "Current Problems in the Full Employment Concept"; and Robert C. Vogel, "The Responsiveness of State and Local Receipts to Changes in Economic Activity: Extending the Concept of the Full Employment Budget."

based on income measured in *dollars*. Clearly, the increases in tax revenues due to inflation do not reflect a change in fiscal policy. But they do affect the full-employment budget measure; the full-employment budget automatically tends to move into surplus as a result of inflation. Therefore, the full-employment budget can be a misleading measure of fiscal *policy* during periods of inflation.

2. Some federal operations are not included in the budget, and therefore both the actual accounting budget and the full-employment budget are incomplete indicators of the impact of the federal government. (Most notably, only the specific budgetary subsidy received by the Postal Service is included; other operations of the Postal Service have been excluded from the budget since 1972.)

3. State and local government expenditures have been rising as a share of total government expenditures in the United States. Thus, the full-employment budget—which measures only *federal* government operations—has become an increasingly incomplete measure of the effects of the government sector on the economy.

4. The full-employment budget treats every dollar of federal expenditures as having the same expansive effect on the economy; and this effect is assumed to be equal in size (but opposite in sign) to every dollar of tax revenue. Yet it is reasonable to argue that some government expenditures—such as purchases for goods and services—will have a greater effect on aggregate demand than will some other expenditures—such as the government payment of interest on the national debt.[6]

5. The full-employment budget is based on the assumption that a 4 percent unemployment rate represents "full employment."

---

[6] If the government spends $1 on road building, then national product is directly increased by the $1 of roads built. There is a second-round effect when workers on the road consume a large fraction of their incomes; and so on. When the government pays out $1 in interest, there is no first-round effect on national product. Furthermore, the recipients of interest may not consume as large a fraction of their income as the workers on the road.

Observe that a $1 government expenditure on roads exactly offsets a $1 tax receipt in its effects on the full-employment budget. Thus, the full-employment budget measure implies that the balanced budget multiplier is zero, in contrast to the balanced budget multiplier of one indicated by Keynesian theory.

For a suggested weighting of various government expenditures and receipts aimed at overcoming this shortcoming of the full-employment budget measure, see Arthur Okun and Nancy Teeters, "The Full Employment Surplus Revisited," *Brookings Papers on Economic Activity*, 1970, vol. 1, p. 85.

Yet there is a heated debate among economists as to whether this low rate of unemployment can be reached on a sustainable basis with our present labor market institutions. (This important— and difficult—problem is put off until Chapter 13.)

The full-employment budget is not, therefore, by any means a perfect measure of the expansive or contractionary nature of government policy. However, most economists would argue that, as a starting point for evaluating fiscal policy, it is clearly superior to the actual budgetary position.[7] But the real world is complex; the expert cannot rely on any simple single figure for budgetary analysis. It is most unlikely that economists will agree on a weighting system which can be used to develop a more refined indicator of fiscal policy. The full-employment budget concept is not very good, but it is the best we have.

The difference between the actual budget of the federal government and the full-employment budget is shown in Figure 4–7. Note that *the full-employment budget has less tendency than the actual budget to swing into deficit during recessions.* This is because recessions do not reduce "full-employment" tax revenues but they *do* reduce actual revenues.

On the basis of the full-employment budget measure, fiscal policymakers must be given a mixed report card. There were two substantial stabilizing actions: The tax surcharge of 1968 acted as a restraint on the overheated economy, and the 1975 tax cut stimulated the economy during the worst recession since the Great Depression of the 1930s. But, on the other hand, the deficits of 1966–68 and 1972 contributed to the overheating of the economy and inflationary pressures.

APPENDIX

MORE COMPLEX MULTIPLIERS

In Chapter 3, we saw that there are two ways of looking at economic equilibrium in a simple economy with only two sectors, con-

---

[7] There are, however, exceptions—for example, Murray Weidenbaum in his essay cited earlier. Warren Smith was also very skeptical regarding the full-employment budget, although for different reasons. See his comment in the *Brookings Papers on Economic Activity*, 1970, vol. 1, p. 91.

Figure 4–7

The federal budget, quarterly, 1947–1977: Actual and full employment (national income accounts basis, seasonally adjusted annual rates)

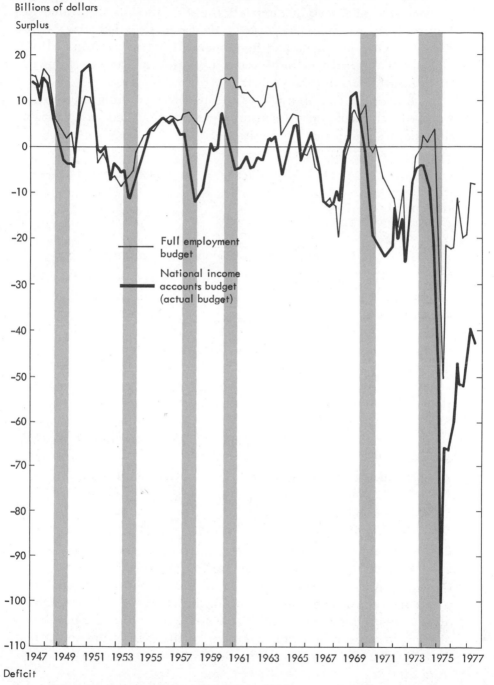

Source: Federal Reserve Bank of St. Louis, *Federal Budget Trends.*

During recessions, the actual budget swings sharply into deficit since a decline in national income automatically causes a reduction in tax collections.

sumption and investment. First, equilibrium occurs where the aggregate demand function intersects the 45° line (as illustrated in Figure 3–3). Alternatively, *exactly the same situation* may be illustrated with the saving and investment diagram; equilibrium occurs when the leakages into saving are equal to the injections of investment demand (Figure 3–4).

Each of these two alternatives has its corresponding multiplier. First, concentrating on the consumption function and on aggregate demand, we found that the multiplier was:

$$\text{Multiplier} = \frac{1}{1 - c} \quad \text{(4–18; repeat of 3–15)}$$

In general,

$$\text{Multiplier} = \frac{1}{1 - \text{Slope of consumption function}} \quad \text{(4–19)}$$

This more general version was applied to an economy with taxes; taxes affect the slope of the consumption function, and therefore the size of the multiplier, as we saw earlier (Equation 4–7).

Consider now the alternative injections-leakages approach. When we deal with a complex economy with many injections and many leakages, this is the most straightforward approach. In the most basic economy, with no taxes and only a single leakage (saving), we saw that:

$$\text{Multiplier} = \frac{1}{s} \quad \text{(4–20; repeat of 3–23)}$$

This equation also may be stated in a more generalized form:

$$\text{Multiplier} = \frac{1}{\text{Marginal rate of leakages}} \quad \text{(4–21)}$$

Concentrating on this equation, let us reconsider the economy with a marginal tax rate of t. As we saw earlier, taxation rotates not only the consumption function clockwise as a function of national income; it does the same for the saving function (see Figure 4A–1, drawn from the last column of Table 4–3). And, just like the slope of the consumption function, the slope of the saving function is reduced by the tax. Specifically, the slope of the saving function falls from s to:

$$\text{Slope of saving function} = s(1 - t) \quad \text{(4–22)}$$

Figure 4A–1
Saving function with a proportional tax

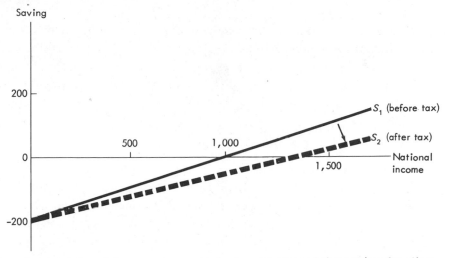

A proportional tax causes a clockwise rotation of the saving function, similar to the effect on the consumption function. (Compare this diagram to Figure 4–6.)

or, alternatively:

$$\text{Slope of saving function} = s - st \qquad (4\text{--}23)$$

However, the multiplier (Equation 4–21) depends not only on the leakage into saving; it depends on *all* leakages from the spending stream. What other leakages are there? Taxation is one such additional leakage. Income extracted from the public in the form of taxation is not used in the next round of consumption. Thus, in an economy with taxation, we must add the marginal rate of taxation, *t*, to the saving leakage in order to get total marginal leakages:

$$\text{Marginal rate of leakages} = s + t - st \qquad (4\text{--}24)$$

But the multiplier is equal to the reciprocal of the marginal rate of leakages; thus:[8]

---

[8] The equivalence of Equation (4–25) and the version based on the consumption function may be proved algebraically. Substituting

$$s = 1 - c$$

into Equation (4–25), we readily derive our earlier multiplier equation:

$$\text{Multiplier} = \frac{1}{1 - c(1 - t)}$$

$$(4\text{--}26; \text{ repeat of } 4\text{--}7)$$

$$\boxed{\text{Multiplier} = \frac{1}{s + t - st}} \qquad (4\text{–}25)$$

Now let us consider an even more complex economy. The complete form of the national income equation is:

$$Y \equiv C + I + G + X - Z \qquad (4\text{–}27; \text{ repeat of } 1\text{–}1)$$

where

X stands for exports of goods and services.
Z stands for imports of goods and services.

Like investment and government spending, *exports* represent an *injection* into the spending stream, on which the multiplier process operates. Those working in export industries derive incomes from the exports; these incomes (after tax subtractions) may be used for purchases of consumer goods, adding to the size of the circular flow of income.

On the leakages side, imports should appear. Insofar as consumers spend for imported shoes, for example, those consumption expenditures do not enter into the *domestic* income stream; the payments go to foreigners. Thus, if we define:

$$\text{Marginal propensity to import} = z = \frac{\Delta Z}{\Delta Y} \qquad (4\text{–}28)$$

we may add the marginal leakage into imports, z, to the other marginal leakages in the denominator of the multiplier, thus obtaining:

$$\text{Multiplier} = \frac{1}{s + t + z - st} \qquad (4\text{–}29)$$

Unfortunately, this is not the end of the complications. For example, corporations may hold part of their profits back, not distributing them to stockholders in the form of dividends. In this case, the multiplier will be further complicated by a leakage into undistributed profits.[9]

KEY POINTS

1. The government can raise aggregate demand to the full-employment level by increasing its expenditures on goods and services

---

[9] For a more elaborate series of multipliers, see Warren L. Smith, *Macroeconomics* (Homewood, Ill.: Richard D. Irwin, Inc., 1970).

by the amount of the recessionary gap. This increase in government spending has a multiplied effect, similar to that which follows from an increase in investment spending.

2. The simple Keynesian model suggests that the effects of a single government expenditure will peter out over time, and the economy will tend to return to its initial equilibrium. For a continuing higher level of aggregate demand, continuing government expenditures may consequently be required.

3. Taxation causes the consumption function to rotate clockwise. Thus:
   a. The *imposition* of taxes lowers the consumption function and consequently reduces aggregate demand.
   b. The *existence* of taxes makes the consumption function flatter (as a function of national income). It thus reduces the size of the multiplier.

4. The lower multiplier may be desirable. It involves *automatic stabilization;* swings in aggregate demand are reduced. But it may also be pernicious, slowing down healthy economic expansion. In this case, the term *fiscal drag* is used.

5. If the government attempts to keep the budget in balance each year, it will cancel out the automatic stabilization, thereby increasing the swings in the economy. Expenditures will be cut or taxes raised during recessions, adding to the downward movement of aggregate demand.

6. Because the actual budget responds automatically to changes in economic activity, it is not a good indicator of fiscal policy. The full-employment budget is a better measure (although it is far from perfect).

QUESTION

1. Consider the simple economy with no government or taxes, and suppose that

$$C = 200 + 0.9Y_d$$

and

$$I^* = 300$$

   a. What will the equilibrium level of national income be?
   b. Now suppose that a government sector is introduced, with

$G = 100$, while taxes remain zero. What will equilibrium
national income become? Comparing this answer with the
answer to part *a,* what value is found for the multiplier?

c. Now suppose that taxes $= \frac{1}{6}Y$. What is the equilibrium
level of national income now?

d. With this consumption function and this rate of taxation,
what is the multiplier? Derive your answer by assuming that
G rises to 200, and compare the new equilibrium to the
equilibrium income found in part *c.*

SUGGESTED READINGS

Council of Economic Advisers, *Annual Report,* 1963, pp. 45–51, section headed "Tax Revision: Impact on Output and Employment"; reprinted under heading "The Workings of the Multiplier" in Arthur M. Okun, *The Battle against Unemployment,*
rev. ed. (New York: W. W. Norton, 1972), pp. 54–62.

Milton Friedman, *Capitalism and Freedom* (Chicago: University of
Chicago Press, 1962), chap. 5, especially pp. 79–84, reprinted
under the heading "Weak Links in the Multiplier Chain" in
Okun, *The Battle against Unemployment,* pp. 63–68.

Chapter 5

Investment in the simple Keynesian equilibrium system: The marginal efficiency of investment, the rate of interest, and liquidity preference

---

The safest way to double your money is to fold it over once and put it in your pocket.

Kin Hubbard

In the preceding chapters, two of the three principal components of aggregate demand were considered: consumption, which depends primarily on the level of disposable income; and government spending, which is determined by public policy. In this early discussion, the level of investment demand was taken as a given constant for simplicity. The determinants of investment demand will now be considered.

In the original, simple Keynesian system, the quantity of desired investment is determined by:[1]

1. The rate of return of investment, that is, the *marginal efficiency of investment (MEI)*.
2. The rate of interest, which is in turn determined by:
   a. The demand for money, or *liquidity preference (L)*.
   b. The stock of money *(M)*.

THE INVESTMENT DEMAND FUNCTION: THE MARGINAL EFFICIENCY OF INVESTMENT

In making a decision whether to invest—by, for example, buying a new machine—businesses weigh the expected costs and benefits. There are two costs:

1. The capital cost of purchasing and installing the machine. This price of capital goods will be designated P_K.
2. The interest charges which will have to be paid on the money borrowed to buy the machine. Alternatively, if the businesses already have the needed money at hand from retained profits or other sources, the use of this money to purchase the machine has an opportunity cost—for example, what they could earn by using the money to purchase interest-bearing securities. The interest rate will be represented by i.

On the other hand, they expect to receive a stream of future benefits from the investment in the form of enhanced productivity, lower labor costs per unit of output, or other benefits attributable to the machine. This stream of expected future returns is designated as $R_1, R_2 \ldots R_n$, where the subscripts stand for consecutive future periods, and the machine is expected to have a useful life of n periods.[2]

---

[1] Present-day economists would not apply this theory in the simple form presented in this chapter, but would rather opt for the more sophisticated treatment of Chapter 6. In all conditions but those of depression—the situation with which Keynes was most concerned—the treatment of the demand for money is inadequate in the simple equilibrium model in this chapter. (Specifically, the transactions demand for money is inadequately dealt with, for reasons which will be explained in Chapter 6.) This simple Keynesian model is presented for two reasons: (1) It was the simple model used by early Keynesian economists; and more important (2) it is a necessary building block, to be used in the development of the more sophisticated model of Chapter 6.

[2] Defined strictly, $R_1, R_2 \ldots R_n$ are the increases in revenues resulting from the purchase of the machine, net of all costs except those from the initial cost of the machine (P_K), and except the interest costs associated with the carrying of the machine. Suppose that, as a result of a purchase of a machine, total revenues in year n would be $1,000 higher, labor and materials costs would be $600 higher (since more would be produced), and repairs on the machine would be $100. Then $R_n = \$300$.

Table 5–1
Compound interest

Value of $100 at end of year	With $i = 10$ percent	Or, in general
1	$110	$100 $(1 + i)$
2	$121	$100 $(1 + i)^2$
3	$133.10	$100 $(1 + i)^3$
.	.	.
.	.	.
.	.	.
n	$100 $\times$ 1.1^n$	$100 $(1 + i)^n$

In weighing the relative costs and benefits of the proposed invest-ment, it is necessary to use the concept of compound interest. For simplicity it is assumed that periods of one year are considered, and that interest payments are made once yearly at simple annual rates. Table 5–1 illustrates the total accumulation from an initial $100, with interest at 10 percent per annum.

If we have $100 now, it will, with interest, be worth $110 at the end of a year. Therefore, if we expect to get $110 at the end of the year, this will have a *present value* of $100. (There is an implicit as-sumption here, that we can borrow at the same rate as we can lend; that is, there is a *single* interest rate.) In general, the expected re-ceipt of a specific number of dollars, R, after n years will have a present value of

$$PV = \frac{R}{(1 + i)^n} \tag{5–1}$$

From this formula, the present value of investment may be calcu-lated:

$$PV = \frac{R_1}{1 + i} + \frac{R_2}{(1 + i)^2} + \frac{R_3}{(1 + i)^3} + \cdots + \frac{R_n + S_n}{(1 + i)^n} \tag{5–2}$$

where

PV is the present value of the investment.
$R_1, R_2 \ldots R_n$ are the expected future returns.
S_n is the scrap or resale or other residual value of the investment at the end of n years.
i is the rate of interest.

This equation can be used for judging whether an investment proj-ect should be undertaken. If the cost of the machine is less than the present value, the investment should be undertaken, provided that appropriate allowance has been made for risk. If the cost is just equal to the present value of the returns, the investment is a matter of indifference; if the cost is greater, the investment should not be undertaken. Put another way, the right side of Equation (5–2) can be used to calculate the *maximum* the business would be willing to pay for the investment project.

In Equation (5–2), the rate of interest (*i*) was taken as given, and the equation was solved for the present value of the machine or other proposed investment. Alternatively, an equation of the same form can be used to calculate the rate of return on a prospective investment, thus:

$$P_K = \frac{R_1}{(1+r)} + \frac{R_2}{(1+r)^2} + \frac{R_3}{(1+r)^3} + \cdots + \frac{R_n + S_n}{(1+r)^n} \quad (5\text{--}3)$$

where

P_K represents the price of the capital good.

r represents the rate of return on the investment.

r is the unknown for which we are solving [in contrast to Equation (5–2), in which *PV* was the unknown].

Equation (5–3) can be used by the business (or by the society)[3] to determine the desirability of undertaking investment projects. Ranking the possible investments for the coming year by the height of their expected return, the business executive might calculate (for

---

[3] Although, if the *social* desirability of a project is to be determined, all the social costs and benefits should be included, not just the costs and benefits to the business. Does the investment cause pollution and, if so, what is the measure of this pollution cost? Does the investment create employment and, if so, what is the social benefit flowing from this effect? And so on.

The important point here is that Equation (5–3) is the relevant basis for calculation, whether the individual is making the investment decision or whether the social desirability is being evaluated. The distinction between the individual and social goals determines which costs and benefits are to be included in the calculation, but does not affect the logic of Equation (5–3).

The logical validity of Equation (5–3) caused headaches for early Soviet planners, who were under strict ideological inhibitions against implying that the concept of interest payment was valid. In dealing with major alternative projects involving quite different lives and, most specifically, in evaluating the relative desirability of hydroelectric plants as compared with thermal power stations (where the initial capital cost is lower but the annual running costs are higher than for hydro plants), Soviet planners tended to get tied in knots, and to settle for logically imperfect substitutes for Equation (5–3), such as the payoff period concept. Their ideological squeamishness, combined with the general Soviet fascination with the heavy and grandiose, led to overcommitment to large and costly hydroelectric projects. In the post-Stalin period, enthusiasm for large projects has waned; in particular, the Soviets became concerned with the rigidities of huge projects. See Raymond Hutchings, *Soviet Economic Development* (Oxford: Basil Blackwell, 1971), pp. 81, 90, 209–12.

example) that a truck costing $10,000 would earn the highest return, 20 percent; that a stamping machine would return 15 percent on an investment of $20,000; that a new set of office machines costing $10,000 would return 10 percent; and that a drilling machine costing $15,000 would earn 5 percent. This will give the investment demand by this business shown in Figure 5–1. Because of the lumpi-

Figure 5–1
Investment demand (individual business in $000)

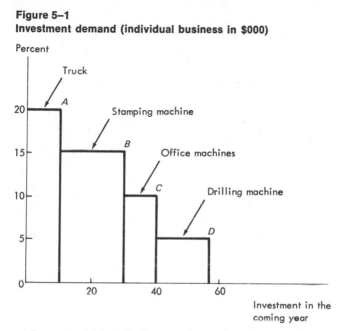

Possible investments may be ordered according to their expected returns. This indicates which investments may be profitably undertaken at various interest rates.

ness of projects, the investment demand of an individual business is represented by a number of specific points (*A, B, C, D* in Figure 5–1) rather than by a smooth, continuous function. When the demands of all businesses are added horizontally, this lumpiness disappears. A continuous investment-demand curve—or marginal efficiency of investment[4] curve—is derived for the economy as a whole

---

[4] Keynes labeled this function the marginal efficiency of capital. However, marginal efficiency of investment is a more precise term, since what is under consideration is the rate of return on *new* investment and not on the *total* stock of capital (which includes capital already in place).

Figure 5–2
Investment demand: The marginal efficiency of investment ($ billions)

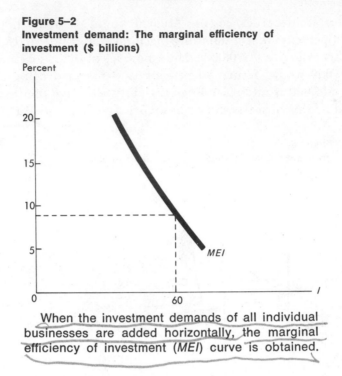

When the investment demands of all individual businesses are added horizontally, the marginal efficiency of investment (*MEI*) curve is obtained.

(Figure 5–2). With this function, the level of desired investment can be determined once the rate of interest is known. If, for example, the rate of interest were 8 percent, the level of desired investment would be $60 billion. For the individual business shown in Figure 5–1, the first three investments would be undertaken, but the drilling machine would not be purchased, since it would not earn enough return to cover the interest costs. If, alternatively, the interest rate were 12 percent, then the individual business would also decide against the purchase of the office machines. For the economy as a whole, a 12 percent interest rate would cause a fall in investment demand to $50 billion.

By changing the interest rate, monetary policy affects investment demand and hence aggregate demand. We now turn to the determination of the interest rate.

THE RATE OF INTEREST

Although the Keynesian system downgraded the importance of

monetary policy, it is important to recognize that in the Keynesian system the interest rate is primarily a *monetary* phenomenon *determined by the demand for and the supply of money*. The "supply of money" in the Keynesian system means the total *stock* of money (M) existing in the economy at any particular time. In line with simple Keynesian expositions, the supply of nominal money is taken as a given constant determined by the central bank.

The "demand for money" is the willingness of people to hold money. There are two major reasons for holding money—the transactions motive and the speculative motive.[5] The *transactions motive* represents the desire to hold money in order to be able to engage in ordinary transactions, buying goods or services. The receipt of income is not perfectly synchronized with the desired time pattern of expenditures; money is held as a convenient way of bridging the time between receipts and expenditures. The desire to hold money for transactions purposes will vary with the level of expected purchases; note that the transactions demand is primarily a function of income.

The transactions motive was inherent in the classical approach to monetary theory. Classical economists argued that money was held so that purchases of goods and services could be made. Consequently, they argued that an increase in M would lead to an increase in purchases (PQ). Hence, the transactions motive represented no particular innovation on Keynes' part. Rather, his innovation lay in his exposition of the *speculative motive* for holding money. The speculative motive concerned the relative attractiveness of money and interest-bearing securities as a means of holding wealth through time.

Consider first a simple economy with only two types of financial assets—money and long-term bonds. If people desire to hold assets through time, should they hold these assets in the form of money or in the form of interest-bearing securities? At first glance, the answer might seem obvious; why should people wish to hold money over and above their transactions needs if they have the alternative of buying bonds and receiving interest payments? But, to Keynes, this was a rhetorical question demanding the wrong answer. People might prefer to hold money because of the *risk* involved in the hold-

---

[5] Keynes also included a third element in the demand for money, the precautionary motive. We ignore this third motive, as it is not essential in understanding the main points of Keynesian theory.

ing of bonds; specifically, the loss from a *fall in the price of bonds* might more than wipe out the returns in the form of coupon payments on the bonds.

The price of bonds can be calculated from an equation similar to Equation (5–2), which was used to calculate the present value of investment projects. The purchaser of a bond gets two types of payments, a coupon payment each period and the repayment of the face value of the bond at the time of maturity. Let us assume for simplicity that coupon payments are made once per year.[6] Then the price of a bond is:

$$P = \frac{C}{1+i} + \frac{C}{(1+i)^2} + \cdots + \frac{C+F}{(1+i)^n} \qquad (5\text{–}4)$$

where

P is the price of the bond.
C is the coupon payment on the bond.
F is face value; that is, the principal to be repaid in year n.
i is the current interest rate or yield on the bond.
n is the number of years to maturity.

Once a bond is issued, the coupon rate, C, is fixed, as is the face value F.[7] As market rates of interest rise, the prices of outstanding bonds fall, as can readily be seen from Equation (5–4). Indeed, the fall in bond prices can be looked on as the other side of the coin to increases in bond yields. It is more accurate to say that a fall in bond prices *is* an increase in yields than it is to say that a fall in bond prices *causes* an increase in yields.

An individual who holds a bond to maturity is guaranteed a positive rate of return, barring the possibility of default. [This rate of return can be calculated from Equation (5–4) by plugging in C, F, and the price paid for the bond, and solving for i.] However, if the

---

[6] In practice, coupons are normally paid semiannually, not annually. This changes the details of Equation (5–4), but not its logic. Consider a 6 percent bond written with semiannual coupon payments of $3 per $100 of face value. If the current market interest rate were 8 percent per annum (that is, 4 percent for each six-month period), then Equation (5–4) could be solved, making $C = 3$, $i = 4\%$, and $n =$ the number of semiannual payments.

[7] This is the usual way in which bond contracts are written, although there have been experiments in recent years with bonds whose coupons vary with market interest rates during the life of the bond.

bond is sold before the maturity date, the original purchaser has no guarantee against loss, even if there is no risk of default by the issuing agency. Suppose, for example, that a bond with a 4 percent coupon and with 10 years to maturity were purchased when market yields were 4 percent; the price of this bond would be $100. Now, suppose that the bond were held for only two years and then sold when yields had risen to 6 percent per annum. The bondholder would receive $8 in coupon payments during the two years the bond was held. But, when the bond was sold, it would be worth only $87.58 [from Equation (5–4), with $C = 4$, $i = 6\%$, and $n = 8$]. The bondholder would have suffered a penalty of $4.42 from owning the bond; the capital loss of $12.42 in selling the bond would have exceeded the coupon receipts of $8.00, and the bondholder would have been better off leaving the money in a checking deposit or in a safety deposit box, earning no interest but risking no capital loss. In deciding whether to purchase bonds or hold money, therefore, it is relevant for the asset holder to address the question of whether interest rates are likely to rise; in other words, whether the prices of outstanding bonds are likely to fall.

As a general proposition, the bond purchaser cannot be sure whether future interest rates will rise, fall, or remain stable. The future is uncertain. However, observed Keynes, there are times when the uncertainties are preponderantly *one-sided;* when there are significant risks of a fall in bond prices (that is, a rise in yields) and little or no chance of a rise in bond prices (fall in yields). This would occur when interest rates on long-term bonds were very low; say, 2 or 2.5 percent. In such a situation, interest rates cannot fall much, if at all. Clearly, interest rates cannot fall to zero, since nobody would buy bonds rather than holding cash if there were no interest incentive. Indeed, there must be some positive interest rate to compensate the bond purchaser for the transactions costs and nuisance of entering the bond market. Therefore, when interest rates are very low (2 or 2.5 percent), the bond purchaser will *know* that there is *no* hope of a sizable increase in the price of outstanding bonds; that is, bond yields *cannot* fall significantly.

There is no such limitation on the other side. Bond yields can go up; and they can go up a great deal: to 3 percent, 4 percent, 5 percent, or higher. With such changes in bond yields, the price of an outstanding bond with 10 years to maturity and with a 2 percent coupon would fall (respectively) to $91.47, $83.78, $76.83, or lower. Thus, when interest rates are very low, the potential purchaser of bonds will face a risk of a sizable fall in the price of bonds. The purchaser's evaluation of the probability that interest rates will, in fact, rise in the future will determine the degree of risk associated with the purchase of a bond.

When interest rates are low and bond prices are high, the uncertainties thus lie predominantly on one side; the chance of a capital loss is greater than the chance of a capital gain. The lower the interest rate falls, the more one-sided the future prospects become. When the interest rate becomes low enough, the risk of a capital loss completely outweighs the current return to a bond, and therefore bond purchasers will retire from the market. If their assets increase, they will be willing to hold *all* their additional wealth in the form of money rather than committing *any* of it to additional bonds. At something like 2 percent or 2.5 percent yields, asset holders will have an unlimited preference for money rather than bonds.

Thus, the speculative demand for money—the willingness to hold money as an alternative to bonds in asset portfolios—will look something like the curve in Figure 5–3, flattening out rapidly as it approaches the 2 to 2.5 percent range.

The strength of this speculative argument depends on the length

Figure 5–3
The speculative demand for money

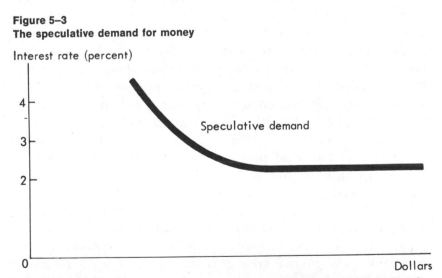

The lower the interest rate, the greater the risk of holding bonds. Thus, at low interest rates, people are willing to hold large amounts of money in preference to buying bonds.

to maturity of the bond. If, for example, the yield on a 10-year bond with a 2 percent coupon were to rise from 2 percent to 3 percent, its price would fall from $100 to $91.47. For a bond with only five years to maturity, in contrast, the price fall would be less precipitous in the face of this rise in yields; the price would fall to only $95.39. For a very short-term security, the price fall would be very small. Consider, for example, a three-month government bill, which has no explicit interest coupon but provides a return to the purchaser as a result of the discount of the bill from its face value. With an interest rate of 2 percent (per annum), the price of a three-month bill would be approximately $99.50 for every $100 of face value. The price would be about $99.25 with a 3 percent yield. Thus, a rise in interest rates causes a much greater change in the prices of long-term bonds than in the prices of shorter-term securities.

The implications of this difference between long- and shorter-term securities are two. First, the prices of long-term securities change more than the prices of short-term securities. But, on the other hand, interest yields on short-term securities are much more volatile than yields on longer-term bonds. The risks of a capital loss on longer-term securities (say, 10 years to maturity) are high; this prevents a fall in yields below the 2 percent to 2.5 percent rate shown in Figure 5–3. In contrast, the risks of loss on a short-term bill are very low. Thus, there is a very little speculative risk to keep up the short-term yields, which may consequently fall to very low levels. (The three-month bill rate fell to less than 0.01 percent per annum during late 1938.) Keynes was interested in the longer-term securities which could be used for financing capital equipment. It is therefore the longer-term yields, resisting a fall below 2 percent, which are shown in Figure 5–3.

The transactions demand for money will be much less sensitive to interest rates. Even at quite high interest rates, people still wish to hold money balances to cover their desired purchases in the near future (Figure 5–4, Panel A). The total demand for money—or *liquidity preference*—is derived by a horizontal addition of the speculative and transactions demands, as illustrated in Figure 5–4. For example, at an interest rate of 5 percent, the transactions demand is shown as L_t and the speculative demand as L_s. Adding these quantities, we find the total demand (L). A similar exercise at other rates of interest allows us to trace out the entire liquidity preference curve.

Figure 5–4
The total demand for money

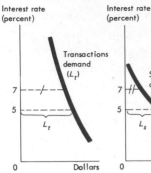

A. The transactions demand

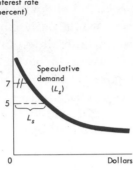

B. The speculative demand

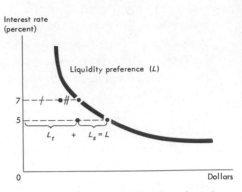

C. The total demand for money (liquidity preference)

A. The transactions demand	B. The speculative demand	C. The total demand for money (liquidity preference)
The amount of money held for transactions purposes depends primarily on income and is relatively insensitive to changes in the rate of interest.	Holdings of money for the speculative motive are sensitive to change in the rate of interest. The curve becomes very flat at a low rate of interest.	The total demand for money is found by a horizontal addition of the transaction demand and the speculative demand.

The equilibrium rate of interest will be at point E in Figure 5–5, at the intersection of the demand for money and the supply (stock) of money. At a higher rate of interest—say, 8 percent—the demand for money (AB) is less than the total actual money holdings of individuals and corporations (AC). People attempt to reduce their money holdings by purchasing bonds. This bids up the price of bonds, and the interest rate is driven down to the equilibrium of 6 percent. Similarly, at an interest rate below the equilibrium, the demand for money (HK) exceeds the actual quantity in the hands of the public (HJ). People attempt to get more money by selling bonds, and the interest rate is driven up to its equilibrium (E). [Observe that, although people are *attempting* to get more money, they do not succeed, since the quantity of money is fixed. What happens then? The interest rate is driven up until people are actually satisfied with the quantity of money that they actually hold (at E).]

Figure 5–5
The equilibrium rate of interest

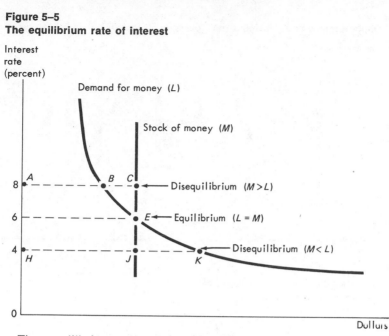

The equilibrium rate of interest exists where the demand for money intersects the stock of money.

THE SIMPLE KEYNESIAN SYSTEM: UNEMPLOYMENT EQUILIBRIUM IN THE FACE OF AN INCREASING SUPPLY OF MONEY

We are now in a position to put the pieces of the analysis together and to illustrate why Keynes believed that a market economy could have a persistently high level of unemployment *even in the face of a very large increase in the money supply*. In order to illustrate Keynes' criticisms of the market economy, we revert to the most simple economy, with only consumption and investment and with no government spending, taxation, or international sector.

The simple Keynesian equilibrium is illustrated in Figure 5–6. In Part A (which repeats Figure 5–5), we see how the equilibrium rate of interest is determined, at the intersection of the demand (L) and supply (M) curves for money. The equilibrium rate of interest i_1 is then carried over to Part B, showing the *MEI* schedule (from Figure 5–2). The rate of interest, together with the *MEI* schedule, determines the quantity of investment demanded (I_1). Investment demand can then be added on to consumption (in Part C) in order

Figure 5–6
The simple Keynesian equilibrium (no government sector)

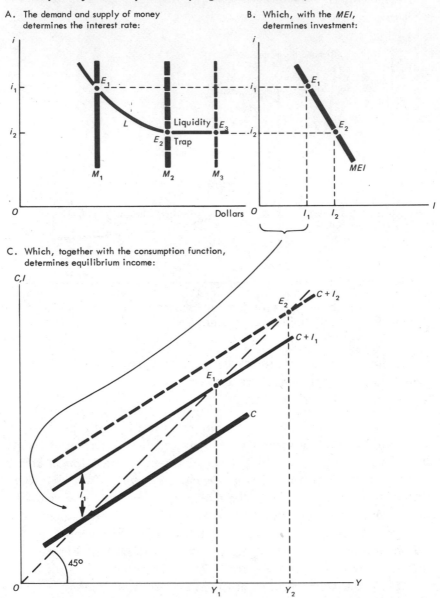

A. The demand and supply of money
   determines the interest rate:

B. Which, with the *MEI*,
   determines investment:

C. Which, together with the consumption function,
   determines equilibrium income:

The simplest complete Keynesian system can now be presented. The investment demand (derived in this chapter) can be added to the equilibrium diagram of previous chapters.

to give the familiar diagram showing equilibrium income at E_1.

Now, consider how a change in monetary policy affects the economy. Suppose that the initial equilibrium involves very high rates of unemployment, and that the central bank decides to engage in an expansive policy in order to stimulate the economy. What happens? As the money supply increases to M_2, the interest rate falls to i_2 (Part A). In turn, this fall in the rate of interest causes an increase in investment demand (Part B). Finally, the higher investment demand causes a rise in equilibrium income from Y_1 to Y_2 (Part C).

So far, so good; the expansive monetary policy has the desired effect of increasing aggregate demand. But suppose that income Y_2 is still below the full-employment level and that the central bank decides to step up its expansive policies, increasing the money supply to M_3. What happens then? Observe that, to the right of money quantity M_2, the demand curve for money flattens out. Thus, an increase in money from M_2 to M_3 has no effect on the rate of interest. With an unchanged interest rate, investment remains unchanged at I_2 and equilibrium income remains stuck at Y_2. In other words, once the horizontal range of the liquidity preference function is reached, further increases in the quantity of money are caught in the *liquidity trap. People simply hold the additional money in the form of idle balances;* interest rates and equilibrium income remain unaffected. Thus, Keynes believed that, while monetary policy could play a useful role in aggregate demand management under normal circumstances, monetary policy might become *completely useless* as a way of stimulating aggregate demand once interest rates had been reduced to a very low level (of 2.5 percent or thereabouts). It might become *essential* to embark on an expansive *fiscal* policy in order to move the economy toward full employment. Government spending should be increased, or taxes could be cut, or both.

It will be noted that in the Keynesian theory, there are *two* steps in the operation of expansive monetary policies: The expansion of the money supply must reduce the rate of interest, and the reduction of the rate of interest must stimulate investment. Although Keynes himself did not dwell on the point, the second step also involves a possible barrier to an effective monetary policy. Suppose for the moment that monetary policy does indeed change the rate of interest significantly. If the *MEI* schedule is close to vertical, indicating that investment does not respond significantly to altered interest rates, then once again monetary policy will be thwarted: A change in the quantity of money will have little affect on aggregate demand. During the late 1930s and 1940s, many of the early followers of Keynes argued that the *MEI* schedule indeed was interest inelastic and that monetary policy therefore was a relatively unimportant demand-management tool, *even during normal periods of relatively high interest rates,* when the central bank had the power to move rates in either direction. Not surprisingly, there is a controversy over the interest elasticity of the *MEI* schedule, with economists in the classical tradition accusing Keynesians of "elasticity pessimism." We will return to the question of the interest elasticity of the *MEI* schedule in the discussion of monetary policy in Chapter 9.

In summary, for monetary policy to be effective in the simple Keynesian system, both of two conditions must be met:

1. The demand and supply of money must intersect to the left of the liquidity trap in Part A of Figure 5–6; that is, the interest rate must respond to changes in the quantity of money.
2. The *MEI* schedule must not approach a vertical position; that is, investment must respond to changes in the interest rate.

APPENDIX

UNEMPLOYMENT WITH FLEXIBLE WAGES AND PRICES AND A FIXED NOMINAL MONEY SUPPLY

> *A downward swoop of the level of prices*
> *reveals like a flare a line of struggling*
> *figures, caught in their own commitments*
> *as in a barbed-wire entanglement.**
>
> D. H. Robertson

The debate between Keynes and classical economists had two aspects: one, a debate over the effectiveness of monetary policy as a real-world tool; and the other, a debate over the existence of an unemployment equilibrium as a theoretical possibility. Clearly, the

---

* D. H. Robertson, *Money,* rev. ed. (New York: Harcourt, Brace, 1929) , p. 15.

first of these is the more important for practical economics dealing with policy issues. Nevertheless, as economic theory has a habit of coloring real-world decisionmaking, it is of relevance to pursue further the second, purely theoretical aspect of the Keynesian-classical controversy.

Keynesian and classical economists agreed that, on the theoretical level, downward flexibility of wages and prices is important: it should have *equilibrium* effects similar to the effects of an increase in the nominal quantity of money. The *real* quantity of money will be increased in either case: if the nominal quantity of money increases in the face of wage and price rigidity, or if the nominal quantity of money is constant while wages and prices decline. (The "nominal" quantity of money is the number of dollars. The "real" quantity is the nominal quantity divided by the average level of prices. The real quantity is measured by the goods and services that the money will buy.) The theoretical debate dealt with the effects of a *general* deflation, that is, a deflation in which *all* prices and wages fall by the *same percentage*.

Keynes argued that an increase in the nominal quantity of money would be ineffective in establishing a full-employment equilibrium when the liquidity trap was reached. He also argued that a general price and wage deflation would be ineffective, and for precisely the same reasons. This can be seen by returning to Figure 5–6 and measuring real quantities on the axes. (In drawing Figure 5–6 originally, it was assumed that prices and wages are rigid. Therefore, it was unnecessary to specify whether real or nominal quantities were being measured on the axes; increases in nominal quantities of necessity meant increases in real quantities.) In the deflation case, an increase in the real money supply comes about as a result of a fall in prices rather than as a result of central bank policy, but it has the same effect of shifting out the M function in Part A of Figure 5–6. Beyond point E_2, an increase in the money supply is ineffective in stimulating employment.

As classical economists had disagreed with Keynes over the effects of an increase in the nominal quantity of money, they also disagreed with him over the equilibrium effects of a general deflation. With lower prices, the given nominal stock of money would buy more. People would therefore increase their purchases, and the economy would eventually move back to full employment.

Keynes and the classical theorists agreed that, in *static equilibrium* terms, an increase in the nominal quantity of money was equivalent to a general deflation with the money supply being fixed—although they flatly disagreed as to whether full employment could be assured through such changes. They also had a second major area of agreement. They agreed that, *in practice,* there might be a world of difference between the economic effects of increases in the money supply and decreases in the general level of prices and wages.

In the first place, the simple theoretical assumptions are very difficult to reproduce in the real world. It is easy to assume that all prices and wages drop proportionately; but, in practice, some prices and wages are stickier than others, so that the actual process of deflation is an uneven and uncertain affair. With some prices in fact falling more rapidly than others, the process of deflation involves a disturbance of relative prices, with redistributive effects among various segments of the economy. In addition, deflation redistributes wealth from debtors to lenders. As prices fall, debtors are "caught in the barbed wire" of their commitments; they have to pay back their debts with dollars whose real value has risen. In purely theoretical models, this difficulty is sometimes circumvented by the assumption that debts are revalued downward following deflation, in order to restore their initial real value. Again, this is an easy assumption to make in theory, but it does not correspond to the real world. Bonds are legal contracts specified in nominal monetary units, and these legal commitments cannot be easily brushed aside.

Indeed, the effects of deflation on the real value of bonded indebtedness constitute one of the major reasons against using price reductions as a means of getting out of a depression. As the real value of indebtedness rises, bond issuers become increasingly unable to meet their commitments, and defaults and bankruptcies result. Bankruptcies of business corporations themselves have a disturbing effect on the level of employment. But, worse still, the bankruptcies of businesses may have a domino effect, taking banks into bankruptcy with them and thereby wiping out the assets of bank depositors. Bank demand deposits are part of the money supply. Thus, the process of deflation may in the real world lead to a reduction of the money supply. Indeed, once the process of deflation has begun, there is no assurance that the nominal money supply will not contract *even faster* than prices fall, with a *decline* rather than an increase in the real money supply accompanying the actual process of deflation. Deflation as a means to full employment may thus involve the pursuit of an ever-receding goal. This was a major concern of the classical economists, who saw instability of the money supply as the main source of economic instability during the interwar period. (As a result of the banking disturbances of the early 1930s, steps have been taken to rule out an implosion of the money supply. In particular, bank deposits are guaranteed through the Federal Deposit Insurance Corporation.)

Furthermore, even if it is possible to keep up the nominal supply of money during a deflation, there can be no assurance that deflation will have a stimulative effect on aggregate demand, at least not over considerable periods of time. *Expectations* of a further decline in the price level will have a dampening effect on the level of demand. Why buy a machine or new refrigerator now, or construct a new building, when they may be gotten more cheaply next year? This question, of course, demonstrates the importance of the *static equilibrium* qualification in the classical argument that deflation will increase aggregate demand in real terms. The conclusion is based on the assumption that deflation *has taken place* and has *stopped;* it does not follow *while* the deflationary process is going on, and while expectations of further deflation have a depressing effect on demand.

KEY POINTS

1. A business may increase its profits by undertaking investment for which the present value of future returns exceeds the initial cost of the investment (P_k). The present value is found from Equation (5–2).

2. The rate of interest, together with the schedule of the rates of return on investment (the marginal efficiency of investment schedule) determine the amount of investment that will be undertaken during the period in question.

3. In the Keynesian theoretical system, the rate of interest is determined by the stock of money and the demand for money (liquidity preference). There are two main motives behind the demand for money—the transactions motive and the speculative motive.

4. Because the speculative demand increases very rapidly at low interest rates (that is, the speculative demand approaches a horizontal slope at low interest rates), there is a limit to the downward movement of interest rates that can be caused by monetary

expansion. Therefore, there is a limit to the amount of investment that can be caused by monetary expansion, and consequently a limit to the stimulation of aggregate demand which is
possible through monetary expansion. Thus, *in the Keynesian
theoretical system,* it is possible for the economy to remain in an
unemployment equilibrium even in the face of large increases in
the money supply.

QUESTIONS

1. Assume that the following investment projects may be undertaken, and that they provide a return (R) during next year,
   with no returns thereafter. (There is no scrap value.) Assume
   also that the returns are riskless; it is certain that the investment
   project will provide the return shown.

Project	Initial cost (P_K)	Return (R)
A	$1,000	$1,200
B	2,000	2,300
C	3,000	3,300
D	4,000	4,500

   a. Calculate the percentage rate of return (r) for each of these
      projects.
   b. Assume that the interest rate is 10 percent. Which projects
      will business undertake?

2. Investment demand has historically been one of the least stable
   components of total demand. What is there, in the theory of the
   marginal efficiency of investment, which suggests that investment demand may be unstable through time?

SUGGESTED READING

Alvin Hansen, *A Guide to Keynes* (New York: McGraw-Hill, 1953),
   chaps. 5 and 6.

Chapter 6

A Keynesian-classical synthesis: A Keynesian view

There is no effect without a cause," replied Candide modestly. "All things are necessarily connected and arranged for the best."*

Voltaire

In proposing his theoretical model of the economy in the *General Theory,* Keynes attacked the classical argument that the economy could be in equilibrium only at full employment. In particular, Keynes criticized the mechanism which classical economists believed would lead to an equilibrium between desired investment and saving.

SAVING AND INVESTMENT IN THE CLASSICAL SYSTEM

There was no disagreement between Keynes and the classicists that saving and desired investment would be equal in equilibrium; rather the difference was over how the equilibrium would come about. Keynes foresaw the equilibrium between saving and desired investment coming as a result of *changes in the level of income.* If saving were greater than desired investment, the level of income would fall until the public wished to save no more than the current

* From *Candide.*

117

Figure 6–1
The equilibrium of saving and investment: The classical
system

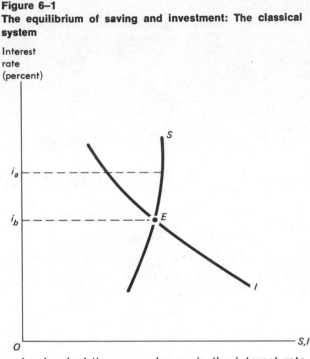

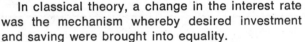

In classical theory, a change in the interest rate
was the mechanism whereby desired investment
and saving were brought into equality.

level of desired investment. (This fall in income was described in
Chapter 3, with Figure 3–4.)

Not so, said classical economists. If there were a tendency for
saving to exceed investment demand, the rate of interest would fall,
establishing an equilibrium as illustrated in Figure 6–1.[1] As usual,
classicists saw equilibrium occurring as a result of a change in price,
the "price" in this case being the rate of interest. In the classical
framework, interest rates performed an important function in bringing together the desired levels of investment and saving.

Keynes' objection

The problem with this, said Keynes, is that the classical economists implicitly assumed away the most important variable of all;

---

[1] The investment demand function—that is, the *MEI* curve of Chapter 5—is labeled
simply *I* in the diagrams in this chapter.

in constructing the saving and investment schedules, they assumed full employment. That is, the points on the S schedule in Figure 6–1 represent the levels of saving with various rates of interest, but for all points a situation of full employment is assumed. This is *Hamlet* without the prince.

The Keynesian objection may be driven home with a question. What assurance do the classical economists have that the saving and investment functions will intersect at a *positive* rate of interest? Keynes' answer: None whatsoever.[2] Unemployment will result if the full-employment saving and investment functions intersect at a negative rate of interest, or, indeed, if they intersect at any point below the minimum interest rate determined by liquidity preference.

Keynes' objection is illustrated in Figure 6–2. (This figure is based on the *only* diagram in *General Theory*. By singling out the

Figure 6–2
The classical *S* and *I* equilibrium: Keynes' objection

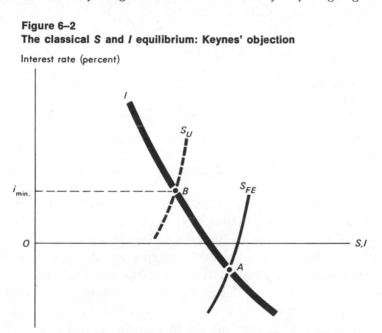

Keynes argued that classical economists overlooked one critical problem: The full-employment saving and investment schedules need not intersect at a positive interest rate.

---

[2] In his booklet, *Keynes and the Classics* (London: Institute of Economic Affairs, 1971), p. 21, Axel Leijonhufvud has flatly denied that the *General Theory* contains the proposition that "the trouble is that at no positive interest rate would saving equal investment." Therefore, Keynes' proposition should be footnoted. It *is* in the *General Theory*, on p. 182: "There is no guarantee that a given Y-curve [saving curve] will intersect a given X-curve [investment curve] anywhere at all."

classical theory of interest in this way, Keynes clearly indicated that he thought it was *gravely* deficient.) With the full-employment saving and investment schedules intersecting at A, a negative rate of interest, there will be unemployment. The freedom of asset holders to choose between money and bonds will keep the interest rate from falling below i_{min}, the minimum rate of interest established by the liquidity trap. The interest rate cannot change enough to equate desired investment and saving at the full-employment level. The desire of the public to save more than is invested at the minimum rate of interest leads to a reduction in the level of aggregate demand and employment. As incomes fall, people want to save less; the saving function in Figure 6–2 shifts to the left. Income continues to fall and unemployment continues to rise, until the saving function has shifted all the way to S_u. A fall in the rate of interest cannot be counted on to ensure full employment.

A KEYNESIAN-CLASSICAL SYNTHESIS

The trouble with classical interest theory, said Keynes, was that it assumed the fixity of the key economic variable. The level of employment was assumed fixed at full employment when the saving function was drawn (Figure 6–1). But, said J. R. Hicks and Alvin Hansen, exactly the same type of logical problem arises regarding the simple Keynesian theory of interest presented in Chapter 5.[3] In the simple Keynesian theory of income determination (Figure 5–6), L (the demand for money) and M (its supply) determine the rate of interest; this, in conjunction with the *MEI*, determines the level of investment; which, in conjunction with the consumption schedule, in turn determines the level of aggregate demand and equilibrium income. The trouble with this sequence: Until the level of income is determined, the demand for money cannot be determined and the liquidity preference curve (L) cannot be drawn. Specifically, the transactions demand for money depends directly on the level of income. The higher the level of peoples' incomes, the more money they will wish (on average) to hold as a means of bridging the time between receipts and expenditures. Therefore, one cannot determine the rate of interest until the level of income is *already* known. A logical problem arises in working through the simple Keynesian system in the sequence specified in Chapter 5.

---

    [3] J. R. Hicks, "Mr. Keynes and the 'Classics'; A Suggested Interpretation," *Econometrica*, April 1937, pp. 147–59; Alvin Hansen, *A Guide to Keynes* (New York: McGraw-Hill, 1953), chap. 7.

The level of interest cannot be determined until the level of income is known, and the level of income cannot be determined until the interest rate is known. What is needed, therefore, is some way of determining the rate of interest and the level of income simultaneously. Hicks and Hansen proposed a way to bring together the four parts of the puzzle—investment demand, saving, the demand for money, and the quantity of money. They showed how these four items *jointly* determine national income and the rate of interest.

Equilibrium in the goods market: The investment-saving curve

First, let us bring together saving and investment. A fundamental condition for equilibrium is that desired investment and saving must be equal. The importance of this condition in determining the equilibrium income and interest rate is illustrated in Figure 6–3. In Part 1, the investment demand function is illustrated. Part 2 shows the equilibrium condition—saving must equal investment demand. With saving and investment on the two axes, the equilibrium condition of $S = I$ is shown as a 45° line from the origin. In Part 3, Keynes' objection is, met: This panel reintroduces the diagram of earlier chapters, which shows how *saving* is related to *income*.[4] Part 4 is what we are after—the investment-saving (*IS*) curve which can be derived from Parts 1, 2, and 3.

To show how the *IS* curve is derived, let us begin in Part 1, taking any point, A_1. The interest rate at this point—6 percent—may be carried directly across the page to Part 4, giving the *height* of the corresponding point, A, on the *IS* curve.

But, of course, we do not yet know the income level of point A. It is found as follows. Returning to Part 1, we note that point A_1 represents not only a rate of interest, but also the corresponding quantity of investment demand ($100 billion). This investment demand is carried vertically to point A_2 in Part 2. Here we see that, for equilibrium, saving must also equal $100 billion (measured on the vertical axis). This $100 billion in saving may be carried over to Part 3 which shows that saving will be $100 bilion when income

_____

[4] When we present saving in this manner—as a function of income—we ignore any effect which the interest rate might have on saving; this effect would show up in the classical theory of interest-rate determination in Figure 6–1. There is, however, little cost in omitting any possible influence of the interest rate on saving. Keynes was very skeptical that the interest rate would affect saving. And classical economists were very uncertain even of the *direction* in which saving would change in the event of a rise in the rate of interest. Among the factors that determine saving, the interest rate is well down on the list; it may be ignored.

Figure 6–3
Deriving the *IS* curve

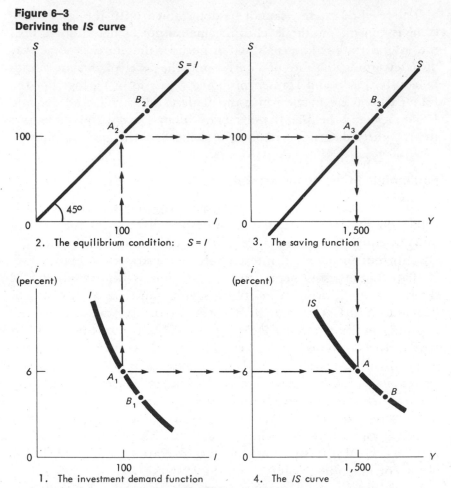

2. The equilibrium condition: *S = I*   3. The saving function

1. The investment demand function   4. The *IS* curve

The IS curve—representing points of equilibrium in the goods market—is derived from the investment demand function, the saving function, and the equilibrium condition (that *S = I*). Note that the *IS* graph
has the interest rate on one axis and the level of income on the other.

is $1,500 billion. We now have the quantity of income ($1,500 billion), which can be carried down to Part 4. Together with the 6
percent rate of interest, we now have enough information to plot
point *A* on the *IS* curve.

Other points on the *IS* curve can be derived in a similar manner.
For example, beginning with point B_1 in Part 1, we can derive
point *B* on the *IS* curve in Part 4.

The *IS* curve shows *the combinations of income and interest rates at which desired investment and saving are equal.* But the saving function is an alternative way of showing the consumption function. Thus, the *IS* curve represents equilibrium in the market for consumer and investment goods; it represents *equilibrium in the goods market.*

Equilibrium in the financial sector: The *LM* curve

Now, let us bring together the other two components of the puzzle, namely, the demand for and the supply of money which Keynes used in his theory of interest. With a procedure similar to that used to derive the *IS* curve, we may derive the *LM* curve, which shows *the combinations of income and interest rates at which the demand for money equals the quantity of money in the economy.*

This is done in Figure 6–4. In Part 1, the speculative demand for money (L_s) is shown; A_1 is any point on this demand curve. Again, by going directly to the right across the diagram, we can find the height of corresponding point A on the *LM* curve which we are deriving in Part 4. But once again, to get the income level for point A, we must take a circuitous route around Figure 6–4.

Beginning again in Part 1, we take the quantity of money demanded for speculative purposes ($100 billion) vertically upward from point A_1 to point A_2 in Part 2. Part 2 gives two pieces of information:

1. It states the equilibrium condition; namely, that the demand for money $(L_s + L_t)$ must equal the quantity of money (M).
2. It shows the quantity of money in the economy. In Figure 6–4, this is $300 billion.

Observe that these two bits of information together give the line shown in part B, which represents the equation:

$$L_s + L_t = M = \$300 \tag{6-1}$$

At point A_2, $100 billion is demanded for speculative purposes. For there to be equilibrium in the financial sector, the remaining $200 billion must be demanded for transactions purposes, as shown by the height of point A_2. This $200 billion is carried to the right, to Part 3, which shows the transactions demand for money. This demand depends primarily on the level of income; it is represented by a straight line from the origin. (When the transactions demand is shown as a function of income, then the Hicks-Hansen objection

Figure 6–4
Deriving the *LM* curve

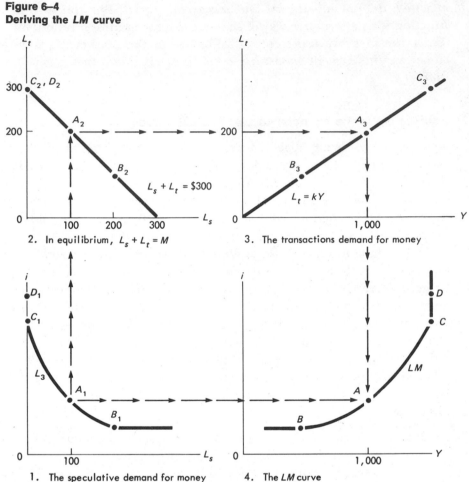

2. In equilibrium, $L_s + L_t = M$

3. The transactions demand for money

1. The speculative demand for money

4. The *LM* curve

The *LM* curve—representing points of equilibrium in the financial market—is derived from the two demands for money and from the quantity of money in the economy. Like the *IS* graph, the *LM* graph has the rate of interest on one axis and the level of income on the other.

to Keynes' theory of interest has been satisfied.) At point A_3, we see that the transactions demand for money will be $200 billion when income is $1,000 billion; this income level is carried down to Part 4 to give us point A on the *LM* curve.

Other points on the *LM* curve can be derived in a similar manner, for example, point B. Observe that, in the liquidity trap to the right of point B in Part 1, interest rates cannot fall further no matter how great the quantity of money available for speculative purposes. This liquidity trap also shows up in the *LM* curve: *The equilibrium level of the rate of interest cannot fall below a minimum, no matter how low the level of income.*

At the other end, the *LM* curve—as we have drawn it—becomes perfectly vertical at interest rates above point *C*. Above some interest rate (perhaps 6 or 7 percent), the speculative demand for money becomes zero. Although potential bondholders still face the risk that interest rates may rise further and bond prices consequently fall, the uncertainties cease to be predominantly one-sided. (Recall that it was the *one-sidedness* of uncertainties that lay behind the speculative demand for money.) Bond prices may fall; but, on the other hand, they may rise, providing a capital gain to bondholders. And there is a large return to bondholders in the form of the high yield. No longer does the risk of a loss from the fall in bond prices outweigh the high interest to be earned; no longer does it make sense to hold assets in the form of money rather than bonds. Because no money is tied up as a way of holding an asset (at point *C* or above), it is all free to be used for transactions purposes; there will be equilibrium only when the income level is sufficiently high that all the whole money stock of $300 billion is demanded for transactions purposes. So long as the money stock remains fixed, no more money can become available for transactions purposes no matter how high the interest rate rises. (For example, at D_1 and D_2, there is still the same $300 billion available for transactions.) Consequently, the level of income cannot rise further, even if interest rates rise.[5] Above *C*, the *LM* curve is vertical. Because the transactions demand for money is dominant, the section above point *C* is known as the "classical" range of the *LM* curve.

The equilibrium income and interest rate

We may now bring together the *LM* curve, which represents equilibrium in the financial sector, and the *IS* curve, representing equilibrium in the markets for goods and services. When this is

---

[5] Note what we have said: Income cannot rise unless the money supply rises, regardless of what happens to interest rates. This implies that the transactions demand for money is a function *only* of the level of income and is *not* influenced *at all* by interest rates. This tacit assumption is made when Part 3 of Figure 6–4 is used.

This will turn out to be an important assumption, to which we shall return in Chapter 12. (For simplicity, we stick to the standard *LM* presentation here.) To anticipate the conclusion of Chapter 12: Once we take into account the responsiveness of the transactions demand to interest rate changes, then there is no perfectly vertical section of the *LM* curve.

Figure 6–5
The *LM* and *IS* curves: Overall equilibrium

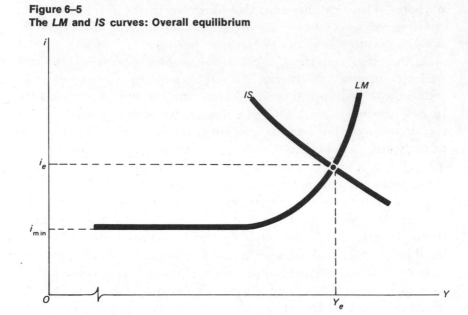

The equilibrium interest rate and income are determined simultaneously at the intersection of the *IS* and *LM* curves.

done (Figure 6–5), the rate of interest and the equilibrium level of
income are determined simultaneously. The common problem of
both classical and Keynesian economics is solved; no longer is the
interest rate determined independently of the determination of the
level of income.

To summarize, we recall that the following things lie behind the
equilibrium illustrated by the intersection of the *IS* and *LM* curves:

First, there are four fundamental functions:

1. Investment as a function of the rate of interest (Figure 6–3,
   Part 1).
2. Saving as a function of income (Figure 6–3, Part 3).
3. The speculative demand for money as a function of the interest
   rate (Figure 6–4, Part 1).
4. The transactions demand for money as a function of income
   (Figure 6–4, Part 3).

Second, we have a given:

5. The quantity of money, determined by the central bank
   (Figure 6–4, Part 2).

Finally, we have two equilibrium conditions:

6. Desired investment equals saving (Figure 6–3, Part 2).
7. The demand for money equals the quantity of money (Figure 6–4, Part 2).

FISCAL POLICY IN THE *IS/LM* FRAMEWORK

For the analysis of fiscal and monetary policies, the *IS* and *LM* curves present a more sophisticated framework than the simple Keynesian system outlined in Chapters 3–5. In particular, the *IS/LM* analysis draws attention to the effects of fiscal and monetary policies on interest rates as well as on the level of national income.

In considering the effect of fiscal policy on the level of economic activity and on interest rates, we must elaborate on the simple two-sector (consumption and investment) model described earlier. In that simple world, desired investment and saving are equal in equilibrium. In the more complex world with government spending, we must turn to the more general statement of equilibrium: It requires that total injections into the spending stream be equal to total leakages. In order to keep our illustration simple, we will follow the procedure of Chapter 4, and initially consider an admittedly unrealistic economy with government spending but no taxes.

The effects of $100 billion of government spending are illustrated in Figure 6–6. Government spending involves an injection into the spending stream; it is added (horizontally) to investment in Part 1. The condition for equilibrium in this artificial world, with government spending and no taxation, is that $I + G = S$, as shown in Part 2. Point B_2 may now be carried over to Part 3, which shows that saving will increase by $100 billion when national income rises by $500 billion. The $2,000 billion level of income at point B_3 may now be carried down to point B on the new *IS* curve in Part 4.[6]

Observe that the increase in government spending causes the *IS* curve to shift to the right *by the amount of government spending times* $(1/s)$, that is, by the amount suggested by the multiplier formula of Chapter 3. But now observe that a complication arises when we carry down the new *IS* curve to the Part 5, which shows the overall equilibrium of the economy. Although the *IS* curve shifts to the right by the full amount indicated by the multiplier formula (Multiplier $= 1/s$), national income rises by *less* than this

---

[6] Perhaps we should relabel this the *IGS* curve now that it represents the equilibrium of *I*, *G*, and *S*. However, the terminology would become cumbersome in this case. By convention, the injections-leakages curve retains the simple *IS* label even for more complex economic models with many injections and many leakages.

Figure 6–6
Fiscal policy in the *IS*/*LM* framework

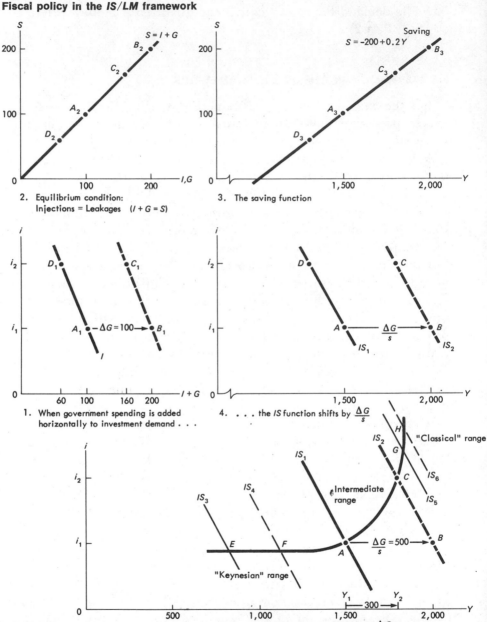

1. When government spending is added
   horizontally to investment demand . . .

2. Equilibrium condition:
   Injections = Leakages $(I + G = S)$

3. The saving function

4. . . . the *IS* function shifts by $\frac{\Delta G}{s}$

5. When the *IS* curve shifts, equilibrium income rises, but by less than $\frac{\Delta G}{s}$.

When government spending is added, the *IS* curve shifts to the right by
$\Delta G/MPS$. Except in the "Keynesian" range of the *LM* curve, this rightward shift
causes an increase in income of less than $\Delta G/MPS$.

amount. Specifically, it rises only by the $300 billion between income levels Y_1 and Y_2.

How can this be? Why do we get less than a full multiplier response? The answer is that as the *IS* curve shifts to the right and the economy moves along the *LM* curve, interest rates rise. The new equilibrium on the *IS* curve is not *B,* but rather *C.* These higher interest rates cause a reduction in investment demand (from A_1 to D_1 in Part 1). In other words, the deficit spending of the government *crowds out* private investment spending.

The extent to which private investment is crowded out depends on the slope of the *LM* curve. In the range we have been considering—between *A* and *C* in Part 5—there is only a moderate crowding out; the $100 billion of government spending crowds out $40 billion in investment. And crowding out might be even less. If the initial equilibrium were at *E*—in the liquidity trap or the Keynesian range of the *LM* curve—then a rightward shift of the *IS* curve would have no effect on interest rates. There would be no crowding out and the multiplier would have its full effects. On the other hand, if the economy were initially at a point in the vertical section of the *LM* curve—that is, if it were in the classical range— then an increase in government spending would have *zero* effect on aggregate demand. Every dollar of government spending would crowd out $1 in private investment, and fiscal policy would be useless as a tool for controlling aggregate demand.[7]

In more complex economies with other leakages (such as taxes), the more complicated multipliers discussed in the appendix to Chapter 4 become relevant. Once again, however, these multiplier formulas measure the amount by which the *IS* curve shifts *horizontally.* Only in the Keynesian range of the *LM* curve will this shift result in an equivalent increase in aggregate demand. In other cases—where interest rates rise—investment will be crowded out, and the effects on aggregate demand will consequently be reduced.

MONETARY POLICY: SHIFTS IN THE *LM* CURVE

Consider now the effects of an increase in the quantity of money, illustrated in Figure 6–7 (which involves an elaboration of Figure

---

[7] In Footnote 5 to this chapter we noted the very special assumption behind the vertical range of the *LM* curve. The grounds for skepticism regarding a perfectly vertical range in the *LM* curve will be considered in Chapter 12.

Figure 6–7
Monetary policy

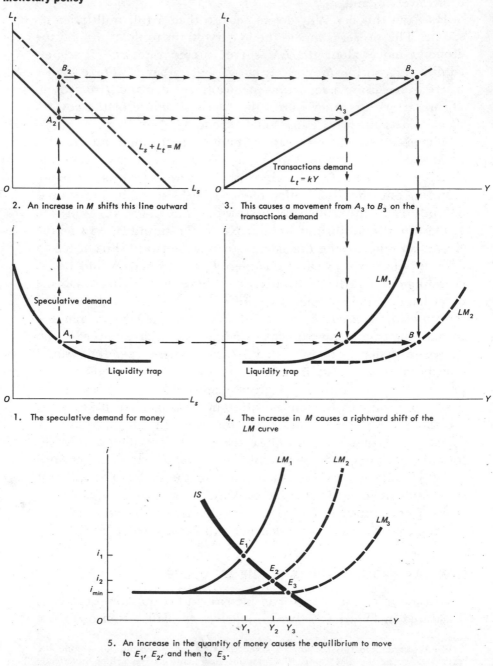

2. An increase in *M* shifts this line outward

3. This causes a movement from A_3 to B_3 on the transactions demand

1. The speculative demand for money

4. The increase in *M* causes a rightward shift of the *LM* curve

5. An increase in the quantity of money causes the equilibrium to move to E_1, E_2, and then to E_3.

Expansive monetary policy causes interest rates to fall and incomes to rise, until E_3 is reached. Thereafter, expansive monetary policies have no further effect within this basic *IS/LM* framework.

6–4) . The increase in the quantity of money causes an outward shift in the money line in Part 2. As a consequence, the LM curve is shifted to the right, from LM_1 to LM_2.

Where the initial equilibrium is either in the classical range or in the intermediate range of the LM curve (illustrated at E_1 in Part 5) , then an increase in the quantity of money has two effects: a reduction in the interest rate, and an increase in equilibrium national income. Once the LM curve has moved as far as LM_3, however, all the expansive effects of monetary policy have been felt; a further monetary expansion will have *no* effect on either the rate of interest or the level of aggregate demand and national income. Again, this is the Keynesian range. The economy can languish in a continuing state of unemployment unless the government takes steps to shift the IS curve to the right through fiscal action.

Thus, in the IS/LM framework, the main theoretical proposition of the Keynesian revolution continues to hold: It is possible for an economy to be in equilibrium with less than full employment, even if the money supply is increased without limit. Money loses its expansive power once the liquidity trap is reached. While the IS/LM analysis contains elements of both Keynesian and classical economics, it represents Keynes triumphant.

APPENDIX

AN ALGEBRAIC VERSION OF THE *IS/LM* FRAMEWORK

The IS/LM framework has been presented in the form of graphs; this makes the argument easiest to follow. It may also be presented algebraically.

There is some difficulty in doing so, as not all of the relationships are linear. Most obviously, the speculative demand for money is not a straight line. And the particular form of the speculative demand is important, since it strongly influences the shape of the LM curve and involves the liquidity trap, which is crucial to the Keynesian argument that an unemployment equilibrium can exist even when the money supply is increased without limit.

For simplicity, however, we must limit our example to the straight lines which give uncomplicated equations.[8] Important character-

---

[8] The specific numbers used in this appendix are illustrative.

istics of the demand for money may nevertheless be retained by specifying three separate ranges for the speculative demand, L_s:

1. First, in the intermediate range:

$$L_s = 600 - 100i \text{ (for 2 percent} < i < 6 \text{ percent)} \quad (6\text{--}2a)$$

2. Second, in the classical range:

$$L_s = 0 \text{ (for } i \geq 6 \text{ percent)} \quad (6\text{--}2b)$$

3. And, finally, in the Keynesian range:

$$i = 2 \text{ percent (for } L_s \geq 400) \quad (6\text{--}2c)$$

To derive the *LM* curve, we also need an equation for the transactions demand for money:

$$L_t = 0.25y \quad (6\text{--}3)$$

and the quantity of money

$$M = 700 \quad (6\text{--}4)$$

and the equilibrium condition:

$$L_s + L_t = M \quad (6\text{--}5)$$

Putting these three equations (6–3, 6–4, and 6–5) together with Equation (6–2a), we may derive the intermediate range of the *LM* curve:

$$y = 400i + 400 \quad (6\text{--}6)$$

Similarly, the *IS* curve may be derived from the underlying equations:[9]

$$
\begin{align}
I &= 140 - 10i & (6\text{--}7)\\
G &= 100 & (6\text{--}8)\\
I + G &= S & (6\text{--}9)\\
S &= 0.2y - 200 & (6\text{--}10)
\end{align}
$$

These may be combined and solved to find the *IS* curve:

$$y = 2,200 - 50i \quad (6\text{--}11)$$

Combining Equations (6–6) and (6–11), we find the intersection at:

$$
\begin{align}
y &= 2,000 & (6\text{--}12)\\
i &= 4 & (6\text{--}13)
\end{align}
$$

---

[9] An important assumption should be repeated—that there is government spending, but no taxation. With taxes, Equation (6–9) would be modified to:

$$I + G = S + T$$

Since this solution meets the side condition for Equation (6-2a) (namely, 2 percent $< i <$ 6 percent), we know that the *IS* curve intersects the *LM* curve in its intermediate range, and we have found the equilibrium national income and the interest rate.

[If the solution of Equations (6-6) and (6-11) gave $i > 6$ percent, we would have to go back and substitute Equation (6-2b) for (6-2a); the solution would be in the classical range. On the other hand, if Equations (6-6) and (6-11) gave $i < 2$ percent, the equilibrium would be in the Keynesian range, and it could be found directly from Equations (6-2c) and (6-11).]

KEY POINTS

1. In the classical theoretical system, interest rates perform a function in equating desired investment and saving at full employment. If desired investment falls short of saving at the full-employment level, interest rates will fall, stimulating investment (and possibly discouraging saving).

2. Keynes argued that this interest rate mechanism might be inadequate to ensure full employment. In particular, there was no assurance that the saving and investment schedules would intersect at a positive interest rate. Yet, because of the liquidity motive for holding money, the level of interest rates would have to remain at a positive level. Thus, if there were a gap between desired investment and saving at the full-employment level, and if this gap persisted after interest rates had fallen to their minima, then the adjustment between desired investment and saving would come about as a result of a decline in the level of income. Incomes would fall until saving was no greater than desired investment. In other words, it was important to recognize that saving is a function of *income*. The classical theory of interest rate determination (Figure 6-1) was severely inadequate in that it ignored the importance of income as a determinant of saving.

3. A somewhat similar objection may be made to the very simple version of the Keynesian theory of interest rate determination presented in Chapter 5 (Figure 5-6). In this simple version, the importance of the level of income on the demand for money is ignored.

4. Hicks and Hansen suggested a way of avoiding these limitations of the classical and Keynesian theories of the rate of interest. The *IS* curve may be derived, showing various combinations of interest rates and incomes at which saving and investment will be in equilibrium. Similarly, the *LM* curve shows the various combinations of interest rates and incomes at which the demand for money equals its existing stock. The *IS* and *LM* curves may be brought together to determine the equilibrium income and interest rate simultaneously.

5. Although the *IS/LM* framework contains elements of both classical and Keynesian interest rate theories, the analysis is fundamentally Keynesian, in the sense that equilibrium can exist with income below the full-employment level.

QUESTION

1. Consider an initial equilibrium with the interest rate at a minimum in Figure 6–7, with the *LM* curve initially in position LM_3.
    a. If the money supply is increased by 10 percent, what will be the effects on (*i*) the equilibrium level of national income, and (*ii*) the velocity of money?
    b. Suppose one wishes to reject answer (*i*) in part *a* above, and argues that expansive monetary policy is effective in stimulating the level of aggregate demand. What must be argued about the shape or movability of the *IS* or *LM* curve?

SUGGESTED READING

Alvin Hansen, *A Guide to Keynes* (New York: McGraw-Hill, 1953), chap. 7.

Chapter 7

A classical rebuttal

Hey Diddle Diddle
Distribute the Middle
The Premise controls the Conclusion. . . .[*]

Frederick Winsor

The previous chapter presented a theoretical system more comprehensive than either the simple Keynesian or simple classical system, but with elements of each. The *IS/LM* analysis may therefore be considered a partial integration of Keynesian and classical economics. But in one important respect, the Keynesian and classical systems cannot be integrated or compromised, since they lead to flatly contradictory conclusions. Beginning with the fundamental equation, $MV = PQ$, classical economists concluded that there could be a lasting unemployment equilibrium only in the most unusual case. Two restrictive assumptions would *both* have to be valid. Specifically, prices would have to be rigid in a downward direction, and the quantity of money would have to be fixed at an amount that was inadequate to provide for a full-employment level of aggregate demand. Because they believed that V was reasonably stable, clas-

[*] From Frederick Winsor and Marian Parry, *The Space Child's Mother Goose* (New York: Simon and Schuster, 1958). Copyright © 1956, 1957, 1958 by Frederick Winsor and Marian Parry. Reprinted by permission of Simon and Schuster, Inc.

sical economists also believed that a full-employment level of output Q could be restored by *either* of two responses, that is, either by a sufficient increase in M or by a sufficient fall in P (or by a combined increase in M and fall in P). This Keynes denied. In the liquidity trap, unemployment could persist *regardless* of how much the money supply was increased (or regardless of how much prices fell). An increase in M would simply be offset by a decrease in V; output Q would remain unchanged. The Keynesian and classical views are clearly oil and water—they cannot be mixed or compromised.

The *IS/LM* analysis holds out the possibility of an equilibrium with less than full employment, even in the event of an unlimited increase in the quantity of money. It is therefore fundamentally a Keynesian analysis, although it does contain some of the elements of the classical theory. Therefore, either the *IS/LM* analysis must be subject to a rebuttal from the classical viewpoint, or Keynesian economics must be granted a sweeping victory in the theoretical debate. This chapter presents the classical rebuttal.

Keynes attacked classical theory on the ground that the capital markets might prove inadequate; specifically, he argued that if the full-employment saving schedule intersected the full-employment investment schedule at a negative rate of interest, there would be unemployment, since the nature of money and the capital markets ruled out the possibility of a negative interest rate (Figure 6–2). However, the equalization of full-employment saving and investment through changes in the rates of interest represented *only one of two* classical mechanisms for ensuring full employment in equilibrium. The other, which Keynes ignored, provided the basis for the classical counterattack.

THE QUANTITY THEORY AND THE REAL-BALANCE EFFECT

Suppose we reconsider the simplest classical quantity theory ($MV = PQ$, with V reasonably stable). If the economy begins with large-scale unemployment, then output Q will increase in response to either a rise in M or a fall in P; in either case, the *real quantity of money* will increase.[1] (The real quantity of money is defined as

---

[1] As we emphasized in the appendix to Chapter 5, a general deflation is equivalent to an increase in the nominal quantity of money M only *if* positions of *equilibrium* are being considered. In the real world, the deflationary *process* can adversely affect expectations, depress investment demand, and cause a further decline in output.

Because of the complications that expectations create, classical writers at times stressed that, in discussing deflation, they were attacking the purely theoretical side

the purchasing power of the money stock; that is, M/P.) What is the logic of the classical case?

What the classicists held, simply, was that if people have more real money, they will buy more goods and services. If their wealth in the form of money increases, they will be in a position to increase their levels of consumption, and they will do so. In other words, classical economists argued that *something is left out of the Keynesian consumption function*, namely, the effect of increases in individuals' money holdings on their consumption behavior. Classical economists believed that, if people are provided with *enough* money, there is *no limit* to the amount they are willing to consume, since consumer wants are unlimited; full employment can therefore be assured by a sufficiently large increase in the quantity of money.

The effect of a change in the real stock of money on the level of consumption is known by a variety of names: the real-balance effect, the wealth effect, or the Pigou effect.[2] The theoretical significance of the real-balance effect is fundamental: If increases in the (real) money supply do indeed stimulate consumption, then the Keynesian liquidity trap is invalid. Additional quantities of money are not caught in this trap and prevented from affecting the level of aggregate demand; rather, they stimulate aggregate demand by shifting the consumption function upward.

The real-balance effect and the *IS/LM* analysis

The *IS/LM* analysis divides the economy into two markets: the product market, with the *IS* function showing the locus of equilibrium points for this market, and the financial market, with the *LM* curve showing the equilibrium points for this second market. If the real-balance argument is accepted, *this dichotomy must be rejected. The product and financial markets are not separable.* Rather, an increase in the (real) quantity of money will cause consumption

---

of Keynes' argument; they were not proposing an actual policy of deflation. For example, in the preface to *Lapses from Full Employment* (London: Macmillan, 1945), p. v, classical standard-bearer A. C. Pigou cautioned: "Professor Dennis Robertson, who has very kindly read my proofs, has warned me that the form of this book may suggest that I am in favour of attacking the problem of unemployment by manipulating wages rather than by manipulating aggregate demand. I wish, therefore, to say clearly that this is not so." Nevertheless, Pigou and other classical writers were not always so careful, and their writings at times suggested that wage and price cuts were, indeed, an appropriate antidepression measure.

[2] Because of A. C. Pigou's early attack on Keynesian theory, "The Classical Stationary State," *Economic Journal*, 1943, pp. 343–51.

to shift upward as a function of income. But the saving function
can be derived directly from the consumption function; it represents the same information in a different guise. Thus, the classical
position can be restated: An increase in the quantity of money will
cause the saving function to shift *down*. (If people consume *more*
out of any level of income, they must save *less,* since saving is *defined*
as $Y_d - C$.) The significance of this is illustrated in Figure 7–1. *As
a result of the increase in the quantity of money,* the saving function

Figure 7–1
The real-balance effect: The rightward shift of the *IS* curve

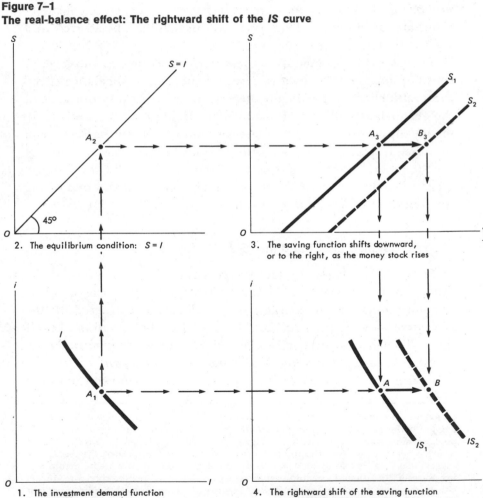

2. The equilibrium condition: $S = I$

3. The saving function shifts downward,
   or to the right, as the money stock rises

1. The investment demand function

4. The rightward shift of the saving function
   causes a similar shift in the *IS* curve

According to classical economists, an increase in the money supply shifts not
only the *LM* curve but also the *IS* curve.

in Part 3 shifts down; as a consequence, *the IS curve shifts to the right*.

Once the *IS* function is permitted to shift in response to changes in the money supply, the Keynesian range of the *LM* function ceases to act as a trap preventing any increase in the money stock from increasing aggregate demand. Rather, an increase in the money stock will cause *both* the *LM* and the *IS* functions to move to the right: the *LM* function because the money supply is used directly in the derivation of this function, and the *IS* function because of the real-balance effect on the saving function (Figure 7–2) .[3] In the classical theoretical system, wants are unlimited, and there is therefore no limit to how far the *IS* curve can be shifted to the right if there is a sufficient increase in the quantity of money. Unemployment cannot exist in equilibrium if the money supply is increased enough. Classical economists have a powerful theoretical rebuttal to Keynes' demonstration of an unemployment equilibrium.

From the viewpoint of practical real-world policies, the *IS/LM*

Figure 7–2
***IS/LM* analysis: Effect of increase in money supply with real-balance effect**

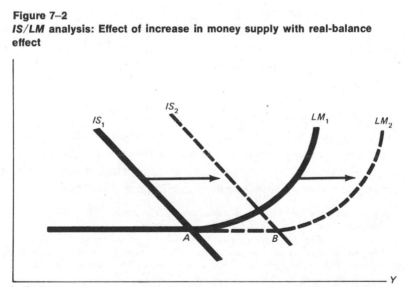

According to classical theory, an increase in the money supply will stimulate consumption. It will therefore cause the *IS* curve to shift to the right. Even if the interest rate is initially at its minimum, national income will rise.

---

[3] On the rightward movement of the *IS* curve as a result of the real-balance effect, see Don Patinkin, "Rejoinder to J. R. Hicks," *Economic Journal,* September 1959, pp. 582–87.

analysis can no longer be used to conclude that monetary policy becomes ineffective during a depression, when interest rates are at or close to their minimums. (The reader is warned against jumping to the opposite conclusion, that monetary policy *is* effective in such circumstances. This is a complicated question, which will be deferred until Chapter 9.)

SAY'S LAW AND THE INCONSISTENCY IN CLASSICAL THEORY[4]

Keynes was a brilliant economist, steeped in the classical tradition which he attacked in his *General Theory*. It is therefore somewhat paradoxical—and, indeed, may at first glance seem downright astounding—that he should look at only one half of the classical mechanism when he launched his attack on the classical proposition that equilibrium could exist only at full employment. [He attacked the classical argument that the rate of interest would change so as to equate full-employment saving and desired investment (Figure 6–1), but he ignored the classical argument that changes in the real quantity of money would affect saving.][5] Keynes' omission of the real-balance effect becomes more understandable, however, when it is recognized that the classical economists were not consistent regarding the real-balance effect and, indeed, held views which were contradictory.

The difficulty apparently grew out of a natural confusion between propositions that were true *only in equilibrium,* and those that were *invariably* true whether the economy was in equilibrium or not.

Classical economists looked on money as a veil, behind which real goods and services were *ultimately* exchanged for other real goods

---

[4] This section may be skipped without loss of continuity. (It will, however, be needed by those who read the appendix to this chapter.)

[5] Actually, it is not *precisely* correct to say that Keynes completely ignored the classical argument that an increase in the quantity of money can ensure full employment. On page 235 of the *General Theory,* he explicitly attributed unemployment to an inadequate supply of money:

Unemployment develops, that is to say, because people want the moon;—men cannot be employed when the object of desire (i.e., money) is something which cannot be produced and the demand for which cannot be readily choked off. There is no remedy but to persuade the public that green cheese is practically the same thing and to have a green cheese factory (i.e., a central bank) under public control.

This "green cheese" quotation is difficult to reconcile with the rest of the *General Theory* and, in particular, with Keynes' argument that the economy might reach an equilibrium at less than full employment.

and services. The butcher, the baker, the candlestick maker, it is true, sold their goods for money in the first instance, but the reason they did so was in order to have the money to buy the shoes and sealing wax they wanted. Money, of course, was important in oiling the wheels of commerce, making it possible to sell in large batches and to engage in complex transactions involving many individuals which would have been cumbersome or impossible in a barter economy. Money made the system work smoothly, but it was not what the game was all about. People were selling goods in order *ultimately* to get other goods.

In careless hands, this line of argument was extended until it got some classical economists into trouble. In particular, J. B. Say (who became one of Keynes' favorite whipping boys) argued along the following lines in the early part of the 19th century. People sell goods to get other goods. (Note that the word "ultimately" has been dropped from this statement; this is important, as will be seen shortly.) Therefore, the supply of one good involves the demand for some other good. (For example, when $100 worth of wheat is offered for sale, the farmer is thereby demanding $100 worth of gasoline, fertilizer, clothing, or whatever.) Therefore, for the economy as a whole, the supply of all goods must be equal to the demand for all goods. (Incidentally, services are included throughout this argument, and the word "goods" should be taken as meaning "goods and services.") *Supply creates its own demand,* and there can *never* be a general oversupply of goods. It is true that there may be an oversupply, say, of meat, and therefore distress in the meat industry. But what this meant, according to Say, is that there was a corresponding excess demand for some other product—bread, shoes, or whatever.

This conclusion, *Say's Law,* may be put formally, thus:

$$P_1 S_2 + P_2 S_2 + \cdots + P_n S_n \equiv P_1 D_1 + P_2 D_2 + \cdots + P_n D_n \quad (7\text{--}1)$$

That is,

$$\sum_{i=1}^{n} P_i S_i \equiv \sum_{i=1}^{n} P_i D_i \qquad (7\text{--}2)$$

where:

P_i is the price of the ith good.
S_i is the quantity of the ith good supplied.
D_i is the quantity of the ith good demanded.

There are n goods in the economy, 1, 2, . . . , n.

Σ, the Greek letter sigma, stands for "sum."

$\equiv$ means "is always equal to."

The important point of identity (7–2) : Say was arguing that the supply of all goods was of necessity always equal to the demand for all goods, *regardless of the general price level.*

As implied above, this formulation leads to trouble. In order to explain why this is so, it is necessary to digress briefly to the work of 19th century economist Leon Walras. Walras noted that, if *money is taken into account,* then any supply does indeed involve a demand. In the ordinary transaction involving money, the supplier of a good is "demanding" money in return. The demander of a good is offering ("supplying") money in exchange. In other words, supply does involve demand, and therefore the total supply and total demand in the economy must invariably be equal *if the demand and supply of money are included in total demand and supply.* Formally, where money is identified as the $n + 1$st item, *Walras' Law* may be written:

$$\sum_{i=1}^{n+1} P_i S_i \equiv \sum_{i=1}^{n+1} P_i D_i \qquad (7\text{–}3)$$

Walras' Law is correct; total demand is indeed equal to total supply, provided that the demand and supply of money are included.[6]

However, the quantities demanded and supplied of *each* item need not invariably be equal. If the price is higher than the equilibrium level for a particular good, then the quantity demanded will be less than the quantity supplied. Demand and supply for a specific good are equal, *but only at the equilibrium price.* This may be put in the familiar diagram of microeconomic textbooks (Figure 7–3).

Now, according to the Walrasian argument, exactly the same type of proposition applies to the $n + 1$st item, money. If the supply of money is taken as given, then the demand and supply of money look like the functions in Figure 7–4. The value of money is its purchasing power: The *higher* the general price index, the *lower* the value of money in terms of goods. Thus, the reciprocal of the general price index, $1/P$, is put on the vertical axis when illustrating

---

[6] For simplicity, this exposition is in terms of goods and money. To be complete, it would have to include goods, services, money, and *other financial assets.* For an extensive elaboration of the Walrasian model to include other financial assets, see Don Patinkin, *Money, Interest, and Prices,* 2d ed. (New York: Harper & Row, 1965).

the demand and supply curves for money. Because the *reciprocal* of the price index appears on the vertical axis, *lower* points are observed as prices *rise*.

The formulation of Figure 7–4 is consistent with the quantity theory of money. The demand and supply of money are equal, *but only when the general price level is at its equilibrium*. With an initial supply of money of S_1, the initial equilibrium price level is P_e. If prices are above this level (that is, if prices are at P_2, giving an

Figure 7–3
Demand and supply: An individual good

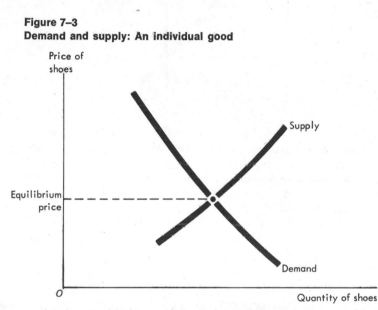

At the equilibrium price, the quantity demanded and the quantity supplied are equal.

observation *below* the equilibrium height of $1/P_e$ in Figure 7–4), then the demand for money (OB) exceeds the supply (OA); or, put another way, the supply of goods exceeds their demand and there will be unemployment. The indicated solutions: Increase the quantity of money (to S_2), or allow the general price level to fall to its equilibrium level (P_e). These, of course, represent the standard classical responses to unemployment.

But let us return to Say's Law, and the problem which it raises. The implications of Say's Law may be seen by subtracting Say's Law (Equation 7–2) from the correct formulation, namely, Walras' Law (Equation 7–3). This gives:

Figure 7–4
Demand and supply of money

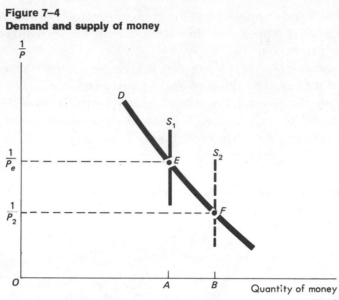

When the purchasing power of money is at its equilibrium level—that is, when the general price level is at its equilibrium —then the quantity of money demanded is equal to its supply. For example, there is an equilibrium at point *E* when the quantity of money is *OA*.

$$P_m S_m \equiv P_m D_m \qquad (7\text{--}4)$$

where the subscript m stands for money. By convention, money is the "numeraire" in the economy; prices are quoted in dollar terms. But the price of a dollar is \$1; the price of money is one.[7] Thus, Equation (7–4) reduces to:

$$S_m \equiv D_m \qquad (7\text{--}5)$$

Say's Law thus implies that the quantity of money demanded *must equal the quantity supplied, regardless of the general price level.*[8]

---

[7] Note that we are making a distinction between the price and the value of money. The price of money is a bookkeeping concept; as the books are kept in dollar terms, the price of money is one. The *value* of money, however, depends on how much a dollar will buy; as the prices of goods rise, the value of the dollar declines. The desirability of money—and hence the quantity of money demanded—depends on money's *value;* thus, 1/P is shown on the vertical axis of Figure 7–4.

[8] This was pointed out explicitly by Oscar Lange, "Say's Law: A Restatement and Criticism," in Lange, Francis McIntyre, and Theodore O. Yntema, eds., *Studies in Mathematical Economics and Econometrics* (Chicago: University of Chicago Press, 1942), pp. 52–53.

The problem is this. Say's Law (implying Equation 7–5) is inconsistent with the quantity theory which states that, if we begin at an equilibrium with full employment and with equilibrium prices (P_e in Figure 7–4), and then we increase the quantity of money (from S_1 to S_2), there will be an *excess supply* of money at the existing price level (P_e), and when consumers attempt to spend this money, the general price level will be bid up to its new equilibrium (P_2). With the quantity of money at S_2 and with the prices at P_e, there will be an excess supply of money: The demand for money (OA) will be less than the supply (OB). So states the quantity theory. In contrast, with Say's Law (and consequently with Equation 7–5), there can be no excess demand or supply of money; the quantity theory cannot apply.

Say's Law thus introduces a dichotomy into classical theory, a dichotomy between equilibrium in the real goods sector and what is happening in the monetary sector. Say's writings, therefore, blurred the logic behind the real-balance effect; Say's Law by implication denied the effect of the money supply on the demand for goods and services. It is not surprising that, in attacking Say's Law, Keynes propounded a theory which ignored the real-balance effect. The division between the goods sector and the financial sector was continued into the *IS/LM* analysis presented in the last chapter (but was amended in the *IS/LM* presentation in Figure 7–2). This dichotomy is, however, inconsistent with the quantity theory and with the real-balance effect; in order to be sure of full employment in equilibrium, a classical economist must argue that an increase in the supply of money will affect the aggregate demand for goods. He must argue that there is a demand and supply for money which are *not necessarily* equal, but which have the general characteristics shown in Figure 7–4 and are equal only when the price level is at equilibrium.[9]

It was at first glance surprising that Keynes focused only on one half of the classical mechanism and ignored the real-balance effect in putting forward his case that unemployment might exist in equilibrium. The explanation, as we have seen, was that classical economists, and particularly J. B. Say, had laid the basis for Keynes'

---

[9] Because a quantity theorist must reject the Say-Keynes dichotomy between the real and monetary sector, and because he must look at the (microeconomic) demand and supply of money, modern classical economists object to the sharp separation between macroeconomic theory and microeconomic theory. It is also why Patinkin picked the subtitle he did for his *Money, Interest, and Prices,* namely: *An Integration of Monetary and Value Theory.*

theoretical approach by splitting the theory of the demand and supply of goods and services from the theory of the demand and supply of money. It may seem even more astounding that classical economists should create this split, and at times ignore the effect of the real quantity of money when investigating the markets for goods and services. After all, the quantity theory of money—which lay at the heart of their analysis of aggregate demand—required that the money supply affect the aggregate demand for goods and services. But once again there is an answer; the classical economists were not simply stupid. Rather, they were frequently concerned with a problem quite different from the unemployment problem addressed by Keynes. Specifically, they were concerned with government policies that restricted international trade with tariffs and other devices. In part, trade restrictions were based on a crude mercantilist proposition that the wealth of nations depended on their holdings of gold, and that, therefore, trade restrictions were desirable as a means for increasing the quantity of gold in a country. In arguing against this crude merchantilist thesis, Say and many other classical economists[10] insisted that the wealth of nations lay, not in their holdings of precious metal, but in their ability to produce goods and services to satisfy the wants of their people. In so doing, some of them tended to simplify—a procedure fully justified by the very elementary level of much of the tariff debate. In the process of simplification, they argued that money did not represent real wealth—an accurate statement at a high level of simplification. The fine points of monetary theory got lost; a dichotomy was put forward which laid the groundwork for Keynes' skipping over the real-balance effect in his demonstration of an unemployment equilibrium.

THE MULTIPLIER AND THE REAL-BALANCE EFFECT

The argument of this chapter thus far has been highly theoretical and abstract, dealing with the nature of equilibrium in the economy. As yet, it seems to have little practical application, although it does point to one very important conclusion, namely that Keynesian theory may lead us to an overly hasty rejection of the importance of monetary policy. (See the discussion of Figure 7–2.) It is important that we get back to something with a clearer relationship to the real

---

[10] Including the most famous of them all, Adam Smith, *An Inquiry into the Nature and Causes of the Wealth of Nations,* 1776. Available in the Modern Library Series, Edwin Cannan, ed. (New York: Random House, 1937).

world. To this we turn: a closer look at the argument behind the Keynesian multiplier.

In Chapters 3 and 4, a number of alternative derivations of the Keynesian multiplier were given with the use of diagrams, algebra, and a period analysis. In this section, attention will be focused on the period analysis. It is the most useful for going through the blow-by-blow causal argument behind the multiplier theory, and for drawing out the behavioral assumptions. In going through the step-by-step process, we will throw into question the "normal psychological law" which Keynes saw determining consumer behavior and which was the basis of the multiplier theory.[11]

Suppose we look more closely at the multiplier model. Suppose, further, that we introduce an initial spending in the simplest possible way—the government engages in a one-time expenditure of $100 million for road building, acquiring the money by borrowing from the central bank (that is, the road building is financed with newly printed money). Then, with an *MPC* of 0.8, the standard illustration of the simple multiplier is shown in Table 7–1. The questions which arise are these: Why do income earners spend only $80 million of their additional $100 million in period 2? What do they do with the remainder, and why? The first answer, of course, is that the remaining $20 million is saved. In what form? As currency, bank deposits, or bonds. (With money created in the first round, *someone* will be holding additional money. Individual savers

Table 7–1
The multiplier: Single government expenditure

Time period	Assumed government spending G	Effects on spending for: C	I	Total
1..............	100	0	0	100
2..............	0	80	0	80
3..............	0	64	0	64
4..............	0	51.2	0	51.2
....	.	.	.	.
....	.	.	.	.
....	.	.	.	.
n..............	0	$100 \times 0.8^{n-1}$	0	$100 \times 0.8^{n-1}$
....	.	.	.	.
....	.	.	.	.
....	.	.	.	.
$\to \infty$..........	0	$\to 0$	0	$\to 0$
Sum.......	100	400	0	500

[11] Keynes, *General Theory*, pp. 114–15.

need not, however, hold their savings in the form of money; they can exchange money for bonds with some other members of the economy.) Good enough; why is it saved? To have something on hand for a rainy day (for contingencies, to buy a large-ticket item, etc.). Fine. When is the rainy day (when do the unforeseen contingencies arise, etc.)?

At this point, the logic of the simple multiplier becomes clear; the savings of period 2 are assumed *never* to influence future consumption *at all*. What happens in this simple multiplier analysis is that the $20 million of monetary wealth created in the first round but not actually spent in the second round ceases to have any affect on the level of aggregate demand; similarly, the $16 million saved during the third period is assumed to have no further effect on aggregate demand; and so on. To put it glibly, what happens in the Keynesian system is that, when the period ends, a whistle blows, a trap door opens, and through it fall all wealth accumulations from the saving process; they are assumed never to influence consumers' behavior again.[12]

It is difficult to find people who say that their own consumption is utterly unaffected by past savings. The questions raised in this section, therefore, throw doubts on whether the standard multiplier analysis is based on a reasonable "normal psychological law." On the contrary, it seems reasonable to argue that consumption depends in part on wealth, and that, in other words, past savings will tend to leak back into the spending stream.

It is, however, very important to recognize what this criticism does and does not mean. Most important, it does *not* mean that no multiplier-type process is at work. Rather, it means that, as accumulated past saving (wealth) stimulates consumption, then the multiplier process is stronger than indicated by the simple Keynesian analysis. Any tendency of consumers to spend their saving of period 2 during period 3, 5, 10, or whenever will increase the total level of aggregate spending ultimately resulting from the initial government spending. This illustration has suggested that the inclusion of the effect of wealth on the level of consumption requires an *upward* revision of the multiplier.

The event which began the multiplier process—a single-shot government expenditure financed with the creation of new money in

---

[12] Or, in the words of Lloyd Atkinson, "A penny saved is a penny burned."

our illustration—involved two simultaneous changes in the economy. It involved a flow of income to the public, in the form of additional government expenditures. And, as a part of the same process, the money wealth of the public was increased. The multiplier analysis focuses on the first of these changes, an income increase whose effect tends to peter out with the passage of time. But, if attention is focused on the second change—the increase in money wealth— then there is no similar reason to expect a vanishing effect; the money, once created, stays in the economic system to influence spending behavior indefinitely into the future. In Keynesian theory, attention is focused on the change in income; a single injection of spending is seen to peter out over time, returning the economy to its initial equilibrium (Figure 4–3). The classical quantity theory, however, focuses on the increase in the quantity of money. A *single* increase in the money stock will influence the level of aggregate demand indefinitely into the future; a single injection of money into the system will *permanently* increase the level of aggregate demand; a single injection will increase the *equilibrium* level of aggregate demand.

This illustration was chosen in order to draw the line most sharply between Keynesian and classical theory; the government expenditures stressed by Keynesian theory were financed by the money creation stressed in classical theory. What we have done is introduce real money into the system in a much more realistic manner than the price-wage reduction method which dominated the debate between Keynes and the classical economists. In doing so, we have put the real-balance effect into a context in which it has a relevance of real-world issues: Will a *single* program of government spending financed with newly created money lead to a *permanent* change in the level of demand? Our answer: Yes.

The above illustration—with government spending financed with newly created money—drew the line most sharply between multiplier analysis and classical thinking. The same general question can, however, also be raised for other types of injections into the spending stream which initiate a multiplier process. Consider a government expenditure financed by selling bonds to the public. The government obtains $100 million of the public's money by issuing $100 million in bonds. When the government spends the $100 million (for example, to build roads), then the public's money balances are restored to their initial level. As a result of the government expenditure, there is a net increase in the public's assets—they now hold the $100 million in government bonds. As a result, future consumption should be higher. Alternatively, consider investment expenditures. As investment spending proceeds, the real capital stock of the nation rises. Someone owns that capital stock. Society as a whole owns greater wealth. A plausible result: a stimulus to consumption into the indefinite future.

Wealth and the size of the multiplier: A classical interpretation

Suppose that we return to the initial example, of a government expenditure financed with newly created money. According to classical economists, the real money balances of the public should influence their consumption expenditure. As a result of the money created to finance the single-shot government expenditure, the money supply is permanently higher than it otherwise would have been. As a result, the level of demand is permanently higher than the initial level. Thus, the effects of the government expenditure (originally shown in Figure 4–3) must be modified, as illustrated in Figure 7–5. The height of the equilibrium change in demand will be related to the velocity of money. If, for example, the time period shown in Figure 7–5 is one month, and the equilibrium annual income velocity of money is four, then the equilibrium monthly change in aggregate demand will be one-third the change in the money stock. (One third is found by dividing the annual velocity, 4, by the number of months in the year, 12.) Thus, with an initial government expenditure of $100 million financed with the creation of new money, equilibrium monthly aggregate demand will rise by $33.3 million. If one follows a rather rigid quantity theory of money, with velocity being highly stable, then the equilibrium ($33.3 million) change in aggregate demand will be quickly approached.

For more sophisticated classical treatments, the possibility of a change in the velocity of money must be considered. This complication arises if the initial government spending is financed with the issue of bonds. In this case, the wealth of the public also increases with the initial government spending, but the money stock does not. As consumers' wealth has permanently increased, their consumption (as a function of current income) should be permanently higher than it would have been in the absence of the government spending. Again, the income increase attributable to the initial government spending will not completely evaporate with the pas-

Figure 7–5
The multiplier process: Period analysis with real-balance effect
(single government spending financed by central bank)

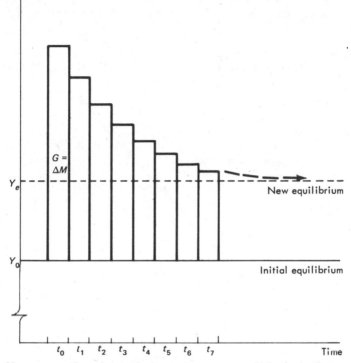

Aggregate demand
and its components

$G = \Delta M$

Y_e — New equilibrium

Y_0 Initial equilibrium

t_0 t_1 t_2 t_3 t_4 t_5 t_6 t_7 Time

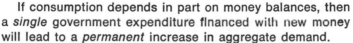

If consumption depends in part on money balances, then
a *single* government expenditure financed with new money
will lead to a *permanent* increase in aggregate demand.

sage of time; there will be a higher equilibrium level of income—
although the increase in this case will be less than in the event of
an initial money creation.[13]

With the initial injection permanently increasing the level of demand (Figure 7–5), the size of the multiplier calculated in the

---

[13] With consumption spending higher, there will be a greater demand for the given
stock of money balances. Interest rates as a consequence will be higher, with the consumption spending increase therefore being partially offset by a reduction in investment. With interest rates higher, the average money balances which individuals and
corporations wish to hold at any level of income will be reduced; the velocity of money
will rise. (This rise is obviously necessary if income is to rise with a fixed stock of
money.) The relationship between the demand for money and interest rates is investigated in Chapter 12.

standard way—as a series summed over an infinite number of periods—will become infinite; infinity times any minimum constant equals infinity. The question of the size of the multiplier in the classical system therefore becomes uninteresting, and attention in the classical theoretical system is rather focused on the *amount* by which the equilibrium level of income changes (that is, the distance

Figure 7–6
The multiplier process: Continuing government spending financed by central bank

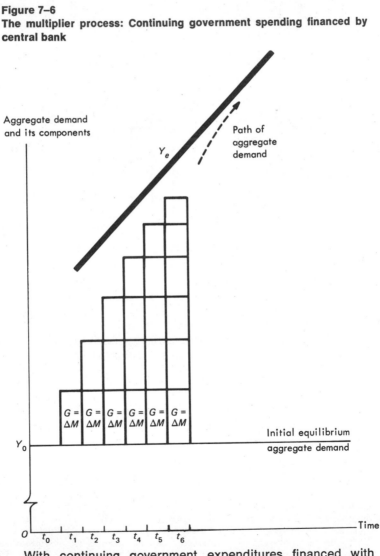

With continuing government expenditures financed with continuing additions to the money stock, aggregate demand will rise continuously.

between Y_o and Y_e in Figure 7–5). For public policy, the relevant question is the change in aggregate demand over some specified finite time period—such as three years—as a result of an initial injection into the system.

The previous illustrations assumed a *single* government expenditure. Assume, alternatively, a *continuing* government expenditure financed with continuing money creation. Then, if consumption is a function of wealth, aggregate demand will continue to grow without limit, as shown in Figure 7–6.[14] (Compare to Figure 4–4.) This is, of course, what one would expect from a simple application of the quantity theory: If the money supply increases indefinitely, so will aggregate demand. Such a continuing injection will not lead to any new, stable "equilibrium" level of aggregate demand, although there will be an equilibrium *growth path* of aggregate demand.

Following the assumptions of the simple multiplier discussion of Chapters 3 and 4, it has been assumed throughout this analysis that there are unemployed resources in the economy, and that real output changes in response to changes in demand, with prices stable. Where the economy is at full employment, the previous analysis must clearly take that into account. A rise in prices will result if aggregate demand increases (or, more precisely, if aggregate demand increases at a rate faster than the increase in productive capacity of the economy). In such cases, increases in demand financed by money creation need not involve an increase in the *real* value of the total quantity of money; rather, they may simply involve increases in prices.

STOCKS AND FLOWS AND THE PROBLEM OF THE KEYNESIAN EQUILIBRIUM

The real-balance or wealth effect objection to the Keynesian concept of an equilibrium level of demand may be reiterated in slightly different terms, concentrating on the distinction between *stocks* and *flows*. A stock is a quantity of something which exists at a point in time: We can speak of the money stock (the amount of money that exists in the economy); the capital stock (the quantity of equipment and other forms of capital that exist); and so on. Expenditure flows —consumption, investment, and so on—involve a time element;

---

[14] Figure 7–6 is similar to the curve illustrating the wealth effect in Franco Modigliani, "Monetary Policy and Consumption," *Consumer Spending and Monetary Policy: The Linkages* (Federal Reserve Bank of Boston, Conference Series No. 5, 1971), p. 28.

they represent a "quantity per time period." It makes no sense to speak of consumption at noon on January 1. Rather, a time dimension must be specified: We can talk of consumption during 1974; or during the first quarter of that year; or during the month of January. The quantity of water in Lake Erie at noon today is a stock; the amount of water that goes over Niagara Falls per month is a flow.

Keynesian economics concentrates on flows, particularly aggregate demand and its components. The difficulty with this, as seen from the classical viewpoint, is that stocks and flows are interrelated. The flow of water going over Niagara Falls will be affected by the stock of water in Lake Erie. In turn, the flow over Niagara Falls will affect the stock of water in Lake Ontario. In macroeconomics, the flow of saving involves a change in the stock of wealth as time passes.

For a general equilibrium to exist, there must be an equilibrium of both stocks and flows, since dissatisfaction with either can lead to a change in the other. If people are dissatisfied with their total wealth, they may try to build up their wealth by saving more. If they have a high level of wealth, they may consume more and save less; that is, the *stock* of wealth may affect the *flow* of saving, and hence the equilibrium aggregate demand (a flow). This last observation, of course, is a restatement of the real-balance effect. Keynesian economics, charge the classicists, concentrates on the equilibrium of flows without reference to what is happening to stocks; this shows up in the emphasis on income as a determinant of consumption and a tendency to dismiss the importance of wealth. The Keynesian equilibrium consists of flows. Out of any level of income, people save, adding to their stock of wealth. The implicit assumption in the simple Keynesian system is that this accumulation of wealth does not affect future flows.

(From the very early period, however, Keynesian economists did generally recognize and integrate into their thinking a second stock problem. Specifically, in an economy in which investment is taking place, the stock of capital will be rising, and therefore the full-employment level of production of the economy will also be increasing. This means that, for a continuing condition of full employment, aggregate demand must rise as time passes.)

Whatever its failings, classical economics does handle the stock-flow interconnection in a satisfactory manner. Money is a stock. If it is increased from an initial point of equilibrium, people will have an undesirably large stock and will respond by spending it. Thus, the aggregate demand flow will adjust to a disequilibrium in a stock.

PROBLEMS WITH THE KEYNESIAN EQUILIBRIUM AND WITH THE MULTIPLIER ANALYSIS: THEIR SIGNIFICANCE[15]

On the basis of the real-balance effect, a strong classical counter-attack may be made on the Keynesian theory of an unemployment *equilibrium,* in general, and on the Keynesian concept of an equilibrium multiplier, in particular. Multiplier expressions such as $1/MPS$ are based on the fundamental assumption that at the end of a period a whistle blows and wealth acquired in the saving process disappears. Since the accumulation of wealth is an inherent part of the saving process, and since the saving process is fundamental to the multiplier, this elimination of wealth from consideration may be viewed as an internal contradiction within the multiplier theory.

To adhere to Keynesian equilibrium theory taken to its ultimate logical consequences, it is necessary to argue by implication that individuals are completely unresponsive to accumulations of real money wealth. A diehard Keynesian believes in fat mattresses: People are willing to squirrel away unlimited quantities of idle money without modifying their consumption patterns. That is the implication of the liquidity trap, which is necessary to demonstrate the theoretical possibility of an unemployment equilibrium with flexible wages and prices, or, what is the same thing in static theoretical terms, with stable prices and increasing quantities of nominal money.

This theoretical attack on the multiplier, showing the logical difficulties of a process extended to an infinite number of periods into the future, does not, however, give us much clue to the practical limitations of Keynesian theory as a guide to policy. If Keynesian theory runs into difficulties in its conclusions regarding the long-run

---

[15] While the criticisms of the multiplier in the earlier section are intimately related to the key theoretical issue between classical and Keynesian economists (namely, the possible existence of an unemployment equilibrium), they by no means represent a comprehensive or complete criticism of the multiplier theory. For other criticisms, see, for example, Gottfried Haberler, "Mr. Keynes' Theory of the 'Multiplier': A Methodological Criticism," in American Economic Association, *Readings in Business Cycle Theory* (Homewood, Ill.: Richard D. Irwin, 1951), p. 193–202; and Milton Friedman, *Capitalism and Freedom* (Chicago: University of Chicago Press, 1962), chap. 5. For a policy-oriented exposition of the multiplier, see Council of Economic Advisers, *Annual Report,* January 1963, pp. 45–52.

equilibrium, why should this be of concern in establishing short-run policy?

Keynesian economics: The long run and the short

The simplest answer, which will for the moment be conditionally acceptable, is that it does not really make much difference. Keynes was concerned with short-run policymaking, and, in particular, with the policies necessary to stabilize the economy at full employment. This concern was nowhere more clearly demonstrated than in his dismissal of long-run equilibrium theorizing by economists: "This *long run* is a misleading guide to current affairs. *In the long run* we are all dead."[16] The elaborate—and questionable—theoretical structure which Keynes presented to demonstrate the existence of an unemployment equilibrium was not necessary to make his case for a policy of short-term fiscal expansion; but it was most helpful in convincing economists steeped in equilibrium theory that action was necessary. The Keynesian recommendations of increases in government spending and tax cuts during depressions do not fall as a result of theoretical problems with the nature of the long-term equilibrium.

In a situation such as the depressed 1930s, the objections that were made above to the simple multiplier do not throw doubt on the advisability of fiscal expansion, although they may indicate that, in cases where only mild stimulation is needed to restore full employment, some adjustment should be made in the degree of fiscal expansion in order to take account of feedbacks of saving into the spending stream. The only immediately obvious implication of the above discussion is that it is inadvisable, in a situation of depression or recession, to make sizable *long*-term spending commitments in the belief that they will clearly be required for a long-term achievement of full employment. Keynesian theory, although appearing in the guise of long-term equilibrium, should be applied only to short-term problems. It is no less important for this limitation.

For the development of practical economic policies, two aspects of the Keynesian-classical controversy are important. First, classical theory suggests that consumption should be significantly influenced by wealth, and that wealth effects should therefore be taken into account when estimating the future course of demand. More will be

---

[16] J. M. Keynes, *Monetary Reform* (New York: Harcourt, Brace, 1924), p. 88. (Italics in original.)

said about wealth effects in detail in Chapter 14; suffice it for the moment to note that wealth effects are not easily identified in spite of their logical importance in the theoretical controversy between Keynes and the classical economists.[17]

Second, the discussion of the classical counterattack casts doubt on the precedence given by Keynesian theory to fiscal policy as contrasted to monetary policy, particularly as a cure for depression. The theoretical Keynesian structure dismisses the importance of money in a manner that is not altogether plausible—particularly with the liquidity trap. There is something intrinsic in the Keynesian intel-

---

[17] Suppose we wish to investigate the Keynesian consumption function statistically. There is no necessary connection between the "periods" of multiplier theory and the periods for which statistics are gathered. Within the Keynesian framework, it is therefore reasonable to specify consumption as a function of "recent" income—that is, income of this period and the previous period. But it is also reasonable to assume that people are also influenced by habit, and that therefore previous consumption (in period $t-1$) should also be used to explain current consumption (in period t). Thus, the consumption function is readily extended within the Keynesian framework to include the following variables:

$$C_t = f(Y_t, Y_{t-1}, C_{t-1}) \qquad (7-6)$$

Now, what is the classical objection to the Keynesian consumption function? It is that Keynesian theory ignores the effect of wealth on consumption. To return to the very simple criticisms of the multiplier presented above, the classical objection to Keynesian theory is that people in future periods should be affected by the saving or the changes in wealth during the present period. In other words, the logic of the classical position is that Equation (7-6) must be amended to include S_{t-1}, thus:

$$C_t = f(Y_t, Y_{t-1}, C_{t-1}, S_{t-1}) \qquad (7-7)$$

where S_{t-1}, the saving of the previous period, is put in as a measure of the change in wealth.

The problem is that the consumption function has now become a statistical monstrosity. Specifically, from the view of the fitting of statistical functions, it makes no sense to include Y_{t-1}, C_{t-1}, and S_{t-1} all as independent variables in the equation, since they are not only closely related, but S_{t-1} may be *directly* derived from the *definitional* relationship among the three variables:

$$S_{t-1} \equiv Y_{t-1} - C_{t-1} \qquad (7-8)$$

We get no statistical mileage by putting S_{t-1} into Equation (7-7); the central *theoretical* issue between Keynes and the classics is not amenable to such a simple statistical test.

This does not mean, however, that wealth concepts are irrelevant in the empirical investigation of the consumption function. Something will be said on this subject in Chapter 14. For the moment, it suffices to note that, when wealth is introduced statistically into the consumption function, measures *not* directly related to saving of the previous period (as commonly defined) are used. For example, in the MPS (Massachusetts Institute of Technology/University of Pennsylvania/Social Science Research Council) model of the economy, capital gains accrued in the stock market are included as an explanatory variable in the consumption function.

The effect of wealth held in the form of corporation stocks is also examined in Barry Bosworth, "The Stock Market and the Economy," *Brookings Papers on Economic Activity,* 1975, vol. 2, pp. 257–90.

lectual framework which reiterates to the unwary economist that "money is not very important; money is not very important." (Just as, on the other side, the quantity theory suggests to the unwary economist that "money is the key; money is the key.") If a judgment is to be made about the *relative* merits of fiscal and monetary policy, a much closer look will have to be taken at the manner in which money affects the economy. In the contest between fiscal and monetary policy, the prize cannot be awarded after considering only the first contestant. In the coming chapters, the second contestant— monetary policy—will be studied.

APPENDIX

THE *GENERAL THEORY* AS THE ECONOMICS OF DISEQUILIBRIUM: CLOWER AND LEIJONHUFVUD

> *Like us, Keynes does not in any way deny the generality of orthodox equilibrium analysis; he only denies that orthodox economics provides an adequate account of disequilibrium phenomena.*[*]
>
> Robert Clower

For more than four decades, the existence of an *unemployment equilibrium* has been considered a principal theoretical innovation of Keynes in his *General Theory*. Certainly Chapters 3–6 of this book outline the standard textbook version of Keynes—a version that also forms the intellectual foundation for much of the more advanced literature on macroeconomics. But, regardless of its usefulness as a framework for analyzing short-term stabilization policies of the real world, the continuing popularity of Keynesian theory is perhaps puzzling in light of the strength of the classical counterattack. The Keynesian unemployment equilibrium depends on the implausible assumption that consumption is unaffected by wealth held in the form of money.

Among others, Professors Robert Clower and Axel Leijonhufvud have been bothered by the problems in Keynesian equilibrium

---

[*] Robert Clower, "The Keynesian Counterrevolution: A Theoretical Appraisal," in F. H. Hahn and F. P. R. Brechling, eds., *The Theory of Interest Rates* (New York: St. Martin's, 1965), p. 109.

theory. Leijonhufvud goes so far as to question whether Keynes was "a theoretical charlatan," and to speak of the

> shadow-life that Keynes' [equilibrium] theory leads. Properly speaking, there is no such theory. Not one that could serve for your advanced graduate theory courses, at any rate. But there is this "apparatus" (of which you do not speak to your theorist friends for fear of being sneered at), which serves so admirably in the proper care and feeding of undergraduates.[18]

But Clower and Leijonhufvud do not reject Keynes. They believe that, like a troublesome juvenile, Keynes was not bad, but just misunderstood.[19] Specifically, a generation of economists have misinterpreted Keynes' *General Theory;* Keynes' innovation lay not in the demonstration of an unemployment *equilibrium,* but rather in the analysis of *disequilibrium.* In the *General Theory,* "we should look for descriptions of *processes,* rather than of states."[20]

---

[18] Axel Leijonhufvud, *Keynes and the Classics* (London: Institute of Economic Affairs, 1971), p. 19. Leijonhufvud's views are explained in greater detail in his book, *On Keynesian Economics and the Economics of Keynes: A Study in Monetary Theory* (New York: Oxford University Press, 1968). (Leijonhufvud's Swedish name is less forbidding when translated into its English equivalent, "lion's head.")

[19] See, for example, Robert Clower, "The Keynesian Counterrevolution," p. 111.

[20] Leijonhufvud, *Keynes and the Classics,* p. 29 (italics in original). As I read their works, Leijonhufvud takes a stronger view than does Clower that Keynes has been misconstrued, and that their alternative explanation was what Keynes really meant. Indeed, Clower's article might be interpreted as Clower's view of what he *thinks* Keynes had in mind. Consider, for example, Clower's statement (p. 115, italics added) that he is describing "the route which Keynes *apparently* travelled." Or consider this passage (p. 120): "It is another question whether Keynes can reasonably be considered to have a dual decision theory [which forms the basis for Clower's dynamic explanation] . . . in mind when he wrote the *General Theory.* For my part, I [Clower] do not think there can be any serious doubt that he did, although I can find no direct evidence in any of his writings to show that he ever thought explicitly in these terms." To this, Coddington objects that Clower has read "not so much between the lines as off the edge of the page." (Alan Coddington, "Keynesian Economics: The Search for First Principles," *Journal of Economic Literature,* December 1976, p. 1268.)

[It is perhaps a tribute to the subtlety of the *General Theory* (or to the complexity of the subject material with which Keynes was dealing) that economists have tended to find their own strong views in the *General Theory*—even over the objections of Keynes himself. Thus, Joan Robinson complained that "there were moments when we had some trouble in getting Maynard [Keynes] to see what the point of his revolution really was . . ." (Robinson, "What has become of the Keynesian Revolution?" in Robinson, ed., *After Keynes,* Oxford: Basil Blackwell, 1973, p. 3).]

I do not agree with the charge—leveled particularly by Leijonhufvud—that Hansen, Samuelson, and countless other economists who have written about the Keynesian unemployment equilibrium have gravely misinterpreted Keynes. The now-popular unemployment equilibrium model is indeed to be found in the *General Theory.* But that was not *all* that was in the *General Theory*—a book that is at once delightful yet aggravating in its subtleties and complexities. Certainly discussions of disequilibrium may be found on many pages of the *General Theory.* Thus, in the *General Theory,*

So far as it goes, there is nothing logically wrong with the classical theory of general equilibrium as developed by Walras and others. A full-employment general equilibrium can exist, with the price of each good (including money) at the level at which the quantity demanded and the quantity supplied are equal. But, in the dynamic setting of the real world—with changes continuously occurring in demand and supply conditions, there is a problem of getting to the equilibrium pattern of prices, and of changing this pattern as the underlying conditions in the economy change. Walras formally solved this problem with two devices. First, he assumed that time can be divided into a number of discrete periods, within which demand and supply conditions do not change. Second, he introduced the artificial concept of an auctioneer, whose function it was to discover the market-clearing set of prices. (A market "clears" when the quantity demanded and the quantity supplied are equal at the quoted prices.)

The auctioneer begins the period by crying out a suggested list of prices to market participants, who respond by proclaiming their desires to buy or sell at those prices. As yet, however, no actual transactions take place. These initial prices called out by the auctioneer need not be the equilibrium set; indeed, they will represent equilibrium only with the greatest good fortune. Most likely, the demand and supply of some goods will be out of line. The auctioneer then calls out a new set of prices, raising the prices of goods whose demand exceeds supply, and lowering the prices of goods whose supply exceeds demand. Once more, the market participants respond with their desired sales and purchases at these new prices. Through this process of "tatonnement"—a step-by-step trial and error—the auctioneer gropes toward the equilibrium set of prices. Once he has found it, he announces the prices as final for that period. Transactions now are carried out at the prices that ensure that demand equals supply for each good and service.

However satisfactory the device of the auctioneer may be for solving the theoretical problem, it has distinct limitations when applied to the real world. Time is continuous, not discrete, and changes in underlying demand and supply conditions can take place at any time. Market participants do not wait until they have the

---

the basis may be found *both* for the traditional equilibrium interpretation and for the Clower-Leijonhufvud interpretation.

For the rest of this appendix, I shall refrain from niggling footnotes over what Keynes did or did not say; a simplified version of the Clower-Leijonhufvud thesis is presented without further harrassment.

perfect information supplied by Walras' mythical auctioneer. Rather, they respond to prices actually in existence—whether these prices represent equilibrium or not. At any time, these prices tend to be closely related to prices of the preceding time interval. On the basis of existing prices, market participants act. In the real world, false trading takes place, that is, transactions at prices that do not result in an equality of the quantity demanded and the quantity supplied.[21] Some participants are disappointed. Some might wish to buy at the prevailing price, but find that the store has sold out; others might be willing to sell, but find they have no buyer.

Consider a specific illustration—the market for hotel rooms in a large city in which there are a large number of reasonably similar hotels.[22] If there were a Walrasian auctioneer who communicated current conditions to all market participants, then the occupancy rate of hotels would be high and reasonably stable; prices would fluctuate in response to changes in the demand for hotel rooms. No individual hotel owner would be able to hold out for a "reasonable" or traditional price, since the marginal cost of having a room actually occupied is negligible, and because customers would be redirected to other hotels by the auctioneer in the event that any single hotel held out for a price above the market-clearing equilibrium.

But, in fact, nothing of the sort is observed in the hotel business. Excluding the obvious exception of resort hotels with peak-season prices, we observe that hotels, in fact, keep reasonably stable room prices. Day-to-day, week-to-week, and month-to-month fluctuations in demand show up, not primarily in price fluctuations, but in fluctuations in the occupancy rate.

In part, this can be attributed to uncertainty regarding demand. At the beginning of any day, hotel owners do not have precise knowledge of the number of customers who will show up to rent rooms. But this surely is not the only explanation. If hotels were seriously searching for the market-clearing price, they could adjust prices on a day-to-day basis, and extended periods of low occupancy interspersed with extended periods of high occupancy would not be observed.

Something else is needed to explain hotel owners' behavior.

---

[21] See Clower's "The Keynesian Counterrevolution," pp. 111–15, which draws heavily on J. R. Hicks, *Value and Capital*, 2d ed. (Oxford: Clarendon, 1946), pp. 119–29.

[22] This example is drawn from Arthur M. Okun, "Inflation: Its Mechanics and Welfare Costs," *Brookings Papers on Economic Activity*, 1975, vol. 2, pp. 360–61.

There is a distinct advantage in keeping prices relatively stable. Why? Because hotel owners hope to build up a clientele of customers who will return regularly to the hotel. Customers are likely to come back if they have a reasonably accurate idea of what the price will be. They want to be able to make their plans without a time-consuming and irksome canvassing of hotels to see which one is currently giving the lowest price. By keeping prices reasonably stable, hotels provide some assurance that arrangements that were considered satisfactory during past visits will be repeated on future visits. In other words, price stability has a positive utility to hotel patrons: it cuts down on the need to search continuously for the best price.

Something similar happens in the labor market. A newly un-employed worker does not know where the best job is to be found; he must search for it. In searching, he does not take the first job available, regardless of the wage offered. He sets some minimum acceptable wage, which he believes he will be able to obtain within a reasonable search time. This minimum wage will be heavily in-fluenced by what the worker is used to, that is, his wage in his most recent job. During a recession, of course, jobs are hard to come by and the search may be long and frustrating.

What does this all mean? Even though there is a theoretical full-employment equilibrium for the economy which could be reached if there were a Walrasian auctioneer, no such auctioneer exists in practice. In response to changes in demand and supply conditions, there will be extended periods of nonclearing markets, when hotel owners have extra rooms which they would be delighted to rent at the going rate, and when many workers are out of jobs even though they would be delighted to work for the going wage. Actual prices and actual transactions are not determined by the intersection of the demand and supply curves, where the quantities demanded and supplied are equal. Rather, prices adjust only slowly to gaps between demand and supply, and current prices are heavily influenced by tradition and previous prices. Actual transactions are determined by the lesser of the quantity demanded and the quantity supplied at the current price. Changes in demand tend to show up initially in the form of changes in output; prices adjust only slowly. Extended recessions are possible in the face of declining aggregate demand.

According to Clower and Leijonhufvud, the failure of market signals is the main message of the *General Theory*. To understand

Keynes, one must study disequilibrium, and the dynamics of change in an economy.[23]

In the following chapters, three major dynamic issues will be considered. In Part Three (Chapters 8–12), we will study the short-run effects of monetary and fiscal policies and the complex interactions among monetary changes, fiscal changes, and changes in aggregate demand. In Chapter 13, we will look at the dynamics of inflation and of the labor market. In Chapters 14 and 15, we will consider consumption and investment demand in more detail; in particular, we will study how consumption and investment respond *gradually* to changes in income and other variables.

KEY POINTS

1. According to classical theory, the dichotomy between the product market (the *IS* curve) and the financial market (the *LM* curve) must be rejected. An increase in the quantity of money held by the public will increase their level of consumption out of any given amount of income. Thus, it will shift the saving function down, and shift the *IS* curve to the right. An increase in the quantity of money directly affects *both* the *LM* and *IS* curves.

2. Consequently, the "liquidity trap" argument becomes invalid if consumption responds to additions in real money holdings of the public (the real-balance effect). Increases in the real money stock will increase aggregate demand. The economy does not remain in an unemployment equilibrium regardless of increases in real money balances.

3. Once we recognize the potential effect of increases in the quantity of money (or other forms of wealth) on consumption, then the multiplier process becomes more complicated. For example, a one-shot government spending financed by newly created money will involve a *permanent* increase in the equilibrium

---

[23] The literature on dynamics is extensive; Clower and Leijonhufvud were considered here because of their thesis that disequilibrum and dynamics constituted the basic point of the *General Theory*.

Other works on dynamics include Robert J. Barro and Herschel I. Grossman, "A General Disequilibrium Model of Income and Employment," *American Economic Review*, March 1971, pp. 82–93; and many of the works cited in Chapters 9–16.

level of national income; the effects do not peter out asymptoti-
cally toward zero as foreseen in the simple multiplier theory.

QUESTION

1. In Chapter 3, consumption was introduced as a function of income. We have now introduced a second determinant of consumption demand, namely, money wealth (and other forms of
wealth). What other variables might be expected to influence
consumption demand?

SUGGESTED READING

Don Patinkin, *Money, Interest, and Prices; An Integration of
Monetary and Value Theory,* 2d ed. (New York: Harper &
Row, 1965), chaps. 1–4. (For advanced students only.)

PART THREE

AGGREGATE DEMAND POLICIES IN A DYNAMIC AND UNCERTAIN ENVIRONMENT

Highbrow opinion is like a hunted hare;
if you stand still long enough,
it will come back to the place it started from.

Dennis Robertson

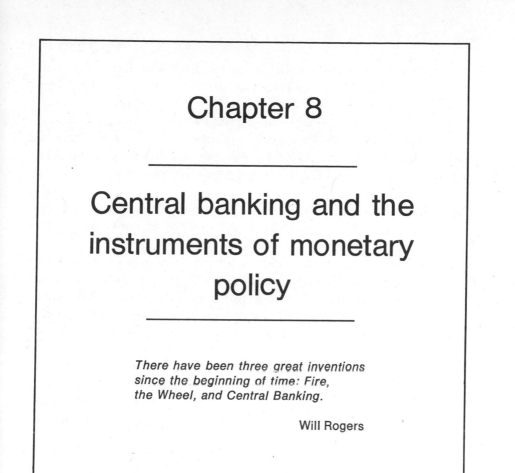

Chapter 8

Central banking and the instruments of monetary policy

There have been three great inventions since the beginning of time: Fire, the Wheel, and Central Banking.

Will Rogers

In the previous chapters, we have considered the policy proposals and the theoretical controversies introduced by Keynes' *General Theory*. On the policy side, we have concentrated on the tool that Keynes himself emphasized—the use of fiscal policy to stabilize aggregate demand at a level high enough to provide full employment, but not so high as to generate inflation. On the theoretical side, the focus has been on the possible existence of an unemployment equilibrium.

Toward the end of Chapter 7, the theoretical discussion reached a dead end. The Keynesian unemployment equilibrium does not survive careful examination; it is based on the implausible assumption that consumers do not respond to accumulations of wealth.

But it is not to kick a dead horse that a textbook should be written. The unemployment equilibrium is dead, but Keynesian economics lives. Large-scale unemployment may not represent a situation of long-run equilibrium. But large-scale unemployment can exist for an extended time span; unemployment is a very real and painful problem. And Keynesian economics provides a program to deal with this problem: adjust aggregate demand in order to achieve a higher and more stable level of economic activity.

This policy issue—the management of aggregate demand—will be the topic of the coming chapters. Having cut ourselves away from the comfortable—but unsatisfactory— concept of equilibrium, we are left with the realistic—but messy—questions which must be addressed by the policymaker. How is aggregate demand policy to be made in a dynamic, changing economy? What are we to do if we do not know the position of the consumption function (and other economic relationships) with any degree of precision? What do we do if we cannot be certain of the speed and magnitude of the economy's response to policy initiatives?

In dealing with these questions, we are drawn toward the conclusion that policymakers should not depend upon a single policy weapon. Monetary policy and fiscal policy should not be looked upon as competitive tools; the issue is not whether we use monetary policy *or* fiscal policy. Rather, both monetary *and* fiscal tools should be used in an overall policy strategy. This proposition is the main topic of Chapter 10.

As a preliminary, however, we must look in more detail at monetary policy. In earlier chapters—particularly Chapter 4—we studied how fiscal policy affects aggregate demand. As yet we have not looked at the detailed effects of monetary policies. Before turning to the interrelationships between fiscal and monetary policies, we should study monetary policy itself; this is done in the present chapter and in Chapter 9. It is particularly appropriate to look at monetary policy now that our focus has shifted from equilibrium to the problems of a dynamic economy. Regarding monetary policy, the major issue is not *whether* it works—it does—but *how quickly* and *how predictably* it works; and whether it has painful side effects.

MONEY IN THE U.S. ECONOMY

The money supply, as usually defined, is made up of two components: currency (coins and paper currency) held by the public and checking deposits owned by the public. Each of these clearly qualifies under the most obvious criterion of money: Each is used by the public in the purchase of goods and services.

Demand deposits form by far the largest component of the money stock—about three fourths of the total (Table 8–1). These deposits are assets to the corporation or individual who has made the deposit; they represent "money in the bank," against which checks can be written in order to make purchases or pay bills. But, from the viewpoint of the commercial banks, the deposits represent liabilities: The banks are committed to pay on the demand of the depositor. Money may therefore be looked on either as an asset (to the individual or corporation that holds it) or as a liability (from the viewpoint of the bank). This is true not only of demand de-

Table 8–1
Components of the money stock (December 1976)

Component	Billions of dollars	Percent of total
Demand deposits	231.2	74.1
Currency	80.7	25.9
Total	311.9	100.0

Most money is held in the form of demand deposits, that is, deposits against which checks can be written.

posit money, but also of currency, which consists mainly of the Federal Reserve notes (dollar bills) which people carry in their wallets. (Coins are also a component of currency.) Federal Reserve notes are an asset of the public, but a liability of the Federal Reserve.

Because money represents the liabilities of the banking system— either of the commercial banks (in the case of demand deposits) or of the Federal Reserve (in the case of Federal Reserve notes) — changes in the quantity of money may be studied by looking at the balance sheets of the banks. The quantity of money in our economy is subject to control by the Federal Reserve, the central bank of the United States.[1]

---

[1] The Federal Reserve has a peculiar organization. Although it is technically owned by the private commercial banks which are members, the "Fed" is a government agency. It is managed by a Board of Governors nominated by the President and subject to congressional confirmation. (The presidents of the 12 regional Federal Reserve banks also play an important decisionmaking role.) Although the Fed works in close consultation with the U.S. Treasury, it is technically not part of the executive branch. It was created by Congress to fulfill the constitutionally mandated congressional re-

OPEN MARKET OPERATIONS

If the Federal Reserve wishes to increase the money supply, its most important tool is the purchase of government securities in the open market. If the Federal Reserve purchases a $100,000 bond from a commercial bank (bank A),[2] the initial effects on the balance sheets of the two institutions will be those shown in Table 8–2. In exchange for the government security, the commercial bank receives a reserve deposit in the Federal Reserve. At this initial stage, no change has yet taken place in the money supply. Demand deposits are counted as part of the money supply only if they are held by the general public; interbank deposits (including deposits of commercial banks in the Federal Reserve) are not counted as part of

Table 8–2
Open market purchase by Federal Reserve: Initial effects (first-round balance sheet changes; in $000)

Federal Reserve

Assets	Liabilities
Government securities +100	Reserve deposits of commercial banks +100

Commercial Bank A

Assets	Liabilities
Reserve deposits in Federal Reserve +100 Government securities −100	No change

When the Federal Reserve purchases securities on the open market, the reserve deposits of commercial banks are increased.

---

sponsibility "to coin Money, [and] regulate the Value thereof" (Art. 1, sect. 8); and the Federal Reserve is answerable to the Congress.

A substantial degree of independence is provided by the 14-year terms to which the members of the Board of Governors are appointed. (One of the seven positions on the board becomes vacant every two years.) The Chairman of the Board serves a four-year term, beginning on February 1 of the year following the beginning of the President's term. In order to provide for greater coordination with the President's policies, suggestions have been made that this one-year lag be eliminated, with the chairman's term being made coincident with that of the President. Others object, arguing that it would be undesirable to reduce the Fed's independence from the President.

[2] Since it is operating on the open market, the Federal Reserve has no control over who the seller is; the seller will be anyone or any organization willing to sell at the bid placed by the Federal Reserve. Below, we will consider the alternative example, where the Federal Reserve buys from a seller other than a commercial bank.

the money supply. This definition, incidentally, makes sense: We are interested in the effects of the changes in the money supply on the behavior of the public, and therefore it is only the changes in the deposits or currency held by the public that are relevant.

While no direct increase in the money supply takes place immediately as a result of this open market transaction in which the bond is sold by a commercial bank, the stage is set for a change in the money supply. Commercial bank A now has excess reserves, and is permitted to make additional loans.

Commercial banks are required to keep reserves equal to a fraction of their demand (and time) deposits; these reserves are made up of reserve deposits which the commercial banks hold in the Federal Reserve, plus the commercial banks' holdings of currency. As of mid-1977, these reserve requirements on demand deposits ranged from 7 percent to 16.25 percent, depending on the size of the bank's deposits.[3] Clearly, if the correct figures are used for required reserve percentages, the illustrations will become hopelessly bogged down in fractions. Messy fractions will be avoided by the simple assumption of a single, required reserve of 20 percent of demand deposits.

Since its demand liabilities have not been changed by the open market operation, commercial bank A's required reserves likewise will not have been changed; it will therefore have $100,000 in excess reserves which it can lend out. Suppose that it lends the full $100,000 to a bicycle manufacturer. The bank does not, however, normally give the borrower currency in exchange for an IOU; rather, the bank credits the $100,000 to the demand deposit of the bicycle manufacturer. The loan by commercial bank A has the effects shown in Table 8–3. Now there has been an increase in the money stock; it has gone up by the $100,000 held by the bicycle company in its demand deposit.

This is not the end of the story, however. The bicycle maker has not borrowed just to let the money sit in a demand deposit. Rather, the borrowing in all likelihood was for a specific purpose; let us suppose for purchasing steel. The bicycle company pays for the steel with a check, which the steel company deposits in its bank (bank B). The check now enters the check-clearing process, as illustrated in Table 8–4. As a result, bank A loses its reserve deposits. The total effects, as seen by bank A, are rather simple: it

---

[3] Prior to 1972, the required reserve ratio also depended on the location of the bank (see Table 8–12).

Table 8–3
The commercial bank lends its excess reserves (in $000)

1. Balance-sheet effects of the loan

Commercial Bank A

Assets		*Liabilities*	
Loan	+100	Demand deposit of bicycle company	+100

Bicycle Manufacturer

Assets		*Liabilities*	
Demand deposit	+100	Bank loan	+100

2. Net effects to date on commercial bank A (open market operation plus loan)

Commercial Bank A

Assets		*Liabilities*	
Reserve deposits in Federal Reserve	+100	Demand deposits	+100
Government securities	−100		
Loans	+100		

A commercial bank can safely lend an amount
equal to its excess reserves; in this case $100,000.

has sold a government security and has loaned the proceeds to the bicycle company (Table 8–5).

As a result of the steel company's deposit, bank B now has excess reserves—but this time, less than the $100,000. Bank B's total reserves, it is true, have gone up by $100,000 (Table 8–6). But its demand deposit liabilities have gone up by $100,000, and therefore its required reserves have risen by $20,000. Therefore, its excess reserves are only $80,000. Bank B can safely lend this $80,000; when it does so, then the money supply rises by $80,000 (Panel 2 of Table 8–6). When the proceeds of this loan are spent, then another bank—bank C—will receive the $80,000 in deposits and will get $80,000 in reserves as a result of the check-clearing process. This bank, in turn, will have excess reserves—of $64,000—and will be able to lend that amount.

The process can continue. The result is a series of increases in the money supply shown in Table 8–7. This is a series of the form

Table 8–4
The clearing of checks (balance sheet effects; in $000)

Federal Reserve

Assets	Liabilities
No change	Reserve deposits
	of Bank A −100
	of Bank B +100

STEP 3.
Federal Reserve sends check along to bank A, subtracting $100,000 from bank A's reserve deposit.

STEP 2.
Bank B sends check along to the Federal Reserve and gets a reserve deposit.

Bank A

Assets	Liabilities
Reserves −100	Demand deposit of bicycle company −100

Bank B

Assets	Liabilities
Reserves +100	Demand deposit of steel company +100

STEP 4.
Bank A deducts $100,000 from deposit against which check was drawn.

STEP 1.
Steel company deposits check.

In the process of check clearing, Bank A loses an amount of reserves equal to the loan it has made. It is for this reason that the bank can safely lend only the amount of its excess reserves.

Table 8–5
Net effects on commercial bank A (open market operation, plus loan, plus check clearing, in $000)

Assets		Liabilities	
Reserves	0	Demand deposits	0
Government			
securities	−100		
Loans	+100		

Bank A no longer has excess reserves. It has sold a government security and loaned the proceeds to the bicycle company.

Table 8–6
Effects on commercial bank B (in $000)

1. When steel company's check is deposited

Assets		*Liabilities*	
Reserves	+100	Demand deposits	+100

2. When bank B makes loan

Assets		*Liabilities*	
Loans	+80	Demand deposits	+80

3. When proceeds of loan are spent and cleared

Assets		*Liabilities*	
Reserves	−80	Demand deposits	−80

4. Net effect of above three transactions

Assets		*Liabilities*	
Reserves	+20	Demand deposits	+100
Loans	+80		

Commercial bank B can safely lend its excess reserves of $80,000. When it does so (at Step 2), the money stock is increased by $80,000.

Table 8–7
Effects of open market operation (in $000)

As a result of loans by	*Money supply increases by*
Bank A...........................	$100
B...........................	80
C...........................	64
D...........................	51.2
....	.
....	.
....	.
→ ∞	→0
Total................	$500

The banking system *as a whole* can create $500,000 in demand deposits on the base of the $100,000 reserve.

100, 100 (0.8) , 100 (0.8) ^{2}, 100 (0.8) ^{3} . . . . If the series is summed to an infinite number of terms, the *maximum* increase in the money supply is $500,000 [that is, $100,000 ÷ (1 − 0.8)] as a result of the initial $100,000 open market purchase of the Federal Reserve. The final balance-sheet effects on the commercial banking *system*—that is, all commercial banks taken as a group—are shown in Table 8–8.

As the above example shows, commercial banks may lend out their excess reserves, increasing the money supply in the process. Alternatively, they may purchase bonds or short-term securities with their excess reserves. Where the nonbank public is the seller of such securities, the money supply will also be increased as a result of the

Table 8–8
The commercial banking system (in $000)

Assets		Liabilities	
Reserves	+100	Demand deposits	+500
Government securities	−100		
Loans	+500		

The commercial banking system *as a whole* can do what no individual bank can do—lend five times as much as the increase in reserves.

acquisition of bonds (or other securities) by the commercial banks.[4] Reconsider the illustration in Table 8–6. Rather than lending its customer the $80,000, bank B might use its excess reserves to buy $80,000 in bonds, providing the seller with $80,000 in demand deposits. The effects on the money supply are the same; the money supply will increase by $80,000 at this point. When the seller of the bond spends the proceeds—for example, by purchasing goods from a customer of bank C—the $80,000 in reserves will be transferred to bank C in the check-clearing process. The process of monetary expansion can continue. Loans or security purchases by banks—or any combination of the two—can take place during each round of monetary expansion.

Thus far, it has been assumed that the process of monetary creation began when the Federal Reserve bought a bond that was sold by a commercial bank. This need not, however, be the case; a mem-

---

[4] If the security is sold by another bank rather than by the nonbank public, then no monetary expansion will take place as a direct result of the purchase. However, the other bank will now acquire the reserves, and when it makes loans, the money supply will increase.

ber of the nonbank public might be the seller. In this instance, there would be an increase in the money supply in the initial round. If the seller deposits the proceeds from the bond in his demand deposit in commercial bank A, the results are as shown in Table 8–9. Here, the money supply goes up by $100,000 as a direct result of the open market purchase by the Fed. The amount that

Table 8–9
Open market purchase by Federal Reserve: Bond sold by nonbank public (initial effects, in $000)

Federal Reserve

Assets		*Liabilities*	
Government securities	+100	Reserve deposits of commercial banks	+100

Commercial Bank A

Assets		*Liabilities*	
Reserve deposits in Federal Reserve	+100	Demand deposit	+100

Mr. Smith (nonbank public)

Assets		*Liabilities*
Government securities	−100	No change
Demand deposit	+100	

If the Federal Researve purchases a security from a member of the public, then the *initial* effects include an increase in the money stock.

bank A can lend out, however, is now only $80,000, since its demand deposit liabilities have risen by $100,000, and therefore its required reserves have increased by $20,000. Therefore, when bank A lends its excess reserves, the money supply will increase by only $80,000. Although the timing is different, the overall results in terms of the maximum increase in the money supply are the same as in the first example, in which a commercial bank sold the bond. Whether the commercial banks or the nonbank public sell the bonds that the Federal Reserve purchases in the first round, the maximum increase in the money supply will be five times the size of the open market operation, provided that the required reserve ratio is 20 percent. In general,

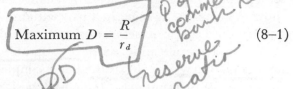

$$\text{Maximum } D = \frac{R}{r_d} \qquad (8\text{--}1)$$

where

D stands for demand deposits.
R is the quantity of commercial bank reserves.
r_d is the required reserve ratio applying to demand deposits.

These examples have shown how the money supply can *increase* as a result of an open market *purchase* by the Federal Reserve. If the Federal Reserve wanted to *decrease* the money supply, it would take the opposite action, *selling* securities on the open market. In our growing economy, however, an actual decrease in the money supply would represent a *very* restrictive policy. Restraint is generally exercised in a more moderate fashion, that is, by a *decrease in the rate of growth* of the money stock rather than as an absolute decline.

MONEY CREATION IS LESS THAN THE MAXIMUM

The above illustration—showing the *maximum* increase in the money supply that can occur as the result of an open market operation—makes it appear as if the Federal Reserve exercises a precise control over the money supply; the commercial banks and the public appear to be puppets dancing to the Fed's tune. However, this mechanical illustration represents an oversimplification. In fact, there are decisions to be made both by the public and by the commercial banks. As a result of these decisions, the increase in the money supply which actually takes place can be significantly less than suggested by the earlier illustration.

In the first place, as people's holdings of money increase, they may decide to hold part of the increase in the form of currency. How do they get this currency? By going to the bank and making withdrawals from their deposits (Table 8–10). When the banks hand over the currency, their reserves are decreased, since banks' currency is included (together with their deposits in the Fed) in calculating their reserves. As a consequence, the banks' ability to make loans is decreased—and with it, their ability to expand the money stock. (From the viewpoint of a bank, vault cash and reserve deposits in the Fed are interchangeable. When a bank runs short of currency, it may, in turn, withdraw currency from its deposit in the Federal Reserve, as shown in Table 8–11.)

A second complication arises if the public decides to hold more savings or other time deposits.[5] For example, the steel company in the earlier illustration may decide to deposit the $100,000 check in a time deposit rather than in a demand deposit. In this event, two

Table 8–10
A withdrawal of currency by the public
(balance sheet changes; in $000)

Public

Assets		Liabilities
Demand deposits	−50	No change
Currency	+50	

Commercial Banks

Assets		Liabilities	
Reserves:		Demand deposits	−50
Deposits in Fed	0		
Currency	−50		

As a result of a change in the *composition* of the public's money holdings, bank reserves are reduced.

points should be noted. First, as required reserves are less for time deposits than for demand deposits, the total expansion of bank deposits—including *both* time and demand deposits—will be larger than if the public had decided to hold only demand deposits. But, on the other hand, the change in the quantity of *money* will be less, since time deposits are not included in the money stock—at least not according to the usual definition.

Finally, in the illustration at the beginning of this chapter, we assumed that when a bank *can* make a loan or purchase a security, it actually *does* so. This need not be the case, however. The bank may prefer to hold excess reserves; that is, reserves above and be-

---

[5] As a general rule, savings deposits are held by individuals; other time deposits are held by businesses.

yond those required by law. Once again, the expansion of the money supply will be less than suggested by our earlier example.

Because of these three complications, the demand deposit equation becomes rather complex. In purchasing $100 million in securities on the open market, the Federal Reserve causes a $100 million increase in the *monetary base*—that is, commercial bank reserves (either in the form of reserve deposits or in the form of

Table 8–11
The banks replenish their currency holdings
(balance sheet changes; in $000)

Commercial Banks

Assets		Liabilities
Reserves:		No change
Deposits in Fed	−50	
Currency	+50	

Federal Reserve

Assets	Liabilities	
No change	Reserve deposits	−50
	Federal Reserve notes (currency) outstanding	+50

If and when the commercial banks decide to replenish their currency holdings by withdrawals from their deposits in the Fed, the *composition* of their reserves changes, but there is no further change in the quantity of reserves.

Federal Reserve notes) plus currency held by the public. The Federal Reserve does not control the composition or the use of the monetary base, however; this depends on the decisions of the commercial banks and the public. Rather than being used entirely as required reserves for demand deposits, the additional monetary base has four possible uses:

1. Reserves required for demand deposits.
2. Reserves required for savings (or time) deposits.
3. Excess reserves.
4. Currency in the hands of the public.

Suppose we look only at one of the complications: currency holdings of the public. If the required reserve against demand deposits is 20 percent, and people wish to hold $0.30 in currency for every additional $1 in demand deposits, then a $100 increase in the monetary base from an open market purchase will lead to the following:

$$\text{Increase in demand deposits} = \frac{\$100}{0.2 + 0.3} = \$200$$

$$\text{Increase in required reserves} = \$40$$
$$\text{Increase in currency of public} = \$60$$

In this illustration, the $100 increase in the monetary base is reflected in an increase of $60 in currency holdings by the public and $40 in bank reserves.

As long as the uses of the monetary base are defined as fractions of demand deposits, then the various uses can simply be added to give the denominator of the demand deposit equation:

$$D = \frac{B}{r_d + (t \times r_t) + e + c} \tag{8–2}$$

where

D is demand deposits.

B is the monetary base (that is, commercial bank reserves of deposits plus currency, plus the public's holdings of currency).

t is time deposits which the public holds, as a fraction of their demand deposits.

r_d is required reserve ratio applying to demand deposits.

r_t is required reserve ratio applying to time deposits.

e is excess reserves that banks hold, as a fraction of their demand deposit liabilities

c is currency that the public holds, as a fraction of their demand deposits.

Thus, the money stock is:

$$M = \text{Demand deposits plus currency held by the public}$$
$$= D + c \cdot D = D \, (1 + c)$$

$$M = \frac{B(1 + c)}{r_d + (t \times r_t) + e + c} \tag{8–3}$$

where

M is the money supply (defined as demand deposits plus currency held by the public).

As a first approximation, it is reasonable to assume that c, t, and e are more or less stable fractions. As the total quantity of money goes up, for example, it seems reasonable to assume that the fraction held as currency will not change much (and that, therefore, c will be reasonably stable). But there is clearly no logical requirement that c, t, and e *must* be constants. Indeed, much of advanced monetary research focuses on the responsiveness of these fractions to economic variables such as interest rate changes. If these fractions become subject to rapid and unpredictable change, then the Federal Reserve will have difficulty in controlling the quantity of money with any degree of precision. Changes in the fractions—particularly those that occur during a depression—will be considered in Chapters 9 and 11. In more normal times, the fractions will be more nearly stable, and the money supply will therefore respond in a more nearly predictable manner to changes in the monetary base. Indeed, one of the items—excess reserves—has become so small as to be almost a negligible complication in recent years. Because of the development of such short-term markets as the Federal Funds Market (a market in which banks lend or borrow reserves from other banks), it is possible for banks to manage with very narrow margins of excess reserves, even though the exact pattern of their deposit withdrawals cannot be predicted.

MONEY CREATION IS NOT MAGIC

The process of money creation illustrated in the early part of this chapter is sometimes spoken of as the creation of money "with the stroke of a pen." Such phrases should not be permitted to become the basis for the misconception that the process of money creation has endowed the commercial banker with some sort of magical or arbitrary power to create money out of thin air. To the banker, the transactions illustrated in the examples in this chapter appear perfectly normal. Consider bank A in the first illustration. What has it done? It has sold government securities in order to be able to make additional loans (Table 8–5). There is no magic here. And what about bank B? One of its customers comes in with a check for $100,000 to deposit, and having taken the check in deposit, bank B is now in a position to lend money out—but not the whole $100,000, just $80,000. It does not see itself "magically" creating money; indeed, it is lending out less than has been deposited by its customer.

The important thing to recognize here is that a normal financial transaction is taking place; not a sleight of hand. It gains particular attention because the type of liability being created is considered part of the money supply. Indeed, you or I can "create" liabilities in the same general way as a commercial bank, although we cannot create the same *type* of financial liabilities (demand deposits). I can borrow money from my neighbor in order to fix my roof, giving him my IOU. I have thereby, with a stroke of the pen, created a financial liability (my IOU) in the same general way as the banking system—although the terminology is quite different. My neighbor would scarcely say that he has "deposited" money with me. I have created my IOU. The bank similarly "creates" its IOUs, although in this case the IOUs take on special significance because, being demand deposits, they can be used directly for the purchase of goods and services. This difference in the nature of liabilities provides the compelling case for close regulation of banks by governmental authorities; but there is nothing magical about the process of liability creation itself.

OTHER INSTRUMENTS OF MONETARY CONTROL

Open market operations constitute the most important method of monetary control. The monetary base can be increased by the Federal Reserve by open market purchases, or decreased by open market sales if booming demand threatens to cause inflation. But this is not the only weapon in the hands of the Federal Reserve.

The amount of money that will be created on any given base depends on a number of variables (Equation 8–3), prominent among which are the reserve ratios required for demand and time deposits. As an alternative to open market operations (or as a supporting action), the Federal Reserve can change the reserve requirements. In theory, this is a very powerful weapon: an increase from 15 percent to 20 percent, for example, would reduce the maximum money supply by a quarter. But, because of its very power, this weapon should be used with circumspection, particularly in a restrictive direction. A large increase may put very severe pressures on commercial banks to liquidate their loans and investments in order to meet their reserve requirements. Therefore, as can be seen from Table 8–12, changes in required reserves are generally small. (This has not always been the case, however. Between August 1936 and May 1937, required reserve percentages were *doubled*—an interest-

Table 8–12
Reserve requirements on deposits of member banks of Federal Reserve System (deposit intervals in $ millions; requirements in percent of deposits)

	Net demand				Time (all classes of banks)		
	Reserve city banks		Other banks			Other time	
Effective date	0–5	Over 5	0–5	Over 5	Savings	0–5	Over 5
In effect							
Jan. 1, 1963	16½	—	12	—	4	4	4
1966							
July 14, 21	—	—	—	—	—	—	5
Sept. 8, 15	—	—	—	—	—	—	6
1967							
Mar. 2	—	—	—	—	3½	3½	—
Mar. 16	—	—	—	—	3	3	—
1968							
Jan. 11, 18	16½	17	12	12½	—	—	—
1969							
Apr. 17	17	17½	12½	13	—	—	—
1970							
Oct. 1	—	—	—	—	—	—	5

	Net demand					Time		
							Other time	
← Deposits, in millions of dollars →	0–2	2–10	10–100	100–400	Over 400	Savings	0–5	Over 5
In effect								
1972								
Nov. 9	8	10	12	16½	17½	3	3	5
Nov. 16	—	—	—	13	—	—	—	—
1973								
July 19	—	10½	12½	13½	18	—	—	—
1974								
Dec. 12	—	—	—	—	17½	—	—	3–6*
1975								
Feb. 13	7½	10	12	13	16½	—	—	—
Oct. 30	—	—	—	—	—	—	1–3*	1–6*
1976								
Dec. 30	7	9½	11¾	12¾	16¼	—	—	—
In effect								
Sept. 1977	7	9½	11¾	12¾	16¼	3	1–3*	1–6*

Present legal limits (1977)	Minimum	Maximum
Net demand deposits, reserve city banks	10	22
Net demand deposits, other banks	7	14
Time deposits	3†	10

* Since December 1974, reserve requirements on time deposits have depended on their maturity, with higher requirements applied to shorter-term deposits.
† The average of reserves on time deposits must be at least 3 percent, the minimum specified by law. (For details, see footnotes in *Federal Reserve Bulletin*.)
Source: *Federal Reserve Bulletin*.

Changes in reserve requirements are usually small—½ or ¼ percent.

ing experiment, but one that can scarcely be recommended. It contributed to the derailment of the economic recovery then underway, and to the economic decline in the last half of 1937.)

Third, the Federal Reserve can change its discount rate. This is the rate at which the Federal Reserve makes loans to the member banks. Such loans increase the reserve base; therefore, steps by the Federal Reserve to discourage loans by raising the discount rate constitute a restrictive measure. The discount rate was also at one time considered to be significant because of its announcement effect, with a rise in the discount rate being taken as a signal that the Federal Reserve considered monetary restriction in order. With the rapid changes in market interest rates and in the discount rate in recent years, however, relatively little significance is now attached to the announcement effect.

The Federal Reserve also has the power to set margin requirements on loans for the purchase or carrying of securities. The objective of margin requirements is to reduce instability in the securities markets, especially the stock market. Several decades ago, there were also selective controls on consumer credit (1941–47 and again during the Korean War) and on real estate credit (during the Korean War). Moral suasion—recommendations to banks and financial markets—is sometimes also listed as a method of Federal Reserve control, and, indeed, the Federal Reserve authorities have on occasion made such recommendations. The scope for moral suasion is, however, much less in the United States than in some other countries, such as Britain or Canada. In the United States, there are many independent banks. In Britain or Canada, in contrast, there are relatively few banks (with these banks having a large number of branches scattered throughout the country, providing banking services to the public). In Britain or Canada, therefore, it is possible for the central bank to keep in direct and close touch with the top management of *all* the banks—something that is not feasible in the United States.

ALTERNATIVE CONCEPTS OF "MONEY"

According to the common, traditional definition, the money supply consists of currency and demand deposits held by the public. This definition—M_1—is the most straightforward: it defines as money those items actually used in everyday commerce to make payments.

But this is not the only way of defining money. Economists are interested not only in the great convenience which money provides as a means of payment. They are also interested in the way in which money affects aggregate demand. There is, of course, a basic economic proposition—which may be traced back through classical literature—that people will tend to spend more if they have more currency and demand deposits (M_1). But, as a means of encouraging spending, money defined in the traditional way is far from unique; there are close substitutes. Savings deposits, in particular, can be easily switched into demand deposits. Thus, while we would expect people to spend more if they have more narrowly defined money (M_1), it is also reasonable to expect that they would spend more if they had additional savings deposits. If we are concerned about the relationship between money and aggregate demand, we may thus wish to define "money" more broadly than M_1, to include close substitutes. The second major definition of money, M_2, includes M_1 plus time deposits (excluding large, negotiable certificates of deposit).[6]

Monetary economists differ as to whether it is better to focus on M_1 or M_2 in studying the effects of monetary policy on aggregate demand. Here, we might note that, in the past two decades, there has been little noticeable trend in the income velocity (GNP/M_2) when M_2 is taken as the measure of money, while the ratio of national income to M_1 has trended significantly upward (Figure 8–1).[7] As the ratio of time deposits to demand deposits has risen, the turnover of demand deposits has increased.

The relative merits of M_1 and M_2 as *the* definition of money have been a matter of controversy for several decades. In the past few years, a further complication has been introduced, with the blurring of distinctions between demand and savings deposits. In the early 1970s, savings banks in New England began to experiment with "negotiable orders of withdrawal"; in effect, these were checks drawn on savings deposits. More recently, some savings institutions have undertaken to act as bill-paying agents for their depositors, charging the payments against savings deposits.

As savings deposits have begun to be used as the actual means of

---

[6] These large "CDs"—which are held mainly by business corporations—are more similar to short-term marketable securities (such as short-term government bills) than they are to the savings deposits that the ordinary citizen might hold.

[7] M_3 is M_2 plus deposits in mutual savings banks, plus shares (deposits) in savings and loan associations, plus shares in credit unions.

Figure 8–1
Income velocity of money (annually, 1910–1946; seasonally adjusted, quarterly, 1947–1976)

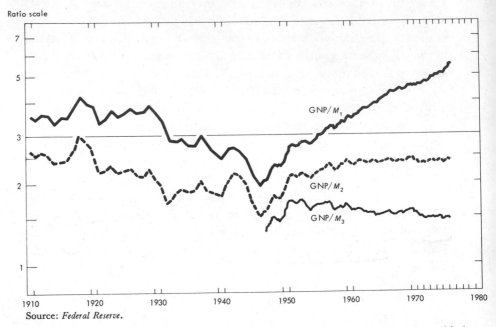

Source: *Federal Reserve.*

During the past three decades, velocity has trended upward—when M_1 is taken as the definition of "money." The income velocity of M_2 has shown no trend since 1960.

payments in some instances, the Federal Reserve has argued that the narrow definition of money (M_1) has become less meaningful and that it is appropriate to have a less rapid rate of expansion of M_1 than has occurred in the past.[8] Furthermore, once the line between demand and savings deposits has been blurred, the question arises as to whether we should not also consider other close substitutes. Consequently, the Federal Reserve regularly publishes not just two measures of the money supply, but five.[9] In order to avoid confusion, this book will use the term "money" to refer to M_1, unless otherwise specified.

---

[8] See statement of Federal Reserve Board Chairman Arthur F. Burns to the U.S. Congress, reprinted in the *Federal Reserve Bulletin,* November 1976, pp. 906–12, especially pp. 908–909.

[9] M_4 is M_2 plus large negotiable certificates of deposit. M_5 is M_3 plus large negotiable CDs.

KEY POINTS

1. The Federal Reserve can increase the level of reserves in the banking system through an open market purchase. Because the banks are required to maintain reserves of only a fraction of their deposit liability, the expansion of the money stock which can result from an increase in reserves is a multiple (Equation 8–1) of the increase in reserves.

2. In practice, however, the expansion of the money stock does not equal the maximum permitted by the required reserve ratio. (Refer back to Equation 8–3.)

3. While the banking system as a whole can create a multiplied quantity of money on the basis of an injection of additional reserves, this is not true of an individual bank. Indeed, where the individual bank receives reserves as a result of a deposit of one of its customers, it can lend out less than the increase in reserves (since it is required to keep part of the reserves, in accordance with the required reserve ratio). Where the individual bank acquires reserves as the result of a sale of assets (for example, a sale of government bonds), it can lend out the full increase in reserves (since its reserve liabilities have not changed, and therefore its required reserves have not changed).

QUESTION

1. Excess reserves have recently been very small. This has not always been the case, however. If you were a banker, what would determine your holdings of excess reserves?

SUGGESTED READING

Board of Governors, Federal Reserve System, *The Federal Reserve System; Purposes and Functions,* 6th ed. (Washington, D.C.: Federal Reserve, 1974).

Chapter 9

The effectiveness of monetary policy

Glendower: *I can call spirits from the vasty deep.*

Hotspur: *Why, so can I, or so can any man;*
but will they come when you do call for them?

Shakespeare*

There is a temptation, when studying money, to approach the subject in an overly mechanical way. There is a temptation—against which we have warned in the previous chapter—to look at the process of money creation as a mechanical response of the banks and the public to an open market purchase by the Federal Reserve. And, in the classical tradition at least, there is a tendency to look at aggregate demand as responding in a more or less mechanical way to a change in the quantity of money. If people have more money, they will spend more; if they have twice as much money, they may be expected to spend twice as much, more or less. Thus is money raised to its place of primacy as a determinant of aggregate demand in the classical theory.

As a basis for policy, this mechanical approach is inadequate. If

---

* From *King Henry IV*.

we are to have confidence in money as a tool for economic stabilization, we should have some idea of *how* monetary policy works. If money is to affect aggregate demand, then it must affect one or more of the components of demand—investment, consumption, government spending, or net exports. The major topic of this chapter will be the ways in which monetary policy can affect the components of aggregate demand, particularly investment and consumption. (The interrelationships between monetary policy and federal government spending, and between monetary policy and the balance of international payments, will be deferred to Chapter 10.)

But, before we turn to this topic, we should deal with a preliminary. The debate of recent decades regarding monetary policy was touched off by Keynes, who argued that monetary policy might be ineffective during a depression, since an increase in the quantity of money will not depress interest rates, and therefore will not stimulate investment. Because of the importance of the depression in the evolution of macroeconomic theory, we should double back to deal with a *second* potential problem of a depression: monetary policy may be inadequate as a means of stimulating recovery because the Federal Reserve may have *difficulty in causing an increase in the money supply.*

CAN MONEY BE CREATED DURING A DEPRESSION? FAST ENOUGH?

As we saw in Chapter 8, the Federal Reserve can purchase securities on the open market and thus increase the reserves of the commercial banks. As a result, the banks will be *able* to expand the money supply by increasing their loans and their holdings of other earning assets. But the Federal Reserve cannot *make* the banks add to their earning assets—they cannot *force* an increase in the money supply. There may, in particular, be a problem during a depression, when banks may choose to hold significant amounts of excess reserves when the reserve base increases.

To see how this can be so, it is necessary to go into the behavior of banks in some detail. Apart from the required reserves, banks hold a whole spectrum of assets: excess reserves, federal government bonds and shorter-term obligations, state and local government securities, corporation bonds, commercial and industrial loans, real estate loans, and loans to individuals. In order to make the problem manageable, attention will be confined to three possibilities: excess reserves, commercial and industrial loans, and federal government securities. Loans and federal government securities are the two most important earning assets of banks, and they are quite far apart in the spectrum in two important respects: There is a risk of default on loans, while federal government securities are essentially free from such risk; and federal government securities are readily marketable, while loans are not.

When the reserves of banks rise, they may choose one of the following options, or any combination thereof: They may opt to hold additional excess reserves; they may expand their loans; or they may increase their holdings of marketable securities, such as government bonds. In making the choice, banks will be influenced by a number of factors, including:

1. The interest rates on loans and government securities.
2. The risk of loss.
3. The demand for loans.

During good times, there is a brisk demand for loans from businesses, and the risk of default is modest. As the reserve base increases, therefore, commercial banks are willing to increase their loans significantly, adding to the money supply as outlined in Chapter 8. They may also acquire additional government bonds. The money supply will therefore expand quite rapidly toward the maximum permitted by the size of the reserve base, and large amounts of excess reserves are unlikely to be held for any length of time.

During a depression, however, conditions are quite different. When business is bad, there may be a crisis of confidence. Demand falls, employment falls, prices decline, and there may be general fears that worse is yet to come. If, in such conditions, commercial banks find their excess reserves rising, it is not certain that they will expand their loans rapidly. It is not obvious that the net return on additional loans will be positive. The considerable risk of default if the borrower goes bankrupt will have to be weighed against the interest payment on the loan. Furthermore, even if the bank were willing to lend additional amounts, the demand for loans may be quite slack: The depression is a time for retrenchment, when businesses have relatively few prospects for profitable expansion. The volume of loans may therefore not respond quickly to increases in reserves.

But loan expansion is not the only way in which monetary expansion can take place; it will also occur if the banks purchase securities from the public. With rising excess reserves, the banks will increase their bids for government securities—thereby driving up their prices and reducing their yields. As the yields on government bonds drop, the banks must begin to wonder about the risks involved: While government bonds are free from the risk of default, they will fall in price if interest rates move upward, inflicting a capital loss on the holder. Thus, the banks may have a speculative demand for excess reserves similar to the public's speculative demand for money in Keynesian theory: Banks are willing to hold additional amounts of a zero-interest asset (excess reserves) rather than take the risks inherent in acquiring an interest-bearing security when yields are very low. The banks' willingness to hold excess reserves depends on interest rates, and increases very rapidly as interest rates fall to low levels.

As in the case of the Keynesian liquidity trap—in which monetary policy becomes ineffective as a stimulant during a depression because of the willingness of the public to hold additional quantities of money as idle balances—so monetary policy becomes ineffective if increases in reserves are caught in the excess reserve trap, with banks holding additional reserves without much change in their acquisitions of loans and securities.[1]

So much for the theoretical excess reserve trap argument. There was a debate over its importance, even during the 1930s. The high level of excess reserves after the Depression hit its bottom in 1933 does, however, suggest that there were limits to the speed of monetary expansion which could be induced by increases in bank reserves.[2] During 1934–35, and again in 1939–40, excess reserves were very large (Figure 9–1), amounting to *almost half of the total bank reserves* during much of those years. (They would have been

---

[1] Because of the similarity of the arguments, they are often both classified under the same "liquidity trap" heading. See, for example, Karl Brunner and Allan H. Meltzer, "Liquidity Traps for Money, Bank Credit, and Interest Rates," *Journal of Political Economy*, January–February 1968, pp. 1–37. Brunner and Meltzer distinguish six versions of the liquidity trap (broadly defined).

[2] For a different view, see Milton Friedman and Anna J. Schwartz, *A Monetary History of the United States, 1867–1960* (Princeton: Princeton University Press, 1963). In their introduction to the chapter on the depression, they argue (p. 301): "It is true also, as we shall see, that different and feasible actions by the monetary authorities could have prevented the decline in the stock of money—indeed, could have produced almost *any* desired increase in the monetary stock." (Italics added.) As I read their chapter, this conclusion applies not only to the Depression as a whole, but also to every major subperiod of it. Not all readers may agree, however. (See, for example, the very brief reference to excess reserves on pp. 313–14 of the Friedman-Schwartz study.)

Figure 9–1
Excess reserves and borrowings of member banks ($ billions, monthly averages of daily figures)

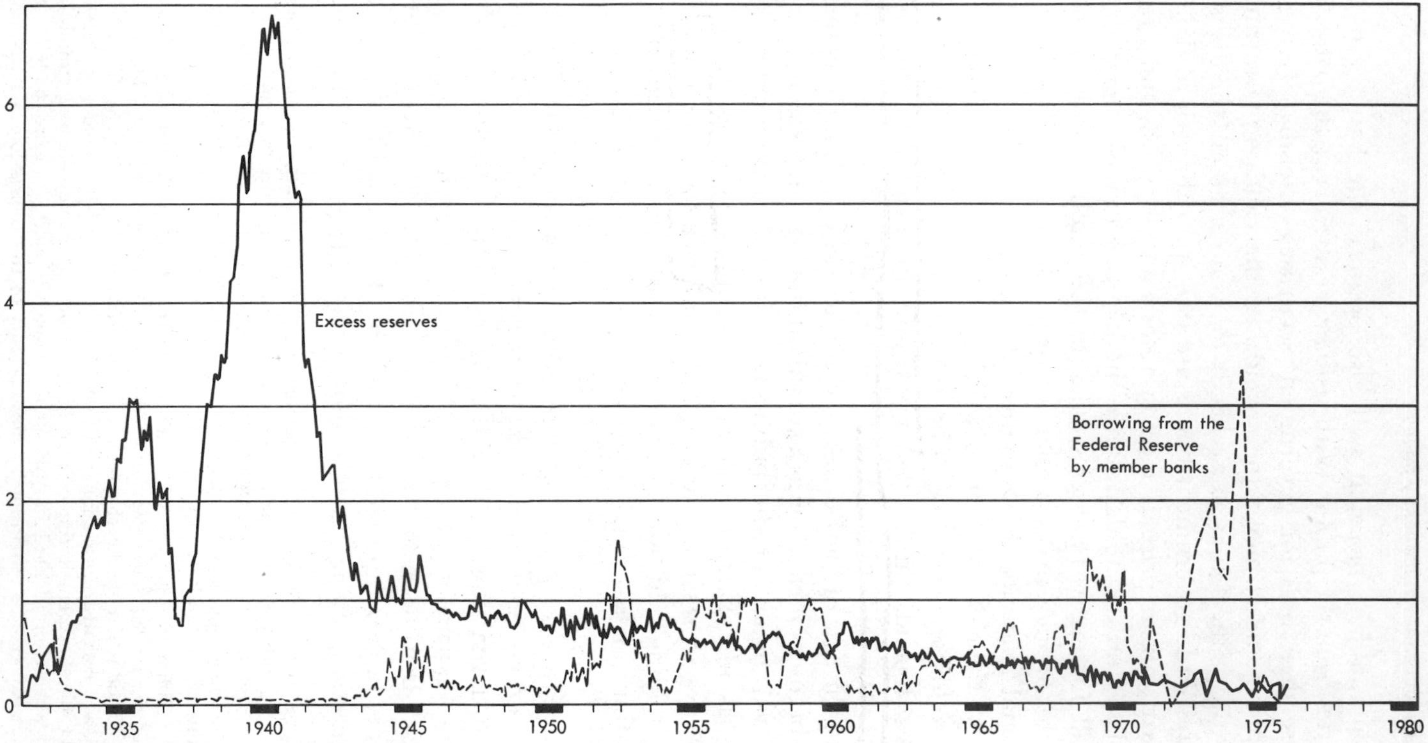

Excess reserves

Borrowing from the Federal Reserve by member banks

Source: Federal Reserve, *Historical Chart Book.*

Excess reserves were very large during the middle 1930s. In recent decades, in contrast, they have been small—smaller, on average, than bank borrowings (discounts) from the Federal Reserve.

high throughout the slow recovery period, had not the Federal Reserve increased the required reserve ratios in 1936–37.)

Care should, however, be taken to avoid overly broad generalizations about the Depression. It was a complex phenomenon. In particular, the 1930s *did not represent a decade-long period of expansive but ineffective monetary policies.* On the contrary, there were critical periods when excess reserves declined sharply—particularly during 1931–32 when the reserve base declined, and during 1936–37 when reserve requirements were hiked. The former period coincided with the downward slide toward the depths of the Depression, while the latter preceded the interruption of the recovery in 1937–38. While the high level of excess reserves in 1934–35 and 1939–40 does suggest that there are limits to the quick effectiveness of expansive monetary policies during a depression, the history of the Depression also indicates that *inappropriate* movements in the reserve positions of banks were a contributing factor to the extent of the economic collapse. Taken as a whole, the Depression *is not* a clear demonstration of the ineffectiveness of monetary policy. (In Chapter 11, the *causes* behind the changes in reserves in the early 1930s will be studied; here we are dealing with the *effects* of changes in reserves.)

The excess reserve trap and the liquidity trap: Some distinctions

Some similarities have been noted between the Keynesian liquidity trap and the excess reserve trap argument. In particular, each suggests that monetary policy may become ineffective as a stimulant during a depression, and each involves very low interest rates on high-grade securities free from default.

But if there is a similarity between the two arguments, there are also sharp differences.

1. The liquidity trap argument is flatly inconsistent with the quantity theory of money; the excess reserve trap argument is not. The first suggests that monetary policy may be ineffective because changes in the money supply are in themselves ineffective in stimulating the economy. The second suggests that a problem may exist in getting an actual expansion of the money supply through the normal banking procedure.
2. Because of this distinction, observed similarities between busi-

ness conditions and the historical pattern of changes in the quantity of money tend to undercut the Keynesian argument that money is not very important;[3] but they provide no leverage on the "excess reserve trap" argument. In this latter argument, the slippage in monetary policy takes place *before* money is created.

3. The liquidity preference argument is often put in static equilibrium terms.[4] It therefore becomes the basis of the conclusion that once the economy gets into a depression, this may become a chronic condition which can *only* be corrected by massive and continuing government deficits. In contrast, the short-term transitory nature of the problem is stressed in the excess reserve trap argument. There may be a difficulty, but it is due to a collapse of confidence. The question of whether the money supply can be expanded *at all* therefore becomes quite secondary. The issue rather becomes whether the money supply can be expanded *rapidly enough* during the depths of a depression in order to meet short-term goals. When the trap is sufficiently severe to lead to a negative response to this question, then the stage is set for short-term fiscal expansion—even within a narrowly defined classical (quantity theory) world. Most obviously, when a government spends newly printed money borrowed from the central bank, then additional money is put directly into the hands of the public.

Rationality for an individual bank does not equal rationality for the system

It is one of the characteristics of a depression that the types of action which would be beneficial if followed in concert by all are suicidal for the individual who follows them alone.*

Jacob Viner

---

[3] But fall *far* short of making a conclusive case. See Chapter 12.

[4] For a logical problem with the liquidity trap in a static equilibrium framework, see the appendix to this chapter.

* From *Balanced Deflation, Inflation, or More Depression* (Minneapolis: University of Minnesota Press, 1933), p. 11. Viner's statement might be contrasted to Adam Smith's "invisible hand" [in *An Inquiry into the Nature and Causes of the Wealth of Nations* (New York: Modern Library edition, 1937), p. 423]:

. . . it is only for the sake of profit that any man employs a capital in the support of industry; and he will always, therefore, endeavour to employ it in the

The possibility of an excess reserve trap illustrates a very important general principle about the economy: Decisions that make sense for an individual decisionmaking unit do not necessarily lead to desirable results for the economy as a whole. Consider the position of banks with large excess reserves during a depression. If they were *all* to use their excess reserves to expand loans rapidly, business would improve, the rate of bankruptcies would decline, and banks would be earning interest payments on a higher portfolio of loans whose average default rate would be lower. But the general prosperity of business depends on the overall lending behavior of banks, not on the loans of an individual bank. If an individual bank were to expand its loans in spite of the riskiness of business, it might be contributing its modest share to the restoration of prosperity, but it might also be committing suicide in the process. With other banks declining to follow suit, it might be faced with a high default rate on its loans.

In such circumstances, the job for public policy is to create conditions in which the self-interest of banks leads to a desirable outcome for the economy as a whole. Where an excess reserve trap limits the effectiveness of an expansive monetary policy, the indicated policy is one of fiscal pump priming. By improving economic conditions and cutting down on the risk of default, it will create the conditions under which it is in the interest of banks to expand their loans more rapidly.

MONETARY POLICY AND INVESTMENT:
THE MARGINAL EFFICIENCY OF INVESTMENT
AND THE AVAILABILITY THESIS

In the Keynesian framework, the first step in evaluating the effects of monetary policy consists of determining the change (if any) in

---

support of that industry of which the produce is likely to be of the greatest value. . . .
. . . by directing that industry in such a manner as its produce may be of the greatest value, he intends only his own gain, and he is in this, as in many other cases, led by an invisible hand to promote an end which was no part of his intention. . . . By pursuing his own interest he frequently promotes that of the society more effectually than when he really intends to promote it. I have never known much good done by those who affected trade for the public good.

Viner's point is, of course, related to the Keynesian paradox of thrift (Chapter 3).

the interest rate resulting from a change in the money supply. The second step lies in estimating the interest elasticity of the marginal efficiency of investment, that is, in estimating the responsiveness of investment demand to changes in the interest rate.

Surprisingly enough, it is not easy to determine the interest elasticity of the investment schedule even within rather broad limits. Empirical studies conducted during the early Keynesian period suggested that the interest responsiveness of investment demand might be quite low, thus adding to the prevailing pessimism regarding the effectiveness of monetary policy. The validity of these studies was, however, thrown into question by the existence of several important and difficult methodological problems:

1.   The marginal efficiency of investment (*MEI*) tends to *shift* to the right during periods of prosperity, when buoyant demand creates a need for additional plant and equipment. In order to finance greater investment, businesses borrow in the bond markets (by issuing new bonds) and they also increase their bank borrowings. The additional demand for credit tends to push up interest rates. Similarly, when business is bad, the *MEI* curve shifts to the left, the demand for borrowing declines, and interest rates fall. Because of these *shifts* in the *MEI* curve, high interest rates historically have tended to be associated with a high rate of investment, and low interest rates with a low rate of investment. This can introduce a bias into statistical estimates of the *MEI* function, making the estimated function less elastic than the true function.[5]

2.   When the early studies were done, the economy had experienced an extended period of low and stable interest rates on high-

---

[5] This is illustrated in the accompanying figure where points *A* and *B* are the two historical observations, *A* occurring during a recession when the investment demand schedule is depressed (at MEI_R) and *B* occurring during prosperity, after the investment demand schedule has shifted out to MEI_P. Drawing a function through the two observed points *A* and *B* does not give the true *MEI* curve; indeed, it gives a function sloping upward to the right.

Such a curve, going through *A* and *B*, raises obvious problems: it is implausible to expect the *MEI* curve to have such a slope, implying higher rates of interest will cause a higher level of investment. Clearly, there is a statistical problem of adjusting point *B* for the shift in the marginal efficiency of investment schedule, so that the true *MEI* schedule, *CA*, can be found. Unfortunately, however, it is difficult to make accurate and complete adjustments for the shifts in the function. A partial adjustment will give an estimated *MEI* of *DA*, which is less elastic than the true curve *CA*. This problem— of *identifying* the effects of interest rate changes on the level of investment when other variables also affect investment—is an example of the general *identification problem* which is one of the most important difficulties in economic statistics. A classic article on the identification problem and related statistical difficulties is Guy Orcutt, "Meas-

quality securities. This added to the difficulty of estimating the effects of interest rate changes on investment. When people in business were asked to rank the important variables in their investment decisions, interest rates tended to be ranked low; as interest rates were stable at low levels, they were not an important input into investment decisions.[6]

The determinants of investment are an important subject in macroeconomics and warrant a chapter of their own (Chapter 15). Having noted the difficulties in estimating the *MEI* schedule, we will sidestep the problems. We will simply *assume* that the investment demand function (*MEI*) is relatively interest inelastic, and investigate the consequences for monetary policy.

---

urement of Price Elasticities in International Trade," *Review of Economics and Statistics*, May 1950, pp. 117–82.

The marginal efficiency of investment: The identification problem

Not as interest inelastic as it is assumes

[6] The early survey studies were criticized by W. H. White, "Interest Inelasticity of Investment Demand," *American Economic Review*, September 1956, pp. 565–87. White judged the surveys to be so defective that conclusions based on them were essentially worthless.

The availability thesis

If the *MEI* schedule is interest inelastic, it might seem that monetary policy cannot be effective. Even if monetary expansion or contraction succeeds in appreciably changing the interest rate, the level of investment will not be appreciably affected if the elasticity of the *MEI* schedule is low. This was a view commonly held during the 1940s.

During the 1950s, however, an alternative method of operation of monetary policy was suggested, the *availability thesis.* According to this thesis, banks and other lenders ration their loanable funds among potential borrowers, particularly during periods of restrictive central bank operations when such funds are scarce. Thus, during such periods of tight money, it was argued, businesses might not severely curtail their demand for investment loans in the face of higher interest rates, but they might still be prevented from making the investment by their *inability* to borrow the money at the prevailing rates of interest. The limit to investment might come

Figure 9–2
The availability thesis: The effectiveness of tight money

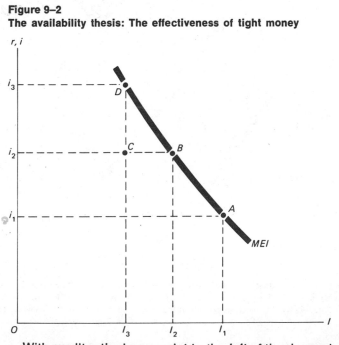

With credit rationing, a point to the *left* of the demand curve is observed.

from the unwillingness of lenders to expand their loans, rather than from a lack of demand from borrowers. The availability of money to potential investors rather than its cost would become the constraint to additional investment.

Consider in graphic terms (Figure 9–2) what this means. With a tightening of monetary conditions, interest rates rise from i_1 to i_2. But, according to the availability thesis, B is not the new observed point; rather, the new observed level of investment is at C, to the left of the MEI curve. The effects of tight money can be looked on as having two components: the reduction in investment (from I_1 to I_2) due to the rise in interest rates from i_1 to i_2, and the reduction in investment (from I_2 to I_3) due to the rationing of loans by banks and other lenders.

Because there would be rationing of credit, with the observed level of investment to the left of the MEI schedule, the availability thesis clearly assumes that disequilibrium conditions can exist in the financial markets, with a gap existing between the demand and supply of loans. But this raises a question: Is it plausible to argue that there can be any extended period of disequilibrium? Put another way: If the conditions postulated by the availability thesis did in fact exist, why would not the interest rates simply rise to the equilibrium level? If banks, for example, are prevented by their reserve restraint from lending any more funds than needed to finance investment level OI_3 (Figure 9–2), why do not they raise their interest rate to the equilibrium level, i_3? With higher interest on the volume of loans permitted by the reserve base, they would be in a position to increase their short-run profits.

The response: Banks are interested not just in short-term profits, which could indeed be increased by a rise in the lending rate to i_3, but also—and even more fundamentally—in their long-term profit prospects. A bank's customers may look more favorably on their association with the bank as a continuing source of funds if interest rates charged by the bank are kept reasonably stable. During periods of monetary stringency, of course, something *must* give: The bank cannot continue to lend freely at old rates of interest. But, in order to avoid really irate customers, it feels a need to make some compromise between a rise in interest rates and the rationing of credit. (This argument assumes that customers prefer some credit rationing by the bank to a situation where soaring interest rates perform the sole allocative function in determining which lenders obtain the scarce funds. If the demand for loans is indeed quite interest inelastic, this is a reasonable preference for bank borrowers to have. Otherwise, their interest costs might become extremely high, rising to point D in Figure 9–2.) That banks may be willing to forego short-term profits in order to maintain their relations with customers is a matter of record. During the credit stringency of 1969 and 1974, banks suffered (short-term) losses on marginal loans by borrowing at very high interest rates and lending at lower rates to their customers. (Some of this borrowing was in the Eurodollar market—a European financial market in which loans are denominated in U.S. dollars rather than in the currency of the host country.)

Any hesitation that banks may have to push up lending rates very rapidly may be reinforced by fears of official action. Such fears played a part in the prime interest rate charged by banks in late 1972, for example. A number of banks had been using "floating" prime lending rates which reflected changes in the yields on short-term marketable securities. As their prime rates approached 6 percent, and as pressures grew from Washington to keep down interest rates as a contribution to the price-control program then in existence, a number of these banks altered their method of setting their prime rates to keep the rates from reaching 6 percent.

Similarly, there may be rationing in other segments of the capital market. For example, bond underwriters (institutions which market new issues of bonds) may ask—or insist—that their customers delay the floating of new securities in order not to congest the markets and to facilitate the sales of bonds that the underwriters already have on hand. The borrower may be willing to go along with the delay because of the long-term value of an established relationship with an underwriter. And the borrower may have no alternative: His traditional underwriter may flatly refuse to schedule a new issue, and other underwriters may decline new business when bonds are hard to sell.

The availability thesis is basically a one-way argument. It suggests that tighter monetary policy may be effective, but that more expansive monetary policy may continue to be ineffective in the face of an inelastic MEI. Nevertheless, to the extent that there initially is some credit rationing rather than a point on the MEI schedule, expansive monetary policy may also gain effectiveness by reducing the degree of credit rationing.

THE UNEVEN IMPACT OF TIGHT MONEY ON DIFFERENT SECTORS: IS TIGHT MONEY DISCRIMINATORY?

It is sometimes argued that monetary policy is one of the most general tools, affecting demand throughout the economy and avoiding the necessity—inherent in fiscal policy—of choosing which specific expenditures to raise or lower, or which taxes to change. Nevertheless, the use of tight money as a means of restraining a boom in aggregate demand has been criticized on the ground that the restrictive effects fall particularly severely on specific sectors of the economy. Specific sectors may be hard hit if they are particularly sensitive to the normal interest rate pressures accompanying tight money; alternatively, some sectors may be especially subject to credit rationing.

A persistent charge, but one that is very difficult to evaluate, is the argument that, when credit rationing begins, banks are particularly solicitous of the needs of their larger customers and cut back drastically on the funds they make available to the smaller borrower. The debate is complicated by the unequal dependence of large and small companies on bank funds, with the larger companies being in a position to issue their short-term marketable liabilities as an alternative source of financing.

Two sectors of the economy—housing and state and local governments—are at the center of the controversy over the uneven effects of tight money.

Housing

There can be little doubt that tight monetary conditions have a particularly heavy impact on housing. In the past 15 years, there have been three periods of especially tight money—1966, 1969, and 1974. In each case, housing starts declined significantly, particularly in 1974 (Table 9–1).

To demonstrate that housing starts declined during periods of tight money does not, however, in itself make an air tight case that monetary policy has adverse side effects. If the economy is overheating, it is necessary that the production of *something* be restrained. A case can be made that it is particularly important to restrain long-term investment, of which housing is an example. Because a house is used over such a long period of time, there is little short-term connection between the quantity of housing and the rate of new construction. The consumption of nondurables (services, milk, vegetables, etc.), in contrast, is closely tied to current production. If, therefore, a long-term investment like housing can be made to move down in a boom and up during a recession, then the level of total production of all goods can be stabilized without greatly disturbing current consumption. Put another way: Interest rates can be used as a way of signalling the scarcity of productive resources. When the economy overheats, productive resources

Table 9–1
Private housing starts (thousands of units)

	Total	Single family houses	Two or more family units
1963	1,610	1,021	589
1964	1,529	970	559
1965	1,473	964	509
1966*	1,165	778	387
1967	1,292	844	448
1968	1,508	899	609
1969*	1,467	811	656
1970	1,434	813	621
1971	2,052	1,151	901
1972	2,357	1,309	1,048
1973	2,045	1,132	913
1974*	1,338	888	450
1975	1,160	892	268
1976	1,540	1,163	377

* Years of tight money.
Source: *Federal Reserve Bulletin.*

are scarce. If the demand for new housing is very responsive to high interest rates during such periods of overheating, and if construction falls, then there is a case to be made that this is a desirable place to cut back temporarily while excess demand is restrained.

Nevertheless, there are several grounds on which it may be argued that tight money had an *undesirably* restrictive effect on housing in 1966–67, 1969–70, and 1974. The fall in housing starts was due not only to the responsiveness of demand to higher interest rates, but also to the unavailability of housing loans. Even at the high interest rates (which reflected the scarcity of productive resources), people wanted more housing than they could get. The fall in housing starts was undesirably sharp, given the willingness of the public to pay the high interest rates for mortgages. Furthermore, the rationing of funds was selective, falling more heavily on housing than on other types of long-term investment. This selectivity was the result of the institutional and legal characteristics of housing finance: A large percentage is financed through savings and loan associations, which were prevented from competing for funds by the legal ceilings on the interest rates they were permitted to pay depositors. There was an incentive for depositors to look elsewhere for higher rates of return during the financial squeeze. With the rapid rise in market interest rates, the increase in deposits at savings and loan associations and mutual savings banks fell by more than half between 1967 and 1969. (In order to alleviate the periodic squeeze on housing finance, the limits on interest rates payable by savings and loan associations were relaxed during the early 1970s. Nevertheless, the high interest rates of 1974 and the recession of 1974–75 combined to cause a very sharp contraction in new housing starts.) [7]

A second argument is that housing has a social significance which goes beyond the willingness and ability of individual families to pay for it; while the family that dwells in the newly constructed housing is the major gainer, there is an additional gain to society as a whole. Therefore, it is particularly important that housing not be depressed by public policies. The social significance of housing constitutes an important argument. It does not, however, completely undercut the case for following countercyclical monetary policies involving a cutback in housing construction during booms. To judge a high level of housing to be socially desirable does not settle the question as to how a high average level of housing construction should be distributed throughout the business cycle.

State and local governments

The case that tight money is unfortunate because of its effects on state and local governments rests on the same two basic arguments noted with regard to housing: Tight money may be accompanied by rationing which particularly excludes some classes of borrowers who would be willing to borrow even at the prevailing high interest rates; and tight money may adversely affect sectors of the economy that are deemed to have a particularly great social significance.

---

[7] The instability of deposit inflows and other problems of housing finance are discussed in *Ways to Moderate Fluctuations in Housing Construction* (Washington, D.C.: Board of Governors of the Federal Reserve System, 1972).

Table 9–2
State and local government securities (in $ millions)

Year	Total	Education	Roads and bridges	Utilities	Housing	Other purposes	State and local government obligation held by large banks (first Wednesday of December)
			Use of proceeds				
1965	10,471	3,619	900	1,965	626	3,361	n.a.
1966*	11,303	3,738	1,476	1,880	533	3,667	23,437
1967	14,643	4,473	1,254	2,404	645	5,867	29,147
1968	16,489	4,820	1,526	2,833	787	6,523	33,886
1969*	11,838	3,252	1,432	1,734	543	4,884	31,902
1970	18,110	5,062	1,532	3,532	466	7,526	37,032
1971	24,495	5,278	2,642	5,214	2,068	9,293	44,591
1972	22,079	4,981	1,689	4,714	1,910	8,785	46,805
1973	22,397	4,311	1,458	5,654	2,639	8,335	46,563
1974*	23,508	4,730	768	5,634	1,064	11,312	47,182
1975	29,495	4,689	1,277	7,209	647	15,673	46,339

The columns under "State and local government issues for new capital" span Total through Other purposes.

n.a. = Not available.
* Years of tight money.
Source: *Federal Reserve Bulletin.*

On the first score, there does indeed seem to have been a problem, particularly in 1969. Some governments were prevented from competing for funds by the existence of legal ceilings on the rates they could pay. Partly as a consequence, new issues by state and local governments fell off sharply during 1969 (see Table 9–2). Financial problems of the states and localities were complicated by the liquidation of about $2 billion of their securities by the large commercial banks in 1969, which contributed to the congestion in the markets for state and local securities.

During the tight money period of 1974, there was no repeat of the sharp reduction in the volume of new issues of state and local government securities. During the mid-1970s, there was indeed a grave financial problem for a number of local governments—but it became most severe *after* the period of tightening money in 1974. During 1975, as the economy slid down into the worst recession in more than three decades, tax revenues fell off sharply, causing severe financial strains in a number of cities. Most notably, New York City teetered on the brink of bankruptcy and was forced to turn to the state and federal governments for emergency assistance. While this represented by far the worst financial crisis for the cities in recent decades, it does *not* make a case against the use of monetary policy for economic stabilization purposes. Rather, it indicates that, when stabilization policies fail and a sharp recession occurs, severe strains can occur in the cities.

On the second question—that of the particular social significance of state and local expenditures—opinions differ widely. On the one hand, taxpayer revolts and rejections of bond referenda reflect a view that people want to retain their incomes for their own use, and not to turn them over to the government for public projects. On the other hand, some observers argue that the U.S. system tends to be biased against public expenditure—toward private affluence and public penury.[8] Clearly, there are complex and subtle issues which cannot be settled here. Two observations are, however, in order. First, however much state and local government spending may have fallen short of the social optimum in the past, this short-fall should have been reduced in recent years. Between 1968 and 1975, state and local government spending rose by more than 100 percent, and from 11.6 percent to 13.9 percent of GNP. Second, the most severe problem seems to be *unevenness* of resources—between the impoverished inner cities and the relatively affluent suburbs—rather than a general inadequacy of resources for the states and localities as a group.

The impact on housing and other sectors, and the effectiveness of monetary policy

To demonstrate that tight money has a strong effect on a specific sector of the economy does not, obviously, indicate that monetary policy is ineffective; quite the contrary, it indicates that monetary policy does indeed have an impact on aggregate demand. The sectoral impact may, nevertheless, be included among doubts about the usefulness of monetary policy. Insofar as the impact falls on areas of particular political sensitivity—housing and local governments—the Federal Reserve may be very reluctant to engage in a vigorous monetary policy.

There are several ways to deal with sectoral problems. First, the weight of stabilization policy may be shifted away from monetary policy and toward fiscal policy. If tighter fiscal policies are instituted,

---

[8] The best-known argument that government spending is below the optimum is found in John Kenneth Galbraith, *The Affluent Society* (Boston: Houghton-Mifflin, 1958).

an overly buoyant aggregate demand may be reduced without very high interest rates. (Cooperative monetary and fiscal policies will be studied in Chapter 10.) Second, steps may be taken to soften the blow to particularly sensitive areas. The housing programs of the federal government are an illustration of this approach.

On the other hand, a reduction of government interference in the economy may be suggested as a way of dealing with the sectoral problem. The clearest case of undesirable sectoral effects can be found when there is a particularly severe rationing of credit and not simply a reduction in demand in the face of higher interest rates. Severe rationing may be at least partly a result of regulations—such as the ceilings on interest rates which savings and loan associations may pay. During the 1970s, there has been a partial deregulation; the ceilings on some interest rates which may be paid by banks and savings and loan associations have been raised, and others eliminated.

Special government programs for housing and deregulation of interest rates are not mutually exclusive approaches. The case can be made for more government in some areas and less government in other respects.

MONETARY POLICY AND CONSUMPTION: DOES MONEY CREATION ADD TO WEALTH?

Monetary economists criticize the Keynesian liquidity trap, in which additional quantities of money have no effect on spending. This is unreasonable, say classical economists, because if people have more money they will have additional wealth and, therefore, will be in a position to consume more. Therefore, it is argued, it is not unreasonable to look to a link between *monetary policy and consumption* as well as between monetary policy and investment. In the Keynesian system, of course, there is an *indirect* linkage between money and consumption: If investment increases, then consumption will consequently increase (the multiplier process). But, in the Keynesian system, this linkage depends on the money-investment linkage: If increases in the money supply have no stimulative effect on investment, they will not stimulate consumption either. An economist in the classical tradition will deny this, seeing a direct linkage from money to consumption.[9] This issue goes back to the earliest debates between Keynes and the classicists,

---

[9] On this controversy, see *Consumer Spending and Monetary Policy: the Linkages* (Federal Reserve Bank of Boston, Proceedings of a Monetary Conference, June 1971).

when Pigou argued that the Keynesian concept of an unemployment equilibrium was defective, since Keynes ignored the effect of additional (real) money balances on consumption.

If people have more money, *ceteris paribus,* then they will also have more wealth; money is one type of asset. The *ceteris paribus* assumption—that other things remain unchanged—is important. In the discussion of the real-balance effect, we have thus far avoided difficulties on this score by considering two specific illustrations in which other forms of wealth are held constant while the real quantity of money is increased:

1. A general deflation, with the nominal quantity of money fixed. (This was the example on which Pigou himself concentrated.)
2. An increase in the money supply which results when the government spends money borrowed from the central bank (that is, the government spending puts newly created money into circulation).

While the first of these involves an increase in real monetary wealth without any corresponding decrease in other types of wealth, it also involves a major real-world complication. The *process* of deflation can have adverse effects on *expectations* and therefore depress investment. Therefore, this deflation example is highly abstract and theoretical, and need not be further considered in a discussion of real-world monetary policy. The second method is realistic enough, and indeed was the basis for casting doubt on the Keynesian concept of an equilibrium multiplier (Chapter 7). But it, too, lacks something in a discussion of monetary policy proper, since it involves a combined fiscal action (government spending) and monetary action (increase in the money supply).

In looking at monetary policy proper—open market operations —we immediately run into a problem. While an open market purchase creates money, it does *not* leave other forms of wealth unchanged. Rather, it involves an *exchange:* The Federal Reserve provides money to the public, but in exchange it gets government bonds from the public. The public exchanges one asset (bonds) for another (money). It is not obvious that the public is wealthier. Furthermore, the same general argument applies to the expansion of bank loans: It involves increases in public holdings of an asset (namely money) but there are corresponding increases in the liabilities of the public (namely, their debts to the banks).

Nevertheless, there are several grounds for believing that an open market purchase may increase the public's wealth. As the demand for bonds is increased, bond prices will tend to rise (interest rates fall). Insofar as the public is a net holder of bonds, the current value of its assets will therefore rise.

An open market purchase may also affect the public's wealth by increasing the value of its portfolios of common stocks. The Federal Reserve does not buy stocks directly, but rather confines its operations to government securities. As interest rates fall, however, this may tend to increase the value of stocks. The present value of stocks, like bonds, reflects the discounted value of a future stream of payments (although in the case of stocks, the stream of expected earnings is of very uncertain magnitude). As interest rates fall, the rate at which all future income streams are discounted may be reduced; that is, stock prices may rise. Put another way, those who are making the choice between purchasing a stock and a bond may be induced to buy a stock if bond prices have already risen; thus, increases in bond prices may spread to the stock market. In addition, the stock market may be quite sensitive to changes in tightness of financial markets, the extent of credit rationing, and so on. Furthermore, the stock market can act as an amplifier of policy. If expansive monetary policy is generally expected to stimulate the economy, then it will have a *double* effect on stock prices: Not only will the rate of discounting used in the present value calculation be reduced, but the expected future flow of earnings from the stock will be revised upward. Monetary policy can therefore have an effect on the wealth represented by stocks—although many other forces also operate in determining stock prices.

There is also a third method by which an open market purchase may increase the public's wealth, but one that takes time. Insofar as the open market purchase leads to an increase in investment (either because of lower interest rates or greater credit availability, or both), then the wealth of the public will rise. Investment involves the accumulation of real assets.

This third possibility for wealth effects—through the increase in the real capital stock (that is, investment)—is quite different from the first two in its potential implications. Its potential significance is for the *long run*, since real capital formation takes time. For the evaluation of the effectiveness of monetary policy as a means of controlling the level of demand in the relatively short run, it is the first two, short-run, wealth effects on which attention must be focused.

There is some statistical evidence to support the view that changes in wealth constitute a significant channel for the operation of monetary policy. Of the major econometric (statistical) models, the MPS (MIT/Penn/Social Science Research Council) model investigates most thoroughly the channels through which monetary policy can operate, specifically attempting to identify monetary effects working through:

1. Interest rates, and hence on the rate of investment expenditures. This is the basic Keynesian channel for monetary policy and is included in practically all econometric models.[10]
2. Credit rationing, which shows up as important in the MPS model only in the housing sector.
3. Changes in wealth, and hence in consumption.

Of the total effects of monetary policy on aggregate demand, the MPS model finds over one third attributable to the wealth effects of monetary policy in the relatively short run (four quarters) and an even higher fraction in the longer run. Although econometric model building is still in an experimental stage, tentative conclusions are possible; namely, that if wealth effects are ignored, the effectiveness of monetary policy may be significantly underestimated.[11]

It should be noted, however, that the wealth effect operates through changes in interest rates, which directly involve changes

---

[10] The monetarist models, discussed in Chapter 12, are a notable exception. They investigate the tendency of the money stock and aggregate demand to move together, without addressing the problem of how money affects aggregate demand.

[11] In his paper on "The Stock Market and the Economy," Brookings Papers on Economic Activity, 1975, vol. 2, pp. 257–90, Barry Bosworth concludes that a $1 change in the value of stocks can affect the annual rate of consumption by as much as 5¢. Thus, the decline in the market value of stocks by more than $500 billion during the bear market of 1973–74 may have been a significant contributor to the recession of 1974–75. This finding is not, however, a direct indicator of the effectiveness of monetary policy. As Bosworth notes (p. 279), "it is questionable that any observed correlation between stock prices and consumption over the postwar period can be used to deduce the effect on consumption of monetary policy." Among other problems, the change in the price of stocks clearly cannot be attributed solely to changes in monetary policy; stock prices are affected by a whole host of forces and are notoriously unpredictable. The conclusion that can be drawn from Bosworth's paper is quite weak: His findings are consistent with the view that an important channel of monetary policy involves a change in stock prices, and thence affects consumption.

On the stock market's effect on consumption, see also Irwin Friend and Charles Lieberman, "Short-Run Asset Effects on Household Saving and Consumption: The Cross-Section Evidence," American Economic Review, September 1975, pp. 624–33; Robert H. Rasche, "Impact of the Stock Market on Private Demand," American Economic Review, May 1972, pp. 224–28.

in the value of bonds, and whose effects can percolate through the stock market. In considering the problem of the effectiveness of monetary policy during the depression when interest rates are at or near their minimums and are therefore not subject to significant reduction by central bank policy, the wealth effect cannot be counted on to give strength to an otherwise weak monetary tool for the stimulation of aggregate demand.

APPENDIX

A THEORETICAL PROBLEM WITH THE LIQUIDITY TRAP

[*In Keynes' Theory*] *the rate of interest is what it is because it is ex-pected to become other than it is; if it is not expected to become other than it is there is nothing left to tell us why it is what it is. The organ which secretes it has been amputated, and yet it somehow exists—"a grin without a cat."**

Dennis Robertson

Within the static equilibrium framework of the simple Keynesian system, there is a problem of theoretical significance (although of little policy importance) with the liquidity preference argument. Specifically, there is a fundamental logical problem in assuming continuing expectations of an upward movement of interest rates— expectations which were crucial in establishing the Keynesian minimum rate of interest at about 2 or 2.5 percent. In a static equilibrium it is assumed that people expect nothing to change from the established equilibrium. But, as depressed conditions and very low interest rates last for a longer and longer time, asset holders will increasingly come to look on low interest rates as the normal state of affairs, and they will therefore come increasingly to discount the risk of an upward movement of interest rates (that is, a fall in the price of bonds). Therefore, the one-way expectations that estab-lish the minimum of about 2 or 2.5 percent for the interest rate in the Keynesian system are not really consistent with a static equilib-rium framework.

The downward slide of long-term interest rates on default-free federal government securities during the Depression suggests that the "minimum" rate may indeed be subject to downward revision as a depression persists. There were very large excess reserves in both

---

* From *Essays in Monetary Theory* (London: P. S. King and Son, 1940), p. 25.

1935 and 1940, indicating that the banks in both years had reached the point where the fears of capital losses inhibited the acquisition of additional government bonds. In 1940, however, the interest rate on long-term U.S. government bonds averaged about 2.2 percent, lower than the 2.8 percent rate of 1935.

While there is a logical problem with the liquidity trap in a static equilibrium framework, there are two compelling reasons why this objection to Keynesian theory should be consigned to the trash heap of intellectual curiosa. While it may be true that, if a depression were to last for a hundred years, expectations would be revised and the monetary authorities would then be able to push the interest rate on long-term securities down to 1 percent, it is difficult to see what practical significance this can conceivably have for public affairs. Here, Keynes' aphorism has particular force: In the long run we are all dead.

The second counterargument in defense of the Keynesian theory is that it does not really matter to the overall structure of the theory if one-way expectations establish a minimum interest rate of 2 percent or not. Suppose that there are *no* expectations of changes in interest rates, and, to make the case against the Keynesian minimum as strong as possible, assume also that there are no transactions costs in buying or selling bonds. What then will the demand function for money look like? The answer: the same as it did in the simple Keynesian system (Figure 5–5), except that the curve will flatten out at an interest rate no lower than zero. Once interest rates reach zero, no potential bondholder will be foolish enough to put in a bid that would push bond prices even higher and give him a negative interest rate. He would be better off simply to hold cash. The liquidity preference function flattens out; one may debate the exact level, but not the flattening out itself. The Keynesian liquidity trap argument is left substantially unaffected. Once the interest rate has been driven to its minimum (now 0 percent), monetary policy becomes completely ineffective in reducing interest rates further and therefore, in the Keynesian system, in having *any* stimulative effect on the economy.

KEY POINTS

1. If there is a crisis of confidence, an increase in reserves may to a significant extent show up as an increase in excess reserves, with the effects on the money supply being delayed. The excess

reserve increases of 1934–35 and 1939–40 illustrated the possibility of the economy responding slowly to an increase in total reserves. This experience was, however, abnormal, in the sense that it was the result of widespread fears of bankruptcy. These fears inhibited a rapid expansion of loans by the banks.

2. It has also been argued that monetary policy may be ineffective because investment is not very sensitive to the rate of interest. If the Marginal Efficiency of Investment is interest-inelastic, expansive monetary policy may have only a small effect on aggregate demand, even if it succeeds in pushing down interest rates. The interest elasticity of the *MEI* is not, however, easily discovered because of statistical problems.

3. Even if the *MEI* function is interest inelastic, monetary policy may have a large effect on investment by altering the *availability* of loans to potential borrowers.

4. Monetary authorities may be hesitant to use tight monetary policies to restrain aggregate demand because of the harsh effects on some sectors of the economy, most notably housing.

5. The classical approach to monetary theory suggests that monetary policy may have part of its effect by changing the wealth of the public, and thereby influencing consumer behavior. One problem with this line of argument is that an open market purchase does not lead to an increase in the money stock, *ceteris paribus*. Rather, the public exchanges an asset (government securities) for another (money), so that wealth does not increase by the amount of the money creation. Nevertheless, wealth may be affected: An open market purchase directly pushes up the price of bonds, and the buoyant effects may spread to the stock market, raising the total market value of stocks. The empirical results of the MPS model suggest that a significant proportion of the total effects of monetary policy depend on the effects operating through changes in wealth and thence through changes in consumption.

QUESTIONS

1. Suppose that there were two alternative "worlds," with changes in the availability of loans being important in one, and with no

credit rationing occurring in the other (with funds always being available at the market-determined interest rate for those with good credit ratings). If you were in business, how would your holdings of money differ in the two cases? Your holdings of short-term assets? Your desired distribution of liabilities among short-term liabilities and long-term bonds?

2. Because the *MEI* schedule tends to shift toward the right during periods of prosperity, and since interest rates tend to be high during periods of prosperity, a time series showing the historical relationship between investment and the rate of interest will slope upward to the right. Thus, there is an "identification problem" in statistically estimating the elasticity of the true *MEI* curve, which slopes downward to the right. What other illustrations might be suggested of a time series that gives a set of points moving upward to the right through time, while the true demand curve may be expected to slope downward to the right?

3. An open market purchase by the Federal Reserve involves an exchange in assets, with the public (or a commercial bank) giving up a bond and receiving a demand deposit in exchange. Thus, there is no direct effect on wealth, except insofar as the value of outstanding bonds increases as interest rates fall, and except insofar as there is a sympathetic movement of the stock market toward higher stock prices. Now consider the second- and third-round expansions of the money supply. In particular, consider a second- or third-round expansion of the money supply associated with an increase in loans to businesses. Will such loans be associated with an increase in the total wealth of the public?

SUGGESTED READINGS

John R. Boorman and Thomas M. Havrilesky, *Money Supply, Money Demand, and Macroeconomic Models* (Arlington Heights, Ill.: AHM Publishing Co., 1972).

Lawrence S. Ritter and William Silber, *Money,* 3d ed. (New York: Basic Books, 1977), chaps. 5–18.

Dwayne Wrightsman, *An Introduction to Monetary Theory and Policy,* 2d ed. (New York: The Free Press, 1976), pt 2.

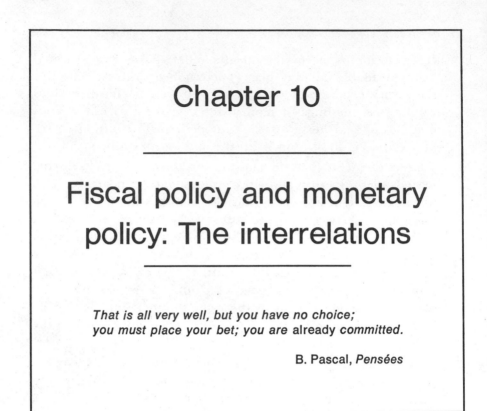

Chapter 10

Fiscal policy and monetary policy: The interrelations

That is all very well, but you have no choice;
you must place your bet; you are already *committed.*

B. Pascal, *Pensées*

In the preceding chapters, much attention has been paid to the debate between Keynesians and classicists over the relative importance of fiscal and monetary policies. Debates are intrinsically interesting and can be helpful in clarifying difficult points. But preoccupation with a debate can itself give a distorted view: It tends to give undue attention to sharply contrasting views, to the neglect of intermediate positions. While there are still substantial differences between neo-Keynesian and neo-classical economists over the relative importance of monetary and fiscal policies, many—and indeed most—current economists take an intermediate, eclectic view. They look on *both* monetary and fiscal policies as important tools in the hands of policymakers. For those in a middle-of-the-road position, the way in which monetary and fiscal policies are fitted together into a coherent overall macroeconomic strategy is an important matter. It is the topic of this chapter.

214

MONETARY POLICY IN SUPPORT OF FISCAL POLICY: AN ACCOMMODATIVE MONETARY POLICY

In Chapter 6, we saw how a rise in the interest rate could reduce the effectiveness of an expansive fiscal policy. As a result of an increase in government spending, the *IS* curve shifts to the right by G/MPS.[1] However, except in the special case of the liquidity trap, the increase in aggregate demand is less than the rightward shift of the *IS* curve. In Figure 10–1 (which repeats Part 5 of Figure 6–6),

Figure 10–1
An accommodative monetary policy

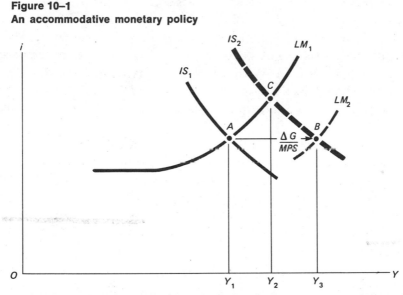

With pure fiscal policy, income rises only from Y_1 to Y_2. With an accommodative monetary policy, the *LM* curve is shifted out to LM_2 and income rises to Y_3.

we observe that the new equilibrium is at *C* rather than *B;* aggregate demand goes up by only the distance Y_1Y_2. When the government issues bonds to finance its deficit spending, bond prices are depressed and interest rates are pushed up. The higher interest rates act as a depressant to investment, reducing the overall expansive effect of the fiscal policy.

Such is the result of the use of *pure fiscal policy;* that is, a change

---

[1] This simple version is applicable only in an economy in which saving is the only leakage from the spending stream. In more complex economies with taxation and imports, we must use the more complex multiplier formulas developed toward the end of Chapter 4.

in the government's budgetary policy with no change in the quantity of money. *If the economy is in need of a substantial stimulation,* this drag on the effectiveness of fiscal policy is unfortunate. In this case, the central bank can restore the effectiveness of fiscal policy by an *accommodative* monetary policy. In order to prevent the adverse effect on investment, the central bank can create the credit necessary to *accommodate* the increasing demand for funds without an increase in the interest rate. How does it do this? By purchasing bonds whenever bond prices begin to fall. (It will be recalled that a fall in the price of bonds and an increase in the rate of interest are opposite sides of the same coin.) When the central bank purchases bonds, it creates money, thereby shifting the LM curve to the right. (Recall the discussion of shifts in the LM curve in Chapter 6; see especially Figure 6–7.) With an accommodative policy which prevents any change in the rate of interest, the LM curve shifts out to LM_2 (Figure 10–1), and there is an increase in aggregate demand to Y_3.

In this case, monetary policy makes a significant contribution to the increase in aggregate demand. However, the Federal Reserve is operating in a manner quite different from that discussed in earlier chapters. Rather than aiming at a specific increase in the quantity of money, the Federal Reserve follows a *passive, accommodative* policy, stabilizing interest rates and allowing the quantity of money to respond to the pressures in the financial markets created by the expansive fiscal policy.

FISCAL POLICY IN SUPPORT OF MONETARY POLICY

Just as monetary policy can contribute to the operation of fiscal policy, so too fiscal policy can make important contributions to the operation of monetary policy.

One of the principal examples of this proposition was touched upon in the previous chapter, in the section on the excess reserve trap. During a depression, when interest rates are very low, the wheels of normal monetary policy may spin; open market purchases may simply add to the reserves of banks and have little short-run effect on the quantity of money or aggregate demand. In such circumstances, fiscal policy can be a tool for making monetary policy work. By borrowing from the central bank and spending the money, the government can put new money into circulation.

In more normal circumstances, fiscal policy has a less critical, but nevertheless important role in the monetary-fiscal combination. Consider the difficult problem of restraining an inflationary boom. Restrictive policies are in order; and these will cause discomfort to participants in the economy. Suppose that a reduction in aggregate demand from Y_1 to Y_2 is desired (Figure 10–2) . This can be achieved

Figure 10–2
Fiscal policy in support of monetary policy

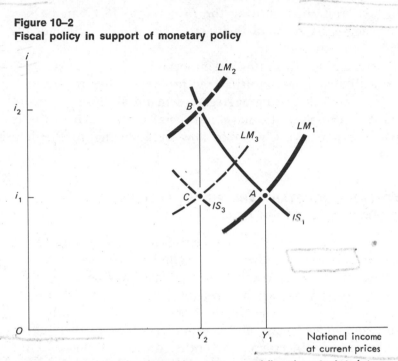

By using a combination of monetary *and* fiscal restraint, interest rates can be kept lower (at *C*) than if the whole burden of restraint had fallen on monetary policy (at *B*).

by various combinations of policies. One option is to place the whole weight of restraint on monetary policy, reducing the quantity of money enough to shift the *LM* curve to *LM*₂.[2] While this policy will have the desired effect of reducing aggregate demand to its target level, it will place severe strains on the financial markets,

---

[2] For simplicity, we here use the basic *IS/LM* approach, in which fiscal policy affects only the *IS* curve and monetary policy affects only the *LM* curve. For a more sophisticated treatment, we would have to take into account the effects of monetary policy on wealth, and hence on the saving function and the *IS* curve. If this complication were taken into account, it would not substantially alter the conclusions of this chapter; it is therefore ignored.

pushing interest rates all the way up to i_2. This may be accompanied by credit rationing and distress in particular sectors of the economy, such as housing. This distress may be alleviated, and the pain of the restrictive policies more broadly distributed, if part of the burden of restraint is placed on fiscal policy. For example, a more moderate monetary restriction (moving the *LM* curve to LM_3) combined with fiscal restraint (shifting the *IS* curve to IS_3) can be used to reduce aggregate demand to its target level (Y_2) without any increase in the interest rate.

This example illustrates an important point. Policymakers are faced with a complex, multifaceted problem. They pursue not just the single goal of getting aggregate demand as close as possible to its target path; they also have additional goals—such as the maintenance of a reasonably stable flow of financing to the housing market.

OFFSETTING MONETARY AND FISCAL ACTIONS: THE PURSUIT OF OTHER GOALS

Indeed, these other goals may be sufficiently important to make a case for *offsetting*—rather than complementary—monetary and fiscal actions. More restrictive fiscal policies may be combined with more expansive monetary policies (or vice versa); while the policies tend to offset one another in their effects on demand, they do not offset—and indeed may reinforce one another—in their effects on other economic objectives. The "other objectives" most frequently mentioned in this regard are growth, important government spending programs, and the balance of international payments.

Growth

Suppose that a society wished to increase its rate of growth. To achieve this goal, a *low interest rate* would be helpful: It would stimulate the investment that contributes to an increase in the productive capacity of the economy. To achieve this low interest rate without a large, inflationary increase in aggregate demand, a tighter fiscal policy may be combined with a more expansive monetary policy; the *IS* curve would be shifted to the left and the *LM* curve to the right (Figure 10–3).

A government that spends less than it collects in taxes will thereby reduce the pressure of demand on productive capacity. Even if the

Figure 10–3
A high-growth strategy

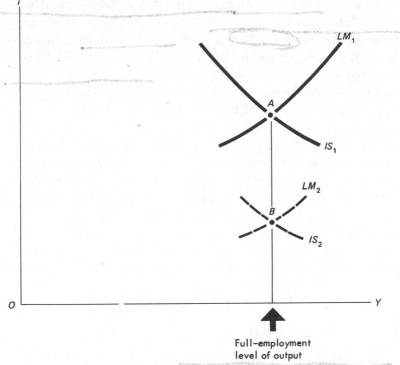

Full–employment
level of output

By following a tight fiscal policy and an expansive monetary policy, the authorities can decrease the rate of interest associated with the full-employment level of aggregate demand. With lower interest rates, investment is stimulated and growth promoted.

economy began at full employment (at point *A* in Figure 10–3), resources can be made available for use in additional investment projects without causing inflation.

Government spending programs

Quite a different outcome will result if the government considers spending programs to be of critical importance; the goods and services that can be provided through large government spending are themselves a major policy objective. Of course, increases in government spending do not necessarily cause excess aggregate demand. During a depression, new government projects have a desirable effect, moving the economy toward full employment. But, during more normal times, large increases in government spending have inflationary consequences unless offset with other aggregate demand policies. One offset is an increase in taxes, which removes disposable income from the hands of the public, thereby depressing consumption. A second alternative is a tighter monetary policy. In other words, tighter money may be combined with more government spending in order to redirect the resources of society toward the things the government provides.

It should be recognized that this combination is *exactly the opposite* of the high-growth policy described in the preceding section. Because of the tight money, the resources for the new government programs will come in substantial degree from the investment sector, and thus the rate of growth will be depressed. Over the longer run, this approach therefore raises a question: Will the future productive capacity of the economy be great enough to provide the rising level of government services and private goods which the public is likely to demand?

The balance of payments

An expanding aggregate demand—whether caused by monetary or fiscal stimulation—tends to make the balance of international payments move in a negative direction. As incomes rise and people buy more goods, some of those goods are imported from foreign countries.

But, while expansive monetary and fiscal policies have similar effects on the merchandise balance, they have quite different effects on the capital components of the balance of payments. Fiscal expansion—involving government borrowing on the financial markets to finance deficit spending—tends to push up interest rates, and thus encourage foreigners to buy U.S. securities; and the payments by foreigners for these securities tends to balance the U.S. expenditures for merchandise imports. Monetary expansion, on the other hand, depresses U.S. interest rates and discourages foreign purchases of U.S. securities (and encourages U.S. residents to buy foreign rather than U.S. securities). Thus, the negative movement of the balance of payments is more pronounced with an expansive monetary policy than with an expansive fiscal policy.

During the 1960s, there were proposals that this differential impact of monetary and fiscal policies on the balance of payments be used to ease the U.S. balance-of-payments problem. Specifically, suggestions were made that fiscal *expansion* be accompanied by relative *tightness* on the monetary side, in order to push up interest rates and attract foreign capital (that is, in order to encourage foreigners to buy U.S. securities). Put somewhat differently, suggestions were made that fiscal policy be directed toward the domestic objective of an appropriate level of aggregate demand, while monetary policy be directed toward a balance of the international accounts.[3]

The trouble with this strategy is that a relatively tight monetary policy (aimed at keeping up interest rates and thus protecting the balance of payments) combined with a relatively expansive fiscal policy (aimed at the appropriate level of aggregate demand) would once again have adverse effects on investment and hence on the growth of productive capacity; and the 1960s was a period when growth was given a very high priority indeed. Thus, there was a major policy problem. There were three objectives—the appropriate level of aggregate demand, growth, and a balance of the international accounts. All three objectives could not be pursued if policymakers had only two weapons (fiscal policy and monetary policy) at their disposal. What was needed was a third policy tool.

One suggestion was that monetary policy be divided into two. While economists frequently speak of *the* interest rate, this is clearly a simplification; there is a whole series of interest rates in the market. The proposal was for the Federal Reserve to purchase long-term bonds, thus pushing down the long-term interest rates which were important for investment. At the same time, short-term securities would be sold, pushing up the short-term interest rates which were considered particularly important as a determinant of international capital flows.[4] By thus "twisting" the pattern of interest rates—pushing rates on short-term securities up and rates on long-term securities down—it was hoped that balance-of-payments and growth objectives might both be met.

Operation Twist was not pursued vigorously by the Federal Reserve. The attraction of short-term funds to the United States might temporarily ease the payments problem, but there were long-run, fundamental defects in the international financial system. The de-

[3] Robert Mundell, "The Appropriate Use of Monetary and Fiscal Policy for Internal and External Stability," *International Monetary Fund Staff Papers,* March 1962.

[4] Walter W. Heller, *New Dimensions of Political Economy* (New York: W. W. Norton, 1966), p. 75.

nouement came in the early 1970s, when the United States suspended the convertibility of gold, and exchange rates were permitted to fluctuate in response to the demand and supply for foreign exchange. (An exchange rate is the price of one national currency in terms of another; for example, $1\pounds = \$1.60$. Foreign exchange is currency of another country. For example, the German mark is foreign exchange for Americans; the U.S. dollar is foreign exchange to Germans.) Fluctuating exchange rates may be looked on either as the acquisition of another tool (namely, movements in exchange rates) or as the elimination of one objective (namely, the maintenance of fixed or "pegged" exchange rates). At any rate, the relationship between tools and goals was brought into better balance.

TARGETS AND INSTRUMENTS: AN INTRODUCTION TO THE THEORY OF ECONOMIC POLICY

These examples illustrate that if policymakers wish to achieve additional goals or *targets* they will need additional policy tools or *instruments* For example, if a balance-of-payments target is added to aggregate demand and growth objectives, then the two basic policies (monetary and fiscal) will generally not be sufficient; a third policy tool will be needed.[5] Dutch economist and Nobel prize-winner Jan Tinbergen has demonstrated a fundamental proposition: In order to achieve N targets, N policy instruments are necessary.[6]

Furthermore, these policy tools must be independent; that is, they must have different effects on different targets. In this sense, monetary and fiscal policies are independent. If we look at two policies—monetary and fiscal—which have the same effect on aggregate demand, they will have different effects on interest rates (and therefore on investment and growth). Because of this differential effect on interest rates, the mix of monetary and fiscal policies aimed at any specific level of aggregate demand may be adjusted to help achieve the growth objective. As we noted in the previous section, a tighter fiscal policy may be combined with a more ex-

---

[5] In particularly fortunate circumstances, two policies may be sufficient. It is possible that, by a stroke of luck, the monetary and fiscal policies designed to meet the aggregate demand and growth objectives will just happen to give the desired balance of payments.

[6] Jan Tinbergen, *On the Theory of Economic Policy*, 2d ed. (Amsterdam: North-Holland, 1952); Tinbergen, *Economic Policy: Principles and Design* (Amsterdam: North-Holland, 1956).

pansive monetary policy in order to reduce interest rates and thus promote investment and growth.

THE EFFECTIVENESS OF FISCAL AND MONETARY POLICIES: THE "BANG FOR THE BUCK" AND OTHER CRITERIA

The complexity of the objectives facing policymakers demonstrates that there is more to choosing an instrument than judging its power, that is, judging how much "bang" in terms of a change in aggregate demand will come from a buck's change in government spending (or taxation, or monetary policy). Indeed, upon reflection, it is not so clear that the "bang for the buck" is a good criterion, or even a good starting point. It is true that, in an extreme case, the bang for the buck criterion is relevant: In dealing with the Keynesian liquidity trap argument that monetary policy may have zero effect on aggregate demand, it is necessary to establish whether there is any bang before proceeding to other issues. But, outside the extreme case where zero effectiveness is at issue, it is not clear that the size of the bang makes an a priori case for the use of an instrument.

This is particularly so if expansive actions are under consideration. What are the mechanics of monetary expansion? The Federal Reserve buys government debt, thereby in a fundamental sense reducing the outstanding national debt (since the Federal Reserve is in fact part of the federal government, and all incremental interest earnings of the Federal Reserve are returned to the U.S. Treasury). Interest rates are driven down. The reduction of interest rates and the government debt are side effects that are widely considered desirable. Therefore, it can be argued that expansive monetary policies should be particularly relied on if they are relatively ineffective (that is, have a low bang per buck). If they have but little power, we will be able to get a *lot* of the things we want—lower interest rates, a repayment of the government debt—for any quantity of aggregate demand stimulation.

This is also the case with expansive fiscal policies. They take the form of things that are even more ardently admired: tax cuts and increases in government spending. If these can be accomplished with only a small multiplier effect on aggregate demand, then so much the better. Just think how nice it would be to reduce taxes drastically—which could be done without fear of adverse consequences during a recession if the effects on aggregate demand really were small. Here again, a low bang per buck would make a good case for the use of the policy, not for its avoidance.

In short, the authorities do all sorts of miserable things—collect taxes, keep down government spending, pay interest on the national debt—which would be unnecessary if expansive fiscal and monetary policies had little stimulative effect. But alas, there is indeed a sizable bang to expansive monetary and fiscal policies; we will have to live with the miserable reality of taxes, etc.

If the bang for the buck is not a good criterion for choosing among various policies, to what do we look? In the face of changing economic conditions, policy tools claim attention insofar as they have the following desirable characteristics:

1. ~~Speed.~~ The more changeable underlying conditions are, the more important speed of the policy instrument is.
2. ~~Predictability~~. If we are going to get to a desired level of aggregate demand without overshooting the target, it is important that the effects of policy actions be predictable.
3. ~~Reversability~~. Since we do not continuously face the unchanged need to either stimulate or restrain aggregate demand, reversability is vital.
4. ~~Desirable side-effect characteristics~~. A policy may have either desirable side effects—as noted in the above illustrations of tax cuts—or undesirable ones. A good policy is one for which the net side effects have as great a positive (or as small a negative) value as possible.

Insofar as the bang for the buck measure has any validity at all, it is as a subcomponent of one or more of these four main criteria. There is, presumably, some connection between strength and speed, and also between strength and predictability.

TIME LAGS AND THE EFFECTIVENESS OF MONETARY AND FISCAL POLICIES

There are a number of delays in the operation of discretionary monetary and/or fiscal policies. There is, first, a delay in realizing exactly what is going on in the economy. Policy judgments must be based in large part on statistical evidence, and there is some lag before statistics can be collected and put into a coherent and usable form. Then, too, because of random errors in statistical collection and the existence of short-run perturbations in economic conditions which are independent of any significant trend, policymakers must avoid responding to every little monthly jiggle in unemployment or prices.

As a result, there may be a significant lag between the change in fundamental economic conditions and the recognition that something should be done. This is the *recognition lag.*

There is a close connection between the length of the recognition lag and the ability of government economists to predict. If it were possible to predict a significant period into the future with a high degree of precision, the recognition lag could be eliminated, and even made negative. Action could be taken on the basis of predicted changes in economic conditions which had not yet actually occurred. It is therefore difficult to say much in general about the length—or even the sign—of the recognition lag; it depends on the strength and predictability of the underlying economic changes.

After the need for action is recognized, there is a lag in implementing the needed policies—the *action lag.* Again, it is difficult to be specific about the probable length of this lag; it depends on the clarity with which the need for change is recognized and the process of policy adjustment. (The recognition and action lags may therefore obviously overlap and blend into one another.)

The two lags—the recognition lag and the action lag—which occur before action is taken together constitute what is usually known as the *inside lag;* it is the lag that takes place *inside* the policymaking process. This is not the end of the problem, however. After the action is taken, there will be another lag before the substantial effects of the policy are felt. For fiscal policy, there will be a lag between tax changes and the consequent changes of consumer behavior. For monetary policy, there will be a lag between the open market operation and the increase in the money supply, and between the increase in the money supply and changes in spending. Because the events that mark the beginning or ending of lags are themselves likely to occur over a span of time—the gradual recognition that a problem exists, for example, or the gradual effects on aggregate demand once an action has been taken—the lags themselves have fuzzy ending times, as illustrated in Figure 10–4.

Lags can vary greatly from one instance to another. For example, the length of time required for congressional approval of a tax change will depend on the nature of the change, the clarity with which a need for fiscal action is recognized, the degree of cooperation between the administration and Congress, and so on. The lag between the conception and passage of the major tax cut of 1964 was measured in years; in contrast, the tax reduction of 1975 was passed quickly. Because of such discrepancies—and because the economy responds gradually to policy actions—it is difficult to generalize about the length of lags. Nevertheless, there are some grounds for

Figure 10–4
Policy lags

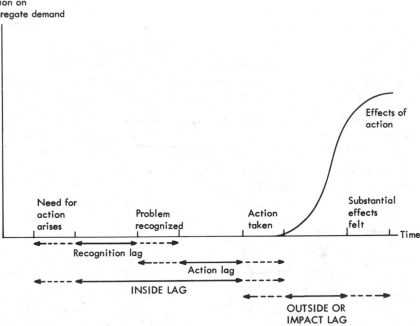

Because of a combination of lags, there is a substantial interval between the time when problems arise and the time when corrective actions become effective.

believing that the lags may be shorter with tax changes than with public works programs, particularly if the tax changes can be kept simple in order to hasten their passage through Congress. Tax rebates can be distributed to the public relatively rapidly. To design and execute a public works program, on the other hand, takes time —unless spending is considered so pressing that little thought is given to the design and probable usefulness of the public projects. (A *restrictive* fiscal policy, involving a rapid *reduction* in public works spending, is even more problematic. Projects left half completed clearly involve a waste of resources.) Because of the problems with public works, the incoming Carter administration in early 1977 designed its stimulative package around a tax rebate. (The tax rebate proposal was later withdrawn.)

Time lags may be shorter with monetary policies than with fiscal policies; indeed, this constitutes one of the traditional arguments for the use of monetary policies. All that is needed to institute a change in monetary policy is a decision by the Open Market Committee of the Federal Reserve, which meets regularly, once every month. In contrast, most significant fiscal policy changes must go through the whole legislative process. (This point is made with particular reference to the United States. In parliamentary systems such as that of the United Kingdom, the argument loses its force. Tax changes become effective with the budget speech of the Chancellor of the Exchequer, and both the legislative and the executive branches are controlled by the same party and the same individuals. Thus, the reasons for some of the delays in fiscal policy are absent.)

Two broad proposals have been made to reduce the inside lag in the initiation of corrective fiscal actions. First, taxation and spending policies may be designed around automatic, built-in stabilizers, so that the fiscal posture changes in a desired direction without any specific decision by the government. (Automatic stabilizers were considered in Chapter 4.) Second, the decisionmaking process may be speeded up by granting discretionary power to the executive branch.

EXECUTIVE DISCRETION?

The President has some discretion to determine the timing of government expenditures. Even on the taxation side, there is an element of control exercised by the executive. During early 1972, for example, the government urged the public to apply for a reduced rate of income tax withholding in order to avoid the drag on the economy which would come from overwithholding of taxes.

But such changes in withholding provide minor room for maneuver on the taxation side. During the 1960s, stabilization policy was complicated by delays in getting tax changes. The tax cut needed for stimulation in the early 1960s did not actually come until 1964. By this time it was beginning to be too late, as the Vietnam expenditures were beginning to push the economy toward excess aggregate demand. Later, when restraint was needed, there was a similar delay in getting tax changes; the surcharge was not enacted until mid-1968.[7]

In order to reduce the action lag and lay the groundwork for a more active and useful fiscal policy, the Kennedy administration recommended that the President be given the authority to reduce taxes within limits, subject to a congressional veto. To minimize the executive excursion into the area of congressional prerogative, the administration confined its proposals to personal income taxes, and then asked only for authority for *across-the-board* cuts of not more than 5 percent. At the beginning of 1969, this request was reiterated by the outgoing Johnson administration, which broadened the request to include authority for an upward, across-the-board change of not more than 5 percent.

Congress has, however, been reluctant to grant such power over the purse. And the case for executive discretion was set back in the early days of the Ford administration in 1974. One of the first major steps of the new administration was to ask for a tax *increase*. But the economy was already on the way downward into recession; the Congress responded by *cutting* taxes in early 1975. Congress felt that it could not trust the executive to get even the *sign* of a change in taxes right; the concept of executive power over taxes faded even further into the background.

[Discretionary proposals have involved simple, across-the-board changes in taxes, in order to avoid the complicated issue of tax equity. The desire to avoid debates over equity was also a reason for adhering to a relatively simple, across-the-board formula when the Johnson administration recommended the surcharge which was enacted in 1968. To try to change the structure of taxes and simultaneously increase taxes, it was felt, was just out of the question. On the other hand, when the Kennedy administration put forward the proposals that ultimately led to the tax cut of 1964, there was a modest effort at tax reform. The point suggested by these two experiences: It may be easier to get tax reform when the overall level of taxes is being reduced than when it is being increased. This point was not lost on the incoming Carter administration in January of 1977. In explaining why the administration had made a *temporary* tax cut the major component of its initial proposals aimed at stimu-

---

[7] The action lag is given as the major reason for fiscal failure by Charles E. McLure, Jr., *Fiscal Failure: Lessons of the Sixties* (Washington, D.C.: American Enterprise Institute, 1972).

lating the economy, the chairman-designate of the Council of Economic Advisers (Charles Schultze) noted that a permanent cut would involve "giving away . . . revenues that we're going to need later to grease the skids for tax reform. . . ."][8]

POLICY TARGETS, POLICY INSTRUMENTS, AND THE PROBLEM OF UNCERTAINTY

Lags constitute a major complication of policy, and *unpredictability* is another. Thus far, we have slid over this problem, assuming that the policymakers have a precise idea of where the various curves lie (for example, in Figure 10–2), and how much each curve is shifted by any given change in monetary or fiscal policies. Such a world—in which there is no uncertainty—may be complex, involving many goals for which many policy tools are needed. Yet it leads to the relatively straightforward and strong conclusion noted in the earlier section on the theory of policy: As long as policymakers have N independent policy tools, they should be able to achieve N policy goals. Indeed, if they have more tools than goals, then some tools become superfluous; they may be discarded by policymakers as unnecessary for the achievement of their goals.

Clearly, this theory of policy is useful and relevant for the real world; for example, it gives important insights regarding the appropriate mix of fiscal and monetary policies if investment is to be encouraged. But clearly, also, there is something missing: We do not live in a world in which policymakers can achieve their goals, with some tools to spare. In part, this is due to the large numbers of goals to which policymakers pay attention. But also, it is due to *uncertainty* regarding the effects of policy actions. For example, when tax cuts were made in 1964 and 1975, and a tax surcharge imposed in 1968, policymakers were uncertain regarding the size of the multipliers; thus, they were uncertain regarding the *strength* of the response of the economy. And, if anything, policymakers are less certain now than they were during the optimistic days of Kennedy's Camelot, when the first large-scale application of fiscal management was being planned. In particular, the tax surcharge of 1968 had much less effect on aggregate demand than had been expected, and led to doubts about the economy's response to fiscal policies.

In the face of uncertainty regarding the effectiveness of policy

[8] As quoted in *The Wall Street Journal,* January 19, 1977.

actions, important modifications are in order in the strategy of policy. Specifically,

1. Where a single policy is being used to pursue a single goal, then policymakers should aim short of the target.
2. Where policymakers have more than one policy instrument available for use on a single goal, they should use them all, thereby cutting down on the uncertainty of the outcome. No tools are superfluous.

And the second proposition has a corollary:

3. The use of offsetting policies to meet secondary goals has a cost, in terms of increasing the uncertainty with respect to the achievement of the primary goal.

The second and third propositions are the most important; to them we now turn. (The first proposition is explained in Appendix A of Chapter 10.)

One target, two instruments: Both instruments should be used

In a world of uncertainty, the economy's response to a policy action will not necessarily fall directly on the target; there will be a whole range of possible outcomes. In order to *illustrate* the problem of uncertainty as simply as possible,[9] let us assume a very simple case (shown in Figure 10–5) where there is a 50–50 chance that the effects of fiscal policy will be as expected (outcome *A*), one chance in four that the response will be 50 percent too great (outcome *B*), and one chance in four that the response will be 50 percent too small (outcome *C*).

Figure 10–5, it should be stressed, applies to a specific time interval. Points along the horizontal axis do *not* represent later and later time periods. Rather, they measure the *amount* of fiscal policy used during any single time period. Thus, if the policymakers were aiming fiscal policy for an increase of $100 billion in aggregate demand, they would use five units of fiscal expansion; to aim for a $200 billion increase, they would use a fiscal policy twice as vigorous (ten units) during the current period. If they do, indeed, want to in-

---

[9] *Proofs* of propositions 1 and 2 are given in William Brainard, "Uncertainty and the Effectiveness of Policy," *American Economic Review,* May 1967, pp. 411–25. (These proofs require a familiarity with statistical theory.)

Figure 10–5
Uncertainty: An illustration

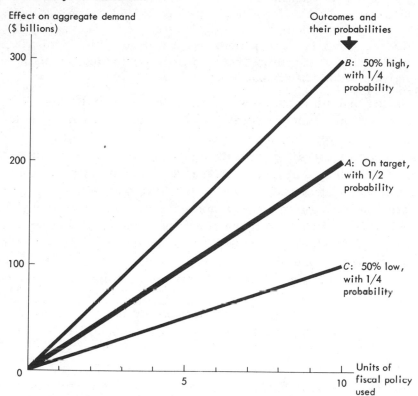

In an uncertain world, the response of the economy may correspond to the best estimate, A. But the response may be stronger (at B), or weaker (at C).

crease aggregate demand by $200 billion and use only fiscal policy, then the expected results are shown in Figure 10–5: They have only one chance in two of being on target, and one chance in two of being either 50 percent too high (at $300 billion) or 50 percent too low (at $100 billion).

Now, suppose they can use a combination of fiscal *and* monetary policy. For simplicity, assume that monetary policy is neither more precise nor more crude than fiscal policy; assume, in other words, that it gives the same pattern of uncertainty as fiscal policy (one chance in four of being 50 percent too strong, one chance in four of being 50 percent too weak). For the problem to be manageable, we must also make an additional important assumption.

Key assumption: That the use of monetary policy does not change our uncertainty regarding the effects of fiscal policy. That is, we assume that if monetary expansion is undertaken together with fiscal expansion, the effects of fiscal policy itself on aggregate demand follow the same pattern shown in Figure 10–5. Similarly, fiscal policy actions are assumed not to affect the uncertainty associated with monetary policy.

Rather than using ten units of fiscal policy, assume that the policy-makers use five units of fiscal policy and five units of monetary expansion during the current period. The fiscal policy, shown in Part 1 of Figure 10–6, repeats Figure 10–5. The five units of monetary policy, shown in Part 2, give a similar set of outcomes, with monetary policy indicated by the lowercase letters *(a, b, c)*. Because we are assuming that neither policy interferes with the predictability of the other, the effects of monetary policy may be simply *added* to fiscal policy, as shown in Figure 10–7. Regardless of whether the outcome from fiscal policy is *A, B,* or *C,* there will be three possible outcomes from monetary policy—high *(b)*, low *(c)*, or accurate *(a)*. (While monetary policy is shown as being added to fiscal policy, we reiterate that these do *not* happen sequentially, with fiscal policy being used first and then monetary policy being

Figure 10–6
Uncertainty: Two policy tools

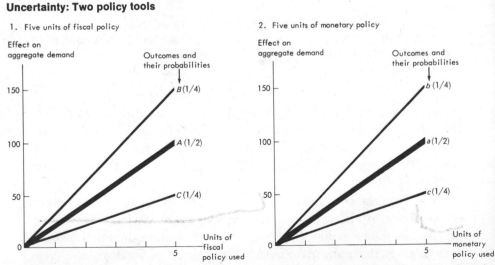

1. Five units of fiscal policy

2. Five units of monetary policy

If the use of monetary policy does not affect our uncertainty regarding fiscal policy (and vice versa), then five units of each policy—shown here—can be added to derive Figure 10–7.

Figure 10–7
A combination of monetary and fiscal policies

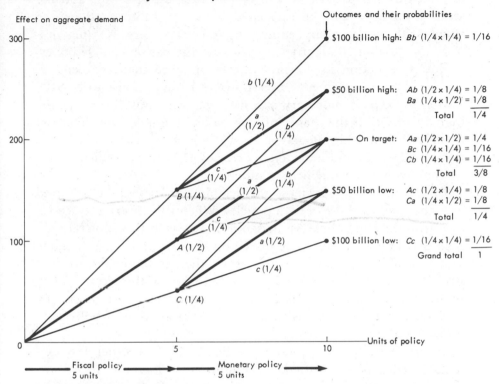

With a combination of fiscal *and* monetary policies, the dispersion of results is reduced. Policymakers can have greater confidence of coming close to the target level of aggregate demand.

added. Rather, *both* monetary and fiscal policies are used *during the same period,* aiming at a specific change in aggregate demand within a specified time framework.)

Now, observe what happens to the overall uncertainty associated with the combined fiscal-monetary policy. Because there is one chance in two that fiscal policy will be accurate, and a similar chance that monetary policy will be accurate, there is only one chance in four that both monetary policy and fiscal policy will together be accurate, resulting in a "hit" on the target (outcome *Aa*). But that is not the only way that the economy may end up on target. The wandering of fiscal and monetary policies may offset, leading to a hit. Fiscal effects may be too high and monetary effects too low (outcome *Bc*), or vice versa (*Cb*). Because each policy has one chance in four of wandering in a specific direction, the probability of a hit through pattern Bc will be $\frac{1}{16}$ (that is, $\frac{1}{4} \times \frac{1}{4}$) ; and the same probability will be associated with Cb. In total, then, the chances of the economy ending up on target are $\frac{3}{8}$ (or $\frac{1}{4} + \frac{1}{16} + \frac{1}{16}$) —that is, slightly less than with the use of a single policy.

But, a reduction in the probable error more than compensates for this adverse outcome.[10] Observe that, for the response to be $100 billion high, *both* monetary and fiscal policies must be off in the high direction. As the chance of each being high is $\frac{1}{4}$, the chance of them both being high together is only $\frac{1}{16}$ (outcome (Bb). Much more likely is the more moderate error of $50 billion, which occurs when only one of the policies wanders.

In general, then, the most predictable results will be achieved with the combined use of both policies. When the uncertainty associated with the two policies is the same (as it was in this illustration), then equal reliance should be placed on the two policies. When one policy is more accurate than the other, then it should be used in stronger doses than the second policy, but some of the second policy should nevertheless be used. For any set of uncertainties regarding individual policies, there is an optimum combination of policies to minimize overall uncertainty.[11]

Where the application of one policy makes the other less predictable (that is, when the key assumption is violated), then these results are undermined and the policy problem is made substantially more complicated; but in the absence of much more detailed knowledge than we now possess, we are nevertheless left with a presumption in favor of the combined application of available policies.

One final—and important—point should be noted. The uncertainty considered in this section is *only one* of two quite different types of uncertainty:

1. Uncertainty over the *response* of the economy to *changes in policy*. (This is the uncertainty considered in the previous pages.) For example, if we cut taxes now, we do not know pre-

---

[10] The adverse result—involving a slight reduction of the probability of a direct hit in the target area—is a peculiarity of our simplified method, in which only three specific outcomes are possible with a single tool. In the more general case, where the outcome may be anywhere in the general vicinity of the target, then the adverse result does not hold. The use of more than one policy tool both increases the chance of a direct hit in the target area and reduces the dispersion of expected outcomes around the target. See Brainard, "Uncertainty and the Effectiveness of Policy."

[11] For a proof, see Brainard, "Uncertainty and the Effectiveness of Policy," pp. 418–21.

cisely *how much* effect will this have on aggregate demand over the next six months.

2. Uncertainty about *how much* adjustment in aggregate demand is *desirable*. We are uncertain about the *precise position of the economy* at present, and even more *uncertain* about *where the economy will go in the absence of policy actions*. Thus, even if there were no type 1 uncertainty—for example, *even if* we had the policies to make aggregate demand in six months precisely $10 billion higher than it otherwise would be—we could not be sure if it is wise to use such policies.

This distinction may perhaps be clarified by an analogy. Consider a submarine that is trying to torpedo a ship. The first type of uncertainty arises because the torpedoes are imperfect; they do not run precisely true. The second type of uncertainty arises because the submarine commander does not know exactly where the ship will be when the torpedo arrives in the target area. The range finder on the submarine may not be very good, or the target may be shrouded in mist, or the current speed and direction of the ship may not be known with precision. (In economic terms, we don't have precise statistics on where the economy is today, nor do we know precisely what the underlying trends are.) Furthermore, while the torpedo is running, the ship may change course. (After the initiation of the policy, but before its major effects occur, the path of the economy may be disturbed by a blizzard, a change in foreign demand for our exports, or other factors.)

The *first type* of uncertainty can be reduced by using a *combination of policies* as explained earlier. (This makes our "torpedoes" better.) But, a combination of policies cannot deal with the second type of uncertainty.

Indeed, if there were uncertainty regarding *only* the course of the economy in the absence of policy changes (type 2), then there would be *no gain* from the use of a second policy tool. (In terms of our analogy, the torpedo always goes precisely where it is aimed; the trouble is, the ship may not be there.) A single policy would cause a precise response; two tools could do no better. Additional tools would not help in the choice of a target; *we would have to pick the best point we could* and aim for that—even though it might not turn out to be what we wanted in the light of unfolding events. Thus, a world in which there is uncertainty concerning only the position of the target may be analyzed as a world of "certainty equivalence."[12] The basic theory of policy again becomes relevant; to aim for N targets, instruments beyond the first N independent tools are superfluous.

Of course, in the real world, *both* types of uncertainty—regarding the strength of policies and the position of the target—may occur together. In this case, the use of all policy tools is desirable; it will help to reduce uncertainty *regarding the response of the economy to changes in policy* (type 1). However, no combination of policies will deal with the second type of uncertainty; combinations will not reduce our uncertainty over where the economy is going *in the absence of changes in policy*. Thus, we are left with troublesome uncertainty about whether policy changes are needed or not.

A corollary: The cost of using offsetting policies to seek secondary goals

Uncertainty gives us a reason to use policies in cooperation; and, for similar reasons, it imposes a cost—in terms of additional dispersion of the outcomes—if two policies are used in an *offsetting* manner in order to achieve secondary goals.

Reconsider the example described earlier in the chapter, where restrictive fiscal policies are combined with expansive monetary policies in order to bring down interest rates and therefore promote growth. The problem in an uncertain world is illustrated in Figure 10–8, which continues the assumptions of uncertainty used in Figure 10–7. Now, however, five units of *restrictive* fiscal policies are used, together with the 15 units of *expansive* monetary policies that are needed to offset the fiscal policies and aim for the targeted increase of $200 billion in aggregate demand. The effects of monetary policy (a, b, c) may again be added to the fiscal effects (A, B, C). Observe that the dispersion of outcomes is not only greater than when the two policies are used in combination (Figure 10–7), but also greater than when a single policy is used (Figure 10–5). The objective of lower interest rates and higher growth is bought at a cost—the cost of an increase in the uncertainty regarding aggregate demand.

In some circumstances, this cost may not be excessive. Such may be the case, for example, with respect to growth. (The question of whether we should indeed wish to stimulate growth will be deferred

---

[12] Brainard, "Uncertainty and the Effectiveness of Policy," p. 411; Henri Theil, *Optimal Decision Rules for Government and Industry* (Chicago: Rand McNally, 1964).

Figure 10–8
Uncertainty: The problem of offsetting policies

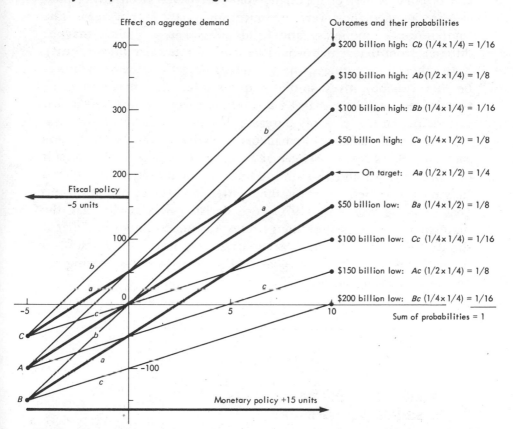

If offsetting aggregate demand policies are used, with the objective of achieving some second goal, then the uncertainty with respect to the achievement of the aggregate demand target will be increased.

until Chapter 16.) Growth takes time and pays its dividends over a long period; it makes little sense to place a high priority on an abrupt shift to a high-growth policy. In these circumstances, the change in policy mix may be approached slowly with a trial-and-error method. If only small changes in the mix are attempted during any brief time span, then corrections to aggregate demand policies may be made as experience unfolds; the costs in terms of added uncertainty may be quite small. Indeed, over a number of business cycles, actual offsetting policies may not be needed to change the policy mix. During boom periods, fiscal policies may be the centerpiece of restrictive actions; and, during periods of slack, the emphasis may be placed on monetary expansion. In this manner, the mix of policies may be gradually changed. (Even if offsetting policies are avoided, however, the uncertainty cost is not zero. The composition of monetary and fiscal policies at any time may be different from that which would be used to minimize uncertainty.)

In other circumstances, the secondary objectives themselves may be short-run objectives; and if a quick attempt is made to reach these objectives, there may be a substantial cost in terms of added uncertainty in the path of aggregate demand. Such apparently was the case for the balance-of-payments objective of the 1960s. Where such a conflict arises—between reducing uncertainty in the pursuit of a primary goal and also aiming for a secondary objective—then a judgment is needed regarding the relative importance of the various goals. During the early 1970s, the decision was made that the maintenance of pegged exchange rates was not so important that it should be permitted to substantially complicate the pursuit of domestic aggregate demand goals. The result was the floating exchange rate system of the 1970s.

APPENDIX A

ONE TARGET AND ONE INSTRUMENT: THE CASE FOR AIMING SHORT

To illustrate the first uncertainty proposition—that policymakers should aim *short* of their objective—we must depart from the simplifying assumption that any single policy can have only three specific outcomes (50 percent high, 50 percent low, or on target). We must deal with the more realistic case, where a policy aimed at a point may hit anywhere in the vicinity of the point, with the probability that a position will be hit declining continuously as we move further away from the aiming point (A), as illustrated in Figure 10A–1. The *aiming point* is defined as the most likely outcome from a given policy setting; that is, it is the point at which the probability distribution is at its peak (P).

As stronger and stronger policy is used—that is, as the distance between the starting point and the aiming point is increased—the greater will be the dispersion of outcomes; the curve representing the distribution of probabilities will become lower and wider, as

Figure 10A–1
Probability distribution

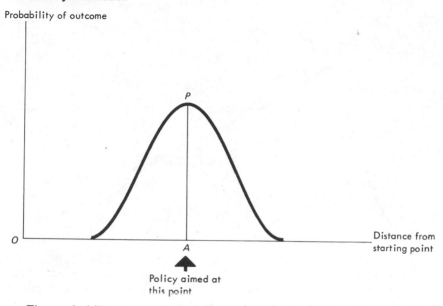

The probability is greatest at the point of aim (*A*). In other words, the curve reaches its peak (*P*) directly above this point.

illustrated in Figure 10A–2. Only three such curves (C_1, C_2, C_3) are shown, but there is an infinite number. Policymakers may use policy of any strength; that is, they may aim anywhere along the continuous horizontal axis.

For this family of curves, an "envelope curve" may be drawn. At any distance to the right, the point on the envelope curve represents the highest point that can be chosen from any of the underlying curves. Observe that the envelope curve touches each of the underlying probability distribution curves (C_1, C_2, C_3) *to the right* of the point of aim; for example, the point of tangency T_1 is to the right of aiming point A_1. Why is this so? The envelope curve must slope *downward to the right,* since the probability distribution curves are lower and wider as the aim moves to the right. But, a probability distribution curve is horizontal at its peak (P), directly above the aiming point (A). Clearly, if the envelope curve (which slopes downward) were to go through the peak, it would have to *cut* the probability distribution curve (which is horizontal at that point). The envelope curve is not tangent at the peak but at a point to the

Figure 10A–2
Aim short of objective

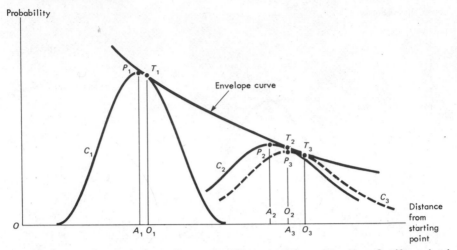

Aiming at A_3 maximizes the probability of hitting objective O_3. If we had wanted to hit A_3, it would have been better to aim for A_2 (giving probability T_2 of a hit) rather than to aim directly for A_3 (which would give a probability of only P_3).

right.[13] Thus, in order to maximize the probability of ending up at objective O_3, policy should be *aimed* at point A_3, that is, somewhat short.

---

[13] This mathematical problem has been belabored because of its intrinsic difficulty —and because a failure to understand it led to a famous error by Jacob Viner. A U-shaped short-run cost curve of a firm is constructed on the assumption that the capital equipment of the firm is fixed. Logically, there is a whole family of such short-run cost curves, one for each quantity of capital. Viner was interested in the relationship between this family of short-run cost curves and the long-run cost curve, that is, the curve that represents the lowest-cost method of production when the quantity of capital can be varied. Viner instructed his draftsman to draw the long-run cost curve as an envelope curve around the family of short-run cost curves; he also instructed the draftsman to draw the curve through the *lowest* point of each individual short-run cost curve. The draftsman demurred; his instructions were contradictory. Viner insisted. The draftsman presented a diagram with the envelope curve clearly going through the minimum points on the short-run curves, but also clearly *cutting* these curves. Much to the amusement of his colleagues, Viner published this diagram, with complaints about his obstinate draftsman who "saw some mathematical objection . . . which I could not succeed in understanding. I could not persuade him to disregard his scruples . . . and to follow my instructions." [Jacob Viner, "Cost Curves and Supply Curves," *Zeitschrift für Nationalökonomie*, 1931; reprinted in George J. Stigler and Kenneth E. Boulding, *Readings in Price Theory* (Homewood, Ill.: Richard D. Irwin, 1952) , p. 214.]

His students were even more amused. A brash young undergraduate at the University of Chicago—Paul Samuelson—observed that the draftsman could have followed instructions; he just needed a thick enough pencil. In order that future teachers and students would be able to enjoy his embarrassment, Viner allowed the original diagram to remain when the article was republished.

This constitutes a general statistical result, which is applicable to a number of problems. For example, if a shore battery is trying to sink a ship, it should aim slightly short. However, because modern artillery pieces are well rifled, the dispersion of shots is small, each of the probability distributions is very narrow and high, the distances between each A and O are small, and therefore this is an unimportant problem for artillery. Economic weapons are, however, not so well rifled; the "shots" fall in a more erratic pattern, with the probability distributions being relatively low and wide, and the distance between each A and the corresponding O therefore relatively large. Thus, the question of aiming short is not trivial for an economic policymaker.

Uncertainty propositions 1 and 2 may be combined. By using more than one tool in the pursuit of a goal, policymakers may reduce the dispersion of results, and thus reduce the amount by which they should aim short of their target.

APPENDIX B

MONETARY AND FISCAL POLICIES WITH FIXED AND FLEXIBLE EXCHANGE RATES

In Chapter 9, the ways in which monetary policy may affect investment and consumption were studied; in the present chapter we have looked at the relationship between monetary policies and government spending (fiscal policy). We now consider the relationship between the last component of national income—net imports—and monetary and fiscal policies.

As we noted in the body of this chapter, monetary and fiscal policies have differential effects on interest rates and therefore on international capital flows. In order to eliminate this complication, we first consider a world of zero capital flows, where interest rates are unimportant for the balance of payments.

As expansive monetary and fiscal policies are applied in such a world, aggregate demand will rise and imports consequently will rise too. *With fixed exchange rates,* the balance of trade will deteriorate (unless even more rapid expansion is occurring abroad, raising our exports more rapidly than our imports are rising). The effectiveness of both monetary and fiscal policies will be reduced by the leakages into imports, which will reduce the size of the multiplier. (Recall the multiplier formulas in the appendix to Chapter 4.)

If, now, exchange rates are allowed to fluctuate in response to demand and supply in the foreign exchange markets, then the tendency of imports to rise will cause the price of our currency to decline on the foreign exchange markets. (In order to buy more imports, we will need more foreign currency. The rise in our demand for foreign currency will push up its price in terms of our currency; that is, it will reduce the price of our currency in terms of foreign currencies.) As exchange rates change, our goods become less expensive to foreigners (as measured in their currencies), and foreign goods become more expensive to us (when measured in dollars).[14] Consequently, we will tend to import less, and foreigners will import more of our goods (that is, we will export more). This process should continue until the initial balance of trade is restored. Thus, exchange rate flexibility will add to the effectiveness of both monetary and fiscal policies, in the sense that it will remove the external leakage and increase the size of the multiplier (the bang for the buck).

There is also a second reason why exchange rate flexibility may improve the effectiveness of both monetary and fiscal policies. By reducing the importance attributed to balance-of-payments goals, it may make authorities feel more free to follow relatively vigorous policies.

Capital flows

When capital flows are introduced, exchange rate flexibility adds to the effectiveness of *monetary* policy for a third reason. (Unlike the first two reasons, this does not apply to fiscal policy.) As expansive monetary policies are pursued, interest rates will fall; this will encourage U.S. residents to switch out of U.S. securities into foreign securities with their more attractive interest rates. (Again, the outcome depends not only on what is happening in the United States, but also on what is happening abroad. That is, it depends on the *relative* strength of movements in the United States as compared to foreign countries.) In order to buy more foreign securities, we

---

[14] At an exchange rate of £1 = $2, a U.S. machine selling for $20,000 would cost £10,000 in Britain; a British car costing £2,000 would sell for $4,000 (plus transportation costs, etc.) in the United States. After the exchange rate moves to £1 = $2.50, the U.S. machine would cost only £8,000 in Britain; the British car would sell for $5,000 in the United States.

will need more foreign currency; the price of foreign currencies will be bid up even higher. Thus, our imports will be discouraged and exports stimulated by an additional amount. Indeed, an expansive monetary policy will tend to cause a positive trade balance under a flexible exchange rate system with mobile capital, and on that account monetary policy will gain additional potency as a tool for stimulating aggregate demand. (Exchange rate flexibility similarly adds to the effectiveness of restrictive monetary policies. The argument is the same, with the signs changed.)

On the other hand, capital flows tend to reduce the short-run effectiveness of fiscal policies under a flexible exchange rate system. As the government engages in deficit spending, it borrows on the securities markets, pushing up interest rates. Foreign capital tends to be attracted and the demand for our currency raised. This result is, however, not altogether certain. If fiscal policy is considered irresponsibly expansive by foreign investors and taken as a forewarning of future inflation and currency depreciations, then there may be a capital flight, putting *downward* pressure on the price of the dollar on the foreign exchanges.

It is difficult to generalize about the relationhip between fiscal policy and exchange rate flexibility because we cannot be certain *which way* a flexible exchange rate will move in the face of expansive fiscal policies. A tendency toward *depreciation* of the home currency will be created by the increase in the demand for imports which accompanies the general increase in aggregate demand. Capital inflows—if they indeed materialize—will tend to *strengthen* the currency. The net effects of these two forces may differ from time to time and from country to country; no general conclusion is possible. Thus, exchange rate flexibility may complicate the use of fiscal policy by making its consequences more unpredictable.

KEY POINTS

1. If the money stock is held constant, then the effects of an expansive fiscal policy will be eroded (except in the special liquidity trap case). Government borrowing on the financial markets will push up interest rates, and higher interest rates will discourage investment. This drag on the effectiveness of fiscal policy may be eliminated if the central bank follows an *accom-*

modative policy; that is, if the central bank stabilizes the interest rate by purchasing government securities.

2. Just as monetary policy may be designed to assist fiscal policy, so fiscal policy may be designed to assist monetary policy. In particular, during an inflationary boom, it is appropriate for some of the restriction to come from the fiscal side in order to prevent excessively high interest rates and distress in the housing market.

3. While monetary and fiscal policies may be used cooperatively in order to achieve a target level of aggregate demand, they may also be used in offsetting directions. For example, tight fiscal policies may be combined with expansive monetary policies in order to stimulate investment and growth without creating excessive aggregate demand.

4. In a world of certainty, a government may achieve N goals, provided that it has N independent policy tools.

5. The bang for the buck is a very imperfect criterion for measuring the usefulness of a policy tool. More important criteria are: (*a*) speed, (*b*) predictability, (*c*) reversability, and (*d*) desirable side effects.

6. Lags in the implementation and operation of policies add to the difficulties of determining appropriate aggregate demand policies.

7. In a world of uncertainty, the most predictable results will be achieved if a combination of monetary and fiscal policies is used to move aggregate demand toward its target.

8. In a world of uncertainty, the use of offsetting aggregate demand policies—such as a tight fiscal policy combined with an expansive monetary policy—will generally reduce the predictability of aggregate demand.

QUESTIONS

1. A tight fiscal policy might be accompanied by an expansive monetary policy in order to keep interest rates low and stimulate investment and growth. Under what circumstances (if any) would it be appropriate to combine an expansive fiscal policy with monetary tightness?

2. If you were in Congress, would you be willing to grant the President the authority to impose an across-the-board income tax surcharge of up to 5 percent, or grant an across-the-board tax rebate of up to 5 percent? Why or why not? Are such across-the-board changes equitable? Why or why not? (Note: A 5 percent surcharge involves an increase of 5 percent in income taxes which must be paid; it does *not* mean an increase in taxes equal to 5 percent of income. Similarly, a tax rebate of 5 percent means a return to the taxpayer of 5 percent of the taxes paid.)

SUGGESTED READING

William Brainard, "Uncertainty and the Effectiveness of Policy," *American Economic Review,* May 1967, pp. 411–25. (This article is recommended *only* for students who are at ease with statistics.)

Chapter 11

Money misbehaving: The monetary explanation of economic instability

To suffer either the solicitation of merchants, or the wishes of government, to determine the measure of the bank issues, is unquestionably to adopt a very false principle of conduct.*

Henry Thornton

Economists in the classical monetary tradition have three inter-related reservations regarding Keynesian theory. The primary short-coming, in their view, is that Keynesian economics underplays the importance of changes in the money supply as a causal force de-termining aggregate demand. To a classical economist steeped in the quantity theory, changes in the quantity of money are the key to understanding changes in aggregate demand. Second, Keynesian theory emphasizes the instability of private markets, and leads to the conclusion that the government must actively manage aggregate

---

* From *An Enquiry into the Nature and Effects of the Paper Credit of Great Britain* (1802). In modern terminology, the "measure of the bank issues" means the quantity of currency.

demand if a high and stable rate of employment is to exist.[1] Those in the classical tradition, in contrast, generally argue that the market economy will be reasonably stable—provided that the money supply is reasonably stable.

The third classical objection is based on the first two. Keynesian theory, as classicists see it, does not give sufficient weight to monetary disturbances as a causal force in business cycles, recessions, and depressions. In the classical view, money is the key determinant of aggregate demand. Therefore, in understanding why business cycles, inflations, and depressions have occurred, it is crucial to investigate the possibility that the monetary system may misbehave, creating either very large increases in the money supply sufficient to explain the inflation, or significant reductions in the money supply capable of producing the declines in aggregate demand which are the hallmark of recessions and depressions. In previous chapters, we have studied how monetary policy can be used as part of an overall stabilization strategy. This chapter will address a more disquieting topic—the possibility that the misbehavior of the monetary system may be a significant cause of instability.

There are several reasons why the money supply might change in a manner such as to disturb the economy:

1. It is possible that small, random disturbances may cause an uneven growth in the money supply. While this is an interesting possibility and should be carefully considered in any detailed

---

[1] These two propositions—that the private economy is basically unstable and that money is relatively unimportant—were held much more strongly by early Keynesians than by present-day economists in the Keynesian tradition; there has been a tendency for modern economists to move toward a middle ground. Thus, modern econometric (statistical) models built on a Keynesian framework generally show a reasonably high degree of stability; and a significant role is played by money. A moderately technical survey of these models may be found in Lawrence R. Klein and Edwin Burmeister, eds., *Econometric Model Performance* (Philadelphia: University of Pennsylvania Press, 1976). Nevertheless, there are still substantial differences between economists in the Keynesian and classical traditions—as we shall see in Chapter 12.

The most conspicuous example of an unstable early Keynesian model was that of Roy Harrod, which will be critically evaluated in an appendix to Chapter 15. This model—in which money plays no role—gives a wildly unstable path of demand when the economy approaches full employment.

The dismissal of monetary policy by some prominent Keynesians continued for at least two decades after the appearance of the *General Theory*. For example, in a study for the Congress in 1959, Professor Warren Smith of the University of Michigan concluded that "General [monetary] controls are a mirage and a delusion" [*Staff Report on Employment, Growth, and Price Levels* (Washington, DC: Joint Economic Committee, U.S. Congress, 1959), p. 401]. By "general" controls, Smith meant open market operations or changes in reserve requirements. (He was less negative regarding selective controls, such as those over consumer installment credit.)

investigation of monetary events, it is not very important in the present context. If the money supply is affected by minor but truly random events, this may cause small disturbances in the money supply; but it will not cause changes sufficiently great to explain the large, spectacular inflations and depressions which rightly claim the central attention in macroeconomics.

2. The monetary system may be disturbed by strong, continuing forces originating outside the monetary sector. The clearest example of this occurs during wartime. The government, pressed by the need to finance armaments, may either engage directly in the process of money creation, or borrow large amounts of newly created money from the central bank. The result: a large and continuing creation of money during wartime periods, with inflationary results. This type of continuing, strong, external disturbance to the monetary system is very important for understanding the history of inflations.

3. There may be something within the monetary system itself which causes continuing movements in the money supply in one direction following an initial disturbance. Once the process gets going, changes in aggregate demand and changes in the money supply may feed upon and reinforce one another. Thus, even though an initial disturbance may be small, the cumulative effects may be large.

This third possibility will be the principal topic of this chapter. It will be elaborated in some detail below, but the major points of the argument may be put quite succinctly:

1. Changes in aggregate demand are reflected in changes in the desire to borrow. During a boom in aggregate demand, for example, the demand to borrow will be high and rising.

2. The money supply may respond to changes in the demand for borrowed funds. For example, an increase in the demand for borrowed funds may result in an increase in bank loans, with the money supply increasing in the process.

3. As a result of the increase in the money supply, aggregate demand will be augmented further, reinforcing the initial trend.

In other words, large economic disturbances may occur because of the *two-way* causal relationship between money and aggregate demand. Changes in the quantity of money are a *causal* force behind changes in aggregate demand, and money may also *respond* to changes in aggregate demand, with the initial disturbances thus

being amplified. The monetary theory of economic disturbances is
based on the proposition that the money supply is not only an active
determinant of aggregate demand but it may also be a *passive*
respondent to changes in aggregate demand. And, if the monetary
explanation is accepted as valid, the general lines of the solution
to pathological demand conditions are clear: Break the reverse
causation from aggregate demand changes to changes in the money
supply. Do not allow the money supply to respond strongly to
changes in aggregate demand. Do not allow the rate of monetary
expansion to be significantly determined by the demand for borrowed funds.

THE PATHOLOGY OF MONEY: THE
MONETARY DYNAMICS OF WICKSELL

The process of monetary creation was seen as a key factor in
economic disturbances and unemployment by pre-Keynesian economists. As they held that unemployment could not exist in equilibrium, their discussion of unemployment dealt of necessity with
the dynamic process of change within the economy. Major problems
of unemployment or inflation required either a large, continuing
outside shock—such as a war—or sympathetic responses of the monetary system to initial changes in aggregate demand. If the monetary
supply tended to contract in response to a decline in aggregate demand, or increase in response to an increase in aggregate demand,
then initial disturbances would be amplified. Of the early writings
on monetary dynamics, the turn-of-the-century works of Swedish
economist Knut Wicksell stand out for their theoretical interest and
continuing influence.

Wicksell's theory centered on the forces operating in the capital
markets. As in other markets, prices are established in the financial
capital markets in response to the forces of demand and supply;
that is, interest rates are determined by the supply of loanable funds
and the demand for these funds. The demand for loanable funds
is related to the desired level of investment: During an investment
boom, there will be a strong demand for borrowed funds to help
finance new plants and equipment. (While the demand for loanable
funds is largely derived from the desire to invest, the two series do
not move precisely together. Investment may be financed from
sources other than borrowings on the capital markets; for example,
by the use of retained corporate earnings. And there may be a de-

mand for loanable funds not related to investment; for example, the demand arising when consumers borrow money for the purchase of durable goods or for other expenditures.)

The supply of loanable funds—or, in other words, the demand for bonds and other interest-bearing financial assets—flows from a number of sources. Individuals may purchase bonds from their current saving, from their past accumulations of money, or from the proceeds from the sale of other assets. Financial institutions—banks, savings and loan associations, etc.—make loans and purchase bonds with part of their resources arising from the deposits of the public; they act as intermediaries, taking demand or short-term, interest-bearing deposits, and acquiring longer-term assets. The relationship between the deposits of the public and the supply of loanable funds by the financial institutions is not fixed or rigid, however; banks and other financial institutions may hold cash reserves in excess of legal requirements.

The flexibility of bank reserves played a key role in Wicksell's theory. In the face of increases in the demand for loans, banks increase their volume of loans while keeping interest rates reasonably stable. They can do so by running down their reserve positions. Thus, Wicksell saw bank credit as responding flexibly to changes in the demand for funds. Boom conditions would cause the volume of loans and the money supply to expand. There was a two-way causation between increases in the money supply and increases in aggregate demand.

In explaining the tendency for bank lending and the money supply to expand during periods of boom and a high demand for loanable funds, Wicksell introduced the concept of the *natural rate of interest.* This was defined by Wicksell as the "rate of interest at which *the demand for loan capital and the supply of savings* exactly agree."[2] It is the rate consistent with a stable money supply and stable prices.[3]

The trouble, as Wicksell saw it, was that the natural rate need not

---

[2] Knut Wicksell, *Lectures on Political Economy* (New York: Augustus M. Kelly Reprints of Economic Classics, 1967), vol. 2, p. 193. (Italics in original.) The summary of Wicksell's views is drawn from pp. 127–208. A more comprehensive exposition was presented in Wicksell's *Interest and Prices* (1898).

[3] There is a logical problem in Wicksell's theory here, since a stable price level does not necessarily involve a stable supply of money. Indeed, in a growing economy, aggregate demand in money terms will have to grow for the average level of prices to remain stable. This suggests that the money supply should grow moderately through time for prices to remain stable.

This logical problem does not, however, undercut Wicksell's main point: that the money supply may *respond* to business conditions, thus contributing to economic instability.

be the same as the interest rate that actually exists in the financial markets. Indeed, it would be surprising if the market rate and the natural rate corresponded for any extended period of time. The natural rate is determined in part by the demand for loans, which depends on the *expected* profitability of investment. Thus, the natural rate of interest changes in response to all sorts of disturbances which affect the expected profitability of investment. New methods of production, changes in domestic or foreign demand, etc.,[4] can change the expected profitability of investment, and therefore the natural rate of interest. But the market rate of interest tends to be sticky, responding only slowly and with a delay to changes in the demand for funds.

Consider an illustration. Suppose that, in an initial equilibrium, the market rate and the natural rate of interest coincide at i_1 in Figure 11–1. D_1 is the demand for loanable funds and S is the supply of loanable funds with a constant money supply. (That is, S *excludes any supply of funds which comes from the process of monetary expansion*.) Suppose, now, that the demand for loanable funds increases from D_1 to D_2 as a result of an increase in the expected profitability of investment. If the market rate adjusted immediately to the new natural rate, i_2, then, according to Wicksell, there would be no progressive upswing in the economy. But the market rate does not respond immediately. The supply of bank funds available for lending is elastic. As banks normally possess excess reserves, they are able to increase their lending at existing rates of interest. Banks usually consider it desirable to have relatively stable lending rates over considerable periods of time as a convenience to customers. Moreover, even if it wanted to, a bank would not be in a good position to calculate precisely the natural rate of interest. The net result: When the natural rate rises, a gap is opened up between the natural rate and the rate charged by banks. In the face of the increasing investment demand and the sticky lending rate of banks, there is an increase in bank loans and in the money supply. In Figure 11–1, for example, when the natural rate increases to i_2, while the market rate remains at i_1, there is an expansion of AB in bank loans and an increase in the money supply.[5] Demand rises, particularly the de-

---

[4] We will come back to the "etc." in Chapter 15, on the determinants of investment demand.

[5] It was noted earlier that the demand and supply of loanable funds determines the market rate of interest. It may therefore seem puzzling how the interest rate can remain at i_1 when the demand and supply are D_2 and S, respectively. The answer: S is not the *total* supply of funds; it excludes loanable funds generated in the process of monetary expansion. At interest rate i_1, the supply is OA from the S curve, and an

Figure 11–1
The gap between the market rate and the natural rate of interest: The expansion of bank credit

Rate of interest

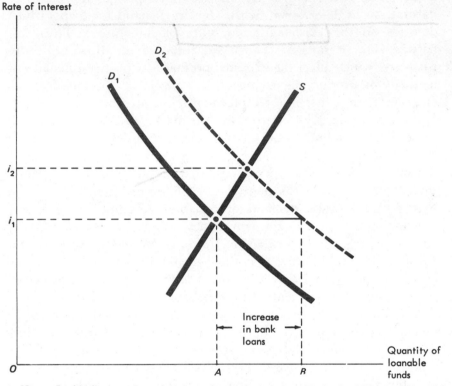

Note: In this diagram, the supply curve does *not* include loanable funds which are generated by the banks in the process of money creation.

If banks keep their lending rate stable in the face of an increase in the demand for loans, then loans will increase and the money supply will rise.

mand for capital goods, and pressures are put on the markets for goods and services.

If there is slack in the economy, the increase in demand may result in an increase in real output rather than a rise in prices. In good classical tradition, however, Wicksell argued that "as a first approximation, we are entitled to assume that all production forces are already fully employed,"[6] so that the increasing money demand is reflected principally in an increase in prices rather than an in-

---

additional AB from monetary expansion. Thus, at i_1, the total supply and demand are equal, at *OB*.

[6] Wicksell, *Lectures,* vol. 2, p. 195.

crease in output. The stickiness of the bank lending rate in the face of an increasing investment demand causes a rise in prices.

But this is not the end of it. The rising level of prices will become the basis for judging the future profitability of investments, and therefore the investment demand is likely to shift outward again. The process of inflation will be cumulative—at least so long as the actual rate of interest remains below the natural rate. In practice, however, there is a limit to the expansion of money and cumulative inflation: The reserve positions of the banks will sooner or later become precarious.[7] Their response: an increase in their lending rates and a curtailment of their loans.

Any tendency for the banks to overreact in the face of a declining reserve position would lead to a market interest rate *higher* than the natural rate. Just as a market rate below the natural rate would cause a progressive increase in demand and rise in prices, so a market rate above the natural rate would lead to a progressive decline in demand and prices. Swings in aggregate demand are accompanied by —and, indeed, are *caused* by—expansions and contractions of bank credit. These in turn are caused by market rates of interest which are periodically lower and then higher than the natural rate.

In brief, business disturbances are caused by the passivity of the banks, and in particular by the inertia of their interest rates on loans. Modern monetary explanations of business disturbances are the descendants of Wicksell's views.

THE PATHOLOGY OF MONEY: CHANGES IN RESERVES

As long as the quantity of commercial bank reserves remains stable, then economic fluctuations due to the misbehavior of the monetary system are unlikely to be large; monetary expansion during booms will be confined by the available quantity of reserves. But if reserves themselves move in the same direction as economic

---

[7] Writing in the late 19th century, Wicksell saw the international gold standard playing an important part in ending the monetary expansion. Banks would be able to continue an indefinite expansion of credit only if there were a continuous inflow to them of new gold (that is, an increase in reserves). But the process of inflation would work in the other direction—toward a diminution of gold held by the banks. As inflation continued, there would be an outflow of gold coins to the public, since the public would wish to hold more currency in the face of higher prices. In addition, if the price level were rising more rapidly than in other countries, exports would tend to be priced out of world markets, the balance of trade would become unfavorable, and gold would tend to flow abroad. Because of the internal and external gold drains and the increase in their deposit liabilities, banks would find their reserve positions threatened.

activity, then the potential destabilizing effect will be greatly magnified. Many monetary theorists consider the instability of reserves to be a significant source of instability of aggregate demand.[8] The depth of the Great Depression, in particular, has been attributed to *instability of bank reserves,* which contributed to the instability of the commercial banking system itself.

For several reasons, there may be some tendency for commercial bank reserves to move perversely, expanding in response to boom conditions and contracting during hard times.

1. The central bank itself may follow policies along the lines suggested by Wicksell's argument. Commercial bank reserves may be increased in response to the rising demand for loans during good times, and decreased as the demand for loans falls off during recessions. (This may be particularly so if the central bank attempts to stabilize interest rates. During a boom, the high demand for loanable funds will push up interest rates. If the central bank responds by purchasing bonds to prevent the rise in interest rates, then reserves of the commercial banks will rise. Similarly, commercial bank reserves will fall if the Federal Reserve sells bonds during a recession in order to keep bond prices from rising.)

2. During a depression, there may be a crisis of confidence, leading the public to withdraw their deposits from banks. If this happens, there will be downward pressure on the money supply. While the public will hold $1 extra in currency for each $1 withdrawn from deposits, it will thereby remove $1 in "high-powered" reserves from the banking system; this $1 reduction in reserves will require a multiple reduction of demand-deposit money. [In the money equation (Equation 8–3), the quantity of M falls as the propensity to hold currency (c) rises.]

3. Under the old gold standard, a crisis of confidence and a withdrawal of gold to foreign countries might occur during a depression. This would tend to reduce bank reserves.

---

[8] For example, Wesley C. Mitchell, *Business Cycles* (1913); A. C. Pigou, *Industrial Fluctuations* (1927), pt. 1; R. G. Hawtrey, *Currency and Credit,* 3d ed. (1928); Clark Warburton, "The Quantity and Frequency of Use of Money in the United States, 1915–45," *Journal of Political Economy,* October 1946, pp. 442–50; Milton Friedman and Anna Schwartz, *A Monetary History of the United States, 1867–1960* (Princeton: Princeton University Press, 1963). For a skeptical view, see Peter Temin, *Did Monetary Forces Cause the Great Depression?* (New York: W. W. Norton, 1976).

MONETARY PROBLEMS DURING THE GREAT DEPRESSION

*We have now entered calmer waters. So
the writer* [Robertson] *assured his readers
in 1928; and so many, with wiser heads than
his, then hoped and believed.**

D. H. Robertson

Each of the three problems contributed to monetary disturbances during the Great Depression. As the economy slid downward between 1929 and 1933—with *GNP* measured in dollars declining by almost 50 percent—the quantity of money fell by over 25 percent (Table 11-1). Clearly, it is too strong to interpret the Depression as an illustration of the simplest type of quantity theory. Since *GNP* fell by much more than the quantity of money, velocity was far from stable. (Indeed, the fall in *GNP* reflected a significant slowing of the rate at which the average dollar was spent.) But clearly, also, one need not be an uncompromising classicist to consider the decline in the money stock as a contributor to the Depression.

Federal Reserve policy

As economic activity fell off at the beginning of the 1930s, Federal Reserve policy was marred by doubts, indecision, and an adherence to outmoded and fallacious theories. In the face of the decline in business, the quantity of money should have been increased. With the strong contractionary forces at work, large-scale open market purchases of government securities by the Federal Reserve were in order as a means of augmenting the reserves of commercial banks. Yet the Federal Reserve looked on the purchase of government securities as being unsound. [There were historical reasons for this belief. In the past, large-scale inflation had occurred when money had been created to finance large government deficits, especially during wartime. Furthermore, the inflationary experience of a number of countries (particularly Germany) during the early 1920s had underlined the dangers of unlimited monetary creation as a means of financing government deficits. But these were the problems of the past. By the early 1930s, the money supply was far from excessive.] Because of the view that central bank purchases of government securities were unsound, the Federal Reserve engaged

---

* D. H. Robertson, "Money in the Second Great Muddle," *Money*, rev. ed. (Cambridge University Press, 1948), chap. 9, p. 183.

Table 11–1
The money supply and reserves, 1929–1941 (in $ millions; GNP in $ billions)*

Year	(1) GNP	(2) Money stock (col. 3+4)	(3) Currency outside banks	(4) Demand deposits	(5) Time deposits	(6) Total bank reserves†	(7) Excess reserves†	(8) Gold stock	(9) Reserve bank credit‡	(10) U.S. government securities held by Federal Reserves§
1929	104.4	26,179	3,639	22,540	28,611	2,358	43	3,996	1,459	208
1930	91.1	25,075	3,369	21,706	28,992	2,379	55	4,173	1,087	564
1931	76.3	23,483	3,651	19,832	28,961	2,323	89	4,417	1,274	669
1932	58.5	20,241	4,616	15,625	24,756	2,114	256	3,952	2,077	1,461
1933	56.0	19,172	4,761	14,411	21,656	2,343	528	4,059	2,429	2,052
1934	65.0	21,353	4,659	16,694	22,875	3,676	1,564	7,512	2,502	2,432
1935	72.5	25,216	4,783	20,433	23,854	5,001	2,469	9,059	2,475	2,431
1936	82.7	29,002	5,222	23,780	24,908	5,989	2,512	10,578	2,481	2,431
1937	90.8	30,687	5,489	25,198	25,905	6,830	1,220	12,162	2,554	2,504
1938	85.2	29,730	5,417	24,313	26,236	7,935	2,522	13,250	2,600	2,565
1939	91.1	33,360	6,005	27,355	26,791	10,352	4,392	16,085	2,628	2,584
1940	100.6	38,661	6,699	31,962	27,463	13,249	6,326	19,865	2,487	2,417
1941	125.8	45,521	8,204	37,317	27,879	13,404	5,324	22,546	2,293	2,187

* *GNP* for the year; Money stock (cols. 2–4) as of June 30; other data are annual averages of daily figures.
† Federal Reserve member banks only.
‡ Bills discounted and bought by Federal Reserve; U.S. government securities owned by Federal Reserve; and minor miscellaneous items.
§ Col. 10 is a component of col. 9.
Sources: Col. 1: Council of Economic Advisers; *Annual Report*, 1962, p. 207; cols. 2–10: Board of Governors of Federal Reserve System, *Banking and Monetary Statistics* (1943), pp. 34–35, 368.

Between 1929 and 1933, the money stock fell as the economy collapsed. Demand deposits decreased rapidly, but the public's holdings of currency rose.

in open market purchases only hesitantly and half-heartedly, in response to outside pressure. (In the column 10 of Table 11–1, note how small is the growth of the Fed's holdings of Federal government securities between 1929 and 1931, while the economy was sliding downward.)

The distaste for open market operations was reinforced by a peculiar view of banking—known as the "commercial loan theory of credit"—which had played an important role in British and American banking history.[9] According to this theory, the money supply should be elastic, in order to *meet the needs of trade.* This meant that, in the face of an increase in the demand for loans—when money seems to be *needed*—the money supply should be expanded. And, when the economy turns down—when the demand for loans is low and money does not seem to be *needed* by businesses—this approach leads to a decline in the quantity of money.

As long as the commercial loan theory is the basis solely for the lending policies of commercial banks, it is likely to be a relatively minor destabilizer to the economy. But if it is the basis for *central* bank policy, it becomes a recipe for disaster. It then will lay the groundwork for mutually reinforcing instability of aggregate demand and the money supply. Indeed, if one wished to generate economic instability, it is hard to imagine a better way than convincing central bankers of the validity of the commercial loan theory.[10] (Convincing the government of the need to balance the budget every single year might be just as good; it would lead to destabilizing fiscal policies.)[11] Unfortunately for the United States, the theory was an

---

[9] The "commercial loan theory of credit," also known as the "real bills doctrine," was the subject of Lloyd W. Mints, *A History of Banking Theory in Great Britain and the United States* (Chicago: University of Chicago Press, 1945). A subtitle might be suggested for the Mints book: "A Hundred and Fifty Years of Nonsense."

[10] Because of the historical flirtation of central bankers with the commercial loan theory or real bills doctrine, critics of the doctrine are not as a general rule great admirers of central bankers. In his opening statement (pp. 1–2), Mints observed that "The real bills doctrine has been a most persistent one. . . . It was as comforting to the Federal Reserve Board following the depression of 1921 as it had been a century earlier to the directors of the Bank of England."

Writing in 1873, Walter Bagehot was even more biting about the Bank of England's defense of its actions in 1810 along real-bills lines. The reasons provided by the bank's directors, said Bagehot, had "become almost classical by their nonsense" [*Lombard Street* (Homewood, Ill.: Richard D. Irwin, 1962 paper edition), p. 86].

The view that it is a mistake to allow the money supply to respond to the demand for loans may be traced back at least to Thornton's works at the beginning of the 19th century. (Refer back to the quotation that introduced this chapter.)

[11] A desire to balance the budget motivated the tax increase of 1932, which contributed to the depth of the Depression. (Recall the discussion of Chapter 4.) Thus, major blunders in both fiscal *and* monetary policies made the Depression worse. In a grim sort of way, this is reassuring. If we don't repeat the blunders of the early

important component of the original Federal Reserve Act (1913) and of Federal Reserve operations during the first two decades. The disaster came in the early 1930s.

The commercial loan theory was a culprit in the decline in the quantity of money in the early Depression for two reasons. First, the theory was reflected in the legal requirements which the Federal Reserve had to meet, and these legal requirements inhibited open market purchases.[12] Even more importantly, the doctrine was the basis for much opposition to open market purchases even after the legal requirements were relaxed by the Glass-Steagall Act of 1932; the commercial loan theory lived on in men's minds. The natural tendencies of a divided Federal Reserve System to act cautiously as the economy collapsed into the Depression were fortified by the view that open market operations were intrinsically unsound, and that the only proper function of the Federal Reserve was to discount eligible commercial paper. (In effect, such discounts amount to loans to commercial banks, secured by the loans which these banks in turn have made to businesses.)

A crisis of confidence and withdrawals of deposits

Normally, we would expect the fraction of total money held as currency to be quite stable; it is relatively convenient to use currency for some transactions (especially small ones), and checks for others. This is not to say that the ratio will be completely stable. It may change slowly, for example, as employers switch from cash to

---

1930s, hopefully we will avoid a repetition of the Depression. If the Depression had occurred *in spite of* good policies, then we would have cause for alarm: There might be no way to avoid a repetition.

[12] For the Federal Reserve notes (currency) outstanding, the Federal Reserve was required to keep a gold reserve of 40 percent, and an additional 60 percent "collateral" of either gold or short-term paper arising from commercial loans. In the early 1930s, the public became uneasy regarding its deposits in uninsured banks and began to withdraw currency. With the Federal Reserve notes in circulation increasing, the Federal Reserve began to bump against its collateral requirement, with the small supply of commercial paper contributing to its problem. The Federal Reserve increasingly felt unable to combat the Depression with open market operations, with matters coming to a head in February 1932. A tumultuous conference was held in the President's office; Senator Glass later confessed that he "was very much afraid that he swore at the President of the United States." The outcome was the Glass-Steagall Act of February 1932, which removed the collateral requirement.

This footnote follows E. A. Goldenweiser, *American Monetary Policy* (New York: McGraw-Hill, 1951), pp. 121–29. (Goldenweiser was for many years Director of the Division of Research and Statistics at the Federal Reserve Board.) For a different interpretation, see Friedman and Schwartz, *A Monetary History of the United States*, pp. 399–406.

checks for their payroll payments, or as the public makes greater use of charge accounts (which they generally pay with regular monthly checks).

There is one circumstance, however, in which the ratio can change quite rapidly—when questions arise about the continuing value of one of the types of money. This occurred during the early part of the Depression. As the number of banks sliding into bankruptcy increased in the early 1930s, inflicting losses on deposit holders, the public became alarmed and attempted to protect itself by withdrawing deposits. (See the changes in the relative positions of currency and demand deposits in Table 11–1, columns 3 and 4.)

Such a drain of deposits reduces the reserves of commercial banks, thus creating pressures for a multiple contraction of the money supply. It is a highly dangerous occurrence, coming at a time when bankruptcies are already high and when, therefore, a reduction in the money supply is particularly likely to cause trouble. The appropriate policies to deal with such a drain are two:

1. *Offset the loss of bank reserves through open market purchases.*
    If the public wants dollar bills in exchange for demand deposits, then give them dollar bills. The Federal Reserve should be willing to print *any* amount the public wishes to exchange. In normally prosperous times, very large open market purchases are generally considered unsound because they lay the basis for a rapid, inflationary increase in the money supply. When a run on the banks is in progress, however, it is fundamentally unsound *not* to undertake open market purchases sufficiently massive to at least offset the currency run. Such open market operations do not lead to a large increase in the money supply; rather, they prevent a decrease.

    During the currency drains of the early 1930s, the Federal Reserve failed to make the necessary vigorous open market purchases. Bankruptcies came thick and fast; between 1930 and 1933 inclusive, over 9,000 banks failed, including almost 2,000 national banks. As Roosevelt entered the presidency in March 1933, the banking system was in a state of collapse.

2. *Insure the deposits of banks.* This will not only prevent losses to depositors in the event of failure, but will make failures much less likely in the first place, since the public will lose its incentive to run on the banks. It will remove the sharp conflict between private incentives and the public good which exists

during a period of bank runs. A run on banks tends to destroy the banking framework, inflicting widespread losses throughout the economy; but if a run is in progress, it is in each individual's clear interest to get as close to the front of the line as possible.

In 1933, a temporary bank insurance plan was instituted, to be superceded in 1935 by the Federal Deposit Insurance Corporation. This innovation has perhaps done as much as any other single act to rule out a repetition of the Depression of the 1930s. Between 1934 and 1940, only 312 banks (and only 16 national banks) were suspended (that is, closed because of financial difficulties). These figures contrast to a total of 4,000 in 1933 alone (of which 1,101 were national banks).

Gold

*You have to choose (as a voter) between trusting to the natural stability of gold and the honesty and intelligence of the members of government. And with due respect for these gentlemen, I advise you, as long as the capitalist system lasts, to vote for gold.**

George Bernard Shaw

During the period when gold played an important role in settling imbalances in the international payments of the United States, it was at times a source of instability in bank reserves. When gold flowed in from abroad—for example, as a result of an excess of U.S. exports over U.S. imports—then there were significant monetary consequences, shown in Table 11–2 on page 261.

1. The money supply was directly increased by the amount of the gold inflow; observe that demand deposits rise.
2. While commercial bank deposit liabilities were increased by the amount of the gold inflow, their reserves were also increased by a similar amount. Thus, the gold inflow resulted in excess reserves and made possible additional bank loans and a further expansion of the money supply.
3. Federal Reserve reserve deposit liabilities and holdings of gold were increased by an equivalent amount.

With fractional reserve banking, the monetary system may be looked upon as an inverted pyramid: The banks can create a large

* From *The Intelligent Woman's Guide to Capitalism and Socialism* (London: Constable, 1928), p. 263.

Table 11–2
A gold inflow from abroad (in $000)

Federal Reserve

Assets		Liabilities	
Gold account	+100	Reserve deposits of commercial banks	+100

Commercial Bank A

Assets		Liabilities	
Reserve deposit	+100	Demand deposit of machinery manufacturer	+100

Machinery Manufacturer

Assets		Liabilities
Demand deposit	+100	No change
Inventory of machinery	−100	

These balance sheet changes result when a U.S. company exports machinery, and the foreign country pays in gold. The consequences are the same *as if* the manufacturer had received the gold and deposited it in his bank account, and the bank in turn had deposited the gold in the Federal Reserve. (In practice, the manufacturer was unlikely to handle the gold, even prior to 1933 when he was legally permitted to do so. The financial transactions were normally handled by the banking system, with the manufacturer receiving the deposit without actually handling the gold.)

superstructure of demand deposit money on the basis of a relatively small amount of reserves, with the relationship between the superstructure and the base depending on the required reserve ratio. Under the old gold standard, there was also one further level in the pyramid (as illustrated in Figure 11–2). As the Federal Reserve was originally set up, it was required to keep reserves of gold amounting to specified percentages of its reserve deposit liabilities and Federal Reserve notes outstanding. Thus, the amount of liabilities that the Federal Reserve could create (in the form of commercial bank reserves and Federal Reserve notes) was larger than its gold holdings. If the reserve deposits at the middle level of the pyramid may be considered high-powered money, on which a multiple expansion of bank deposits could take place, then gold is super high-powered money. In response to a gold inflow into the United

Figure 11–2
The pre-1933 gold standard pyramid (simplified)

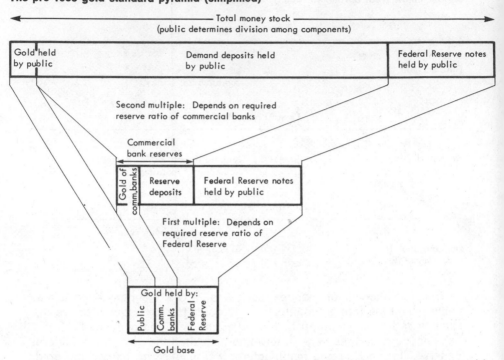

Under the old gold standard, the monetary system was a two-staged pyramid. On the basis of its gold holdings, the Federal Reserve could create a superstructure of liabilities in the form of reserve deposits and Federal Reserve notes. On the basis of its reserves, the commercial banks could create a superstructure of demand deposits.

States, two multiple expansions were possible: a multiple expansion of reserve deposits on the basis of the Federal Reserve's gold holdings, and a multiple expansion of commercial bank deposits on the basis of their reserve deposits. (While the Federal Reserve was legally *enabled* to engage in a multiple expansion of its liabilities, it did not always do so because of the potential inflationary consequences. Indeed, during most of its history, it did not allow the money supply to respond strongly as gold flowed into the country.)

The gold standard had certain advantages. By legally limiting the amount of money that could be created, it placed a restraint on the inflationary pressures that could be generated by official policies. And the gold standard played a role in bringing international payments back into balance.[13] But, under certain circumstances, the monetary pyramid could be the source of instability.

Since gold was the ultimate money—free from the dangers of default and bankruptcy—there was a tendency for the public to switch to gold in the face of grave uncertainties. There was a particularly sharp spurt in gold holdings by the U.S. public in early 1933, as the banking crisis developed. (Prior to Roosevelt's inauguration in March of 1933, the U.S. public was permitted to hold unlimited amounts of gold.) This switch had the same general effect as a switch of the public from demand deposits to Federal Reserve notes: By removing reserves from the base of the system, it tended to create strong pressures for a monetary contraction.

A second complication came from international flows of gold. Flows of gold to foreign countries responded to changes in confidence in a manner somewhat similar to the domestic drains of currency from the banking system; gold tended to flow to the least troubled country. (Gold also responded to the fundamental balance-of-payments situation; a country that exported more than it imported tended to be a recipient of gold inflows.)

Because international gold flows depend on the relative positions of the various countries, there is no general presumption that a country will tend to lose gold abroad during a cyclical downswing. It is possible for all countries to suffer bad times together—and, indeed, the Great Depression was truly international in scope—yet

---

[13] As the money stock increases in the surplus country (the one receiving gold), aggregate demand and prices will tend to rise. As a consequence, imports will also rise. In the deficit country, the money supply and aggregate demand will be depressed by the gold outflow. Consequently, its imports will fall. These changes in trade will reduce the original imbalance in international payments.

There are, however, several problems with this mechanism. While the gold inflow itself causes an increase in the money stock of the surplus country, this increase may be offset by a central bank which is concerned about inflation. In other words, the gold inflow may be "sterilized" by open market sales or other restrictive actions. The deficit country will be less free to offset the deflationary consequences of the gold outflow. If it does so, there may be no international adjustment mechanism left, and the deficit country may progressively lose its gold. In order to prevent a complete loss of its gold, the deficit country may feel *forced* to go through a deflationary period. Thus, the gold standard may put the burden of adjustment on the deficit country and create a deflationary bias in the international economy as a whole.

During the 1920s, European countries complained that the U.S. sterilization of gold inflows put the burden of adjustment on them, making it difficult for them to repay their debts to the United States contracted during the World War I. (Increases in U.S. tariffs added to the European difficulties.)

During the 1960s, the situation was reversed: The United States was the deficit country, and it felt that it had to bear the brunt of international adjustment. In order to reduce pressures for a quick adjustment and to ease tensions in the international monetary system, the International Monetary Fund introduced Special Drawing Rights (SDRs) —or paper gold—at the end of the 1960s.

it is clearly not possible for all countries simultaneously to lose gold to all other countries. Thus, while international gold flows *may* contribute to instability of the reserve base of the banking system, there is no general presumption that they *will* in fact do so.

Indeed, during the early part of the Great Depression, international gold flows eased monetary difficulties in the United States, particularly following the May 1931 failure of the Kreditanstalt, Austria's largest private bank. Shock waves from that failure spread throughout Europe: German banks were closed in mid-July; British short-term assets in Germany were frozen; an intergovernmental debt moratorium was negotiated, as was a standstill agreement among commercial banks not to press for the repayment of short-term loans. There was a flight of capital to the United States, swelling U.S. gold stocks. This had the effect of offsetting some of the monetary consequences of the switching of U.S. domestic depositors out of bank deposits and into currency.

But this good fortune for the United States was not to continue. The climax of the European monetary muddle came in September 1931, when Britain became the target of the speculative panic, and was forced to abandon the gold standard (that is, Britain suspended her commitment to redeem British currency with gold). The fear spread that the United States might follow suit, and foreign central banks and private holders of U.S. dollar assets rushed to buy gold with their dollars while they still had the chance. Between the middle of September and the end of October 1931, the U.S. gold stock fell by more than $700 million. This external drain was accompanied by an intensification of the internal drain of domestic deposit holders switching into currency and gold.

The effects of drains on the reserve positions of banks might have been offset by the Federal Reserve if it had engaged in vigorous open market purchases. The Federal Reserve did not respond to the massive drains with massive open market purchases, however. On the contrary, *it took steps to tighten monetary conditions in an attempt to protect the gold reserves of the United States.* During October 1931, the discount rate was raised in two quick, large jumps from 1.5 percent to 3.5 percent. The Federal Reserve's holdings of government securities were actually reduced slightly between mid-September and mid-December 1931. The monetary tightness was accompanied by a spectacular increase in bank failures; monetary conditions were set for a further deepening of the Depression. The international gold standard proved to be a fair-weather friend.

The gold outflow continued through 1932 and early 1933. When Roosevelt entered the presidency, one of his first acts was to suspend the gold standard, prohibiting the export of gold, forbidding banks to pay out gold domestically, and ordering the public to sell its gold to the Treasury. (The holding of old coins was permitted, as was the use of gold for artistic and industrial purposes.) In late 1933, the government bought gold at increasing premiums over the earlier official price of $20.67, and in early 1934 the new official price of $35 per ounce was established. Throughout the remainder of the ⌣ Depression, gold was no problem for the United States. Indeed, there was a veritable avalanche of gold inflows, increasing the monetary gold stock from $4.0 billion in mid-1933 to $17.6 billion by the end of 1939, and contributing to the rise in bank reserves and the money supply.

(The prohibition against the holding of gold by U.S. citizens continued until the beginning of 1975, that is, until after the elimination of the role of gold as the foundation of the U.S. monetary system and as an important means of settling imbalances in international payments. By the end of 1974, the U.S. government took the position that gold had ceased to be the ultimate money, and that it should be considered just like any other commodity, such as copper. Because the public could no longer undercut the foundation of the monetary system by demanding gold, there was no reason to continue the prohibition.) [14]

MORE RECENT EXPERIENCES

The Great Depression represented the most spectacular economic breakdown in American history; it is to the 1930s that we must turn for the clearest, most dramatic lessons. Because of a number of institutional changes made during the Depression—including deposit insurance and the prohibition on private holdings of gold—the monetary system has been protected against a repeat of that debacle.

---

[14] This was the view of the Congress and the administration, and most notably the Treasury. For a contrasting view, see the testimony before Congress of Federal Reserve Chairman Arthur Burns, December 5, 1974, reprinted in the *Federal Reserve Bulletin*, December 1974, pp. 835–37. While he believed that, with good management, "we shall be reasonably successful," he nevertheless recommended that the prohibition not be lifted at that time, declaring that it was his duty "to point out that prompt removal of present restrictions on private trading in gold could complicate a financial situation that is already beset by strains and stresses." (This fear turned out to be unjustified. The American public greeted the new gold market with a yawn.)

In addition, some painful and important policy lessons were learned. Specifically, ~~two popular views of the 1920s and 1930s were found to be policy traps~~. On the monetary side, the commercial loan theory—including the view that the money supply should be elastic in response to changes in the demand for money—was found to be a source of instability. On the fiscal side, the view that sound finance required an annually balanced budget was also discredited. It led to the tax increase of 1932, which contributed to the depth of the Depression. Indeed, pointing out the potential destabilizing effects of an annually balanced budget was one of the principal contributions of the Keynesian revolution.

In spite of the improvements in our understanding of economics, weak similarities to the 1930s may be found in the monetary conditions that accompanied economic fluctuations during the past three decades. For example, the growing concern with the balance of payments and with U.S. gold reserves was apparently a factor in the monetary restraint which contributed to two quick (but relatively mild) recessions in the late 1950s. But, with the elimination of the last vestiges of the gold standard and with the coming of exchange rate flexibility in the early 1970s, gold standard problems are of historical interest only.

Of more lasting concern is the relationship between interest rates and monetary policy. Specifically, if the Federal Reserve attempts to stabilize interest rates, it may behave in the manner suggested by Wicksell, increasing the money supply in response to a boom in the demand for credit, and allowing the money supply to decline during periods of slack. We will consider two episodes. One, during the 1940s, is relatively straightforward and clear: The Federal Reserve followed an explicit policy of keeping interest rates low and stable. The second—involving the business upswing of 1972–73 and the sharp and deep recession of 1974–75—is more complex and ambiguous.

The pegging of interest rates in the 1940s

The 1930s were a period of inadequate demand; the 1940s were a period of high demand brought on by World War II. At the beginning of the war, it was clear that the government would have very large financial requirements, far in excess of its tax receipts. The primary function of the Federal Reserve became the facilitation of the war effort.

During World War I, interest rates had moved up with successive issues of government bonds. At the beginning of World War II, the government was determined to prevent a repeat of this experience, which might discourage the purchase of bonds: Why should people buy bonds now, if they could hope for bonds with higher interest rates in the relatively near future? The Federal Reserve therefore undertook to peg the existing level of yields on government securities—2.5 percent on the longest-term issues and even less on shorter-term maturities (down to ⅜ of 1 percent on 90-day bills). In order to keep down the rate of monetary expansion, the Treasury carried on extensive campaigns to sell bonds to the public, enrolling the services of movie stars and other celebrities in advertising campaigns and introducing payroll deduction plans. Nevertheless, with the Treasury deficits averaging over $40 billion per year, large amounts of Treasury securities were bought by the Federal Reserve as part of the pegging program, and the money supply consequently rose significantly; large quantities of government bonds were also bought by the commercial banks.

All the prerequisites for excessive demand and inflation were present: large government spending and deficits, low interest rates, and a rapid increase in the money supply. And the average level of prices did rise by more than 30 percent by the end of 1945. But the increase would undoubtedly have been greater had no direct preventive steps been taken. Ceilings were placed on prices, rents, and wages. Extensive controls over production and the purchase of materials were introduced.

After the end of the war, the price ceilings and other controls were dismantled (with rent ceilings remaining a partial exception). Strong demand pressures—built up in part as a result of the wartime accumulations of financial assets and wearing out of consumer durables—then resulted in an overt inflation, with consumer prices rising by 18 percent in 1946 alone. Nevertheless, under pressures from the Treasury, the Federal Reserve continued to peg interest rates at the rates established in the depressed 1930s. There were reasons for what may, in retrospect, seem like a strange and shortsighted policy:

1. There were great fears of a postwar depression. The memories of the 1930s were strong; the rudimentary economic models of the time were almost unanimous in their predictions of recession or worse; and the historical precedent of the worldwide depression of 1921–22 suggested that the early postwar period would be dangerous.

2. With the recent revolution in economic thought, there was some doubt as to the importance of monetary policy: If it didn't matter much, why not have the advantages of low interest rates?
3. There was concern over the effects on the solvency of financial institutions if interest rates were allowed to rise rapidly, depressing the market value of existing portfolios of bonds.
4. The Treasury was concerned about the budgetary effects of an increase in interest payments. Significant chunks of the large outstanding government debt were coming due and would have to be refinanced at higher interest rates unless the low pegged rates were retained.

These four factors were responsible for the continuation of the pegging policy for almost six years after the end of the war. During that period, the average level of consumer prices rose by 43 percent. In retrospect, the most surprising thing perhaps is that price increases were not even greater, in view of the depression-level interest rates prevailing. Indeed, the recession of 1948–49, with its 3.9 percent decline in consumer prices (between June 1948 and March 1950), took place in spite of the low interest rates and the passive open market policies of the Federal Reserve. That the postwar inflation was so mild in the face of such monetary conditions was a tribute to the depth of the impression which the hard times of the 1930s had left on people's minds, and to the continuing nagging worries that it was necessary to keep the personal and corporate financial hatches battened down in anticipation of a coming storm. There was a widespread hesitance to take a plunge with cheap borrowed funds.

With the coming of the Korean conflict and the associated inflationary pressures, the conflict between the Federal Reserve and the Treasury over the pegging policy became acute. After a tense period of public assertion and public denial, in which the President himself became involved on the side of the Treasury, the Treasury–Federal Reserve Accord of March 1951 was reached. It ended the Fed's commitment to pegged interest rates.

The early 1970s

The history of the early 1970s is more complex; during this period, the Federal Reserve followed an active open market policy and was not bound by any formal commitment to keep interest rates stable. Nevertheless, there is some ground for believing that the desire for reasonably stable interest rates may have contributed to monetary instability and hence to instability of the economy.

The facts are basically these. Between the first quarter of 1972 and the second quarter of 1973, the increase in the money supply was relatively rapid. (M_1 increased at an annual rate of about 8 percent, compared to an average annual rate of little more than 5 percent during the preceding three years.) This was accompanied by a rapid expansion of aggregate demand and by growing inflationary pressures. Then, the rate of increase in the money supply was significantly reduced. Between the second quarter of 1974 and the first quarter of 1975, the annual rate of growth of M_1 was only 3 percent. This relatively slow growth accompanied the slide of the economy down into the worst recession in three decades.

However, two problems of interpretation arise. First, it is not clear how important the instability of the money supply was as a cause of the business cycle of 1972–75.[15] Second, it is not clear how important a desire to stabilize interest rates may have been as a determinant of Federal Reserve policies.

There are some bits of evidence that point the finger of suspicion at interest rate stabilization. In early 1971, Federal Reserve Chairman Arthur Burns had advocated an incomes policy—that is, government restraints on wage and price increases—as a way of slowing down inflation. At the time, this suggestion was most unwelcome to the Nixon administration. It added to political pressures for price controls, which continued to mount until the administration abruptly switched policy and instituted controls in August 1971. One problem with price and wage controls is that they may be considered unfair. In particular, labor unions object strongly to wage controls unless other incomes—including interest and dividends—are also controlled. The task of supervising interest and dividends went to Burns. Unfortunately, Burns was now wearing two hats, and the two jobs were in conflict. As part of the wage-price program, his responsibility was to keep interest rates from rising. But, as the chairman of the Federal Reserve, he had the responsibility for control over the money supply. If the Fed were to attempt to keep down interest rates in the face of a rising demand for loans,

---

[15] This question will be one of the subjects of Chapter 12. For the view that monetary disturbances were relatively unimportant, see Franco Modigliani, "The Monetarist Controversy or, Should We Forsake Stabilization Policies?" *American Economic Review,* March 1977, pp. 1–19.

then the money supply might shoot rapidly upward. And a rapid increase in the money supply did, in fact, occur.

However, we cannot be sure that this is the right explanation for the increase in the money supply in 1972 and early 1973, since there are plausible alternatives. First, the Federal Reserve may have underestimated the inflationary potential in 1972–73; the unemployment rate was still high (5.6 percent in 1972) by the standards of past recoveries, suggesting that there was still considerably slack in the economy. Second, the Fed was working with imperfect statistics. The currently available data on the money supply in 1972–73 showed a less rapid rate of growth than the revised statistics. (While the Fed has good current statistics from its member banks, it does not have such good information from the commercial banks that are not members of the Federal Reserve System. With the decline in membership in the Fed in recent years, this statistical problem has grown worse.) Third, allegations have been made that Burns was anxious to stimulate the economy in 1972 in order to aid in the reelection of Richard Nixon.[16]

It is hard to sort out these reasons; motivation is complex and difficult to demonstrate. But the 1972–73 experience does provide cause for emphasizing the trap of interest stabilization and the potential for economic instability which such a policy holds. Furthermore, it suggests a disturbing set of questions. Are wage and price controls politically acceptable if they do not include a ceiling on interest rates? If such a ceiling is imposed, will this lead to rapid monetary expansion, whose inflationary consequences will demolish the control mechanism? Willingness to answer these questions may be taken as a test of whether proponents of wage and price controls are serious.

During the latter part of 1974, a somewhat different issue arose. This was a time of recession, when interest rates in the normal course of events would be on the way down. There is no great political problem in allowing such a change in interest rates to take place (unlike the situation in a boom, when there is widespread dislike of rising interest rates). The problem arose because of the

---

[16] This allegation was made most explicitly by Sanford Rose, "The Agony of the Federal Reserve," *Fortune*, July 1974, pp. 186–88. This allegation is difficult to evaluate because of inaccuracies in the Rose article. For a strong denial, see the letter from Federal Reserve Board member Andrew Brimmer, *Fortune*, August 1974, p. 113. (Brimmer, an appointee of President Johnson, was known for his high degree of independence as a board member.) The politics of the business cycle will be briefly considered in Chapter 13.

double objective of the open market committee: At each monthly meeting, the committee decided on both an interest rate objective and a money supply objective. (Each objective is a range, rather than a single point.) But these objectives are not independent; an open market operation aimed at an increase in the money supply will also have an effect on interest rates. In practice, the Federal Reserve may choose an interest rate target which is inconsistent with their money supply target. And that is what happened. During the last half of 1974, the Federal Reserve generally picked an interest rate which was too high for the money supply target. (This suggests that the committee overestimated the demand for loans at each interest rate, and thus underestimated the downward momentum of the economy.) The open market desk in New York apparently paid more attention to the interest rate objective than to the money supply objective (Figure 11–3). While the interest rate objective was generally achieved, the actual increase in the money supply fell short of the target. There was criticism of the Federal Reserve from a wide range of economists, from Keynesian Paul Samuelson, who argued that "if we do go into a depression, the Fed will justly bear much of the blame," to neo-classicist Milton Friedman, who charged that the Fed's policy in 1974 and early 1975 "has already deepened the recession."[17]

This is a problem of considerable gravity. When the Federal Reserve underestimates the strength of a downswing—which is presumably most likely to occur during a sharp recession such as in 1974—then the granting of precedence to the interest rate objective will tend to make the money supply too small, and thus con-

---

[17] The quotations are from *Newsweek* columns: Samuelson's on March 3, 1975, entitled, "A Burns Depression?" and Friedman's on March 10, 1975, entitled, "What is the Federal Reserve Doing?"

While there was strong criticism of the Fed from a wide spectrum of economists, there was less unanimity that the problem resulted from a Federal Reserve preoccupation with interest rates. Friedman took an explicitly Wicksellian position, arguing (in his testimony, Senate Committee on Banking, Housing, and Urban Affairs, *Monetary Policy Oversight*, February 1975, p. 60) that the Federal Reserve could not stabilize monetary growth and the economy "if it insists on operating as it now does by controlling an interest rate such as the Federal Funds rate." In contrast, Franco Modigliani argued (in his testimony, Joint Economic Committee, *The 1975 Economic Report of the President*, February 1975, p. 542):

I think the mistakes of last year came from the fact that the Fed was looking at the money supply instead of looking at what really bites the economy. No one, no one except a few fools perhaps on Wall Street are directly affected by the money supply, but people do pay higher interest rates, people do have to pay higher mortgage rates, and that is where monetary policy bites, not through the change of the money supply.

Figure 11–3
Federal Reserve targets and results, 1974–early 1975

A. Federal open market committee range for the interest rate on federal funds

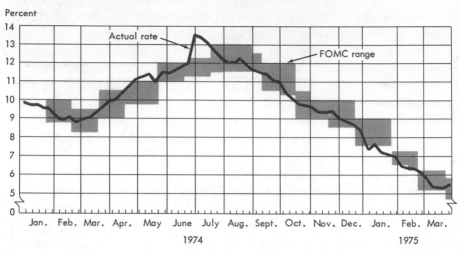

B. Federal open market committee ranges of tolerance for changes in M_1 and M_2

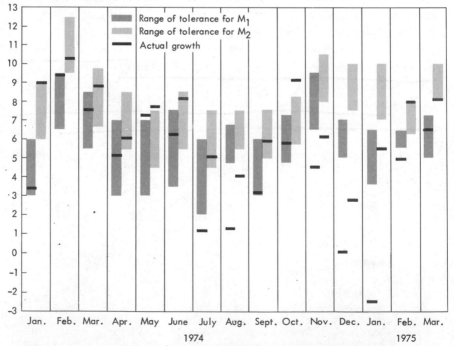

As the economy slid into recession in late 1974, the Federal Reserve misjudged the demand for money. Interest rates were kept within their targeted limits, but the increase in the money supply was much less than desired.

tribute to a further downswing. The indicated solution: give more prominence to the money supply objective. (Beginning in 1975, the Federal Reserve did so, as a result of strong pressure from a Congress dissatisfied with the monetary instability of previous years.)

But, in the very short run, this solution itself raises problems. While the Fed knows precisely what interest rates are on a day-to-day (or even a minute-to-minute) basis, its current estimates of the money supply are far from precise (as we observed in our discussion about 1972–73). Thus, on a day-to-day basis, aiming at a monetary objective might be a chancy business. Furthermore, even if one accepts the case for a steady growth of the money supply over relatively lengthy periods, such a policy is most unwise on a day-to-day basis. There may be short, sharp disturbances in the demand for money. For example, the demand for money to finance new-car purchases may rise sharply during a sunny week. It is hard to find any useful purpose—and easy to envisage harm—if interest rates were to shoot up in such a circumstance (as might happen if there were a rigid control on the money stock). Even if it were achievable, the aim of monetary policy should not be to smooth out sales on a week-to-week basis; rather, its function is to provide reasonable stability in the economy over more extended periods.

We are thus left with an ill-defined conclusion. While the Federal Reserve must of necessity pay considerable attention to interest rates in its day-to-day operations, there is a danger of instability in the economy if interest rates become the preoccupation. If money supply targets are consistently undershot or overshot during a series of months, then it becomes increasingly important to pay attention to the quantity of money, to bring it back on target and lessen the possibility of a cumulative swing in the economy. (In line with this conclusion, the Congress in 1975 did not insist that the Fed meet a monetary target on a month-to-month basis. Rather, it insisted that the Fed declare a monetary target for the coming year, and attempt either to meet this target or to explain why the target should be changed.) [18]

One final observation is in order. In this chapter, we have stressed the dangers of an accommodative policy on the part of the Fed, with

---

[18] For details on the targets, see J. A. Cacy, "Is the Federal Reserve Hitting Its Money Supply Targets?" *Federal Reserve Bank of Kansas City Monthly Review*, February 1976, pp. 3–10; Nancy Jianakoplos, "The FOMC [Federal Open Market Committee] in 1975: Announcing Monetary Targets," *Federal Reserve Bank of St. Louis Review*, March 1976, pp. 8–22; and William Poole, "Interpreting the Fed's Monetary Targets," *Brookings Papers on Economic Activity*, 1976, vol. 1, pp. 247–59.

interest rates being held stable and with the money supply responding to the demand for funds. Therefore, this chapter seems to conflict with Chapter 10, which emphasized the importance of monetary-
fiscal cooperation and monetary accommodation. The apparent inconsistency is related to a similar paradox on the fiscal side (discussed in Chapter 4). Two different terms—*automatic stabilizer*
and *fiscal drag*—are applied to the same thing, namely, the tendency
for tax revenues to rise as the economy expands, thus reducing the
strength of the upswing. Both the monetary and the fiscal paradox
can be resolved in the same way; in each case, it depends on the
situation in the economy. *If the economy is recovering from a deep
recession or depression,* then a strong and continuing upswing is
desirable for an extended period. In such circumstances, the automatic restraint exercised by the tax system is a *drag;* and accommodative policies that monetize both the government's deficit spending and the increases in private investment demand are desirable,
up to a point. On the other hand, *if the major economic problem
is one of instability* rather than the *level* of aggregate demand, then
automatic fiscal stabilizers play a constructive role and accommodative monetary policies constitute a potential trap.

APPENDIX

INTEREST RATES AND THE QUANTITY OF MONEY
IN THE *IS/LM* FRAMEWORK

The argument that a central bank should focus its attention on
the quantity of money—rather than on interest rates— can be traced
back to the 19th century. More recently, during the past decade,
there has been a more formal discussion of the relative merits of
the two approaches (concentrating either on interest rates or on
the quantity of money) in a world of uncertainty.[19]

In dealing with the relative merits of the two approaches, uncertainty is important. Without uncertainty, there is no question to
be answered.[20] In a world of certainty, the *IS* and *LM* curves are

[19] William Poole, "Optimal Choice of Monetary Policy Instruments in a Simple
Stochastic Model," *Quarterly Journal of Economics,* May 1970, pp. 197–216. (To read
this article, a familiarity with statistical theory is required.)

[20] Recall that uncertainty was important in Wicksell's writings. Banks are not in a
good position to know just what the natural rate of interest is.

known. In order to achieve the target rate of demand (Y^*) in the coming period (Figure 11A–1), the central bank may either engage in whatever open market operations are necessary to keep the interest rate at r_1, or aim open market operations at the quantity of money required for the curve LM_1. (For simplicity, we continue the assumption of Chapter 10, that monetary policy affects only the LM curve and not the IS curve also.) Both of these approaches will result in exactly the same outcome: an interest rate of r_1, the money stock used in the derivation of curve LM_1, and the target rate of income, Y^*.

Now consider a world of uncertainty. To make the problem manageable, let us *initially assume away the dynamic feedback problem* which concerned Wicksell, and deal only with the policies relevant for a single period. Suppose, to begin with, that there is uncertainty regarding the exact position of the IS curve. With given fiscal policy settings, it may fall anywhere in the range IS_2 to IS_3, which surrounds the best guess of IS_1 (Figure 11A–2). If the monetary authorities set interest rates at r_1, designed to give target income Y^*, they will be successful if the IS curve does indeed coincide with the

Figure 11A–1
Monetary policy in a world of certainty

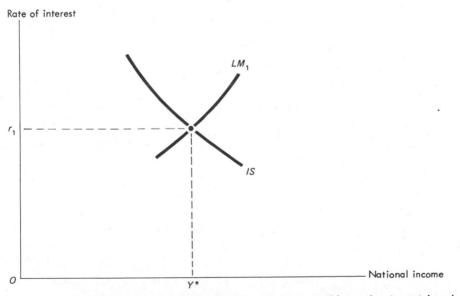

Rate of interest

r_1

LM_1

IS

O Y^* National income

In a world of certainty, monetary managers may achieve the target level of national income, Y^*, either by picking interest rate r_1 or by choosing the quantity of money behind curve LM_1.

Figure 11A–2
Uncertainty regarding the position of the *IS* curve

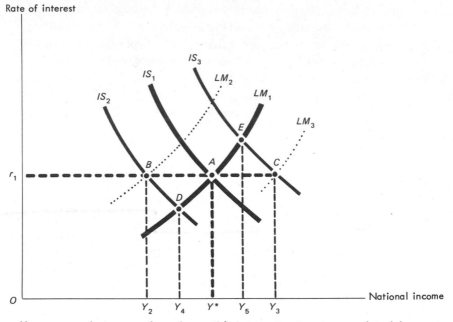

If open market operations keep the interest rate at r_1, national income may fall anywhere in the range between Y_2 and Y_3. With the alternative strategy of choosing the money supply to give LM_1, the range of possible outcomes is smaller—only Y_4 to Y_5. In this case, the choice of a money stock by the central bank is better than the choice of an interest rate.

best guess. But, suppose that the curve turns out to be at IS_2. Pegging the interest rate will give outcome *B*, that is, income Y_2. (It will also result in the quantity of money required to derive curve LM_2. However, this quantity of money will not be the objective of monetary policy; indeed, it will not be known ahead of time, since the outcome, *B*, is not known ahead of time. Rather, it will be the quantity of money that results when the open market desk follows its instructions to buy or sell whatever securities are necessary to keep interest rates at r_1.) Similarly, if the *IS* curve turns out to be IS_3, then income will be Y_3, greater than the target rate.

If, alternatively, the monetary authorities choose the quantity of money rather than the interest rate, they will pick the quantity behind LM_1, aiming for income Y^*. (In Figure 11A–2, it is assumed that there is no uncertainty regarding the position of the *LM* curve, once the quantity of money is chosen.) With an *IS* curve in the range IS_2 to IS_3, the outcome will lie in the range between D and E; that is, income will fall between Y_4 and Y_5. This is a smaller range than if the interest rate is chosen as the policy guide. Thus, *if there is uncertainty only over the position of the IS curve*, picking a money supply will give a more predictable—and therefore better—outcome than picking an interest rate.

Now, consider another situation, where the position of the *IS* curve is known with certainty, but the position of the *LM* curve is not. With a specific quantity of money, the position of the *LM* curve need not be LM_1, the best guess (Figure 11A–3). Rather, it may lie anywhere between LM_2 and LM_3. If open market operations are aimed at achieving this specific quantity of money, then income may fall anywhere in the range Y_2 to Y_3. In this circumstance, the choice of interest rate r_1 constitutes a better policy; it will result in income Y^*, precisely on target. (The amount of money needed to keep interest rates at r_1 and therefore to achieve the target Y^* will not, however, be known ahead of time.)

Figure 11A–3
Uncertainty regarding the position of the *LM* curve

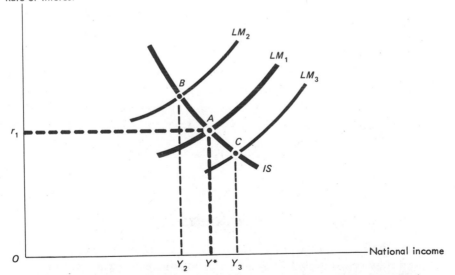

If, with a specific quantity of money, the *LM* curve may lie anywhere between LM_2 and LM_3, then the choice of that money stock by the central bank will result in income in the range Y_2 to Y_3. In this case, the choice of interest rate r_1 is preferable; it will result in income Y^*, precisely on target.

In the more general case, where there is uncertainty regarding both the *IS* curves and *LM* curves, no firm, general rule can be developed regarding the relative merits of choosing an interest rate or a money stock. The solution depends on the relative degree of uncertainty regarding the two curves, and on the slopes of the curves. A mathematical solution can be derived, which indicates that in many cases the best option is for the central bank to follow a combined policy.[21] Thus, support is given to the position of the "fence-sitters," who "argue that the monetary authorities should use both the money stock and the interest rates as instruments." Furthermore, this mathematical formula allows the fence-sitters to be explicit, and avoid their traditional weakness of offering "nothing more than a plea for wise behavior by the authorities."[22]

The trouble is, the use of this formula requires a judgment as to just how uncertain we are regarding the *IS* and *LM* curves. Furthermore, the formula is complicated (and is therefore not reproduced here); so complicated, indeed, that "intuition in this matter is to be distrusted; a combination [of interest rate and money stock policies] based on intuition may be worse than either of the pure policies."[23]

This analytic swamp occurs, moreover, even in the very simple case we have been considering of only one period, with the dynamic feedback problems (such as those of Wicksell) being ignored. When such problems are introduced, the central bank's choice of an interest rate may lead to a dynamically unstable result, with aggregate demand moving progressively in one direction, as explained earlier in this chapter. Thus, although it is clear that we are dealing with a very complicated problem, the general presumption in favor of concentrating on the money stock (rather than interest rates) survives this discussion of uncertainty.

KEY POINTS

1. In the earlier chapters, the effects of changes in the quantity of money on the level of economic activity were studied. The subject of this chapter is the possibility of causal forces working in the opposite direction, that is, from changes in economic ac-

21 Poole, "Optimal Choice of Monetary Policy Instruments," pp. 208–9.

22 Poole, "Optimal Choice of Monetary Policy Instruments," p. 199.

23 Poole, "Optimal Choice of Monetary Policy Instruments," p. 209.

tivity to changes in the money supply. If there are significant causal forces operating in both directions, then the stage is set for swings in economic activity associated with the operation of the monetary system: Increases in aggregate demand will lead to increases in the money supply, which in turn will cause further increases in aggregate demand.

2. Changes in the money supply are associated with the process of bank lending. The demand of businesses for loans is high during periods of prosperity, when prospects for profitable investments are good. Thus, from the side of the demand for loans, the stage is set for a response of the money supply to changes in business conditions.

3. On the supply side, Wicksell suggested that banks would respond to increases in demand during prosperity by extending additional loans, running down their reserve positions. In particular, they have a tendency to keep interest stable in the short run, increasing their lending when the demand for loans increases.

4. As long as bank reserves follow a pattern of moderate expansion (in line with the needs of a gradually growing economy), the excesses that can arise because of point 3 are limited: The reserve base will limit the ability of banks to expand loans. As they bump against the reserve limit, they will have to curtail the expansion of loans by raising interest rates or rationing their loans (or both).

5. Therefore, if economic swings attributable to monetary causes are to be large, the *reserve base* will also have to be responsive to changes in aggregate demand. Adherence to the *commercial loan theory* will tend to make the reserve base responsive; the commercial loan theory is therefore a recipe for disaster. The theory contributed to the policy errors of the 1930s.

6. More broadly, a policy of *interest-rate stabilization* on the part of the central bank in the face of changing economic conditions may make the monetary base responsive to changes in aggregate demand, thus adding instability to the economy.

QUESTION

1. Suppose that there is a run on the commercial banks, with the public withdrawing demand deposits in large quantities and holding cash. What will be the effects of this change in the com-

position of the public's holding of money on the total stock of money? Why? What policy should the Federal Reserve follow in such a case? To what extent should this policy be pursued?

SUGGESTED READINGS

E. A. Goldenweiser, *American Monetary Policy* (New York: McGraw-Hill, 1951), pp. 148–82.

Knut Wicksell, *Lectures on Political Economy* (New York: Augustus M. Kelly Reprints of Economic Classics, 1967), vol. 2, pp. 127–208.

Edward J. Kane, "New Congressional Restraints and Federal Reserve Independence," *Challenge,* November 1975, pp. 37–44.

Chapter 12

Monetary policy versus fiscal policy: The monetarist challenge

I came to the Council [of Economic Advisers]
with the determination to be a monetarist,
if anybody provided me with the flimsiest
evidence. And Willie [Fellner] *provided it.*

Herbert Stein*

The view that money is an important determinant of aggregate demand is held by practically all contemporary economists, but views on just *how* important it is cover a wide spectrum. A group of economists commonly identified as the monetarists hold down one end of the spectrum, arguing that money is not only important but is the key determinant of aggregate demand. Professor Milton Friedman of the University of Chicago is the most prominent of this group, with the Federal Reserve Bank of St. Louis contributing considerable statistical ammunition.

The monetarist position involves four major propositions:

---

* From remarks of the former chairman of the Council of Economic Advisers in honor of retiring CEA member William Fellner, February 1975.

1. Monetary policy is much more important than fiscal policy as a determinant of aggregate demand.

2. Indeed, "pure" fiscal policy is of small or even negligible importance as a determinant of aggregate demand, with the possible exception of the short run (the first few quarters after the fiscal stimulus or contraction is exerted) . By "pure" fiscal policy is meant a change in taxation or government spending *unaccompanied by* a change in the rate of growth of the money supply. Where a change in government spending (or taxation) is financed by an accommodating change in the rate of growth of the money supply, aggregate demand will be significantly affected; but it is the change in the money supply, not the government spending which is the important thing.

3. In spite of the importance of money, the authorities should not attempt to control the economy with discretionary monetary policies. In doing so, they are more likely to destabilize the economy than to stabilize it, for two major reasons:

    a. There are significant and variable lags between changes in the money supply and changes in aggregate demand which make short-run control of the economy difficult or impossible. Because the economy does not respond quickly to changes in policy, the authorities tend to overreact to current problems.

    b. Policymakers exercising discretion are likely to watch the wrong thing. In particular, there is a continuing temptation to try to stabilize interest rates rather than the rate of growth of the money supply. Where policymakers yield to this temptation, they are likely to destabilize the economy (see Chapter 11) .

    Professor Friedman's views are summarized:

    Is fiscal policy being oversold? Is monetary policy being oversold? I want to stress that my answer is yes to both of those questions. I believe monetary policy is being oversold. I believe fiscal policy is being oversold. What I believe is that fine tuning has been oversold.[1]

---

[1] Milton Friedman and Walter Heller, *Monetary vs Fiscal Policy: A Dialogue* (New York: W. W. Norton, paperback, 1969) , p. 47. (Although this booklet is now dated, it remains one of the clearest and most readable presentations of the differences between the classical monetary tradition and the Keynesian fiscal tradition.) See also Friedman, "Have Fiscal-Monetary Policies Failed?" *American Economic Review,* May 1972, p. 17: "I believe that we economists in recent years have done vast harm—to society at large and to our profession in particular—by claiming more than we can deliver."

4. Discarding discretionary policies, monetarists suggest that a *monetary rule* be adopted, with the central bank aiming for a *steady* increase in the money supply of 4 percent or 5 percent per year, to permit aggregate demand to expand in line with the growth of productive capacity. The *steadiness* of the growth is considered more important than the exact figure. If aggregate demand grows steadily at a rate that exceeds the growth of capacity by 1 percent, 2 percent, or even more, no great harm will result: The economy will adjust well to a *steady small rate* of price increase.

Those in the Keynesian tradition disagree with each of these four monetarist propositions. Although modern Keynesians are much less negative regarding monetary policy than were early Keynesians, a significant gap remains between them and the monetarists over the importance of changes in the quantity of money.[2] Because they

---

[2] Some of those in the Keynesian tradition suggest that money is no longer an important point of dispute between Keynesians and monetarists. For example, the following passage appears in the discussion of monetarism by Alan S. Blinder and Robert M Solow—who classify themselves as "eclectic Keynesians":

> The monetarist critique is sometimes described by its proponents as a defense of the proposition that monetary policy matters against the "Keynesian" belief that it does not. But since contemporary Keynesians do in fact believe in the effectiveness of monetary policy, the monetarist argument usually turns out to be a defense of the proposition that fiscal policy does not matter against the Keynesian belief that it does.

[From "Analytical Foundations of Fiscal Policy," in Blinder, Solow, George F. Break, Peter O. Steiner, and Dick Netzer, *The Economics of Public Finance* (Washington, DC: Brookings Institution, 1974) , p. 9.]

Nevertheless, a second passage (from p. 41 of the Blinder-Solow article) might be quoted in support of the proposition that important disagreements remain regarding the effects of the quantity of money on aggregate demand:

> It is hard to quarrel with such a position [of the Committee for Economic Development (CED) , that there is no need for persistent deficits or surpluses in the government's full-employment budget], especially if it is admitted as a corollary that *if* private saving and private investment *do not* equalize at full employment, the government should do something about it. If investment is *chronically* too high (despite Federal Reserve policy and everything else) , then the full-employment budget should run a surplus to combat inflation. Conversely, *chronically* low investment will imply a full-employment deficit as a *necessary* means to achieve full employment.

(Italics were added to *chronically* and *necessary;* other italics in original.)

It is hard to imagine someone in the classical monetary tradition writing—or agreeing with—this passage. What does it imply? That there may be *chronic* unemployment *regardless* of how much the money supply is increased. Furthermore, it is based on the original proposition of Keynes (discussed earlier in Chapter 6) that investment may be chronically less than saving *regardless* of the expansion of the money supply. To those in the classical tradition, this is heresy. Indeed, in his famous article introducing the "Pigou effect," A. C. Pigou argued that if the quantity of money were increased enough, then consumption could be continuously expanded until saving fell

are skeptical regarding the stability of velocity, modern Keynesians are likewise skeptical regarding a policy "rule," aiming for a constant rate of growth of the money stock. Modern Keynesians believe that discretionary policies should be used—although they acknowledge that monetary as well as fiscal policies should be important components in the overall aggregate demand strategy, and they are generally less confident than the Keynesians of the 1960s that the economy can be fine tuned to a high degree of stability.

Of the four monetarist propositions, the first two are the most important; the final proposition depends directly on the first two. Unless money is the preponderant determinant of aggregate demand, the rule of stable monetary growth will not result in a stable growth of aggregate demand. The presentation and evaluation of the evidence which monetarists offer to substantiate points 1 and 2 must therefore be the first order of business.

THE FRIEDMAN-MEISELMAN STUDY

The Keynesian view was predominant in the economics profession during the 1940s and 1950s, although it was a view softened from the simplest Keynesian theoretical structure (being based primarily on the *IS/LM* framework of Chapter 6 rather than the very simple Keynesian theory outlined in Chapters 3–5).[3] This is not to suggest that all pockets of intellectual resistance had been mopped up. Clark Warburton continued to view money as the key to understanding changes in aggregate demand;[4] a strong monetary view persisted at the University of Chicago; and a number of the most respected senior economists—of whom Jacob Viner was perhaps the most outstanding—declined to follow the Keynesian bandwagon.

During the 1960s, there was a major monetary counterattack. Three events stand out: the *Monetary History of the United States,*

---

to *zero;* saving would then equal the *zero* investment which would occur in a no-growth (stationary) economy. (Recall that the title of Pigou's 1943 *Economic Journal* article was "The Classical Stationary State.")

From the Blinder-Solow passage, we once again see that Keynesian theory—eclectic or otherwise—tends to lead to the conclusion that there may be severe limits on the effectiveness of monetary policy as a means of stimulating aggregate demand, *even in the very long run* (and even when the theory is in the hands of two of the most perceptive and thoughtful practitioners).

[3] There were also very significant modifications of the simple Keynesian consumption and investment functions. These will be studied in Chapters 14 and 15.

[4] "The Quantity and Frequency of Use of Money in the United States, 1915–45," *Journal of Political Economy,* October 1946, pp. 442–50.

1867–1960 by Milton Friedman and Anna J. Schwartz, published in 1963; the statistical evaluation of "The Relative Stability of Monetary Velocity and the Investment Multiplier in the United States" by Milton Friedman and David Meiselman, also published in 1963;[5] and the more recent work on money by the Federal Reserve Bank of St. Louis.[6] Reference was made to the Friedman-Schwartz work in Chapter 11; for the sake of brevity, attention will here be focused on the Friedman-Meiselman paper and the St. Louis Fed studies.

Friedman and Meiselman argued that Keynesian theory had gained popularity at the expense of the monetary view on the basis of very little empirical evidence. Their objective was to correct this shortcoming by a statistical comparison of the two theories, which they briefly summarized as follows:[7]

> The view that the quantity of money matters little is typically held for either of two reasons: one, because the quantity of money is regarded as adapting to "the needs of trade," and hence is regarded as a passive element in the economic system, determined by and responsive to other economic and noneconomic factors, but incapable of being a source of disturbances; the other, because the ratio of money to other assets is regarded as variable and pliable, and hence the economic effects of changes in the quantity of money are regarded as highly unpredictable.
>
> The alternative view holds that the quantity of money does matter, and for three reasons: one, because the quantity of money is capable of being controlled fairly accurately by deliberate policy; two, because changes in the quantity of money can produce substantial changes in the flow of income, prices, and other important variables; three, because the relationships between the stock of money and other assets are relatively stable and dependable.

---

[5] In Commission on Money and Credit, *Stabilization Policies* (Englewood Cliffs, N.J.: Prentice-Hall, 1963), pp. 168–268.

[6] Leonall C. Andersen and Jerry Jordan, "Monetary and Fiscal Actions: A Test of Their Relative Importance in Economic Stabilization," *Federal Reserve Bank of St. Louis Review*, November 1968, pp. 11–16; Andersen and Keith M. Carlson, "A Monetarist Model for Economic Stabilization," *Federal Reserve Bank of St. Louis Review*, April 1970, pp. 7–25; Andersen and Carlson, "St. Louis Model Revisited," in Lawrence R. Klein and Edwin Burmeister, *Econometric Model Performance* (Philadelphia: University of Pennsylvania Press, 1976), pp. 47–69.

[7] Friedman and Meiselman, "Relative Stability," pp. 166–67. The points raised by Friedman and Meiselman in the first paragraph have been studied in earlier chapters. The "needs of trade" and the possible passivity of the money supply were investigated in Chapter 11, and Chapter 5 presented the liquidity trap argument—that the demand for money is sufficiently interest elastic that an increase in the money supply will cause an offsetting decrease in velocity, with aggregate demand remaining unaffected.

To do an adequate job of sorting out the comparative empirical validity of the two theories would be a complex task: The world is not a simple place and theories are capable of detailed elaboration to take care of real-world complexities. (For example, the distribution of income might influence the propensity to consume in a complex Keynesian model, as might the composition of taxation.) Because of time and data constraints, Friedman and Meiselman chose to test the comparative validity of the two theories in a simplified form; this procedure was justified because the issue which divides the profession "is extremely basic and one which should lend itself to a common answer over a wide range of circumstances."[8]

In its simplest form, the quantity theory suggests that there should be a stable and predictable relationship between the money supply and aggregate demand. Thus, the quantity theory suggests that there should be a good statistical fit for the equation:[9]

$$Y = vM \qquad (12\text{--}1)$$

where velocity v is written as a lowercase letter representing a constant. The question is how close a correspondence there is between: (1) $M \times$ a constant, and (2) observed income.

In the quantity theory, money is the major engine of changes in aggregate demand. In the Keynesian theory, changes in "autonomous expenditures"—investment, government spending, and net exports—are the major source of demand changes. Therefore, in simplified form, the Keynesian equivalent to the quantity theorist's Equation (12–1) is the following equation:

$$Y = a + bA \qquad (12\text{--}2)$$

where

A is equal to "autonomous expenditures,"
    that is, net private domestic investment, plus government expenditures on income and product account, plus exports minus imports.[10]

---

[8] Friedman and Meiselman, "Relative Stability," p. 170.

[9] For an introductory exposition of the statistical technique of fitting an equation, see Thomas H. Wonnacott and Ronald J. Wonnacott, *Introductory Statistics for Business and Economics,* 2d ed. (Santa Barbara: Wiley-Hamilton, 1977).

[10] Because it provided a better statistical fit, the Keynesian equation with government *deficits* rather than government *expenditures* was used by Friedman and Meiselman when they made their statistical comparison between Keynesian theory and the quantity theory. See Friedman and Meiselman, "Relative Stability," pp. 183–84 and 246–56.

In the form given, Equation (12–2) is not obviously the same as any of the simple Keynesian equations presented in earlier chapters. However, by algebraic manipulation,[11] it can be shown to be the equivalent of the simple Keynesian consumption function:

$$C = a_1 + cY \qquad (12\text{–}8)$$

Friedman and Meiselman, however, perceived a problem in the way in which Equation (12–2) is stated. In this form, the equation is inappropriate for a statistical test because autonomous expenditures constitute a component of income (see Equation 12–5), and therefore fitting the Equation (12–2) would in part involve fitting a set of data to itself. Therefore, they argued, it is appropriate to exclude from the left side the variables already included on the right. This may be done by subtracting A from both sides of Equation (12–2), giving:

$$C = a + kA \qquad (12\text{–}9)$$

where

$$k = b - 1.$$

In order to make the two equations as comparable as possible for statistical tests, Friedman and Meiselman put the quantity theory Equation (12–1) in the same form as the Keynesian Equation (12–9), thus:

$$C = \alpha + vM \qquad (12\text{–}10)$$

When Friedman and Meiselman switched the dependent variable in the quantity theory equation from income (Equation 12–1) to

---

[11] From Equation (12–2), it follows that

$$\frac{1}{b} Y = \frac{a}{b} + A \qquad (12\text{–}3)$$

and, subtracting each side of Equation (12–3) from Y gives

$$\left(1 - \frac{1}{b}\right) Y = (Y - A) - \frac{a}{b} \qquad (12\text{–}4)$$

But, by definition,

$$Y \equiv C + A \qquad (12\text{–}5)$$

which, when substituted into Equation (12–4) gives

$$\left(1 - \frac{1}{b}\right) Y = C - \frac{a}{b} \qquad (12\text{–}6)$$

or

$$C = \left(1 - \frac{1}{b}\right) Y + \frac{a}{b} \qquad (12\text{–}7)$$

which is the same form as Equation (12–8).

consumption (Equation 12–10), they thought that this would introduce a bias against the quantity theory, since that theory is usually
framed in terms of total income rather than any of its components.
Indeed, quantity theorists often argue that money will have a more
stable relationship to total spending than to its components; any
tendency for spending in one particular area to drop will leave
spending power which will tend to find an outlet in other areas.
Nevertheless, this substitution did not make the quantity equation
appear inferior when data were fitted to it; indeed, the fit for Equation (12–10) was somewhat better than that for Equation (12–1).

As between the simple Keynesian Equation (12–9) and the simple quantity theory Equation (12–10), the empirical results of
Friedman and Meiselman were "remarkably consistent and un-
ambiguous. The evidence is so one-sided that its import is clear
without the nice balancing of conflicting bits of evidence. . . ."[12]
The velocity of money was found to be consistently and decidedly
more stable than k (in Equation 12–9) with the exception of only
the period of the Great Depression of the 1930s. Thus, Keynes did
not write a "general theory" at all; rather, he put forward a special
theory applicable to the tormented 1930s.[13] Overall, Friedman and
Meiselman found the simple Keynesian equation to be "almost
completely useless as a description of stable empirical relationships,
as judged by six decades of experience in the United States."[14]

The conclusions of Friedman and Meiselman were basically two:
First, the profession had swung over to the inferior Keynesian explanation of real-world phenomena on the basis of a very special
and relatively short-lived experience during the 1930s, when the
problems of aggregate demand were critical and when the Keynesian
explanation did indeed have an apparently closer relationship to the
facts than the quantity theory; second, for economic policy, their
findings "indicate that control over the stock of money is a far more

[12] Friedman and Meiselman, "Relative Stability," p. 186. In the Friedman-Meiselman
study, M_2 (including time deposits) provided better statistical results than M_1, and M_2
accordingly was taken as the basic definition of "money" (pp. 184, 246).

[13] Keynes had declared his work to be "general" to contrast it with the classical
theory, which he believed was applicable to only the special case of full employment.

A. A. Walters carried out an experiment similar to that of Friedman and Meiselman
with British data and came to a similar conclusion: The interwar period, 1921–38,
constituted an exceptional Keynesian interlude [Walters, *Money in Boom and Slump*
(London: Institute of Economic Affairs, Hobart Paper 44, 1969)].

(In the United States, the 1920s were generally prosperous, with the Depression
coming in the 1930s. In Britain, the 1920s too were a time of depression. Incidentally,
this British head start with the Depression may partially explain why the *General
Theory* was written by an Englishman.)

[14] Friedman and Meiselman, "Relative Stability," p. 187.

useful tool for affecting the level of aggregate money demand than control over autonomous expenditures."[15] Thus, if the national authorities wish to alter aggregate demand, they should change the monetary base rather than look for ways in which to change investment, government expenditures, taxation, or net exports.

The Friedman-Meiselman study clearly represents a fundamental attack on Keynesian economics and on the basic intellectual framework of most postwar economists in approaching problems of aggregate demand. Either the framework presented in Chapters 3–5 will have to be substantially discarded, or the Friedman-Meiselman study will have to be subjected to fundamental criticisms. In this sense, our discussion has come to a place similar to that reached at the end of Chapter 6, but on the opposite side: There will have to be a counterattack, or the victory will have to be granted to one of the two competing views. Just as in the earlier case—when a classical response was found (Chapter 7) to the Keynesian insistence on the possible existence of an unemployment equilibrium—so here also there is a powerful counterattack which should rule out the granting of a sweeping victory to one side in the macroeconomic debate.

The Friedman-Meiselman study: Some objections

"The cause of lightning," Alice said very decidedly, for she felt quite sure about this, "is the thunder—no, no!" she hastily corrected herself, "I meant it the other way."

"It's too late to correct it," said the Red Queen. "When you've once said a thing, that fixes it, and you must take the consequences."

Lewis Carroll

Friedman and Meiselman have run a horse race between two competing theories to see which performs better. They came to an unambiguous conclusion: One horse breezed across the finish line while the other contestant was still stuck at the starting gate (being found to be "almost completely useless"). The major objection: It's an unfair race—the fiscal "horse" is laboring under an unfair disadvantage, with the statistical methods favoring the monetary "horse."

Three objections are worth particular note:

1. A simple equation is taken as a representative of each theory. This biases the statistical test because the "simple" quantity theory is, in effect, *the* quantity theory. The quantity theory, in

---

[15] Friedman and Meiselman, "Relative Stability," p. 213.

other words, has its primary incarnation as a *very* simple theory and, indeed, is incapable of very great elaboration. In contrast, the Keynesian theory invites elaboration and, indeed, is usually put forward in its simplified form only as an expositional device. When real-world phenomena are under consideration, a significantly more complex version is called for.

2. The test is biased because there is significant *two-way* causation between money and aggregate demand. An increase in the money supply leads to an increase in aggregate demand, and vice versa. The Keynesian-classical controversy is confined to the *causal* role of money; yet the statistical correlations show an association regardless of which way the cause-effect relationship runs. In contrast, there is no presumption that whatever reverse causation operates between aggregate demand and autonomous expenditures will bias the correlations in an upward direction. Increases in aggregate demand or consumption may lead to increases in autonomous expenditures; but they may alternatively lead to decreases. (Increases in consumption, for example, will attract imports and lead to a fall in net exports.) Statistical noise rather than a clear upward bias is introduced into the test of the Keynesian equation by reverse causation.

3. The quantity theorists do not specify in detail *how* monetary policy is expected to work; statistical correlations are taken as a conclusive case. In contrast, Keynesians spell out how fiscal— or monetary—policy may be expected to influence aggregate demand. Until the linkages between money and economic activity are spelled out and tested, statistical claims of monetarists must be discounted as guides to policy.

Each of these points represent a major battleground between Keynesian and monetary economists; each is worthy of elaboration.

The problem of a simple test of the Keynesian system

Keynesian theorists agree that, indeed, autonomous expenditures should influence the level of consumption. However, it is just incredible to apply data to such a simple equation as Equation (12–9).[16] While very simple models with only one or two types of leakages (S, imports) are the standard basis for simple expositions

---

[16] Albert Ando and Franco Modigliani objected that Friedman and Meiselman grossly misspecified the Keynesian model, making their statistical results "essentially worthless." See "The Relative Stability of Monetary Velocity and the Investment Multiplier," *American Economic Review,* September 1965, p. 694.

of Keynesian theory, a rather extensive list of leakages must be considered if the model is to approach an applicable form; this is recognized even in relatively elementary undergraduate presentations.[17] In addition to individual saving and income taxes, for example, leakages from the spending stream in a relatively simple Keynesian model would include undistributed profits and corporation taxes.

Furthermore, Keynesian economists long ago recognized that the simple consumption function (Equation 12–8) is inadequate. Indeed, much effort has been expended in the past 30 years to develop better—and more complex—consumption functions, as will be seen in some detail in Chapter 14. The simple Friedman-Meiselman specification of the Keynesian system ignores these developments which have become a central segment of the Keynesian approach to aggregate demand.

There is a fundamental difference between the Keynesian and monetarist approach to aggregate demand which makes a simple test show the monetary argument at its strongest and the Keynesian argument at its weakest. The Keynesian approach is to take the major components of aggregate demand—consumption, investment, government expenditures, and net exports—and develop increasingly elaborate (and hopefully precise) explanations of their determinants; the results can then be combined to give the total level of demand. On the other hand, the quantity theory suggests no such improvement in the overall results if the system is disaggregated and investigated in segments. Indeed, monetary economists operate on the general presumption that it is easier to predict the overall level of demand than the demand of any subcomponent.

In short, reply the critics, a simple test is by its very nature a biased test.[18]

Reverse causation

From Wicksell and even before, economists have been concerned with two-way causation between money and aggregate demand. Indeed, the elasticity of the money supply in the face of increasing demand was seen as a major source of economic instability.

Friedman and Meiselman recognize the possibility of reverse

---

[17] For example, John Lindauer, *Macroeconomics*, 2d ed. (New York: John Wiley, 1971), p. 179, where the multiplier equation contains 11 variables; or Edward Shapiro, *Macroeconomic Analysis*, 3d ed. (New York: Harcourt, Brace, Jovanovich, 1974), pp. 113–14.

[18] On the problem of using single-equation models to test theories, see Blinder and Solow, "Analytical Foundations of Fiscal Policy," pp. 63–71.

causation. In their introductory statement of the two competing theories, they observe that the antimonetarist position involves the argument that money may simply be adapting passively to the "needs of trade." However, while noted, this argument is not adequately dealt with before Friedman and Meiselman proceed to their statistical work.

As Friedman and Meiselman recognize, the causal problem cannot possibly receive an adequate test as a result of statistical correlations. Correlations tell which events were associated; they tell practically nothing about which *caused* which. Thus, the Friedman-Meiselman argument that the causation runs primarily from money to aggregate demand rather than in the opposite direction is based on grounds that are largely independent of statistical correlations. There is one exception: *time lags*. Friedman and Meiselman found that changes in the money supply tended to precede changes in the level of aggregate demand. Therefore, there is a presumption that the causal relationship from money to economic activity was stronger than the opposite causal relationship.

This is a presumption, but certainly not a strong one, as Friedman and Meiselman note.[19] It might seem like a surprising admission, as it might certainly seem reasonable to assume that a cause would precede its effect; but this is not necessarily so. Consider for a moment the determinants of prices in the stock market. Corporation profits are certainly a major one: the higher profits are, the higher stock prices will tend to be. But it is not so clear that profits will rise before stock prices rather than the other way around. Indeed, stock prices may well go up first. Participants in the stock market identify the forces which are likely to cause an upward movement of profits, and thereupon bid up stock prices before profits actually go up. Time lags do not demonstrate causality.

Because of the inconclusiveness of time lags, Friedman and Meiselman also based their proposition that the causal relationship ran from money to demand on the following argument:

> Even if changes in the stock of money tend to precede changes in income, the direction of influence need not be from money to income. . . . Therefore, other kinds of studies are needed to judge

---

[19] Friedman and Meiselman, "Relative Stability," p. 179. In response to an attack by James Tobin, Friedman emphasized that his conclusion (that causation was primarily from money to aggregate demand rather than vice versa) was *not* based primarily on time lags. See James Tobin, "Money and Income: Post Hoc Ergo Propter Hoc?" *Quarterly Journal of Economics*, May 1970, pp. 301–17; Friedman, "Comment," pp. 318–27; and Tobin, "Rejoinder," pp. 328–29.

with any confidence the direction of influence. Historical studies of particular episodes are especially valuable in this connection. The reason is that, in many episodes, attendant circumstances give strong evidence that changes in one or more variables were independent in origin. For example, a change in the supply of money brought about by currency reforms, gold discoveries, and the like, can hardly be attributed to contemporary changes in income.[20]

But, as a way of disposing with the bias issue based on two-way causation, this argument of Friedman and Meiselman will simply not do. It is true that, if all that is needed is to demolish the naïve super-Keynesian position that money never matters, then it is sufficient to demonstrate that there may have been historical instances of autonomous changes in money which led to changes in aggregate demand. But the Friedman-Meiselman objective is surely more than to flog this naive proposition. Their goal is something much more ambitious: to test whether, *year in and year out,* velocity *on average* is more stable than the Keynesian multiplier. A few historical illustrations that money behaved in an autonomous manner (in unusual circumstances, such as currency reforms) does not rule out the possibility that, for much of the 1897–1958 period covered by their statistical studies,[21] a significant causal chain ran from changes in aggregate demand to changes in the money supply. Thus, the problem of possible bias remains significant.

Nor does the related argument of the two authors act as a reassurance in this matter. For example, they argue (p. 178) that "it is plausible to suppose the major direction of influence to run from M to Y or C. . . . This is partly because M, the stock of money in nominal terms, *is or can be* under the control of the monetary authority, which can make it anything it wishes within very narrow limits." (Italics added.) But what the central bank *can* do is irrelevant in sorting out the significance of historical statistics; the only relevant thing is what they *did* do. Within the monetary framework, it is pretty difficult to explain how the Depression actually happened without introducing causal relationships running from

---

[20] Friedman and Meiselman, "Relative Stability," p. 179.

[21] Friedman and Meiselman footnote their reference to historical episodes, giving four studies as substantiation. Only one of these, the Friedman-Schwartz volume, overlaps the 1897–1958 period covered by the Friedman-Meiselman statistical study. On the lack of support given by the Friedman-Schwartz volume to the Friedman-Meiselman causal argument, see footnote 22, below. Because three of their four historical citations refer to periods outside the scope of their statistical work, and because of the lack of strong support provided by the fourth, the Friedman-Meiselman appeal to historical studies cannot be considered a strong defense.

aggregate demand to the money supply as well as in the opposite direction. To do so is to explain the changes in the money supply on the basis of pure caprice on the part of the monetary authorities rather than on their adherence to theories which were wanting (such as the commercial loan theory, which introduces a reverse causation.) [22]

Indeed, Friedman's line of attack on central bankers belies his dismissal here of the reverse causation problem. Central bankers, he argues, are likely to make significant blunders if left to their own discretion, first responding more or less passively to changes in aggregate demand in an attempt to keep interest rates more or less stable, and then overreacting when they perceive a pressing problem in the trend of aggregate demand. That they do on occasion act strongly and autonomously does not detract from the possibility that, year in and year out, they on average allow the monetary supply to respond to demand conditions. Friedman cannot have it both ways. He cannot downgrade the reverse causation argument in his statistical studies, and yet fault the central bankers for responding passively to demand.

How does monetary policy work?

In the absence of an explicit statement as to how the monetary policy influences aggregate demand, the statistical relationship

---

[22] The two points just mentioned are by no means the only arguments of Friedman on the direction of causation. See especially Friedman and Schwartz in their summary chapter in *A Monetary History*, p. 695 (italics added):

> While the influence running from money to economic activity has been predominant, there have clearly also been influences running the other way, particularly during the shorter-run movements associated with the business cycle. The cyclical pattern of the deposit-reserve ratio is one example. The resumption and silver episodes, the 1919 inflation, and the 1929–33 contraction reveal clearly other aspects of the reflex influence of business on money. Changes in the money stock are therefore a consequence as well as an independent source of change in money income and prices, though, once they occur, they produce in their turn still further effects on income and prices. Mutual interaction, but with money rather clearly the senior partner in longer-run movements and in major cyclical movements, and *more nearly an equal partner with money income and prices in shorter-run and milder movements*—this is the generalization suggested by our evidence.

What does this say? That if short-run statistical correlations are run (such as the tests with quarterly data which form part of the Friedman-Meiselman study), then the causal relationship is about equal (?) between the money supply and aggregate demand. Thus, the Friedman-Meiselman quarterly correlations are picking up the two-way causal forces in about equal proportion (?); the test of money as a causal force is clearly biased.

which Friedman and Meiselman found between money and aggregate demand forms a poor basis for the conclusion that monetary policy is the preferred policy tool. Friedman and Meiselman have declined to give any such detailed explanation. Money works in a mysterious manner, its wonders to perform.

But a detailed explanation of the nature of the causal relationship is important for policy. Suppose for example that, as a result of historical investigations, the research director of the Democratic party discovered that a certain town had *always* voted on the winning side in presidential elections. He might note the perfect correlation and suggest that the party concentrate on this town, forgetting the rest of the country and resting assured that it could be statistically demonstrated that if they took this town, their chances of winning the country would be very high indeed. Not very good advice.

To work from a statistical regularity to a policy prescription requires some view—explicit or implicit—as to the basis for the statistical connection. An attempt to control one of the variables (the money supply; the voting of Middletown, USA) may in itself break the connection between the two variables. Before policy changes are made, it is relevant to ask whether an attempt to control one of the variables is likely in fact to break the connection. This point, of course, is related to the second one, regarding the causal relationships between money and aggregate demand.

In contrast to the Friedman-Meiselman approach, Keynesian-based models attempt to identify and measure the channels through which monetary policy works. The most elaborate model, the Massachusetts Institute of Technology/University of Pennsylvania/Social Science Research Council (MPS) model, evaluates the effects of open market operations in terms of:[23]

1. Changes in the reserves of banks. (Monetary policy initially affects the reserve base.)
2. Changes in interest rates, in the availability of money to borrowers, and in the value of common stocks (the latter of which is a component of the wealth of consumers).

----

[23] This is a simplified version. For details, see Frank de Leeuw and Edward M. Gramlich, "The Channels of Monetary Policy," *Federal Reserve Bulletin,* June 1969, especially p. 484; Franco Modigliani, "Monetary Policy and Consumption: Linkages via Interest Rates and Wealth Effects," in Federal Reserve Bank of Boston, *Consumer Spending and Monetary Policy: the Linkages,* 1971, pp. 9–58; Douglas Battenberg, Jared Enzler, and Arthur Havenner, "MINNIE: A Small Version of the MIT-Penn-SSRC Econometric Model," *Federal Reserve Bulletin,* November 1975, pp. 721–27; and the book on the MPS model by Albert Ando and Modigliani, to appear in the late 1970s.

3.   Changes in business investment, housing construction, state and local expenditures, and consumption expenditures, which follow from point 2.
4.   The effects of changes in point 3 on consumption (the multiplier process).

THE ST. LOUIS FED MODEL

On Revolution: Revolutions revolve 360 degrees.*

Charles Issawi

Beginning in the late 1960s, a group of economists at the Federal Reserve Bank of St. Louis built upon the work of Friedman and Meiselman, introducing monetary and fiscal variables as determinants of the level of aggregate demand in a simple set of equations.[24] They "tested three commonly held propositions. . . . The response of economic activity to fiscal actions relative to that of monetary actions is (I) greater, (II) more predictable, and (III) faster." They found the opposite to be the case: "The response of economic activity to monetary actions compared with that of fiscal

---

* From "Laws of Social Motion," *Columbia Forum* (New York: Columbia University, 1970).

[24] A typical equation, in simplified form, is:

$$\Delta Y_t = 1.57^*\Delta M_t + 1.94^*\Delta M_{t-1} + 1.80^*\Delta M_{t-2}$$
$$+ 1.28\Delta M_{t-3} + 0.15\Delta(E - R)_t$$
$$+0.20\Delta(E - R)_{t-1} - 0.10\Delta(E - R)_{t-2} \qquad (12\text{--}11)$$
$$-0.47^*\Delta(E - R)_{t-3} + 1.99$$

where

Y_t is nominal GNP in quarter t, measured at annual rates.
M is the money supply (defined narrowly as M_1, that is, currency plus demand deposits only).
E represents high-employment government expenditures, at annual rates.
R represents high-employment government receipts, at annual rates.

Thus $(E - R)$ represents the high-employment government deficit, at annual rates. Also the t subscripts indicate successive yearly quarters, Δ means "change in," and (*) signifies that the coefficient is statistically significant at the 5 percent level.
[Source: Andersen and Jordan, "Monetary and Fiscal Actions: A Test of Their Relative Importance in Economic Stabilization," Equation (1–1).]

These equations contrast with the Keynesian approach, which begins with the equation:

$$Y = C + I + G + X - Z \qquad (12\text{--}12)$$

and investigates in detail the determinants of the items on the right side of this equation.

actions is (I′) larger, (II′) more predictable, and (III′) faster."[25]

Indeed, if the early St. Louis Fed results are compared to the results of Keynesian-based econometric models (which investigate the *components* of aggregate demand, namely consumption, investment, government spending, and net exports), the difference is found to be not simply a minor disagreement over the effectiveness of monetary and fiscal policies, but rather a great gulf. This shows up clearly in Figures 12–1 and 12–2, which give the effects of monetary and fiscal policies on aggregate demand as estimated by the St. Louis model and three well-known Keynesian models—the Data Resources,

Figure 12–1
The estimated effects of monetary policy

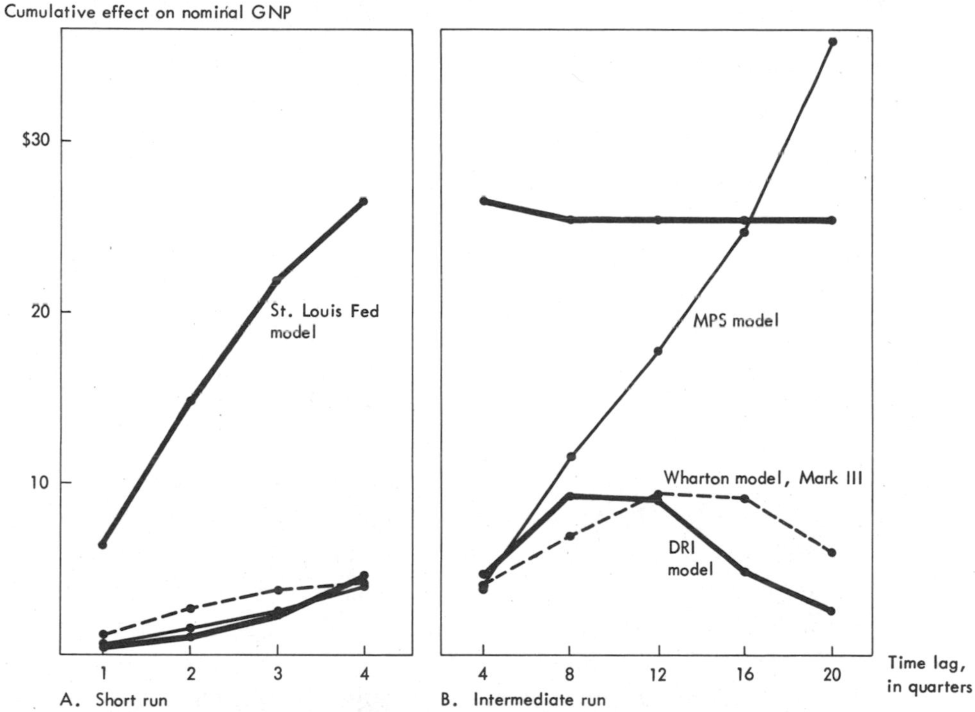

Cumulative effect on nominal GNP
$30
20
10
St. Louis Fed model
MPS model
Wharton model, Mark III
DRI model
1
2
3
4
4
8
12
16
20
Time lag, in quarters
A. Short run
B. Intermediate run

Note: For the MPS, Wharton, and DRI models, this diagram shows the effect of a $1 change in unborrowed reserves. The St. Louis Fed model deals with the effects of changes in M_1, not changes in unborrowed reserves. To make the model results roughly comparable, the figure shows the effects of a $5 change in M_1 for the St. Louis Fed model.

The St. Louis Fed model shows a much stronger effect of monetary policy than do the other three models—with the exception of the MPS model in the long run.

---

[25] Andersen and Jordan, "Monetary and Fiscal Actions: A Test of Their Relative Importance in Economic Stabilization," pp. 11, 22.

Figure 12–2
The estimated effects of fiscal policy

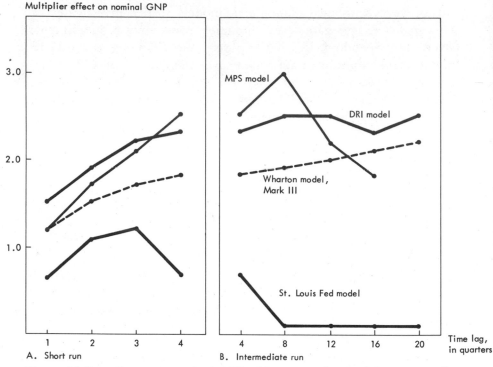

Multiplier effect on nominal GNP

A. Short run

B. Intermediate run

Time lag, in quarters

The multiplier effects on nominal *GNP* of increases in nondefense spending are reasonably similar for the Keynesian-based models, at least during the first year. The St. Louis Fed model shows a much weaker effect of fiscal policy.

Inc. (DRI) model, the MIT/Pennsylvania/Social Science Research Council (MPS) model, and the Wharton Mark III model.[26]

On the monetary side (Figure 12–1), the results are not strictly comparable, since the St. Louis Fed model measures monetary policy in terms of the effect of the change in the quantity of money, while the other three models take a change in (unborrowed) reserves as the starting point of monetary policy. Because reserve changes on average precede changes in the quantity of money, this different starting point tends to make the response of monetary

---

[26] Figures 12–1 and 12–2 are drawn from the data in Gary Fromm and Lawrence R. Klein, "The NBER/NSF [National Bureau of Economic Research/National Science Foundation] Model Comparison Seminar: An Analysis of Results," in Klein and Burmeister, *Econometric Model Performance,* pp. 402, 405.

policy quicker in the St. Louis Fed model.[27] Nevertheless, the major impressions given by Figure 12–1 are accurate. The St. Louis Fed model indicates that monetary policy operates much more quickly than in the Keynesian models. And the St. Louis Fed model indicates that monetary policy is much stronger than in the Keynesian models (with the exception of the MPS model, where the effects are delayed, but powerful).

Perhaps surprisingly, there are substantial disagreements among the Keynesian models—sufficiently strong, indeed, to provoke a negative conclusion from Carl F. Christ:

> Though the models forecast well over horizons of four to six quarters, they disagree so strongly about the effects of important monetary and fiscal policies that they cannot be considered reliable guides to such policy effects, until it can be determined which of them are wrong in this respect and which (if any) are right.[28]

There is some reason to give particular weight to the MPS results, since that model was designed in cooperation with the Federal Reserve with the explicit objectives of measuring the strength of monetary policy and identifying the channels through which that policy operates. Nevertheless, *this great dispersion of results does underline a problem discussed in Chapter 10: Policymakers live in a world of uncertainty.*[29]

On the fiscal side, there is a strong contrast between the early results of the St. Louis Fed model, on the one hand, and the Keynesian models as a group, on the other. In response to a rise in the rate of government expenditures by $100 *and a continuation* of the expenditures at the higher level, the Keynesian models show a gen-

----

[27] Because of the fractional reserve banking system (described in Chapter 8), the money stock can increase by a multiple of the change in reserves. In order to make an adjustment for this complication, the St. Louis Fed results (which relate to a change in the *money stock*) have been multiplied by five, to make them roughly comparable to the results of other models (which show the effects of a change in *reserves*).

[28] Christ, "Judging the Performance of Econometric Models of the U.S. Economy," in Klein and Burmeister, *Econometric Model Performance*, p. 322.

Christ's statement might seem puzzling, since we might expect that a model that provides good forecasts of aggregate demand should also provide an accurate measure of the effects of policy. This is, however, not necessarily so. For example, a model might give good forecasts of investment by using surveys of business investment intentions; yet this model might not provide a good measure of how monetary policy affects investment.

[29] Furthermore, as Christ's quotation indicates, the uncertainty over the *effects of policy* is greater than the uncertainty over the future course of aggregate demand. Thus, this uncertainty is of the type for which Brainard's analysis is relevant. (Refer back to Chapter 10.)

erally rising level of aggregate demand. In contrast, the St. Louis Fed model indicates only a *temporary* effect of government expenditures on aggregate demand. *GNP* rises by a maximum of $120 during the third quarter but then recedes rapidly, so that the effects of fiscal policy vanish after the fourth quarter. After a relatively brief interlude of higher income, government expenditures result in approximately offsetting reductions in private expenditures.

The revolution had revolved 360°. The early St. Louis Fed model took us back to the old British Treasury view of the early depression: Fiscal policy is essentially useless as a means of stimulating the economy, since additional government spending will simply crowd out a more or less equivalent amount of nongovernment spending, leaving the overall level of aggregate demand more or less unchanged.[30] It was against this very strong antifiscalist view that Keynes had directed his *General Theory*.

The monetarist counterrevolution met with only partial success. The St. Louis Fed model was subjected to criticisms similar to those directed at the Friedman-Meiselman study (discussed earlier). After an auspicious beginning, the St. Louis Fed model performed unevenly. And the strong antifiscal conclusions of the early monetarist models were open to question. The demand for money which this viewpoint implied was at once implausible on theoretical grounds, and contrary to a substantial body of empirical evidence—including the empirical results that were obtained when the St. Louis Fed model was reestimated with data from the 1970s.

THE UNEVEN HISTORY OF THE ST. LOUIS FED MODEL

From the viewpoint of its proponents, the St. Louis Fed model was introduced at a fortunate time—in 1968. In order to cool down the inflation associated with the Vietnam conflict, Congress in the

---

[30] This conclusion would not apply, *if* the fiscal policy were accompanied by a change in the quantity of money. In this case, the change in aggregate demand would be attributed to monetary policy, not to fiscal policy.

Here, there is a problem of separating the semantic difference between monetarists and Keynesians from the difference in substance. Keynesians prefer to consider government spending financed by monetary expansion as fiscal policy and are exasperated by the monetarist insistence on calling this monetary policy.

If the central bank follows a Wicksellian policy of interest rate stabilization, then an increase in government deficit spending will indeed tend to cause a rise in the money supply. For this reason (among others) monetarists believe that fiscal policy is important—even though it will have little effect on aggregate demand if the money supply is unaffected. See Darryl R. Francis, "How and Why Fiscal Actions Matter to a Monetarist," *Federal Reserve Bank of St. Louis Review*, May 1974, pp. 2–7.

middle of 1968 had imposed an income tax surcharge and placed a limitation on federal government spending. On the basis of Keynesian models then in use, there were widespread fears that the Congress had engaged in fiscal overkill, and that a recession would be caused by the magnitude of the fiscal restraint. In order to soften the expected recessionary effect of fiscal policy, the Federal Reserve eased monetary policy. [The money stock (M_1) grew at a very rapid rate of 7.8 percent during 1968.] Thus, monetary and fiscal policies were pointed in opposite directions: Monetary policy was strongly expansionary, while fiscal policies involved substantial restraint.[31] In contrast to the Keynesian models, which suggested that aggregate demand would weaken, the St. Louis Fed model indicated that the fiscal restraint would be swamped by the expansion effects of monetary growth. And what happened? The economy continued to boom through late 1968 and until after very tight monetary policies were introduced in early 1969. The buoyancy of the economy in late 1968 gave credibility to the monetarist approach and caused consternation among fiscalists. In the words of Blinder and Solow, "If the aftermath of the Revenue Act of 1964 made household heroes of [Keynesian] macroeconomists, then the aftermath of the Revenue and Expenditure Control Act of 1968 bid fair to send them scurrying back to their universities with their doctrinal tales [sic] between their legs."[32]

---

[31] In fact, fiscal policy turned out to be somewhat less restrictive than had been expected when the Revenue and Expenditure Control Act was passed in mid-1968. In spite of the limitation on federal government expenditures in the act, federal spending rose by $8.8 billion during 1968, and state and local government expenditures were unexpectedly strong. For details on fiscal policy—and for a balanced evaluation of the 1968 episode—see Blinder and Solow, "Analytical Foundations of Fiscal Policy," pp. 102–15, especially pp. 111–12.

For the argument that the 1968 surcharge was indeed powerful in restraining demand, see Arthur Okun, "The Personal Tax Surcharge and Consumer Demand, 1968–70," *Brookings Papers on Economic Activity*, vol. 1, 1971, pp. 167–200, especially p. 198: "These detailed statistical findings stand in marked contrast to some intuitive conclusions that the surcharge was ineffective in curbing consumer outlays."

[32] Blinder and Solow, "Analytical Foundations of Fiscal Policy," p. 10. The 1964 act involved a substantial tax cut and was followed by the predicted and welcomed expansion of the economy, which continued almost uninterrupted until the end of the decade (with only a very minor pause in the first quarter of 1967). In the mid-1960s, Keynesian economists were indeed household heroes—the issue of *Time* magazine for December 31, 1965 contained a cover story on Keynes.

One economist who conspicuously declined to scurry away with his "tale" between his legs after 1968 was Arthur Okun, the chairman of the Council of Economic Advisers when the 1968 tax act was passsed. On the contrary, Okun concluded that the 1968 episode "provides further confirmation of the general efficacy and continued desirability of flexible changes in personal income tax rates—upward or downward, permanent or temporary" [Okun, "The Personal Tax Surcharge and Consumer Demand, 1968," *Brookings Papers on Economic Activity*, 1971, vol. 1, p. 200].

In spite of its impressive beginning, the St. Louis Fed model in turn was soon thrown into question. During 1970, for example, the economy responded to the expanding money supply much more weakly than forecast by the model. And, during the early 1970s, the model's projections were sufficiently inaccurate that its designers concluded that the St. Louis Fed model "is not suitable for exact quarter-to-quarter forecasting, or even for periods of two or three quarters."[33] Indeed, Andersen and Carlson declared that the objective of the model "was not to forecast economic events, but rather, to assess the impact of alternative monetary and fiscal policies."[34]

Furthermore, the strong antifiscalist conclusions of the St. Louis Fed model began to dissipate as it was reestimated with new data from the 1970s. For example, when Andersen and Carlson reestimated the model using data from 1953–73 (rather than the 1953–68 data used in an earlier version), they found that the estimated demand effect over four quarters of a $100 increase in government spending rose to $54 (compared to their earlier estimate of $5).[35] And, when Benjamin Friedman used even more recent data running into 1976, he found a cumulative first-year government spending multiplier of about 1.5—a result "not very dissimilar to the values reported in familiar nonmonetarist models." He concluded that "Even the St. Louis model now believes in fiscal policy."[36]

In spite of the uneven history of the St. Louis Fed model, the debate over the relative importance of monetary and fiscal policies is likely to be with us for some time to come. It is important to look not only at the empirical evidence—which changes as new data become available—but also at the theoretical problems with the strong antifiscalist position.

THE ANTIFISCAL POSITION: ITS LOGICAL IMPLICATIONS

The proposition that fiscal policy may have a zero effect on aggregate demand deserves a careful evaluation for two reasons. First, monetarists have suggested that fiscal policy may have little effect on aggregate demand. Second, the simple *IS/LM* framework, which is a popular theoretical structure for the analysis of macroeconomic

---

[33] Andersen and Carlson, "St. Louis Model Revisited," p. 55.

[34] Andersen and Carlson, "St. Louis Model Revisited," p. 48.

[35] Andersen and Carlson, "St. Louis Model Revisited," p. 67, Equations 1A and 1B.

[36] Benjamin M. Friedman, "Even the St. Louis Model Now Believes in Fiscal Policy," *Journal of Money, Credit, and Banking*, May 1977, pp. 365–67.

questions, suggests that the effects of fiscal policy will be zero once the interest rate has risen high enough to reduce the speculative demand for money to zero. Presumably, this demand will become zero once interest rates on long-term federal government bonds have risen above the 5 percent to 7 percent range, and once short-term interest rates exceed 2 percent or thereabouts.[37] As interest rates have consistently been at or above these figures in recent years, a straightforward application of the *IS/LM* framework therefore suggests that fiscal policy should have had little, or even zero, effect in recent years. In an earlier chapter, we warned against such a straightforward application; it is now time to explain why.

Reconsider the derivation of the classical range of the *LM* function, originally presented as Figure 6–4 and repeated here as Figure 12–3. The *LM* curve becomes vertical once interest rates have risen above the point at which the speculative demand for money becomes zero, at point *C* in Part D. Once this occurs, there is only one demand for money—the transactions demand. In this simple presentation, the transactions demand (L_t) is a function of national income, and national income only; that is,

$$L_t = kY \tag{12-13}$$

If this equation represents the only demand for money, and if it is rigidly applied, then a rigid version of the quantity theory of money is obtained. In equilibrium, the demand for money equals its supply. M may be substituted for L_t and Equation (12–13) rewritten as:

$$M = kY \tag{12-14}$$

This, of course, is very close to the basic quantity theory Equation (12–1), with k being equal to $1/v$.[38] The income velocity of money will be rigid if the demand for money is a rigid function of national income.

In such a world, aggregate demand depends on money and money alone; fiscal policy has no role to play in the determination of aggregate demand once the speculative demand has disappeared. The question is, how plausible is it to postulate the rigid relationship

---

[37] Since long-term bonds will fall in price more than short-term securities in the event of an upward movement of interest rates, the long-term interest rate needed to compensate for the risk of a capital loss—and therefore needed for the disappearance of the speculative demand for money—will be higher than the short-term interest rate.

[38] Indeed, Equation (12–14) was used by classical economists as an alternative to Equation (12–1), and was known as the Cambridge (England) version of the quantity theory.

Figure 12–3
The *LM* curve

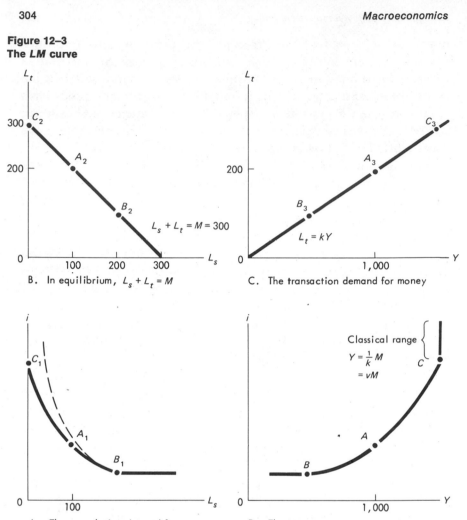

B. In equilibrium, $L_s + L_t = M$

C. The transaction demand for money

A. The speculative demand for money

D. The *LM* curve

The basic *IS/LM* approach suggests a rigid quantity theory, once the speculative demand has reached zero (at point *C*).

between income and the transactions demand represented by Equation (12–13)?

The answer: not very. While it is reasonable to argue that the transactions demand for money depends on income, as shown in Equation (12–13), this equation is *incomplete.* The transactions demand may *also* depend *on other things,* and these things can be affected by fiscal policy. Specifically, the transactions demand for money may also depend on: (1) the composition of aggregate demand, and (2) the interest rate.

Consider the first point. Individuals and institutions hold money as a convenience; the amount they wish to hold will tend to rise as their expected expenditures rise. Thus, it is plausible to argue—in line with Equation (12–13)—that the demand for money depends on the size of national income. But money is not an equal convenience to all individuals and institutions. If borrowing is difficult, time consuming, or irksome—as it is for you or me—then we may wish on average to hold relatively large quantities of money relative to our expenditures. The government, in contrast, has easy, continuing, and well-developed access to the capital markets. Thus, the government can conveniently spend large amounts compared to its average cash balances; if it runs out of cash, it has easy access to borrowed funds. Thus, the government's demand for cash balances may be low compared to its expenditures, causing the velocity of money[39] to be high as it passes through the government's hands. Put another way, when the government increases its spending, it may thereby increase aggregate demand without creating a proportionate demand for money balances. Thus, even if we begin from a classical money supply/money demand starting point, we may plausibly argue that fiscal policy can affect aggregate demand—provided that we are willing to look beyond the very simplest version of money demand.

But, for the present discussion, the second point is even more important, since interest rates already appear explicitly in the *IS/LM* framework. The amount of money that people and institutions on average wish to hold should depend on the opportunity cost of holding money, that is, on the interest foregone by holding cash rather than an interest-bearing asset. The higher the interest rate, the lower should be the demand for transactions balances: At high interest rates, people should manage with less money and be willing to put up with the bother of more trips to and from the savings bank in order to earn interest.

If the transactions demand for money is indeed responsive to changes in the rate of interest, then a significant modification must be made of the *LM* curve in Figure 12–3 and the antifiscal implications of its vertical, classical range. Even after a disappearance of the

---

[39] There is also a definitional complication, which reinforces the conclusion of this paragraph. Cash balances held by the federal government are not included in the measured money stock. Thus, the federal government spends large amounts without technically holding any "money" at all. The larger government spending is (as a percentage of *GNP*), the higher therefore should be the velocity of the measured money stock.

speculative demand for money, expansive fiscal policy will have an effect on aggregate demand. The fiscal expansion will cause a right-ward movement of the *IS* curve. This will push up interest rates. At higher interest rates, the demand for money associated with any given national income will be lower. With a lower demand for money, the existing stock of money will support a higher level of spending; aggregate demand will rise. Put another way, *the responsiveness of the transactions demand to changes in interest rates will eliminate the vertical, strictly classical range of the LM curve; the LM curve will continue to slope gradually upward to the right.*[40] Fiscal policy continues to have an impact on aggregate demand.

There is unanimity among economists that the transactions demand for money *should* respond to interest rate changes. Even Friedman, who takes the strongest classical position, agrees that the theoretical case is persuasive. But in his empirical work, he finds no statistically significant evidence that the interest rate does, in fact, affect the demand for money.[41] In Friedman's view, the effectiveness of fiscal policy cannot be demonstrated along these lines. Friedman's antifiscal position is firm: "I come to the main point—in my opinion, the budget itself has no significant effect on the course of nomi-

---

[40] It is not possible to show the derivation of the correct, upward sloping *LM* curve with a two-dimensional diagram such as Figure 12–3. In Part C, we can show the relationship between the quantity of money demanded and only *one* other variable. Since income is the most important determinant of the transactions demand, it is reasonable to focus on income as that single variable; thus, the effect of interest rates on the transactions demand is ignored.

There is one way of partially dealing with this problem. In Part A, we may show the effect of the interest rate not only on the speculative demand, but also on the transactions demand. This will give a curve of the general form of the light dashes in Figure 12–3, from which a continuously upward-sloping *LM* curve can be derived.

While this approach avoids the major pitfall of Figure 12–3, it is not entirely satisfactory, since the amount of change in the transactions demand in response to a change in the rate of interest depends on the level of the transactions demand; that is, it depends on the level of national income. Strictly speaking, it is not legitimate to divide the transactions demand into two separate parts, one part dependent on income (and shown in Part C) and one part dependent on interest (and included with the speculative demand in Part A). Thus, it is not legitimate to draw the dashed curve in Part A until we already know what the level of income is; we cannot go methodically from one panel to the next. For a strictly legitimate derivation, we must either struggle with the horrors of a three-dimensional diagram, or use algebra.

[41] Milton Friedman, "The Demand for Money: Some Theoretical and Empirical Results," *Journal of Political Economy,* August 1959, p. 329: "In our experiments, the rate of interest had an effect in the direction to be expected but too small to be statistically significant." Friedman's position on the demand for money is not altogether un-ambiguous, however. Contrast the preceding quotation with Milton Friedman, "A Theoretical Framework for Monetary Analysis," *Journal of Political Economy,* March–April 1970, p. 216: "We have been interpreted, wrongly, I believe, as saying that *k* is completely independent of interest rates." (*k* is the *k* of Equation 12–13.)

nal income, on inflation, on deflation, or on cyclical fluctuations."[42]

The views of Friedman's critics on this point have been neatly summarized by Arthur Okun in the bibliography on money and interest appended to his *Political Economy of Prosperity*. The appendix is divided under two headings, the first being: "The following articles report empirical results showing a negative relation between the demand for money and the rate of interest." There follows a list of 25 studies, from the work of Bronfenbrenner and Mayer to that of James Tobin, covering the period from 1939 to 1967. The second part of the appendix, in full:[43]

> The following article reports empirical results showing no relationship between the demand for money and the rate of interest:
> Friedman, Milton. "The Demand for Money: Some Theoretical and Empirical Results," *Journal of Political Economy*, August 1959, pp. 327–51.

A majority does not, of course, define truth; but it is reasonable to proceed on the assumption that the demand for money does, indeed, respond to the rate of interest.[44] Students (and others, too!) should be skeptical of any elasticity that is held to be either zero (as perhaps it is in Friedman's demand for money function) or infinite (as in the Keynesian liquidity trap). Most elasticities lie somewhere between. An effect of fiscal policy on aggregate demand is both plausible on theoretical grounds and supported by the overwhelming body of empirical evidence.

---

[42] Milton Friedman and Walter Heller, *Monetary vs. Fiscal Policy* (New York: W. W. Norton, paperback, 1969), p. 51. In spite of this strong statement, Friedman's exact position on the effectiveness of fiscal policy is open to question. The statement might be compared to his argument in "The Role of Monetary Policy," *American Economic Review*, March 1968, p. 14: "If, as now, an explosive federal budget threatens unprecedented deficits, monetary policy can hold any inflationary dangers in check by a slower rate of growth than would otherwise be desirable." This implies (at least to me) that fiscal changes do affect aggregate demand even if unaccompanied by changes in the rate of growth of the money stock.

[43] Arthur Okun, *The Political Economy of Prosperity* (New York: W. W. Norton, paper, 1970), pp. 146–47. Okun's attribution to Friedman of "empirical results showing *no* relationship . . ." might be compared to Friedman's more cautious statement in the cited article that the interest rate effects were "in the direction to be expected but *too small* to be *statistically significant*." (Italics added in both quotations.)

[44] Regarding statistical problems in the Friedman study, see David E. W. Laidler, *Demand for Money: Theories and Evidence* (Scranton, Pa.: International Textbook Co., 1969), p. 96.

For a more recent discussion of the demand for money—including an analysis of changes in the demand during the mid-1970s—see Stephen M. Goldfeld, "The Case of the Missing Money," *Brookings Papers in Economic Activity*, 1976, vol. 3; and Jared Enzler, Lewis Johnson, and John Paulus, "Some Problems of Money Demand," *Brookings Papers in Economic Activity*, 1973, vol. 1, pp. 261–80.

THE CASE FOR A MONETARY RULE

The belief that money is the key to understanding changes in aggregate demand is only one of the two major views that distinguish monetarists. The other is the belief that a fixed policy rule, involving a steady, stable increase in the money supply, is preferable to discretionary short-term monetary and fiscal policies aimed at stabilizing the economy at a high level of employment and at stable prices.[45]

There are a number of grounds for the monetarist advocacy of a fixed rule for monetary policy. First is the belief that the velocity of money is stable and that money is the most important determinant of aggregate demand. Evidence such as that presented in the Friedman-Meiselman and the St. Louis Fed studies is therefore a major input into the argument for a monetary rule. (It is, however, definitely not a prerequisite; the advocacy of a steady, fixed increase in the money supply greatly antedates the recent monetarist statistical studies.) Second is the view that, in the absence of monetary disturbances, the private economy is basically stable. Here the monetarists differ sharply with the Keynesian view that the private economy is basically unstable, and that full employment can be maintained only with continuing government intervention to maintain a high level of aggregate demand. Third is the view that, left to their own devices, central bankers may concentrate on the wrong thing. In particular, there is a continuing temptation to try to stabilize interest rates. Watching interest rates is a trap; the reserve base and the quantity of money may thereby be subjected to swings (Chapter 11). Fourth is the view that, even if central bankers have a sophisticated understanding of the role of interest rates and changes in the money supply, they may nevertheless destabilize the economy because there are significant and unpredictable lags in the operation of policy; by responding to current conditions, they may destabilize

---

[45] The view that a monetary rule is desirable does not follow directly from the belief that money is important. A person might with perfect consistency argue that money is the most important determinant of aggregate demand, yet at the same time believe that a discretionary monetary policy should be followed in an attempt to stabilize the economy. Nevertheless, as Blinder and Solow note ("Analytical Foundations of Fiscal Policy," p. 63), "belief in monetarism and belief in rules are quite strongly correlated. Why that should be so is an interesting question for a sociologist of science." There is a similar, strong association between the belief that fiscal policy is powerful and the belief that discretionary policies should be used, although once again there is no necessary connection. (One might, for example, argue that fiscal policy is an important determinant of aggregate demand, yet also argue that a rule is desirable—for example, a rule of a balanced full-employment budget. For a discussion of such a fiscal rule, see Blinder and Solow, "Analytical Foundations of Fiscal Policy," pp. 36–45.)

the economy. Fifth is the view that short-run discretionary policies are politically undesirable, and that policy *rules* are more in keeping with a free society.

The first three of these points have been discussed earlier; to the last two we now turn.

Lags in the operation of policy

In Chapter 10, the length of the lags involved in monetary and fiscal policies was recognized as a problem which might detract from the effectiveness of these policies as a means for keeping the economy moving along a high-employment path. In Professor Friedman's view, the length and unpredictability of the lags weigh powerfully against the use of discretionary short-run policies.

The problem is that policymakers may respond in what seems to be a correct manner to contemporary conditions or to those of the recent past, but their policies will influence the economy at some unpredictable future time when they may make matters worse, not better. The possible destabilizing consequences of policy actions are illustrated in Figure 12–4. The solid curve through the figure represents the course of aggregate demand if policy is in some fundamental sense "neutral." Now, suppose that an active policy is followed, and also, in the Friedman tradition, suppose that changes in the money supply are a dominant cause of changes in aggregate demand.

The possible horror scenario runs as follows. Between times *A* and *B*, the Federal Reserve has no firm idea as to the course of the economy. It therefore does what comes easiest, watching interest rates and other conditions in financial markets and acting to stabilize them. In doing so, it allows the money supply to respond to the upward swing of aggregate demand; steam is therefore added to the expansion. Sooner or later, however, it becomes clear that inflationary forces are getting out of hand, and the Federal Reserve takes action to restrain demand—and the Fed overreacts. The restrictive policy followed between times *B* and *C* does not immediately have its major impact, however. Rather, there is a lag until time period *D* to *E,* when the depressing effects of the tight policy make the economic situation worse. The Fed then becomes alarmed at the unemployment rate, and overreacts to lay the basis for the next period of inflation.

This, of course, puts the case in its worst light. But, to argue in favor of a rule, one need not believe that the Federal Reserve *always*

Figure 12–4
Discretionary policy and the problem of lags

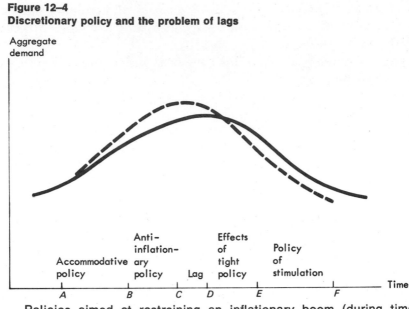

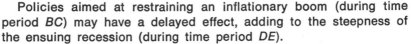

Policies aimed at restraining an inflationary boom (during time
period *BC*) may have a delayed effect, adding to the steepness of
the ensuing recession (during time period *DE*).

does the wrong thing; one need argue only that discretionary policies
on average destabilize the economy. In support of this contention,
a number of historical examples may be cited, of which 1968–69 and
1972–74 are the most interesting. The argument goes as follows.
In the middle of 1968, the long-awaited anti-inflationary tax surcharge was passed. However, the government and the Federal Reserve had only a very imperfect knowledge of the effects of the fiscal
action and exaggerated its importance. Particularly as the tax increase had been accompanied by an expenditure ceiling, there were
fears that the economy might become the victim of fiscal overkill.
To prevent an overreaction of the economy and the onset of a recession, the money supply was allowed to expand rapidly. But demand continued to boom; the increasing money supply set the stage
for continuing inflation in spite of official assurances that "the
corner has been turned" in the anti-inflationary fight. Then, as the
Federal Reserve became increasingly alarmed by the spread of inflationary expectations, they determined to prove that they were
men, and cracked down hard on the rate of monetary expansion in
1969. Following the increase of 7.8 percent in 1968, the money
supply (M_1) expanded by only 3.1 percent during 1969—and at a
seasonally adjusted annual rate of only 1.2 percent in the last half of

1969. (If time deposits are included in the money supply, the contrast between 1968 and 1969 becomes even more dramatic. On this definition, the money supply increased by 9.7 percent during 1968, and *decreased* by 1 percent in 1969.) The result of this overreaction: the recession of 1970.

Then, according to this line of argument, the error was repeated in the early 1970s. Watching a sticky and slowly declining rate of unemployment, the Fed allowed the money stock to expand rapidly in 1972 and early 1973. Inflationary momentum gathered steam. Then, when the inflation rate jumped into double digits (above 10 percent per annum), the Federal Reserve became alarmed and severely restricted the money supply, particularly during the last half of 1974. The result: The worst postwar recession occurred in 1974–75.

This is an argumentative interpretation of the events of 1968–75, and one to which many economists have significant objections.[46] Without getting into the fine points, it suffices here to note that there is clearly enough to the monetarist argument so that it must be treated seriously and not simply dismissed out of hand.[47]

---

[46] Including Arthur Okun, the chairman of the Council of Economic Advisers in 1968. See his "The Personal Tax Surcharge and Consumer Demand, 1968–70," *Brookings Papers on Economic Activity*, 1971, vol. 1, pp. 167–204. Many economists would argue that any summary is grossly incomplete if it makes no mention of the quadrupling of prices by the Organization of Petroleum Exporting Countries (OPEC) in 1973–74. (This episode will be discussed in Chapter 13.)

[47] Monetary policy is the focus of discussion, since the most vigorous debate is over the desirability of a *monetary* rule. However, the same issue may be raised regarding fiscal policies. Have they on average stabilized the economy? Or would adherence to a rule of a stable full-employment budget be better?

Experience with fiscal policies has not been very reassuring. In his study of fiscal policies in seven countries, Bent Hansen found that discretionary policies had on average been destabilizing in three of them, and these destabilizing effects were quite large. (See Table below. Only the discretionary policies in the first column are relevant

Percentage of business cycle eliminated by discretionary and by automatic stabilization policies, 1955–1965

Country	Eliminated by discretionary policy	Eliminated by automatic policy	Total percentage eliminated
Belgium	5	16	21
France*	−35	48	13
Germany*	14	12	26
Italy†	−17	32	15
Sweden	5	n.a.	n.a.
United Kingdom	−10	−3	−13
United States	17	32	49

n.a. = Not available.
* 1958–65.
† 1956–65.
Source: Bent Hansen, *Fiscal Policy in Seven Countries, 1955–1965* (Paris: Organization for Economic Co-operation and Development, 1969), Table 2.6, p. 69. The figures pertain to central governments only.

Economic freedom: Rules versus authority

One of the tenets of conservative political philosophy (or, if you prefer, "liberal" political philosophy in the 19th century sense) is that we should be governed by laws, not men. Reasonably simple and understandable rules should be set down for the guidance of the public, and the area of discretion on the part of the government should be circumscribed, lest power be misused.

The current monetarist proposal for a steady increase in the money supply is based in part on this philosophical viewpoint. Indeed, the desire for a monetary rule may be traced back through the literature, particularly to the 1936 article of Professor Henry C. Simons of the University of Chicago on "Rules vs. Authorities in Monetary Policy."[48] According to Simons,

> In a free enterprise system we obviously need highly definite and stable rules of the game, especially as to money. The monetary rules must be compatible with the reasonably smooth working of the system. Once established, however, they should work mechanically, with the chips falling where they may. To put our present problem as a paradox—we need to design and establish with the greatest intelligence a monetary system good enough so that, hereafter, we may hold to it unrationally—on faith—as a religion, if you please.

The search for such a rule leads to the proposal that the money supply be increased steadily, by a fixed percentage year after year.

THE CASE AGAINST A MONETARY RULE[49]

The philosophical case for the rule is the easiest to dispose of. Upon examination, the apparently sharp distinction between "rules" and "authority" disappears: As Professor Paul Samuelson has ob-

---

to this argument; the automatic effects would still occur if a rule of a stable high-employment budget were followed.) Keynesian Otto Eckstein concluded that "the record of the 1960s seems to repeat the verdict of the 1950s. Discretionary policy did harm as well as good. The automatic [fiscal] policy [rule] developed by the Committee for Economic Development . . . would have done better" [Eckstein, "The 1961–1969 Expansion," in *American Statistical Association, Proceedings of the Business and Economic Statistics Section,* 1969, pp. 327, 329]. For a similar conclusion for Britain, see J. C. R. Dow, *The Management of the British Economy* (Cambridge: Cambridge University Press, 1964), p. 384.

[48] *Journal of Political Economy,* February 1936, pp. 1–30; reprinted in Henry C. Simons, *Economic Policy for a Free Society* (Chicago: University of Chicago Press, 1948), pp. 160–83. The quoted passage is from p. 169.

[49] For a discussion of policy rules, see Arthur M. Okun, "Fiscal-Monetary Activism: Some Analytical Issues," *Brookings Papers on Economic Activity,* 1972, vol. 1, pp. 123–64.

served, a set of rules "is set up by discretion, is abandoned by discretion, and is interfered with by discretion."[50] Indeed, the attempt to draw an unwarranted sharp line between rules and authority led Simons into a logical contradiction. Directly after proclaiming that the monetary rules would have to be followed irrationally, as a religion, "with the chips falling where they may," Simons observed that "the utter inadequacy of the old gold standard, either as a definite system of rules or as the basis of monetary religion, seems beyond intelligent dispute." Precisely. The gold standard caused too many chips to fly—painfully—in the 1930s; its abolition was in order in the light of unfolding events. It was inappropriate to adhere to this rule irrationally, as a religion. The proclaiming of a set of rules does not lift from future generations the responsibility (and, indeed, the *freedom*) to reevaluate the desirability of the rules in the light of their current circumstances.

Thus, there is no sharp logical distinction between "rules" and "discretion." The debate does, however, reflect important differences regarding the appropriate approach to policy. A stress on discretion implies relatively frequent changes in policy; it implies relatively high hopes for the performance of the economy, with fine tuning being used to smooth out relatively modest fluctuations in economic activity. Those who stress the desirability of a monetary rule, on the other hand, emphasize the chances of making a mistake if policies are changed frequently and stress the dangers of attempting to achieve an unattainable degree of prosperity. It is the apparent

---

[50] *The Collected Scientific Papers of Paul A. Samuelson* (Cambridge, Mass.: The MIT Press, 1966), vol. 2, p. 1278. The quotation is from a 1951 essay, "Principles and Rules in Modern Fiscal Policy." The same point is made by Blinder and Solow, "Analytical Foundations of Fiscal Policy," p. 9: "We tend to regard the debate between rules and discretion as more or less pointless, in the sense that it is more or less pointless to debate whether a growing boy should abstain completely from eating between meals; talk is one thing, but nobody can actually keep a young boy's hand out of the cookie jar." The point is repeated on p. 38: "If Congress can make a rule, Congress can break it."

Even if it could be clearly demonstrated that a rule leads to a more stable economy than do discretionary policies, Congress still could—and should—consider departures from the rule from time to time. Stability is not the only objective; Congress has the responsibility to weigh it against other objectives. For example, large military spending was justified in order to defeat Hitler, even though the inflationary consequences were predictable.

Because Congress, the administration, and the Federal Reserve cannot be counted on to "keep their hands out of the cookie jar," we should refine the conditions that must be met to make the case for a rule. To justify a rule, one need argue that monetary and fiscal policies followed by discretionary policymakers will on average lead to a less stable economy than the policies which would in fact be followed if a rule were taken as the starting point for policymaking. This condition clearly makes the debate complex.

willingness of monetarists to settle for relatively modest standards of performance, together with their clear view that the fine tuners are not half as smart as they think they are, which adds spice—and a degree of heat—to the debate over a monetary rule.

The practical question is a relatively simple one: Would the path of aggregate demand be more stable, and would it permit a higher average level of output and employment, if the monetary base were increased steadily, or would these goals be more nearly achieved with continued use of short-term discretionary policies? But if the question is simple, the answer is not. An answer requires, among other things, an agreement over the way in which monetary and fiscal policies affect the economy. But, as is clear from the earlier sections of this chapter, there is a great conflict in views over the determinants of aggregate demand.

But if the answer cannot be categorical, the grounds for rejecting the monetarist prescription are impressive. The monetarist policy rule depends on a reasonably stable velocity; otherwise, a stable growth in the money stock will not assure a stable growth in demand. Yet the experience of the 1970s—as illustrated by the mediocre forecasting performance of the St. Louis Fed model—has cast doubt on the stability of velocity.[51] Equally impressive is the experience of the 1950s, a period when monetary explanations of aggregate demand did poorly. Indeed, using a Friedman monetary equation, Lyle Gramley found an average error of over 3 percent in predicting *GNP* during the 1950s. And this overall average error included a number of notable shortcomings in individual years:

> Annual percentage changes in current income predicted by Friedman's equation are about equal for the three years 1953–55, though

---

[51] In the empirical discussions of this chapter, we have focused on comparative studies which are several years out of date. More recent data strengthen doubts about the stability of velocity. In the mid-1970s, actual observations wandered substantially from the predictions of money demand equations, even when these equations were expanded from a simple dependence on income to include such plausible variables as interest rates. See Goldfeld, "The Case of the Missing Money."

Even if velocity *had* been very stable in the past, we might still have doubts about its future stability because of major changes in the financial system. (Stable past relationships need not continue into the future—as we shall see in another context in our chapter on consumption.) The growing use of savings deposits in making payments, and the current debate over the payment of interest on demand deposits, blurs the distinction between money and other financial assets. It raises questions about the proper definition of money (which would obviously have to be settled if money—however defined—were to be held to a stable growth path) and casts doubt as to whether any single measure of money is adequate for policymaking. See Board of Governors of the Federal Reserve System, *Improving the Monetary Aggegates. Report of the Advisory Committee on Monetary Statistics* (processed, March 1976) .

you will remember that income growth turned negative in the recession year 1954 and rose sharply in 1955. His equation also predicts an acceleration of income growth in the recession year 1958 and a slight reduction in the boom year 1959. And if its description of short-term economic changes leaves something to be desired, its longer term predictions are even more astonishing. The predicted growth of nominal income over the ten years 1952–61 as a whole is only a bit over one half as large as the actual growth that took place.

If these results surprise you, they shouldn't since there has always been a good deal of variability in the M_2-GNP relation. The facts are there to read in Professor Friedman's *Monetary History of the United States*. Annual variations of 3 percent or more in the income velocity of M_2 are the rule, not the exception. They occur in two thirds of the some 90-odd years covered by the study. Even if the first 12 years of this period of history are thrown out on grounds of unreliable data, as Friedman suggests, and if the years of the Great Depression and the two world wars are also discarded, for reasons that are not so clear, annual velocity changes of 3 percent or more still occur in more than one half of the remaining years.[52]

The case for the rule is simply not proven. And the burden of proof must lie with the proponents of a monetary rule—even if references to falling chips and steadfast religion are duly discounted. Three things of importance have, however, come out of the monetarist controversy:

1. There has been a needed antidote to the tendency of economists steeped in the Keynesian tradition to downgrade the importance of monetary policies.
2. Attention has been once more focused on the traps which face the monetary policymaker, and, in particular, the unfortunate consequences which may follow if the stabilization of interest rates becomes the primary short-run policy objective.
3. There has been a general, and desirable, presumption created that, *unless there are good reasons to the contrary,* monetary expansion should be kept within reasonably narrow limits. Thus, the Federal Reserve has acquiesced to strong congressional pressure to state monetary growth objectives and to aim for those

[52] Lyle E. Gramley, "Guidelines for Monetary Policy—the Case against Simple Rules," mimeographed (1969); reprinted in Warren L. Smith and R. L. Teigen, *Readings in Money, National Income, and Stabilization Policy,* 3d ed. (Homewood, Ill.: Richard D. Irwin, 1974), pp. 422–426. (In 1977, Gramley became a member of the Council of Economic Advisers.)

objectives. Targets for the growth of the money stock have also been enunciated in a number of foreign countries, such as Canada and Germany.[53]

KEY POINTS

1. According to monetarists:
   a. Monetary policy is much more important than fiscal policy as a determinant of aggregate demand.
   b. Because of the lengthy and unpredictable lags in the operation of monetary and fiscal policies, it is inadvisable for the authorities to fine tune the level of aggregate demand with frequent adjustments in aggregate demand policies. Rather, they should follow a basic, stable policy aimed at a consistent increase in the money supply. For example, they should follow a "monetary rule," aiming at a steady increase in the money supply by, say, 4 percent per annum.
2. In their statistical study, Friedman and Meiselman found that velocity has been more stable than the multiplier in the United States. Hence, they concluded that monetary policy was a more stable and dependable tool than fiscal policy for influencing aggregate demand.
3. Three major objections may be made to the Friedman-Meiselman findings:
   a. Since they were observing the statistical tendency of money and aggregate demand changes to occur together, they were picking up the effects of both (i) changes in the money supply on aggregate demand, and (ii) changes in aggregate demand on the money supply. In the evaluation of the effects of monetary policy on aggregate demand, only (i) and not (ii) is relevant. Since the statistics reflect causation in both directions, the statistical results give an exaggerated view of the strength of effect (i).
   b. A simple equation is taken as representative of each theory by Friedman and Meiselman. This provides an adequate presentation of the quantity theory, which is very clean and

---

[53] On the Canadian experience, see Thomas J. Courchene, *Monetarism and Controls: The Inflation Fighters* (Montreal: C. D. Howe Research Institute, December 1976), especially chap. 3, "Embracing Monetarism."

simple. However, in practical applications, rather complicated versions of the Keynesian theory are normally used.
Thus, it can be argued that Friedman and Meiselman have
provided an oversimplified and inadequate test of Keynesian
fiscal theory.

   c. Quantity theorists do not specify in detail how monetary
policy is expected to work, and the Friedman-Meiselman
study does not provide a test of the detailed steps in the
operation of monetary policy.

4. As contrasted to statistical models incorporating Keynesian views
(such as the MPS model), the model developed by Andersen
and Jordan and the Federal Reserve Bank of St. Louis indicated
that monetary policy has a much greater effect on aggregate demand, and fiscal policy has a much smaller effect (Figure 12–2).
The controversy over the Andersen-Jordan model is broadly
similar to the controversy over the Friedman-Meiselman study.

5. Recent data have undercut the antifiscalist conclusions of the
early St. Louis Fed model. Furthermore, the strong antifiscalist
position is implausible on theoretical grounds. It presupposes
(among other things) that the interest elasticity of the demand
for money is very low.

6. On the policy side, targets have been announced for money
growth in a number of countries, for example, in Canada, Germany, and the United States.

QUESTIONS

1. Suppose that the following events are observed. What should
we conclude about the causal relationships when:

   a. The sale of gasoline is high in countries where automobile
sales are high.

   b. The sales of shoes in the United States tend to be high
during the years when the sales of dishwashers are also high.

   c. The crop of wheat tends to be high during years when the
rainfall the preceding spring is high.

   d. The crop of corn in Kansas is large in the same years in
which there is a large corn crop in Missouri.

   e. There was a large number of upsets in the National Football League last Sunday. Of the seven matches between previously high-ranked teams and previously low-ranked teams, the low-ranked teams were winners in five of the cases.

2. Suppose that we also know something about the time sequence in cases *a* and *b* above. Suppose:

   a. A boom in automobile sales *precedes* a boom in gasoline sales in all countries observed.

   b. High sales of shoes *precede* high sales of dishwashers.

   How, if at all, does this affect the causal conclusions we can reach in these two cases?

3. Suppose that a strong relationship is found statistically between increases in the money stock and increases in national income two quarters later. Does this demonstrate that the primary causation runs from money to income, and not the other way? Is it possible to argue, in spite of the time sequence, that money stock changes respond passively to changes in national income?

SUGGESTED READINGS

Alan S. Blinder and Robert M. Solow, "Analytical Foundations of Fiscal Policy," in Blinder, et al., *The Economics of Public Finance* (Washington, DC: Brookings Institution, 1974), pp. 3–115.

Milton Friedman and Anna J. Schwartz, *A Monetary History of the United States, 1867–1960* (Princeton: Princeton University Press, 1963), chapters 7, 13.

Lyle E. Gramley, "Guidelines for Monetary Policy—The Case against Simple Rules," in Warren L. Smith and R. L. Teigen, *Readings in Money, National Income, and Stabilization Policy,* 3d ed. (Homewood, Ill.: Richard D. Irwin, 1974), pp. 422–26.

Arthur M. Okun, "Fiscal-Monetary Activism: Some Analytical Issues," *Brookings Papers on Economic Activity,* 1972, vol. 1, pp. 123–64.

PART FOUR

CONSUMPTION, INVESTMENT, AND AGGREGATE SUPPLY: A CLOSER LOOK

Real people
have a funny habit
of not doing
what economists presume they do.

Franklin M. Fisher

Chapter 13

Aggregate supply and the inflation-unemployment dilemma

The connection between [unemployment and inflation] . . . is the principal domestic burden of presidents and prime ministers, and the major area of controversy and ignorance in macroeconomics.*

James Tobin

In the early chapters, simple functions have been used to represent rather complex economic phenomena. The response of the economy to changes in aggregate demand was assumed to be very simple and straightforward. Increases in demand up to a well-defined point of full employment result in an increase in real output, with no change in the average price level. Beyond the point of full employment, increases in demand cause a rise in prices, with no change in real output. This gave a simple aggregate supply function, originally shown in Figure 2–3 and reproduced here as Figure 13–1. Similarly, consumption and investment were represented by very simple functions (Chapters 3–5). The purpose of this series of chapters is to look much more closely at each of these functions.

---

* From "Inflation and Unemployment," *American Economic Review*, March 1972, p. 1.

Figure 13–1
The simple Keynesian aggregate supply function

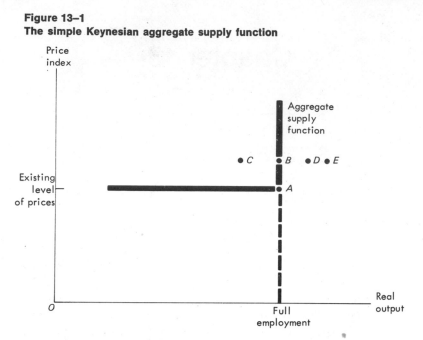

In simple Keynesian theory, this aggregate supply function was usually assumed. Up to the point of full employment (*A*), an increase in demand will cause an increase in output, with no change in the average level of prices. Thereafter, an increase in demand will cause inflation.

AGGREGATE SUPPLY

In the previous chapters, attention has been focused on aggregate demand and on the ways in which monetary and fiscal policies influence demand. But the behavior of the economy depends not only on aggregate demand; aggregate supply is also important. An increase in aggregate demand may cause an increase in output, or an increase in prices, or a combination of the two, depending on supply conditions.

In the first two decades after the appearance of Keynes' *General Theory* in 1936, macroeconomists were preoccupied with aggregate demand and its determinants. Because of the overriding concern with demand, macroeconomists usually assumed the simple function of Figure 13–1.[1] Once such a function was assumed, the objective of

[1] Even in the earliest days of the Keynesian revolution, this was recognized as an oversimplification. One complication was that prices might not be absolutely rigid in a downward direction. But the possibility of deflation was not considered very im-

macroeconomic policy became simple: manage aggregate demand to get as close as possible to point *A*, where there would be full employment and stable prices. (It was, however, recognized that the *achievement* of this objective might not be simple. Because of destabilizing forces in the economy, it would be difficult to get to point *A* and hold the economy consistently at or near that target.)

During the past two decades, the deficiencies of this simple approach to aggregate supply have become increasingly obvious; it doesn't fit the facts. Most notable was the behavior of the economy during the recession of 1974–75: The unemployment rate shot upward, while prices continued to rise at a rapid rate. The economy suffered simultaneously from high unemployment and a high rate of inflation.

In order to look in detail at the experience of recent decades, it is helpful to modify the simple Keynesian diagram (Figure 13–1), relabeling the axes with the two major macroeconomic problems— unemployment and inflation. When this is done, the backward L of Figure 13–1 flips over to become the normal L of Figure 13–2. Since

Figure 13–2
The simple Keynesian aggregate supply function: A translation

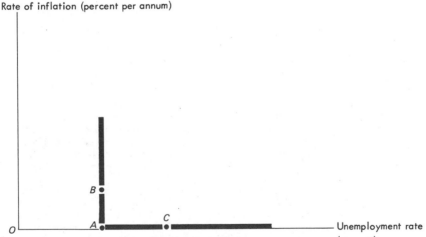

The simple Keynesian aggregate supply function of Figure 13–1 can be translated into this diagram, with unemployment and inflation on the two axes.

portant, since Keynes had demonstrated to most economists' satisfaction that price reductions were basically irrelevant as a way of getting out of a depression.

For a more complex early Keynesian aggregate supply function—but one that still assumes downward inflexibility of wages and prices—see Appendix A to this chapter.

the *rate of change of prices* (that is, the rate of inflation) is put on the vertical axis, the horizontal part of the function falls along the X-axis; so long as prices are at their existing level, the rate of inflation is zero. And, when unemployment (rather than output) is put on the X-axis, an increase in demand will cause the economy to move to the left, toward *A*. Once full employment is reached, any additional increase in demand will cause inflation; the economy will move up the vertical section of the function toward *B*. (Full employment does not mean that the unemployment rate is *zero*. Frictional unemployment cannot be eliminated by increases in aggregate demand.) Thus, if Figure 13–1 is valid, then real-world observations should fall on or near the L-shaped function in Figure 13–2.[2]

THE FACTS

When we look at the observations for the past several decades, a disaster results (Figure 13–3). Not only do the historical observations fail to lie along a well-defined L-shaped function, but it is hard to discern any systematic relationship at all between inflation and unemployment.

The importance of this problem for macroeconomic policy can scarcely be exaggerated. If the economy does not respond in a predictable way to changes in aggregate demand, then the foundation for aggregate demand management is severely shaken. An increase in demand that is aimed at increasing real output and employment

---

[2] In addition to focusing on the two main macroeconomic problems, Figure 13–2 avoids major difficulties which would arise if historical observations were plotted directly on a diagram such as Figure 13–1. Even if the theory were precisely correct, there might be observations both above and to the left of point *A*, and above and to the right of point *A* (Figure 13–1); the data would not necessarily fall along a well-defined function.

Why? Suppose that, starting at the full-employment position *A* in Figure 13–1, aggregate demand increases. Prices will increase to B; thus, a new price level becomes established. Now, if aggregate demand falls, prices will not go back down to their original level; by assumption, they are inflexible downward. Rather, the economy will move to point *C*, with unemployment and with prices remaining at their high level. Then, if aggregate demand rises to full employment and grows enough to maintain full employment, points such as *D* and *E* will be observed. In a growing economy, the full-employment level of output moves progressively to the right.

These difficulties are avoided in Figure 13–2. If, after an inflationary surge to *B*, aggregate demand falls, then the economy will move to *C* (provided that the theory is right). While *prices* have not fallen back to their original level, the *rate of inflation* has receded to zero; *C* is on the original L-shaped function. And, as the economy grows, points of stable prices and low unemployment will coincide. The *D* and *E* of Figure 13–1 will fall on point *A* in Figure 13–2.

Figure 13–3
Inflation and unemployment: The facts

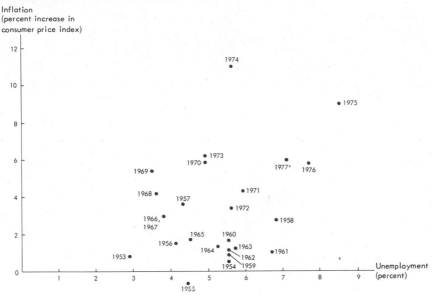

* Preliminary.

The observations of the past two and a half decades form no clear pattern.

may cause a price rise instead. And demand restraint aimed at price stabilization may result instead in a fall in real output. Making sense of Figure 13–3 therefore is one of the major tasks facing macroeconomists; it has occupied an increasing share of their time over the past two decades.

By joining the points chronologically (Figure 13–4), we can take the first step toward making sense of the historical observations. And we can identify three consecutive puzzles which faced economic theorists:

1. During the late 1950s (and most notably in 1958), prices continued to rise even during periods of high unemployment. Inflation could no longer be seen as a simple result of too much demand chasing too few goods.
2. During the 1960s, the economy moved along a reasonably smooth curve, known as a Phillips curve.
3. During the 1970s, observations were above and to the right of

Figure 13–4
Inflation and unemployment: Making sense

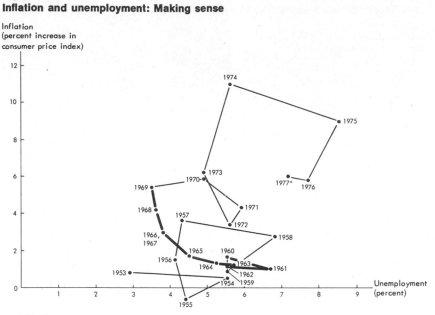

* Preliminary.

When the points are joined, three things may be observed:

1. Inflation and unemployment got worse in the late 1950s.
2. The 1960s traced out a curve.
3. The combined problems of unemployment and inflation were much worse in the 1970s than in the 1960s.

the curve for the 1960s. The twin problems of inflation and unemployment became more acute.

Each of these sets of observations inspired considerable theoretical work and led to controversial policy proposals. To provide order to a confusing and difficult topic, we will consider each of these three points in historical sequence.

PRICE INCREASES WITH UNEMPLOYMENT:
COST-PUSH INFLATION

. . . the age of Keynesian economics is over; the macroeconomic revolution in fiscal and monetary management we owe to Keynes has run afoul of the microeconomic revolution in trade union and corporate power.

John Kenneth Galbraith

As the economy slid down into the recession in 1957–58, inflation persisted. This coincidence of inflation and unemployment suggested that there must be some explanation for inflation other than the upward "pull" on prices from an excessive aggregate demand. With relatively high rates of unemployment, the increase in prices could not be attributed simply to too much demand. An alternative explanation was therefore put forward: Inflation was caused by the upward *push* of costs.

The cost-push argument quickly became rather confused, but its central proposition was straightforward.[3] There were groups within the economy which had significant power to set prices or wages, and they continued to push prices and wages upward even in the absence of a high or rising level of demand. This proposition clearly invited the search for culprits.[4] The same basic argument appeared in widely differing incarnations: Labor blamed the powerful corporations for pushing up prices in their greed for "fantastic profits," while business executives blamed the aggressive and "irresponsible" bargaining of labor unions, which raised their costs and put them in a position where they were impelled to raise prices in order to make ends meet.

The policy implications of the cost-push argument were very disturbing. In particular, aggregate demand policies as a means of controlling inflation were thrown into question. Suppose for the moment that the cost-push argument is essentially correct; the push from the cost side is the predominant cause of inflation. Suppose, also, that the Federal Reserve responds to inflation by a tightening of monetary policy. What happens? Interest rates are pushed up by the tighter monetary policy. But interest payments are an element of business costs. If the upward march of costs is the major reason for inflation, the increase in interest costs will tend to *add* to inflation, not ease it. Alternatively, suppose that the government attempts to stop inflation by an increase in taxation. If the additional taxes take the form of sales taxes or taxes on business, they will add to the costs of products, pushing up prices. In general, the cost-push inflation argument suggests that monetary *expansion* and tax *cuts* may be the appropriate policies to stop inflation, since such policies will reduce the costs of bringing goods and services to the market.

---

[3] A readable and detailed account is given in William G. Bowen, *The Wage-Price Issue: A Theoretical Analysis* (Princeton: Princeton University Press, 1960).

[4] Paul McCracken, who served as the chairman of the Council of Economic Advisers from 1969 to 1971, has sadly observed that "one of the less impressive characteristics of this age is a recidivistic tendency towards demonology."

This is clearly the direct opposite of policy prescriptions based on aggregate demand analysis.

There are, however, several reasons for discounting the upside-down aggregate demand prescriptions of the cost-push argument. First, much of the evidence used to substantiate the existence of cost-push forces does not, upon reflection, make a very good case. For example, the large increases in negotiated wage settlements during periods of inflation are sometimes presented as evidence of strong cost pressures originating from the power of labor unions. Yet, even if there were no union power whatsoever and inflation were completely the result of demand pull, wage rates might be expected to increase rapidly during inflationary periods. An excess demand inflation will tend to pull up prices across a broad spectrum —including the price of labor.[5]

The second reason for discounting the upside-down aggregate demand policy prescriptions of the cost-push thesis is even more important. The cost-push forces which do exist in the economy may be the result of *lags in the response of the economy* to changing aggregate demand conditions. Suppose, for example, that excess demand causes a significant upward movement of prices. Wage contracts will come to reflect expectations of future prices; a wage increase will be built into the labor contract for the coming three years or so. Now, if the growth of demand slows down, there may be a period of unemployment, while wages continue to increase in line with the previously negotiated contract. Cost-push is the apparent problem. But this is a very partial view; the present cost-push is the result of *earlier* excess demand. If cost-push is taken as the basic or sole reason for inflation, and if monetary policy is eased and taxes cut, the basis for a continuing demand inflation will be laid.

Cost-push may thus reflect the importance of *lags* in the response of the economy to changes in aggregate demand. In the face of an increase in aggregate demand, output will tend to respond most quickly; as demand rises, the initial reaction is to produce more. As time passes, however, the increase in demand will be reflected in rising prices and wages. On the other side, when demand declines, output will again respond first. Output will decline, even though prices and wages will continue upward, based on previously negotiated contracts. Only relatively slowly will wages and prices respond to the changing demand conditions.

---

[5] On the problems of interpreting the evidence on cost-push, see Paul A. Samuelson and Robert M. Solow, "Analytical Aspects of Anti-Inflation Policy," *American Economic Review,* May 1960, pp. 177–94.

The cost-push problem therefore underlines the discussion of earlier chapters regarding lags in the operation of aggregate demand policy. It underlines the desirability of policies designed for a moderate, continuous, *steady* expansion of aggregate demand.

Two other policy implications of the cost-push argument might be noted. A policy dilemma arises if cost-push elements are a significant contributing force in inflation. Costs will be pushed up— and the short-run inflation exacerbated—if an attempt is made to deal with the long-run problem by restraining aggregate demand with tight monetary policies or with increases in taxes. There is, however, one way of restraining aggregate demand which does not contribute to short-run cost increases, namely, a reduction of government spending. Where cost-push forces are judged to be strong, *cuts in government spending therefore should be given prominent consideration in the development of anti-inflationary programs.*[6] (In terms of their cost-push consequences, personal income tax increases may be placed in an intermediate category between sales taxes and cuts in spending. Personal income taxes do not directly add to costs in the way sales taxes do; but, when rising income taxes cut into take-home pay, labor unions may be more militant in pushing for higher wage settlements.)[7]

Second, since cost-push forces may be the result of lags, it may be desirable to *speed the transition* to a lower rate of inflation by the imposition of wage and price controls. This presupposes, of course, that an equilibrium is possible with a lower rate of inflation; that is, it presupposes that wage-price controls will be used *in conjunction with restraint* on the aggregate *demand* side, and *not* as a *substitute* for restraint on demand. Wage and price controls will be considered in a later section of this chapter.

Demand-shift inflation

The cost-push argument is also an element in a more complex explanation of inflation, the demand-shift theory of Charles L.

---

[6] The argument of this paragraph is important. It has been particularly stressed by Blinder and Solow. (They declare that its absence from most textbooks is "almost embarrassing," because it is so obvious.) See Alan S. Blinder and Robert M. Solow, "Analytical Foundations of Fiscal Policy," in Blinder, et al., *The Economics of Public Finance* (Washington, DC: Brookings Institution, 1974), pp. 98–101.

[7] Robert J. Gordon has estimated that each 1 percent increase in the personal tax rate will result in about a ⅙ percent increase in wage rates in the short run (Gordon, "Inflation in Recession and Recovery," *Brookings Papers on Economic Activity*, 1971, vol. 1, pp. 105–58).

Schultze.[8] In a rapidly changing economy, in which the composition of demand among various goods and services is significantly shifting, excess demand will occur in some sectors even though the overall level of aggregate demand is not excessive. Prices will be bid up in the sectors of high demand. Prices in the sectors of declining demand may be sticky in a downward direction, and, indeed, there will be upward price pressures from the segments of excess demand, insofar as these products (with their higher prices) are used as inputs in the relatively declining sectors. Furthermore, the expanding sectors may bid up the price of labor and other inputs, adding to the cost-push on the declining sectors. Thus, changes in the composition of demand will lead to an upward movement of prices as a combined result of demand-pull in the expanding sectors, and cost-push in the relatively contracting sectors. The implication of the demand-shift theory: Some level of inflation is the price to be paid for a dynamic and prosperous economy.

THE PRICE-UNEMPLOYMENT DILEMMA: THE PHILLIPS CURVE

But if the demand-shift explanation of inflation blurred the line between "cost-push" and "demand-pull" inflation, the research of A. W. Phillips completely obliterated it. Phillips concluded that there was a *conflict between the objectives of stable prices and full employment.* An increase in demand could reduce the level of unemployment, but this gain would be acquired at the cost of a higher rate of inflation.

Phillips found that the relationship between the rate of change of wages and the unemployment rate had remained quite stable in the United Kingdom during the 1861–1957 period that he studied. The data for 1948–57, for example, came quite close to the curve fitted for 1861–1913, as can be seen in Figure 13–5.[9] Since there is a close (although by no means precise) relationship between changes in wages and changes in prices, a similar curve is observed when the rate of price change is put on the vertical axis (Figure 13–6). In this case, however, the curve will shift down by about two percentage points: Since labor productivity in Britain increases by

---

[8] "Recent Inflation in the United States," Study paper No. 1 of study of *Employment, Growth, and Price Levels* (Washington, DC: Joint Economic Committee, United States Congress, 1959.)

[9] A reproduction of Figure 10 from A. W. Phillips, "The Relation between Unemployment and the Rate of Change of Money Wage Rates in the United Kingdom, 1861–1957," *Economica,* November 1958, pp. 282–99.

Figure 13–5
Wage rate changes and unemployment, United Kingdom, 1948–1957

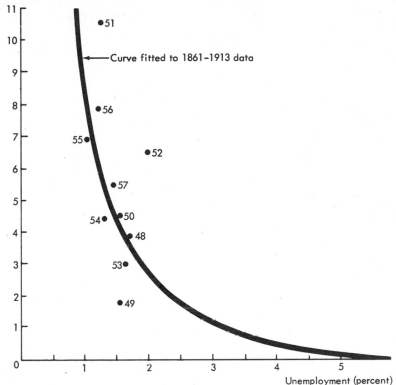

Rate of change of money wages
(percent per year)

Unemployment (percent)

Phillips found that British observations from 1861 to 1957 traced out a smooth, curved relationship between changes in money wages and the unemployment rate. This was the original Phillips curve.

about 2 percent per annum, wage rates can, on average, rise by about 2 percent more than prices. The term "Phillips curve" is applied both to Figures 13–5 and 13–6. A similar curve is traced out by U.S. observations during the 1960s—as was shown in Figure 13–4. (Indeed, Arthur M. Okun has concluded that the data for 1954–68 "fit a hyperbola like a glove.") [10]

---

[10] "Inflation: Its Mechanics and Welfare Costs," *Brookings Papers on Economic Activity*, 1975, vol. 2, p. 354. In 1968–69, Okun served as the chairman of the Council of Economic Advisers. See also, Council of Economic Advisers, *Annual Report*, January 1969, chap. 3.

Figure 13–6
The inflation-unemployment tradeoff: United Kingdom, 1861–1957

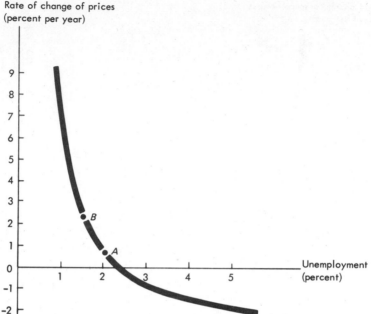

Because productivity increases, money wages rise more than prices. In other words, prices rise less than wages. Thus, this curve—showing the relationship between the rate of price changes (inflation) and unemployment—is lower than the curve of Figure 13–5.

The Phillips curve implied that policymakers face a powerful *dilemma.* The choice of a high level of employment would involve a *continuing* upward movement of prices (for example, at point *B* in Figure 13–6). Furthermore, there was no obvious point to pick, and, indeed, the concept of full employment itself became quantitatively imprecise. The *tradeoff* between the goals of full employment and stable prices was continuous. Demand could be suppressed below that at point *B* (Figure 13–6) in order to restrain price increases, but, if a lower or zero rate of inflation were chosen, this would involve a continuing high rate of unemployment.

Phillips presented his statistical results without any detailed explanation; the Phillips curve has been called "an empirical finding in search of a theory."[11] Most explanations of the Phillips curve include cost-push elements, suggesting that these elements become powerful only when a favorable environment has been created by a high level of demand. (Thus, the distinction between demand-pull and cost-push inflation is obliterated.) For example, it has been suggested that the Phillips curve is the result of the bargaining strategy of labor unions, and of the response of employers to tight market conditions.

The Phillips curve and the labor market

In the labor market, there are always workers looking for jobs. This is true even during periods of very high demand, when some workers voluntarily quit work and accept temporary unemployment while they look for better jobs. On the other side of the market, there are always some unfilled jobs, even during periods of recession. When employees retire, die, or quit, employers may not immediately fill their positions by hiring new workers; there may be some time lag while a search is made for qualified or interested applicants. Thus, there is continuously a process of search going on in the market. There is a group of unemployed workers looking for appropriate jobs; and there are job openings for which appropriate applicants are being sought.

There is, of course, no reason why the number of workers seeking jobs must be equal to the number of available job vacancies. During recessions, the number of job seekers exceeds the number of job vacancies, while the number of vacancies exceeds the number of available workers during periods of boom. (Indeed, one of the suggested definitions of full employment is a situation in which job seekers are equal to job vacancies. This definition is not, however, generally used in empirical work because of the difficulty of defining and measuring job vacancies.) [12]

---

[11] James Tobin, "Inflation and Unemployment," *American Economic Review*, March 1972, p. 9.

[12] The difficulty of defining a job vacancy may be illustrated with an example. The economics department of almost every university in America would have a job opening if a Paul Samuelson or a James Tobin were to indicate an interest. This does not, however, mean that there are job "vacancies" in a relevant market sense. The difficulty in defining "vacancies" is that quality is a continuous variable and the number of vacancies depends in part on the quality of applicants available. This is not to say that evidence is completely lacking on job vacancies. For example, the government publishes an index of the amount of help-wanted advertising.

Thus, there are a number of important variables that determine the state of the labor market. These variables, which are inter-related, include:

1. The time and effort it takes workers to seek out and find appropriate jobs.
2. On the other side of the market, the time and effort it takes employers to find qualified workers to fill their job openings.
3. The "square pegs-round holes" problem; that is, the degree of mismatch between the qualifications of those out of work and the qualifications sought by prospective employers. (This mismatch may work against the highly trained as well as against the unskilled. Employers hesitate to hire an applicant who is overqualified for the available opening, because overqualified employees are likely to continue to look around and leave when better positions become available.)
4. The number of job vacancies compared to the number of available workers; that is, the demand for workers to fill available slots compared to the available supply of labor.

It is reasonable to expect that the rate of change of wages will depend on the pressures in the labor market. The greater is the competition among employers for the available supply of labor, the more difficult it will be for the employer to find an appropriate applicant. As the time of the search lengthens and the costs of leaving the position unoccupied rise, the employer may respond by offering a higher wage. On the other side, the smaller the demand for labor, the more difficult it will be for unemployed workers to find the jobs they want; and they will be under increasing pressure to accept whatever is available, even if they consider the wage unreasonably low. Thus, because of the natural responses of employers and workers, wages will tend to move up more rapidly as the demand for labor increases relative to its supply. This will be a continuous relationship: The greater the demand for labor, the greater will be the wage increase, and the lower will be the unemployment rate.

Consider the response of the labor market to an increase in aggregate demand starting from a high initial rate of unemployment. At first, as job vacancies are created by the rising level of demand, they will be quickly filled. The change in labor market conditions will be reflected primarily in a fall in the unemployment rate, with relatively little effect on wages. As demand continues to rise, however, the effects will be progressively felt in terms of a rise in vacancies; it will be increasingly difficult for employers to fill their vacancies quickly. In order to cut down the costs of search, they will be encouraged to offer higher wages.

On the other side of the market, labor unions must balance their twin objectives of higher wages and job security for their members. When times are generally bad, they give primary attention to job security, and wage rates become a secondary matter. As conditions improve, however, they turn their attention increasingly to the wage objective, and employers become increasingly willing to grant wage increases because of the buoyant demand for their products. These changes do not come suddenly when some specific point of "full employment" is reached. Rather, there is a continuous change in emphasis as unemployment gets smaller and smaller. On theoretical grounds, it is reasonable to expect the responses in the labor market to give a function similar to the Phillips curve. The Phillips curve has found its theory—at least at a simple level.[13]

POLICIES TO DEAL WITH THE PHILLIPS CURVE DILEMMA

It is hard to exaggerate the importance of the dilemma presented by the Phillips curve: It involved a conflict between the goals of full employment and price stability. Policymakers could choose high rates of employment, but this would involve a continuing upward movement of prices; or they could choose stable prices, but this would involve continuously high unemployment.

Policy proposals to deal with the inflation-unemployment dilemma are perhaps even more controversial than is usual in the field of economic policy. The high ratio of heat to light generated in the dilemma debate is due to two major causes: The problem is very important, dealing with the basic social objectives of full employment and stable prices, and it is very imperfectly understood. (As will be seen in the following pages, significant complications and disagreements arise when the simple labor market theory of the Phillips curve is elaborated.)

During the 1960s, when the preponderance of evidence suggested

---

[13] For much more sophisticated and complex treatments, see Robert E. Hall, "The Process of Inflation in the Labor Market," *Brookings Papers on Economic Activity,* 1974, vol. 2, pp. 343–93; Edmund S. Phelps, ed., *Microfoundations of Employment and Inflation Theory* (New York: W. W. Norton, 1970), especially Phelps, "Introduction," pp. 1–23; Charles C. Holt, "Job Search, Phillips' Wage Relation, and Union Influence: Theory and Evidence," pp. 53–123; and Phelps, "Money Wage Dynamics and Labor Market Equilibrium," pp. 124–66.

that there was a well-defined Phillips curve, there were two possible strategies in the face of the inflation-unemployment dilemma:

1. Choose the best point on the existing Phillips curve, picking the least painful combination of inflation and unemployment.
2. Attempt to move to an even better position (below and to the left of the Phillips curve) by restraints or controls on prices and wages, aimed at keeping the inflation rate down as the economy expands toward a high level of unemployment.

Choose the full-employment objective, and learn to live with inflation

The costs of unemployment are much greater and much more obvious than the costs of inflation. Unemployment represents a dead loss to society; productive capacities of the work force are utterly wasted. Unemployment falls unequally on different social, racial, and age groups; it involves social costs beyond the loss of physical production. A rise in prices is less clearly a problem. There is a gainer (the seller) and a loser (the buyer) as a result of each price increase. Thus, one suggested response to the Phillips curve dilemma is to concentrate on the more important employment objective. According to this viewpoint, expansive aggregate demand policies should be chosen in order to achieve a low unemployment rate— even though this will mean living with inflation. For example, the objective of policy might be to aim for a point close to the 1966–67 observations in Figure 13–4. The major objection to this policy—to which we will return in our discussion of the 1970s— is that such a point may be unstable; it may not be possible to remain permanently at such a point by aggregate demand management.

Wage-price guideposts and controls[14]

If the problem is an upward creep of prices and wages prior to the achievement of the employment objective, then an obvious possible solution suggests itself: Take direct steps to prevent the rise in prices and wages. In the United States, there have been a number of efforts along these lines, including the wage-price guideposts of the Kennedy-Johnson administrations, and the wage-price freeze and

[14] For a history of the U.S. experience, see Craufurd D. Goodwin, ed., *Exhortation and Controls: The Search for a Wage-Price Policy, 1945–1971* (Washington, DC: Brookings Institution, 1975).

controls of the Nixon administration. (The United States has also experimented with more extensive price controls, particularly during World War II. However, the objective then was not to ease the dilemma of the wage-price tradeoff, but rather to suppress the price effects of excess aggregate demand.)

The Kennedy and Johnson administrations were concerned that price increases would cause resistance to the expansive policies necessary for the achievement of a high level of employment. (Recognizing the fuzziness of the full-employment concept, they set a reduction of the unemployment level to 4 percent as an "interim" goal.) In order to restrain price and wages increases, guideposts were set for wages and prices:

1. Generally, prices should not be raised.
2. Generally, wages should increase no more than the rate of growth of labor productivity (3.2 percent per annum). This rate would be consistent with stable prices and with a stable labor share of total income.

From the early days of the guideposts, it was recognized that they should not be rigid rules to be invariably applied in all circumstances. Wages should be allowed to increase by more than the guidepost in industries where wages were exceptionally low, or in industries that would otherwise be unable to attract sufficient labor. Price increases should be allowed in industries in which profit levels were insufficient to attract capital; and prices should be reduced in industries where labor costs had fallen or in which excessive market power had resulted in high profit rates.[15]

These exceptions made sense; indeed, it is easy to see how a mechanical application of the guideposts to all situations would lead to trouble. (Consider an industry granting 3.2 percent wage increases, with very little change in productivity and with fixed selling prices.) But, once exceptions are admitted, it becomes difficult in any specific case to have a very firm idea as to whether the proposed wage or price fits within the noninflationary guidepost; the guidepost ceases to be a firm guide to individual decisions. Yet the course of the overall level of prices is nothing more than a weighted average of individual pricing decisions.

The Kennedy administration saw the publication of the guideposts as a way to marshall public opinion against inflationary wage

---

[15] Council of Economic Advisers, *Annual Report,* January 1962, p. 189.

or price increases.[16] "Jawboning" was to be the order of the day, rather than rigid legal price ceilings. In order to add teeth to the "jawbone," the administration was ready to apply direct pressure on corporations or unions. In April of 1962, the President had a direct confrontation with the steel industry when it raised prices in violation of the guideposts. To add insult to injury, the steel price increases came after the secretary of labor had taken an active role in persuading the steel union to accept a noninflationary wage settlement. The President reacted angrily to the announcement of the price increase. The steel industry then backed down, retracting its announced price increases.[17]

There were also frictions between labor and the government over guideposts. Most notably, the Johnson administration was accused of changing the procedure for calculating productivity increases in order to come out with a low guidepost for wage increases.

But it was not friction of this type which caused the breakdown of the guideposts—after all, if guideposts are to induce behavior different from that of private parties following their own interests, then a certain amount of friction and squabbling between the administration and private groups may be no more than a sign that the guideposts are in fact exerting restraint on price and wage decisions. The big problem came when high levels of demand generated broad upward pressures on prices. Once prices had begun to rise, it became less and less reasonable to expect labor to stick to a 3.2 percent wage increase. (After all, *real* productivity is going up by about 3.2 percent, and if labor's share of national income is not to decline, then wages should go up by 3.2 percent *plus* the rate of inflation.)

One way of dealing with this problem would have been to amend the guidepost to include an adjustment for inflation. But, if this had been done, the whole point of the guideposts would have been lost: They would no longer have been a means for stabilizing prices, but rather would have built past inflation into the contracts for the future. Some suggestions were made for guideposts which would permit the reestablishment of stable prices, such as a guidepost permitting a wage increase of 3.2 percent plus some *fraction* (for example, one half) of the rate of past inflation. Businesses might be allowed to raise prices, but not enough to retain their profit margins.

---

[16] Council of Economic Advisers, *Annual Report*, p. 185.

[17] For more details on the steel confrontation, see John Sheahan, *The Wage-Price Guideposts* (Washington, DC: Brookings Institution, 1967), pp. 33–38.

Thus, it was hoped, guideposts might be used to wind down inflation. But these suggestions were discarded as impractical, and the Johnson administration abandoned the guideposts in the face of an upward march of prices and wages.

At the beginning of his term of office, President Nixon declared a hands-off policy regarding the price and wage-making process. The appropriate anti-inflationary policy, he argued, was to deal with the root causes of inflation, and particularly the large government deficits and the associated excess demand. But, even after excess demand had been wrung from the economy during 1969 and 1970, prices continued to increase at a disturbing rate, and in August 1971, there was an abrupt change in policy; a wage and price freeze was initiated in order to break the momentum of inflation.[18] The freeze was followed by successive "phases" of Nixon's economic program, during which controls were gradually abandoned on most products. (Oil was a notable exception; price controls were continued throughout the Nixon presidency, and beyond.)

Although the pressures of events have repeatedly driven reluctant governments toward wage and price guideposts and controls, the experience with such policies provides little ground for optimism that they can greatly alleviate the price-unemployment dilemma; the Phillips curve apparently cannot be shifted downward either easily or by any great amount. Controls and persuasion have been used in a number of countries during the past two decades, with indifferent results.[19] Price increases have continued as a nagging problem in countries using a variety of methods of persuasion and wage-price controls. For example, Britain has had extensive experience with a variety of "incomes policies," aimed at restraining the inflationary scramble of the various economic groups for a larger share of the society's product. These efforts have included negotiations for a "social contract," that is, an agreement among labor, business, and others for mutual restraint in order to reduce inflation. In spite of such efforts, rapid inflation has continued in Britain, particularly during 1974, when prices on average rose by more than 20 percent. Not only did incomes policies fail to lead to a better price-unemploy-

---

[18] For details, see Arnold R. Weber, *In Pursuit of Price Stability: The Wage-Price Freeze of 1971* (Washington, DC: Brookings Institution, 1973).

[19] On the foreign experience, see Lloyd Ulman and Robert J. Flanagan, *Wage Restraint: A Study of Incomes Policies in Western Europe* (Berkeley: University of California Press, 1971). See also Hugh Clegg (a member of the now-defunct British Prices and Incomes Board), *How to Run an Incomes Policy, and Why We Made Such a Mess of the Last One* (London. Heinemann Educational Publishing Co., 1970).

ment tradeoff, but the combined problems of inflation and unemployment became worse. Indeed, by the early 1970s, the country which discovered the Phillips curve had trouble finding any stable price-unemployment relationship.[20]

The continuing shifts in policy in the United States and elsewhere underline the severity of the policy problem. Experience suggests that controls or guideposts have only limited—and debatable—usefulness, yet the price-employment tradeoff posed by the uncontrolled operation of the market drives governments to repeated experiments with controls and guideposts.

The case for controls or guideposts is straightforward: If they can be made to work, they can allow the achievement of a high level of employment with a low rate of inflation. Apart from their debatable effectiveness, controls may be considered objectionable on a number of grounds:

1. If the government imposes price controls, it must obviously set maximum prices for individual products. This raises an immediate difficulty: What is the proper pattern of *relative* prices? The obvious way of solving this problem is to take the pattern of prices when controls are initiated, limiting individual prices to their existing levels (with perhaps some general, limited, across-the-board increase). Yet, as time passes, conditions will change, and a frozen pattern of prices will become increasingly divorced from underlying demand and supply conditions for individual products. As a result, some products may become unavailable at the fixed price. A low price for something you can't readily buy is a small comfort. In theory, of course, a government might have enough information to adjust relative prices to changing conditions, but it is unlikely in fact to be able to do so with sufficient rapidity to prevent distortions from developing in the economy.

The problem of relative prices may be made more manageable by limiting government controls to a relatively small number of products and wages—the prices of products and the wage rates in the highly concentrated industries. An example of policies aimed particularly at the pricing policies of larger companies occurred during Phases II and IV of President Nixon's economic programs in 1972–73. During those phases, large firms with over $100 million in

---

[20] See A. Marin, "The Phillips Curve (Born 1958–Died?)," *Three Banks Review*, December 1972, pp. 28–42. The high rates of inflation and unemployment during the 1970s were an international phenomenon. See Organization for Economic Co-operation and Development, *Towards Full Employment and Price Stability* (Paris: OECD, 1977).

sales were required to submit proposed price increases to the Price Commission for approval. For such limited controls to be effective in restraining the rate of inflation for the economy as a whole, a significant source of the inflation must be cost-push forces in the concentrated sector.

2. The limitation of controls to a relatively small number of products involves dangers of its own, however. There may be a strong political pressure to control the prices of necessities. Where these prices are controlled and others are not, then the production of necessities may become relatively unprofitable. Producers will switch to the production of other goods. Thus, the goods deemed most important and necessary may become increasingly unavailable.

3. As the duration of the controls lengthens, the problem of distortions of relative prices will tend to become more severe. Therefore, a case can be made for limiting controls to a relatively brief period. If prices can be stabilized and the inflationary psychology broken, then the basis may be laid for a stable price level on a continuing basis.

The question of the desirable duration of controls is complicated, however. Precisely the opposite case may also be made, that controls should be continued for an extended period of time. If controls are only temporary and simply suppress price increases, while the underlying causes of inflation remain unaltered, then the abolition of controls may be followed by a wage-price explosion, putting prices and wages back near the path they would have been on if there had been no controls; the controls will have had no lasting effect in slowing inflation. The experience of the 1970s adds force to this point. The substantial elimination of controls in 1973 was followed by a rapid inflation in 1974–75.

4. Guideposts rather than controls may be used as a way for the government to avoid the extremely complex task of specifying prices for individual products. However, guideposts also involve problems. As they are intended as guides and not as mandatory rules, they may be frequently broken. Indeed, it is possible that wage guidelines may make the inflationary situation *worse*. A government-specified guidepost may be taken as a minimum bargaining objective. If the government approves a wage increase of x percent, how can any self-respecting labor leader settle for less?

5. Major policy shifts—such as the imposition of guideposts or controls—should normally be preceded by a public debate. Yet the discussion of guideposts or controls can be counterproductive. Busi-

nesses have an incentive to "jump the gun," raising prices at once in order to establish a high price prior to the imposition of controls.

Such anticipation was widely interpreted as a contributing factor in the steel price increase announced soon after Jimmy Carter's election in November 1976. During the campaign, Carter had indicated his intention to ask Congress for standby authority for wage and price controls. As steel has traditionally been a primary target of controls and guideposts, it made sense for the steel industry to establish higher prices prior to Carter's inauguration.

This episode involved an additional complication, in that it fell in the interval between the election and the inauguration. The lame-duck president took no action; he was skeptical of jawboning, and, at any rate, presidents have traditionally avoided major policy steps after their defeat at the polls. (This reluctance was illustrated in a much more dramatic fashion in early 1933, when President Hoover declined to act, even as the banking system collapsed.) On the other hand, Jimmy Carter had not yet been inaugurated; he could not preempt the powers of the presidency. He did, however, act to reduce anticipatory price increases, declaring that he would not, after all, ask for standby authority to control prices. One of his chief advisers, Bert Lance of the Office of Management and Budget, favored a much less formal approach, involving unobtrusive discussions between business and government prior to price increases. The development of this low-keyed approach was an important element of economic policy in the early days of the Carter administration.

6. Guidelines or controls will be considered unfair unless they apply to all components of income—including profits, dividends, and interest. As we saw in Chapter 11, an effort to peg interest rates can lead the authorities into the Wicksellian trap, increasing the quantity of money in the face of an increase in the demand for loans, thus contributing to the upward pull of demand on prices.

The two cases, pro and con, can be briefly stated. The positive case for controls has been succinctly summarized by John Kenneth Galbraith: "Any idiot can argue the case against controls in the abstract. It is only that there are no alternatives." The negative case is that the proponents of controls and guidelines have committed a logical error in arguing thus:

1. There is a wage-price dilemma.
2. There must be a solution.

3.   Wage-price controls are the only thing we can think of.[21]
4.   Therefore, wage-price controls are the solution.

The problem: Arguments 2 and 4 do not necessarily hold. But if these arguments—and particularly the second—are to be questioned, then the conclusions may be fundamentally pessimistic. A pessimistic evaluation of the Phillips curve dilemma is presented in more detail on pages 348–57.

SHIFTS IN THE PHILLIPS CURVE

The early 1960s were marked by both a worry and a hope. The worry was that the newly discovered Phillips curve had presented the policymaker with a painful dilemma. No longer could macroeconomics be seen in terms of the relatively simple objective of aiming aggregate demand toward the "right" position of full employment and stable prices. The Phillips curve suggested that there was no such well-defined, clearly correct target for demand management. The hope was that wage-price guidelines could be used to ease the dilemma and restrain inflation as the economy was stimulated toward full employment. Thus, it was hoped, a "better" point might be achieved—one below and to the left of the original curve.

In the light of this hope, the 1970s have provided a sobering and saddening experience. The Phillips curve has conspicuously resisted efforts to shift it down. Indeed, the economy has been inflicted simultaneously with high rates of inflation *and* high unemployment. We seem to be getting the worst of both worlds; far from shifting down, the Phillips curve has shifted up—in spite of our efforts. Why?

One possible explanation is that our efforts have not been strong enough. In particular, the incoming Republican administration in 1969 declared a hands-off policy, rejecting guidelines or other direct means of restraining inflation. Then, when it was pushed into a policy of price controls by the force of events in 1971, it pursued the control program with obvious distaste. A successful control program requires public confidence, for which the confidence of the government itself may reasonably be considered a prerequisite. In

---

[21] See the previous quotation from Galbraith. Or David C. Smith, "Incomes Policy," in Richard E. Caves, et al., *Britain's Economic Prospects* (Washington, DC: Brookings Institution, 1968) , p. 106: "The case for an incomes policy has depended on the case against the alternatives."

other words, efforts to shift the Phillips curve down may have failed because they were pursued erratically and half-heartedly.

This is an interesting proposition. But we will not attempt to evaluate it in detail, for two reasons. First, because of its obvious political content, it quickly generates more heat than light. Second, it can scarcely be considered the overriding, or even the major, cause of the problems of the 1970s. Painful bouts of inflation and unemployment have also been suffered in countries which have used incomes policies more strongly and enthusiastically. We are here not dealing with a simple problem which can be quickly and easily solved with the brute force of strong and consistent price controls.

Three additional explanations have been offered for the painful combination of inflation and unemployment in the 1970s:

1. The prices of a number of commodities have risen on world markets, most notably oil. These price increases generated unusually strong cost-push forces in the first half of the 1970s.
2. Changes in the labor market may have made it more difficult to reduce the unemployment rate to a low level.
3. Feedbacks between prices and wages mean that inflation can gather momentum during periods of low unemployment, and can continue even into periods of slack aggregate demand.

COST PUSH: OIL AND OTHER COMMODITIES

During the 1972–74 period when inflation was accelerating most dramatically, major disturbances were occurring in the international commodity markets. First, problems with their harvests drove the USSR into world markets to purchase large quantities of grain, including wheat. As a consequence, the price of grains shot upward. For the American economy, this of course represented a demand pull in the first instance; the export demand for our products rose. However, as the price of wheat increased, costs of wheat-using industries (such as bakeries) were pushed upward, contributing to U.S. inflation. (Again we see the difficulty of sharply separating cost-push and demand-pull forces.)

Even more important was the *quadrupling* of prices by the Organization of Petroleum Exporting Countries (OPEC) in 1973–74. The widespread use of oil in transportation, heating, and chemicals meant that the increases in oil costs were very widely diffused throughout the U.S. economy—and foreign economies, too. Because the price increases were a result of overt decisions by an international cartel, they are about as pure an example of cost push as can be found. (Even here, however, demand forces were not irrelevant, particularly in the timing of the price increases. The international boom of 1973 raised the demand for oil, and OPEC consequently found it relatively easy to make its price increases stick.)

It is difficult to identify precisely the effects of such disturbances on U.S. inflation; to do so, one must know precisely what would have happened in their absence. Reasonable estimates may, however, be made. The staff of the Federal Reserve has estimated that international developments accounted for a large, although not preponderant, share of the inflation of 1971–73. (That is, increases in internationally traded commodity prices, plus the devaluations of the dollar, together accounted for more than one quarter, but less than one half, of total inflation).[22] This does not pick up the major effects of the oil price increases, which spilled over into 1974 and 1975.[23] The inflation of the early 1970s cannot be explained without reference to international commodities; but other forces were also at work.

CHANGES IN LABOR MARKETS

The tightness of the labor market has been used to explain the Phillips curve tradeoff. (A labor market is "tight" when it is hard for an employer to find a worker, and it is easy for a worker to find a job.) As the market becomes tighter, employers are increasingly willing to offer higher wages, and workers demand increasingly higher wages. Because of changes in the composition of the labor force, and because assistance to unemployed workers makes them less desperate to take any job that comes along, the tightness of the labor market associated with any measured rate of unemployment may have increased during recent years, pushing the Phillips curve upward.

----

[22] Richard Berner, Peter Clark, Jared Enzler, and Barbara Lowrey, "International Aspects of Recent Inflation," Paper No. 3 of *Studies in Price Stability and Economic Growth* (Washington, DC: Joint Economic Committee, U.S. Congress, August 1975).

[23] Empirical studies do not give a consistent set of estimates of the inflationary effects of the oil price increases. See George L. Perry, "The United States," in Edward R. Fried and Charles L. Schultze, eds., *Higher Oil Prices and the World Economy: The Adjustment Problem* (Washington, DC: Brookings Institution, 1975), pp. 95–103.

The composition of the labor force

Unemployment touches all segments of the population, but it does not touch them all equally. The unemployment rate for women is consistently higher than that for men (Figure 13–7). In good times and bad, the unemployment rate for blacks is approximately double that of whites. And, most conspicuously of all, the unemployment rate for teenagers is about three times as high as the rate for men age 20 and over.

There are a number of reasons for these differences. Blacks and women may be "last hired, first fired" because of prejudice or convention. (Because layoffs are generally based on seniority, discrimination has a lasting effect. If employers cease to discriminate now in hiring, women and blacks will nevertheless still be laid off first in a recession, since they will have the least seniority.) [24] Women are

Figure 13–7
Selected unemployment rates

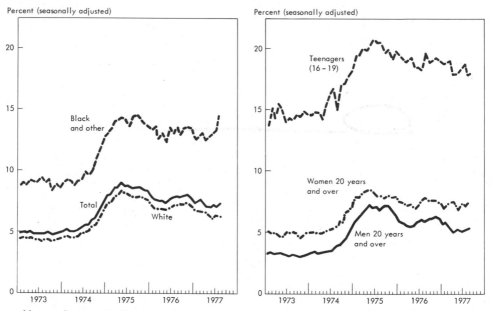

Unemployment affects various groups unevenly, with teenagers having the highest unemployment rate.

---

[24] However, during the recession of 1974–75, the employment losses of women were *smaller* than their share of employment. This apparently was because women were particularly underrepresented in the industries (such as construction) which were hardest hit by the recession. See Ralph E. Smith, "The Impact of Macroeconomic Conditions on Employment Opportunities for Women," Paper No. 6 of studies on *Achiev-*

more likely than men to withdraw from the labor force, to reenter at a later date. Thus, they are more subject to frictional unemployment; they may have a period of unemployment prior to finding a "first" job more than once during a lifetime.

For different reasons, teenagers have a high rate of frictional unemployment. Youth is a time of experimentation before settling down to life's work. Many young people try a number of jobs, with periods of unemployment sometimes occurring between jobs. And the teenage labor force is relatively unskilled. Young workers have had little time to gain experience, and many of the most highly skilled young people remain in school and out of the labor force.

During the past two decades, the composition of the labor force has changed substantially, with women and young people constituting larger fractions. This has been used as an explanation for a higher rate of unemployment by some economists (for example, George Perry of the Brookings Institution).[25] As groups with high unemployment rates become a larger fraction of the labor force, then the weighted average rate of unemployment tends to rise. Put somewhat differently, as the labor force includes proportionately more of those with high frictional unemployment rates, then the degree of labor market tightness tends to be greater for any measured rate of unemployment. Thus, the inflation rate associated with any rate of unemployment tends to be higher, or the rate of unemployment associated with any rate of inflation tends to be greater. In short, the Phillips curve shifts upward.

One must, however, be careful with this argument. Insofar as certain groups have high unemployment rates simply because they are last hired and first fired, then the differential unemployment rates reflect discrimination in the labor market queue, and changes in the composition of the labor market must be discounted as an explanation for the high unemployment rate of recent years.

---

ing the Goals of the Employment Act of 1946 (Washington, DC: Joint Economic Committee, 1977), especially the section entitled "Has the Recession been an Equal Opportunity Disemployer?", pp. 5–15.

[25] George L. Perry, "Changing Labor Markets and Inflation," Brookings Papers on Economic Activity, 1970, vol. 3, pp. 411–41. See also R. A. Gordon, "Some Macroeconomic Aspects of Manpower Policy," in Lloyd Ulman, ed., Manpower Programs in the Policy Mix (Baltimore: John Hopkins, 1973); Charles C. Holt, et al., "Manpower Policies to Reduce Inflation and Unemployment," also in the volume edited by Ulman; and Michael L. Wachter, "The Changing Cyclical Responsiveness of Wage Inflation," Brookings Papers on Economic Activity, 1976, vol. 1, especially pp. 125–33. Wachter estimates that, by the early 1980s, the labor force composition will be changing in the opposite direction, tending to reduce the unemployment rate.

Other labor market changes

Even more controversial is the view that improved unemployment insurance and higher welfare payments have reduced the cost of being unemployed and have consequently lessened the pressures on the unemployed to take the first available job.[26] In some anomalous cases, people may actually be better off not working. The unemployed are less desperate because of assistance programs, and the search time prior to the acceptance of a new position may have increased as a consequence. On the other side of the market, increases in the minimum wage make employers less anxious to hire those with limited skills. Teenage unemployment in particular may be related to the minimum wage: In 1975, the minimum wage of $2.10 per hour was 94 percent of the median wage of teenage workers.[27]

SHIFTS IN THE PHILLIPS CURVE: THE ACCELERATION OF INFLATION

A third explanation of shifts in the Phillips curve is based on the response of the labor force to increases in the cost of living. In the face of rising prices, workers press for wage increases to make up for the effects of inflation on their wages. In other words, workers are concerned with their *real* wages, not simply with their nominal

[26] Peter B. Doeringer and Michael J. Piore, *Internal Labor Markets and Manpower Analysis* (Boston: Heath, 1971); Martin S. Feldstein, "Lowering the Permanent Rate of Unemployment," in *Reducing Unemployment to 2 Percent* (Washington, DC: Joint Economic Committee, 1973); Stephen T. Marston, "The Impact of Unemployment Insurance on Job Search," *Brookings Papers on Economic Activity,* 1975, vol. 1, pp. 13–48. (Marston concluded that the average insured job seeker looks for 16–31 percent longer before obtaining employment than does the average uninsured job seeker.) In his survey, *Unemployment Insurance: Programs, Procedures, and Problems* (Kansas City, Mo.: Federal Reserve Bank of Kansas City, 1977), Stephen P. Zell concludes that "Recent research . . . seems to indicate that UI [unemployment insurance] benefits are responsible for a sizable increase in the duration of unemployment."

In Canada, there were major steps to liberalize unemployment insurance in 1971. These changes added 0.8 percent to the unemployment rate, according to Herbert G. Grubel, Dennis Maki, and Shelley Sax, "Real and Insurance-Induced Unemployment in Canada," *Canadian Journal of Economics,* May 1975, pp. 174–91. An alternative estimate of 0.7 percent has been made by C. Green and J. M. Costineau, *Unemployment in Canada: The Impact of Unemployment Insurance* (Ottawa: Economic Council of Canada, 1976), p. 114.

[27] Edward M. Gramlich, "Impact of Minimum Wages on Other Wages, Employment, and Family Incomes," *Brookings Papers on Economic Activity,* 1976, vol. 2, pp. 409–51; Finis Welch, "Minimum Wage Legislation in the United States," *Economic Inquiry,* September 1974, pp. 285–318.

(money) wages.[28] As a consequence, the Phillips curve—which shows a relationship between the unemployment rate and changes in *nominal* wages (or, alternatively, the relationship between unemployment and the rate of inflation) —*is stable only so long as the rate of inflation is stable.*

The easiest way to explain this argument is to assume initially that prices have been stable for an extended time and are expected to remain so in the future. The economy is in a stable equilibrium at point *G* on the initial Phillips curve, PC_1 (Figure 13–8). The inflation rate is zero. Nominal (and real) wages rise in line with the increase in labor productivity—at a rate of something like 3 percent per annum. In this initial equilibrium, the rate of unemployment is obviously not zero. Young people spend some time looking for their first jobs; some individuals quit one job and spend time looking for something better; and so on. Now, suppose that the authorities decide that this rate of unemployment is unsatisfactory. In order to bring the unemployment rate down to a lower target level, U_T, expansive monetary and fiscal policies are instituted. What happens?

In order to meet the higher demand, producers schedule over-

---

[28] The change of the real wage is defined such that:

$$1 + \frac{\Delta W_r}{W_r} \equiv \frac{1 + \frac{\Delta W_n}{W_n}}{1 + \pi} \tag{13–1}$$

where:

$\Delta W_r / W_r$ is the change in the real wage (as a fraction or percentage).
$\Delta W_n / W_n$ is the change in the nominal money wage (as a fraction or percentage).
π is the change in the average price level (as a fraction or percentage; that is, $\Delta P / P$).

From Equation (13–1) we see that:

$$1 + \frac{\Delta W_n}{W_n} \equiv 1 + \frac{\Delta W_r}{W_r} (1 + \pi) \tag{13–2}$$

From which an alternative statement of the change in the real wage can readily be derived:

$$\frac{\Delta W_n}{W_n} \equiv \frac{\Delta W_r}{W_r} + \pi + \pi \cdot \frac{\Delta W_r}{W_r} \tag{13–3}$$

As long as the change in prices and the change in the real wage are both small, the final term of Equation (13–3) is very small, and can be dropped, leaving:

$$\frac{\Delta W_r}{W_r} \approx \frac{\Delta W_n}{W_n} - \pi \tag{13–4}$$

(For example, if the rate of inflation is 3 percent per annum, and the wage increase is 5 percent per annum in nominal terms, then the *real* wage increase is approximately 2 percent per annum.)

Figure 13–8
The inflationary spiral

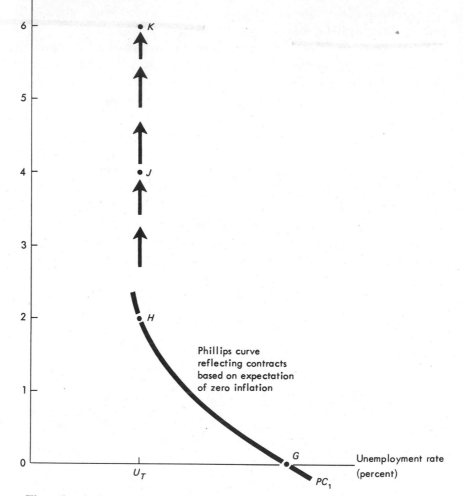

The stimulation of aggregate demand aimed at keeping the unemployment rate very low can result in a wage-price spiral.

time and begin looking for new workers. Job vacancies increase, and
unemployed workers find jobs easily and quickly. Production increases and unemployment falls. In the face of higher demand, producers gradually begin to raise prices. In the early stages of the
inflation, workers continue to offer their labor services at the old
nominal wages, for two reasons. In the first place, as the inflation

begins quite gradually, there may be a delay in perceiving it. After all, relative prices in the past have been flexible, with some prices rising and others falling to give the stable average. When fewer prices decline and more prices rise, this may not immediately be noticed; people do not spend their time calculating price averages, or waiting breathlessly for the monthly announcement of the consumer price index. In the second place, many wages are set contractually, either as a result of union negotiations or as a result of individual bargaining. These contracts last for some time—with three years being a common lifetime for union contracts. And, even where there is no written contract, it may be customary to review wages only periodically. In the face of a 1 or 2 percent increase in prices, people do not head immediately for the boss's office to demand a compensatory wage increase. The short-run consequence, therefore, is a move of the economy to point H (Figure 13–8). Unemployment is low, production is high, inflation is moderate, and wage rates have not yet been appreciably affected.

But this situation does not last; *point H is not stable.* The initial Phillips curve (PC_1) reflects wage contracts *based on the assumption of a stable level of prices.* As time passes, labor contracts run out, and the customary time rolls around for the review of more informal agreements. As the 2 percent rate of inflation (at point H) is increasingly perceived, workers begin to insist not only on the old 3 percent average annual wage increase based on the increase in labor productivity, but also on an additional 2 percent per annum to compensate for inflation. Because sales are high, employers agree. Thus, higher wages are now built into labor contracts.

If the monetary and fiscal authorities are determined to maintain the low target level of unemployment (U_T), demand will be expanded enough to keep markets buoyant. Producers, as a consequence, will be able to pass the higher wage costs along in the form of higher prices; and they will do so. The rate of inflation will accelerate—to point J. With a higher rate of inflation, workers will again demand higher wages when contracts are renegotiated. Still facing buoyant demand, employers will agree; and they will pass their increasing costs along in the form of even higher prices. On and on the price-wage spiral will go, gathering momentum. So long as demand is aimed at keeping the unemployment rate at the low target level (U_T), inflation will continue to accelerate. (Compare points J and K in Figure 13–8 with the observations for 1967, 1968, and 1969 in Figure 13–4.) Thus, the Phillips curve gives the wrong impression. The cost of a very low rate of unemployment is *not* a consistent, moderate rate of inflation. The cost is much greater: an *ever-accelerating inflation*.

Limiting the rate of inflation

Ever-accelerating inflation will eventually put severe strains on the financial system. The usefulness of money depends on some degree of price stability. If prices are galloping upward by 50 or 100 percent per annum (or even faster), then people will increasingly be unwilling to accept money in exchange for goods and services; there will be a tendency to move back toward an inefficient barter system. And substantial resentment is caused even by more moderate rates of inflation of 5 or 10 percent. Sooner or later, the authorities will therefore feel compelled to draw the line on inflation; aggregate demand will no longer be pushed up by whatever amount is needed to maintain low unemployment.

Suppose that this line is drawn sooner, rather than later. Suppose that, once the rate of inflation has reached 2 percent, the authorities change their objective. Rather than aiming demand at the achievement of a low target rate of unemployment, they determine to prevent the acceleration of inflation. The existing 2 percent rate of inflation is accepted, but aggregate demand is restrained by whatever amount is necessary to prevent an even more rapid inflation. What happens?

Workers still push for higher wages. Even the low 2 percent rate of inflation cuts into the purchasing power of their wages, and they attempt to gain higher money wages to compensate. But, unlike the earlier case—where the authorities pushed aggregate demand strongly upward to maintain a booming economy—producers now find their markets limited by the monetary and fiscal restraint. Demand is kept sufficiently tight to prevent producers from passing higher costs along to the consumer. Strong labor demands are met with employer intransigence. Labor strife and strikes result. In the face of the restrained demand, the rate of growth of production decreases and unemployment rises. The economy moves to the right, toward L (Figure 13–9).

A vertical long-run Phillips curve?

An important question is: How far will this rightward movement go? On this point, there are two schools of thought. The most

Figure 13–9
Limiting the rate of inflation

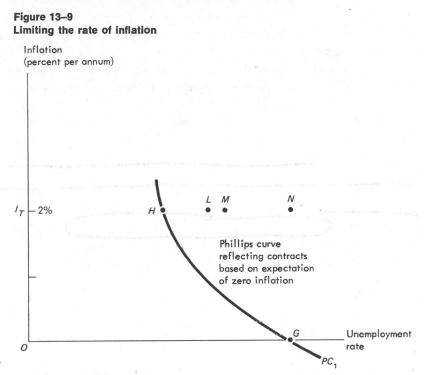

If the rate of increase in aggregate demand is limited in order to prevent the acceleration of inflation, then the economy will move to the right from *H;* the rate of unemployment will rise.

straightforward view is that of Professors Edmund Phelps of Columbia University and Milton Friedman of the University of Chicago.[29] They argue that the economy will move all the way to *N,* to a point directly above the original equilibrium, *G.* Why?

G was a stable equilibrium; producers and workers had a chance to adjust completely to a stable price level over an extended period. If now they get a chance to adjust completely to a constant, steady rate of inflation of 2 percent per annum over a long period of time, they will behave in the same way they did at *G.* Both workers and employers are interested fundamentally in *real* incomes, not money incomes. If the rate of inflation is steady, then their "real" prefer-

---

[29] Milton Friedman "The Role of Monetary Policy," *American Economic Review,* March 1968, pp. 1–17; Edmund S. Phelps, "Money Wage Dynamics and Labor Market Equilibrium," in Phelps, ed., *Microeconomic Foundations of Employment and Inflation Theory* (New York: W. W. Norton, 1970), pp. 124–66; Phelps, "Phillips Curves, Expectations of Inflation and Optimal Unemployment Over Time," *Economica,* August 1967, pp. 254–81.

ences will be accurately reflected in contracts. The economy will move toward its fundamental equilibrium, with unemployment at its equilibrium or *natural* rate of *OG*.

With inflation consistently at 2 percent per annum, the economy will eventually move to *N*, where unemployment and real wages are the same as at *G*. Similarly, if the inflation rate were steady at 4 percent, the economy would gravitate toward *Q* (Figure 13–10), or, with a steady 6 percent inflation, toward *R*. Each of these points is stable; at each, *the actual rate of inflation corresponds to the rate which negotiators expected when they drew up existing contracts.* All of these points lie directly above *G*; thus, the long-run Phillips curve is *vertical.* This brings us back to the old classical position: In the long run, the aggregate supply function is vertical, and changes in demand affect prices, not real output or the unemployment rate.

Through each of the points of long-run equilibrium (*G*, *N*, *Q*, *R*), there is a short-run curve, reflecting contracts based on the respective rates of inflation. For example, the short-run Phillips curve through *N* is based on the expectation by contract negotiators that there will be a continuing rate of inflation of 2 percent per annum. If there is an unexpected increase in aggregate demand, the economy will move along this short-run curve to a point such as *K*. (Even though contract negotiators made a mistake and assumed a continuation of 2 percent inflation, they are generally willing to fulfill their contracts. There are major and obvious advantages in being able to negotiate contracts; contracts serve as the basis for making plans. Such advantages would inhibit the "tearing up" of mistaken contracts, even if there were no legal barriers to doing so.) [30]

But *K* is unstable for exactly the same reason that *H* was unstable. Inflation exceeds the rate expected when contracts were negotiated. Therefore, when contracts again come due for renegotiation, workers push harder for higher nominal wages to make up for inflation.

---

[30] Clearly, the pressures to "tear up" a contract mount in proportion to the magnitude of the error made when the contract was negotiated.

In this discussion, we have concentrated on labor contracts, since labor is the most important single element of cost. However, the same general argument can be applied to other contracts. For example, a contract for the future delivery of steel introduces a stickiness into the cost structure of the steel-using industry.

Perhaps the most dramatic contractual error was made by Westinghouse, which underestimated inflation in general, and the rise in energy prices in particular. Prior to the energy crunch, they entered large fixed-price contracts for the future delivery of uranium. When the price of oil soared, so did the price of uranium, a competing source of energy. Westinghouse's potential losses became so staggering—estimated as high as the total net worth of the company—that they broke their contracts (and they were sued by their customers).

Figure 13–10
A vertical long-run Phillips curve?

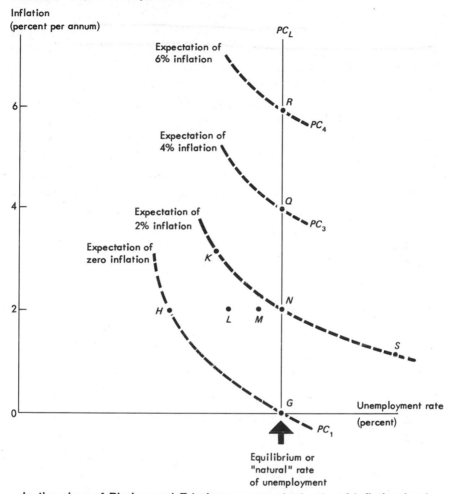

In the view of Phelps and Friedman, a constant rate of inflation leads to a complete adjustment to that rate. The economy will move to its equilibrium (or "natural") rate of unemployment. There is a vertical long-run Phillips curve (PC_L) representing points of equilibrium, that is, points where *actual inflation* equals *expected inflation*. (For example, at point *R*, both actual inflation and expected inflation are 6 percent.)

Again the short-run curve shifts upward to the right. As a consequence, the economy will tend to move back toward a stable point on the long-run Phillips curve (PC_L) —unless the authorities are willing to create enough demand to cause an *ever-accelerating* rate of inflation. Barring this outcome, the economy will move back toward its equilibrium, or "natural," rate of unemployment. In Friedman's words, "There is *always* a *temporary tradeoff* between inflation and unemployment; there is *no permanent tradeoff*."[31] The unemployment-inflation tradeoff depends on contract negotiators being fooled regarding the future rate of inflation. In the long run, the tradeoff does not exist; you can't fool people all the time.[32]

Indeed, this argument can be extended. Even the willingness to accept an ever-accelerating rate of inflation may not be enough to permanently "buy" a rate of unemployment below the natural rate. Once the public perceives the willingness of the authorities to pursue recklessly expansionist demand policies, they will base their contract demands not only on *past* inflation, but also on the *expected* higher rates of *future* inflation. As a result, the short-run Phillips curve will shift up even more rapidly, and the unemployment rate will move toward its natural rate. (The natural rate of unemployment may be defined in either of two ways: as the equi-

---

[31] Milton Friedman, "The Role of Monetary Policy," p. 11.

[32] Since the tradeoff depends on erroneous expectations on the part of contract negotiators, the short-run Phillips curves of Figures 13–10 may be collapsed into a single curve, with "deviations of the rate of inflation from the expected rate" on the vertical axis (Figure 13–11).

Figure 13–11
Deviations of the rate of inflation from the expected rate

Deviations of rate of
inflation from expected rate
(percent per annum)

Unemployment rate
(percent)

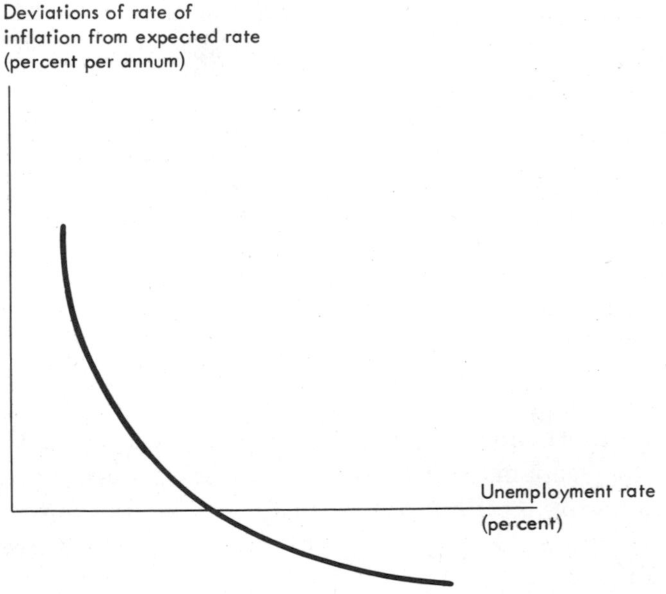

librium rate of unemployment, or as the rate of unemployment that exists when the average contract negotiator correctly anticipates the rate of inflation.)

Alternative views

The proposition that contract negotiators include an allowance for expected inflation is plausible and is supported by empirical evidence. No longer do economists believe that the original Phillips curve represents a stable relationship.[33] On behalf of the dying Phillips school, Arthur Okun conceded: "We are all accelerationists now."[34]

But if all economists are now accelerationists, they are not all accelerationists to the same degree. All would agree that the long-term relationship is steeper than the short-term Phillips curve which reflects contracts built on given inflationary expectations. But not all would agree that the long-run Phillips curve is vertical.

Indeed, many would argue that, while the Phillips curve approaches the vertical at rates of inflation above 2 or 3 percent per annum (for the reasons explained earlier), the long-run relationship curves downward and to the right once inflation falls below that threshold. An illustration of this view is the curve presented by Eckstein and Brinner, reproduced here as Figure 13–12.[35]

---

[33] This raises an obvious paradox. After all, Phillips discovered his curve on the basis of historical evidence covering almost a full century; data for the end of the period fit the curve drawn from 19th century data quite nicely (Figure 13–5). This surely was a long-run relationship, not a transient observation. Yet, soon after its discovery, it shifted. How is this paradox to be resolved?

The explanation is this. Until the last several decades, there was no strong, clear inflationary bias in the economy. Contract negotiators had no strong, clear anticipations of inflation. Inflations had, of course, occurred from time to time; but so had deflations (most notably in the period between the two world wars). Then, with the development of Keynesian aggregate demand tools, and with the Keynesian determination to keep unemployment low, policymakers decided to use the Phillips curve tradeoff, choosing a point of low unemployment and moderate inflation. But such points turned out to be unstable.

[34] "Inflation: Its Mechanics and Welfare Costs," p. 356. Okun was paraphrasing Friedman's celebrated concession to Keynes, quoted earlier on p. 8.

Interestingly, Friedman and Phelps put forward the acceleration argument on the basis of its theoretical plausibility, before the accumulating evidence in the 1970s that the Phillips curve shifts. For their foresight, they received the grudging admiration of Okun ("Inflation: Its Mechanics and Welfare Costs," p. 355): "Accelerationism was a pessimistic forecast rather than an explanation of experience; whatever else one thinks of the theory, the prophetic accuracy of its pessimism has to be admired."

[35] Otto Eckstein and Roger Brinner, *The Inflation Process in the United States* (Washington, DC: Joint Economic Committee, February 1972), p. 5. A similar long-run tradeoff is implied by Robert J. Gordon, "Wage-Price Controls and the Shifting

Figure 13–12
An alternative view

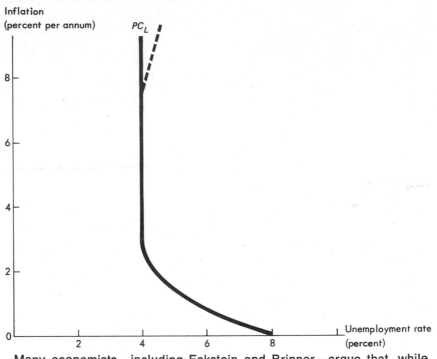

Many economists—including Eckstein and Brinner—argue that, while the long-run Phillips curve may be vertical at high rates of inflation, it curves increasingly to the right as it approaches the horizontal axis.

Such a curve implies two things. First, workers (and others) must be concerned with their real incomes after adjustment for inflation. This proposition is what gives the vertical section of the curve. Second, workers (and others) must be concerned with something *in addition* to their real incomes. This something is what will give the curved lower part of the curve.

What can this something be? Workers are also concerned with money wages; they suffer from *money illusion.* (People suffer money illusion if their behavior changes in the event of a proportionate change in prices, money incomes, and assets valued in money terms.) Specifically, a cut in the money wage is a symbolic

Phillips Curve," *Brookings Papers on Economic Activity,* 1972, vol. 2, pp. 404–6. For a related theoretical argument, see James Tobin, "Inflation and Unemployment," *American Economic Review,* March 1972, p. 11.

step which workers will strongly oppose; a cut in the nominal wage represents a humiliation. To the proposition that workers are concerned primarily with real wages, we must add a qualification: *provided that nominal wages do not actually fall.*[36]

In a growing economy, with rising productivity and rising real wages, this proviso would seem to raise no particular complication. After all, real wages generally rise in line with productivity; thus, even in an economy with *zero* inflation, the average nominal wage will increase. Thus, the issue of a falling nominal wage would seem unlikely to rise.

This conclusion does not, however, necessarily follow; the argument is misleading because it concentrates on the average. Not all industries conform to the average; even in a growing economy, some industries decline. As their demand slackens, they will tend to lay off or discharge workers, thus adding to unemployment. This response can, however, be slowed down if a declining industry cuts its prices relative to other prices in order to hold customers. It will be assisted in doing so, if it can reduce the wage it pays to its workers, relative to the average wage rate. In a zero-inflation economy, its ability to do so will be severely limited. With average wages rising by only about 3 percent (in line with productivity), the wage in the declining industry can be reduced relative to the average wage by only 3 percent, unless the employer is willing to stir up a hornet's nest by attempting to cut money wages. However, with a moderate rate of inflation, of 2 to 3 percent per annum, then average wages will be rising by something like 5 or 6 percent in nominal terms (equal to the 3 percent increase in productivity, plus the 2 to 3 percent increase in prices), and the relative wage in the declining industry can therefore fall by as much as 5 or 6 percent without any reduction in nominal wages. Thus, a moderate rate of inflation can ease the problems of declining industries and consequently reduce the rate of unemployment. According to this line of argument, the economy will tend to have a higher long-run rate of unemployment if the average price level is held steady than if a moderate rate of inflation is allowed.[37] Thus, the long-run Phillips curve slopes down-

---

[36] This proposition—that nominal wages are downwardly rigid—was very important in Keynes' view of the aggregate supply function, as will be seen in Appendix A to this chapter.

[37] Although there is no "long-run" declining industry—since a declining industry will eventually cease to exist—there nevertheless will always be a transient population of declining industries in a dynamic economy.

ward to the right as it approaches the horizontal axis (Figure 13–12).

This argument, it should be noted, is a descendant of Schultze's view that a moderate rate of inflation can ease the problems of transition in a dynamic economy. And it is based on the assumption that workers in a declining industry will accept declining real wages (that is, stable nominal wages in the face of moderately rising prices) in preference to unemployment, even though they would not accept the overt humiliation of a cut in nominal wages during a period of stable prices. In short, it is based on the view that economic behavior is complex, involving cool calculation, on the one hand, and attention to symbols, on the other.

While the lower parts of the long-run Phillips curve have been the center of attention, questions may also be raised as to whether the curve is vertical at high rates of inflation. There are grounds for believing that the curve bends outward to the right as it rises (as shown by the dashed section in Figure 13–12). High rates of inflation may disrupt the financial system, complicating the productive process and contributing to a high rate of unemployment.

The problem of unwinding inflationary expectations

The position of the short-run Phillips curve depends on expectations of inflation. A point is reached on the long-run Phillips curve when actual inflation is equal to expected inflation, for example, at point R in Figure 13–13. Suppose that the monetary authorities decide that this rate of inflation is too high and determine to bring it down by restraining the rate of growth of aggregate demand.

As a consequence, businesses will find their markets less buoyant. Unwanted inventories will accumulate, production will be cut back, and unemployment will rise. The economy will move to a point to the *right* of the long-run Phillips curve (for example, to point S in Figure 13–13). Like a point to the left of the long-run function (for example, *H*), this point is unstable, and for a similar reason. The rate of inflation no longer corresponds to the rate expected when contracts were negotiated. Consequently, new contracts will be revised; because of the lower rate of inflation, workers will be willing to settle for smaller increases in nominal wages. As a result, the economy will gradually work back toward the equilibrium long-run function, moving from S to *T,* then to *U,* and finally to *V.*

Figure 13–13
Reducing the rate of inflation

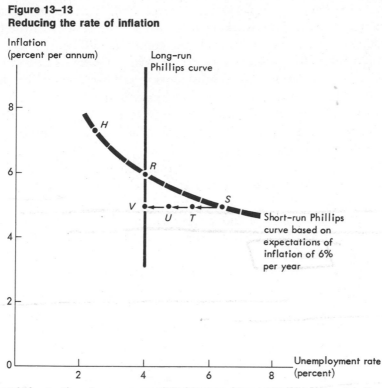

If, starting from an equilibrium position with 6 percent inflation, the demand authorities take restrictive steps to reduce inflation, then the short-run effect will be an abnormally high rate of unemployment.

Cyclical movements

In practice, the path of the economy may be complicated by changes in labor productivity during the business cycle. As the economy moves into a recession, average labor productivity generally falls as total output falls. As the economy recovers from a recession, labor productivity rises.

Why is that so? Because in the face of short-run changes in demand and output, labor costs are partly fixed. Some segments of the labor force work on annual salaries and cannot be easily fired or let off. Nor is the laying off of production-line workers costless: They may get jobs elsewhere and be unavailable when the company wishes to expand production. Because of the costs of hiring and training new workers, a company's labor force represents an investment which may be lost if the workers are laid off. The result: In the face of a short-run decrease in demand, the company will reduce its level of employment by less than its output. Average output per worker declines. This relationship, it must be stressed, applies in the short run. If demand were to stabilize *permanently* at a lower level, then companies would work down their number of employees; without the prospect of an upturn in production, there would be no need to "stockpile" trained workers.

In his investigations of output and unemployment during business cycles, Arthur M. Okun found a stable relationship. A 1 percent change in the unemployment rate was associated with a change (in the opposite direction) of about 3 percent in real *GNP*.[38] This short-run relationship (derived from quarterly observations) has come to be known as *Okun's law.*

What are the implications of this greater variability of output than employment? *As the economy enters a recession, everything will go wrong at the same time.* Employment will fall (though not so much as output), and per unit costs will rise. This will be reflected in a downward movement of profits, on the one hand, and pressures for a continued upward movement of prices, on the other. The initial effects of a weakening demand may be to *worsen* inflation; the gain in terms of a lower rate of inflation may come only after a substantial delay. In contrast to the dismal picture during a recession, the best of all possible worlds will come with the recovery. Employment will rise, profits will rise, and the pressures on prices from the cost side will be relatively weak. Again, there will be delayed price effects: It is only in the later stages of the upswing that the inflationary effects of buoyant demand conditions will become apparent.

These effects show up in the corkscrew pattern of the economy during the past two decades, illustrated in Figure 13–14. During recessions, the economy did not simply move down a well-defined short-run Phillips curve. During the initial stages of a decline, "everything" seemed to go wrong. Thus, in 1970 and 1974, both the unemployment rate and the inflation rate rose. (Annual data are too crude to show similar adverse movements during the early recessions of 1957 and 1960. However, observe that, with respect to both inflation and unemployment, 1961 was worse than 1959, and 1958

---

[38] Arthur M. Okun, *The Political Economy of Prosperity* (New York: W. W. Norton, 1970), pp. 135–38.

Figure 13–14
Inflation and unemployment in the United States, 1953–1977

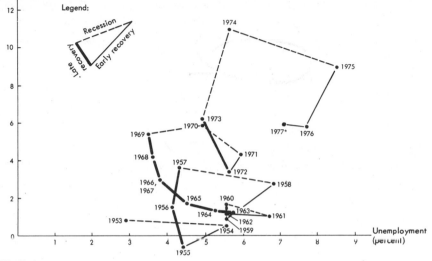

* Preliminary.

During recessions, both unemployment and inflation may get worse. During the early recovery, everything seems to go right, with inflation and unemployment both falling.

was worse than 1956.) Then, during the early stages of recovery, everything went right. Both the unemployment rate and inflation declined in 1954–55, 1958–59, 1971–72, and 1975–76. (This early recovery tendency does not show up for the early recovery of 1961–62, both because of the crudeness of annual data and because the mild cyclical swing of 1959–62 resulted in a small cyclical movement in productivity.) It was only during the later stages of recovery that the inflation rate accelerated with declining unemployment, and the economy moved along a short-run Phillips curve—most notably in the mid-1960s. (There was a movement upward to the left in 1973 and 1956, but in each case the recovery was too short-lived to give a well-defined Phillips curve.)

This cyclical pattern—with periods of bliss (early recovery) being interspersed with periods of pain (recession)—has raised the disturbing possibility that an unscrupulous president might generate a political business cycle to enhance the chances of reelection. The evidence suggests that the economy is an important determinant of voting behavior, and that, moreover, the *trend* of the economy is more important than its *position*.[39] (The economy was still in miserable shape in 1936, but it was getting better; Roosevelt was re-elected by a landslide.) If this is so, then the political game would not be simply to create sustained prosperity; sooner or later, lower and lower unemployment rates will generate inflation. In its crudest form, the game rather is to have an election during the halcyon days of an *early* recovery—when *both* unemployment *and* inflation are declining. But, of course, an early recovery requires a preceding recession. Thus, in the words of Professor Raymond Fair, a vote-maximizing strategy "requires that the economy be first brought into a recession. From the recession trough, the policy is then to stimulate the economy strongly until Election Day."[40]

Speculation along these lines centers on the Nixon administration; his compulsion to win without worrying about the fine points is well documented. Fair summarizes:

Regarding the Nixon and Nixon-Ford administrations,[41] the be-havior of the economy since the beginning of 1969 has been con-

[39] Raymond Fair, *The Effects of Economic Events on Votes for President* (New Haven: Yale University, Cowles Foundation Discussion Paper #418, processed, January 19, 1976).

[40] Fair, "Growth Rates Predict November Winners," *New York Times,* January 25, 1976. On the "political" business cycle, see also Assar Lindbeck, "Stabilization Policy in Open Economies with Endogenous Politicians," *American Economic Review,* May 1976, pp. 1–19, especially p. 14; C. Duncan MacRae, "A Political Model of the Business Cycle," *Journal of Political Economy,* April 1977, pp. 239–63; and W. D. Nordhaus, "The Political Business Cycle," *Review of Economic Studies,* April 1975, pp. 169–90.

[41] Fair's article was written in early 1976, when the economy was recovering rapidly and a continuation of the strong recovery was widely expected. On the basis of this expected recovery, Fair predicted that Ford would be reelected with a sweeping victory of 56 percent of the popular vote.

Fair recognized the rashness of his forecast: "I make this prediction with some trepidation, knowing what happened to the *Literary Digest* after its prediction of victory for Alfred Landon in 1936. If I am never heard from again, you will know what happened." In Fair's behalf, it should be noted that the economy did not develop as expected. After a fast start in 1976, the recovery began to peter out in the summer and fall. In the months directly prior to the election, there was a string of bad news. It is interesting to speculate on what might have happened in the close election had the timing of economic news been different. (Almost immediately after the election—and before the inauguration of Jimmy Carter—economic news improved; Ford was just plain unlucky.)

On the basis of the unexpectedly bad economic news prior to the election, Fair's reputation may be salvaged. Hopefully, we will hear from him again—although he might perhaps like to choose another topic.

And, on the basis of the weak economic performance of mid-1976 and Gerald Ford's loss in the election, Mr. Ford may be removed from the shadow of suspicion—although he might muse that the cost of absolution was rather high. On a more serious note, it is difficult to argue that Ford was manipulating the economy for political purposes. Although he was very slow in perceiving the recession of 1974–75, he did not create it;

sistent with what one could expect its behavior to be under a vote-maximizing policy. . . . Whether the policies . . . were actually motivated to maximize votes . . . I leave for others to decide.[42]

Thus, we have a disturbing possibility, but one on which the evidence is inherently difficult to evaluate.

POLICIES TO DEAL WITH THE SHIFTING PHILLIPS CURVE

The feedback of prices into wage negotiations, and hence into higher labor costs, is widely recognized; "all" economists are accelerationists now. The acceleration thesis has three important, straight-forward policy implications.

First, it suggests that attempts to "buy" very low rates of unemployment with very expansive aggregate demand policies will work only in the short run, and will create headaches for the future.[43] This is not simply a proposition of technical economic literature. It was stated forcefully by British Prime Minister Callaghan to a Labor Party Conference in 1976:

We used to think that you could just spend your way out of a recession and increase employment by cutting taxes and boosting

---

the economy was headed downward when Nixon left office. And Ford did not push for stimulus in 1975–76, prior to the election. Indeed, he frequently opposed attempts of the Democratic Congress to stimulate the economy. In 1976, prior to the election, some Democrats sadly observed that they might have saved Ford's political career by forcing through a tax cut in 1975.

[42] Fair, "Growth Rates Predict November Winners." In a study for the Organization for Economic Co-operation and Development (OECD), a group of experts suggested that the forthcoming elections in a number of countries in 1972 "may have been a common factor making for expansionary policies, and hence for the subsequent synchronization of the business cycle." In 1972, there were elections in Canada, Germany, Italy, Japan, and the United States. In early 1973, France had an election. See OECD, *Towards Full Employment and Price Stability* (Paris: OECD, 1977), p. 52.

[43] In his presidential address to the American Economic Association ("The Role of Monetary Policy"), Friedman argued that, just as pegging the interest rates represents a trap for the monetary policymaker, so an attempt to peg the unemployment rate at a very low rate represents a trap. The analogy to the Wicksellian "natural interest rate" argument was close; indeed, this was the reason for the term, *natural* rate of unemployment. In his address (p. 10), Friedman argued:

As in the interest rate case, the "market" rate can be kept below the "natural" rate [of unemployment] only by inflation. And, as in the interest rate case, too, only by accelerating inflation. . . .
What if the monetary authority chose the "natural" rate—either of interest or unemployment—as its target? One problem is that it cannot know what the "natural" rate is. . . . And the "natural" rate will itself change from time to time.

Because a target rate of unemployment represents an attractive trap, Friedman proposed that policy be aimed at a stable price level.

government spending. I tell you, in all candour, that that option no longer exists, and that insofar as it ever did exist, it only worked by injecting bigger doses of inflation into the economy followed by higher levels of unemployment as the next step. That is the history of the past 20 years.

In its strongest form—as put forward by Friedman—the acceleration argument indicates that there is *nothing* to be gained in the long run in terms of employment by accepting *any* rate of inflation; the long-run Phillips curve is vertical.[44] In more complex versions—such as that of Eckstein and Brinner—there is some money illusion, and some long-run gains may be made on the employment front by accepting a moderate rate of inflation (of something like 2 percent per annum). But beyond this low rate, additional inflation cannot be used as a way of lowering unemployment.

Second, *a stable rate of growth of demand* is important.[45] Indeed, this is *by far the most important conclusion* to flow from the acceleration thesis. Over an extended period, the greater the instability of aggregate demand, the higher the average rate of unemployment will tend to be. This follows from the curvature of the short-run Phillips curve. For example, in Figure 13–10, a year at point K plus a year at point S will average out to a 2 percent rate of inflation, and will therefore be approximately neutral in its effect on inflationary expectations. But the average level of unemployment with one year at K and one at S will be higher than the level with two years at the stable point N. (The short-run Phillips curves *must* curve increasingly steeply upward as we move to the left. No matter *how* much aggregate demand is pushed ahead in the short run, the unemployment rate cannot be pushed to zero; the short-run Phillips curve does not touch the Y-axis.)

Third—and as a corollary of the second point—it is important to

---

[44] In his Nobel lecture, "Inflation and Unemployment" (reprinted in the *Journal of Political Economy,* June 1977, pp. 451–72), Friedman argued that in the intermediate run—involving an extended adjustment period running for a number of years—there may be a *positive* relationship between inflation and unemployment. (That is, the intermediate run Phillips curve might slope upward to the *right*.) Friedman marshalled evidence from a number of industrialized nations to support this view. However, he maintained that over the very long run—after all adjustments have taken place—the relationship should be vertical.

In Appendix B to this chapter, historical evidence is presented which casts doubt on one of Friedman's strong views, that the long-run Phillips curve is vertical all the way down to—and across—the horizontal axis.

[45] On the importance of the stability of the growth of aggregate demand as a way of softening the inflation-unemployment dilemma, see George L. Perry, *Unemployment, Money Wage Rates, and Inflation* (Cambridge, Mass.: MIT, 1966), pp. 118–20.

prevent rapid inflation from persisting for any extended period of time. Once inflationary expectations become built into the decision-making process, they may be very costly to eliminate.

In addition to these relatively simple and straightforward conclusions, there are a number of much more complicated issues. First, the position of the short-run Phillips curve depends on inflationary expectations. By changing such expectations, some policies may result in a shift in the Phillips curve without extended periods of excessive or insufficient aggregate demand. Second, a strong external shock—such as the increase in the international price of oil—provides a reason for modifying the fundamental rule-of-thumb that a steady increase in demand is best. Third, labor market policies can influence the position of the long-run Phillips curve; that is, they can influence the average rate of unemployment which will be observed in a stable economy. To these three issues we now turn.

Inflationary expectations

Past experience with inflation is one of the most powerful determinants of inflationary expectations; people expect inflationary history to repeat itself. But other forces may also mold expectations. Therein lies an opportunity—and a danger.

It may provide an opportunity for breaking the inflationary spiral without the painful costs of an extended period of unemployment. For example, one of the objectives of the wage-price freeze in 1971 was to break the inflationary expectations which contributed to the continued upward march of wages and prices. Similarly, recent price controls in Canada have been aimed at unwinding inflationary expectations without the high costs of soaring unemployment. And a similar objective has been behind the British "social contract," involving restraint on the part of all groups in society in order to break the wage-price spiral.

The issues which such "incomes policies" raise are quite similar, whether the short-run Phillips curve is assumed to be stable (as it was in the 1960s) or unstable. Thus, most of the earlier discussion of the pros and cons of incomes policies is relevant here. There is, however, one additional complication. Insofar as *expectations* of inflation are an important determinant of the position of the short-term Phillips curve, then the *credibility* of government anti-inflation policies is very important. And therein lies the danger. If incomes policies are looked at as a way of "solving" the inflation-unemployment dilemma, and permitting a rapid expansion of aggregate demand to stimulate employment, then the public may be quite skeptical that inflation will, indeed, subside. Thus, incomes policies may be ineffective; they may simply be swept aside in the tide of inflationary expectations.

Furthermore, credibility can become important whether incomes policies are followed or not.[46] Where expectations are stable, then expansive aggregate demand policies can "buy" a low rate of unemployment for some time, until inflation is widely perceived and built into contracts. However, if the economy has already gone through extensive inflationary episodes—as it now has—then expectations may be quite volatile. The determination of the government to follow expansive policies may itself be taken as a sign of future inflation, and therefore as a ground for stepping up contract demands even before the actual inflation occurs. Insofar as this happens, then the period during which aggregate demand policies can "buy" lower unemployment will be shortened; the inflationary response will be speeded up.[47] This was a concern during the early

---

[46] Credibility is the central topic of William Fellner, *Towards a Reconstruction of Macroeconomics: Problems of Theory and Policy* (Washington, DC: American Enterprise Institute, 1976). Fellner argues (p. 116) that the "main difficulty" in macroeconomic policy is "the public's self-justifying skepticism about policymakers."

[47] According to one line of thought—the "rational expectations hypothesis"—lags may collapse toward zero. *If the authorities follow a consistent set of policies,* then both the policy and the effects of this policy on aggregate demand will be anticipated. As a result, the inflationary consequences will also be anticipated and taken into account by contract-writers. Consequently, the Phillips curve will be vertical even in the short run; monetary and fiscal policies will have no effect on output or employment, but only on prices. The only way in which the authorities can affect real output is to behave in an unpredictable (erratic?) manner. In the words of Robert W. Lucas, "To affect real output, the monetary authorities must resort to trickery." (This quotation is taken from the *Business Week* article cited below.)

Regarding rational expectations, see R. J. Barro, "Rational Expectations and the Role of Monetary Policy," *Journal of Monetary Economics,* January 1976, pp. 1–32; Robert E. Lucas, Jr., "Expectations and the Neutrality of Money," *Journal of Economic Theory,* April 1972, pp. 103–24; and Thomas J. Sargent and Neil Wallace, " 'Rational' Expectations, the Optimal Monetary Instrument, and the Optimal Money Supply Rule," *Journal of Political Economy,* April 1975, pp. 241–54. (This literature is rather hard to read. For a popularized version, see "How Expectations Defeat Economic Policy," *Business Week,* November 8, 1976, pp. 74–76.)

The "rational expectations" literature pushes the argument rather far. It attributes to market participants an impressive ability to digest and interpret complex interrelations between economic policy and economic activity. (In "Recent Developments in Monetary Policy," *American Economic Review,* May 1975, p. 164, Stanley Fischer notes that one strong criticism of the rational expectations hypothesis is that "it is absurd to assume individuals can make the necessary calculations since most economists still cannot do so.") Furthermore, changes in demand management policies during the 1970s have rather clearly affected real output and unemployment (particularly the expansive steps of 1971–72 and the restrictive actions of 1974). Thus, unless one wants to write off macroeconomic policy of these years as trickery, the rational expecta-

days of the Carter administration: How much could aggregate demand be stimulated without setting off inflationary expectations?

Aggregate demand management in the face of soaring oil prices

The key conclusion of the acceleration thesis—that policy should be aimed toward a stable, steady rate of growth of demand—is based on the assumption that changes in the expected rate of inflation are the only reason for shifts in the short-run Phillips curve. But this was conspicuously not the case in 1973–74, when strong inflationary forces were generated by the decision of OPEC to quadruple oil prices.

Such an external disturbance greatly exacerbates the policy dilemma. If demand (measured in dollars) is held on a steady course, then the upward shift of the short-term Phillips curve will cause lower output and rising unemployment. Thus, there will be a substantial secondary cost from the oil price increase. (The primary cost consists of the higher payments for oil; this cost cannot be avoided unless the oil cartel is broken and prices kept low.) On the other hand, if aggregate demand is increased in order to prevent an adverse effect on economic activity, then the higher inflation rate will be built into wages and other contracts. In other words, the single external shock from the oil cartel either will result in a *permanently* higher rate of inflation, or will require a future period of controls and/or above-normal unemployment in order to sweat the inflation out of the economy. Furthermore, if the demand management authorities signal their willingness to let the inflation rate rise in order to smooth over the employment and output effects of any disturbance that might occur on the supply side, then their credibility may be shaken. Contract negotiators, as a consequence, may begin to anticipate even higher rates of inflation in the future.

In the real world, decisions are made with a complex combination of events pressing for the policymaker's attention. Nevertheless,

tions hypothesis greatly exaggerates the ability of private markets to adjust to—and defeat—changes in demand management policies.

(For variants of the rational expectations model, in which macro policies may nevertheless be stabilizing, see Stanley Fischer, "Long-Term Contracts, Rational Expectations, and the Optimal Money Supply Rule," *Journal of Political Economy*, February 1977, pp. 191–205; Edmund S. Phelps and John B. Taylor, "Stabilizing Powers of Monetary Policy under Rational Expectations," *Journal of Political Economy*, February 1977, pp. 163–90; and William Poole, "Rational Expectations in the Macro Model," *Brookings Papers on Economic Activity*, 1976, vol. 2, pp. 463–505.)

generalizations are possible regarding the actual policies of 1974–75. In the face of the twin dangers resulting from the oil price increases, the administration and the Federal Reserve placed a relatively heavy weight on limiting the inflationary spiral; the President vetoed a number of spending bills, and the Federal Reserve followed a tight monetary policy, particularly in 1974.[48] On the other hand, Congress was more concerned with the unemployment problem, passing additional spending programs and cutting taxes in early 1975 as the economy fell into the worst recession of recent decades.

The policies of 1974–75 were further complicated because the oil price increases affected *aggregate demand* as well as aggregate supply. Higher payments went to foreign oil producers, who declined to respend the payments for U.S. exports (or did so only with a lag).[49] Thus, there was a leakage from the domestic spending stream, which had a demand effect similar to that of an increase in saving or taxation.[50] As a consequence, policymakers not only faced a difficult decision in picking an aggregate demand target, but they also had an unusually difficult time in estimating the policy adjustments needed to achieve the target. Again, there was a division in Washington. Congress was relatively concerned about the demand effects of the oil price increases, and consequently pushed for stimulus. In contrast, the Ford administration and the Federal Reserve tended to downplay the demand effects, and therefore favored a less expansive demand policy.

---

[48] In Chapter 11, the possibility was considered that monetary expansion in 1974 may have been less than the Federal Reserve wished. Thus, the outcome cannot be taken as an unambiguous measure of policy *intentions*.

[49] On this point, and on other macroeconomic effects, see Perry, "The United States" (in the cited work edited by Fried and Schultze), pp. 88–95. The Fried-Schultze book also has chapters on the effects of oil prices on Western Europe, Japan, and the developing countries.

[50] Because the income tax has progressive rates on *nominal* income, the inflation of 1974–75 automatically increased income tax rates, and thus added to the drag on aggregate demand.

In a noninflationary situation, progressive taxes act as an automatic stabilizer, with tax collections rising as incomes rise and falling as incomes fall. However, during a period of strong inflation and rising unemployment, money income can rise even though real income may be falling. As a consequence, the tax rates on that income will rise, adding to the drag on the economy. Thus, Dernburg argues that the indexation of the personal income tax "would have helped to avert the collapse of 1974." (Indexation involves the changing of the income tax brackets in proportion to changes in the consumer price index.) See Thomas F. Dernburg, "Indexing the Individual Income Tax for Inflation: Will This Help to Stabilize the Economy?" Paper No. 2 of *Studies in Fiscal Policy* (Washington, DC: Joint Economic Committee, December 1976), p. 2. See also James L. Pierce and Jared J. Enzler, "The Implication for Economic Stability of Indexing the Individual Income Tax," in Henry J. Aaron, ed., *Inflation and the Income Tax* (Washington, DC: Brookings Institution, 1976), pp. 173–93.

Labor market policies

The equilibrium rate of unemployment is the rate to which the economy tends in the face of a steady increase in demand (and in the absence of major disturbances on the supply side, such as the oil price increase). This equilibrium rate is not necessarily constant through time; it can be affected by changes in the composition of the labor force, and by changes in policies affecting the labor force.

If the only policy objective were to decrease the unemployment rate, then a number of policy changes would readily follow; for example, the unemployment insurance and welfare programs, which reduce the desperation of the unfortunate members of society, might be cut back in order to increase the willingness of people to take any job that comes along. But clearly, policy should not be made in such a simple-minded context. A humane society—and the alleviation of distress—are important; the reduction of the pain of unemployment should be ranked as a goal, along with the reduction of unemployment itself. Thus, the policy conclusion here is somewhat muted: In designing unemployment and welfare programs, attention should be given to incentives. Work should be rewarded; those who work should end up better off than similarly placed individuals who do not work. But unemployment and welfare programs are complex, and it is hard to envision a major breakthrough in this area.

Other changes might be aimed specifically at lowering the very high unemployment among teenagers. For example, the minimum wage might be made nonapplicable to teenagers; or teenagers might have a lower minimum wage than those over 20.[51] This would provide an incentive to employers to train teenage workers. By accepting low initial wages, teenagers would accept some or all of the costs of training, and would signal their interest in sticking with their jobs. However, proposals to change the minimum wage law have come under strong attack, particularly from union leaders, who object to competition from low-wage labor. There might, indeed, be some problem of 20-year-olds being fired (or not hired) in order to employ low-wage teenagers.

Another approach would be to excuse teenagers from the high social security tax. (In 1977, the employee and employer each had to

---

[51] In his "Impact of Minimum Wages on Other Wages, Employment, and Family Incomes," p. 450, Edward Gramlich addresses the question of "whether the minimum should be differentiated according to the age of the worker. The results here suggest casting a moderately strong vote for a differential. If anything, minimum wages seem too low or about right for adults and too high for teenagers."

pay 5.85 percent social security tax on the first $16,500 of earnings.) The removal of the social security tax from teenage employment could be justified on the ground that such taxes are intended primarily for the financing of retirement benefits; and 20 is early enough for people to be forced to save for retirement. Furthermore, the removal of the social security tax is preferable to alternative proposals to subsidize teenage employment. (It is a very clever government indeed that can both tax and subsidize the same item, and cause a net benefit in the process.) There is, of course, a case to be made on the other side. The social security program is facing large future deficits, which will become worse as the number of elderly rises as a fraction of the population. The elimination of taxes on a segment of the population would obviously make this financial problem worse, and would, as a consequence, probably require payments into the fund from general tax revenues. (Such payments could be defended as preferable to subsidies to teenage employment, paid out of general government funds.)

Finally—and perhaps most important of all—proposals have been made that the government should act as the "employer of last resort," undertaking to offer enough government jobs to substantially eliminate unemployment.[52] This topic promises to be important in the years ahead, and deserves much more careful thought than it has yet received. On the one hand, government employment programs similar to those of the Depression might give useful work to those (particularly teenagers) whose time would otherwise be wasted in idleness. On the other hand, very careful consideration would have to be given to the maintenance of an incentive to enter the private sector, if the government programs were not to become a monster, gradually taking over larger and larger segments of the economy.[53] To design such a program is no mean task; the desire to pay "reasonable" wages to those in the government programs comes into direct

[52] The Humphrey-Hawkins bill of 1976 (which did not pass) would have committed the government to offer enough jobs to reduce the unemployment rate to 3 percent.

For an evaluation of existing public-employment programs, see Michael Wiseman, "Public Employment as Fiscal Policy," *Brookings Papers on Economic Activity*, 1976, vol. 1, pp. 67–104.

[53] In order to limit this danger, Wiseman ("Public Employment as Fiscal Policy," p. 104) recommended that tenure in government employment programs be limited to one year. In a comment on Wiseman's paper, James Tobin wondered "whether a program that placed eligible workers into private or public jobs with a federal wage subsidy might not be a better device for balancing several objectives than are the public-service employment programs."

conflict with the need to keep wages below those in private industry in order to maintain incentives for private employment.[54]

APPENDIX A

THE KEYNESIAN AGGREGATE SUPPLY FUNCTION:
A MORE COMPLEX VERSION

In simple Keynesian presentations—both in the *General Theory* and elsewhere—the reversed L aggregate supply function (Figure 13-1) was used as a first approximation. Below the point of full employment, an increase in demand would cause an increase in real output; beyond the point of full employment, inflation would result.

This function was based on Keynes' view that workers are concerned with money wages and will strongly resist any reduction in the money wage rate.[55] (Keynes' specifically attacked the classical view that workers are preoccupied with real wages—a view that has been revived with Friedman's long-run supply function, which is vertical even in a deflationary range.) With the nominal wage being downwardly inflexible, a fall in the demand for labor will not result in a cut in the wage rate. Furthermore, if there is large-scale unemployment, more workers can be hired at the going wage rate. Thus, in the range of particular interest for the Keynesian analysis—the range significantly short of the full employment level—the supply of labor will be horizontal. Changes in the demand for labor will be reflected in employment, and not in the nominal wage rate.

Here, however, a problem was recognized, and this led to a more complex Keynesian version of the aggregate supply function. To argue that the wage rate will be constant over a range in the face of changes in the demand for labor is not the same as arguing that the

[54] The Humphrey-Hawkins bill placed major emphasis on the payment of reasonable wages in the government programs, with little attention being paid to the problem of incentives. This one-sidedness contributed to the heavy opposition which killed the bill. For example, Charles Schultze (who later became the chairman of the Council of Economic Advisers under President Carter) testified that, if the bill were to become law, individuals might turn down jobs in private industry at $2.50 per hour, in order to get government last-resort jobs at $3.50 to $4.50 per hour.

[55] John Maynard Keynes, *General Theory of Employment, Interest, and Money* (London: Macmillan, 1936), pp. 7–13.

general price level will be stable in the face of changes in aggregate demand. A stable wage rate does not necessarily imply a stable price level; a horizontal section in the supply of labor does not necessarily mean that there will be a horizontal section in the aggregate supply function.

To illustrate this point, suppose that competitive conditions exist in the market for goods. This means that the price faced by a producer of a good will be given; it does not depend on the sales of an individual business. In this situation, the marginal revenue from hiring one more worker will be equal to the marginal product of labor times the price of the good. In order to maximize profits, a firm will hire workers up to the point where the wage rate is equal to the value of the marginal product, thus:

$$W = P \times MP \tag{13--5}$$

Which rearranged becomes:

$$P = \frac{W}{MP} \tag{13--6}$$

where

W is the wage rate.

P is the price of the good.

MP is the marginal product of the worker—that is, the increase in real output resulting from the last worker hired.

Now, what happens as aggregate demand increases and more workers are hired? As the amount of capital equipment is fixed in the short run, it is reasonable to expect that each additional worker will be able to add somewhat less than previous workers added to total output; the marginal product of labor will fall. Thus, from Equation (13–6), it may be concluded that, if the nominal wage rate is constant, prices will have to rise as aggregate demand rises and output increases.

The relationships between wages, marginal productivity of labor, and the aggregate supply function are illustrated with Figures 13A–1, 13A–2, and 13A–3. Figure 13A–1 illustrates the Keynesian assumption regarding money wages: Additional labor is available at the going rate, up to the point of full employment; thereafter increases in the demand for labor will simply bid up the wage rate. Figure 13A–2 illustrates the declining marginal productivity of labor. From these two diagrams, the shape of the corresponding

Figure 13A–1
Keynesian supply of labor

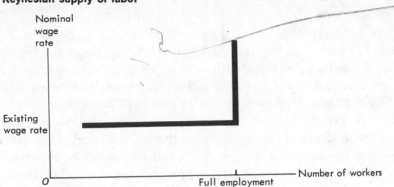

According to Keynes, the nominal wage rate is inflexible in a downward direction. A low demand for workers leads to unemployment, not to a drop in the money wage.

Figure 13A–2
Marginal product of labor

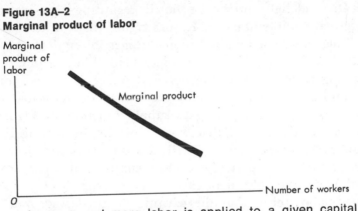

As more and more labor is applied to a given capital stock, the marginal product of labor falls.

Figure 13A–3
Sophisticated Keynesian aggregate supply function

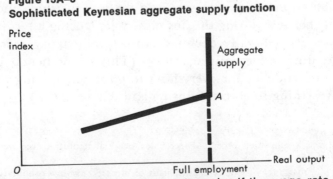

In a competitive system, prices rise if the wage rate is constant and the marginal productivity of labor is falling. This happens as the economy expands toward full employment. Once full employment is reached, further increases in demand cause wages and prices to rise.

aggregate supply function may be deduced, as is done in Figure 13A–3. In the range to the left of the full-employment level of output, increases in demand will lead to additional output and additional workers being employed. The wage rate will remain steady (Figure 13A–1), but the marginal product of labor will fall (Figure 13A–2); therefore, from Equation (13–6), the price level will creep upward as demand increases. Once the point of full employment is reached (point A in Figure 13A–3), output cannot be increased further. Additional increases in demand will result in a bidding up of prices (Figure 13A–3) and wages (Figure 13A–1). Thus, the possibility of a decreasing marginal product of labor—which Keynes himself recognized[56]—leads to a more sophisticated version of the Keynesian aggregate supply function, as shown in Figure 13A–3.

One sidelight might be noted regarding this version of the aggregate supply function. Keynes argued that workers would not be willing to accept nominal money wages lower than the prevailing rates, even in the face of unemployment. They would, however, be willing to work for stable nominal wages as the economy moved toward full employment and prices rose (as indicated by the upward slope on the aggregate supply function in Figure 13A–3). Thus, Keynes argued that workers would be willing to settle for lower *real* wages. Indeed, a willingness to work for lower *real* wages was an intrinsic part of Keynes' definition of unemployment: Involuntary unemployment exists when the supply of workers offering their labor services at the existing nominal wage rate would be greater than the present level of employment, even in the event of a small increase in prices.[57] Finally, it should be noted that, while the Keynesian argument regarding changes in productivity is plausible, it does not correspond to the way in which the economy actually behaves during the business cycle. During a recession, labor productivity generally declines, while productivity increases very rapidly during the early upswing. (This phenomenon helped explain the tendency for everything to go wrong during a recession, and everything to go right during an early recovery.)[58]

---

[56] Keynes, *General Theory*, pp. 299–300.

[57] This is a simplified version. For Keynes' original definition, see Keynes, *General Theory*, p. 15.

[58] While *marginal* productivity is difficult to identify, *average* productivity is readily calculated. Thus, the observed behavior involves average productivity rather than the marginal productivity which played a strategic role in Keynes' aggregate supply function. In spite of this discrepancy, the facts may be considered at variance with Keynes' expectations.

APPENDIX B

THE VERTICAL LONG-RUN PHILLIPS CURVE: THE PROBLEM OF THE 1930s

While "we are all accelerationists now," and economists generally agree that the long-run Phillips curve is steeper than the curve traced out by the short-run responses of the economy to changes in aggregate demand, there is an important difference of opinion as to what happens at low rates of inflation (below 2 percent, or thereabouts). Eckstein, Brinner, and a large number of economists argue that the curve slopes downward to the right at such low rates of inflation. Friedman, in contrast, argues that the long-run Phillips curve falls vertically across the horizontal axis and into the de-flationary quadrant.

In the interpretation of recent history, this difference of opinion is insignificant; the rate of inflation has been too high. But the controversy is important if we are to strive for zero inflation. Many economists argue that this would come at the cost of a permanently higher rate of unemployment. Friedman disputes this view. Furthermore, Friedman goes even farther, arguing that the best policy is not one of *stable* prices, but rather one of moderate, steady *deflation.*[59] Thus, for Friedman's policy recommendations, the lower part

---

[59] Milton Friedman, *The Optimum Quantity of Money and Other Essays* (Chicago: Aldine, 1969), pp. 47–48. In this book, Friedman reversed his earlier stand in favor of a steady increase in the money stock of 5 percent per annum, aimed at a zero rate of inflation. Rather, he came out in favor of a 2 percent per annum growth in the money stock, involving a secular deflation of something like 3 percent per annum.

Friedman's conclusion followed from the proposition that the optimum quantity of an item will be produced when its marginal social cost is equal to its marginal utility. In a competitive economy, production of goods will approximate this target (in the absence of externalities). Money, however, is special. The costs of printing money are approximately zero. (That, of course, is why the government must maintain a monopoly in the printing of currency, and throw counterfeiters into prison.) Yet, money has a positive marginal utility, represented by the rate of interest. People forego interest payments as a cost of holding money; they hold money only so long as its marginal utility exceeds the rate of interest.

An optimum can be approached if the price of money—that is, the interest rate—is reduced toward the marginal cost of zero. The rate of interest includes an adjustment for expected inflation. (During inflationary periods, lenders recognize that they will be repaid in money of less value; they therefore demand compensation in the form of higher nominal interest rates.) A low rate of inflation results in low interest rates; a mild deflation results in lower interest rates still, and is therefore better, according to Friedman.

Note two things about this argument (in addition to its dependence on a vertical long-run Phillips curve which crosses down into the deflationary quadrant). First, it

of the long-run Phillips curve becomes a matter of prime importance.

Because of the predominantly inflationary trend during recent decades, the shape of the lower section of the Phillips curve cannot be settled by an appeal to recent history. Rather, we must go back to the 1930s, when demand was low, unemployment rates were high, and prices fell (at least in some of the years). Figure 13B-1 illustrates the implications of the theory that the long-run rate of unemployment is unaffected by the trend of demand (that is, the theory that the long-run Phillips curve is vertical). Just as the point *B* is unstable, leading either to an accelerating inflation (if unemployment is held low) or to a movement back toward the natural rate of unemployment (if inflation is held constant), so a point such as *G* is unstable. With prices falling, workers will find that their real incomes are more than they bargained for originally. With a high rate of unemployment, they will therefore be willing to settle for a smaller increase—or for a decrease—in money wages during the next wage negotiations. But this will allow prices to fall even faster. Thus, if the unemployment rate is kept high, by restrictive demand policies, then deflation should continue, and *at an accelerating rate*. Alternatively, if demand is stabilized, the unemployment rate should move toward its equilibrium, natural rate. In either case, the economy moves from point *G*—either progressively downward or to the left.

For some time, it has been recognized that the experience of the 1930s creates difficulties for this hypothesis.[60] During that decade, the unemployment rate was consistently above 14 percent. Yet, during the years 1935–40, prices were reasonably stable. In particular, there was no tendency toward accelerating deflation. Thus, one (or a combination) of the following propositions must be accepted:

1. The long-run Phillips curve is not vertical, but bends quite sharply to the right as the inflation rate falls toward zero. (This is another way of saying that the basic Keynesian aggregate sup-

---

implicitly dismisses the Keynesian liquidity trap argument (and thereby involves the proposition that the hoarding of money will not be a significant contributor to instability). Second, its importance depends on the responsiveness of the demand for money to changes in the rate of interest. (If people hold very little additional money as interest rates fall, then the argument is trivial.) Yet elsewhere, Friedman stands practically alone in casting doubt on the interest elasticity of the demand for money. Thus, Friedman's argument for mild deflation is inconsistent with his view that there is no strong evidence that the demand for money responds to interest rates.

[60] For example, Robert J. Gordon, "The Welfare Costs of Higher Unemployment," *Brookings Papers on Economic Activity*, 1973, vol. 1, p. 135.

Figure 13B–1
The theory of the vertical long-run Phillips curve

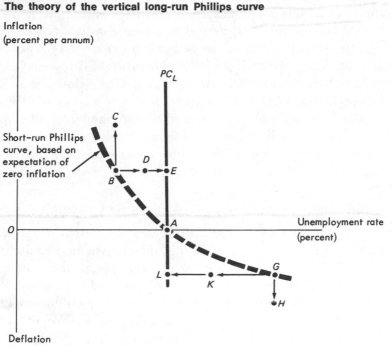

Inflation
(percent per annum)

Short-run Phillips
curve, based on
expectation of
zero inflation

Deflation
(percent per annum)

If there is a vertical long-run Phillips curve—that is, if the equilibrium amount of unemployment is not affected at all by the rate of inflation—then we should observe the following:

A point such as *B*, with a very low rate of unemployment, should be unstable. Either inflation will accelerate or unemployment will rise (toward point *E*).

Likewise, a point such as *G*, with a very high rate of unemployment, should also be unstable. Either deflation should accelerate or unemployment should fall (toward point *L*).

ply curve of Figure 13–1 was quite plausible in the light of the facts available up until the mid-1950s.)

2. There was some strong force—independent of the path of aggregate demand—which raised the natural rate of unemployment very high (to 15 or 20 percent) during the 1930s. This is implausible; it is hard to imagine what such a force might have been. Furthermore, this conclusion is very damaging to the free enterprise philosophy. If markets can result in an equilibrium rate of unemployment of 15 or 20 percent, then we ought to look around for an alternative to the market system.

3. The delays in adjusting contracts downward by any appreciable
    amount are very long (since there was no noticeable tendency
    toward accelerating deflation after *a whole decade* of very high
    unemployment). The lag in perceiving deflationary tendencies
    may be long; alternatively, the short-run Phillips curve may
    quickly become almost horizontal as it falls below the axis in
    Figure 13B–1. With long delays, the costs of adjusting to Fried-
    man's deflationary objective would be extremely high. And, as a
    more pressing matter, the costs of winding down our present in-
    flation may be very painful. (This conclusion can be avoided if
    any of the other three propositions is chosen in preference to
    proposition 3.)
4. There is something wrong with the statistics for the 1930s.

Professor Michael Darby has investigated the fourth proposition,
noting that the manner of calculating unemployment was different
in the 1930s than it is now.[61] Specifically, the official unemployment
statistics were taken as a measure of the magnitude of the job creation that would be required to restore a normal economy. Thus,
those employed in special government job programs of the 1930s
(such as the Civilian Conservation Corps) were included with those
actually out of a job in generating the unemployment statistics. But,
from the point of view of estimating pressures in the labor market,
those working for the government have different significance from
those actually out of work.

Darby adjusted the unemployment figures to eliminate those
working in special government job programs. His revised estimates
are used to plot the points in Figure 13B–2. While these results are
not so bluntly in contrast to the natural unemployment rate theory
as are the raw figures, they still show persistently high unemployment without any tendency toward progressive deflation. Thus,
they still require the choice among the first three propositions above,
albeit in modified form. (For example, in proposition 2, one need
argue "only" that the natural rate of unemployment had risen to
the neighborhood of the 10 percent shown by the adjusted figures
for the late 1930s.) [62] We have substantial grounds for doubting that
the long-run Phillips curve is vertical right down to the axis. A

---

[61] Michael R. Darby, "Three-and-a-Half Million U.S. Employees Have Been Mislaid; Or, an Explanation of Unemployment, 1934–1941," *Journal of Political Economy*,
February 1976, pp. 1–16.

[62] This "eyeball" conclusion from Figure 13–1 is confirmed by Darby's equations,
which suggest an equilibrium rate of unemployment in the 8.5 to 10 percent range in
the 1930s. Darby, "Three-and-a-Half Million U.S. Employees Have Been Mislaid,"
p. 13.

Figure 13B–2
. . . And the facts

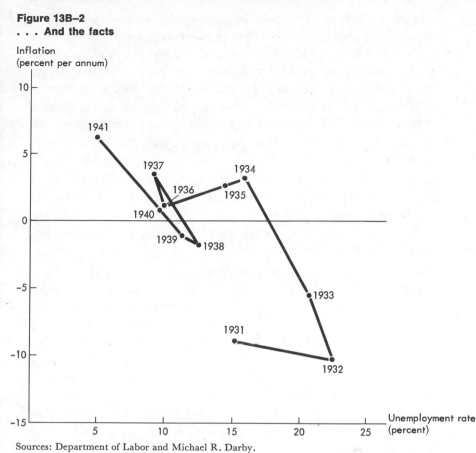

Sources: Department of Labor and Michael R. Darby.

But the facts are inconsistent with the theory that there is a vertical long-run Phillips curve, running down to and across the axis. Deflation did not accelerate, in spite of the very high unemployment rates (even after adjustment for emergency employment). And unemployment remained stuck near 10 percent between 1936 and 1940.

minor amount of inflation (2 percent?) may be accepted as a reasonable price to pay for a low long-run rate of unemployment. Friedman's deflationary proposal may be rejected as dangerous.

KEY POINTS

1. In elementary presentations of Keynesian theory, the response of the economy to changes in aggregate demand is assumed to be very simple. As long as the economy is operating below the full-

employment level, changes in aggregate demand will cause changes in real output while prices remain stable. After the economy reaches full employment, a further increase in aggregate demand will cause a rise in prices, with real output remaining constant (Figure 13–1). With this aggregate supply function, the desirable policy objective is clear: Raise aggregate demand to the full-employment level, but do not push it beyond.

2. During the late 1950s, this aggregate supply function was increasingly considered to be inadequate. In particular, it was inconsistent with the upward movement of prices and the high level of unemployment of 1958. This resulted in a broadening of the discussion of inflation from a demand-pull argument to include: (*a*) the cost-push argument, (*b*) the demand-shift argument, and (*c*) the Phillips curve.

3. The Phillips curve illustrates the historical relationship between inflation and the unemployment rate. This historical relationship suggests that there is no well defined point of full employment. As the economy moves toward higher and higher rates of employment, there is a tendency for the rate of inflation to become higher and higher. The policymaker faces a *dilemma:* A high rate of employment can be "bought," but it will come at the cost of a *continuing* rise in prices.

4. During recent years, points above and to the right of the historical Phillips curve have been observed. This has led to several possible explanations:

    a. There has been a strong cost push, especially from the higher prices of oil.

    b. The Phillips curve has shifted upward because of changes in the labor market.

    c. The Phillips curve ignores the feedback of higher prices on wages. But workers are concerned with their *real* wages. In the face of rising prices, they demand higher money wages.

5. According to this line of argument, an attempt to keep unemployment at a very low level through expansive aggregate demand policies will lead to a continuous acceleration of inflation.

6. Furthermore, since expectations of future inflation play a key role in wage negotiations, this line of argument suggests that even an acceptance of a continuously accelerating inflation will not be enough to "buy" an abnormally low level of unemploy-

ment. Once an *acceleration* of inflation is itself anticipated, the unemployment rate will gravitate toward its natural rate. It is only *unanticipated* inflation which is associated with unusually low rates of unemployment.

7. Nevertheless, if there is "money illusion" on the part of wage earners and others, then there may be some long-run tradeoff between unemployment and inflation, at least up to an inflation rate of 2 percent or thereabouts (Figure 13–12).

QUESTIONS

1. Suppose that wage negotiators on both the labor and management sides negotiate over real wages; expectations of future inflation are included in the nominal money settlement. In much of this chapter, it has been assumed that the expected rate of inflation is equal to the actual rate of inflation of the recent past.

    a. If expected inflation does indeed equal past inflation, what are the implications, in terms of increases in prices, of a policy aimed at stimulating aggregate demand enough to keep the unemployment rate constant at a very low level?

    b. Now suppose that expectations regarding future inflation are dependent not only on the recent rate of inflation, but also on past changes in the rate of inflation and on public perceptions regarding aggregate demand policies. What will be the effects of aiming for a very low rate of unemployment under these circumstances?

2. The "acceleration" thesis suggests that the Phillips curve has shifted upward through time. Yet Phillips' original study was based on a very long period of almost a full century (1861–1957). On the basis of the British data for a very long period, Phillips concluded that the functional relationship was stable between nominal wage changes and the unemployment rate. How can the "acceleration" thesis be maintained in the light of this long-run British experience? Is there any way in which it might be argued that the British experience is consistent with the "acceleration" thesis?

SUGGESTED READINGS

Milton Friedman, "The Role of Monetary Policy," *American Economic Review,* March 1968, pp. 1–17.

Craufurd D. Goodwin, ed., *Exhortation and Controls: The Search for a Wage-Price Policy, 1945–1971* (Washington DC: Brookings Institution, 1975).

Organization for Economic Co-operation and Development, *Towards Full Employment and Price Stability* (Paris: OECD, 1977).

A. W. Phillips, "The Relation between Unemployment and the Rate of Change of Money Wage Rates in the United Kingdom, 1951–1957," *Economica,* November 1958, pp. 282–99.

James Tobin, "Inflation and Unemployment," *American Economic Review,* March 1972, pp. 1–18.

Chapter 14

The consumption function

The study of the consumption function has undoubtedly yielded some of the highest correlations as well as some of the most embarrassing forecasts in the history of economics.*

Franco Modigliani and Richard Brumberg

In the third chapter, a simple consumption function was presented, with the form

$$C = a + cY_d \qquad \text{(14–1; a generalized form of Equation 3–3)}$$

where

    c represents the marginal propensity to consume.

    Y_d is disposable income.

    a, the constant term, represents the height at which the consumption function meets the vertical axis.

Equation (14–1) was the cornerstone of the early Keynesian literature on consumption, for three major reasons:

---

* "Utility Analysis and the Consumption Function," in Kenneth K. Kurihara, ed., *Post-Keynesian Economics* (New Brunswick, N.J.: Rutgers University Press, 1954), p. 388.

Figure 14–1
The consumption function using a time series, 1929–1944 (per capita figures measured in 1972 dollars)

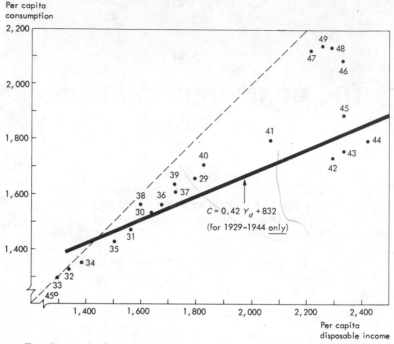

For the period 1929–44, per capita consumption fits a relatively flat consumption function.

1. It is a relatively simple function. (For this reason, the function is still used in introductory textbook expositions, such as that of Chapter 3 of this book; and it is still used in simple theoretical models.)

2. It is a plausible form for the consumption function to take. Keynes spoke in terms of a "normal psychological law" governing consumer behavior;[1] it was reasonable to expect consumers to increase consumption as income increases, but by less than the increase in income. This "normal psychological law" was consistent with the simple function of Equation (14–1).

3. The early empirical studies supported the belief that the consumption function had the general form of Equation (14–1).

---

[1] John Maynard Keynes, *General Theory of Employment, Interest, and Money* (London: Macmillan, 1936), p. 114.

There were two distinct sets of data used in these early empirical studies. One was the information on consumption and disposable income for the years 1929–44 (1929 was the first year for which official national income accounts were available). The 1929–44 figures fit the linear consumption function drawn in Figure 14–1 reasonably well. As of the end of World War II, observed consumption over a 15-year period was consistent with a function of the form of Equation (14–1).

The second set of evidence came from budget studies for the years 1935–36 and 1941–42. In a budget study, a cross-section of the popu-

Figure 14–2
The consumption function using a time series, 1950–1976 (per capita figures measured in 1972 dollars)

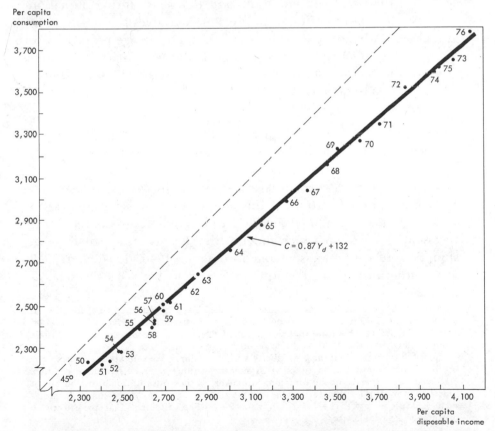

In contrast to the 1929–44 data, observations over the past two and a half decades trace out a relatively steep consumption function, passing close to the origin.

lation is investigated; the population is divided according to income groups, with the consumption of families in the different income groups at one particular period of time being compared. Thus, the points in Figure 14–3 show the consumption of different income groups at one particular period (1935–36). In contrast, the points on Figure 14–1 give the total consumption for all groups in the economy, with each point giving data for a different year.

The consumption functions drawn in these two diagrams gave a similar picture of consumer behavior. According to both the time series (Figure 14–1) and cross-section budget figures (Figure 14–3):

1. A straight line consumption function gives a passably good fit to the consumption data.[2]
2. The intercept of the consumption function on the vertical axis is positive and of significant size. That is, fitting Equation (14–1) to either of these two sets of data gives an *"a"* which is significantly positive. This means that the average propensity to consume (C/Y_d) becomes smaller as the level of income rises; and the saving rate or the average propensity to save (S/Y_d) correspondingly increases.

In the mid-1940s, then, there were three reasons for using the consumption function of Equation (14–1). It was simple, it was theoretically plausible, and two sets of empirical data were broadly consistent with it.[3]

During the late 1940s, however, it became increasingly clear that the consumption function in this simple form was not very satisfactory. It had been used in numerous predictions of a postwar recession, a recession which did not develop as anticipated.[4] Consumption relative to disposable income in 1946, 1947, and 1948 was significantly above the function fitted to the 1929–44 data, as

---

[2] Although cross-section data suggest that the "correct" consumption function is not a straight line, but rather becomes flatter as incomes rise. That is, the plotted points in Figure 14–3 indicate that the marginal propensity to consume of high-income groups is less than the *MPC* of the lower-income groups.

In much of early literature, simplicity was a dominant consideration dictating the use of a linear consumption function. A nonlinear function is clearly more complex mathematically than a linear function. Moreover, if the consumption function is not linear, then multiplier illustrations become very messy. One cannot use simple formulas such as Multiplier $= 1/(1 - MPC)$ in situations where the marginal propensity to consume is a variable.

[3] See Appendix A for an evaluation of the "secular stagnation" thesis which was built largely on this simple consumption function.

[4] There was a recession in 1949, but it was later and much milder than forecasted with the economic models used at the end of the war.

Figure 14–3
The consumption function using a budget study, 1935–1936 (current dollars)

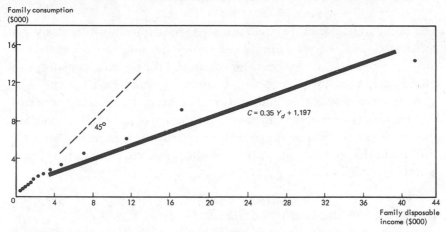

Cross-section data give a relatively flat consumption function. Those in high income brackets save a much higher percent of their incomes than do the poor.

can be seen from Figure 14–1. Furthermore, the historical statistics on income and saving collected by Simon Kuznets (the 1971 Nobel prize winner in economics) clearly indicated that the 1929–44 line could not be extended to the left without conflicting with historical data. His data for 1869–1929 indicated that there was no significant long-run change in the rate of saving as a proportion of income (although there was cyclical variation, with the saving rate being high during periods of boom and low during recessions). Thus, the long-run historical data running back into the 19th century were not consistent with a consumption function which had a significant constant term (*a* in Equation 14–1). Long-run data suggested a function running (approximately) through the origin.

By the late 1940s, then, the search was on for better consumption functions, more consistent with the increasing body of information becoming available. In particular, there was a need to develop a more sophisticated consumption function which would be consistent with both:

1. Kuznets' long-run time series data on income and consumption running back into the 19th century (which suggested that the consumption function goes through the origin).

2. Short-run time series for 1929–44 and cross-section budget

studies, both of which indicated that there was a significant positive term in the consumption function.

The search for more sophisticated consumption functions has continued and is continuing to the present day, related closely to the development of forecasting models. While the consumption function is very much a major subject of study in its own right, most current work is an elaboration of one of three basic theories: the relative income hypothesis developed by James Duesenberry, the permanent income hypothesis of Milton Friedman, and the life cycle hypothesis of Albert Ando, Richard Brumberg, and Franco Modigliani.

THE RELATIVE INCOME HYPOTHESIS (Duesenberry)

> *There lived a King, as I've been told,*
> *In the wonder-working days of old,*
> *When hearts were twice as good as gold,*
> *And twenty times as mellow. . . .*
>
> *He wished all men as rich as he*
> *(And he was rich as rich could be),*
> *So to the top of every tree*
> *Promoted everybody. . . .*
>
> *Lord Chancellors were cheap as sprats,*
> *And Bishops in their shovel hats,*
> *Were plentiful as tabby cats—*
> *In point of fact, too many. . . .*
>
> *In short, whoever you may be,*
> *To this conclusion you'll agree,*
> *When every one is somebodee,*
> *Then no one's anybody.* *
>
> Gilbert and Sullivan

In the late 1940s, Duesenberry presented his reconciliation of Kuznets' historical data with the flatter consumption functions suggested by the post-1929 data and the budget studies. In doing so, he discarded as invalid two fundamental assumptions which had previously been at the base of consumption theory.[5] These assumptions were:

---

* From *The Gondoliers*.

[5] James S. Duesenberry, *Income, Saving, and the Theory of Consumer Behavior* (Cambridge, Mass.: Harvard University Press, 1949), p. 1.

1. Every family's consumption behavior is a reflection of its own wants, independent of the consumption patterns of other families.

2. Consumption relationships are reversible in time; or, put another way, consumption depends on current income independently of past consumption behavior.

The importance of previous behavior: The ratchet effect

Kuznets' historical data indicated that, while the average fraction of income consumed did not vary much over long periods of time, there was nevertheless considerable variation within business cycles. Consumption as a fraction of income tended to be low during periods of boom and high during periods of economic slump.

Duesenberry explained these phenomena on the ground that consumers tend to follow their habitual patterns of behavior. As income rises quickly, they consume more, but not as much more as one might expect from long-run historical relationships. The reason: They are held back by their relatively low habitual patterns of consumption and adjust only slowly to their new affluence. On the other hand, when incomes drop, they find it difficult to adjust their consumption patterns downward; they have become accustomed to the good life. Thus, during periods of declining income, consumption rises as a fraction of income. In contrast to the standard assumption (point 2 above), which he rejected, Duesenberry's fundamental psychological postulate was that "it is harder for a family to reduce its expenditures from a high level than for a family to refrain from making high expenditures in the first place."[6]

In order to take consumers' previous experience into account in statistically fitting a consumption function, Duesenberry introduced the previous high level of disposable income into the consumption equation, and obtained:[7]

---

[6] "Income-Consumption Relations and their Implications," in *Income, Employment, and Public Policy,* Essays in Honor of Alvin H. Hansen (New York: W. W. Norton, 1948); reprinted in M. G. Mueller ed., *Readings in Macroeconomics,* 2d ed. (New York: Holt, Rinehart and Winston, 1971), p. 70.

[7] Duesenberry, *Income, Saving, and the Theory of Consumer Behavior,* p. 4, gives the following equation:

$$\frac{S_t}{Y_t} = 0.25 \frac{Y_t}{Y_0} - 0.196$$

It has been presented in the alternative form shown as Equation (14–2) because the focus of the discussion here is on consumption rather than saving.

$$\frac{C_t}{Y_t} = 1.196 - 0.25\frac{Y_t}{Y_0} \tag{14-2}$$

where

C_t is current consumption in year t.

Y_t is current disposable income in year t.

Y_0 is highest disposable income attained previous to the year t. All the variables are corrected for price and population changes.

Consider first the implications of Equation (14–2) for the long-run average rate of consumption. If the economy moves steadily along the long-run growth path, with per capita real disposable income increasing at a rate of about 2.5 percent per annum, Y_t would consistently equal $1.025Y_0$, and Equation (14–2) would reduce algebraically to:[8]

$$\frac{C_t}{Y_t} = 0.93975 \tag{14-3}$$

which, rounded off, can be restated:

$$C_t = 0.94Y_t \tag{14-4}$$

As a long-run average, consumption is a constant 94 percent share of disposable income. Duesenberry's equation is consistent with the long-run constancy of the average propensity to consume suggested by Kuznets' historical data.

If incomes grow steadily through time, only points along the long-run consumption function (Equation 14–4) will be observed. However, if the rate of growth of disposable income deviates from its long-run average—in either direction—then points off the long-run function will be observed. During a depression, disposable income (Y_t) is low relative to the highest previous disposable income (Y_0); therefore, according to Duesenberry's Equation (14–2), consumption is high as a fraction of income. In contrast, during a boom, when income is growing at a rate more rapid than the long-

---

[8] With

$$Y_t = 1.025Y_0$$

then

$$\frac{Y_t}{Y_0} = 1.025$$

and Equation (14–2) becomes

$$\frac{C_t}{Y_t} = 1.196 - 0.25 \times 1.025$$

from which Equation (14–3) follows directly.

run average, then the ratio Y_t/Y_0 is high, reducing consumption as a fraction of income below its long-run average. Equation (14–2) is therefore consistent with the cyclical behavior of the consumption rate observed by Kuznets.

The effects of short-run deviations in the rate of growth of income may be stated more formally. Reconsider Equation (14–2), which may be rewritten:

$$C_t = 1.196 Y_t - \frac{0.25}{Y_0} Y_t^2 \tag{14–5}$$

At the beginning of any year, the previous high income Y_0 is given. As far as the short-run responses of that year are concerned, therefore, Y_0 may be entered as a constant; this gives a short-run consumption function as shown in Figure 14–4.[9] As the years pass, of course, Y_0 will rise in growing economy, and the short-run consumption function will shift upward. Because Y_0 represents the previous high income, regardless of when it occurred, the short-run function (Equation 14–5) does not shift back down if the economy declines; it rather remains at the previous high level. Thus, the short-run consumption function is subject to a *ratchet effect.* It ratchets upward in response to the achievement of new all-time high levels of real per capita disposable income, but it does not fall back downward in response to declines in income.

Because the short-run function ratchets upward through time in response to the achievement of new highs in per capita real income, economists were misled when they looked only at the 1929–44 data. During the early 1930s, income was low by past standards; the points representing the depression years therefore fell on or near a single one of the short-run consumption functions to the left of the long-run consumption line. For the war years, the consumption points fell below and to the right of the long-run consumption line, since the rate of increase of income was greater than the historical average. (Rationing and the shortage of goods also kept down wartime consumption.) The 1929–44 data therefore gave a consumption

---

[9] Equation (14–5) obviously is not linear. The changing marginal propensity to consume may be found by elementary calculus:

$$\frac{dC_t}{dY_t} = 1.196 - \frac{0.50}{Y_0} Y_t$$

Thus, in Dusenberry's equation, the short-run *MPC* falls as the level of income (Y_t) rises. Also, for all relevant ranges, the short-run *MPC* is less than the long-run *MPC* of 0.94. (It becomes larger only if the absurd case is considered where Y_t is less than 51 percent of Y_0.) As the function (Equation 14–5) crosses the long-run growth path, it has a slope or *MPC* of 0.68.

Figure 14–4
The ratchet effect

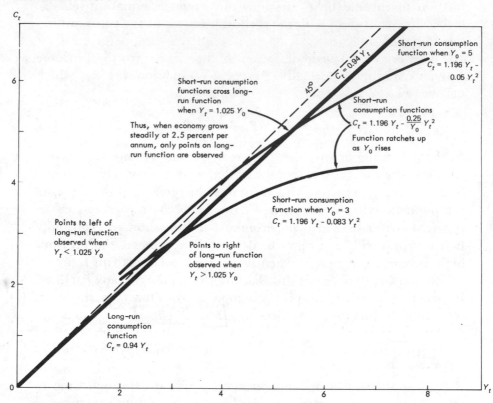

As people become accustomed to a higher standard of living, the shortrun consumption function ratchets upward.

function much flatter than Equation (14–4) $(C_t = 0.94Y_t)$; the 1929–44 data gave a misleading impression of the long-run consumption function.

The interdependence of consumer wants:
Keeping up with the Joneses

The long-run data of Kuznets indicated that the consumption function went through the origin. Two other sets of data—the short-term 1929–44 time series and the budget data—indicated that the consumption function had a significant positive constant, intersecting the vertical axis well above the origin. By the ratchet effect, Duesenberry explained the apparent contradiction between the

1929–44 data and Kuznets' historical time series. There remained, however, the problem of explaining the cross-section budget data, which indicated that families in the high-income groups saved a larger fraction of their incomes than families with low incomes. As average incomes of the population at large had risen significantly during the past century, how could budget data be reconciled with Kuznets' discovery that average saving rates did not increase over long periods of time?

The explanation, said Duesenberry, lay in the interdependence of consumer wants; the basic assumption of independence must be rejected. Consumption depends not only on the level of income which the family itself has, but also on its *relative position* in society. Those in the higher income ranges have no trouble keeping up with the standards of their associates, and indeed can do so while saving a considerable fraction of their incomes. Those with relatively low incomes attempt to keep up with the Joneses, running through most or all of their disposable income and possibly even dissaving. By consuming at a high absolute level and demonstrating the pleasures of a high standard of consumption, the richer groups set a pattern for the poorer groups to emulate; this Duesenberry called the *demonstration effect*.[10]

Thus, consumption depends not only on the absolute level of real income, but also on the family's income *relative* to the incomes of other families. As the average income of society increases, the whole consumption function shown in Figure 14–3 shifts upward. The Joneses are moving ahead, and it is necessary to spend more than previously in order to keep up with (or ahead of) them. Thus, the apparent contradiction between budget studies and the long-term time series is explained.

THE PERMANENT INCOME HYPOTHESIS

> *The very rich are different from you and me.*
> F. Scott Fitzgerald

> *Yes, they have more money.*
> Ernest Hemingway

In order to reconcile three sets of apparently contradictory data (budget studies, short-term series, and Kuznets' data), Duesenberry was led to reject the fundamental postulates of consumer theory.

---

[10] Duesenberry, *Income, Saving, and the Theory of Consumer Behavior*, p. 74.

In contrast, in his explanation of the same data, Friedman built on and elaborated the basic theory of the rational consumer.[11]

In the theory of consumer behavior, economists generally postulate that individuals will consume in such a way as to maximize their utility from goods and services. (Although the point is often submerged in simple presentations, it is also assumed that consumers will respond to such things as the relative pleasantness of work, the desire for leisure, etc. The "economic man" is a *maximizer,* not a money-grubbing boor.) In simple, one-period analyses, this maximization principle is illustrated as the choice by the consumer of the point of tangency of the budget line and the highest possible indifference curve.

When more than one period is considered, this analysis must be modified. Individuals generally spend an amount different from their incomes; they save or dissave. This does not, however, mean that the indifference curve analysis must be discarded. Two periods may be considered within the indifference-curve framework, with the individual saving in the first period and dissaving in the second, or vice versa. (The logic of the presentation can be extended to any number of periods algebraically, but, as the printed page has only two dimensions, indifference curves are applied to two periods.)

On one axis is put the consumption of the first period, and on the second axis the consumption of the second (Figure 14–5). The indifference curve now represents a choice not between two specific goods (such as clothes and food), but between consumption in the first period and consumption in the second. The budget line is determined by three factors: the income of the first period, the income of the second period, and the interest rate.[12] Suppose, for the moment, we consider what the individual could consume in the second period if he used all his available income from both periods. He could consume the sum of (a) his income in the second period, Y_2, plus (b) his income in the first period along with the interest

---

[11] Teachers who wish to skip indifference curves may go directly from here to the section beginning on p. 399. The main point of the intervening pages may be briefly summarized. According to Friedman's permanent income hypothesis, people consume in line with their *expected normal income,* not in line with their current measured income. (The one-sentence summary paragraph on p. 398 should also be noted.)

[12] In this analysis, it is usually assumed that there is a single interest rate at which the individual can borrow or lend. This is clearly a simplification. The introduction of a difference between the lending and borrowing rates would not change the analysis in any fundamental way, but it would introduce a complication. There would be a kink in the budget line at the point representing the incomes of the two periods (*H* in Figure 14–5).

Figure 14–5
Consumption and saving using indifference-curve analysis

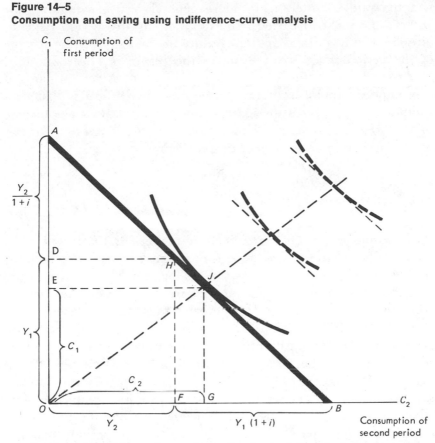

Consumption takes place where the budget line is tangent to the highest possible indifference curve. In this illustration, *DE* is saved in the first period. This amount—plus interest—is dissaved during the second period.

on that first-period income; that is, $Y_1 (1 + i)$. Thus, the budget line will reach the horizontal axis at $Y_2 + Y_1 (1 + i)$, as shown in Figure 14–5. Similarly, the point at which the budget line reaches the vertical axis is the sum of the first-period income plus the discounted value of the second-period income; that is, a total of $Y_1 + Y_2/(1 + i)$. The interest rate determines the slope of the budget line.

What does the indifference-curve analysis suggest? That consumption in the first period does not depend directly on the income of that period, but rather on the combined incomes of the two periods and the rate of interest. In more general terms, extending the analysis beyond two periods, consumption in any period depends on some sort of normal or average income, and not on the income of the period in question. And, as the future is uncertain, it is the *expected* future incomes which are important as determinants of consumption. In formal terms, Friedman's hypothesis is that consumption in the present period depends, *not directly on the income of the current period,* but rather on the *expected normal income,* or, in his terms on *permanent income;*[13] thus:

$$C = f(Y_p, i) \tag{14–6}$$

where

Y_p is permanent income; that is, expected normal income.

If income is unstable from period to period, there will be a tendency for consumers to smooth out their consumption patterns through saving or dissaving, as the case may be. Returning to the diagram illustrating two periods (Figure 14–5), we note that income in the first period (Y_1) is greater than consumption; *DE* is saved. In the second period, *DE* plus interest (that is, *FG* in total) is dissaved, making consumption greater than current income. [Two points of detail might be noted. First, if only two time periods are considered, dissaving of the second period completely uses up the saving of the first; or saving of the second period completely pays back the borrowing of the first. The two periods together are a closed book. For there to be net saving in the two periods together, the analysis must be extended to three or more periods. Second, although there is a *tendency* for consumption to be smoothed out in the face of great year-to-year differences in income, the indifference curve analysis does not imply that consumption will be made *precisely* equal in the two periods; in the above illustration (Figure 14–5), more is consumed during the second period than the first. The precise division of consumption between the two periods depends on the slope of the budget line (that is, on the rate of interest) and on the shape of the indifference curves.]

In brief, *saving and dissaving are used to make the actual time pattern of consumption correspond to the desired time pattern.*

Furthermore, said Friedman, it is reasonable to assume that the

---

[13] For a more formal definition of permanent income and a more formal statement of Friedman's hypothesis regarding the consumption function, see Milton Friedman, *A Theory of the Consumption Function* (Princeton: Princeton University Press, 1957), pp. 9–11 and 25–26.

shapes of other indifference curves are similar to the initial one;[14] any straight line drawn through the origin will cut all indifference curves where they have a common slope (the dotted curves in Figure 14–5). This means that, if the real rate of interest is reasonably stable through time, consumption will be a (reasonably) constant fraction of the growing level of permanent income. Thus, with stable real interest rates, Equation (14–6) reduces to:

$$C = kY_p \qquad\qquad (14\text{--}7)$$

where

k is a constant.

Moreover, Friedman defines permanent income so that it will be equal to measured income *when* measured income is on the long-run growth path.[15] Thus, the *long-run* relationship between consumption and income may be expressed:

$$C = kY \qquad\qquad (14\text{--}8)$$

although, it must be *stressed*, the consumption rate *for any one year* need not fall close to the long-run average unless income in that year is on the long-run trend line.

Equation (14–8) is consistent with Kuznets' long time series of consumption and disposable income. It shows no tendency for the average saving rate to change over long periods of time. (There is no constant term.) Furthermore, Friedman's theoretical foundation is also consistent with the two sets of data giving a consumption function that is considerably flatter than a line going through the origin; namely, the data of the budget studies and the short-run time series for 1929–44. Why this is so will be explained below.

The permanent income hypothesis and short-run time series

During periods of recession, the saving rate out of disposable income tends to be very low; during periods of boom it is high. What is the characteristic of recessions? Incomes have fallen; they are below normal. But the permanent income hypothesis suggests that *expected normal incomes* will be the major determinant of consumer behavior. People consume in line with their *normal*

---

[14] Friedman, *A Theory of the Consumption Function,* initially stated for a riskless universe on p. 12, and carried over to a world of uncertainty on p. 15.

[15] Friedman, *A Theory of the Consumption Function,* p. 144.

incomes; thus, during a recession, they consume a large fraction of their lower-than-normal measured incomes (and consequently they save very little). Similarly, the permanent income hypothesis suggests that the ratio of consumption to measured income will be low during booms, when measured income exceeds normal income; the saving rate consequently will be high.

Friedman found this explanation consistent with historical data. Looking at the period from 1897 to 1949, he found consumption to be unusually high relative to measured disposable income in 1933, 1932, 1934, 1921, 1931, 1935, 1897, and 1938 (ordered from the highest ratio downward). Each of these years was a year of deep depression; there was no year of clearly deep depression that did not appear on the list. Similarly, on the other side, the points of low consumption relative to disposable income were 1942, 1943, 1944, 1945, 1918, 1917, and 1905 (ordered from the lowest upward). Each was a year of abnormally high incomes; and, in addition, the unavailability of consumer goods and patriotic drives tended to depress consumption in every one of these years but 1905.[16]

The permanent income hypothesis and budget studies

Cross-section budget data show that families with relatively high incomes not only save absolutely more than those with low incomes, but also save more as a fraction of their incomes. How is this explained within the permanent income framework?

There are two reasons which combine to explain the membership of the high-income groups. People may have relatively high incomes because they are permanently in that high-income bracket. This permanently rich group should have a saving ratio in line with the saving ratio for the economy as a whole. Alternatively, high-income people may have had an abnormally good year. In this case, the permanent income hypothesis suggests that they will continue to consume in line with their (lower) normal income. They will save much of the windfall to consume over an extended period of time. Because it is made up of both the permanently rich (with moderate saving rates) and the lucky rich (with high saving rates), the high-income stratum on average has a high saving rate.[17]

---

[16] Friedman, *A Theory of the Consumption Function*, pp. 118–19.

[17] Friedman defined consumption to include the *use* of consumer durable goods, but not the *acquisition* of additional consumer durables. Such acquisitions were considered a form of saving. Thus, when incomes were abnormally high, there might be high saving in the form of purchases of consumer durables. See p. 412.

On the other side, families can have membership in the lowest-income groups for similar reasons. Their low incomes may reflect a basically bleak past, present, and future; or they may be temporarily in the low-income bracket because of misfortune or because of an uneven pattern of lifetime earnings. For example, students have very low incomes but can anticipate higher future incomes; the retired may have low current incomes but have accumulated wealth from their working years. In either of these latter cases where individuals will not be or have not been in the low-income group permanently, the permanent income hypothesis suggests that those with low current incomes should tend to dissave, smoothing out their lifetime consumption patterns.

In general, then, there are two sets of people in any income bracket. There are those who are there more or less permanently. According to the permanent income hypothesis, their saving ratio should be about average. On the other hand, there are those who are "transients" in that income class, having come from a higher or lower bracket, or expecting to move on to another class. *Any* income class (including the middle one) may, of course, contain transients. However, the *transients are a biased group*. Those temporarily in the high-income brackets are more likely to belong ordinarily to a lower-income group; those temporarily in the low-income brackets are more likely to belong ordinarily to a higher income group. Their consumption should reflect their permanent income, not their transient membership in a particular income group. Thus, the permanent income hypothesis suggests that those currently in the high-income groups should on average have a high saving rate; those currently in the low-income groups should have a low saving rate. The permanent income hypothesis is consistent with cross-section budget data.

THE LIFE CYCLE HYPOTHESIS

> Life is for living;
> Not for preparing to live.*
> Boris Pasternak

The permanent income hypothesis specifically took into account the possibility of consumer units saving to smooth out consumption over an extended period of time. A similar approach is represented

---

* From *Dr. Zhivago*.

by the life cycle hypothesis of Albert Ando and Franco Modigliani.[18]

Ando and Modigliani argued that the individual wishes to spread lifetime income in such a way as to provide an optimal lifetime pattern of consumption. Typically, income is comparatively low during the early and late years of life. Thus, with an income stream of the general nature shown in Figure 14–6, the individual will aim

Figure 14–6
The life cycle consumption hypothesis

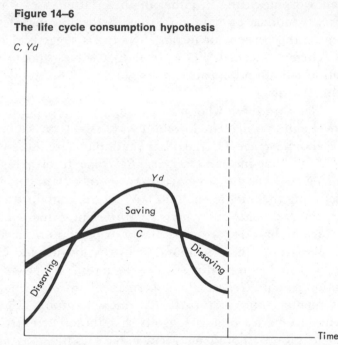

Saving and dissaving are used to smooth out the lifetime pattern of consumption.

for a consumption pattern something like C, dissaving during periods of youth and old age when income is low, and saving during the high-income years. There is, however, no reason for this consumption pattern to be perfectly horizontal. As shown in Figure 14–6, the individual may consume at a high rate during the middle years when family responsibilities are heavy.

At any point in time, the individual's consumption will depend on three things: current income, wealth accumulated from past

---

18 Albert Ando and Franco Modigliani, "The 'Life Cycle' Hypothesis of Saving," *American Economic Review*, March 1963, pp. 55–84.

saving, and the expected pattern of future income. If income is expected to remain high throughout his future lifetime, the individual will consume more currently than if he expects his income to drop off significantly. Similarly, a wealthy individual will consume more than a person with no accumulated savings. This shows up most obviously during the years of retirement, when the savings of a lifetime are called upon to maintain a standard of consumption in excess of current income.

In formal mathematical terms, Ando and Modigliani suggested that the consumption in year t should fit the equation

$$C_t = \alpha_1 Y_t{}^L + \alpha_2 Y_t{}^e + \alpha_3 W_t \qquad (14\text{--}9)$$

where

C_t is consumption in year t.

$Y_t{}^L$ is labor income during year t, net of taxes. Property income —interest, dividends, etc.—is excluded from the income $Y_t{}^L$ because wealth (from which property income is derived) is included separately as the final term of the equation.

$Y_t{}^e$ is expected future labor income. (This is a present value concept, discounted by the interest rate, as in Equation [5–2].)

W_t is wealth at the beginning of year t.

Thus

α_1 is the marginal propensity to consume out of labor income.

α_2 is the marginal propensity to consume out of expected future labor income.

α_3 is the marginal propensity to consume out of wealth.

The difficulty with fitting this equation to statistical data is that there are no observations for expected future incomes. Friedman had faced the same problem with his permanent income hypothesis —expected future incomes were a key determinant of the permanent income. Friedman had solved this problem by assuming that expected future incomes depend on the past pattern of incomes. (This will be explained later in this chapter.) Ando and Modigliani suggested two alternative methods for getting rid of the unobservable expected incomes in Equation (14–9).

1. The simplest—which they labeled their "naïve" hypothesis— was to assume that the expected labor income is directly related

to current labor income. When this is done, the Y_t^e term drops out, and Equation (14–9) becomes simply:[19]

$$C_t = a_1 Y_t{}^L + a_3 W_t \qquad (14\text{--}10)$$

The trouble with this naïve assumption is that it causes important cyclical phenomena to be missed. During the business cycle, the rate of employment varies. It is therefore reasonable to conclude that the relationship between actual income and expected future income will vary cyclically: During recessions, expected future incomes will be relatively high compared to the current level of income.

2. In order to pick up this cyclical effect, Ando and Modigliani introduced unemployment into their equation, getting:

$$C_t = b_1 Y_t{}^L + b_2 \frac{F_t}{E_t} Y_t{}^L + b_3 W_t \qquad (14\text{--}11)$$

where

F_t is the total labor force at time t.
E_t is the number employed.

There are major statistical problems in testing the goodness of fit of equations such as (14–10) or (14–11). Ando and Modigliani therefore used a number of different statistical techniques, the details of which need not detain us. Suffice it to note that in each equation a significant constant term appeared. This was contrary to their theoretical expectations: They believed that, if all resources (current income, expected future incomes, and wealth) were to rise by a common x percent, then consumption should also rise by the same x percent. They discounted the significance of the constant term because of the biases in their statistical methods, and made adjustments to suppress the constant term. When this was done, Ando and Modigliani obtained good fits for the two equations with the following coefficients, using annual data for 1929–59 (excluding 1941–46):

$$C_t = 0.52 Y_t{}^L + 0.072 W_t \qquad (14\text{--}12)$$

and

$$C_t = 0.44 Y_t{}^L + 0.24 \frac{F_t}{E_t} Y_t{}^L + 0.049 W_t \qquad (14\text{--}13)$$

---

[19] With $Y_t{}^e = b Y_t{}^L$, Equation (14–9) becomes:

$$C_t = (\alpha_1 + \alpha_2 b) Y_t{}^L + \alpha_3 W_t$$

with $\alpha_1 + \alpha_2 b$ becoming the a_1 of Equation (14–10).

Wealth showed up significantly in each equation.[20] There was a propensity to consume out of wealth of something like 0.06 (that is somewhere in the neighborhood of the 0.072 of Equation [14–12] and the 0.049 of Equation [14–13]).[21] Since annual data were used in Equations (14–12) and (14–13), consumers were concluded to spend about 6 percent of their accumulated wealth each year. This does *not* mean, however, that they necessarily run down their wealth, since they are simultaneously engaged in saving out of income. What it does indicate, rather, is that the level of consumption rises with higher levels of wealth.

The implication of these functions is a diagram similar to Figure 14–4, which was drawn for Duesenberry's theory. The relatively flat functions now (Figure 14–7), however, represent the consumption pattern if wealth remains unchanged. If wealth grows steadily, the "short-run" consumption function will shift steadily upward. If labor incomes also grow steadily, the only points which will be observed will be along a straight long-run consumption line. During short-run cyclical fluctuations in which assets remain relatively constant, consumption will fall on or near a single one of the short-run consumption functions. (While the level of wealth fell during the Depression, it declined less than income,[22] so that the observed rise in consumption as a percentage of income during the early 1930s is consistent with the Ando-Modigliani specification of the function.)

Ando and Modigliani currently use an updated version of the life cycle hypothesis in their MPS (MIT/Penn/Social Science Research Council) forecasting model. In this version, they substitute total disposable income for labor income, partly because it is difficult to estimate income tax applicable to labor income alone. The cyclical effect is picked up by using lagged as well as current income. Thus, their consumption function now has the form:[23]

---

[20] This conclusion was confirmed by other tests, and the authors summarized (p. 71): ". . . all of the tests seem, by and large, to support the basic hypothesis advanced in this paper, and in particular, the importance of net worth as a determinant of consumption."

[21] And a propensity to consume out of current income of about 0.6.

In Equation (14–12), the coefficient for consumption out of current income is 0.52. Equation (14–13) is less straightforward. It indicates that consumption out of current income is $0.44 + 0.24 \ F_t/E_t$. But F_t/E_t is just a bit more than 1. Therefore, Equation (14–13) indicates a propensity to consume from current income of about 0.7.

[22] The wealth/income ratio rose from 5.96 in 1930 to 6.70 in 1933. See Michael K. Evans, *Macroeconomic Activity* (New York: Harper & Row, 1969), p. 37.

[23] Franco Modigliani, "Monetary Policy and Consumption," in Federal Reserve Bank of Boston, *Consumer Spending and Monetary Policy* (Boston, 1971), especially pp. 14, 75; Albert Ando, "Some Aspects of Stabilization Policies, the Monetarist Con-

Figure 14–7
The life cycle hypothesis (numbers from Equation 14–12)

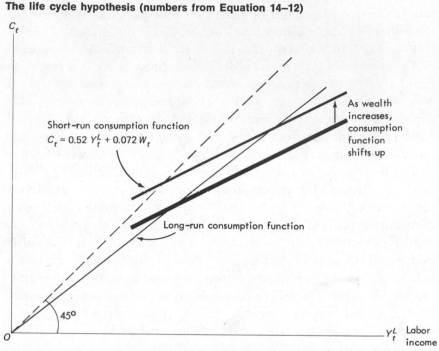

In the life cycle hypothesis, consumption depends both on income and on wealth.

$$C = 0.67 \text{ (weighted average of disposable income over the previous three years)} + 0.053 \text{ (weighted average of consumers' net worth in the previous three years)} \qquad (14\text{--}14)$$

THE THREE CONSUMPTION HYPOTHESES: SOME SIMILARITIES AND DIFFERENCES

There are significant similarities among the three theories. Most obviously, they set out to explain the same observed set of data and, in particular, the apparent discrepancy between the short-term consumption series of 1929–44 and the long-term data of Kuznets. Two of them—the relative income hypothesis (RIH) of Duesenberry

troversy, and the MPS Model," in Lawrence R. Klein and Edwin Burmeister, eds., *Econometric Model Performance* (Philadelphia: University of Pennsylvania Press, 1976), especially pp. 159, 163; and the forthcoming book by Ando and Modigliani on the MPS model.

and the permanent income hypothesis (PIH) of Friedman—also explicitly present an explanation of cross-section data. (The life cycle hypothesis was formulated specifically for the analysis of aggregate data, and therefore does not lead so clearly to an explanation of cross-section data.) [24]

Each of the three theories provides an explanation of why economists were initially misled by the 1929–44 time series data, concluding that the long-run consumption function was relatively flat. The relative income hypothesis and the life cycle hypothesis both have mechanisms causing upward shifts of the consumption function through time, and in each case the Depression prevented or slowed down the upward shift:

1. In the relative income hypothesis, the upward shift results from increasing levels of past income to which consumers have become accustomed. During the early part of the 1929–44 period, income was below the previous high level to which consumers had become accustomed, and therefore the observations were on or near a single one of Duesenberry's short-run consumption functions. During the end of the period, incomes rose very rapidly with the coming of the war, and goods were scarce; both factors tended to suppress the rate of consumption (C/Y_d), putting the observations to the right of the long-run consumption line. The combined effects of the Depression and the ensuing wartime period were therefore to give a relatively flat consumption function for 1929–44.
2. In the life cycle hypothesis, the upward shift of the consumption function occurs as wealth is accumulated. During most of the 1929–44 period, wealth failed to grow at a normal rate; the data for those years were relatively near a single one of the short-run consumption functions shown in Figure 14–7.

In the permanent income hypothesis, there is likewise an explanation of why the 1929–44 period gives an unusually flat line for consumption as a function of measured income. During a period of steady growth, the level of consumption would rise steadily in response to a steady increase in permanent income (Equation 14–8 and the accompanying text). During a depression, however, the

[24] For a related discussion of cross-section data, see Franco Modigliani and Richard Brumberg, "Utility Analysis and the Consumption Function: An Interpretation of Cross-Section Data," in Kenneth K. Kurihara, ed., *Post-Keynesian Economics* (New Brunswick, N.J.: Rutgers University Press, 1954), pp. 388–436. The Modigliani-Brumberg explanation of cross-section data is similar to that of Friedman.

relationship between permanent income (which determines consumption) and measured income is distorted from its normal relationship. Measured incomes fall; they are considered abnormally low. Hence consumption—which is determined by permanent income—becomes abnormally high as a fraction of measured income. Similarly, during a wartime boom incomes are abnormally high, and therefore the consumption rate (C/Y_d) is abnormally low. This explains the flatness of consumption as a function of measured income during the 1929–44 period. In general, permanent income tends to be much more stable than measured income through time, and therefore the short-run consumption function during periods when the growth rate deviates from the long-term average will be flatter than the long-run consumption function. In this respect, the permanent income hypothesis leads to similar expectations as the RIH and the LCH, and for broadly similar reasons: The flatness of short-run consumption (as a function of measured income) *is a result of departures from the long-run average rate of growth of income.*

The RIH and the PIH also include an explanation of the flatness of the consumption function derived from cross-section data. According to the permanent income hypothesis, those in the top brackets of measured income include not only those with consistently high incomes, but also those who have had abnormally good years. This latter component consumes in line with its lower permanent incomes, thus depressing the ratio of consumption to measured income for the group as a whole. Similarly, at the other end of the income distribution spectrum, the low-income group includes individuals whose income is temporarily low and who therefore have high consumption ratios. The relative income hypothesis of Duesenberry ascribes the flatness of the cross-section function to the demonstration effect. Consumption is influenced by the desire to catch up with the Joneses.

But if there are notable similarities in the problems with which the various hypotheses deal, there are also notable differences. Most interesting, perhaps, is the sharp difference in the philosophical implications of the relative income hypothesis, on the one hand, and the other two theories, on the other. The RIH stresses the interdependence and irreversibility of consumer behavior: People strive to keep up with their neighbors and with established patterns of consumption. They are prisoners of social pressures and their own habits. The PIH and the LCH, in contrast, stress the rational basis for behavior. Consumers save with a purpose in mind; saving allows them to smooth out their patterns of consumption and therefore achieve a higher level of satisfaction from their incomes over an extended period of time.

On the basis of the Duesenberry hypothesis, fundamental questions can be asked about the contributions of economic growth to human welfare. If the name of the game is to catch up to or keep ahead of your neighbors, then it is not so clear what contribution will be made to overall human welfare by a simple doubling of all incomes. In the century-old words of Sir William Gilbert, when everybody's somebody, then perhaps still no one will be anybody. Insofar as an individual's utility depends on his comparative place in society, then the normal forces of the market will lead to a greater stress on economic affluence than is socially desirable; no account is taken by the market of the disutility which any individual's increase in consumption will cause for his neighbors in a jealous and status-conscious world.[25] No such philosophical problems are raised by the permanent income or life cycle hypotheses: The basic assumption is that the saving of today is the result of a desire to even out consumption patterns, and that this effort to optimize on the part of individuals has no inherent adverse side effect on others.

In drawing attention to possible adverse side effects of increases in consumption, the RIH suggests that market forces may involve an undue emphasis on economic affluence; the total social gains from increases in income are less than the sum of the gains as seen by individual consumers. Even if one does accept the RIH as being "correct"—in itself a problem when there are (at least) two competing hypotheses—it is important that several qualifications be made. In particular, if "external diseconomies" (adverse side effects)

---

[25] Fred Hirsch believes that this phenomenon explains the apparently paradoxical trend toward collectivism, even at a time when individual freedom of action is especially extolled. He writes:

> Acting alone, each individual seeks to make the best of his or her position. But satisfaction of these individual preferences [for an education or for a country cottage] itself alters the situation that faces others seeking to satisfy similar wants. A round of transactions . . . therefore leaves each individual with a worse bargain than was reckoned. . . .
>
> Advance in society is possible only by moving to a higher place among one's fellows, that is, by improving one's performance in relation to other people's performances. If everyone stands on tiptoe, no one sees better. Where social interaction of this kind is present, individual action is no longer a sure means of fulfilling individual choice: the preferred outcome may be attainable only through collective action. (We all agree explicitly or implicitly not to stand on tiptoe.)

Hirsch, *Social Limits to Growth* (Cambridge, Mass.: Harvard, 1976), pp. 4–5.

are to be considered in evaluating the desirability of economic growth, then the possibilities of external economies (benefits to others) should also be investigated. There are external economies from the process of saving, investment, and the resulting growth.[26] The saver gets back the return from additional capital formation in the form of higher interest and dividend payments, but there is an added benefit to others: Increases in the stock of capital raise the productivity and the wage rate of the labor force. If a balance is struck between these two externalities (and others which rather readily come to mind), it is not clear whether the market places too great or too small a value on economic growth. A second qualification: Although the argument has been put in terms of problems with "market economies," the same issues arise with respect to other economic systems. In "socialist" countries, the stress on growth seems to be at least as great as in "capitalist" countries. Indeed, the Soviet preoccupation with catching up with the West may in itself be an international illustration of Duesenberry's argument that emulation of the rich is an important determinant of economic behavior.[27]

Thus, the RIH and the PIH have quite different philosophical implications, with the former raising fundamental questions about social goals. They also have quite different implications for short-term stabilization policy. In this regard, the RIH of Duesenberry falls within the broad Keynesian tradition. Fiscal policy can remain

---

[26] Note the assumption that additional saving contributes to capital formation and thus to growth. This would not be true in a world of clearly inadequate demand, where the "paradox of thrift" applies. However, it is a reasonable first approximation in an economy in which aggregate demand, on average, has not been inadequate for three decades.

[27] Interestingly, emulation of the rich might lead either to increases in consumption, in order to approach the standard of living established by the rich, or alternatively to increases in saving (*decreases* in current consumption) in order to lay the basis for future incomes approaching those of the relatively rich. Thus, the desire to match others may either raise or lower the rate of consumption out of current income, depending on whether a short- or long-term view is taken. The Soviet government tends to take a long-term view; emulation tends to show up in the form of higher capital formation rather than as increases in current consumption.

Soon after Duesenberry's work on the consumption function, the demonstration effect was seen as a potential problem for developing countries. Even though their absolute incomes might rise through time, they might find it very difficult to save enough to provide the desirable rate of capital accumulation [Ragnar Nurkse, *Problems of Capital Formation in Underdeveloped Countries* (New York: Oxford University Press, 1962), pp. 57–81]. Nurkse concluded that there might be an economic explanation of the "iron curtain" (p. 76): The societies of Eastern Europe wish to promote economic development by reducing international communication, thereby isolating their economies from the demonstration effect. Thus, a higher level of saving and capital formation might be possible.

as the key weapon in the countercyclical fiscal policy arsenal, although the evaluation of the effects of fiscal policies will be complicated. In particular, the difference between the short-run marginal propensity to consume and the larger long-run *MPC* will have to be taken into account when predicting the overall effects of a change in government spending or taxation.

In contrast, the permanent income hypothesis casts doubt on the effectiveness of fiscal policies, and, in particular, on the effectiveness of temporary income tax surcharges or rebates as a means of stabilizing demand. According to the permanent income hypothesis, if the government institutes a tax surcharge which is clearly intended to be temporary, then the surcharge will cause little change in consumers' evaluation of their basic long-run position. As a consequence, the tax surcharge will be reflected mostly in a decrease in saving rather than a decrease in consumption. The temporary tax surcharge will therefore have relatively little effect on aggregate demand.[28] Thus, there were two major features of Friedman's theories which suggested that the failure of the economy to respond quickly to the tax surcharge of 1968 should have come as no great surprise: The surcharge was accompanied by a rapid expansion of the money supply, and the surcharge in any event would have had only a modest effect on consumer behavior because it was clearly intended to be a *temporary* surcharge.[29] Similarly, the PIH suggests that a

---

[28] According to Friedman's statistical estimates, a decrease of measured disposable income of $100 in year t will cause a decrease in consumption of $29 in year t. (See Equation 14–18; $ka = 0.2904$.) This, however, represents an *average* response to changes in measured disposable income—whether a temporary or a permanent change. Friedman's theory suggests that the response of consumption to a tax change which is temporary and reversible should be less than the average response of 29 percent.

On the other hand, the 29 percent does not include purchases of consumer durable goods. In order to get the total effect of a tax change on consumer demand, the changes in consumer durable purchases must be added to Friedman's figures.

[29] The evaluation of historical evidence is a complex matter, which cannot be dealt with adequately here. It is possible to interpret the events of 1968–69 in a quite different manner. See, in particular, Arthur Okun, "The Personal Tax Surcharge and Consumer Demand, 1968," *Brookings Papers on Economic Activity*, 1971, vol. 1, pp. 167–200. Okun concluded (p. 198) that "the evidence of the surcharge period as interpreted by four econometric models indicates that the surcharge curbed consumption nearly as much as was expected, and that *any shortcomings in its effectiveness have no evident connection to the permanent income hypothesis.*" (Italics added.)

William L. Springer worked over the same surcharge period, and arrived at conclusions "exactly the opposite" to those of Okun. In particular, "it was found that the 1968 surcharge did *not* lead to a significant reduction in consumption expenditures." (The surcharge was followed by a drop in the saving rate, consistent with the prediction of the permanent income hypothesis.) Springer, "Did the 1968 Surcharge Really Work?" *American Economic Review*, September 1975, pp. 644–59. (The quotations are from pp. 644–45.)

temporary tax rebate—such as that proposed by President Carter in early 1977—has little effect on consumption. (For a reason why the administration decided on a *temporary* rebate rather than a permanent tax cut as its major fiscal policy proposal, see p. 228).

There is, however, one aspect of Friedman's consumption theory which requires an important modification—and weakening—of this antifiscal policy conclusion. Friedman defined consumption to include only the value of the current use of durable goods and treated purchases of consumer durables as a form of saving.[30] This fits into his general theoretical background: During periods of abnormally high income, people save to enable consumption in following periods to be higher than otherwise. One way of saving for the future: Buy a car or other consumer durable which can be used over an extended period. Thus, if people put abnormally high incomes into consumer durables, it is not inconsistent with this theory. The abnormally high incomes are going into a specific form of saving rather than into current consumption.

Now let us return to the effects of a temporary income tax cut. People will have windfalls of additional disposable income. According to the permanent income hypothesis, this should go predominantly into saving, not consumption. The stimulative effects on aggregate demand would therefore seem to be dissipated. But suppose that they "save" in the form of additional purchases of houses, cars, TV sets, etc. Aggregate demand and production will therefore be stimulated. Similarly, within the PIH framework, the temporary income tax surcharge of 1968 could have a sizable effect on aggregate demand: People might respond to their temporarily depressed disposable incomes by deferring the replacement of consumer durables.

It is perhaps surprising that, after so many years of intensive attention to the consumption function, the economics profession is not yet in a position to make categorical judgments among competing hypotheses. That this has not been possible is in part a testimony to the difficulties of interpreting statistical evidence in a complex and ever-changing world. It is also in part because the various hypotheses predict similar results in many instances; as noted above, this was conspicuously true of the predicted cyclical behavior of consumption. Although there is a philosophical contrast between the permanent income hypothesis (with its emphasis on the rational

---

[30] Friedman, *A Theory of the Consumption Function*, pp. 40, 116.

consumer) and the relative income hypothesis (with its emphasis on the influence of habitual behavior), there is not so much difference between the mathematical representation of the two approaches. Indeed, as will be seen in the section below, the permanent income hypothesis leads to a mathematical specification which is identical to that which can be derived from a straightforward extension of the "habit" argument.

The permanent income hypothesis and the "habit" hypothesis: Their mathematical similarity

In Chapter 7, it was argued that difficulties would arise in distinguishing statistically between a relatively simple Keynesian consumption function, and a consumption function in which individual behavior was influenced by past saving and wealth. Yet the theoretical implications of the two theories are sharply different. In the Keynesian theory, people save without particular thought for what they will do with their accumulated wealth.[31] In classical theory, people save rationally, accumulating wealth for future use, and it is therefore important to include wealth in the consumption function. The Keynesian consumption function with its mindless (?) saving is a key requirement for the demonstration of the theoretical possibility of an unemployment equilibrium; the dependence of consumption on wealth (the "Pigou" effect) is the key to the classical rebuttal, that there can be no equilibrium with unemployment (Chapter 7).

The purpose of this section is to elaborate on the difficulty of statistically distinguishing between the two basic approaches to the consumption function. This is *not* to suggest that *nothing* can be learned about the fundamental theoretical question of wealth as a determinant of consumption. In particular, the life cycle hypothesis includes wealth explicitly in the consumption function (Equations 14–12, 14–13, and 14–14), and does so in a manner that goes a long way to getting around the problem raised in Chapter 7 (p. 157). That is, changes in wealth are defined partially independently of the difference between past income and past saving. Specifically, in

---

[31] In their cited article, p. 407, Modigliani and Brumberg observe: "According to the usual explanation [of saving], which is already to be found in the *General Theory* (p. 97), consumer habits are sticky and only adjust with a lag to the changed circumstances; in the meantime, savings, which are considered as a passive residual, absorb a large share of the changed income."

recent versions of the life cycle hypothesis, forming a key part of the MPS model, changes in wealth include:[32]

1. The value of the increase in the housing stock.
2. The change in the value of the preexisting housing stock and land owned by consumers.
3. The value of the increase in the stock of consumer durables.
4. The change in the value of the preexisting stock of consumer durables.
5. Changes in the market value of corporate equity (stock).

In the MPS model, wealth shows up significantly,[33] suggesting that the controversy should be settled on the classical side; consumers save in a calculated manner, in order to be able to consume more in the future. (Interestingly, the MPS model also provides a much more powerful estimate of monetary policy than do alternative Keynesian-based econometric models. Monetary policy is effective in the MPS model because the model picks up the effect of monetary policy on wealth, and thence on consumption.) However, no such categorical conclusion in favor of the classical viewpoint is possible on the basis of the MPS results. Although the MPS model has at times performed better in predicting the level of consumption (particularly during the third quarter of 1968, right after the income tax surcharge was introduced), its overall predicting record is not clearly superior to other models.[34]

But if the life cycle hypothesis leads to the inclusion of wealth in the consumption function in a manner which is potentially capable of demonstrating wealth's significance (or lack thereof), the wealth issue tends to become blurred elsewhere. This blurring and lack of distinction show up most notably if the statistical implications of two apparently contradictory hypotheses are considered:

1. The permanent income hypothesis. This is based on the assumption that the consumer maximizes utility over an extended

---

[32] For decreases, subtract (for example, item 4 is negative).

[33] The life cycle hypothesis and its variants are not the only consumption functions to include wealth. Wealth also appears, for example, in the consumption functions in H. S. Houthakker and Lester D. Taylor, *Consumer Demand in the United States*, 2d ed. (Cambridge, Mass.: Harvard, 1970); Alan Spiro, "Wealth and the Consumption Function," *Journal of Political Economy*, August 1962, pp. 339–54; and James Tobin, "Relative Income, Absolute Income, and Savings," in *Money, Trade and Economic Growth; Essays in Honor of John Henry Williams* (New York: Macmillan, 1951).

[34] Saul H. Hymans, "Consumption: New Data and Old Puzzles," *Brookings Papers on Economic Activity*, 1970, vol. 1, pp. 117–26.

number of periods. Friedman's permanent income is closely related to the concept of <u>wealth</u>.[35]

2. The hypothesis that consumers are greatly affected by the (irrational?) weight of past habits.

While Duesenberry's work has become the best known exposition of the habit hypothesis, a number of other writers came to substantially similar conclusions. For example, T. M. Brown presented an alternative formulation of the habit hypothesis in his paper, "Habit Persistence and Lags in Consumer Behavior."[36] Suppose we wish to investigate the effects of habit on consumer behavior. Like Brown, we might present a function of the form:

$$C_t = {}_\alpha Y_t + \beta C_{t-1} \tag{14-15}$$

In simplest terms, consumption during this period depends on income in this period and the consumption level established last period.

Now let us turn to the permanent income hypothesis. In the above pages, much has been said about the theoretical underpinnings of the hypothesis and its implications. But little has yet been said about how a key theoretical concept—the consumer's budget constraint—can be measured with available data. This obviously poses a problem. In theory, what we want is a measure of the accumulated past wealth, the current measured income, and expected future incomes in order to be able to determine the total budget constraint of the consumer. But there are obviously no direct measures of expected future income.

Friedman of course recognized this problem. One way of dealing with it, and the one he chose, is to assume that the expected future pattern of income is determined by past experience. It also seems reasonable to give the greatest weight to the most recent experience, and to give successively declining weights to earlier incomes. Thus, the function which Friedman suggested for permanent income (Y_p) in year t had the general form:[37]

$$Y_{pt} = a(Y_t + bY_{t-1} + b^2 Y_{t-2} + \cdots + b^{17} Y_{t-17}) \tag{14-16}$$

---

[35] See Friedman, *A Theory of the Consumption Function,* p. 11.

[36] *Econometrica,* July 1952, pp. 355–71.

[37] This is a simplification. Friedman (pp. 142–47) used a rather complex continuous function. For those with a mathematical bent, the b in Equation (14–16) is a stand-in for his $e^{(\beta-\alpha)}$ where α is the rate of growth. Thus, in Friedman's work, b is a function of the rate of growth.

Now, since the permanent income hypothesis suggests that consumption will be a constant fraction of permanent income,

$$C_t = kY_{pt} \qquad \text{(14–17, from 14–7)}$$

the consumption function to be statistically estimated became:

$$C_t = ka(Y_t + bY_{t-1} + b^2Y_{t-2} + \cdots + b^{17}Y_{t-17})$$
$$\text{(14–18, from 14–16 and 14–17)}$$

This is a simplified version of the function Friedman used with annual data for the nonwar years from 1905 to 1951, finding: $k = 0.88$, $a = 0.33$, and $b = 0.67$.[38]

Thus, the marginal propensity to consume out of income of the current year $(k \times a)$ is about 0.29; income of the current year affects consumption, but only through its effect on permanent income.

Thus far, the possible difficulty with which we started—the potential similarity of the statistical specification of the PIH and the habit hypothesis—has not shown up clearly, although the use of data from the previous 17 years in Friedman's function may raise doubts about whether the effects of habits have been allowed to sneak in the back door. The answer is yes; indeed, the simple habit hypothesis (Equation 14–15) is mathematically identical to the permanent income Equation (14–18).[39] This may be seen as follows. Multiply each side of Equation (14–18) by b, and lag one period; thus:

$$bC_{t-1} = ka(bY_{t-1} + b^2Y_{t-2} + \cdots + b^{18}Y_{t-18}) \qquad \text{(14–19)}$$

And, subtracting Equation (14–19) from (14–18), we get:

$$C_t - bC_{t-1} = ka(Y_t - b^{18}Y_{t-18}) \qquad \text{(14–20)}$$

With b being 0.67, b^{18} becomes exceedingly small (specifically, 0.00074), and the final term of Equation (14–20) may be dropped, giving:

$$C_t - bC_{t-1} = kaY_t \qquad \text{(14–21)}$$

---

[38] Observe that, if Y is constant, and therefore $Y_t = Y_{t-1} = Y_{t-2} \ldots$, then $Y_{pt} = Y_t$ since

$$Y_{pt} = \tfrac{1}{3}(Y_t + \tfrac{2}{3}Y_t + (\tfrac{2}{3})^2Y_t + \cdots)$$
$$= \tfrac{1}{3}(3Y_t) \qquad \text{(using Equation 4–2)}$$
$$= Y_t$$

This is a reasonable outcome. If income is constant, the expected normal income is equal to current income. Thus, it is no accident that $a + b = 1$; indeed, the permanent income study is designed with a assumed equal to $(1 - b)$.

[39] Strictly speaking, the two are identical only when there are an infinite number of periods, and when, therefore, the final term in Equation (14–20) approaches zero.

That is:

$$C_t = kaY_t + bC_{t-1} \qquad (14\text{--}22)$$

which is identical in form to the equation for evaluating the habit hypothesis (Equation 14–15). The derivation of Equation 14–22 from Equation 14–18 is known as the *Koyck transformation* from the procedure used by L. M. Koyck in deriving his investment function.[40]

Thus, while the PIH and the habit hypothesis start out from quite different philosophical viewpoints—with the PIH postulating a coolly calculating consumer maximizing utility over an horizon of many periods, while the habit hypothesis has the consumer responding with little apparent thought to the force of habit—they reduce to the same mathematical formulation when it gets down to the actual fitting of the statistics.[41] [Furthermore, in its recent version the life cycle hypothesis is also similar, using a weighted average of recent income (Equation 14–14). However, the LCH equation retains the distinction of a separate estimate of wealth.]

While the introduction of wealth into the consumption function does allow some light to be shed on the major theoretical differences between Keynesian and classical economists, this excursion into the detailed studies of the consumption function suggests that the basic theoretical and philosophical differences within the profession are not amenable to a simple, clear solution on the basis of statistical evidence. Perhaps this is one of the reasons why there has been a continuing difference in the theoretical framework and the philosophical outlook of Keynesian and classical economists; and also why there has been a tendency for many economists to move toward a middle ground, gaining substantial insights from both bodies of literature without making a total commitment to either. It particularly indicates the desirability of a noncommittal, open-minded approach by beginning students of economics.

The case for remaining noncommittal regarding the "best" theoretical starting point can perhaps be made most clearly by noting the embarrassing questions which must be swept under the rug before either framework can be accepted as entirely valid. These include:

---

[40] L. M. Koyck, *Distributed Lags and Investment Analysis* (Amsterdam: North-Holland, 1954). Koyck's work on investment is outlined in Chapter 15.

[41] For an evaluation of particular evidence regarding the permanent income hypothesis, see Appendix B to this chapter.

1. For Keynesians: Do consumers really save in the apparently un-
    calculating way suggested by Keynesian theory and, in particu-
    lar, by the simple theory of the multiplier and by the habit
    hypothesis? What do they save *for?* Even if they do appear to
    behave in an uncalculating manner in response to short-run
    changes, will they not sooner or later begin to ask questions
    about the purpose of saving? If so, does not a sharp distinction
    have to be made between the usefulness of Keynesian constructs
    for analysis of short-term changes in the economy, and the ques-
    tionable desirability of falling back on Keynesian concepts of
    equilibrium in analyzing the more fundamental, long-run eco-
    nomic problems?

2. For those in the classical tradition, who stress the rationality of
    the consumer and the microanalytic underpinnings of the con-
    sumption function: Do consumers really behave in highly ra-
    tional ways, maximizing over long periods of time? If so, how
    does one explain the behavior of those who save throughout
    their lifetimes, even though their children may be expected to
    have significantly higher incomes? And what about those who
    continuously save even though they have no heirs? Does not the
    desire for power and prestige also provide an explanation for
    saving? Is saving and consumption behavior completely unre-
    lated to the relative position of individuals in society? Are in-
    dividual utility functions really independent?[42]

APPENDIX A

THE CONSUMPTION FUNCTION AND SECULAR STAGNATION

During the early Keynesian period, the discussion of consumption
centered on the relatively simple function:

$$C = a + cY_d \tag{14-1}$$

One of the interesting implications of this function was the support
which it gave to the proposition that the United States was in danger

---

[42] This question is much broader than the points raised by Duesenberry. In particular, the "creation" of wants by business through advertising also is relevant here.
See John Kenneth Galbraith, *The Affluent Society* (Boston: Houghton-Mifflin, 1958).
Galbraith attacks the laissez-faire implications of the theory of the rational, independent consumer.

of *secular stagnation*. The function was one of the major inputs into
the argument that the natural forces of the free market would tend
to make the unemployment problem worse as time passed; the stag-
nant aggregate demand of the 1930s was not a transitory difficulty.[43]

Suppose that we return to the diagram based on Equation (14–1),
and consider the probable position of the economy in 10, 20, or 30
years' time. As technology progresses and productive capacity increases, the level of demand required to ensure full employment becomes greater and greater. In other words, the total amount of consumption, investment, and government spending required for full
employment will rise as time passes. And, to add to the potential
problem, consumption at the full-employment level goes up more
slowly than the total demand required for full employment; as the
full-employment level of output moves to the right with the passage
of time, the gap between C and D becomes larger (Figure 14A–1)
—not only in absolute terms but also *as a fraction* of total demand
required for full employment. Either taxes must be continuously cut
in order to shift the consumption function upward, or a larger and
larger proportion of the total productive capacity of the economy
must be shifted toward investment and the government sector.

In the late 1930s, in particular, economists were not optimistic
about the prospects for a high and growing level of investment demand. The western frontier, which had made continuing demands
on capital resources throughout American history, had come to an
end; indeed, there were no large, rich areas to be occupied anywhere in the entire world. Furthermore, there was no assurance
that there would be a repeat of the great inventions, such as the railroads, which were such significant users of capital in the 19th century. And population showed signs of stabilizing, suggesting an end
to the major investments needed to provide for new people.[44]

The policy implications of this line of analysis are clear: With
investment demand weak and consumption demand rising at a
slower rate than income, then either the United States would
undergo increasing problems of unemployment, or the voting public

---

[43] Professor Alvin H. Hansen of Harvard University was the foremost exponent of
this view. In his *Full Recovery or Stagnation?* (New York: W. W. Norton, 1938), p. 7,
he wrote (italics added): "The relatively full employment enjoyed in this country in
. . . 1923–29 can . . . be explained in large measure in terms of *special conditions.*"

[44] This paragraph draws heavily on Alvin H. Hansen, *Full Recovery or Stagnation?*
pp. 311–18. For a reaffirmation of the stagnation thesis, see Hansen's brief postscript to
the reprinting of his 1939 article, "Economic Progress and Declining Population
Growth," in M. G. Mueller, ed., *Readings in Macroeconomics,* 2d ed. (New York:
Holt, Rinehart and Winston, 1971), p. 276.

Figure 14A–1
Secular stagnation?

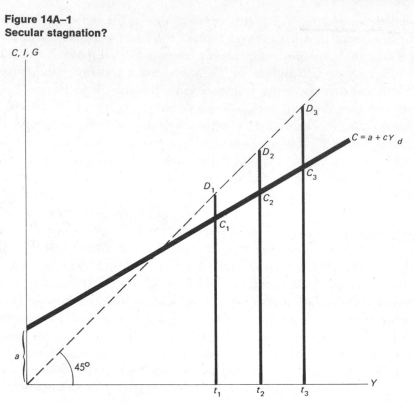

As the productive capacity of a full-employment economy expands through time from t_1 t_2, t_3, and so on, then the gap (*CD*) between consumption demand and the total demand needed for full employment will grow progressively larger.

would have to get used to ever-increasing government deficits. Of these two, big and increasing government deficits were clearly the preferable alternative; increases in government spending, or tax cuts, or a combination of the two were desirable on a continuing basis to counteract the danger of secular stagnation. In the event, of course, the concern over secular stagnation was quickly shunted aside with the coming of World War II. But, toward the end of the war, it revived in the form of predictions by economists of significant slack in the postwar economy. These fears proved greatly exaggerated: The postwar period has generally been one of inflation, not inadequate demand. On behalf of the economists who foresaw demand weakness, however, it might be noted that a number of their fundamental assumptions proved incorrect. Major new investment opportunities opened up, in the airlines and many other industries; there was the demand occasioned by World War II itself, and the need to replace equipment (including private automobiles, etc.) run down during the war; military spending was a continuing source of demand with the Korean conflict, the cold war, and Vietnam; and, last but not least, population growth revived. (This last point is of current interest: Will the recent decline in the birth rate lead to a weakening of investment demand?)

In contrast to the Keynesian view, the logic of the classical theoretical system was that there was no particular level of investment demand or government spending which was *required* to ensure long-run equilibrium; the basic assumptions behind the secular stagnation argument were invalid. According to classical economics, consumption as a function of disposable income is not fixed; it can be shifted. If, for example, the monetary holdings of the public are increased, then consumption out of any given level of income will also increase (the Pigou effect). More broadly, the consumption function responds to changes in wealth in general. The classic view that full employment is possible irrespective of the long-run trend of investment found its strongest expression in the classical theory of the stationary state: As classicists foresaw the ultimate economic equilibrium, there would be no net investment, and consumption (including consumption by the government) would come to equal income at the full-employment level.[45]

Empirical evidence presented in this chapter suggests that, at the least, the early fears of secular stagnation were exaggerated. Kuznets' data, in particular, indicated that the ratio of consumption to disposable income did not change significantly over long periods of time; therefore, there was no reason to believe that the gap between consumption demand and full-employment demand would become *relatively* larger as time passed. (Interestingly, Kuznets' carefully derived data were not necessary to shake confidence in the early Keynesian consumption function. All that was really needed was the correct pointed question regarding Figure 14–1: Approximately where should an average year for the first half of the 19th century be plotted? Precise data are not needed to give a general answer. Income was lower in the earlier 19th century than in the 1930s, yet the saving rate was high enough to finance the rapid capital accumulation that was needed for the economic growth of that era.

---

[45] Recall the title of A. C. Pigou's early attack on Keynes: "The Classical Stationary State," *Economic Journal*, 1943, pp. 343–51.

Therefore, the early 19th century data would fall well below a leftward extension of the 1929–44 consumption function of Figure 14–1. There was something wrong with that consumption function as the basis for long-run projections.)

The empirical evidence of this chapter has not, however, provided a categorical answer to the broader question: Is consumption as a function of income sufficiently subject to shifting to make secular stagnation a relatively minor danger which can be avoided without the large and increasing government deficits deemed necessary by Hansen? As the rate of economic growth declines—as it *eventually* must—and the rate of investment therefore declines, is there a long-term depression and unemployment in the future if the government does not intervene to stimulate demand in a massive way? Can the consumption function really be shifted upward enough so that essentially all the productive capacity of the economy will turn out consumption goods?

No clear answer to this question is provided by the statistical studies of the consumption function discussed in this chapter. And, in a fundamental sense, statistical studies *cannot* provide a categorical answer to such a question. For an answer, what is required is an extension or extrapolation of past statistical evidence well beyond past experience. And, as statistical results are extended beyond the range of observations, the confidence which the conclusions justify becomes increasingly smaller. As growth slackens, the nature of the economy and society will undergo major changes, and in ways which we can only dimly foresee.

Nevertheless, the available evidence weighs against the secular stagnation thesis. Wealth shows up significantly in some of the studies of the consumption function. Furthermore, on theoretical grounds, it is reasonable to argue that consumption will rise as money and other wealth holdings of the public increase. Therefore, as the level of economic activity levels out in the long run and the rate of investment drops, massive and increasing government deficits will not necessarily be needed to prevent aggregate demand from falling below the full-employment level. The wealth effects of accumulated past saving may shift the consumption function up enough for full employment. This conclusion is fortified if there is an expansion of the money supply; and it becomes even stronger if the slowdown in growth takes place gradually, so that habits can be adjusted to higher levels of consumption. As the rate of growth slows down, it should be possible to maintain full-employment levels of demand without massive and increasing government deficits.

APPENDIX B

SOME ADDITIONAL EVIDENCE ON THE PERMANENT INCOME HYPOTHESIS

In the consumption function literature, the principal method of evaluating the various consumption theories has been to derive equations consistent with the theories (for example, Equation 14–2 for the relative income hypothesis and Equation 14–11 for the life cycle hypothesis) and then to see how closely the data fit the equations. The evaluation of the goodness of fit is not a simple matter, raising a number of difficult statistical problems which place it beyond the scope of an introductory macroeconomic study.

There is, in addition, another method for evaluating the validity of a consumption theory; namely, to investigate the implications of the theory and then determine how closely these implications correspond to real-world happenings. In this appendix, two illustrations will be provided of the way in which the implications of the permanent income hypothesis may be used in evaluating that hypothesis. These two illustrations do not in any sense represent a comprehensive evaluation of the PIH; but they are of considerable intrinsic interest because of the light they shed on the permanent income hypothesis. They are also interesting because, in each case, a prominent economist made an error regarding the implications of the permanent income hypothesis. The first illustration involves an invalid argument which Friedman presented in support of the PIH; the second involves an invalid attack on the PIH.

The permanent income hypothesis and the distribution of income

Friedman argued that the PIH gained force because it was consistent with four observations, namely:

1. The rough constancy of the ratio of consumption to disposable income over long periods of time.

2. The evidence provided by the cross-section budget data.
3. The 1929–44 data, which indicated a relatively low marginal propensity to consume, and the high post-1945 consumption rates, which exceeded what might have been expected from the history of 1929–44.
4. "The apparent decline over time in the inequality of income despite the possibility of interpreting the consumption-income relation from time series or budget data as showing that the rich are getting richer and the poor, poorer."[46]

The first three of these points have been discussed at some length in the body of this chapter; it is the fourth which we shall consider here.

Friedman's fourth point may be illustrated by considering the implications of Duesenberry's alternative relative income hypothesis. Let Friedman's argument be spelled out formally and in detail:

a. If Duesenberry's RIH were correct, with the high-income groups consistently saving a high proportion of their income, and the low-income groups consistently saving a low proportion of their income in their effort to "keep up with the Joneses;"
b. And if, also, the composition of the various income groups were to remain reasonably stable; then
c. The upper-income group would accumulate an increasing share of the wealth in the economy, since they would be saving a disproportionately high rate of their incomes.
d. Since wealth produces a flow of income in the form of interest and dividends, point c implies an increasingly less equal distribution of income as time passes. The rich would get richer and the poor, poorer. But, if anything, the trend has been in the other direction, toward more equality of income.
e. Therefore, either assumption a or b must be rejected as inconsistent with the trend in the distribution of income.

Friedman's conclusion was that assumption b should be rejected. According to his permanent income hypothesis, the relatively high saving rate of the high-income group is due entirely to the temporary membership of transients in that group. When these transients move back to their normal membership in a lower-income class, they take their accumulated savings with them. Thus, the high saving rate of the high-income group does not involve an increase

---

[46] Friedman, *A Theory of the Consumption Function,* p. 38.

in the share of the wealth which is held by the upper-income groups.

This is an apparently powerful argument. And it is particularly interesting because it gives a ground for discriminating between the PIH and the relative income hypothesis. In other respects—regarding budget data and the long-run and short-run time series (points 1–3 above) —the two hypotheses lead to similar conclusions. Thus, the observed data in points 1–3 give little ground for choosing one hypothesis over the other. Here, however, in the trend of the distribution of income through time (point 4), the two theories apparently point in different directions.

Unfortunately for Friedman, however, there is a logical weakness in his argument; his conclusion does not follow. The principal difficulty lies in step c. Friedman concludes that, if income groups do not circulate, then the upper income groups will accumulate an increasing share of the total wealth of society. The problem with this conclusion can be illustrated with an example. Consider the top income group, getting 10 percent of the total income of society. Suppose that membership in this income group is stable, and suppose, further, that members save at twice the average rate for society. They will therefore accumulate 20 percent of the additional wealth of society as time passes. This seems to imply that the distribution of wealth becomes less even as time passes. But that conclusion does not necessarily follow. In particular, it does not follow if the top income group *originally* hold 20 percent of the wealth of society. In this case, their share of the income will remain unchanged. In general, step c (the increasing concentration of wealth) does not follow if the initial distribution of wealth is less even than the distribution of income. And, in fact, the distribution of wealth has indeed been less equal than the distribution of income.

Thus, as long as the initial distribution of wealth is less even than the distribution of income, then there is no necessary inconsistency among:

a. A higher saving rate (S/Y_d) of the high-income than of the low-income groups

b. A noncirculating income elite.

c. A stable distribution of income.

The observation of a and c therefore does not in itself make a case for Friedman's conclusion that there are transients in the high-income groups, and that, therefore, point b must be rejected. The failure of income to become more unequally distributed through time does not provide a ground for preferring the PIH over the RIH of Duesenberry.[47]

The permanent income hypothesis and the evidence of occupational groups

According to Friedman's permanent income hypothesis, consumption was determined by permanent income (Y_p) rather than by current measured income (Y). Friedman argued that consumption was *not* influenced by transitory income (Y_T), which is defined as follows:

$$Y_T \equiv Y - Y_p \qquad (14-23)$$

Friedman's hypothesis led to an early controversy over the meaning of income and consumption figures broken down by occupational groupings. In a review of Friedman's book on the consumption function, Professor H. S. Houthakker argued that if the permanent income hypothesis were correct, the cross-section line fitted to the income and consumption patterns for an occupational subgroup of the society should be *flatter* than the consumption function fitted to the cross-section data for all members of the economy. Why? Because the variation of permanent income within an occupational subgroup should be lower than for the economy as a whole. For example, the variation of income among steelworkers is less than the variation of income in the population as a whole; steelworkers tend to have about the same incomes. But, if their permanent incomes are about the same, then the permanent income hypothesis suggests that their consumption should be about the same; thus, a line drawn through their cross-section should be relatively flat. (In an extreme case, with zero variation in permanent income, the line would be perfectly flat.) In brief, argued Houthakker, the perma-

---

[47] Duesenberry did not deny that the income groups might circulate. On the contrary, he explicitly recognized changes in income as a reason for the low saving rate of the low-income groups:

> These families [whose income have fallen because of unemployment] will presumably run substantial deficits immediately after they become unemployed, but as their assets become smaller they will have to adjust to the new situation and presumably balance budgets . . . (Duesenberry, "Income-Consumption Relations," p. 72).

The difference between Duesenberry and Friedman regarding the circulation of the income groups is this. Duesenberry felt that other factors (the desire to keep up with the Joneses) would be major explanatory factors behind observed cross-section data. In Friedman's PIH, the difference in saving rates among income groups is attributed *entirely* to the temporary membership of transients.

nent income hypothesis "implies that the elasticity [of consumption relative to measured income] should be smaller the more narrowly defined the group of households for which it is computed."[48]

Houthakker found the evidence to indicate just the opposite. Taking the major subcategories of the economy—unskilled workers, skilled workers, clerical workers, etc.—he found that for only one subgroup (the self-employed) the slope of the consumption line was flatter than for all groups together. Further breaking down of the groups gave the same general picture: The consumption functions on the whole tended to become steeper, not flatter. Houthakker's conclusion: The permanent income hypothesis was incorrect (p. 404). The marginal propensity to consume out of transitory income, "far from being zero as Friedman maintains, is actually greater than the *MPC* out of permanent income. Thus . . . the lucky winner [at the races] does not run to the bank but to the tavern."[49]

Robert Eisner counterattacked on behalf of the permanent income hypothesis. Suppose that we look more closely at the steelworker example. It is true that the variation of permanent income among steelworkers is relatively low; this would seem to suggest a flat consumption function for the cross-section of steelworkers. But that is not necessarily so. Take a very simple case, where there are only three steelworkers in the sample. Permanent incomes of the three steelworkers are likely to be very similar—*but so are their measured incomes*. So let us assume that their measured incomes are quite close, say $7,000, $10,000, and $13,000. Now what is the likely explanation of the differences among these three measured incomes: Do the differences in measured income reflect differences in transitory income, or differences in permanent income?

The answer, of course, is that the differences may be partly due to each. But the differences are likely to be largely due *to permanent income, not transitory income,* of the three workers. While steelworkers tend to have about the same measured incomes, the differences that do exist among them tend to be due to permanent and not transitory causes. The higher-paid workers live in a generally high-wage area, they have significantly more seniority, they have a more highly skilled job, and so on. What does this mean? If, *in the extreme,* the differences in measured income were *all* due to differences in permanent income, then the consumption of the three steel-

---

[48] H. S. Houthakker, "The Permanent Income Hypothesis: a Review Article," *American Economic Review,* June 1958, p. 400.

[49] Houthakker, "The Permanent Income Hypothesis," p. 404.

workers should be *proportional* to their incomes, according to the
permanent income hypothesis. The consumption function for steelworkers would be *steeper* than the consumption function for all
members of the economy; the consumption function for these three
steelworkers would run through the origin, in contrast to the relatively flat cross-section consumption function for the economy as a
whole (Figure 14B–1).

What is important, then, in determining the flatness of the consumption function is not simply a low variation of permanent in-

Figure 14B–1
**The Houthakker-Eisner debate: The slope of the consumption function of
subgroups (groups of three individuals illustrated, with measured incomes of
$7,000, $10,000, and $13,000)**

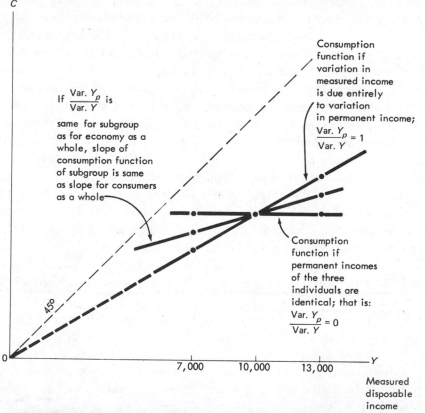

If all steelworkers have approximately the same permanent income,
then the consumption function of steelworkers should be approximately horizontal. On the other hand, if this year's income differences
among steelworkers reflect permanent differences, then the steelworkers' consumption function should be a straight line through the
origin.

come, but a low variation of permanent income *relative to* the variation of measured income, that is, a low ratio of var. Y_p/var. Y. Recall Friedman's explanation of the relatively flat observed consumption function drawn from budget data: Transients in the upper-income groups are a biased lot, coming on average from lower-income groups; similarly, transients in the lower-income groups on average come from higher-income groups; therefore, the variation in actual income exceeds the variation in permanent income; therefore, the cross-section consumption function is relatively flat, containing a positive constant. The lower the ratio of var. Y_p/var. Y, the flatter will be the consumption function. Thus, there was a difficulty in Houthakker's argument. In dividing the population into occupational groupings, he had reduced the variation of permanent income, but, on average, he had reduced the variation of measured income *even more.* Hence, the var. Y_p/var. Y ratios were on average larger for the subgroups than for the economy as a whole, and the consumption functions of the subgroups therefore tended to be steeper than the consumption function drawn for the economy as a whole.

Eisner's criticism was substantiated by a consideration of the particular groupings of the population. For such groups as unskilled workers, skilled workers, etc., the slopes of the consumption lines were relatively steep. These were groupings with low variations of transitory income; their var. Y_p/var. Y ratios were higher than for the population as a whole.

One group, however, was different. The line for self-employed was relatively flat. Precisely. This is the group for which transitory income is all over the place. The var. Y_p/var. Y ratio is therefore lower than for the economy as a whole, and the consumption line therefore flatter. The division of the population into groups does not undercut the permanent income hypothesis, but rather supports it.[50]

KEY POINTS

1. The data for 1929–44, plus the data from cross-section budget studies, fit consumption functions of the form:

---

[50] Robert Eisner, "Comment," *American Economic Review,* December 1958, pp. 972–90; especially p. 985. See also Houthakker, "Reply," *American Economic Review,* December 1958, p. 991.

$$C = a + cY_d$$

in which a is a significant positive constant.

2. The long-run consumption series of Kuznets, plus the observations of the late 1940s which lay above the line fitted to 1929–44 data, suggested that over long periods of time, consumption is approximately a constant proportion of disposable income. In the long run, there is no significant constant a in the consumption function.

3. This apparent contradiction between the long-run historical data and the 1929–44 data led to the development of a number of more complex hypotheses regarding the consumption function, notably: Duesenberry's relative income hypothesis, Friedman's permanent income hypothesis, and the life cycle hypothesis of Ando, Brumberg, and Modigliani.

4. According to Duesenberry, consumption is affected by the previous high level of income; people tend to live according to the style to which they have become accustomed. Thus, consumption as a percentage of income tends to be high when income has fallen, and low when income has risen at an abnormally rapid rate. This explains the relatively "flat" consumption function obtained from 1929–44 data.

5. The explanation of the relative flatness of the cross-section consumption function, according to Duesenberry, lay in the *interdependence* of wants. For example, those at the low end of the income distribution spectrum try to "keep up with the Jones" (the *demonstration* effect), and thus their consumption is high as a fraction of their incomes.

6. According to the permanent income hypothesis, people consume in line with their permanent income, that is, their expected normal income. During recessions, current measured incomes are considered abnormally low. People consume in line with their expectations of their normal income. Hence, consumption as a fraction of current income is high during recessions. Similarly, consumption as a fraction of income is low during booms. In addition, the lower income groups have a disproportionate number of individuals who have had a bad year, or who for other reasons find their incomes below their expected normal (for example, students or retired people). Hence, on average, consumption as a fraction of income is high for the low-income groups. Similarly, consumption as fraction of income is low for

high-income groups. Thus, a single hypothesis can be used to explain why both budget studies and the 1929–44 time series give a relatively flat consumption function, while there is no significant constant in the long-run consumption function.

7. According to the life cycle hypothesis, consumption depends on the total lifetime resources available to individuals. Thus, the hypothesis suggests that consumption should be affected not only by current income, but also by accumulated wealth and expected future income.

QUESTIONS

1. The cross-section budget data of Figure 14–3 suggest that the cross-section consumption function is not linear (although a straight line function was in fact fitted to the data in that figure). Rather, the data suggest that the "true" consumption function becomes flatter at higher levels of income; that is, the marginal propensity to consume of high-income groups is lower than the marginal propensity to consume of lower-income groups. Suppose that this inference is correct. Then a redistribution of income from high-income groups to low-income groups will increase total consumption out of any given total level of disposable income for the economy as a whole. Now suppose that income redistribution is considered as a possible countercyclical policy:

   a. What is the appropriate redistribution of income during a recession, in terms of the goal of increasing employment?
   b. What is the appropriate redistribution of income during an inflationary boom, in terms of the goal of restraining inflationary pressures?
   c. What problems might arise in the use of redistribution policies as a way of stabilizing the economy?
   d. In the light of the answers to the above three parts, what can be said about the desirability of using income redistribution as a countercyclical policy tool?

2. In their article on the life cycle hypothesis, Ando and Modigliani explicitly assumed individuals have no desire to leave inheritances; they intend to spend all their available resources during their lifetimes. Yet, obviously, very sizable inheritances

are left by some, and many individuals leave modest assets for their heirs.

a. How might the existence of inheritances be explained within the theoretical framework which assumes that there is no *desire* to leave inheritances?

b. Does the answer to *a* provide an adequate explanation for inheritances, or should one of the assumptions of the life cycle hypothesis be judged implausible? Explain.

c. Suppose that individuals are assumed to wish to leave inheritances for their children. How might this change the theoretical expectations suggested by the life cycle hypothesis?

SUGGESTED READINGS

James Duesenberry, "Income-Consumption Relations and their Implications," in *Income, Employment and Public Policy,* Essays in Honor of Alvin Hansen (New York: W. W. Norton, 1948) ; reprinted in M. G. Mueller, ed., *Readings in Macroeconomics,* 2d ed. (New York: Holt, Rinehart and Winston, 1971), pp. 61–76.

Robert Ferber, "Consumer Economics, a Survey," *Journal of Economic Literature,* December 1973, pp. 1303–42.

Milton Friedman, *A Theory of the Consumption Function* (Princeton: Princeton University Press, 1957), chaps. 1, 2, 9.

Chapter 15

Investment and economic stability

*You ain't heard
nothin' yet.*

Al Jolson

In macroeconomic theory, investment plays two strategic roles. It is a key part of the growth process. And, because of its short-run variability, investment forms a central part of the study of disturbances in aggregate demand—and of the policy measures which may be taken to smooth out these disturbances. Investment and economic stability will be the subject of this chapter; investment and growth of Chapter 16.

In Keynes' *General Theory,* which introduced the modern macroeconomics discussion, unemployment was seen as the possible result of two quite different sets of problems. First, Keynes was concerned that, in the absence of massive government intervention, the economy would bump along in an unemployment *equilibrium:* The path of demand would be relatively smooth, but the overall level of aggregate demand would be inadequate to get the economy anywhere close to full employment. It was this facet of the unemployment problem which was the focus of Part Two of this book. But there was another, quite different thread running through the *General Theory:* A market economy is inherently *unstable,* and therefore a position of full employment is likely to prove transitory. There is a danger that aggregate demand will fluctuate, creating alternate periods of boom and depression.

In the unemployment *equilibrium* argument, the *consumption function* played the key role. With consumption a stable function of income, an unemployment equilibrium could persist if investment and government expenditures were not sufficient to make up the gap between consumption demand and output at full employment. Because of the continuing high level of aggregate demand over the past three decades, the fear of secular stagnation has receded. Studies of the consumption function suggest that the gap between consumption and the full-employment level of demand will not grow as a proportion of income as the economy grows, and therefore there is no strong reason to anticipate a secular problem of inadequate demand (see Chapter 14, Appendix A). Furthermore, if such a problem were to present itself, the measures to deal with it are readily at hand: secular increases in government spending and the money supply, and cuts in taxation. A secular inadequacy of aggregate demand is not the tough problem before us.

In Keynes' *instability* argument, it was *investment* which took over the center of the stage. Investment depends on the *expectations* of future returns, which depend in large part on expectations regarding the size of future markets. To Keynes, expectations were fragile: An increase in sales could lead to expectations of a further increase and hence to an investment boom; on the other hand, a downturn in sales could lead to expectations of a further decrease and therefore to a reduction in investment and a collapse of aggregate demand. In retrospect, Keynes' fears of a highly unstable economy seem exaggerated. Since 1945, economic activity has been more stable than it was during the interwar period (1919–39) when the *General Theory* was written. But, even so, the problem of instability cannot be laid to rest so easily as that of secular stagnation. In spite of the successes since 1945, there is still a tendency for the growth of aggregate demand to be uneven, with periods of recession succeeding periods of boom. Furthermore, while the experience since 1945 has been a decided improvement over the 1930s, there is no clear *trend* toward greater stability. Indeed, the recession of 1974–75 was the worst in recent decades. In recent economic swings, as in the earlier cycles, the instability of investment demand has been a major cause.

(Somewhat disconcertingly, so have spurts and cuts in government spending.)

Unfortunately, the study of investment is not simple or straight-forward. In part, this is because the important questions—those regarding the *stability* of investment demand—must be considered outside a static equilibrium framework: In order to study the swings in investment demand, changes that occur in a dynamic economy must become the focus of attention. Once the concept of equilibrium is left behind, economists are largely outside their traditional logical framework. And, to compound the problem, the subject of the in-quiry—investment—is sensitive to something neither easily ob-served nor readily measured, namely, expectations of future sales and future profitability. It is not surprising that the study of investment has engaged some of the brightest minds in economics, with hard work leading to ingenious, but contradictory, theoretical models and indifferent empirical results. Compared to the investment literature, the consumption literature is the model of simplicity and clarity.

It is not the objective of this chapter to drag the reader through the morass. The purpose is relatively modest: to hit some of the highlights, and point out some of the major issues and problems in the study of investment.

KEYNES' MARGINAL EFFICIENCY OF INVESTMENT: STOCKS AND FLOWS ONCE AGAIN

In the simple Keynesian equilibrium system, the *flow* of invest-ment is specified as a function of the rate of interest (Chapter 5, esp. Figure 5–2). However, if one assumes that investment is the result of the pursuit of profit-maximizing objectives by business firms, then this view of investment is inadequate and indeed misleading. The firm striving to produce a particular level of output most efficiently will move toward the optimum *stock* of capital.[1]

(Here, the distinctions among the three major concepts should be repeated. The *stock of capital* is the amount of equipment, plant, and inventory which exists at a point in time. *Net investment* is the change in the stock of capital during a period of time. *Gross in-*

---

[1] In a growing economy, with output rising, the optimum stock of capital will grow through time. To acquire the changing optimum stock, firms will aim for a continuing flow of net investment. See Dale W. Jorgenson, "The Theory of Investment Behavior," in Robert Ferber, ed., *Determinants of Investment Behavior* (New York: National Bureau of Economic Research, 1967), pp. 129–55.

vestment is the total production of plant and equipment during a period, plus the change in inventory. Thus, the difference between gross investment and net investment is the depreciation—the wearing out and obsolescence—of plant and equipment during the period. Net investment and gross investment are both flows.)

To illustrate why a firm's basic objective will be for a specific stock of capital rather than for a specific rate of investment, consider an example—an automobile manufacturer. Anticipating sales of, say, 2 million cars in the coming year, the manufacturer will aim for the amount of capital equipment which will help to produce these cars most efficiently—given the current state of technology, the price of labor and capital goods, the rate of interest, etc. These variables, plus the rate of production of cars (2 million per year), provide the basis for calculating the optimum *stock* of capital equipment and and plant. From the demand for cars is derived a demand for a *stock* of capital goods, and not for a continuous *flow* of capital goods.

This proposition—that the business firm's basic aim is not for a flow of investment, but rather for the appropriate stock of capital goods—has been repeatedly stressed in the literature.[2] It was recognized as a necessary modification of the *General Theory* in the early Keynesian writings,[3] and, indeed, was a conspicuous feature of pre-Keynesian works.[4] While many aspects of the investment literature have been highly controversial, this proposition has met with general agreement; in the capital goods area, the importance of the concept of stocks has not been a subject of controversy. Incidentally, this is in sharp contrast to the consumption literature. One of the key disagreements in the early Keynesian controversy involved the classical criticism that Keynes had failed to take account of the stock of real money and other wealth as a factor affecting the flow of consumption. Thus, said the classical critics, there was a basic defect in the Keynesian concept of an unemployment equilibrium, and a basic weakness in the Keynesian argument that monetary policy might be of little value (recall Chapter 7). This criticism was generally dismissed as unimportant by early Keynesian writers.

There is, of course, a relation between stocks and flows: A stock

---

[2] For example, James G. Witte, Jr., "The Microfoundations of the Social Investment Function," *Journal of Political Economy*, October 1963, pp. 441–56.

[3] For example, A. P. Lerner's stock-flow treatment of the theory of investment in *The Economics of Control* (New York: Macmillan, 1944), pp. 323–40; or Samuelson's accelerator-multiplier model, discussed in Appendix A to this chapter.

[4] Specifically, in the pre-Keynesian literature cited below in the section on the accelerator.

(the quantity of capital goods) is adjusted through a flow (that is, net investment). The stress on the importance of the concept of the equilibrium level of capital stock may be therefore rephrased as follows: It is inappropriate to look on an equilibrium *flow* of investment; rather, the flow of investment should be looked upon as the *process of adjusting the capital stock toward its desired level.*

A SIMPLE STOCK ADJUSTMENT MODEL: THE ACCELERATOR

A simple version of a stock adjustment investment model may be traced back decades prior to the writing of the *General Theory,* to the works of Aftalion, Bickerdike, Hawtrey, and Clark during the early years of this century.[5] This version involves the acceleration principle. Although there are difficulties in the accelerator model, in a substantially modified form it provides the basis for much of the recent investment literature.

The accelerator principle may be illustrated with a simple example in Table 15–1. In the first column is given the demand for a consumer good. Assume initially that the demand has been constant at 1,000 units per period for some time. Assume also that a machine is capable of producing ten units of the product per period; thus, the manufacturer needs 100 machines. Assume further that a machine lasts ten periods, and that one tenth of the machinery existing in period 1 was acquired in each of the previous ten periods. This means an initial replacement demand for ten machines per period. With a steady demand for products at 1,000 per year, there will be no desire to change the number of machines; net investment will be zero, and the gross investment in machines will be ten per period,

---

[5] A. Aftalion, "La Réalité des Surproductions Générales," *Revue d'Economie Politique,* 1909; C. F. Bickerdike, "A Non-Monetary Cause of Fluctuations in Employment," *Economic Journal,* 1914, pp. 357–70; R. G. Hawtrey, *Good and Bad Trade* (London: Constable 1913); J. M. Clark, "Business Acceleration and the Law of Demand: A Technical Factor in Economic Cycles," *Journal of Political Economy,* March 1917, pp. 217–35.

In the early chapters of this book, the view that business cycles were the result of monetary disturbances was attributed to classical (pre-Keynesian) economists. As a generalization, this is true. However, the early origins of the accelerator model are worth stressing as an illustration of the breadth and diversity of the views of classical writers. While classical writers stressed monetary causes of business disturbances, they also examined other causes. In this regard, Hawtrey is perhaps especially interesting. He was known as the foremost proponent of the monetary explanation of the business cycle, but also wrote on the accelerator principle.

For a survey of the historical development of the accelerator theory, see G. H. Fisher, "A Survey of the Theory of Induced Investment, 1900–1940," *Southern Economic Journal,* April 1952, pp. 474–94.

Table 15–1
The accelerator principle: The derived demand for investment

Period	(1) Demand for consumer good	(2) Desired stock of machines (col. 1 ÷ 10)	(3) Net investment (col. 2_t − col. 2_{t-1})	(4) Replace- ment (col. 5 for t − 10)	(5) Gross investment (col. 3 + col. 4)
1...............	1,000	100	0	10	10
2...............	1,000	100	0	10	10
3...............	1,100	110	10	10	20
4...............	1,200	120	10	10	20
5...............	1,300	130	10	10	20
6...............	1,300	130	0	10	10
7...............	1,300	130	0	10	10

as shown for the first two periods in the table. (In this table cols. 1, 3, 4, and 5 are flows; col. 2 is a stock.)

Now assume that the demand for the consumer good changes in the third period, rising to 1,100. The manufacturer will need 110 machines. This means an increase—or net investment—of ten units. Together with the replacement demand of ten units, this will involve a total acquisition of 20 machines in period 3. Thus, a relatively modest (10 percent) change in the demand for the final product leads to a magnified or "accelerated" change in the demand for machinery (100 percent in the illustration).

The illustration may readily be extended one step further to find the demand for the machine tools which produce the machinery. The percentage change in the demand for machine tools will be truly spectacular. For example, if it takes one machine tool to produce one machine, the desired stock of machine tools will be numerically the same as the gross investment column of Table 15–1; in the first two periods, the desired stock of machine tools will be 10. If machine tools also last ten periods, the initial demand for machine tools will be one per period; that is, the replacement demand. In period 3, as gross investment in machines rises from 10 to 20, the desired stock of machine tools will likewise rise from 10 to 20, requiring a net addition of 10 machine tools. With a net investment of 10 added to replacement of 1, gross investment in machine tools will rise from 1 to 11, or by 1,000 percent.

But, for simplicity, let us return to the initial illustration of Table 15–1, showing the demand for machinery derived from the demand for the consumer good. If, in periods 4 and 5, the demand for the consumer good continues to grow by 100 per period, the derived demand for machinery will remain constant at 20 per period, that is, 10 units of net investment and 10 for replacement.[6] It is the *initiation of* the growth, not the growth process itself, which leads to the jump in the derived demand for machinery. (The demand for machinery is spoken of as a "derived" or "induced" demand because consumers have no demand for machinery as such. The demand for machinery is derived from the demand for the consumer good. Similarly, the demand for machine tools is derived from the demand for machinery.)

Furthermore, it is not necessary for the demand for the consumer good to drop for the derived demand for capital goods to fall off. Observe the effects of the leveling out of demand at 1,300 during the sixth period. There is no need to increase the stock of machines; net investment drops to zero. As a consequence, gross investment also drops—from 20 to 10 in this illustration. Thus, changes in the demand for investment goods depend on *changes in the growth* of the demand for consumer goods; all that is needed for a decline in investment is a *decline in the rate of growth* of consumer goods, as illustrated in Figure 15–1. This also means that, if the simple accelerator theory is valid, then the turning points of the induced cycles in investment will *precede* the turning points of cycles in the production of consumer goods.[7]

Formally, the simple accelerator theory may be stated in the following equations.

---

[6] Under the assumption we have made that machinery lasts exactly ten periods, the machinery acquired in the third period will be due for replacement in period 13. Thus, the increase of gross investment (col. 5) from 10 to 20 units in the third period will be echoed as an increase from 10 to 20 units in the replacement demand (col. 4) ten periods later. And, as gross investment is the sum of net investment plus replacement, the echo will also show up in the gross investment column ten periods later.

In their study of *The Investment Decision* (Cambridge, Mass.: Harvard, 1957), pp. 91–94, John Meyer and E. Kuh find no evidence of an "echo" in investment demand. A strong echo depends on a specific, invariant life for capital goods; yet it is difficult in practice to identify a specific point at which capital goods are "worn out."

[7] That is, the *effect* (cycles in investment) *precedes* the *cause* (cycles in consumer goods production). Recall the discussion in Chapter 12 on the monetarist models, regarding the question of whether time lags establish the direction of causation.

This aspect of the simple accelerator theory—the prediction that investment cycles will significantly precede cycles in demand for consumer goods—was subject to early attack as being inconsistent with the facts. In his early test of the accelerator, Kuznets found that, while there was a lead in the demand for capital goods, it "is far short of that suggested by the turning points in the net changes in the demand for finished products." Simon Kuznets, "Relation between Capital Goods and Finished Products in the Business Cycle," *Economic Essays in Honor of Wesley Clair Mitchell* (New York: Columbia University Press, 1935), p. 266–67.

Recent literature indicating that investment *lags behind* the demand for finished products is discussed later in this chapter.

Figure 15–1
The accelerator: Changes in output, the capital stock, and net investment

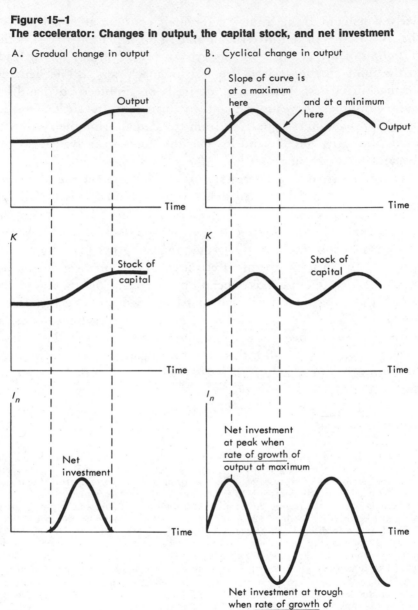

A. Gradual change in output

B. Cyclical change in output

According to the accelerator theory, net investment depends on
the *rate of change* of the output of consumer goods.

$$K^*_t = \alpha O_t \qquad (15\text{–}1)$$

and

$$I_{nt} = K^*_t - K_{t-1} \qquad (15\text{–}2)$$

thus,

$$I_{nt} = \alpha O_t - \alpha O_{t-1} \qquad (15\text{–}3)$$

or alternatively,

$$\boxed{I_n = \alpha \, \Delta O} \qquad (15\text{–}4)$$

and also,

$$\boxed{I_g = \alpha \, \Delta O + R} \qquad (15\text{–}5)$$

where

K^*_t is the desired real capital stock in period t.

O_t is real output in period t; also assumed here to be the real output which was *expected* for period t.

α is the capital-output ratio (0.10 in the illustration), also sometimes known as the "relation" or the "acceleration co-efficient." In this simple model, the average and marginal capital-output ratios are the same; that is, they are both equal to α.

I_{nt} is net real investment in period t.

I_g is gross real investment.

Δ means "change in."

R is replacement.[8]

The key equations are (15–4) and (15–5).

The accelerator is a plausible argument, and examples come readily to mind. When the number of high school students was rising at a rapid rate, there was a great demand for teachers, and many new schools were built. With the *leveling out* of the high school population, new job openings for high school teachers *declined,* and the number of high schools under construction fell off sharply.

But if the accelerator is plausible and consistent with the facts at this level of generality, its detailed application involves problems; a

---

[8] For simplicity, the difference between net and gross investment in this elementary version is taken as the replacement of worn-out machines. This is not exactly the same thing as depreciation.

number of assumptions in the simple accelerator do not correspond closely to the way the world operates. In empirical tests of equations of the form of Equation (15–4), $\alpha \Delta O$ gives an unreliable prediction of investment. The major problems with the simple accelerator include the following:[9]

1. When there is excess capacity, the accelerator does not operate as illustrated. If there is excess capacity, equipment is going unused; output may be expanded without adding to the amount of capital. Thus, the tie between investment and changes in output is broken.

2. On the other hand, when there is full utilization of resources (both capital and labor), then the economy as a whole cannot operate the way the accelerator suggests either. A rise in consumer goods production must squeeze out production of capital goods, and vice versa. Output of consumer goods and capital goods cannot rise simultaneously—except, of course, by the amount attributable to the overall growth of productive capacity in the economy.

    In short, for the economy as a whole the accelerator cannot work as specified in either of the simple cases: that of large-scale unemployment of resources or that of full employment. It is a simple model which cannot work for the economy as a whole in any simple situation. (It may, however, work for a *sector* of a fully employed economy: It is possible to produce more cars and more automobile-producing machinery simultaneously. All that is needed is a transfer of resources from other industries.) Additional problems—some of which are obviously interrelated —are as follows:

3. In the simple accelerator, a fixed capital-output ratio is assumed; a certain fixed amount of capital is considered necessary to produce a given amount of output. Yet this is clearly not the case in any rigid sense. Even though machinery is being efficiently used, it is normally possible to increase output without adding to the amount of machinery, by increasing the amount of overtime or adding additional shifts. (The willingness of the

---

[9] From the time of the early writings on the accelerator, many of these problems have been recognized. For example, points 1 and 7 were stressed by Clark in his cited 1917 article.

For a critical review of the accelerator, see R. S. Eckaus, "The Acceleration Principle Reconsidered," *Quarterly Journal of Economics*, May 1953, pp. 209–30.

firm to do so depends on a number of factors, including the relative prices of machinery and overtime work.)

4.   Furthermore, machinery does not fall apart at some precise point in time; it gradually wears out and becomes obsolete. In the face of an increase in demand, obsolescent equipment may be reactivated, particularly if there is some doubt as to whether the higher level of demand will be sustained.

5.   Machinery is not purchased primarily for the production of current output, but rather for the production of *expected future output*. There is no necessarily close connection between the pattern of actual output and the pattern that was expected.

6.   Businesses do not adjust immediately to their desired level of capital equipment. There is a lag involved in the acquisition of machinery and other capital because of the time required to draw up and approve plans, because of the adjustment problems in breaking in new equipment, etc.

7.   Furthermore, the timing of the acquisition of capital equipment also depends on supply considerations: the availability of equipment, its cost, and the availability and cost of financing.

The simple accelerator Equation (15–4) suggests that the economy may be quite unstable; relatively minor changes in the rate of growth of final demand will be translated into large changes in investment demand. Thus, in the literature, the discussion of the accelerator has generally been included as a part of the analysis of economic disturbances and the business cycle. These seven shortcomings of the accelerator theory suggest, however, that the swings in the demand for capital goods are likely in fact to be considerably smaller than indicated by the simple accelerator theory. Many of the points (indeed, all but point 5)[10] lead to the conclusion that the short-run marginal capital-output ratio will be smaller than the average capital-output ratio, and that the changes in the demand for capital will therefore be smaller than suggested by our illustrative example. And this conclusion has been consistently confirmed by empirical studies. Kuznets' early test of the accelerator, for example,

---

[10] The consequences of the dependence of investment on expectations (point 5) are unclear. If expectations are stable ("inelastic"), then short-run changes in final demand will cause little short-run change in the demand for capital; but if they are unstable ("elastic"), then a large change in the demand for capital may result. (Formally, "elasticity of expectations" is defined as the percentage change in expected output, divided by the percentage change in actual output.)

found that the marginal capital-output ratio in the railroad industry was only one-fifth to one-half as large as the average capital-output ratio;[11] changes in demand led to much smaller changes in investment in the short run than would be expected by looking at the overall level of capital in railroads. Nevertheless, investment historically has still been one of the least stable components of aggregate demand.

The modern study of investment has largely been an effort to deal with these seven complications.[12] This has not been easy; some complications—the determinants of *expected* future sales, for example—are very difficult to pin down.

A RELAXATION OF THE ASSUMPTIONS OF THE SIMPLE ACCELERATOR

In the simple accelerator (Equations 15–4 and 15–5), investment is rigidly tied to changes in output. In order to deal with some of the problems with the simplest accelerator, flexibility may be introduced into an accelerator-type function.

Lags in the response of investment to changes in output: The flexible accelerator

In the simple accelerator theory, the relationship between the desired capital stock and current output is assumed to be a constant (α in Equation 15–1). Furthermore, investment is assumed to bring the capital stock up to its desired level during the current period (Equation 15–2). Neither of these assumptions is very reasonable. As L. M. Koyck observed in his study of lags in investment,[13]

> In a situation of short capacity a tendency of plant expansion may be expected. But an immediate full adjustment is neither technically necessary nor considered possible or advisable from an economic point of view. There may be checks from the side of finance or the lumpiness of investment goods. Moreover, the high level of output may be expected to be temporary, in which case a "wait and see" policy will be followed. . . .

---

[11] Kuznets, "Relation between Capital Goods and Finished Products," p. 262.

[12] For an advanced textbook treatment of investment theory, see Michael K. Evans, *Macroeconomic Activity: Theory, Forecasting, and Control* (New York: Harper & Row, 1969), chaps. 4–8.

[13] **L. M. Koyck,** *Distributed Lags and Investment Analysis* (Amsterdam: North-Holland, 1954), p. 63.

Apart from these factors, causing lags between changes in output and decisions to adjust capacity, there is a lag between a decision to expand capacity and the actual enlargement of the productive capacity of a plant.

In other words, changes in output do not immediately lead to a desire to change the level of the capital stock proportionately; nor is a desire to change the capital stock immediately reflected in actual investment (points 5, 6, and 7 in the above list of problems with the accelerator).

Koyck suggested, rather, that the stock of capital is adjusted not only to current output, but also to past output, with declining weights given to the successively earlier outputs:

$$K_t = \alpha\beta[O_t + (1 - \beta)O_{t-1} + (1 - \beta)^2 O_{t-2} + \cdots] \quad (15\text{–}6)$$

where

β is a fraction, less than one.
α is the average capital-output ratio of the industry.[14]

By a procedure already used above in the consumption chapter—one originally introduced by Koyck—Equation (15–6) may be simplified. Lag Equation (15–6) by one period to get K_{t-1}, and multiply both sides by $(1 - \beta)$, obtaining:

$$(1 - \beta)K_{t-1} = \alpha\beta[(1 - \beta)O_{t-1} + (1 - \beta)^2 O_{t-2}$$
$$+ (1 - \beta)^3 O_{t-3} + \cdots] \quad (15\text{–}7)$$

And, subtracting Equation (15–7) from (15–6), we get

$$K_t - (1 - \beta)K_{t-1} = \alpha\beta O_t \quad (15\text{–}8)$$

that is

$$K_t = \alpha\beta O_t + (1 - \beta)K_{t-1} \quad (15\text{–}9)$$

But, by definition:

$$I_{nt} \equiv K_t - K_{t-1} \quad (15\text{–}10)$$

therefore

$$I_{nt} = \alpha\beta O_t + (1 - \beta)K_{t-1} - K_{t-1} \quad (15\text{–}11)$$

---

[14] In Equation (15–6), note that we must distinguish between a *marginal* capital-output ratio and the long-run *average* capital-output ratio. If there is a sudden change in output, in period t only, then capital rises by only $\alpha\beta$ times the change in output; the marginal capital-output ratio is $\alpha\beta$. However, with a *permanently* higher level of output, with $O_t = O_{t-1} = O_{t-2} \ldots$, then $K_t = \alpha\beta (1/\beta O_t) = \alpha O_t$. (The mathematical derivation here is similar to that in footnote 38, p. 416.) Thus, in a long-run equilibrium, the average capital-output ratio is α.

that is,

$$I_{nt} = \alpha\beta O_t - \beta K_{t-1} \qquad (15-12)$$

This equation may alternatively be written:

$$\boxed{I_{nt} = \beta(\alpha O_t - K_{t-1})} \qquad (15-13)$$

Comparing this equation to Equations (15–1) and (15–2), we observe that, in the current formulation, only a fraction (β) of the investment of the simple accelerator takes place during the current period.

It is also customary in econometric work to depart from the simple replacement assumption made in the initial accelerator model, and specify depreciation as a constant fraction, δ, of existing capital:

$$\text{Depreciation} = \delta K_{t-1} \qquad (15-14)$$

and therefore

$$I_{gt} = \alpha\beta O_t - \beta K_{t-1} + \delta K_{t-1} \qquad (15-15)$$

or alternatively,

$$\boxed{I_{gt} = \alpha\beta O_t - (\beta - \delta) K_{t-1}} \qquad (15-16)$$

Equations (15–12) and (15–16) are each known as the *flexible* accelerator; the relationship between net investment and changes in output during the same period (t) is not given by the average capital-output ratio (α), as it is in the simple accelerator (Equation 15–4) ; rather, it is only a fraction (β) of this ratio.

The mathematical similarity between the Koyck investment function and the Friedman consumption function is close; and there is a theoretical similarity as well. Friedman argued that consumers respond not so much to their current income as to the whole pattern of past incomes; that is, consumption depends on expected normal income, or, in Friedman's terminology, on permanent income. Similarly, Koyck suggests that businesses do not adjust their capital stock simply to the current level of demand for their product, but rather to the whole pattern of past output; that is, they adjust to what might be called *expected normal output.*[15]

Furthermore, making investment a function of "expected normal

---

[15] The similarity between investment theory and Friedman's consumption theory is brought out in Robert Eisner, "A Permanent Income Theory for Investment: Some Empirical Explorations," *American Economic Review,* June 1967, pp. 363–90.

output" has the same consequences for the investment function as for the consumption function. When the capital stock is made a function of past as well as current output, a distinction may be drawn between the short-run,[16] marginal capital-output ratio—$\alpha\beta$ in Equation (15–12)—and the average capital-output ratio (α). (α also represents the long-run, equilibrium amount of capital which will be added for each unit of permanent increase in output in an economy of unchanging technology.) [17] As β is generally much closer to zero than to one (for quarterly data),[18] this distinction is *important;* the investment which is induced in the short run by changes in output is *much* less than suggested by the simple accelerator model in which the capital-output ratio is held constant.

With the short-run responses of investment to changes in output being much less than indicated by the average capital-output ratio, the theoretical expectation is for a more stable pattern of investment through time—and therefore for a more stable overall economy—than is implied by the simple accelerator theory. (This conclusion does *not,* however, tell us that the economy is stable in any absolute sense. It is simply a comparative statement, and tells us as much about the simple accelerator model as it does about the economy itself. Indeed, the simple accelerator model may be used to suggest a spectacularly unstable economy; see the appendix to this chapter.)

---

[16] That is, the ratio representing the response of investment to changes in output during the same time period (t).

[17] For any permanent, steady level of output,

$$O_t = O_{t-1} = O_{t-2} \cdot \cdot \cdot \tag{15-17}$$

in which case Equation (15–6) reduces to

$$K_t = \alpha\beta \left[\frac{1}{\beta} O_t\right] = \alpha O \tag{15-18}$$

This illustrates that α is the long-run equilibrium capital-output ratio. (This text slides over some problems regarding the meaning of α in Equation 1–12, particularly when there are economies of scale. The growth process may also affect the value of α.)

[18] Clearly, the amount of adjustment within a time period depends on the length of the time period; the longer the time period, the more adjustment will take place, and the larger will be the value found empirically for β.

In Kuznets' cited study, a relatively long period—the business cycle—was used. Therefore, the marginal capital-output ratios which he found were larger than would have been the case if he had used quarter-to-quarter changes. Thus, added weight is given to his findings of lower investment rates than suggested by the average capital-output ratios. He used a method which made it possible to find high marginal capital-output ratios; yet he actually found low ratios.

The amount of adjustment depends also on the type of equipment; the adjustment for heavy, complex equipment may be expected to be slower than for simpler, more rapidly produced equipment. Kuznets, for example, found that the actual amplitude of fluctuations in orders for locomotives was only one fifth as large as predicted by the accelerator theory, while it was one half as large for passenger cars.

Figure 15–2
A comparison of the simple and flexible accelerators

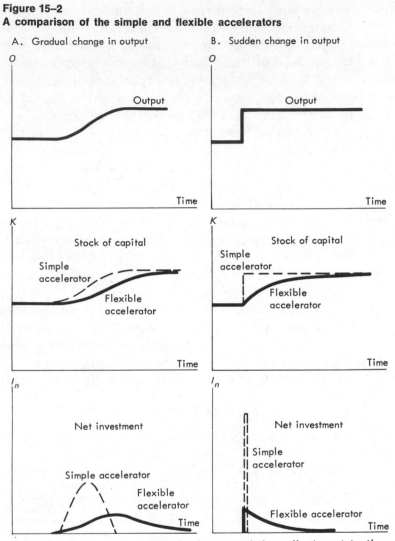

With a flexible accelerator, only part of the adjustment to the desired level of capital takes place during the current period.

The comparison between the simple accelerator and the flexible accelerator is illustrated in Figure 15–2.

Peaked lags in investment

As is shown in Figure 15–2, the flexible accelerator (Equation 15–13) gives a gradual adjustment of the capital stock to a sudden change in output. Net investment is highest in the initial quarter, and gradually declines as time passes.

This view—that the initial net investment resulting from a change in output is greater than later rounds of investment—has also been challenged by many writers. On general theoretical grounds, it is plausible to expect that, if the periods under consideration are rather brief (for example, yearly quarters), then businesses will not have a chance to respond to any great extent during the current period. (Only plant and equipment investment, and not adjustments in inventories, are under consideration here.) It takes time to arrange financing for new machines or buildings, blueprints must be drawn up and approved, orders must be placed, and the equipment or buildings constructed. All this takes time. Thus, the investment induced by a change in sales may build up to a peak gradually; the greatest investment may come several quarters after the change in sales.

A number of mathematical forms have been suggested for the pattern of investment induced by a change in sales, including an inverted U (by Shirley Almon)[19] and an inverted V (by Frank de Leeuw),[20] as illustrated in Figure 15–3. More complex functions have also appeared in the literature.[21] The precise mathematics of these functions need not detain us; what is most important is the empirical results found with these functions. The lag between changes in sales and the peak of induced investment is generally found to be quite long—four to eight quarters, and even longer. The evidence is that, in contrast to the assumption of the simple accelerator model, actual investment in plant and equipment does not respond quickly to changes in sales.

Variability of the equilibrium capital-output ratio

Koyck, de Leeuw, Almon, and others deal with the problem of the speed of the adjustment of the capital stock to changes in output. A second type of flexibility may be introduced into investment models by allowing the equilibrium long-term capital-output ratio—α in the above equations—to itself become a variable.

---

[19] Shirley Almon, "The Distributed Lag between Capital Appropriations and Expenditures," *Econometrica*, January 1965, pp. 178–96.

[20] Frank de Leeuw, "The Demand for Capital Goods by Manufacturers: A Study of Quarterly Time Series," *Econometrica*, July 1962, pp. 407–23.

[21] For an illustrated discussion, see Evans, *Macroeconomic Activity*, pp. 95–105.

Figure 15–3
Lags in the effects of changes in output on net investment

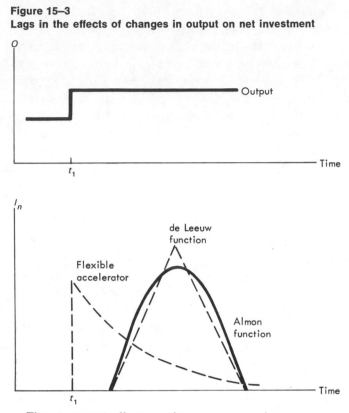

The strongest effects on investment need not occur
immediately; they may be delayed for several quarters.

For the profit-maximizing firm in a competitive economy, capital
will be acquired up to the point where the value of the marginal
product of capital is equal to its marginal cost. In order for the marginal product to be determined in an economic model, a production
function must be specified; a relatively simple form is provided by
the Cobb-Douglas production function:[22]

$$O = \tau K^{a} L^{1-a} \qquad (15\text{–}19)$$

where

---

[22] C. W. Cobb and P. H. Douglas, "A Theory of Production," *American Economic Review*, March 1928, pp. 135–69. An early empirical application of the function is in Paul H. Douglas, *The Theory of Wages* (New York: Macmillan, 1934). Mr. Douglas later became a U.S. senator.

τ is a scale factor which changes with technology.

a is a positive fraction, less than one.

L is the quantity of labor.

This function has some interesting properties, about which more will be said in Chapter 16. For the moment, we are interested in the marginal product of capital, which may be found by elementary calculus:

$$\frac{\partial O}{\partial K} = a\tau K^{a-1}L^{1-a} = \frac{a\tau K^a L^{1-a}}{K} \qquad (15\text{-}20)$$

Or simply

$$\frac{\partial O}{\partial K} = \frac{aO}{K} \qquad (15\text{-}21)$$

where

$\partial O/\partial K$ is the rate of change of output with respect to capital; that is, the marginal product of capital.

For the capital stock to be at its equilibrium in a competitive economy, the value of the marginal product of capital must be equal to the marginal cost of capital. Substituting this equilibrium condition into Equation (15-21), we get:

$$C = \frac{\partial O}{\partial K} \cdot P = \frac{aPO}{K} \qquad (15\text{-}22)$$

where

C is the marginal cost of capital; also sometimes referred to as the "user cost" of capital. It is the amount per period for which capital goods would rent if there were perfect markets for both new and used capital goods. As a first approximation,

C is the sum of the interest costs for carrying the capital good, plus depreciation on new capital equipment.

P is the price of the output.

$\frac{\partial O}{\partial K} \cdot P$ is the value of the marginal product.

Thus, the equilibrium capital-output ratio becomes:

$$\boxed{\frac{K}{O} = a\frac{P}{C}} \qquad (15\text{-}23)$$

With this equation, the equilibrium long-run capital-output ratio need not be constant; it can vary with changes in the cost of capital. (Contrast this with the constant ratio, α, in the earlier equations.) And a study may be made of the effects of monetary and fiscal policies which affect the cost of capital. When this equation is used in conjunction with a lagged-investment function—as, for example, in the work of Hall and Jorgenson[23]—then flexibility has been added in two ways into the simple accelerator model. The equilibrium capital-output ratio has been allowed to vary, and the speed of adjustment has been allowed to vary.

INVESTMENT AND ECONOMIC STABILIZATION POLICIES

The prophesying business is like writing fugues;
it is fatal to everyone save the man of absolute genius.

H. L. Mencken

Investment is important in a study of economic stability in two respects: Investment (including inventory investment) has historically been a relatively unstable component of aggregate demand, and thus may be considered a source of the instability problem; and economic stabilization policies may work through their effects on investment. The first of these points has been the central subject of the previous sections; it is to the second that we now turn.

The effects of monetary policy on investment have already been considered in some detail in Chapter 9; monetary policies change the cost and the availability of financing, and therefore affect the rate at which businesses acquire additional capital.

While the effects of monetary policy on investment have been considered in earlier chapters, the same is not true of fiscal policies. In our earlier discussion of fiscal policy (Chapter 4), the effects of tax changes were traced through in terms of their effects on disposable income, and hence on the consumption component of aggregate demand. On the other side, government purchases of goods and services both added directly to aggregate demand and had secondary effects through their impact on disposable income and hence consumption (the multiplier process). We now turn to an alternative

---

[23] Robert E. Hall and Dale W. Jorgenson, "Application of the Theory of Optimum Capital Accumulation," in Gary Fromm, ed., *Tax Incentives and Capital Spending* (Washington, DC: Brookings Institution, 1971), pp. 9–60. Equation (15–23) is a rearrangement of their Equation (2.23); their Equation (2.29) is related to our Equation (15–16).

channel through which fiscal policies may work; namely, by having an initial, "first-round" effect on investment.

Two tax policies are of primary interest here, having been used as a means of changing the incentives to invest. They are accelerated depreciation and the investment tax credit.

Accelerated depreciation

The calculation of depreciation is important in income tax law. In calculating taxable profits, businesses subtract their costs from the value of their sales; depreciation is one of the deductible costs. A business may minimize its calculated current profit, and therefore its current income taxes, by depreciating its buildings and equipment in the most rapid way permitted by law. (It might seem that there is no gain to the business from a rapid depreciation of its assets; all that it does is *defer* taxes, not avoid them. However, there is a gain from deferred taxes: The business for a time gets the interest-free use of money which would otherwise go currently to the government.) And, in order to prevent rapid depreciation rates from cutting unduly into taxable profits and therefore into tax collections, the income tax law and regulations limit the rates at which businesses may depreciate their buildings and equipment.

The simplest method of calculating depreciation is the straight-line method. If, for example, a machine costing $1,000 has a useful life of ten years, then according to the straight-line method the machine will depreciate by $100 per year.

This method of depreciation may be liberalized in several ways. Rather than using straight-line depreciation, business may be permitted to accelerate depreciation, charging off more than 10 percent of the value of the ten-year asset during the early years.[24] The Internal Revenue Code of 1954 expressly permitted several types of accelerated depreciation, including the double declining balance method. In our above illustration of a $1,000 machine with a life of ten years, the double declining balance method permits annual depreciation of 20 percent of the *remaining* value of the equipment, or $200 the first year, $160 the second (that is, 20 percent of the de-

---

[24] The term "acceleration" has now appeared in three quite distinct contexts, which should be kept clearly separated: the thesis applying to the possible acceleration of inflation (Chapter 13); the acceleration principle, or the accelerator, which suggests that changes in the demand for consumer goods will have an accelerated or amplified effect on the demand for capital goods; and the acceleration of depreciation, a legal concept used here.

preciated value of $800), $128 the third (20 percent of $640), and so on. (Clearly, if 20 percent of the remaining value were depreciated every year, the machine would never be completely depreciated. To permit complete depreciation of the asset during its useful life, businesses are permitted to switch to the straight-line method when the total depreciation on the straight-line method comes to exceed the total under the declining balance method. In the above illustration, the switchover comes in the ninth year.) [25]

Another method for liberalizing depreciation is to shorten the specified lifetimes in the Internal Revenue Code. If, in the example, the lifetime for taxation purposes were reduced from ten to nine years, then current taxable income would be thereby reduced. (Clearly, the useful life is not thereby automatically reduced; a business may keep equipment which has been completely depreciated for tax purposes.) In 1962 and in 1971, the minimum permitted lifetimes of equipment were shortened by administrative action.[26]

The investment tax credit

A further incentive to investment was introduced in 1962, when the Investment Tax Credit (ITC) was enacted. This permitted the purchaser of equipment with a useful life of eight years or more to subtract 7 percent of the cost of the equipment from taxes payable to the government. The tax credit was briefly suspended in 1966–67; it was terminated by the Tax Reform Act of 1969 and was reenacted in 1971. The tax credit was raised to 10 percent as part of the Tax Reduction Act of March 1975. A further increase was proposed by President Carter as part of his initial stimulus package in early 1977, but this was not enacted into law.

The effects of fiscal incentives on investment

A number of studies have been made to measure the effects of such fiscal changes on investment, using advanced theory built upon and

---

[25] An alternative method of accelerated depreciation was also expressly permitted by the 1954 code: the sum-of-the-years-digits method. For an asset with a lifetime of five years, take $1 + 2 + 3 + 4 + 5 = 15$. The depreciation by this method is $5/15$ of the cost in the first year; $4/15$ in the second; $3/15$ in the third; and so on.

[26] With the rapid inflation rates of the early 1970s, there was discussion of the desirability of permitting depreciation on the basis of current replacement cost rather than the actual purchase price. On this complex question, see Edward M. Gramlich, "The Economic and Budgetary Effects of Indexing on the Tax System," in Henry J. Aaron, ed., *Inflation and the Income Tax* (Washington, DC: Brookings Institution, 1976), pp. 271–90; also Aaron's introduction, pp. 10–12.

elaborating the points raised in the previous sections of this chapter. Most notable, perhaps, were four papers presented at a Brookings Institution conference in 1967, and revised for publication in 1971.[27] The four papers were similar, in that they calculated the effects of the tax changes on the cost of using capital (the C in Equation 15–23), and from this calculated the effect on investment. Each of the papers showed considerable ingenuity in dealing with the difficult questions related to the determinants of investment demand. Indeed, as Franklin Fisher commented (p. 243), there would be little left to discuss, "if it were not for the inconvenient fact that the four analyses happen to concern the same problem and happen to contradict each other's findings." In contrast to the consumption function, where there is a general similarity of the statistical results growing out of the application of the different theories, there is no apparent tendency for empirical work on the determinants of investment to produce similar results. Empirical results in the study of investment remain very sensitive to the theoretical underpinnings of the particular model and to the detailed assumptions made in specifying the model.

Hall and Jorgenson find (p. 59) that "tax policy can be highly effective in changing the level and timing of investment expenditures." It also can affect the composition of investment, with accelerated depreciation resulting in a shift toward expenditures on buildings, and the investment tax credit shifting it back toward equipment. (The longer the life of the asset, the greater is the advantage of accelerated depreciation, since the longer is the period for which taxes are deferred. Hence, accelerated depreciation was a particular stimulus to buildings. The ITC, on the other hand, applied only to equipment and not to buildings.) Hall and Jorgenson estimate that, between 1954 and 1961 (inclusive), accelerated depreciation resulted in a total addition of $14.6 billion to net investment (p. 48). Between 1962 and 1965, they find the tax incentives to add a total of $18.0 billion (in 1965 dollars; pp. 48, 52). In contrast, Coen finds that the tax incentives increased net investment by a total of only $1.5 billion up to mid-1962; and by only an additional

---

[27] Gary Fromm, ed., *Tax Incentives and Capital Spending* (Washington, DC: Brookings Institution, 1971). This includes papers by Robert E. Hall and Dale W. Jorgenson, "Application of the Theory of Optimum Capital Accumulation"; Charles W. Bischoff, "The Effect of Alternative Lag Distributions"; Robert M. Coen, "The Effect of Cash Flow on the Speed of Adjustment"; and Lawrence R. Klein and Paul Taubman, "Estimating Effects within a Complete Econometric Model"; and discussion by Franklin M. Fisher and Arnold C. Harberger.

$3.6 billion up to the middle of 1966.[28] His conclusion (p. 179):
"The performance of tax incentives has been quite disappointing."
Bischoff and Klein and Taubman estimate the effects of tax incentives to lie between the Hall-Jorgenson and Coen results.

Many details of the models used by the various authors account
for the differences in their results.[29] Among the more important:

1. As contrasted to the other three papers, Coen stresses the importance of the flow of internal funds as a determinant of the rate
   of adjustment of capital stocks to their desired levels. Coen also
   sticks to the Koyck lag (the flexible accelerator illustrated in
   Figure 15–3, above), while the other three papers use less restrictive lag structures. (The lags of Hall and Jorgenson, and
   Klein and Taubman were similar to the Almon function of
   Figure 15–3.)
2. The Klein-Taubman paper, unlike the other three, allows for
   the feedback of tax policy on interest rates; in this sense it is
   more complete. (It does, however, indirectly raise the question
   of the adjustments in monetary policy which may have been
   caused by tax changes. This is a major difficulty in any attempt
   to identify the effects of a tax change: What would have happened in the absence of the tax changes?)
3. Of the four studies, those by Bischoff and by Hall and Jorgenson
   introduce explicit production functions. The implications of the
   functions in the two studies are, however, quite different. Hall
   and Jorgenson use a function of the form of Equation (15–23).

---

[28] Coen, "The Effect of Cash Flow," pp. 175, 179. Coen's figures, given in 1954
dollars, have been adjusted to 1965 dollars to make them comparable to the figures
of Hall and Jorgenson.

[29] To narrow a very complex discussion arbitrarily, the focus here is on the four
papers in the Brookings volume. The broader literature on investment adds to the
difficulty of coming to a firm view as to the effects of tax changes on investment. For
example, using a variation on the Hall-Jorgenson model, Eisner and Nadiri find almost
no effect of tax policies. Thus, like most investment models, the Hall-Jorgenson model
is very sensitive to changes in assumptions. See Robert Eisner and M. I. Nadiri, "Investment Behavior and Neo-Classical Theory," *Review of Economics and Statistics,*
August 1968, pp. 369–82.

For a more recent study by Hall, in which the ITC is again found to be an effective
stabilization tool, see his "Investment, Interest Rates, and the Effects of Stabilization
Policies," *Brookings Papers on Economic Activity,* 1977, vol. 1. (In this paper, Hall
argues that forces which make general fiscal policy weak tend to make the ITC's effect
strong, and vice versa. Therefore, a package including general policies—that is, tax
and expenditure changes—plus the ITC should have less uncertain results than general
policies alone. This point is related to our discussion in Chapter 10.)

The investment literature is extensive; the 1971 Brookings volume has a selected
bibliography 17 pages long (pp. 280–96).

Bischoff uses a variation, the "putty-clay" model (as contrasted to the "putty-putty" model of Hall and Jorgenson). While capital and labor are readily substitutable in the long run, Bischoff argues that they are not easily substituted in the short run. Before a specific investment is made, productive resources are available in general, flexible form (putty). Once the machine or equipment is constructed, however, flexibility is lost; the capital takes on a specific rigid form; it becomes hardened "clay." The commitment has been made to a specific form of capital; labor and capital are not easily substituted during the lifetime of the machine. This means that changes in the relative cost of labor and capital affect equipment spending only after a long lag; indeed, a lag much longer than that between changes in final output and induced investment. (In the putty-clay model, adjustments are made in the capital-labor input ratio as equipment depreciates and the decision has to be made whether and how to replace it. As equipment depreciates, capital resources become putty again.) [30]

As tax incentives operate by changing the (user) cost of capital, Bischoff therefore finds a much more delayed impact of tax changes than do Hall and Jorgenson. (In Bischoff's model, the effects of reductions in interest rates on the level of investment are also very slow, with no effect until two quarters have passed, and with the resulting level of investment still rising after 12 quarters. This conclusion has obvious implications for monetary policy.)

The divergence of expert opinion regarding the effects of changes in the tax treatment of investment makes the use of such changes for short-term stabilization policy problematical; predictability of results is a major criterion for demand stabilization policies. And short-run stabilization has clearly been one of the objectives of past changes in the investment tax credit—witnessed by the suspension and termination of the tax credit during the boom conditions of 1966 and 1969; its reinstitution when the economy showed weak-

---

[30] It might seem that this argument applies only to *reductions* in the amount of capital—which must await the depreciation of equipment—and not to *additions* to capital. After all, it should be possible to add machines at any time. However, in the Bischoff model, there is inflexibility in both directions. The capital-labor ratio is raised, not by simply adding *more* machines, but by switching to *different*, more complex machines. This is done only as the old machines depreciate and are *replaced* by the more complex machines.

nesses in 1967 and 1971; and its increase in 1975.[31] There were, however, also two other major motives for the use of tax incentives for
investment:

1. To increase the level of demand over a more extended time
    horizon. This was particularly important for the tax incentives
    introduced in 1962. At that time, the problem of "getting the
    economy moving" out of its extended period of slack was seen
    as something that would require extended long-term effort. (It
    is not in the least accidental that this period, in which the in-
    adequacy of aggregate demand was seen as a long-run problem,
    came to be known as the "Age of Keynes.")
2. To change the allocation of resources, directing a greater frac-
    tion of total production into investment, and laying the basis
    for a more rapid growth of the economy. This apparently was
    a motive for President Carter's proposal of a higher tax credit in
    early 1977.

INVENTORY INVESTMENT

Historically, investment has been one of the least stable components of aggregate demand; and changes in inventory have been
one of the least stable components of investment. Except for the
recession of 1970, economic downturns have been marked by sharp
reductions in inventory investment (Figure 15–4) ; indeed, declines

---

[31] Accelerated depreciation has been much less clearly aimed at short-term stabilization of the economy. The case against using accelerated depreciation for this purpose
is strong. In the Hall-Jorgenson study, for example, which gives the strongest results
for tax policies, the peak effect of the 1954 accelerated depreciation did not show up
until 1956 (p. 45). Furthermore, the Hall-Jorgenson study tends to exaggerate the
short-run effectiveness of accelerated depreciation; Hall and Jorgenson in effect assumed that businesses used accelerated depreciation when it became available, and
they then estimated the effects of accelerated depreciation on user cost, and hence
on investment.

However, there was in fact a slowness of businesses to use accelerated depreciation
when it became available in the 1950s. Ture found that, in 1960, about 70 percent of
corporation income tax returns reported no use of accelerated methods of depreciation
[Norman B. Ture, *Accelerated Depreciation in the United States* (New York: Columbia
University Press for the National Bureau of Economic Research, 1967) , p. 36].

Klein and Taubman studied and took account of this failure to use accelerated depreciation in their paper; many businesses reported to them (p. 241) that it was
"hard to determine how much their depreciation expense was currently increased by
the use of acceleration." Observe that, while businesses have a clear incentive to
claim an investment tax credit when it is available (since the credit directly increases their after-tax profit) , accelerated depreciation presents them with something
of a dilemma: In claiming additional depreciation, they depress their current profits
along with their tax payments.

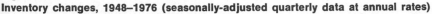

Figure 15–4
Inventory changes, 1948–1976 (seasonally-adjusted quarterly data at annual rates)

Billions of dollars, at 1972 prices

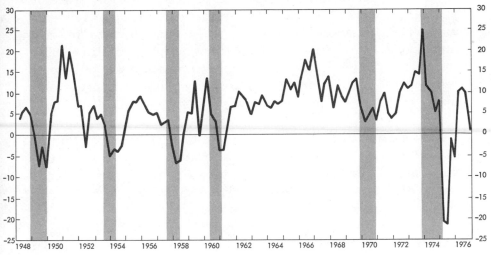

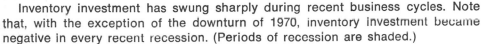

Inventory investment has swung sharply during recent business cycles. Note that, with the exception of the downturn of 1970, inventory investment became negative in every recent recession. (Periods of recession are shaded.)

in inventory investment on average have accounted for about 75 percent of the *total* decline in real *GNP* in the recessions of recent decades. Because of the size of inventory swings compared to total changes in economic activity, post-1945 declines in economic activity have frequently been referred to as "inventory recessions."

Businesses hold inventories in order to avoid losing sales. When customers want goods, they generally do not want to wait for the items to be produced on order. Sales can take place immediately from stocks held on hand as inventories. But there are costs of holding inventories, in the form of interest payments, storage costs, and the possible deterioration in the value of the goods. One cannot say that the more inventories, the better. Rather, here as elsewhere, businesses maximize profits by equating at the margin; inventories should be acquired up to the point where the costs of holding additional inventories come to equal the expected losses in revenues if the additional inventories are not held and sales are lost. And, as future demand is uncertain, it is *expected* future demand which is strategic in the decision to order additional inventories.

Inventories can act as a shock absorber, allowing the economy to continue relatively stable production in the face of day-to-day jiggles in demand. Automobile companies, for example, can schedule smooth production for a period of several weeks without reference to day-to-day changes in demand, which may be due to such capricious events as snow or rain keeping people away from showrooms. Changes in inventories may also be used as a way of keeping production relatively smooth in the face of seasonal changes in demand; the spurt in Christmas buying is reflected in a fall in inventories.

This is illustrated in Part A of Figure 15–5. In the face of jiggles in sales, the pattern of production is relatively smooth. As long as this tendency predominates, with inventories acting as a shock absorber, then inventory investment will stabilize the path of *GNP:* As sales go up, inventories will go down.

Inventory investment may not fulfill this smoothing function, however, as illustrated in Part B of Figure 15–5. Up to time t_2, the experience is the same as in the previous case; the upward movement of sales after t_1 is met out of inventories, with production remaining relatively stable. This is the behavior that would occur if the increase in sales were expected to be temporary; decreases in inventories are used to meet the increase in demand. But the increase in demand does not prove to be temporary; it continues after t_2. There may be some delay (t_2 to t_3) before businesses perceive that the increase in demand is going to hold up; but then they rapidly increase production. The increase in production may now be very rapid, because:

1. Inventories have been run down to dangerously low levels, and it would be desirable to build them up even if sales were to recede back to the level previously considered normal.
2. Expectations of what constitutes normal sales may be revised upward, so that the desired level of inventories is also revised upward. Indeed, businesses may now anticipate a continued upward *trend* of sales, and therefore be particularly anxious to build up inventories.

When the pace of sales levels off (t_4), there may again be a delay in perception; production may be pushed ahead. When the leveling out of demand is perceived (t_5), the rise in production may be abruptly halted. And, if inventories have been built up to very high levels, there may be a sharp cutback in production.

Figure 15–5
Inventory adjustment

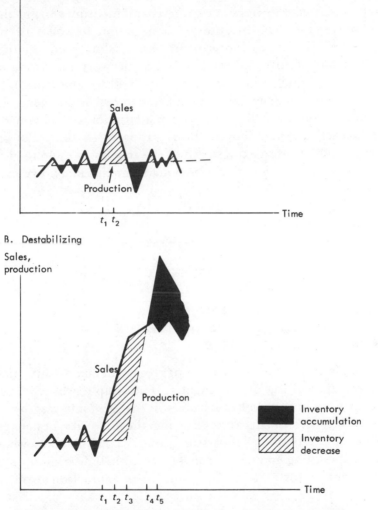

A. Stabilizing

Sales,
production

Sales

Production

t_1 t_2

Time

B. Destabilizing

Sales,
production

Sales

Production

Inventory
accumulation

Inventory
decrease

t_1 t_2 t_3 t_4 t_5

Time

Inventories may act as a shock absorber, permitting smooth production even in the face of unstable sales (Part A). On the other hand, if businesses are slow to perceive a fundamental change in the level of sales, then inventory investment may add to the instability of production (Part B).

This two-stage behavior—with inventories initially absorbing shocks but later adding to instability—showed up clearly in the worst recent recession in 1974–75. As the economy began to soften in the first two quarters of 1974, inventories rose at a seasonally adjusted annual rate of $11 billion, thus cushioning the early downswing. Then, as the recession gathered momentum during the last two quarters of 1974, inventory accumulation fell off to a rate of $7 billion. Finally, as the economy hit its low point in the first two quarters of 1975, inventories fell at the very rapid rate of $21 billion per annum, thus adding to the depth of the trough.[32] It is, however, hard to generalize about inventory investment. In the previous recession (1970), inventory accumulation remained positive in each quarter (Figure 15–4). Indeed, in the wake of that recession, hopes were expressed that the inventory cycle might have "lost its oomph."[33] But that was not to be; the inventory cycle returned in early 1975.

APPENDIX

MODELS OF INSTABILITY: SAMUELSON'S MULTIPLIER-ACCELERATOR MODEL AND THE "RAZOR'S EDGE" OF HARROD

A single important segment of aggregate demand—investment—has been the subject of this chapter. The simple accelerator model demonstrates how mild disturbances in the economy may be magnified by the investment sector. During the early Keynesian period, several more complete (but still quite simple) models were presented, including induced responses in both the consumption and investment sectors. Most important were Samuelson's multiplier-

---

[32] For details on inventory behavior in 1974–75, see Martin Feldstein and Alan Auerbach, "Inventory Behavior in Durable-Goods Manufacturing: The Target-Adjustment Model," *Brookings Papers on Economic Activity*, 1976, vol. 2, pp. 382–85. Feldstein and Auerbach discuss in detail the problems in forecasting inventory accumulation.

[33] Jack Clark Francis, "Has the Inventory Cycle Lost Its Oomph?" *Federal Reserve Bank of Philadelphia Business Review*, February 1973, pp. 19–27. The unpredictability of inventories was one of the major contributors to the poor economic forecasts of 1974–75. See Stephen K. McNees, "The Forecasting Performance in the Early 1970s," *New England Economic Review* (Federal Reserve Bank of Boston, July/August 1976), pp. 35–38.

accelerator model and the growth model of Harrod and Domar.[34] These models underlined the possibility of instability of aggregate demand. (The Harrod-Domar growth model investigated the relationship between growth and instability, with the stress being on instability; it is therefore included in this chapter rather than in Chapter 16 on growth.)

Samuelson's multiplier-accelerator model

In a paper published in 1939, Paul Samuelson demonstrated how the combination of the accelerator and the multiplier can generate a

Table 15A–1
The multiplier-accelerator interaction: Effects of continuing government spending program

Period	Government spending	Consumption $(\Delta C_t = 0.50\,\Delta Y_{t-1})$	I $(I_t = 1.00\,\Delta C_t)$	Resulting change in income
1	100	0	0	100
2	100	50	50	200
3	100	100	50	250
4	100	125	25	250
5	100	125	0	225
6	100	112.5	−12.5	200
7	100	100	−12.5	187.5
8	100	93.75	−6.25	187.5
9	100	93.75	0	193.75
10	100	96.875	3.125	200

Source: Paul A. Samuelson, "Interactions between the Multiplier Analysis and the Principle of Acceleration," *Review of Economic Statistics*, May 1939, Table 1.

cyclical pattern. Consider Samuelson's simple illustration, in which the marginal propensity to consume is 0.50; a $1 change in income in a period causes a 50¢ change in consumption in the next period. Assume, further, a value of one for the desired ratio of capital to production of consumption goods (Samuelson's "relation," that is, the acceleration coefficient α of the simple accelerator model). Thus, an increase of $1 in consumption in any period will induce $1 of investment in the same period. (A decrease in consumption will induce negative investment. This is possible because net investment

---

[34] Paul A. Samuelson, "Interactions between the Multiplier Analysis and the Principle of Acceleration," *Review of Economic Statistics*, May 1939, pp. 75–78; Roy F. Harrod, "An Essay in Dynamic Theory," *Economic Journal*, March 1939, pp. 14–33; Harrod, *Towards a Dynamic Economics* (London: Macmillan, 1948), Lecture 3, pp. 63–100; Evsey D. Domar, "Expansion and Employment," *American Economic Review*, March 1947, pp. 34–55.

may be negative by the amount of depreciation.) Then, if the government institutes a spending program of $100 per period, the results will be those shown in Table 15A–1. The initiation of a steady flow of government spending results in a cyclical path of demand.

Given the assumed values for the *MPC* (0.50) and the acceleration coefficient (1.0), the resulting oscillations in aggregate demand will be dampened, with their amplitude decreasing as time passes, as illustrated by Path$_2$ in Figure 15A–1. This is not, however, the only possible outcome of this model. If, for example, the acceleration coefficient were significantly smaller than the *MPC*, there would be no oscillations, and the model would give an asymptotic approach to the new, higher equilibrium level of income (E_2), as illustrated by Path$_1$. (The multiplier models of Chapters 3 and 4 were a limiting

Figure 15A–1
Multiplier-accelerator model: Possible responses to disturbance

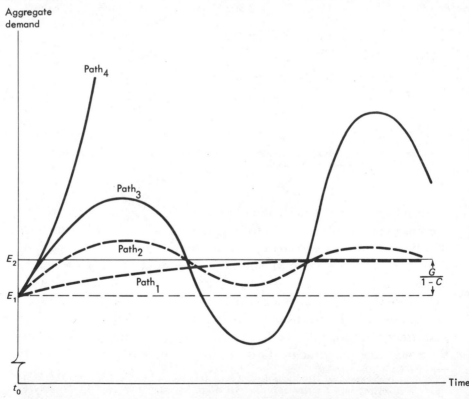

In this diagram, the initiation of a continuing, steady government expenditure is assumed at time t_0. The path that will be followed depends on the size of the acceleration coefficient and on the size of the multiplier.

case; there was no induced investment, and the acceleration coefficient was thus tacitly assumed to be zero.) If the product of the
MPC and the acceleration coefficient exceeds one, the oscillations
become explosive (Path$_3$) ; and if the acceleration coefficient is high
enough, aggregate demand simply explodes without oscillating
(Path$_4$).[35] In general, the higher the acceleration coefficient (α), the
less stable will be the economy.

The Harrod-Domar model

*"A slow sort of a country," said the Queen. "Now, here, you see, it
takes all the running you can do, to keep in the same place. If you
want to get somewhere else, you must run at least twice as fast as
that."*

Lewis Carroll

This quotation from Carroll's *Through the Looking Glass* introduces Domar's famous 1947 article; it neatly sums up the major
point of his paper and the similar argument of Roy Harrod. If the
economy is going to remain at full employment, it must run faster
all the time. If investment does not grow continuously, the economy
will slip off into a depression.

The central concept of the Harrod-Domar model is that of the
equilibrium rate of growth or, in Harrod's terminology, the *warranted* rate of growth, G_w. The equilibrium growth rate is derived
from three underlying equations:

$$S = I \qquad (15\text{--}24)$$

$$S = sY \qquad (15\text{--}25)$$

and

$$\Delta Y = \frac{1}{\alpha} I \qquad (15\text{--}26)$$

---

[35] The conditions may be given more precisely. (These conditions are provided for
reference only. They change if different assumptions are made about lags; for example, they change if it is assumed that investment responds in the period following
the change in output rather than in the same period.)

Path$_1$: $\alpha < 1$ and $c > \dfrac{4\alpha}{(1+\alpha)^2}$

Path$_2$: for $\alpha < 1$, $c < \dfrac{4\alpha}{(1+\alpha)^2}$ and for $\alpha > 1$, $\alpha c < 1$

Path$_3$: $\alpha c > 1$ and $c < \dfrac{4\alpha}{(1+\alpha)^2}$

Path$_4$: $\alpha > 1$ and $c > \dfrac{4\alpha}{(1+\alpha)^2}$

where

ΔY is the change in real income; also assumed to be the change in real income that was *expected*.

I is net real investment—that is, the change in the stock of capital.

S is real saving.

s is the marginal propensity to save.

α is the desired or equilibrium marginal capital-output ratio.

The first two equations come from basic Keynesian theory; the third is a rearrangement of the simple accelerator Equation (15–4).

While the Harrod-Domar model is thus related both to the multiplier (Equation 15–25) and the accelerator (Equation 15–26), there is a significant difference in the emphasis of the Harrod-Domar model and the accelerator. In the accelerator model, investment plays an important role because of its *contribution to aggregate demand;* the accelerator principle illustrates a set of forces which may destabilize the path of demand. The *dual nature* of investment is stressed in the Harrod-Domar model: Investment currently contributes to aggregate demand, and thus promotes employment at the present time; but it adds to the productive capacity of the economy, thereby increasing the amount which will have to be spent in the future to ensure full employment.[36]

But let us return to the warranted or equilibrium rate of growth. It can be derived by a combination of the above three equations, thus:

$$\Delta Y = \frac{1}{\alpha} \cdot sY \qquad (15\text{–}27)$$

that is,

$$\frac{\Delta Y}{Y} = \frac{s}{\alpha} \qquad (15\text{–}28)$$

But these equations represent an equilibrium situation. Therefore,

$$G_w = \frac{s}{\alpha} \qquad (15\text{–}29)$$

where

G_w is the warranted or equilibrium growth rate.

[36] Domar, "Expansion and Employment," pp. 35–39. This proposition was anticipated by Keynes in the *General Theory* (p. 105): "Each time we secure to-day's equilibrium by increasing investment, we are aggravating the difficulty of securing [a full-employment] equilibrium to-morrow." There is also an obvious similarity to the secular stagnation argument of Hansen, discussed in the appendix to Chapter 14.

It must be stressed that the concept of equilibrium is used in a Keynesian sense; there may be *unemployment* in an economy which moves along the equilibrium growth path.

But unemployment is far from the only problem which can occur. In Harrod's version, the economy is highly unstable. It moves along a razor's edge, with any minor deviation in either direction causing a progressive flight from the equilibrium growth path. In Harrod's words, "centrifugal forces are at work, causing the system to depart farther and farther from the required line of advance."[37]

To show why this is so, Harrod considers a case where the actual or realized rate of growth—G—is greater than the equilibrium growth rate, G_w.[38] Given this rapid rate of growth of output, the actual capital-output ratio will fall below the desired ratio. Businesses will respond by increasing their orders for capital goods. But, as incomes rise, the absolute level of saving rises rather slowly; saving constitutes a small fraction of income. Investment demand, however, is drawn up further by the increase in total output; as output increases, businesses order more capital goods. With desired investment remaining greater than desired saving, the economy moves progressively farther away from its equilibrium growth path.

Harrod's argument here seems to get quite close to Samuelson's multiplier-accelerator model, in which aggregate demand explodes when the economy is disturbed in an upward direction and the capital-output ratio and the *MPC* are large. One cannot be certain, however. While Harrod specifically states that the economy moves progressively away from the "required line of advance," he does not explicitly give the reasons why this must be so. He does emphasize a low rate of saving (pp. 79 and 86). But this in itself is inadequate to make the economy move continuously away from the stable growth path; something must simultaneously be said about investment. Indeed, as was seen above in the discussion of Samuelson's multiplier-accelerator model, it is a high acceleration coefficient (α) which is critical in getting a continuous one-way movement. Indeed, as long as the acceleration coefficient is less than one, aggregate de-

---

[37] Harrod, *Towards a Dynamic Economics*, p. 86. The same point is made in Harrod's "Essay in Dynamic Theory," p. 22: "Suppose . . . G exceeds G_w . . . . G, instead of returning to G_w, will move farther from it in an upward direction and the farther it diverges, the greater the stimulus to expansion will be."

[38] Harrod, *Towards a Dynamic Economics*, pp. 85–89. For more detail, see William J. Baumol, *Economic Dynamics*, 3d ed. (London: Macmillan 1970), pp. 37–55; R. G. D. Allen, *Macro-Economic Theory, a Mathematical Treatment* (London: Macmillan, 1967), pp. 184–87.

mand will not explode, no matter how low the *MPS* is. Thus, either Harrod must be implicitly assuming an acceleration coefficient greater than one, or he must have some alternative explosive force in mind, such as unstable expectations which cause investment to respond drastically to initial disturbances. (There will be more about this later.)

On the other hand, consider an initial downward disturbance. If actual growth falls below the warranted rate, businesses will have too much capital; they will cut back on orders, and the economy will move progressively away from the equilibrium growth path on the downward side.

With this tendency for a flight from the equilibrium growth path, instability of the economy will be the normal state of affairs. Stability requires that as a result of the many trial-and-error decisions of large numbers of businesses in ordering capital equipment, the economy by chance lands precisely at the warranted rate of growth, an outcome which would come only with "great luck."[39]

The problem of instability may be illustrated with Figures 15A–2 and 15A–3. We begin at time t_0 with actual income of Y_0. Three paths should be distinguished:

1. The equilibrium growth path, with a growth rate of G_w. (Figures 15A–2 and 15A–3 are constructed with a ratio scale on the vertical axis, so that a constant rate of growth gives a straight line.)
2. The full-employment path, with a growth rate of G_n, or the "natural rate of growth." G_n is determined by the rate of growth of population and the rate of technological change. It has "no direct relation to G_w."[40]
3. The actual path, with a growth rate of G.

If by chance, $G = G_w$, the economy would move along the equilibrium growth path in Figure 15A–2. If, however, G initially were less than G_w, the economy would move progressively farther below the equilibrium path, following illustrated Actual path₁. An initial G above G_w will lead to a continuous upward movement along Actual path₂. If, for some unexplained reason, a disturbance were to occur at point A, depressing the actual growth rate to G_w, then the economy could move along a new equilibrium growth path,

---

[39] Harrod, *Towards a Dynamic Economics,* p. 86.

[40] Harrod, *Towards a Dynamic Economics,* p. 87.

Figure 15A–2
Harrod's economic instability: Warranted growth rate less than natural growth rate

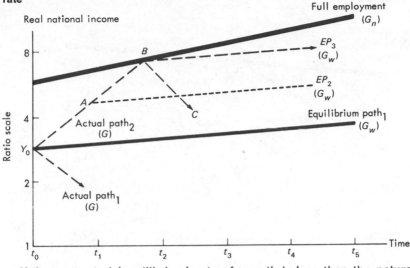

If the warranted (equilibrium) rate of growth is less than the natural (full-employment) rate, then an expanding economy will tend to bounce off the full-employment ceiling and head back into recession.

EP_2; the economy theoretically can start off in the equilibrium direction from any level of employment.

Suppose, however, that there is no such disturbance at *A;* the economy continues along Actual path₂. When the economy gets to full employment at point *B,* it cannot continue along the previous path; the shortage of labor prevents a continued expansion of output at such a rapid rate. Real growth *must* slow down. In the adjustment process, there may be an overreaction; the economy may move back down, toward point *C.* Hopefully, however, that will not occur. It is possible that the economy will slow down only to the warranted rate of growth, moving along a new equilibrium path (EP_3) from point *B.*

But here another problem arises in the Harrod model. The warranted rate of growth is determined independently of the natural rate, and if $G_w < G_n$, as illustrated in Figure 15A–2, the economy will slide back into a state of unemployment even if it manages to keep to the new equilibrium path (EP_3) and not bounce sharply off the full-employment production ceiling. Continuing full employment will occur only in the extremely fortuitous case where

Figure 15A–3
**Harrod's economic instability: Warranted growth rate greater than natural
growth rate**

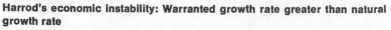

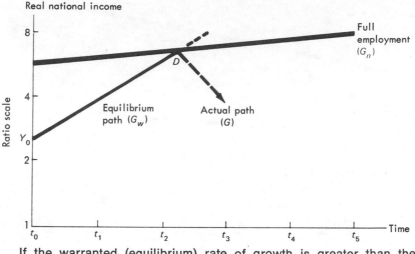

If the warranted (equilibrium) rate of growth is greater than the
natural (full-employment) rate, then a rebound off the full-employment
ceiling is inevitable, according to Harrod.

$G = G_w = G_n$, and where, moreover, this happy coincidence comes
when the economy is already at full employment.

The assumption that the warranted rate of growth is less than the
natural rate led to trouble; but the worst is yet to come. G_w may
exceed G_n. Assume that the economy initially is moving along the
equilibrium growth path (Figure 15A–3). Then, when it reaches full
employment, a continuing equilibrium is impossible; the economy
cannot follow the warranted growth path up beyond D. The "inevitable" outcome:[41] a rebound into unemployment, with real output
falling.

Harrod's model led him to propose pump-priming government
expenditures as a cure for depression. A stimulation of aggregate
demand could give the economy expansive momentum back toward
full employment. (Contrast this with the simple Keynesian model of
Chapter 4, in which pump priming will not give lasting benefits.
The economy simply lapses back toward its unemployment equilibrium as the government spending programs are wound down.) But
his model, with the strong tendency of the economy to rebound

---

[41] Harrod, *Towards a Dynamic Economics*, p. 89.

from the full-employment ceiling, led Harrod to a bizarre proposal for fiscal policy as the economy approaches full employment (p. 75) : ". . . the point at which it will be above all necessary to have a large volume of public works to turn on, perhaps a larger volume than in the original pump-priming phase, is when we approach full employment."

Evaluation

In Samuelson's multiplier-accelerator model, the path of aggregate demand may range anywhere from very stable to spectacularly unstable, depending on the assumptions made about the sizes of the acceleration coefficient and the marginal propensity to consume. In the Harrod-Domar model, the economy is almost certain to be unstable (except in the unlikely case that $G = G_w$) ; and *even in the improbable case of a stable growth, this may involve increasing levels of unemployment* (if $G = G_w < G_n$). Both of these simple models may be criticized on the same ground: They assume fixed capital-output coefficients and fixed marginal propensities to consume.[42]

In Samuelson's illustration in which the multiplier-accelerator interaction gives a dampened oscillatory path in response to an initial disturbance, the marginal propensity to consume is assumed to be 0.50. In dealing with cyclical instability, it is appropriate to consider relatively brief time periods—one or two quarters. For such relatively abbreviated time periods, Samuelson's illustrative *MPC* of 0.50 is not unreasonable; certainly everything in Chapter 14 suggested that the *MPC* for such brief periods will be significantly less than the long-run propensity to consume. Samuelson's assumed *MPC* of 0.50 stands up quite well in the light of more recent work on consumption.

There is, however, a difficulty on the consumption side. The relatively low short-run marginal propensity to consume reflects a slowness of the consumer to respond to higher levels of income; increases in income tend to result in smoothed, lagged responses. Insofar as this is the case, increases in disposable income during the upswings should have some of their stimulative effects on consump-

---

[42] This is not to suggest that the authors were unaware that coefficients and marginal propensities might change. See, for example, Samuelson, "Interactions" p. 78; Harrod, *Towards a Dynamic Economics,* pp. 78–79, 82–83, and 89; and Domar, "Expansion and Unemployment," fn. 19. The possibility of such changes was not, however, integrated into the models; the key relationships were generally assumed to be constants.

tion during the ensuing downswing, thus moderating the amplitude of the cyclical swings suggested by the basic multiplier-accelerator model.

Further stability is introduced into the world if a more complex multiplier process is considered. In Samuelson's model, there is only one leakage from the spending stream, namely saving. This is appropriate for simple illustrations, but the world is obviously more complex. The addition of other leakages, such as taxes and imports, generally adds stability to the course of aggregate demand.

But it is not the multiplier component which is the key determinant of the degree of instability in the multiplier-accelerator model; rather it is the marginal capital-output ratio (α). The instability of the economy becomes much more pronounced as this ratio rises above one. In the simple accelerator model, the capital-output ratio determining short-run responses is assumed to equal or approximately equal the average capital-output ratio, and investment takes place without a lag, during the same period as the change in consumption demand.

Given these assumptions, we immediately run into a problem in considering whether Samuelson's assumed value of 1.0 for the capital-output ratio in his illustration is a reasonable starting point. Business capital amounts to roughly 75 percent of annual *GNP*. (This includes nonresidential structures [30 percent]; producers' durables [28 percent]; and nonfarm inventories [18 percent].) [43] But in the present context, these figures have no particular significance, since capital is a stock and *GNP* is a flow. The (average) capital-output ratio is 0.75 if *annual* output is taken as the denominator; but this is the same as a 1.50 ratio of capital to semiannual output; 3.00 on a quarterly basis; 9.00 on a monthly basis; and so on. Indeed, we can obviously get any particular capital-output ratio we want simply by specifying the "right" time period.

But we can scarcely conclude that the economy is unstable simply by specifying a time period of one month, taking a capital-output ratio of 9.0, and plugging it into a simple multiplier-accelerator model. If we did this, we would be assuming that the stock of capital is adjusted to the equilibrium level within one month. But this makes no sense on general theoretical grounds, and there is considerable empirical evidence that the adjustment of capital is

---

[43] Data for 1958. For these figures and a discussion of the measurement of capital stock, see Dale W. Jorgenson and Zvi Griliches, "Issues in Growth Accounting: A Reply to Edward F. Denison," *Survey of Current Business,* May 1972, pp. 69–74.

quite long—peaking after one to two years in the case of equipment, with longer lags for buildings and shorter lags for inventories.

In brief, it makes sense to address the question of the appropriate capital-output ratio simultaneously with the issue of the time lags in the pattern of investment. As a *very* rough and ready first approximation, this suggests that a period during which a sizable fraction of capital adjustment occurs—something like one and a half years—might be taken as a starting point in applying the simple accelerator, giving a capital-output ratio of about 0.50. With this value for α, fluctuations that come out of the multiplier-accelerator model are not large.

The discussion of the time period in the multiplier-accelerator model does suggest, however, a place to look for a particular source of instability; namely inventories, where adjustment may be much more rapid than for fixed investment. The conspicuous role that inventories have played in postwar business cycles is therefore not surprising. It is, however, difficult to imagine inventories being a strong and continuing source of a one-way movement in an otherwise stable economy; *inventory* cycles are likely to be rather mild.

Reference to the empirical work on investment lags therefore tends to be reassuring regarding the inherent stability of the economy. The more colorful possibilities suggested by the multiplier-accelerator model (Path$_3$ and Path$_4$ of Figure 15A–1) are theoretically interesting, but of little practical significance.

But if we may be reassured regarding the stability of the economy in the face of single, short-run disturbances, the empirical work on the investment and consumption functions is less reassuring in another important respect. In an economy subject to continuous stimulation, a strong momentum may be built up. In the face of a continuing expansive fiscal policy, for example, the initial induced investment during the first several quarters may be quite small. But if the stimulus continues for several years, then the lagged effects of the stimulus on investment will result in a strong total investment demand. Similarly, on the consumption side, a continuing stimulus to disposable income will have a cumulative effect as consumers come to look on their higher levels of income as normal and form new consumption patterns based on their new affluence. The stabilization problem may therefore be not so much one of a basic flightiness of aggregate demand, but, on the contrary, a relative unresponsiveness of the path of aggregate demand to short-run disturbances. Thus, when a strong expansive momentum builds up over an extended period, it may not be readily manageable in the short run by restrictive monetary and fiscal policies. Similarly, a strong downward momentum, once established, may not be readily responsive to stimulative monetary and fiscal policies.

The multiplier-accelerator model deals with real changes in the economy. When the effects of price changes are introduced, the problem of momentum of an expanding or contracting economy may be heightened. In late 1968, for example, the strong expansive forces of the economy continued in spite of the income tax surcharge introduced in the middle of that year. Investment was the major source of strength. In part, this undoubtedly reflected the lagged response of investment to the continuing strong increases in output over the previous years (except for the brief minirecession in 1967). But price expectations also seem to have played an important role. Businesses were anxious to acquire plant and equipment before prices went up.

Highly unstable short-run responses of aggregate demand do not flow automatically or easily out of an accelerator-type model, provided that some attention is paid to the lags in investment decisions. This brings us back to a fundamental problem in Harrod's model; namely, the reason for the "razor's edge," with any movement from the warranted (equilibrium) growth path leading to progressive departures. If, indeed, an implicit multiplier-accelerator model is behind his argument, then he would seem to have made rather strong implicit assumptions about the size of the capital-output ratio and the speed of the response of investment. Specifically, the *minimum* condition for a continuous departure from the equilibrium path is for the increase in the demand for capital goods to exceed the increase in output for the economy. That is, the α in the accelerator must exceed one, where it is redefined to mean the *actual marginal* capital-output ratio, rather than the equilibrium desired ratio.[44] This requires a response which is much speedier than suggested by empirical studies of investment lags. The "razor's edge" remains unexplained, given the ranges of coefficients indicated by empirical work.

Another puzzling feature of the growth model, applying to Domar's version as well as that of Harrod, is the (substantially) fixed capital-output ratio, even in the face of large-scale unemployment.

---

[44] There is no real point in deriving more precise assumptions about α from the specific conditions given in fn. 35, p. 465. Those conditions themselves change when alternative assumptions are made about the lags in the economy.

The quantity of capital determines the level of output along the equilibrium growth path; any additional amount of capital can be combined with readily available labor up to the point of full employment. But surely the capital-output ratio cannot be considered rigid when there is continuing large-scale unemployment of labor. Indeed, the quantity of capital is itself a fuzzy concept: At any period of time, there are older machines near the limit of their useful lives. How long they are kept in service is a matter of considerable flexibility.

The major contribution of the Harrod-Domar model lies in the encouragement which it provided to economists to think methodically about the determinants of growth; but as an explanation of instability, it is not enlightening.

KEY POINTS

1. It is inappropriate to look on investment as being an equilibrium *flow;* rather, the flow of investment should be looked upon as the process of adjusting the capital *stock* toward its desired or equilibrium level.

2. The simplest stock adjustment model involves the acceleration principle (Equation 15–4). In this simple model, the desired capital stock is assumed to be proportional to current output, and net investment fills the gap between the existing stock and the desired stock. In this model, a relatively modest increase in the rate of growth of demand for the final product can lead to a large increase in the demand for investment. On the other hand, an actual decline in the demand for the final product is not a necessary precondition for a decline in investment. Investment can fall as a result of a decline in the *rate of growth* of the demand for the final product.

3. If, in a simple accelerator model, demand for final output moves cyclically, then the demand for investment will also move cyclically, with the peaks and troughs in investment demand *preceding* the peaks and troughs in final demand (Figure 15–1). This is a consequence of the assumption that investment depends on the *rate of change* of demand for final output.

4. A number of criticisms have been made of the simple accelerator theory. It has been argued by Koyck and many others that

businesses adjust their capital stock only gradually. In Koyck's investment function (the flexible accelerator, Equation 15–13), investment makes up only a fraction (β) of the gap between the existing capital stock and the equilibrium desired capital stock. Recall Equation (15–13):

$$I_{nt} = \beta(\alpha O_t - K_{t-1})$$

According to Koyck's function, a disturbance in final demand will have its largest effect during the current period, and then the effect will gradually taper off. If, for example, $\beta = 0.25$, investment in each period will make up one quarter of the gap between the equilibrium capital stock (αO_t) and the existing capital stock (K_{t-1}).

5. In contrast, the functions of other writers (Almon, de Leeuw) give a lagged response, with the greatest effect on investment coming some time after the disturbance in final output (Figure 15–3).

6. Flexibility may also be introduced into the investment function by making the equilibrium capital-output ratio a variable. For example, in the Cobb-Douglas formulation, the α of the accelerator models is supplanted by $a \cdot P/C$ (see Equation 15–23).

7. Statistically, it is not clear which of the investment functions provides the best representation of how the economy actually works. Yet the effects of fiscal changes such as the investment tax credit are very much dependent on the form of the investment function. Thus, the effects of changes in tax policy on aggregate demand cannot be predicted with any high degree of confidence.

8. During postwar recessions, declines in inventory investment have constituted a major fraction of the total decline in output. The unstable behavior of inventories may be attributed to their sensitivity to changes in expectations.

QUESTIONS

1. Suppose that the demand for bicycles in the United States suddenly doubles. Suppose that there is some doubt that this high level of demand for bicycles will continue indefinitely into the future. (After all, the public itself may simply be adjusting to

a higher desired stock of bicycles, and once they reach the desired stock, the demand for bicycles will recede to the level needed to satisfy replacement demand and demand associated with an increase in population.) Explain how the demand for bicycles might be satisfied without a very large production of bicycle-making equipment. (Observe that the simple accelerator theory would require the production of bicycle-manufacturing equipment equal to the total existing stock of bicycle-manufacturing equipment, in order for there to be a doubling of the stock of such equipment.)

2. Suppose that investment has risen rapidly, and that an inflationary boom is feared. Suppose, as a consequence, that the Federal Reserve takes restrictive action which sharply limits the rate of expansion of the money supply. How might this affect the rate of investment? Explain step-by-step how the tighter monetary policy might have this effect. If the tight monetary policy curtails the ability of corporations to finance investment by increasing their bank borrowings, what other sources of funds are open to them? How might these alternative sources be affected by the tight monetary policy?

SUGGESTED READINGS

Michael K. Evans, *Macroeconomic Activity: Theory, Forecasting, and Control* (New York: Harper & Row, 1969), chaps. 4–8, 13–15, and 17. (Evans' treatment is much more detailed, advanced, and difficult than the presentation in this book.)

James G. Witte, Jr. "The Microfoundations of the Social Investment Function," *Journal of Political Economy*, October 1963, pp. 441–56.

Chapter 16

Growth

Not to go back, is somewhat to advance,
And men must walk, at least, before they dance.

Alexander Pope

In the first chapter, three goals were given for macroeconomic policy: full employment, stable prices, and a satisfactory rate of growth. Full employment and price stability have been the theme of the first 15 chapters. At long last, the time has come to study growth.

In the beginning pages of this chapter, the sources or causes of economic growth will be studied, and the possibilities of changing the rate of growth through public policy will be considered. Then a fundamental question will be addressed: What, if any, objective *should* there be for growth? Regarding employment and prices, the goals were relatively simple—although in practice there might be major difficulties in actually achieving the goals. The employment objective should be to provide an adequate supply of jobs, so that job seekers can obtain employment within a reasonable period of searching. The price objective should be a reasonably stable average level of prices through time, although it might be desirable to compromise this goal somewhat in order to achieve other objectives (Chapter 13). The growth objective is not self-evident. One cannot assume that, the more growth, the better. There clearly should be some limits to the amount by which we skimp and save in order that our children and grandchildren may live in luxury.

In the final sections of the chapter, the measurement of growth is taken up. The simple measure of growth—the increase in the real national income through time—is opened to question, with additional indicators of economic progress being considered.

A SIMPLE GROWTH EQUATION: THE COBB-DOUGLAS FUNCTION

To begin, however, let us assume the simplest measure of growth: the rate of change in real national income through time. In this chapter, the focus is on the *supply* side of the economy and specifically on the forces that affect the productive *capacity* of the economy. Left behind are the determinants of aggregate demand and the forces that may cause an economy to operate at a low rate of capacity utilization.

A starting point for much of the growth literature is the Cobb-Douglas production function introduced in the previous chapter. This assumes a competitive economy, with two homogeneous factors of production, capital (K) and labor (L):

$$Y = \tau K^a L^{1-a} \qquad (16\text{-}1; \text{ repeat of } 15\text{-}19)$$

where

Y is real national income.[1]

τ is a scale factor which changes with technology.

a is a positive fraction, less than one.

From this, the marginal product of capital was derived:

$$\frac{\delta Y}{\delta K} = \frac{aY}{K} \qquad (16\text{-}2; \text{ repeat of } 15\text{-}21)$$

where

$\partial Y / \partial K$ is the rate of change of output with respect to capital; that is, the marginal productivity of capital.

Since a competitive economy is assumed, each unit of a productive factor will be paid its marginal product. This means that the total

---

[1] In the previous chapter, the focus was on the capital-output ratio, normally given symbolically as K/O. Here the focus is on changes in real national income, normally given as Y. Hence, although Equations (15–19) and (16–1) are really the same equation, the symbols are slightly changed, with Y here being substituted for the O of Chapter 15.

income going to capital will be equal to the marginal product of capital times the number of units of capital:

$$Y_K = \frac{aY}{K} \cdot K = aY \qquad (16\text{--}3)$$

or, rearranging,

$$\frac{Y_K}{Y} = a \qquad (16\text{--}4)$$

where

Y_K is the total income going to capital.

Thus, *the share of total income going to capital is given by the fraction a.* Similarly, the share of total income going to labor is $(1 - a)$.

Observe that, according to the Cobb-Douglas function, the fraction of total income going to capital, *a,* does *not* change as the quantity of capital grows in relation to the quantity of labor. If each worker has more capital to work with, the marginal product of each unit of capital will go down. But there will be more units of capital, each receiving the new, lower marginal product. These two forces—the decline in the marginal product of capital, and the increase in the number of units of capital—will exactly offset one another, in the sense that the share going to capital will remain unchanged. Thus, perhaps surprisingly, labor gets a constant fraction of the increase in total production $(1 - a)$, even if the increase in production comes from a greater use of capital with the labor supply fixed.

In this Cobb-Douglas formulation, technology (τ) is a scale factor. That is, an improvement in technology permits the production of, say, 10 percent more with any given amount of capital and labor. It is assumed that technological change increases the total amount which can be produced *without altering* the relative marginal products of capital and labor. In other words, the illustrative increase in technology would increase the marginal product of both capital and labor by 10 percent.

Assuming that technological change is thus *neutral*—leaving the relative marginal productivities of labor and capital unchanged while raising them both in absolute terms—the relative shares of national income going to capital and labor will remain unchanged at a and $(1 - a)$, respectively, as the economy grows.

Other major assumptions in the Cobb-Douglas function:

1. There are constant *returns to scale.* If, at any given level of technology (τ), *both* inputs are increased by x percent, then

total output will also be increased by the same x percent. (In technical terms, the function is homogeneous of degree one.)

2. There are *diminishing returns* to the individual factors. If, at any given level of technology, *one* factor of production is increased while the other is held constant, then the marginal product of the first factor will decline as its quantity rises.

(The distinction between *constant* returns to scale and *diminishing* returns may be briefly reiterated. Output goes up proportionately if *both* labor and capital inputs go up by the same fraction. But if only *one* input increases, then the additions to output will become progressively smaller for each additional unit of that input.)

Now let us return to the overall growth of the economy, which will be:

$$G_Y = aG_K + (1 - a)G_L + G_r \qquad (16\text{--}5)$$

where the letter G with the appropriate subscript is used to represent the rate of growth of an economic magnitude through time. For example: G_Y is the rate of growth of real national productive capacity—that is, the rate of growth of full-employment real national income; and G_L is the rate of growth of the labor supply;[2] and so on.

In words, the rate of growth of productive capacity is equal to the sum of the rate of growth of the capital stock times the share of income going to capital, plus the rate of growth of the labor supply times the share of income going to labor, plus the rate of growth of technology.[3] In the simple case, where technology does not change

---

[2] Formally,

$$G_Y \equiv (dY/dt)/Y \qquad (16\text{--}6)$$
$$G_L \equiv (dL/dt)/L \qquad (16\text{--}7)$$

where t is time.

[3] Equation (16–5) may be derived by taking the natural logs (ln) of equation (16–1):

$$\ln Y = \ln r + a \ln K + (1 - a) \ln L \qquad (16\text{--}8)$$

Differentiating with respect to time, we get:

$$\frac{Y'}{Y} = \frac{r'}{r} + a\frac{K'}{K} + (1 - a)\frac{L'}{L} \qquad (16\text{--}9)$$

That is,

$$G_Y = G_r + aG_K + (1 - a)G_L \qquad (16\text{--}5)$$

Those unfamiliar with calculus may derive the general point of Equation (16–5) by algebraic manipulation, in the simple case where technology is constant ($G_r = 0$):

$$\Delta Y = \Delta K \times (\text{marg. prod. of } K) + \Delta L \times (\text{marg. prod. of } L) \qquad (16\text{--}10)$$

Which, from Equation (16–2), gives:

and the rate of growth of the capital stock and the labor supply is the same (x percent), then the rate of growth of output will also be the same (x percent). This, of course, is a repeat of point 1 above regarding the constant returns to scale in the Cobb-Douglas function. A statistical application of Equation (16–5) permits a separation of the growth of output attributable to an increase in the inputs of capital and labor from the growth in output attributable to technological improvement.

THE APPLICATION OF GROWTH EQUATIONS: IS TECHNOLOGICAL CHANGE "EMBODIED"?

According to the Cobb-Douglas growth equation (16–5), the rate of growth of output depends on the rates of growth of capital and labor, and on technological change. Technological change appears in a peculiar way. It does not depend on changes in the inputs of capital or labor; in other words, it is "disembodied." This equation and variations on it have been used by Professor Robert Solow of M.I.T. in estimating the determinants of growth. For the simple Cobb-Douglas function, Solow obtained the following results using annual data for 1929–61 for *GNP* originating in the business sector, adjusted for price changes:[4]

$$G_Y = 0.11G_K + 0.89G_L + 2.5 \text{ percent} \qquad (16\text{–}13)$$

(One adjustment of Solow should be noted. Since this type of production function is used to estimate the growth of productive *capacity,* not the growth of actual output, Solow adjusted for slack in the economy in estimating Equation 16–13.)

According to this equation, the growth rate of the economy is almost entirely the result of technological change, with changes in the quantities of capital and labor inputs contributing little. On theoretical grounds, Solow (p. 77) did not consider this a very plausible approach. Technological change is not independent of investment

---

$$\Delta Y = \Delta K \times \frac{aY}{K} + \Delta L \times \frac{(1-a)Y}{L} \qquad (16\text{–}11)$$

$$\frac{\Delta Y}{Y} = a\frac{\Delta K}{K} + (1-a)\frac{\Delta L}{L} \qquad (16\text{–}12)$$

provided $G_T = 0$.

[4] Robert M. Solow, "Technical Progress, Capital Formation, and Economic Growth," *American Economic Review,* May 1962, pp. 76–86; specifically his equation 5. Solow's specific measure of output (p. 79) was *GNP* minus the product originating in the following: general government, government enterprises, households and institutions, rest of world and services of houses.

in new equipment, and it is illegitimate to separate the growth attributable to technological change from the growth attributable to increases in capital stock, as is done in Equation (16–13). Rather, technological change takes place only when new equipment is installed. Technological change is *embodied* in capital equipment; it is not disembodied as suggested by Equation (16–13).

In order to correct this defect, Solow "embodied" technological change in his capital equipment. He assumed that newer capital equipment embodied more recent and improved technology, and therefore its contribution to the capital stock should be given greater weight than that of older equipment. Using such weighting, Solow derived a new estimate for the size of the capital stock adjusted for technological change. Technological change therefore became an intrinsic part of the capital equipment. Otherwise, however, a function of the same Cobb-Douglas form was used.

With the "embodiment" of technological change in capital equipment, Solow's statistical results changed drastically. In the previous disembodied capital Equation (16–13), national income would continue to grow at a significant (2.5 percent) growth rate even in the absence of capital accumulation or population growth; but, on the other hand, the growth rate could not be increased much by an increase in the capital stock. (Observe from Equation 16–13 that a 1 percent increase in the rate of growth of the capital stock will increase the rate of growth of income by only 0.11 percent.) Thus, to increase the rate of growth of the U.S. economy from 3.5 percent to 4 percent per annum would require a tremendous investment effort; gross investment by business would have to rise from about 10 or 11 percent of total business output to about 20 percent. In contrast, when technology is embodied in capital goods, investment becomes a much more strategic element in growth. Since new capital embodies a higher level of technology than old capital, then the measure of capital including embodied technology will grow faster than the measure of capital excluding technological improvements. Growth becomes more responsive to the acquisition of capital equipment, with its advanced technology. The growth rate of the economy could be raised from 3.5 percent to 4 percent by a relatively modest increase of gross investment from about 10 or 11 percent to about 12 percent of total business output, and to 4.5 percent by an increase in investment to about 14 percent of total business output.

This line of analysis suggested the feasibility of the significant increase in the rate of growth widely desired in the early 1960s. It was the analysis favored by Solow, on the ground that embodied technological change is much more important than disembodied change. Unfortunately, however, his statistical results did not allow him to tie down a final answer. The statistical tests did not signal a clear preference for the equations in which technology was embodied.

THE SOURCES OF ECONOMIC GROWTH: DENISON

The tale of the kingdom lost for want of a nail appears in poetry, not in economic history.

Edward F. Denison

The basic Cobb-Douglas function with its disembodied technological change suggested that raising the rate of growth in the U.S. economy by 0.5 percent by means of more rapid capital accumulation would be a monumental task, and an increase by as much as 1 percent would be practically impossible. In contrast, the Solow results with the embodied technological change indicated that a 1 percent increase in the growth rate was feasible. An intermediate position—that an increase in the rate of growth by as much as 1 percent would be difficult, but not impossible—was taken by Edward F. Denison in his 1962 study, *The Sources of Economic Growth in the United States and the Alternatives Before Us,* a study which was updated in 1974.[5] [The 1962 study had two topics—the sources of growth and the "menu of choices available to increase the growth rate" (p. 275). The 1974 study was more sophisticated statistically, but was confined to the sources of growth.]

In estimating the sources of the growth over the 1929–69 period, Denison began from a point similar to that of the Cobb-Douglas function, assuming a competitive economy in which actual payments to factors measure their respective marginal productivities. From that point, however, his analysis became much more detailed than the simple assumptions of the Cobb-Douglas approach. Rather than throwing all increases in output per unit of input into a catchall category of increases in technology into which most of the increase

---

[5] Edward F. Denison, *The Sources of Economic Growth in the United States and the Alternatives Before Us* (New York: Committee for Economic Development, 1962) ; and Denison, *Accounting for United States Economic Growth, 1929–1969* (Washington, DC: Brookings Institution, 1974). See also Denison with the assistance of Jean-Pierre Poullier, *Why Growth Rates Differ: Postwar Experience in Nine Western Countries* (Washington, DC: Brookings Institution, 1967) ; and Denison and William K. Chung, *How Japan's Economy Grew So Fast* (Washington, DC: Brookings Institution, 1976) .

in growth would fall,[6] Denison made estimates of the contribution to growth of various specific improvements, such as changes in the quality of the labor force. A summary of his conclusions is given in Table 16–1.

Denison concluded that the increase in the number of workers in the labor force contributed about 1.1 percent to the total growth of 3.4 percent per annum in the 1929–69 period. (This 3.4 percent represents growth in capacity, or *potential* output.)[7] The improve-

Table 16–1
Sources of growth of real national income, 1929–1969 (contributions to growth rate in percentage points)*

	1929–69	1953–64	1964–69
Growth rate of potential national income	3.41	3.20	4.85
Increase in total factor inputs	1.82	1.52	2.79
Labor	1.32	0.83	1.85
Employment	1.09	0.81	1.81
Average hours	−0.49	−0.38	−0.36
Education	0.41	0.41	0.43
Other	0.31	−0.01	−0.03
Capital	0.50	0.69	0.94
Land	0.00	0.00	0.00
Increase in output per unit of input	1.59	1.68	2.06
Advances in knowledge and items not elsewhere classified	0.92	1.12	1.17
Improved resource allocation	0.30	0.28	0.30
Economies of scale	0.36	0.31	0.57

* Columns may not add precisely because of minor omissions.
Source: Edward F. Denison, *Accounting for United States Economic Growth, 1929–1969* (Washington, DC: Brookings Institution, 1974), pp. 127, 139.

ment in the quality of the labor force through education accounted for another 0.4 percent, but this was offset by the shorter work week.

While Denison explicitly considered the increased education and other improvements in the quality of the labor force, he assumed that technological change was not embodied in capital equipment. Taking the average share of reproducible capital in the national income, and multiplying it by the rate of growth of the capital stock,

---

[6] Recall that, in Solow's fit of the disembodied technology function (Equation 16–13), growth of 2.5 percent per annum was attributed to the final catchall term.

[7] For Denison's method of computing potential output, see *Accounting for United States Economic Growth*, Chapter 7 and Appendix Q.

Denison estimated the contribution of capital to the total growth at a relatively modest 0.5 percent.[8]

In addition to the estimates of the changes in the quality of the labor force, a major innovation of Denison was to estimate the effects of economies of scale, which he judged to account for 0.36 percent in the growth rate. (If all inputs rise by x percent, and output as a result increases by more than x percent, then the increase in output in excess of x percent is due to "economies of scale." Both the Cobb-Douglas formulation and the Solow variation on it assume constant returns to scale, and therefore are incapable of identifying any economies of scale which may have contributed to the growth of production.)

In estimating the contributions of economies of scale and improvements in the quality of the labor force, Denison arrives at conclusions quite different from either the Cobb-Douglas formulation or the Solow variant. *In contrast to the Cobb-Douglas formulation* of Equation (16–5), Denison does not find a large residual attributable to technological change; rather, the growth rate is explained by a large number of contributing causes. In the Cobb-Douglas approach, most of the growth just "happens";[9] but in Denison's framework the growth rate becomes subject to significant change as a result of alterations in policy. *In contrast to Solow's formulation,* in which technological change is embodied in capital and therefore investment becomes the key to growth, capital is banished to a relatively minor role in Denison's hierarchy. Whereas technological change is embodied *in capital equipment* in the Solow study, in Denison's work some of the "technological" advance is "embodied" *in the labor force* in the form of improved education. Changes in the quality of the labor force become an important determinant of the rate of growth.

---

[8] Denison, *Accounting for United States Economic Growth, 1929–1969,* Chapter 5 and Appendix L. Observe that this method is the same as in the disembodied technology formulation, Equation (16–5).

[9] In concentrating on one or two major issues, the above discussion has slid over other important aspects of the determinants of growth. In particular, we have not here dealt with the economics of the *creation* of technological change, that is, research and development. On this important topic, see Edwin Mansfield, *The Economics of Technological Change* (New York: W. W. Norton, 1968); Richard R. Nelson, Merton J. Peck, and Edward D. Kolachek, *Technology, Economic Growth, and Public Policy* (Washington, DC: Brookings Institution, 1967). For an historical survey, see David S. Landes, *The Unbound Prometheus: Technological Change and Industrial Development in Western Europe from 1750 to the Present* (Cambridge: Cambridge University Press, 1969).

Denison's early suggestions for increasing the growth rate by 1 percent

During the early 1960s, when more rapid growth was widely re-garded as an important objective, Denison suggested that the growth rate might be increased by as such as 1 percent by a com-bination of the following policies:[10]

1. Immigration could be raised in order to increase the labor force; Denison (p. 71) considered it "among the most sensible means of stimulating growth." Annual net immigration had averaged 0.6 percent of the population in the early part of the 20th cen-tury, but has now been restricted to about 0.2 percent. This figure could be doubled by changing immigration laws, thereby adding 0.10 percent to the growth of output.
2. Slow the trend toward a shorter work week, keeping the average reduction to one hour per week rather than the four hours which would occur if past trends were to continue over the next 20 years (an addition of 0.28 percent).
3. Add one additional year to the average amount of schooling (0.07 percent).
4. Add 0.20 to the growth rate by increasing the net investment rate substantially, so that the capital stock increases by a total of 95 percent over the coming 20 years rather than by the projected 64 percent. Policies to increase net saving and investment might include surpluses in the federal budget. (This would require a more expansive monetary policy, aimed at offsetting the ag-gregate demand effects of the government surpluses in order to maintain full employment. Recall the discussion of Chapter 10 on changes in the monetary-fiscal mix to stimulate growth.)
5. Miscellaneous additional policies to add another 0.35 percent, including the reduction of barriers to an efficient use of pro-ductive resources, namely, discrimination against blacks, resale price maintenance laws (which make retailing less efficient), barriers to freer trade, and so on.

(The above percentages seem to be very small, and it may seem that this is a discussion of trivia. However, this is not so. An increase

---

[10] Edward F. Denison, "How to Raise the High-Employment Growth Rate by One Percentage Point," *American Economic Review*, May 1962, pp. 67–75.

It is easier to raise the growth rate for a brief period than for an extended period. Denison's article dealt with the policies necessary to raise growth by 1 percent per annum over an intermediate period of 20 years.

of 1 percent in the growth rate from 3.33 percent to 4.33 percent is an increase of almost *one third*. After 20 years, an economy growing at the more rapid rate will have grown by a total of 134 percent, compared to only 93 percent at the lower rate.)

Following the flurry of interest in growth in the early 1960s, the U.S. growth rate did indeed accelerate. In the period 1964–69, Denison estimates that U.S. potential output rose at an annual rate of 4.85 percent, in contrast to the 3.20 percent of the preceding decade. It is interesting to see how the experience of the 1960s corresponded to Denison's "menu" of possible growth policies. The most notable change—accounting for more than half (1.0 percent) of the increase in the rate of growth—did indeed involve an increase in the labor force (Table 16–1). However, this resulted not from major changes in immigration policy, but from changes in labor force participation, particularly on the part of women. The trend toward a shorter work week was not slowed down, but continued without notable change. Capital formation increased, contributing an additional 0.25 percent to the growth rate. And output per unit of input also improved, although increases in economies of scale were the key factor here.

Denison had presented his list in response to the widespread search for a rapid growth policy during the early 1960s. He did not consider more rapid growth necessarily desirable. Indeed, he stressed that it could be achieved only at a considerable cost, and believed that the public probably could not be persuaded to pay the price unless appeals were made to the "external situation facing the country."[11] On domestic economic grounds, such an increase in the growth rate was probably undesirable.

SHOULD THERE BE A GROWTH OBJECTIVE?

Indeed, a strong case can be put forward that the government should follow a laissez-faire attitude with respect to growth, accepting as the appropriate outcome the growth rate which results from individual saving and investment decisions in the market economy. (Here we consider only the possible desirability of steps to encourage the rate of saving and investment. The policies related to efficiency should be judged on their own merits and are not shaken by the proposition that the government should not have a strong growth objective.) The discussion here applies only to the United

---

[11] "How to Raise the High-Employment Growth Rate," p. 69.

Figure 16–1
Consumption and saving

Consumption of
first period

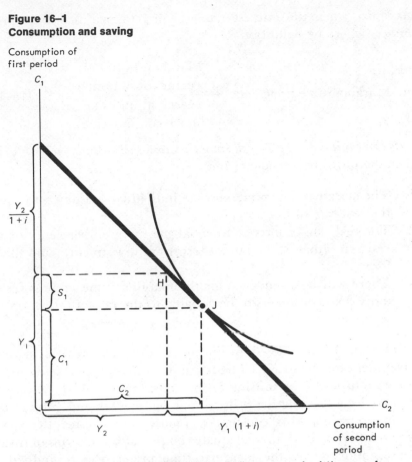

The saving-consumption decision reflects marginal time preference.

States and other relatively affluent countries and should not be extended to the less developed countries without modification.

The laissez-faire case may be outlined by referring to the analysis
of consumption in Chapter 14 with the use of indifference curves, as
repeated in Figure 16–1.[12] Individuals consume and save in accordance with their relative marginal utilities of present and future consumption, and the relative "prices" of present and future consumption (that is, the real rate of interest). The individual will maximize
when his indifference curve is tangent to the budget line in Figure
16–1. This condition may be restated as follows: The individual will

---

[12] The indifference curve analysis may be skipped. To do so, go directly to the paragraph on p. 490, beginning, "This point is worth restating in less formal terms. . . ."

maximize when the interest rate is equal to marginal time preference, where by definition

$$\text{Marginal time preference} \equiv \frac{\text{Marginal utility of present consumption}}{\text{Marginal utility of future consumption}} - 1 \quad (16\text{-}14)$$

If the capital markets work smoothly in a fully employed economy, then there will be a tendency for:

1. The marginal time preferences of individual consumers to equal the real rate of interest (i) ;
2. The real rate of interest to equal the marginal efficiency of investment (that is, the rate of return on investment) ; and therefore
3. There will be a tendency for the marginal time preferences of individual consumers to be equated to the rate of return on investment.

This can be considered an optimum amount of real saving and investment for the society. The last unit of investment yields an expected return of i, permitting future consumption of $(1 + i)$ units. This reflects the relative utilities put on present and future consumption by individual consumers. If more were invested, the return would fall, providing an inadequate compensation in terms of future consumption, given the marginal time preferences of individual consumers.

This point is worth restating in less formal terms, since it is often simply assumed that the more growth the better. (A conflicting simple assumption, the less growth the better, will be considered at a later point.) Yet it is not clear that an individual is better off by saving more. Why should an individual go an extra year now without a new Ford, just so that he can buy a new Cadillac every year during his retirement? The same general question arises for society, and between generations. Why should I skimp and save now, so that my children or grandchildren can live in relative luxury?

If indeed the capital markets do operate relatively smoothly, then a presumption has been established for laissez-faire in the saving-investment-growth decision. There are, however, a number of problems in applying this theory to the real world.

1. Capital markets and the price system in general do not work perfectly. If there is unemployment due to an inadequacy of aggregate demand, there is a case for expansive policies. In such circumstances, present and future consumption are not alternatives; the economy may produce more of *both* consumer and investment goods. A "paradox of thrift" exists. The nature of this problem, and the policies to deal with it, have of course been the central subjects of the earlier chapters.

2. The government and central bank are part of the economic environment. It must be assumed that they exist. Even if the case for a neutral or "hands off" policy is accepted, therefore, a question arises: *What* monetary and fiscal policies are "neutral" regarding saving, investment, and growth?

3. Individuals may be irrational. For example, they may show an unreasonable desire to live for the moment, spending excessively, and causing a lower rate of growth than would be chosen if they had given more thought to the future.

4. The market system may work imperfectly because of externalities of the growth process. An "externality" exists when one individual's behavior puts another individual in a position which is either better (a "positive" externality) or worse (a "negative" externality).

The possibility of externalities applies to any market decision (for example, an individual's decision to buy a car); it is not confined to the saving-investment-growth issue. However, there is one major ground for thinking that externalities may be particularly important regarding intertemporal decisions. In significant part, the benefits of our present saving will go to *future* generations; that is, to individuals who obviously cannot be involved in the current decision-making process.

What is a neutral policy?

In abstracting from monetary questions, the analysis presented in Figure 16–1 omits the effect which the monetary system may have on the amount of saving of society. But the process of money creation in the first instance tends to stimulate investment. Money is created by the purchase of bonds on the open market, driving down interest rates. Businesses therefore borrow more to acquire additional capital goods. The increase in the demand for capital goods raises their prices relative to the prices of consumers goods. Resources are attracted out of the production of consumer goods into the production of capital goods. The society saves more and invests more.

Money is created costlessly by the central bank, yet the individual who wishes to hold additional money must acquire it by providing productive services. In the first instance, production is directed mostly toward investment. Perhaps too much is being invested as a result of central bank activity.

On the other hand, other policies of the central authorities may discourage investment. The overall effects of government action are complex, and their net effects on growth difficult to disentangle. We concentrate therefore on a single illustration of how government activity may keep down the growth rate, thus counteracting the effects of monetary expansion.

The basic proposition of Figure 16–1 is that the marginal time preference of consumers should be equated to the marginal return on capital. If the tax system is to be neutral in this decision, it should tax present and future consumption at equal rates, leaving the saving decision undistorted. For example, present consumption could be taxed at a 30 percent rate, and future consumption also at a 30 percent rate. In practice, however, the tax system involves levies not only on present consumption and future consumption, but also on income flowing from investments; that is, on interest and profit receipts. In doing so, it reduces the return on saving, creating an incentive for present consumption as compared to future consumption.[13] The implication of this line of argument: *Consumption* rather than *income* should be the basis of taxation, in order to leave the saving decision undistorted.

On the other side, however, a number of arguments may be made against the taxation of consumption only. In considering public policy, it is necessary to take a broad overview and not be overly concerned with eliminating possible distortions one by one. In the present case, it may be that the bias against saving and investment arising from the taxation system may be no greater than—and perhaps even less than—the redirection toward investment resulting from the expansion of the money supply. Thus, the overall effect of

---

[13] For a further discussion, see Martin J. Bailey, "The Optimal Full-Employment Surplus," *Journal of Political Economy*, July/August 1972, pp. 649–61, esp. 658–59. Bailey considers the distortions introduced by the taxation of saving as significant and a solid basis for his proposal to encourage growth by combining a policy of fiscal tightness with monetary expansion.

public policy may be of uncertain sign and trivial size. As it seems unfeasible and undesirable to stop the expansion of the money supply, the case for removing the countervailing distortion from the taxation side therefore becomes questionable.[14]

Furthermore, if taxation applies only to consumed income and not to saving, then the tax system would appear to be inequitable, particularly so as those who have high saving have a high ability to pay according to one obvious criterion. (They save; therefore in some sense their "needs" fall significantly short of their incomes.) This view is fortified by the tendency of those with high incomes to save a proportionately higher level of their incomes than those with low incomes, although this tendency is not nearly so strong as implied by annual statistics on income and saving (and indeed, as will be recalled from Chapter 14, Friedman attributes *all* of the tendency for the high-income groups to have high saving rates to transitory rather than fundamental, long-run forces).

In principle, however, it should be possible to get as much progressivity as desired into the taxation system by taxing *consumption* at progressive rates. But here, a practical problem arises. As the base for taxation is reduced (in this case, by eliminating saving from taxable income), the tax rates on the remaining base must become higher in order to raise any given amount of total tax revenue. As tax rates are raised higher on the remaining base, other distortions become progressively more important. For example, if taxes are very high on consumption expenditures, then there may be some tendency to work less, "consuming" leisure which escapes taxation.

In addressing the question of the "neutrality" of public policy regarding the proportion of income invested, we have opened a Pandora's Box. Neutrality is an illusive concept, and it is difficult to say, on balance, whether the existence of the government sector and the central bank discourages or encourages a high rate of investment.

Is the saving decision irrational?

In a word, yes. But the difficulty is this. There are enough irrationalities on both sides that it is unclear whether saving is irrationally large or irrationally small for the economy as a whole.

---

[14] The *theory of the second best* is the term applied to the study of the desirability of removing one distortion in the economic system when other distortions exist and cannot be removed.

Through literature runs the tale of the wastrel. The moral here is clear: Some give too little heed for the morrow. Yet others seem to have an irrational desire to save, accumulating for the joy of accumulation. The miser takes his place beside the prodigal son, leaving an obscure picture as to the net irrationality in the system. It is not clear whether too little is saved, or too much.

In principle, this leaves the government in a position where it should make the decision for society, encouraging the "optimum" rate of growth. But this is no easy solution to the problem. Growth takes time, and therefore decisions should be made in a long-term context. Yet the discussions of the past two decades suggest that the political debate is subject to great emotional swings regarding growth, from the view that we have to run harder to keep ahead of the Russians, to the view that growth has got to stop, lest our world become unlivable. On the basis of past experience, the case can be made for restraint in the development of public policies aimed at altering the growth rate. (It should be stressed once again that in this chapter we are addressing the question of the *growth of capacity*, not changes in real *GNP* which reflect changing unemployment rates.)

Externalities

Why should I think about pollution? I'm used to it.
Archie Bunker

The great change in attitudes toward growth has accompanied the increasing awareness of environmental problems. An increase in growth may be associated with more smoking chimneys and an accelerated degradation of the environment. It has become fashionable to refer to *GNP* as "Gross National Pollution."

The existence of negative externalities—the harm that comes to others as the result of production or use of goods such as automobiles—raises a number of issues:

1. How public policies may discourage activities that involve negative externalities.
2. The population question. In our concern for the welfare of future generations, what goals, if any, should there be regarding the number of people in future generations?
3. Whether it is desirable to adjust the measure of national pro-

duction to include the effects of externalities; and how this may be done.

As the growth process tends to be associated with increasing pollution and other undesirable side effects, it is sometimes argued that the rate of growth of *GNP* should be sharply curtailed. In its strongest form, this becomes a plea for "zero economic growth." (In order that zero economic growth should not involve a decline in the standard of living, it is usually combined with a proposal for "zero population growth." The population question is considered in the next section.) Clearly, population and output cannot continue to grow indefinitely at the rates of the past century; sooner or later, we will run out of standing room. Uncertainty regarding the supply of natural resources—which was dramatized by the quadrupling of international oil prices in 1973–74—has added to doubts about the desirability of a rapid rate of growth.

Concerns over the environment and natural resources were illustrated most strongly in a 1972 study by Donella Meadows and others at the Massachusetts Institute of Technology, under the auspices of the "Club of Rome."[15] Projecting past trends into the 21st century, this group foresees disaster. Population, industrial production, and pollution will rise sharply to a climax in the mid-21st century, at which time the debasement of the environment and the strain on food production and natural resources will cause an explosion of the death rate. Disaster will be upon us—or, more precisely, upon our children and grandchildren.

While this study is an interesting exercise, it should be treated with caution. A mechanical extrapolation of any series which has grown at rapid rates in the past will lead to spectacular results if carried far enough, and the computer has the great advantage—or disadvantage—of mechanically cranking out projections with great efficiency, unhampered by the second thoughts about common sense which hopefully restrain human computations.[16] In the real world,

---

[15] Donella L. Meadows, et al., *The Limits to Growth* (New York: Universe Books, 1972).

[16] "The computer that cried wolf," said Carl Kaysen of the Institute for Advanced Studies at Princeton, dismissing the Club of Rome study.

In his *Economics,* 10th ed. (New York: McGraw-Hill, 1976), p. 815, Paul Samuelson was more charitable toward the Club of Rome study (although he may have been damning it with faint praise) : "Sometimes to sell you must oversell. An antidote to complacency can be provided by hysteria."

For criticisms of the Meadows' book, see H. S. D. Cole and others, *Models of Doom* (New York: Universe Books, 1973).

rapid rates of growth have a natural tendency to slow down as time passes. (Investors, do not count on IBM growing at past rates for the next century. There are unlikely to be ten computers in every basement.) A measured evaluation is in order, not an hysterical search for policies to limit growth.

This is particularly so because economic growth is a complex phenomenon, with many conflicting external effects. While it is obviously true that, *ceteris paribus,* the more steel is produced, the more pollution will come from steel mills, it is also true that economic growth may be used to produce not only more steel, but more pollution control equipment. If we are interested in controlling pollution, the *type* of production becomes more important than the *amount* of production; if we are interested in conserving natural resources for the benefit of future generations, then the development of processes which economize on the use of resources may be more effective than cutting down on production. Growth per se is not the central issue.

There are forces at work within the economic system which help to ease some of the future problems. As raw materials become scarcer, for example, their prices tend to rise, and the search for substitutes is encouraged. Thus, the rise in the price of oil has inspired efforts to save fuel and to search for alternative sources of energy. The adjustment may, of course, be painful—as we are finding out. Nevertheless, the price mechanism does mean that a mechanical extension of past trends is unrealistic. The market provides incentives to economize on scarce raw materials.

But, externalities such as pollution by their very nature are not dealt with by the unfettered operation of markets. The driver of an automobile has no clear incentive to clean up his exhaust for the benefit of the occupants of the cars behind, no matter how much individual motorists and others might wish that all cars had efficient pollution controls.

But if the market does not automatically lead to a desirable outcome, and, indeed, will tend to lead to a less-than-optimum result if a laissez-faire policy is pursued, the market may be *used* to encourage positive externalities and discourage negative externalities. Specifically, the market may be used to approach an optimum outcome by subsidizing activities that produce positive externalities, and by taxing activities that involve negative externalities by an amount equivalent to the social cost of the externality.

This proposition, which has been a fundamental economic

theorem for decades,[17] frequently leads to a strong objection on the grounds that industries should not be given a "license to pollute" by paying the taxes designed to discourage pollution. But its logic is unassailable; the only (but not minor!) problems lie in the calculation of the size of externalities, in the political process by which the appropriate taxes are levied, and in the technical difficulties in collecting the appropriate taxes.

The case for taxing pollution and other "bads" is strengthened by the practical difficulties in designing a system of controls and prohibitions. In particular, it is difficult to design an *efficient* system of controls. Clearly, the objective should not be to eliminate all types of pollution completely; to do so would be prohibitively expensive. Rather, controls generally limit the amount of pollutants. But, faced with such limits, factory managers have no incentive to do better, even if they could do so at relatively little cost. For some other factories, it may be extremely expensive to meet the specified standards. It would be economically efficient for the first group to pollute somewhat less (at a low additional cost), while the second group pollutes somewhat more (thereby saving large amounts). Such an outcome is encouraged by a tax on pollution.[18] The government does not have unlimited ingenuity to design controls, nor are there unlimited numbers of competent and dedicated administrators. There is a substantial case for the government to rely on the market and tax pollution wherever feasible, in order to conserve its scarce resources of time and personnel for the specific items—such as atomic wastes—whose extreme hazards require either outright prohibition or careful control.

POPULATION

Saving, investment, and growth affect the welfare of future generations as well as those of the present. Obviously, there is a problem with making a choice here, since the future generations can scarcely speak for themselves. But the problem is worse than this: How many

---

[17] Particularly, A. C. Pigou, "Wealth and Welfare," *Quarterly Journal of Economics,* 1913, pp. 672–86; A. C. Pigou, *The Economics of Welfare,* 1st ed. (London, 1920). (This is the Pigou of the Pigou effect.) For a more recent work, see Francis M. Bator, "The Anatomy of Market Failure," *Quarterly Journal of Economics,* August 1958, pp. 351–79. The discussion of this text passes over some important distinctions which should be made in an advanced treatment of externalities.

[18] This proposition is explained in detail in Allen V. Kneese and Charles L. Schultze, *Pollution, Prices, and Public Policy* (Washington, DC: Brookings Institution, 1975).

people will be in the future generations is itself a variable, subject to current population control policies.

The rate of population growth clearly can have implications for the per capita level of income, since the more rapidly the population grows, the more thinly will be spread the available raw material supplies and the existing stock of capital. Thus, in the way of an illustration, the average U.S. material standard of living in the year 2000 might be 50 percent higher than at present with a population growth to 240 million, but only 40 percent higher with a growth of population to 260 million.[19] Which of these outcomes is preferable is a fundamental philosophical question with no clear answer. Economists are trained to estimate what the choices before society are; that is, to estimate the quantitative effect on the per capita real national income of a change in the rate of population growth. But they have no particular tools or skills which would help determine which of the above outcomes is "better." There is nothing in economic analysis which can deal with the question of whether one life under certain circumstances is "worth" 1.1 lives under other circumstances. As knowledge of population control methods becomes more generally disseminated, it may be that the rate of population change resulting from the free choice of parents will be satisfactory by any reasonable standard.

In the United States, the reproduction rate by the early 1970s had fallen to the level consistent with the long-run stability of population—just over two children per couple. (At this rate, population will not stabilize quickly, but will gradually approach a stable total in the early 21st century. This is because the current number of births still exceeds the rate of births in the first half of this century. Thus, while the younger age groups of the population have approximately stabilized, the older groups will continue to increase in number as those born in the high-birth years grow older.) The United States is apparently approaching the long-run equilibrium of zero population growth with little difficulty. (Indeed, by 1975, the U.S. reproduction rate had fallen even lower, to 1.8 per couple— that is, below the rate needed for long-run stability of population.)

---

[19] It is possible that, because of economies of scale in production, a higher rate of population growth will cause a *higher* rather than a lower growth of per capita income. However, at some level of population and rate of growth of population, there will be a tradeoff between population growth and per capita real income. In the United States, with its very large internal market and relatively free access to world markets, many of the economies of scale have already been achieved. It is reasonable to assume that, if future rates of growth of population exceed the rates of recent decades, then real per capita income will be adversely affected.

A number of the less-developed countries, however, are in a much less fortunate position. There tends to be a vicious circle of poverty. High population growth makes it difficult to raise the low standard of living. And people in a precarious economic position may insist on raising large families: Their children may provide their only hope for security in their old age. Official population control programs hold out little prospect for easy solutions. On the contrary, they may generate strong opposition. Resentment against government sterilization programs was apparently a factor in the defeat of India's Prime Minister Indira Gandhi at the polls in 1977.

THE MEASURE OF ECONOMIC WELFARE

What is life if, full of care,
We have no time to stand and stare.

W. H. Davies

Changes in real national product as measured by the Department of Commerce are generally taken as the basis for measuring economic growth.[20] However, national product provides a very imperfect measure of welfare. The efficiency and success of the economic system should be measured not simply by the goods and services which come out of the productive pipeline and which are included in *GNP* statistics. To measure welfare, it is important also to take into account the "bads" generated in the productive process —such as the pollution discharged into the air and water. Furthermore, it is relevant to consider how hard the labor force has to work to produce the goods and services. A sweatshop society may produce a lot of goods and services; but it can be inferior to one that produces fewer goods and services, while providing leisure for the enjoyment of the good things of life. In addition, economic performance is not the only measure of the success of a society—indeed, it is not the most important. The good society provides political and personal freedom, justice, and cultural riches. *GNP* is clearly an incomplete measure of welfare.

Two approaches have been suggested to deal with the limitations of *GNP*. The first approach—which is promising—is to develop *additional* measures of performance, which may be used by the policymaker (along with *GNP*) as the basis for decisions. The second approach is more ambitious and more problematical. It in-

---

[20] The problem of adjusting national income figures for price changes—thus making them a measure of real income—is considered in Chapter 17.

volves the development of a more *comprehensive single* measure, which includes *GNP,* but also includes adjustments for leisure, pollution, and so on.

Additional social indicators

The first approach downplays *GNP,* and relegates it to the status simply of one of a number of important social indicators. In the United States and elsewhere, a number of studies have presented estimates of economic and social indicators which can together provide the basis for informed policymaking. In addition to per capita real *GNP,* important social indicators include such things as infant mortality rates, the availability and quality of health care, life expectancy, the quality of air and water, the degree of urban crowding, crime, and so on.[21]

A comprehensive measure of welfare

The more ambitious approach involves the integration of various measures into a single index of welfare. Several years ago, Professors William Nordhaus and James Tobin of Yale University presented their measure of economic welfare *(MEW)*, whose primary components were per capita national product, leisure, and externalities (such as pollution).[22] More recently, the Overseas Development Council has calculated a physical quality of life index *(PQLI)* for a large group of countries. This index combines life expectancy, infant mortality, and literacy into a single measure.[23]

The problems involved in the development of such comprehensive measures are formidable—indeed, they are so formidable and intractable that these interesting efforts may be judged to be failures.

---

[21] See, for example, Economic Council of Canada, *Eleventh Annual Review: Economic Targets and Social Indicators* (Ottawa, 1974) ; Economic Planning Agency of the Japanese Government, *The Japanese and Their Society* (Part 2 of the *Report on National Life,* Tokyo, 1972) , in English; U.S. Department of Health, Education and Welfare, *Toward a Social Report* (Washington, DC, 1969) ; and Burkhard Strumpel, *Economic Means for Human Needs: Social Indicators of Well-Being and Discontent* (Ann Arbor: Institute for Social Research, 1976) .

[22] William Nordhaus and James Tobin, "Is Growth Obsolete?" in National Bureau of Economic Research, *Economic Growth, Fiftieth Anniversary Colloquium* (New York, 1972) .

[23] John W. Sewell and the staff of the Overseas Development Council, *The United States and World Development: Agenda 1977* (New York: Praeger, 1977) , especially pp. 147–54.

To see why, consider the Nordhaus-Tobin measure of economic welfare *(MEW)*. Of the two major adjustments which Nordhaus and Tobin made to per capita national product—namely, disamenities (pollution, etc.) and leisure—leisure was by far the more important. While real per capita product rose by 90 percent between 1929 and 1965, leisure went up by an estimated 22 percent.

The question is, how are these two changes to be combined into an overall index of growth? Specifically, which of the following two conclusions is correct?

1. Production per person went up by 90 percent, and the increasing output was produced with a shorter work week. Since we produced 90 percent more and had more leisure, too, then our economic position improved by *more* than 90 percent.
2. Production increased by 90 percent, but leisure went up by only 22 percent. Thus, economic welfare rose by some weighted average of the 90 percent and the 22 percent. That is, economic welfare improved by *less* than the increase in per capita national product.

Which of these conclusions is correct is unclear. Nordhaus and Tobin therefore did two sets of calculations (shown as MEW_1 and MEW_2 in Figure 16–2). In their initial estimates (MEW_1), they, in effect, added[24] the increase in leisure to the increase in output, leading to the conclusion that economic welfare "climbed somewhat faster on average than official figures for the Gross National Product. . . . The national accounts, therefore, seem to understate—not overstate—the increase in economic welfare experienced in the United States."[25] However, this led to the objection that conclusion 2 might be more appropriate, and Nordhaus and Tobin accordingly featured MEW_2 in their final report—showing a relatively slow rate of growth of economic welfare.[26]

---

[24] Technically, the choice between conclusions 1 and 2 came when a price was placed on leisure. If leisure is valued at its current market price—that is, at the wage rate which is currently being given up when one additional hour's leisure is taken—then the value of each hour's leisure goes up at the same rate as the real wage rate, and economic welfare goes up by more than national product (conclusion 1). If, on the other hand, one hour of leisure in 1965 is judged to be equal in value to one hour of leisure in 1929, then economic welfare goes up by less than national product (conclusion 2).

[25] National Bureau of Economic Research, press release announcing the Nordhaus-Tobin study, December 10, 1970, p. 2.

[26] Disamenities—measured as the income differentials required to hold people in locations with high population densities—did not appreciably affect the Nordhaus-Tobin estimates. Indeed, somewhat paradoxically, disamenities *raised* the rate of

Because of such ambiguities, a fundamental question can be raised about the development of comprehensive indexes of welfare. In the presentation of indexes, underlying information (on leisure, etc.) is lost; as a consequence, the results may be misinterpreted.[27] Furthermore, the statement that "Per capita product rose by 90 percent, while leisure rose by 22 percent," is clearer—and as brief—as the results of the Nordhaus-Tobin study, which may be summarized: "Economic welfare rose by 120 percent (MEW_1) ; or maybe we should make that 40 percent (MEW_2) ." Similarly, the *PQLI* of the Overseas Development Council involves serious problems of weighting; for example, it is not clear how one percentage point increase in literacy should be weighted in comparison to a one percentage point decrease in infant mortality.

Thus, it is doubtful whether such exercises are worth pursuing in greater detail. Certainly, policymakers should be concerned with such important matters as literacy, life expectancy, and pollution. And it is important to measure these things carefully. For example, to estimate the optimum tax on pollution, a dollar estimate must be made of the social costs of pollution. But the policy problem is to get the right pattern of taxes and other policies to *discourage* pollution and other negative externalities. The development of a comprehensive measure of economic welfare is not necessary for the achievement of this objective.

Indeed, the search for a comprehensive *MEW* starts from the wrong premise. It starts from the assumption that, when the appropriate measure of *MEW* is found, then the faster it grows the better. But it is questionable that such an assumption should be made. In particular, it suggests that the higher the rate of saving

---

growth of measured economic welfare. This is because disamenities involve a subtraction from welfare, and they rose more slowly than national product. (When a slowly growing series is subtracted from a more rapidly growing series, the series that results will grow more rapidly than the initial series. Suppose, for example, that output per capita rises from 100 to 200, while per capita disamenities rise from 20 to 30. Then welfare corrected for disamenities grows from 80 to 170, that is, by 112.5 percent, compared to the growth of output of only 100 percent.)

[27] For example, in the last two editions of his famous textbook, Paul Samuelson strongly implies that pollution (rather than the treatment of leisure) is the cause of the slow growth of MEW_2. In a section entitled "Minuses: hidden pollution and ecological costs," Samuelson concludes: ". . . we see that *NEW* [Samuelson's relabeling of MEW_2] grows more slowly than *GNP*. This is more or less inevitable in a densely populated world." Samuelson, *Economics* (New York: McGraw-Hill) , 9th ed., 1973, pp. 195–96; 10th ed. 1976, pp. 195–96.

But, as we noted in the previous footnote, disamenities had nothing to do with the slow growth of MEW_2; indeed, disamenities tended to *accelerate* the measured rate of growth of economic welfare.

Figure 16–2
Measures of economic welfare, various years, 1929–1965—as percent of
1929 (real per capita figures)

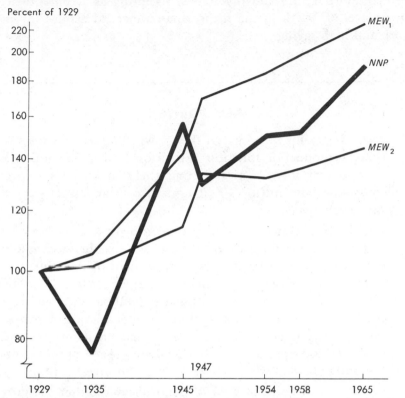

Source: From Table 1 of William Nordhaus and James Tobin, "Is Growth Obsolete?" in *Economic, Growth, Fiftieth Anniversary Colloquium* (New York: National Bureau of Economic Research, 1972), pp. 10–11.

The Nordhaus-Tobin measure of economic welfare is *very* sensitive to the treatment of leisure.

MEW_1 is based on the view that welfare has gone up by *more* than national product, since we have produced more and had more leisure, too.

MEW_2 is based on the view that the measure of welfare should rise by a weighted average of the increase in product and the increase in leisure. Since leisure rose at a slower rate than product, MEW_2 increased less than per capita national product.

and investment and the higher the growth of *MEW*, the better the economy is performing. But this is contrary to the above discussion of the optimum rate of saving (Figure 16–1) ; it is a hangover from the "high growth is intrinsically good" viewpoint. Logically, it is not possible to determine whether a higher rate of growth of *MEW* is better than a lower rate, unless something is known about the marginal time preferences of the public.[28] It may be a good thing if we take more leisure and invest less, accepting as a consequence a lower level of *MEW* in the future than we could achieve by hard work and high saving.

KEY POINTS

1. A starting point for much of the growth literature is the Cobb-Douglas production function (Equation 16–1). One of the characteristics of this function is that the shares of total income going to labor and to capital remain constant at $(1 - a)$ and (a), respectively.

2. When the effects of investment on growth are evaluated statistically, the results are very sensitive to whether technological improvement is assumed to be independent of investment (disembodied technological change) or is assumed to be incorporated in new capital equipment (embodied technological change). If the former assumption is made, the rate of growth of the economy is not very sensitive to changes in investment; if the latter assumption is made, the rate of growth of the economy is found to be highly sensitive to changes in investment.

3. From a social point of view, it is not clear whether the growth that comes from the operation of a market economy is too high, too low, or about right; there are both positive and negative externalities resulting from the growth process.

4. One way of reducing negative externalities is to tax their production. In logic, the appropriate tax is equal to the marginal social cost of the externality, although it may not in practice be feasible to impose taxation in a way which closely corresponds to the social cost.

5. There have been attempts to adjust *GNP* to get a more comprehensive measure of economic welfare. These attempts have, how-

---

[28] *MEW* may be rescued from this criticism by declaring that the rate of growth of *MEW* through time will not be taken as a measure of progress, but rather the goal will be the maximization of the present value of all future *MEW*s discounted by the appropriate social rate of time preference (following the mechanics of equation 5–2). This "present value" approach was not used by Nordhaus and Tobin. Rather, they took the growth of MEW through time as a measure of the performance of the economy.

ever, run into very difficult methodological problems. In particular, the measure of economic welfare is very sensitive to the treatment of leisure; and the "correct" treatment is by no means clear. A comprehensive and acceptable measure of economic welfare is not, however, a necessary prerequisite for the development of policies to deal with pollution and other externalities.

6. While comprehensive measures of economic welfare are unpromising, it is important for policymakers to avoid preoccupation with the growth of national income, narrowly defined. Other social objectives—pollution abatement, justice, etc.—are also important.

QUESTION

1. Suppose that the utility of individuals is dependent not only on their own consumption, but on the consumption of others. Two alternative assumptions might be made: (a) that the total utility of an individual falls as the consumption levels of other people rise; that is, the individual is unhappy when others catch up to him or surpass him; or (b) that the total utility of an individual rises as the consumption levels of other people rise. In other words, he gains pleasure from observing the prosperity of others. What implications would these assumptions have for the theoretical proposition that a laissez-faire rate of growth is the optimum?

SUGGESTED READINGS

"The No-Growth Society," *Daedalus* (Journal of the American Academy of Arts and Sciences), Fall 1973, especially the articles by Kenneth E. Boulding, "The Shadow of the Stationary State," pp. 89–101; Richard Zeckhauser, "The Risks of Growth," pp. 102–18; Roland N. McKean, "Growth vs. No Growth: An Evaluation," pp. 207–27; and Mancur Olson, Hans H. Landsberg, and Joseph L. Fisher, "Epilogue," pp. 229–41.

Edward F. Denison and William K. Chung, *How Japan's Economy Grew So Fast* (Washington, DC: Brookings Institution, 1976).

Simon Kuznets, "Two Centuries of Economic Growth: Reflections on U.S. Experience," *American Economic Review*, February 1977, pp. 1–14.

Tibor Scitovsky, *The Joyless Economy* (London: Oxford University Press, 1976), especially chap. 7, "Income and Happiness."

PART FIVE

THE MEASUREMENT
OF ECONOMIC
AGGREGATES

"The time has come,"
the Walrus said,
"To talk of many things:
Of shoes, and ships,
and sealing wax;
Of cabbages, and kings."

Lewis Carroll

Chapter 17

The national income and product accounts[*]

Never ask of money spent
Where the spender thinks it went.
Nobody was ever meant
To remember or invent
What he did with every cent.

Robert Frost

In Chapter 1, a brief description was given of *GNP* and its major components. This chapter provides more detail.

The national product is the total amount of final goods and services produced by the country. Each transaction involves a buyer and a seller; in studying the final transactions, the focus may be on either the buyers' side or that of the sellers. If we look at the buyers' side, attention is centered on the components of aggregate demand —consumption, investment, government purchases, and net exports. When we look at the buyers' side, we are looking at where the flow of monetary demand comes from.

On the sellers' side, the focus is on where the money payments go

---

[*] This chapter is not dependent on the chapters of Parts Two, Three, or Four, and may be studied directly after Chapter 1.

Figure 17–1
National product

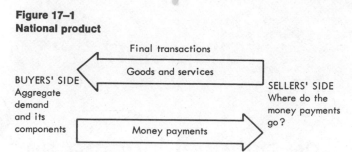

(Figure 17–1). The flow of monetary payments may be broken down into categories either of two ways: by the productive factor which receives the payment—wages, profits, rents, etc.; or by the economic sector which receives the payment—the auto industry, the dry cleaning industry, etc.

These alternative ways of categorizing the payments flowing from final purchases may be illustrated by an example. Consider a component of final output, say a consumer durable selling for $1,000. Assume that the item is sold by the manufacturer to the retailer for $800; that the manufacturer purchases $400 in parts; and that the parts producer in turn purchases $100 of steel. Then the $1,000 from the sale of the consumer durable might be divided up as illustrated in the simple example in Table 17–1.

The difference between the receipts from sales and the costs of goods and services purchased from other businesses is the *value added* of the industry in question. The value added at the retail level is $200 (that is, sales of $1,000 less purchases of $800); in the assembly process, $400 (or $800 − $400); and so on, as given in the total value added column of Table 17–1. The value of the final product ($1,000) is the sum of the value added by the industries involved in bringing the good to market.

Within each industry, the total value added is divided among the

Table 17–1
Hypothetical division of receipts from sale of $1,000 consumer durable

| | Factor payments | | | Total value added | Addendum: Value of sales |
Industry	Wages	Profits	Other		
Retailer..........................	$100	$ 60	$ 40	$ 200	$1,000
Assembler........................	300	70	30	400	800
Parts producer...................	220	60	20	300	400
Steel producer...................	80	10	10	100	100
Total factor payments.........	700	200	100	1,000	

factors of production, mainly wages and profits. The total $200 value added at the retail level is divided among wages ($100), profits ($60), and other ($40). Of the value of $1,000 of the final sale, the total amount that goes to wages ($700) may be found by adding up the first column of Table 17–1.

This is obviously a simplified example and ignores some important points, such as taxation. But it does illustrate the three basic approaches. We may look on what we produce as:

1. The value of the *final product,* that is, the $1,000 sale at the retail level.
2. The *sum* of the *values added* at all stages of production. This also totals $1,000, as illustrated in the value added column.
3. The *sum* of the *factor payments.* This also totals $1,000, as illustrated in the final row.

The first point approaches national product and income from the buyers' side: What is spent? The last two points illustrate the two alternative views from the sellers' side: Where does the money go? Furthermore, this simple table illustrates a basic error to be avoided. Although we may calculate the national income by measuring the *value added* at all stages of production (the second to the last column), we must *not* add the total *sales* at all stages. Thus, national income or product is *not* the sum of $2,300, which would be found by adding the final column. This sum involves the *double counting of intermediate product.* For example, the $100 in steel is counted at the initial stage, and it is counted again as part of the final product. This is wrong. In the national product accounts, all products should be counted *once and only once.*[1]

With this background, we may now look at the actual accounts for a recent year (1976).[2] The major classifications are given in Figure 17–2. The first column gives the components of national

---

[1] In Table 17–1, only the surface is scratched regarding the flow of inputs and payments from one industry to another. Specifically, it is assumed that there is a clear hierarchy of industries, with the steelmaker supplying the parts producer, the parts producer supplying the assembler, and so on. Yet the world is not this simple; there is a complex interrelation among industries. Steel is used as an input by the machinery industry, and machinery is used as an input in the steel industry. The study of these interrelationships is the subject of input-output, a major field of economic accounting and analysis. (One word of caution to those who have been introduced to input-output analysis: Table 17–1 is *not* a simple input-output table, in spite of its somewhat similar form of presentation.)

[2] Each June or July, comprehensive data on the previous year's national income accounts appear in the *Survey of Current Business,* a publication of the U.S. Department of Commerce. Historical series are published in the biennial supplements to the *Survey.*

Figure 17-2
National income accounts, 1976 (simplified, in $ billions)

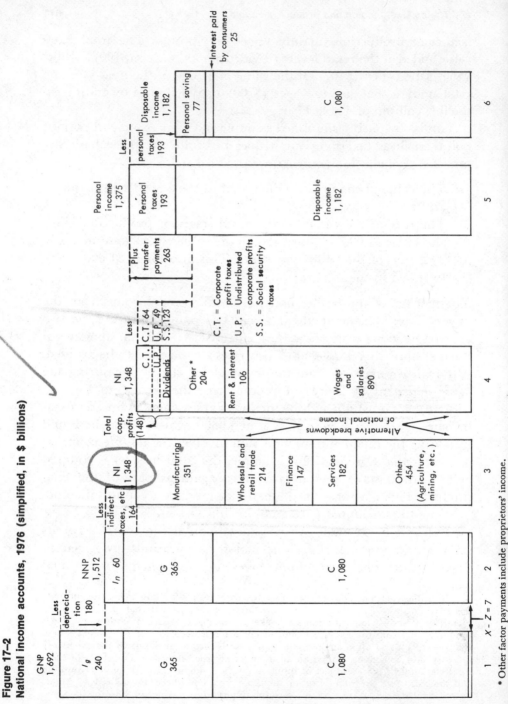

* Other factor payments include proprietors' income.

product looked on from the demand side: personal consumption, government purchases of goods and services, gross private domestic investment, and net exports of goods and services; together these make up *gross national product (GNP)*. When depreciation (capital consumption allowances) is subtracted from *GNP*, the result is *net national product* (col. 2).

Having looked at the demand or buyers' side of final transactions, we may alternatively look to the sellers' side: Where do the money payments go? How are the total payments divided among income recipients? Here, an immediate complication must be taken into account. Part of the payments for final goods and services does not go to any of the income recipients at all; part is extracted during the selling process in the form of indirect (sales) taxes.[3] In order to get the income which goes to the factors of production (wages, profits, etc.), indirect taxes must be subtracted from net national product (and other minor adjustments made),[4] leaving *national income (NI)*, used in its narrow, specific sense. (The term *national income* can be used broadly, to refer to any of the aggregate measures— *GNP, NNP*, or the narrower concept of *NI*. In its narrower sense, national income means the total earnings of labor and property from the production of goods and services.)

We now have national income—the total payments made for the

---

[3] The term "indirect" has traditionally been applied to sales taxes, and "direct" to income taxes. The reason: While sales taxes are collected from the business selling the good, it was assumed that they are passed on in the form of higher prices to the purchasers. Thus, they are "indirect" taxes because the person who ultimately pays them (the consumer) is not the one (the business) from whom they are initially collected. On the other hand, incomes taxes were labeled "direct," since it was assumed that they could not be passed along, and the individual or corporation which initially pays them also pays them in the final analysis.

The question of shifting of taxes—or who ultimately pays—is not simple; it forms one of the major topics in the study of public finance. The simple assumption behind the terms "indirect" and "direct"—that sales taxes are shifted to the buyer while income taxes are not shifted—is of dubious validity, but the terms "indirect taxes" and "direct taxes" survive as a way of classifying sales taxes and income taxes respectively.

[4] In precise terms,

$$NI \equiv NNP - \text{(Indirect business tax and nontax liability)}$$
$$- \text{(Business transfer payments)}$$
$$+ \text{(Subsidies less current surplus of government enterprises)}$$
$$\pm \text{(Statistical discrepancy)} \qquad (17\text{-}1)$$

Of these adjustments, the first (indirect business tax and nontax liability) is by far the largest. In 1976, the four adjustments were, respectively, $149.7 billion, $7.1 billion, $1.2 billion, and $7.7 billion.

The statistical discrepancy arises because the measurement of the national accounts is not precise. Taking *NNP* and making the first three adjustments of Equation (17–1) should give the same as adding up the components of national income (col. 3 or 4 of Figure 17–2). But it does not; hence the statistical discrepancy item in Equation (17–1).

production of goods and services—amounting to $1,348 billion in 1976 (Figure 17–2). This is analagous to the $1,000 payment for consumer durables in Table 17–1, in that it may be broken down either of two ways—among the various industries (the fourth column of Table 17–1), or among the factors of production (the last row). These two alternatives are shown in Figure 17–2 as columns 3 and 4, respectively. Of the factor incomes (col. 4), wages and salaries make up by far the largest component—$890 billion.

In addition to *GNP, NNP,* and *NI,* there are several other important concepts, particularly *personal income* and *disposable income.* Personal income is derived from national income as follows. Profits which corporations make but which are not passed on to their stockholders are subtracted (although dividend payments remain as part of personal income). Specifically, the corporation income taxes that go to the government and the undistributed corporate profits are subtracted. Likewise, social security taxes are subtracted. They go to the government rather than to individuals.[5] But there are also additions. As part of their personal income, individuals receive transfer payments from the government—payments which are not included originally in national income because they are not paid in exchange for productive services.[6] Thus, personal income may be derived by making the subtractions and additions illustrated in Figure 17–2.

People are not free to spend total personal income, however. The government extracts a share in the form of personal taxes. These taxes are deducted from personal income to get *disposable income,* a strategic concept in the theory of consumer behavior.

SELECTED PROBLEMS IN NATIONAL INCOME ACCOUNTING[7]

National income accounts measure the value of the final product of the economy. Three basic questions arise. What exactly is to be

---

[5] This item covers both the employers' and employees' social security payments.

[6] In this transfer item are also included transfers from business and interest received from consumers and from the government. Net interest payments made by businesses are included earlier as part of the rent and interest component of national income.

[7] On the conceptual and statistical problems in national income accounting, see Simon Kuznets, *National Income and Its Composition, 1919–1938* (New York: National Bureau of Economic Research, 1941); Nancy Ruggles and Richard Ruggles, *The Design of Economic Accounts* (New York: National Bureau of Economic Research, 1970); Department of Commerce, *National Income, 1954 Edition* (Supplement to the *Survey of Current Business*); *U.S. Income and Output* (Supplement to *SCB*, 1958); *SCB*, August 1965; and *SCB: 50th Anniversary Issue; The Economic Accounts of the United States: Retrospect and Prospect,* July 1971.

measured? How is it to be measured? And what is the significance of the measure when we get it? The marketplace is the starting point in answering the first two questions: Basically, the final goods and services going through the marketplace constitute the national product being measured, and they are measured at their market prices. To this general answer, however, there are a number of important exceptions and complications. Some goods and services never go through the marketplace, yet are included in *GNP*. And the definition of just what constitutes "final" product raises a number of difficulties.

Nonmarket transactions included in consumption: Imputations of rent, etc.

The objective of the *GNP* accounts is to measure the flow of goods and services being produced in the economy during the year. A particular conceptual difficulty arises regarding the treatment of housing. What should we measure? The amount of housing constructed during the last year? Or the quantity of housing services which the public consumes during the year? The latter clearly depends largely on the housing in existence when the year began.

One possible way of dealing with this question—*not* the one actually used in the national income accounts—would be to simply accept and measure what happens in the marketplace. Part of the housing supply (mainly apartments) is owned as a profit-making venture and rented out to tenants. Another major part is owned by the residents of the housing. It would be possible to treat rental housing as any other business enterprise, including the *construction* of new rental apartments in gross *investment,* and the *current rental* as the sale of a final service, that is, as a component of *consumption.* On the other hand, the construction of new houses for occupation by the owner could be considered the sale of a final product to a consumer, with the sales of newly constructed housing in any year simply included in the consumption sector of *GNP.*

There is a major problem with this approach, which is sufficiently grave to cause it to be ruled out. If such an approach were used, then *GNP* would become sensitive to changes in the rate of home ownership. If people increasingly owned the houses they live in, with the rental sector declining relatively, then there would be a downward drag on measured *GNP,* since owner-occupied housing would be included only once (as consumption, when it was newly constructed), while rental housing would be entered both as investment during the year of construction and as a flow of services (rentals) to consumers over the rental lifetime. Yet surely a movement toward home ownership should be considered either a good thing, or at the least neutral. It should not depress measured *GNP*.

In order to get around this difficulty, owner-occupied housing is treated *as if* it were rental housing in the *GNP* accounts. Sales of newly constructed housing are included in gross investment. And *imputed rents*—the amount homeowners would have had to pay if they had rented equivalent housing—are included in the consumption sector, even though no such rents are actually paid.[8]

The same procedure might conceivably also be applied to other durables purchased by the user—automobiles, refrigerators, etc. These goods might be treated as investment in the year of their production, with imputed rents entered in the consumption sector during the lifetime of the good. For two reasons, this procedure is not, however, followed for nonhousing durables in the national income accounts.[9] First, a line must be drawn somewhere, and the difference between housing and other major durables such as automobiles is relatively large. (Suppose autos were treated initially as investment. Then how about refrigerators? Furniture? Clothing?) [10] Second, there is an active and large rental market for houses, and therefore the overall level of *GNP* would be potentially sensitive to changes in the percentage of owner-occupied housing if new owner-

---

[8] To make the accounts come out right, depreciation of owner-occupied housing is included in the total depreciation subtracted to move from *GNP* to *NNP*. Taxes on owner-occupied housing (together with taxes on actual rental property) are included in the indirect taxes subtracted from *NNP* to get national income. And net imputed rental income (that is, gross imputed rents less depreciation and taxes) is included in national income.

[9] In some of the consumption literature, however, autos and other consumer durables are initially treated as investment and subsequently as imputed flows of services. For example: Milton Friedman, *A Theory of the Consumption Function,* (Princeton: Princeton University Press, 1957) , p. 40.

[10] Even the dividing line between housing and automobiles is not as large as it might first appear. How are mobile homes to be treated? (The answer of the national income accountants: Include purchases of mobile homes with automobiles and parts, in the consumer durables category.)

The line between durables and nondurables cannot, of course, be completely avoided. It must be drawn when consumption is divided into its subcomponents of consumer durables, nondurables, and services. (Refrigerators and furniture are included as durables in the national income accounts, and clothing as nondurables.) But the avoidance of fuzzy edges is less important between subcomponents of consumption than between the major components of *GNP;* that is, between consumption and investment. The *total* level of *GNP* is sensitive to this latter division between consumption and investment, but not to the division among subcomponents of consumption. (The treatment of new owner-occupied houses as investment rather than as consumption increases measured *GNP*, since imputed rents for housing are also included in *GNP*.)

occupied housing were entered as consumption. This problem is relatively trivial in the cases of automobiles and other consumer durables. While there is a rental market in automobiles, it is much less important than in housing.

In addition to imputed rent for owner-occupied housing, a number of other imputations are included in the consumption component of *GNP*. Some workers receive room and board from their employers, and an imputation for such room and board is included in consumption. Similarly, where a producer retains part of his output for his own consumption, this is included as part of *GNP*. This is particularly important in the agricultural sector. (Such imputations are far from complete. No imputation is made for the handyman who fixes his own car, for example.)

Excluded final market transactions: Illegal activities

On the other hand, a final "service" is excluded from *GNP*— even though it goes through the marketplace—if it is illegal. Having decided that certain activities are illegal and represent social "bads" rather than social "goods," the government excludes all such activities from the national product.

Some debatable cases

Although imputations are included in the *GNP* for some items that do not involve market transactions, and although illegal transactions are excluded from *GNP,* the *GNP* accounts nevertheless retain a strong market orientation. The farther one gets from market transactions, the less likely is a product to be included in *GNP*. Many household activities are consequently excluded.

This leads to certain anomalies. If a woman takes a job outside the house and hires a maid to look after the children and do other household work, then the measured national income rises by both her salary and the income of the maid. Yet not that much more is being done than previously. The housework previously got done; the wife did it. The only real increase in the amount of goods and services produced is represented by the new salary of the woman going outside her house to work. The national income accounts thus put a premium on market activity. If housework is done commercially, it is included in national income. If not, it is excluded. Thus, there is an upward bias in the growth of measured *GNP* when women go to work. Two conceivable changes that might be made in the *GNP* accounts to eliminate this anomaly: Either exclude the maid's income as an "intermediate" payment, on the ground that it is a necessary input in the working wife's production;[11] or alternatively, include the work of housewives in the national income in the first place. Either of these decisions would open up new areas of debate, however. (If housewives' work is to be included, how is it to be valued? And should a woman's care of her own children really be reduced to such crass commercial terms?)

There are many marginal areas, where "final product" and "intermediate product" blend into one another. Some travel is clearly for entertainment; some is clearly for business and only business. But business travel may be entertaining, too. Should there be an imputation in *GNP* for the entertainment or consumption value of business travel? (There is in fact no such imputation.) And what about the business executive who takes a prospective client to a football game? The list could rather easily be extended.

Government

Three major conceptual questions may be raised regarding the handling of government expenditures in the national accounts:

1. Which government expenditures are intermediate, and which are for final goods and services?
2. Which government expenditures are current or consumption expenditures, and which are capital expenditures?
3. Since government goods and services are generally not sold in the marketplace, at what value should they be entered in the national accounts?

Each is a basically insoluble question. In actual practice, simple answers are assumed in the national income accounts:

1. All currently produced government purchases of goods and services are assumed to be final; none is intermediate.[12] All are

---

[11] Obviously, there is a relationship here between national income accounting issues and taxation issues: Should a mother working outside the home be allowed to subtract the cost of a maid from her taxable income? However, while these questions overlap, the national income accounts need not follow the tax law. They generally do, but there are exceptions. For example, imputed rent to the homeowner is included in *GNP* but not in taxable personal income. (Until recently such imputations were made in Britain in calculating taxable income. The definition of taxable income, like that of national income, is a matter of continuing debate.)

[12] If the government purchases land or buildings which were contructed in the past, such purchases are not included in *GNP*. They are not part of current production.

therefore included in *GNP*. (Government transfer payments such as social security and interest payments are, however, excluded from *GNP*.)

2. All purchases by the government are assumed to be "current." There is no attempt to capitalize such government expenditures as roads and to impute a continuing flow of user benefits during their lifetime. (Contrast this with the imputed rental treatment of owner-occupied housing.)

3. Government purchases of goods and services are included at the monetary cost to the government. The wages and salaries of government employees are included in the *GNP* as a measure of the services provided to the public by the government.

Each of these simple solutions slides over difficult conceptual problems, and is a potential source of bias in the *GNP* accounts.

Clearly, it is an exaggeration to say that all government purchases of goods and services involve a final product. A road is used by vacationers and by trucks. One represents a final use, and the other an intermediate use. Many of the services provided by government are aimed at assisting the business community, and might therefore better be considered as an input in the productive process, and thus an intermediate service excludable from *GNP*. The inclusion of all government services in *GNP* means that there is a potential upward bias in the *GNP* accounts if the government takes over additional duties. If, for example, the government begins collecting and disseminating statistical information previously collected by businesses at their own expense, then, according to the conventions used in *GNP* accounting, the service ceases to be intermediate and becomes "final." The measured real *GNP* rises by the cost of the government statistical services, even though no more is actually being produced by the economy. (The question of bias in the *GNP* accounts is *quite separate* from the issue of whether the government *should* undertake additional duties. It is possible that the government may be much more efficient in some activities, which it should assume; and much less efficient in others, which it should avoid.)

On the other hand, investment activities by the government involve an underestimate of *GNP,* as compared to investment activities by the private sector. The argument here is related to the above discussion of housing. If the private sector constructs buildings and equipment, then they are originally included in the *GNP,* and subsequently the flow of services from this capital is also included in

GNP. Not so for government investment. If the government builds a new school, the building appears only once, during the period of its construction.

But the really knotty problem comes with the values attributed to government-provided services: They are included at cost. There is one compelling argument for this treatment. It avoids a hopeless task of trying to develop a better method of evaluation. It might on general grounds be argued that government services are under-valued in the *GNP* accounts. Business products are valued at their cost, plus a profit. No such profit is included in the valuation of the government services. On the other side, some might argue that it is fanciful to expect the government to operate efficiently enough to actually make a profit if it were subjected to the test of the market-place; therefore costs overstate the value of government services.

This question is fundamentally insoluble within the framework of the national accounts. The issues here go much deeper. Consider a specific example, the acquisition of an aircraft for $1 million by the Air Force. This shows up as a $1 million contribution to *GNP*. Yet the possible arguments regarding the "real" value of the aircraft to the society cover a vast spectrum. Is the airplane "really" worth:

1. $1 million, on the ground that the government is a maximizing institution, and acquires aircraft and other equipment up to the point where the marginal value of aircraft is equal to their marginal cost; or
2. $20 million, on the ground that the existence of a strong Air Force reduces the chance of a conflict, with its potentially staggering costs; or
3. $0, on the ground that, as the taxpayer is footing the bill, the Air Force asks for as many planes as it can possibly use, up to the point of zero marginal utility; or
4. —$20 million, on the ground that, once the Air Force has additional planes, the government will want to play with them, increasing the possibility of a conflict; thus giving a large figure for the same reason as in point 2), but with a negative sign; or
5. Some other figure?

Clearly this is an important matter, and one that can quickly lead to a heated debate. It is appropriate that the debate take place in Congress, and not in the Bureau of Economic Analysis of the Department of Commerce. It is not a question to be solved within the national accounting framework. The appropriate accounting of government expenditures is at their cost.

Investment

Conceptually, depreciation is perhaps the most troublesome component of the national income accounts. Indeed, the logical difficulties in determining the rate at which existing buildings and equipment lose their economic usefulness is the reason why *GNP* is the most frequently used economic aggregate, when net national product is conceptually more nearly the measure of what the society is producing.

Under the best circumstances, the estimation of depreciation is difficult. But additional problems arise during periods of inflation. Business depreciation records are the basis for the estimates of depreciation in the *GNP* accounts. And business depreciation is calculated on the basis of the actual dollar cost of the plant or equipment when it was acquired, not on the basis of the current replacement prices. Suppose that, in the process of production during the current year, one tenth of a machine is worn out. Suppose, further, that this machine was acquired five years ago at $1,000, but that its current replacement value has risen to $1,200 as a result of general inflation. Depreciation is calculated at $100, or one tenth the original cost.[13] But the value of the capital equipment used up in the productive process is $120 at current prices, not $100. The net product is overestimated, since depreciation appears in the national income accounts *not* on the basis of current prices, but rather on the basis of original acquisition costs. (On the other hand, it also means that the estimate of net *disinvestment* of $6.2 billion during the depression year of 1933 is an overestimate. Depreciation was calculated on the basis of acquisition costs rather than the depressed prices of 1933.)

THE GNP PRICE DEFLATOR AND OTHER PRICE INDEXES

Current-dollar *GNP* figures do not provide a measure of the growth of production in the economy. To obtain such a measure, an

---

[13] It is assumed here that the accounting rates of depreciation correspond to the "real" wear and tear and obsolescence of the equipment. In practice, of course, both problems may occur simultaneously: accounting rates of depreciation which do not correspond to actual rates of depreciation (whatever they are), and distortions caused by the inflation of prices since the acquisition of the capital goods.

adjustment must be made for price changes. This is done by measuring GNP at the prices that existed during a base year. Taking the current-dollar GNP divided by the constant-dollar GNP for the same year (and multiplying by 100 to translate into an index), we get the *Implicit GNP Price Deflator.*[14] Thus:

$$\frac{\text{Current-dollar } GNP}{\text{Constant-dollar } GNP} \equiv \frac{\text{Implicit } GNP \text{ price deflator}}{100} \quad (17\text{--}2)$$

On the conceptual problems involved in the measurement of average price changes through time, perhaps the most difficult is that raised by new products. (Changes in quality involve the same general problem, to a smaller degree.) The change in the price of a bushel of wheat may be readily measured. But how is the change in the price of televisions over the past 50 years to be measured? Fifty years ago, television had not yet been invented. In practice, what can be done in such instances is to include television sets in a category containing reasonably similar products (say, radios), and thus implicitly assume that the price behavior of television sets has been the same as the price changes of radios. This procedure involves an upward bias in price indexes through time. Current consumers are better off in the sense that they have a greater choice of products, yet this greater choice is not picked up in the price indexes.

The television example is difficult enough. But for television, at least, there is some other product (radio) with somewhat similar characteristics. What do we do with something like penicillin? Should we try to put a price on the value of the lives thereby saved? (The GNP accounts do not attempt to do so.) The conclusion: As new inventions become available, indexes of price changes tend to overstate the degree to which money has lost its value.

In addition to the implicit GNP price deflator, there are two other commonly used general price indexes: the consumer price index (CPI) and the wholesale price index (WPI). The implicit price deflator is the most broadly based index, covering price changes in all types of current production, including capital goods. (It is therefore perhaps the most vulnerable to problems associated with new products and changes in quality. Think of the problems in trying to specify relative prices of computers over the past 20 years.) The consumer price index measures the change in the cost of a

---

[14] By convention, indexes use a base of 100. For example, if prices have increased by 20 percent since the base year, the index stands at 120.

typical set of purchases of goods and services by an average urban worker, including not only consumer purchases as defined in the GNP accounts, but also housing.[15] Of the three major price measures, the wholesale price index is the narrowest in its coverage, excluding services and retailing markups and covering only the cost of a basket of commodities at the wholesale level.

Not very surprisingly, the three indexes tend to move together, although there are some differences (Table 17–2). During the 1950s and 1960s, the WPI tended to rise somewhat more slowly than the other two. This was attributable to the exclusion of services from this index—productivity in many service industries rises rather

Table 17–2
Annual rates of change of prices

Period	Implicit GNP price deflator (percent)	Consumer price index (percent)	Wholesale price index (percent)
1954–57	2.8	1.6	2.2
1958–64	1.4	1.2	0.0
1965–69	3.7	3.8	2.5
1970–76	6.4	6.5	8.0

slowly, while changes in wages and salaries are not greatly out of line with changes in wages and salaries in other sectors of the economy. With the rapid rise of international commodity prices (especially oil) during the 1970s, this pattern has been broken, however, and the *WPI* has spurted ahead at a more rapid rate than either of the other two general indexes.

THE SIGNIFICANCE OF THE GROSS NATIONAL PRODUCT

In current-dollar figures, the gross national product indicates the level of aggregate demand. In adjusting monetary and fiscal policies,

---

[15] Primarily because of the treatment of housing, the *CPI* should be called by its correct title, and the term "cost-of-living" index avoided. The *CPI* covers the current price of housing, including owner-occupied housing. The price included for such housing is the price which people would have to pay if they were to go on the market currently to buy their houses. Thus, in effect, the *CPI* assumes that homeowners repurchase and refinance their houses each month. Hence, the *CPI* is sensitive to increases in interest rates on home mortgages.

This procedure is valid for a *price* index. If people want to buy a new house, it includes what they will have to pay. But it is not a valid procedure in estimating the cost of living. When mortgage interest rates are rising, the cost of living of those who stay in their own homes does not automatically rise. Thus the *CPI* gives an upward-biased estimate of the cost of living. Similarly, when interest rates are falling, the *CPI* gives a downward-biased picture of changes in the cost of living.

the government authorities affect the level of monetary *GNP*. When *GNP* figures are put on a constant-dollar basis, they provide a measure of the growth of real output through time.

Even when estimated on a constant-dollar basis, however, the *GNP* gives only a very partial measure of the performance of the economy. Changes in real *GNP* do not directly indicate how the economy is performing in terms of providing jobs for its labor force. Unemployment may be high or rising even when real *GNP* is increasing. Furthermore, there are many other important aspects of the performance of the economy which are not included in *GNP* measures. One of the ways in which the economy has performed better through recent decades has been to provide a greater flow of production with *less effort*. The labor force has taken economic gains in the form of a shorter average work week as well as in the form of more goods and services. Only the latter is included in *GNP*, and the increase in leisure is left out. On the other side, the "bads" created in the process of production—pollution, noise, and tensions—are left out of the *GNP* measure. *GNP* measures *production*, not social welfare.

These omissions from *GNP* have led to suggestions that the national accounts be extended to include other important goals (Chapter 16). *GNP*, it is argued, gives a misleading view of how we are doing. It is better to have a poor measure of what is really important to the society than to have a good measure of something that is of secondary importance.

It can scarcely be questioned that *GNP* is severely deficient as a measure of social welfare. A government that simply attempted to maximize real *GNP* would be derelict in its duty to the public. Yet it does not thereby follow that the national income accounts should be expanded to include other socially desirable objectives. While man does not live by bread alone, the volume of real production of the society is an important concept. What follows, rather, is that gross national product should be considered as *one* of the important social indicators. The achievement of a high level of *GNP* is only *one* of the important social goals—and not the most important. The function of the political process and of public debate is to weigh the various social goals in the complex and ever-changing pursuit of the ultimate objective of human happiness and well-being. No matter how important is *this* goal, it will never be subject to numerical quantification. Precise numbers should be used only when they mean something. The *GNP* accounts are meaningful and valid in their present form.

KEY POINTS

1. National product transactions may be looked on either from the buyer's side or from the sellers' side; that is, either in terms of the type of purchase (consumption, investment, and government purchases) or in terms of where the money payments go. The destination of the money payments in turn may be looked on either of two ways: in terms of the payments to productive factors (wages, salaries, profits, rent, and so forth), or in terms of the value added of the various industries (manufacturing, farming, and so on).

2. In general, national income accounts focus on transactions which pass through the marketplace. No imputation is made, for example, of the housework done by wives or of the "do it yourself" additions and improvements made to homes. There is, however, one important set of imputations: Owner-occupied homes are initially included in investment when they are constructed, and the national income accounts include imputations for the rental value of owner-occupied homes. This procedure has the effect of making the measured *GNP* higher than it would be if houses were considered simply as "consumer durables." It has the major advantage that it makes the rate of growth of measured *GNP* insensitive to changes in the percentage of the population who own their homes rather than renting.

3. All government purchases of goods and services are assumed to represent final purchases and are therefore included in *GNP*.

EXERCISE

1. Obtain figures for a recent year for the national income accounts items shown in Figure 17–2. (Recent national income

accounts may be found in a recent issue of the *Survey of Current Business,* published by the U.S. Department of Commerce.)

SUGGESTED READING

Richard Ruggles and Nancy D. Ruggles, *National Income Accounts and National Income Analysis,* 2d. ed. (New York: McGraw-Hill, 1956) . pt. I.

Answers to
odd-numbered questions

Chapter 2

1. The quantity equation is correct, by definition; that is, V is defined as PQ/M. Thus, MV always equals PQ. If an increase in M leaves PQ unchanged, then the increase in M must be associated with an equivalent movement in V in the opposite direction.

Chapter 3

1. The two identities shown in the question give *actual* magnitudes. The *actual* magnitudes are always equal:

$$I \equiv S$$

On the other hand, Figure 3–4 illustrates *desired* investment and saving. These two need not be equal; they are equal only when the economy is in equilibrium. For example, at an output greater than the equilibrum output, saving will exceed investment *demand*. To restate this point, *actual investment* (which always equals saving) will exceed investment *demand*. There will be undesired or "un-demanded" inventory accumulation. Output will decline to the equilibrium level.

Chapter 4

1. *a.* 5,000
    b. 6,000; 10
    c. 2,400 [Note: $Y = 600 + (\frac{9}{10} \times \frac{5}{6}) Y$]
    d. New equilibrium is 2,800; therefore, multiplier is 4.

Chapter 5

1. *a.*

| | Rate of return |
Project	(in percent)
A......................	20
B......................	15
C......................	10
D......................	12.5

    b. A, B, and D. It is a matter of indifference whether C is undertaken. It is a "marginal" investment.

Chapter 6

1. *a.* The equilibrium level of income will be unchanged. Since the money stock rises by 10 percent and the equilibrium aggregate demand does not change, then income velocity must decline by one tenth. (More precisely, income velocity must decline to 100/110 of its initial value, in order for aggregate demand to remain unchanged.)
    b. One must either argue that the *LM* curve does not flatten out at a minimum rate of interest, or the *IS* curve must also shift to the right as the result of an expansion of the money supply.
    (Note to instructor: This question, and particularly part *b*, may be used to introduce Chapter 7.)

Chapter 7

1. The determinants of consumption will be considered in some detail in Chapter 14. Some of the relevant items which might affect aggregate consumption include:

    a. Expected future income (since people may reduce their saving out of current income if they expect high future incomes).

b. Past income and consumption patterns; that is, present consumption may be influenced by the habits inherited from the past.
c. The relative position of an individual in society may affect personal consumption. Those whose income is low compared to their neighbors or friends, or compared to the general average of society, may consume their total income and even run down their assets or accumulate liabilities in their attempt to "keep up with the Joneses."

Chapter 8

1. Excess reserves might reasonably be responsive to the following:

a. The variability of deposit withdrawals. The more volatile are deposits, the more reasonable it is for a banker to keep a large cushion of excess reserves to cover the withdrawals. (A withdrawal of a deposit reduces required reserves as well as actual reserves, of course. But the actual reserves fall by the full amount of the withdrawal, while required reserves fall only by the amount of the withdrawal times the required reserve ratio. Therefore, a withdrawal reduces excess reserves.)
b. As an alternative to holding excess reserves, a bank may hold easily marketable assets as a cushion against the risk of deposit withdrawals. Thus, the amount of excess reserves may be influenced by the availability of earning assets which are easily marketable at a relatively fixed money price. (The price is important, because the banker does not want to risk the necessity of selling assets at a significant loss in the event of a withdrawal of deposits.) A short-term government security ("government bill") is a prime example of a security which is easily salable at a stable price.
c. The buoyancy of the demand for loans. The higher the demand for loans, the more the bank is likely to lend, and the lower may be its reserves.
d. The stability and predictability of the demand for loans. The more stable and predictable is the demand for bank loans, the less incentive there will be for the banker to hold excess reserves. If, on the other hand, valuable customers are in the habit of appearing unannounced to apply for loans, the banker may wish to have a cushion of excess reserves in order to be able to accommodate these customers without trouble.
e. The risk associated with loans and other earning assets. The riskier the loans, the less anxious the banker will be to extend the loans, and the more excess reserves the bank will hold.

f. The interest rate on loans and other earning assets. The higher the interest rate, the more expensive it is in terms of earnings foregone (the "opportunity cost") for the banker to hold excess reserves, and the smaller are excess reserves therefore likely to be.

A further question grows out of these points: In the light of these determinants of excess reserves, what would you expect to happen to excess reserves during a depression? (This question anticipates the discussion of Chapters 9 and 11.)

Chapter 9

1. Credit rationing occurs when the interest rate is held below the equilibrium rate. The demand for funds exceeds their supply, and the rationing mechanism comes into play as a way of allocating the relatively scarce funds among the various demands. Therefore, in the world of credit rationing, the interest rate will tend to be lower than in a world of no credit rationing. Thus the opportunity cost of holding cash is lower, and cash balances on this account will tend to be higher. Also, the risks of not being able to borrow at all are greater (since the business may find that it has been rationed out of the market when it approaches the lending institutions), and therefore on this account the demand to hold cash should also be higher.

While cash holdings are one way of protecting against the inability to borrow during periods of credit stringency, an alternative method is to hold short-term, high-quality securities, such as government bills. These will be readily salable at a relatively stable price. (The prices of short-term securities fall much less than the prices of longer-term securities during periods of rising interest rates.) Thus, in situations where credit rationing is important, there will be a tendency of businesses to prefer short-term assets rather than longer-term assets.

On the other hand, there will be an incentive to borrow long term rather than short term. Where short-term borrowings are undertaken, there will be a risk of being caught in a squeeze, if the borrower is unable to refinance borrowings during periods of credit stringency.

Observe the different pressures on the borrower and the lender. The lender will have an incentive to hold short-term rather than long-term assets. The borrower will have an incentive to issue long-term rather than short-term liabilities. This will tend to depress average short-term interest rates compared to average long-term interest rates. (That is, the "liquidity premium" on short-term securities will rise.) This will broaden the scope for "financial intermediaries"; that is, for institutions which hold longer-term securities financed with shorter-term obligations.

3. Their principal initial effect is an exchange of assets and liabilities, with the business obtaining an asset (money) in exchange for a liability (the promissory note given to the bank when the loan is obtained). The initial effects on wealth will be similar to those of the "first round" open market operation of the Federal Reserve. That is, the willingness of banks to increase their lending will tend to depress interest rates, increasing the value of outstanding bonds and possibly causing sympathetic movements in the stock market.

In the longer run, another wealth effect may be important. An increase in bank lending and a fall in interest rates should stimulate investment. "Investment" is another way of saying "an increase in the stock of real capital." This increase in real capital represents an increase in wealth.

(The distinction between the shorter run and the longer run is made for the following reason. The exchange of assets and liabilities occurs at a point of time; the interest rate effects may be simultaneous or may follow quickly thereafter. On the other hand, capital formation by its very nature takes time.)

Chapter 10

1. An expansive fiscal policy, combined with a tight monetary policy, will tend to cause a high rate of interest. This may be justified in either of two circumstances:

    a. If the higher interest rate helps to achieve some desired objective (for example, the desired balance of international payments).
    b. If the expansive fiscal policy is aimed at the achievement of important goals. The government spending programs associated with an expansive fiscal stance may in some circumstances be considered more important than the growth which would come as a result of the low interest rate.

Chapter 11

1. Unless there are large excess reserves to begin with, the withdrawals of the public will put the banks in a precarious reserve position, creating pressures on them to reduce their outstanding loans and other earning assets, and thus creating pressures for a contraction of the money stock. (With a 20 percent required reserve ratio, every withdrawal of $1 from banks will reduce actual reserves by $1, but required reserves by only 20 cents.)

    If the run occurs when there is a crisis of confidence and the threat of a recession, then it is important that the Federal Reserve offset the restrictive effects of the flight into currency. As a first approximation, it should be willing to purchase securities on the open market *to whatever degree* is necessary to prevent a fall in the money stock. Such open market purchases, even though they may be massive, are not inflationary. Rather, they are antideflationary, offsetting downward pressures on the money supply which can result in a depression.

More precisely, the Federal Reserve should engage in open market purchases to whatever extent needed to get aggregate demand close to the target path (which should be chosen with the goals of full employment and price stability in mind).

Chapter 12

1. In each case, causation is *not* demonstrated by the statistical relationship. From our existing knowledge of the interrelationships in the economy, it is reasonable to argue that:

   a. The high level of gasoline and automobile sales may both be the result of a common cause, generally high incomes. In addition, it is reasonable to argue that more direct causal forces are also at work, operating both ways. The availability of fuel encourages the purchase of automobiles, and purchases of automobiles cause an increase in the consumption of gasoline.

   b. There is probably little or no direct causal relationship between the sales of shoes and of dishwashers. The tendency of the sales to occur together can be explained by attributing both increases in shoe sales and increases in dishwasher sales to a common cause, namely, general prosperity.

   c. A causal relationship exists; high rainfalls cause large crops.

   d. There is no direct causal relationship, but the two crops respond to similar forces. (Thus, this answer is similar to the answer for *b* above.) Weather in Kansas and Missouri is related; the two states tend to have hot, humid weather simultaneously. Also, when high corn prices are expected, farmers in both Kansas and Missouri respond by planting more corn and using more fertilizer.

   e. Quite probably a coincidence. In general, not much attention should be paid to single observations. More significant is the percentage of upsets during the whole football season. It is, however, possible that there might be some minor causal interrelationship at work. If the games are played simultaneously, the half-time scores of the other games may have become generally available to the players. Hearing that other underdogs are rising to the occasion, some of the weaker teams may have taken inspiration. On the other hand, seeing their close competitors for leadership going down to defeat may have caused some of the high-ranking teams to relax their efforts.

3. The lags increase the strength of the argument that the causal relationship runs primarily from money to economic activity. They do not, however, make a conclusive case. Suppose, for example, that increases in investment demand are the primary cause for increases in the money stock. Having made a decision to increase the magnitude of their operations, businesses may take the preliminary step of borrowing from the banks and increasing their cash holdings in the expectation of larger operations and larger capital expenditures. Thus, the money supply may increase first, even though it was a *result* of the decision to invest and expand. (This example does, however, underline the difficulty of separating out the causal strands: If businesses had not been able to borrow and increase their cash holdings, would they have deferred their capital expansion? If increases in cash reserves are considered desirable for a prudent expansion of business, does not the available supply of money also acquire a causal importance in this example?)

Chapter 13

1. *a.* Inflation will accelerate by a constant amount each period (see Figure 13–8).
   b. Inflation will accelerate by an increasing amount each period, as the negotiators take into account not only the high prices of the preceding period, but also the trend toward an ever-accelerating inflation. Indeed, if wage negotiators become convinced that the authorities are determined to increase aggregate demand sufficiently to keep unemployment very low, no matter how great that increase in demand might be, and if negotiators also take the effects of this determination completely into account, then wages and prices will become highly unstable. (In effect, there will be no equilibrium rate of inflation, and no equilibrium rate for the acceleration of inflation.)

Chapter 14

1. *a.* It is appropriate to redistribute income from the higher-income groups to the lower-income groups. Since the latter are judged to have higher marginal propensities to consume than the higher-income groups, the redistribution will increase total consumption out of any level of income, thus contributing to total demand and employment.

b.   In terms of the goal of restraining inflation, it is appropriate to redistribute income away from the low-income groups toward the higher-income groups, thereby reducing total consumption and the inflationary pressures.

c.   The policies outlined in the first two parts are likely to be very controversial. Even on the assumption that such policies would be successful (and the success depends on the uncertain difference between the marginal propensities of the various income groups), it will be difficult to get quick action on such policies, since the debate over the desirable distribution of income may come to dominate the attention of legislators.

d.   It is probably inappropriate to use income redistribution as a countercyclical tool. Rather, income redistribution policies should be developed with longer-run considerations in mind, and, in particular, with the goal of social justice in mind. (This clearly is a controversial matter, on which there are significant disagreements, and on which the attitudes of the society are likely to change over time.)

Chapter 15

1.   Bicycle production may be increased with the present equipment by adding overtime or additional shifts, or by using the equipment more intensively in other ways. Equipment which otherwise would have been due for retirement may be kept on the production line. Equipment previously used in other industries may be adapted for bicycle production. Part of the increase in demand may be satisfied by running down the inventories of bicycles held by manufacturers, wholesalers, and retailers.

Chapter 16

1.   If an increase in the consumption of one individual decreases the happiness of others, then the increase in the aggregate utility of all individuals which results from the consumption of one additional unit of goods by one individual is less than the amount that the individual is willing to pay for the unit of goods. On the other hand, if the consumption of one individual contributes to the pleasure of others, then the increase in total utility of society exceeds the amount which the consuming individual is willing to pay.

Under assumption *a*, it may be argued that there is too much consumption; under assumption *b*, too little. This does not, however, have direct implications for the optimum rate of growth. The transfer of additional resources from present consumption into investment and growth has as its purpose the possibility for higher levels of *future* consumption; it involves the comparative utilities or desirability of present and future consumption. The possibility of "externalities" in consumption may apply equally to present and future consumption, and thus not affect the optimum growth rate.

Rather, the question of externalities may influence the optimum division between work and leisure. Where the utilities of other people are adversely affected by my consumption, the amount by which I will work and consume if left to my own choices may be too great. The social optimum might involve my taking more leisure and less consumption. Thus, it might be desirable for government policy to encourage leisure rather than work at the margin. (If, however, others are equally jealous of my leisure as they are of my consumption of goods, then the work-leisure choice may be optimal without policy action.) On the other hand, under assumption *b*, policies aimed at encouraging work rather than leisure may be in order.

Index

This book has been set in 11 and 10 point Baskerville, leaded 2 points. Part and chapter numbers and titles are in 24 point (small) Helvetica. The size of the type page is 27 by 46 picas.